GREEN JOBS
FOR A NEW
ECONOMY

PETERSON'S

A nelnet COMPANY

PETERSON'S
A nelnet COMPANY

About Peterson's

To succeed on your lifelong educational journey, you will need accurate, dependable, and practical tools and resources. That is why Peterson's is everywhere education happens. Because whenever and however you need education content delivered, you can rely on Peterson's to provide the information, know-how, and guidance to help you reach your goals. Tools to match the right students with the right school. It's here. Personalized resources and expert guidance. It's here. Comprehensive and dependable education content—delivered whenever and however you need it. It's all here.

For more information, contact Peterson's, 2000 Lenox Drive, Lawrenceville, NJ 08648; 800-338-3282; or find us on the World Wide Web at: www.petersons.com.

By producing this book on recycled paper (40% post-consumer waste) 154 trees were saved.

CONTENTS

PART II: COLLEGES AND UNION ORGANIZATIONS WITH GREEN GREEN PROGRAMS

PART III: WORKFORCE TRAINING

PART IV: PROFILES OF SUSTAINABILITY PROGRAMS

PART V: APPENDIXES

Green Jobs for a New Economy

A NOTE FROM THE PETERSON'S EDITORS

If you are a high school or college student thinking about your future—and the future of our planet—or if you are a career changer wondering what you need to do to get a job in today's new "green" economy, you've picked the right guide. *Peterson's Green Jobs for a New Economy* can offer you an array of possibilities in a wide variety of programs offered at two-year schools, four-year colleges and universities, and graduate and professional institutions and through trade unions and specialized organizations.

To gain a better understanding of what being green or living a green lifestyle means and how to begin your search for a green job, "What Does Being Green Mean?" is the place to start. Here, you'll find out why we're seeing an increase in the current interest in sustainability, what the New Energy for America Plan and the 2009 Stimulus Plan mean in terms of your green job search, how to find and search "green" job boards, and how to "green" your vocabulary. You'll also find a list of organizations in the United States and abroad that support sustainability through education, research, and activities.

In "Essays on the Importance of Sustainability," you'll find insightful and inspirational articles by individuals who are at the forefront of this exciting field:

- Anthony D. Cortese, Sc.D., President of Second Nature–Education for Sustainability; co-organizer of the American College & University Presidents' Climate Commitment; co-founder of the Association for the Advancement of Sustainability in Higher Education; and co-founder/co-coordinator of the Higher Education Associations Sustainability Consortium
- Juliana Williams, Sierra Student Coalition
- Heather Henriksen, Director of the Office for Sustainability at Harvard University
- Sarah Boll, member of the Office of Energy and Sustainability at NYU
- Tony Ash, Director of Operations, Earth911.com
- Jennifer Berry, Public and Strategic Relations, Earth911.com
- Rachel Gutter, Director of the Education Sector at the U.S. Green Building Council

If you are seeking a professional or skilled job in the new green economy, check out **Part I** for a listing of the top in-demand jobs. In chapters 1 and 2, you can search by field for information on job trends, work environment, career paths, earning potential, education/licensure requirements, and organizations to contact for further information. Each job profile includes professional and trade associations that may have special interest groups or sections related to sustainability.

To locate some of the great four-year and/or graduate programs or some of the outstanding two-year (including community colleges) and union programs, check out **Part II.** The fifty colleges and universities profiled in chapter 3 support innovative programs in environmental or sustainability studies, have vibrant on-campus sustainability programs and organizations, and have made a commitment to making their campus communities sustainable. Chapter 4 features twenty-two community colleges that confer "green" degrees and certificates, seven labor unions that offer apprenticeship and training programs to upgrade members' skills for the green economy, and the National Labor College, which grants undergraduate degrees and certificates to AFL-CIO members. Both chapters highlight degrees offered, including distance learning opportunities, and green campus organizations and activities.

In **Part III,** you'll discover what each of the fifty states' one-stop career centers can offer in terms of help with job search, resume writing, training programs, and more. Simply find your state, and you'll uncover a wealth of information, including phone numbers and Web sites.

Additional "green" information on colleges and universities (two-year and four-year) can be found in **Part IV.** Organized by state, these college and university profiles offer pertinent details on two- and four-year schools' sustainability initiatives, academics, student services and green events, food, transportation, buildings and grounds, recycling, and more—as well as important contact information.

Throughout the book, you'll find feature pages offering extra "green" tips and advice, with such topics as the *Top 10 Greenest Places to Live and Work, Top 10 Green Tips for Campus Life,* and *How Green is a Prospective Employer?* In addition, "About" boxes that are scattered throughout the chapters provide even more information and explanations to help you succeed on your way to a green job—and a green life.

What does sustainability mean to Peterson's? As a leading publisher, we are aware that our business has a direct impact on vital resources—most especially, the trees that are used to make our books. Peterson's is proud that its products are certified by the Sustainable Forestry Initiative (SFI) and that all of its books are printed on paper that is 40 percent post-consumer waste. As part of the new green economy, Peterson's continually strives to find ways to incorporate sustainability throughout all aspects of our business.

For more than 40 years, Peterson's has given students the most comprehensive, up-to-date information on private schools and undergraduate and graduate programs in the United States and abroad, as well as test-prep assistance and career guidance.

Peterson's publications can be found at high school guidance offices, college and university career centers, and your local bookstore or library. Coming soon, you'll also be able to purchase e-books from Peterson's. Continue to check our Web site, www.petersons.com, for more information about our e-book program.

We welcome any comments or suggestions you may have about this publication and invite you to complete our online survey at www.petersons.com/booksurvey. Your feedback will help us make your educational dreams possible.

Colleges and universities will be pleased to know that Peterson's helped you in your selection. Admissions and Sustainability Office staff members are more than happy to answer questions and help in any way they can. The editors at Peterson's wish you great success in your search for a great *green* job in the new economy!

WHAT DOES BEING GREEN MEAN?

WHAT IS THE NEW GREEN ECONOMY?

Once upon a time, the only thing that was green was Kermit the Frog. Now, it seems as though everywhere you turn, all you see and hear is "green." Eat organically grown food. Use only low- or no-VOC paint. (What's VOC?) Trade in your gas-guzzler for a hybrid. Have a fuel-efficient car? Buy an even more fuel-efficient car. Wear clothes made from renewable sources such as cotton or bamboo. (Bamboo? For clothes?) Recycle your computer, your cell phone, and even your sneakers. On and on goes the list of do's and don'ts in this new sustainable, eco-friendly, twenty-first century. But what does it mean to you—the student, the worker, the consumer, and the citizen?

Why the Interest in Sustainability Now?

First, the fear of global warming and climate change as well as national security issues are driving the push to conserve energy and become less dependent on foreign oil. Second, the recession that began in 2007 turned the spotlight on the consumption patterns of Americans. Our savings rate had fallen into the negative zone as we borrowed against the equity in our homes to buy boats, electronics, the latest hot trends in clothes, gas-hungry SUVs and crossovers—generally whatever we wanted until we reached our credit limits. And when we did, some of us just got another credit card. Whereas our great-grandparents may have darned a hole in a sock, shortened a hem on a dress, or had their shoes resoled, we just tossed out old items and bought new ones.

New Energy for America

Certainly a number of Americans did practice "recycle, reuse, reduce" since the first Earth Day in 1970, but the nation as a whole had not embraced the mantra of conservationists and environmentalists until the recent recession—which brings us to the third point. The election of Barack Obama in 2008 served to crystallize the need to do something about our profligate attitude toward the environment. As a candidate, President Obama had promised to reduce the nation's dependence on nonrenewable sources of energy and fight climate change. As President, he launched his "New Energy for America" program that is intended to

- "Chart a new energy future: . . . by embracing alternative and renewable energy, ending our addiction to foreign oil, addressing the global climate crisis, and creating millions of new jobs that can't be shipped overseas."

- "Invest in clean, renewable energy: To achieve our goal of generating 25 percent of our energy from renewable sources by 2025, we will make unprecedented investments in clean, renewable energy—solar, wind, biofuels, and geothermal power."

- "Fight climate change: We will invest in energy efficiency and conservation, two sure-fire ways to decrease deadly pollution and drive down demand. . . ."

The 2009 Stimulus Plan

Within a month of Obama's inauguration, Congress passed a $787-billion stimulus package, officially called the American Recovery and Reinvestment Act of 2009, to help the nation dig itself out of the recession. One goal of the act was to put the nation on course to achieve the President's energy plan for the nation, including creating 3.5 million "green jobs." Among the programs included in the stimulus package were the following:

- $32 billion to transform the nation's energy transmission, distribution, and production system
- $6 billion to weatherize low-income homes
- $16 billion to repair and retrofit public housing for energy efficiency
- $30 billion for highway construction
- $31 billion to modernize federal and other public buildings for energy efficiency
- $19 billion for clean water, flood control, and environmental restoration
- $10 billion for transit and rail expansion
- $20 billion for health information technology
- $1.5 billion for biomedical research
- $3.95 billion for the Workforce Investment Act, which includes money available to community colleges for worker-training programs
- $25 billion in Recovery Zone bonds to states with high unemployment rates for job training, infrastructure construction and repair, and economic development
- $20 billion in tax incentives for installing solar and wind systems in homes and businesses

In July 2009, the President proposed another $12 billion to fund workforce training through the nation's network of community colleges. In his speech at Macomb Community College in Warren, Michigan, Obama said, "This is training to install solar panels and build those wind turbines and develop a smarter electricity grid. And this is the kind of education that more and more Americans are using to improve their skills and broaden their horizons." (http://www.whitehouse.gov/the_press_office/Remarks-by-the-President-on-the-American-Graduation-Initiative-in-Warren-MI/)

Focusing much of the stimulus package on energy conservation, infrastructure, and workforce training has meant an immediate impact on people's lives. It also has helped to reorient our thinking about how the choices we make about food, clothing, housing, and discretionary income affect others and the environment.

ALL ABOUT GREEN JOB BOARDS

Once upon a time—actually, just a few years ago, if you were looking for a job, you'd read the want ads in the newspaper or in trade and association publications. Today, most job listings have migrated to the Internet where you will find hundreds of job boards. How do you decide which ones to search and what to look for? Here are a few ideas to help you concentrate your search in the best places.

Remember that job boards are not just for searching when you are looking for a job. They can be helpful when you are deciding on a career to pursue. Analyzing job titles related to your interests; the regions of the country where particular jobs are most common, for example, the Plains states and the Southwest for wind-power jobs; types of employers such as public or private, nonprofit, small companies, or large corporations; and salaries can help direct your career choice.

Where to Look?

Major Internet sites for jobs are monster.com, careerbuilder.com, and hotjobs.yahoo.com. Type in your job area, such as "architectural designer," and see what jobs come up. You can search for jobs in a specific city or nationwide. Monster.com has a green careers section. Green For All and Yahoo! Hotjobs have partnered to create a Green Jobs page at hotjobs.yahoo.com. Green For All is not a job board; it is a great resource for information about green-collar jobs for skilled workers, especially for those in urban centers and for returning veterans. Green For All is a national organization working to build a wide-ranging green economy, one strong enough to lift people out of poverty.

There are a number of job boards that are specific to green jobs. Type "green job boards" into a search engine and more than two dozen will pop up. The following came up in researching this book:

- http://careercenter.usgbc.org/home
- http://www.americangreenjobs.com
- http://www.brightgreentalent.com
- http://www.careersinwind.com
- http://www.careeronestop.org (sponsored by the U.S. Department of Labor)
- http://www.cleanedgejobs.com
- http://www.coolclimatejobs.com
- http://www.eco.org
- http://www.ecojobs.com
- http://www.environmentalcareer.com
- http://www.greenbiz.com
- http://www.greendreamjobs.com
- http://www.greenjobs.net
- http://www.greenjobsalliance.org
- http://www.greenjobsearch.org
- http://www.healthcarejobstore.com
- http://www.jobs.treehugger.com
- http://www.renewableenergyjobs.net
- http://www.solarjobs.com
- http://www.sustainjobs.com
- http://www.sustainlane.com/green-jobs
- http://www.veteransgreenjobs.org

Other Sources for Job Boards

You can also look at the Web sites of the professional organizations and trade associations that you belong to. Many of them have job boards, and their postings will be the most closely aligned with the group's specialties.

Don't overlook your college or university career counseling and job placement offices. Many schools today offer their services to alumni and alumnae, not just to seniors and graduate students. If you graduated from a large university, your department may have its own career services link on its Web site or may have links to other job boards.

"GREEN" YOUR VOCABULARY FOR A SUSTAINABLE FUTURE

Just about everywhere you turn these days, you see and hear the lingo of the new green economy: biofuel, carbon footprint, geothermal, LEED, just to name a few. Understanding what these words actually mean will certainly help you in your green job search—and in your everyday life. Here's a list of some key green terms and their definitions to get you started on your way to a sustainable future.

alternative energy/renewable energy: energy derived from natural resources that aren't used up over time, such as wind and sun

biodegradable: able to decompose by natural forces and without harming the environment

biofuel: produced from biological sources such as biomass and treated waste rather than from nonrenewable fossil fuel such as oil

biomass: agricultural waste, plant material, and vegetation used as an energy source

cap-and-trade: system of pollution credits established by the government and based on the amount of air pollution created in a region that enables a company that doesn't use all of its pollution credits to sell unused ones to companies that pollute more than the credits allotted to them by the government

carbon emissions: carbon dioxide and carbon monoxide gases released by motor vehicles and industrial production that pollute the atmosphere

carbon footprint: way to measure the impact of human activity on the environment; uses units of carbon dioxide to calculate amount of greenhouse gases produced

carbon neutral: not adding to carbon dioxide emissions

carbon trading: process by which companies can sell their unused pollution credits; see *cap-and-trade*

ecotravel: traveling responsibly, especially to natural areas, in a way "that conserves the environment and improves the well-being of local people" (The International Ecotourism Society)

energy audit: assessment of energy use to determine ways to conserve energy; first step is *weatherization;* (see page 5)

energy efficient: denotes a product that is as good as or better than standard products but uses less energy and costs less to operate

Energy Star: U.S. Department of Energy and EPA joint program to increase the energy efficiency of household appliances and electronic devices; adopted by other nations, including the European Union (www.energystar.gov)

ethanol: alternate fuel made from corn or sugarcane

Fair Trade: agreement by countries in international trade to live up to standards for the fair and just treatment of labor and the environment in the production of goods; goods manufactured and sold under the agreement

geothermal: energy source; uses heat from the Earth as a clean, renewable source of electricity

global warming: increase in the average temperature of the Earth's atmosphere resulting in climate change

green-collar career/job: a career/job that promotes stewardship of the environment now and for the future

green design: creating materials, products, buildings, services, and experiences that are energy efficient and environmentally friendly

hybrid: motor vehicle that runs on gasoline and an electric battery

LEED: acronym for Leadership in Energy and Environmental Design Green Building Rating System developed by the U.S. Green Building Council (USGBC); LEED-certified denotes that new construction, renovation, building operations, etc., meet the USGBC guidelines for building sustainability

organic: product made solely from natural ingredients; farming without the use of synthetic pesticides and fertilizers

photovoltaic cell: device that turns sunlight directly into electricity

PCW: stands for Post-Consumer Waste; denotes product made from recycled materials

solar energy system: one of two types of power systems: photovoltaic uses sunlight to produce electricity directly and the solar water heating system uses sunlight to heat water

solar panel/solar array: device that collects the heat of the sun for use in various types of solar energy systems

solar thermal collector: device that uses energy from sunlight to heat substances like water for use in heating

STARS: acronym for Sustainability Tracking Assessment & Rating System for colleges and universities established by the Association for the Advancement of Sustainability in Higher Education, a consortium of U.S. colleges and universities

sustainability: "meeting the needs of the present without compromising the ability of future generations to meet their own needs" [World Commission on Environment and Development, 1987]

USDA organic: The U.S. Department of Agriculture's National Organic Program's seal of certification (found on cosmetics and food) given to any farm, wild crop harvesting, or handling operation that meets certain standards for ecologically based practices, such as cultural and biological pest management and exclusion of all synthetic chemicals, antibiotics, and hormones

VOC: stands for volatile organic compounds; carbon-based molecules that vaporize as gases and enter the atmosphere; ingredient in paint, paint thinners, paint strippers, furniture, and household cleaning products that cause the odor

waste audit: assessment of the amount of waste generated at a home or business

wastewater recycling: treatment of wastewater for recycling for industrial uses and agriculture

waste reduction: reusing materials; reducing or eliminating the amount of waste at its source by buying less; reducing the amount of toxicity in waste by using environmentally safe products

weatherization: improving the energy efficiency of a building by sealing off air leaks

wind turbine: device for harnessing the wind to create electricity

U.S. AND GLOBAL ORGANIZATIONS THAT SUPPORT SUSTAINABILITY

In addition to the organizations listed following each of the job profiles in chapters 1 and 2 as well as the college, university, and training program profiles in chapters 3 and 4, there are other organizations specifically for students interested in preserving the environment and improving the quality of life.

The following list is by no means exhaustive, but it provides a sampling of organizations in the United States and abroad that support sustainability through education, research, and activities:

- **1Sky:** http://www.1sky.org
- **Audubon Society:** http://www.audubonsociety.org

- **Campus Consortium for Environmental Education:** http://www.c2e2.org
- **Climate Challenge** (check the Campus Climate Challenge): http://www.climatechallenge.org
- **Defenders of Wildlife Green Jobs and Wildlife Initiative:** http://www.defenders.org
- **Earth911.com:** http://www.earth911.com
- **Energy Action Coalition:** http://www.energyactioncoalition.org
- **Environmental Defense Fund:** http://www.environmentaldefensefund.org
- **Green For All:** http://www.greenforall.org
- **Greenpeace:** http://www.greenpeace.org
- **The International Ecotourism Society:** http://www.ecotourism.org
- **National Hispanic Environmental Council:** http://www.nheec.org
- **National Parks Conservation Association:** http://www.npca.org
- **National Wildlife Federation:** http://www.nwf.org
- **Natural Resources Defense Council (NRDC):** http://nrdc.org
- **PennFuture** (Pennsylvania-focused)*: http://www.pennfuture.org
- **Practice Green Health:** http://www.practicegreenhealth.org
- **RecycleMania:** http://www.recyclemania.org
- **Second Nature:** http://www.secondnature.org
- **Sierra Club:** http://www.sierraclub.org
- **Sierra Student Coalition:** http://ssc.sierraclub.org/
- **Student Conservation Association:** http://www.thesca.org

Look for similar organizations in your own state. Often you will find them as part of local or area-wide business councils.

- **The Climate Project:**
  http://theclimateproject.org
- **U.S. Green Building Council:**
  http://www.usgbc.org
- **U.S. Partnership for Education for Sustainable Development:**
  http://www.uspartnership.org
- **Waterkeeper Alliance:**
  http://www.waterkeeper.org

- **World Business Council for Sustainable Development** (click on U.S. Office):
  http://www.wbcsd.org
- **World Wildlife Fund:**
  http://www.worldwildlife.org
- **Youth and Environment Europe:**
  http://www.yeenet.eu

ESSAYS ON THE IMPORTANCE OF SUSTAINABILITY

HIGHER EDUCATION'S TRUE ROLE: CREATING A HEALTHY, JUST, AND SUSTAINABLE SOCIETY

by Anthony D. Cortese, Sc.D.
President, Second Nature

Higher education leaders, especially the 655 college and university presidents in fifty states who have signed the American College & University Presidents' Climate Commitment, recognize that providing sustainability education and modeling sustainable behavior are critical to meeting their social responsibility to provide the knowledge and educated citizenry for a thriving civil society.

Higher education is facing its greatest challenge in meeting its responsibility because humanity is at an unprecedented crossroads. Despite all the work we have done on environmental protection, all living systems are in long-term decline and are declining at an increasing rate. We are severely disrupting the stability of the climate, and there are huge social and public health challenges worldwide. This is happening because 25 percent of the world's population is consuming 70–80 percent of the world's resources. How will we ensure that current and future human beings will be healthy and that there will be thriving communities and economic opportunities for all in a world that *will* have 9 billion people by 2050? This is the greatest moral and social challenge human civilization has ever faced.

As Einstein said, "We can't solve today's problems with the same level of thinking at which they were created." We need a transformative shift in the way we think and act. We currently view health, social, economic, political, security, population, environmental, and other major societal issues as separate, competing, and hierarchical when they are really systemic and interdependent. For example, we do not have environmental problems, per se. We have negative environmental consequences due to the way we have designed our social, economic, and political system. *We have a de facto systems design failure.* The challenges of the twenty-first century must be addressed in a systemic, integrated, collaborative, and holistic fashion.

7

Unfortunately, the current educational system is largely reinforcing the current unhealthy, inequitable, and unsustainable path that society is pursuing. This is not intentional—it is because of disciplinary predominance and an implicit assumption that the Earth will be the gift that keeps on giving—providing us with resources and assimilating our wastes and negative impacts, ad infinitum.

We need to redesign the human economy to emulate nature, operating on renewable energy and creating a circular production economy in which the concept of 'waste' is eliminated because all waste products are raw materials or nutrients for the industrial economy. We must manage human activities in a way that uses natural resources only at the rate that they can self-regenerate—the ideas embodied in sustainable forestry, fishing, and agriculture. A growing consensus of business, government, labor, and other leaders believes that a clean, green economy based on these principles is the only way to restore American economic leadership, create millions of jobs, and help solve global health and environmental problems.

Walmart is now requiring all its 64,000 suppliers worldwide to report on and minimize their "greenhouse gas" footprint and reduce the environmental impact of their packaging. In response, Proctor & Gamble and other laundry detergent manufacturers have produced detergent that is twice as concentrated. If this were done with all laundry detergents in the United States, it would remove 140 million pounds of material and eliminate 42 million distribution miles. DuPont has reduced its greenhouse gas emissions by 72 percent over its 1990 levels and saved more than $3 billion in energy costs. This is the future of business and society, for which we will need a newly educated workforce.

What if higher education were to take a leadership role in helping to make this a reality? *The context of learning* would make the human/environment interdependence, values, and ethics a seamless and central part of teaching of all the disciplines. *The content of learning* would reflect interdisciplinary systems thinking, dynamics, and analysis for all majors and disciplines with the same *lateral rigor* across the disciplines as the *vertical rigor* within. *The process of education* would emphasize active, experiential, inquiry-based learning and real-world problem solving *on the campus* and *in the larger community.* Higher education would **practice sustainability** in *operations, planning, facility design, purchasing, and investments* connected with the formal curriculum. Higher Education would form **partnerships with local and regional communities** to help make them sustainable as an integral part of higher education's mission and the student experience.

Fortunately, there are hundreds of examples of changes in all five of the above areas of higher education, especially in the last few years. Exciting environmental studies and graduate programs that incorporate sustainability in scientific, engineering, social science, business, law, public health, ethics, and religion disciplines are abundant and growing. Progress on modeling sustainability has happened at an even faster rate. Higher education has embraced programs for energy and water conservation, renewable energy, waste minimization and recycling, green buildings and purchasing, alternative transportation, local and organic food growing, and 'sustainable' purchasing—saving both the environment and money. The rate of increase is unmatched by any other sector of society. The student environmental movement is the best-organized, largest, and most sophisticated student movement since the anti-war movement of the 1960s.

In the last few years, these efforts have been greatly accelerated by three large social innovations. The Association for the Advancement of Sustainability in Higher Education created a large learning community of faculty, students, administrators, and operations staff members at over 900 colleges and universities to provide resources, professional development, and best practices to accelerate education and practice for sustainability. The aforementioned American College & University Presidents' Climate Commitment is a high-visibility commitment by more than 650 colleges and universities to reduce and eventually eliminate their campus greenhouse gas emissions from electricity use, heating and cooling, and transportation and provide the educated graduates to help all of society to do the same. Higher education is the first societal sector to commit to become climate neutral. In addition, over thirty-five student organizations have formed the Energy Action Coalition involving nearly a million students in advocating for federal and state policy and campus actions for clean energy and actions to avoid catastrophic climate disruption.

Frank Rhodes, former president of Cornell University, suggests that the concept of sustainability offers "a new foundation for the liberal arts and sciences." The students must take advantage of and further push schools to provide them with the right education that will help them excel in a clean green economy. Indeed, humanity is depending on us to get this right.

Anthony D. Cortese is the President of Second Nature and a co-organizer of the American College & University Presidents' Climate Commitment. He is co-founder of the Association for the Advancement of Sustainability in Higher Education and co-founder and co-coordinator of the Higher Education Associations Sustainability Consortium. He was formerly the Commissioner of the Massachusetts Department of Environmental Protection and the first Dean of Environmental Programs at Tufts University. He has a B.S. and M.S. from Tufts University and a doctorate from the Harvard School of Public Health.

Second Nature

Second Nature's mission is to accelerate movement toward a sustainable future by serving and supporting senior college and university leaders in making healthy, just, and sustainable living the foundation of all learning and practice in higher education. Since its founding in Boston in 1993 by Dr. Anthony D. Cortese, Senator John F. Kerry (D-MA), Teresa Heinz Kerry, Bruce Droste, and others, Second Nature has worked with over 4,000 faculty members and administrators at more than 500 colleges and universities to help make the principles of sustainability fundamental to every aspect of higher education. Its successes include advancing Education for Sustainability (EFS) networks at the state, regional, and national levels.

INNOVATION AND COLLABORATION: THE WAY TO A CLEAN ENERGY ECONOMY

by Juliana Williams

We are at the beginning of a beautiful transition, from powering our society on extraction and exploitation to powering it with innovation and collaboration. But because we are in the midst of this transition, no one really knows how to do it yet. There is no blueprint for building a green economy. And this is great news for young people. We may not have the business experience of older generations, but we are also not limited by previous expectations of how things are done. We have immense potential to create our own opportunities.

My own experience with the new economy began in 2004, during my first year of college. At that point, the American public was focused on Iraq, swift-boating, and moral values. Energy just wasn't a major issue. I attended Whitman College in Washington State, and no colleges or universities in the state used renewable energy. It was a non-starter, even in the Northwest.

After a field trip one day to the Stateline Wind Farm 30 miles from campus, I was hooked. Clean energy is such an elegant solution with multiple benefits to society. Besides, the geek in me simply thought the technology was really cool. When I began organizing to get my school to purchase renewable energy, I found myself needing to explain why using renewable energy was a good idea. This was before Katrina, before *An Inconvenient Truth,* before the public cared about clean energy. Within a few months, Whitman became the first school in the state to purchase renewable energy.

Today, the public understands the economic, security, and health benefits of clean energy. In turn, we can spend less time convincing decision makers that a green economy is a good thing and spend more time making it happen.

The trick to making the green economy a reality is innovation. By this I don't mean just technological innovation, but also nontraditional partnerships, creative business models, and new approaches to engaging the public. Although green concepts have previously been considered the domain of environmentalists, they are increasingly being adopted by other parts of society as profitable and beneficial. One example of building nontraditional partnerships comes from Iowa, where I worked for the Sierra Student Coalition. Known primarily for its abundance of corn, Iowa is also home to many high-caliber colleges and universities. One result of this is that students come to the state from all over the Midwest, particularly from Chicago, Madison, and Minneapolis. However, there were few transportation options available to Iowa—plane flights are usually too expensive to be worth such a short distance, but driving takes 4 to 8 hours.

Beginning a year ago, folks in Iowa began advocating for passenger rail service to connect Iowa to the Midwest High Speed Rail network. After building broad support from local business partnerships, road builders, farmers, labor unions, students, environmental groups, and members of Congress, the State of Iowa approved funding to begin construction of a passenger rail line leading to Chicago. The glue that held this campaign together was the work of grassroots organizers reaching out to diverse groups, all of whom benefit from the project.

In order to bring in support from nontraditional groups, you need to have a model or project that will work, especially in the current economic climate. Energy efficiency is the largest untapped source of energy in this country, and young people are mobilizing in truly innovative ways to harness its potential. In Minnesota, students in the Twin Cities are developing a project called Cooperative Energy Futures, which is a community-based energy-efficiency cooperative. What that means is that homeowners from across a neighborhood pool together their resources to fund energy audits and retrofits. The homeowners commit to paying the initial level of their electricity bills, and the savings go back to the community to fund upgrades for other homes. Similarly, folks in Washington, D.C., have used this approach to place solar panels on homes, which will help cut energy use by 25 percent.

While the public supports clean energy, many people don't know where to start to make a difference. One exciting way to engage members of a community, and even an entire state, is to work through the community colleges. Although they tend to receive less recognition than four-year colleges and universities, community colleges provide a crucial link between the local economy and resources for the green economy: they can be a training ground for local green jobs. Several years ago, Iowa Lakes Community College pushed for federal funding to start its Wind Energy and Technology Program. This track trains students to become wind turbine engineers, familiar with installing and maintaining the turbines. This program not only produces graduates highly skilled in a booming field in need of more employees, but it also gives the state a workforce that's able to expand its wind industry. As a result of the skilled workforce, Iowa has been able to secure contracts from wind turbine manufacturers to build plants in the state, which then creates an even higher demand for workers.

While the examples above are only a few cases out of thousands of innovative approaches to building the clean energy economy, they all stemmed from the initiative of a few individuals who wanted to start something big. Whether you want to create job opportunities for yourself and your community, transition to clean energy, or promote cutting-edge technology, remember that innovation comes in many forms. By looking for new opportunities, partnerships, and models, we can not only switch to clean energy, but also strengthen the social fabric of our country. All it takes is for you to start.

Juliana Williams is a youth organizer and writer focused on the transition to a clean energy economy. She graduated from Whitman College in 2007 with a degree in geology and is currently attending the University of Maryland pursuing a Master's in Public Policy, with a concentration on energy issues. She became involved with the Sierra Student Coalition (SSC) in college and began organizing around clean energy initiatives in the Northwest. Through the SSC, she attended the U.N. climate negotiations in Montreal in 2005 and became involved with the Energy Action Coalition. Following graduation, she moved to Iowa to work as the SSC's Great Plains organizer, supporting students in five states in the Midwest working on energy issues. After living in Iowa, Juliana worked as a fellow at the Breakthrough Institute, researching the factors that make clean energy cheap and the policies that drive them. Juliana is an experienced trainer in grassroots organizing and is a contributor to several blogs, including It's Getting Hot in Here, WattHead, *and* Breakthrough Generation.

MY JOURNEY: FROM ILLNESS TO A GREEN CAREER

by Heather Henriksen, Director
Harvard University's Office for Sustainability

Eight years ago I was diagnosed with mercury poisoning from a decade of substantial fish consumption. This experience was my personal "wakeup call" to the dangerous impact of everyday toxins on public health. I quickly saw the need to implement policies to reduce this health risk and address broader contributing environmental problems. Having spent fifteen years working in the private and nonprofit sectors, I sought and found mentors in the environmental policy arena who helped me leverage my business background to make a positive impact on the environment.

I volunteered with the Natural Resources Defense Council (NRDC) and Environmental Entrepreneurs (E2), a national group of business people who seek to protect the environment while increasing economic prosperity. I joined in E2's work of bipartisan advocacy for the adoption of sound environmental policy at the local, state, and national levels. This work introduced me to leading scientists, policy makers, and business leaders, who inspired me to further my education. I decided to pursue a Masters in Public Administration (with a focus on energy and environmental policy) at the Harvard Kennedy School (HKS). While at HKS, I helped lead a student push for a greenhouse gas reduction commitment. After serving on the Harvard University Task Force on Greenhouse Gas Emissions—along with talented faculty members, administrators, and 3 other students—I was asked to lead Harvard's Office for Sustainability.

This Office consists of 20 dedicated sustainability professionals who work with Harvard's ten schools and numerous units to green our campus operations. Our team is passionately committed to finding environmentally sound solutions to how we conduct business and live our lives. We work actively with the University's leaders in the fields of behavior, public health, geology, environmental policy, engineering, and many others to translate the knowledge this University produces into concrete action on campus.

My current focus is on implementing Harvard's voluntary greenhouse gas (GHG) reduction goal of reducing emissions 30 percent below 2006 levels by 2016, including growth. This aggressive goal presents many issues in an institution as big as Harvard: how to identify and support energy conservation measures, how to further lower the GHG intensity of Harvard's energy supply, how to imbue sustainability into the campus culture, how to structure and implement a life-cycle costing calculator that provides building operators with the most useful set of financial metrics, and how to communicate all of these efforts across the campus and to many audiences—students, faculty, staff, and alumni members. Each of these facets, and more, has led me to engage with a different group of professionals: building managers, power plant operators, student life coordinators, financial deans, professors, communications professionals, human resource personnel, and others. Harvard could not possibly make progress on its goals without the buy-in, support, and ideas of hundreds of people across the University. My team is dedicated to organizing these various constituencies in order to drive our sustainability success.

When I reflect on my advocacy work with E2, my study of environmental and energy policy, and my current work on Harvard's sustainability efforts, I am grateful that my profound personal experience with mercury poisoning put me on such a challenging and fulfilling career path. Now, I have a dream job, and I work to help the environment every day. Anyone else who is driven by this same passion should take heart, because sustainability positions are opening in every field, and opportunities for life-changing careers abound.

In addition, the opportunities are broader still. As Harvard's sustainability efforts illustrate, for every person who makes the switch to become a full-time sustainability leader, we need 100 or even 200 people who bring that same passion to reforming the systems they touch in their everyday jobs. Just as we do at Harvard, the nation and the world will rely on a diversity of roles to drive down energy usage and greenhouse gas emissions. We need governments to send the appropriate market signals, businesses to respond to them, universities and entrepreneurs to innovate new solutions, and venture capitalists to fund them. Within each of these organizations, in turn, there will be a handful of leaders who may not have changed their lives or careers, but who can make dramatic changes in their own sphere. Just as at Harvard, these individuals are the key to our environmental progress.

In short, the "Green Jobs for a New Economy" that you seek will be found in a multitude of areas. They may not have the word "sustainability" in the title, but they will all require new learning, new energy, and new skills. Most important, they will all contribute to your own fulfillment and help solve the pressing environmental problems that threaten our health and prosperity.

Heather Henriksen is the Director of the Office for Sustainability at Harvard University. She holds a Master's in Public Administration, with a focus on energy and environment from the Harvard Kennedy School (HKS). Since 2003, Heather has been a partner of Environmental Entrepreneurs (E2), a national community of businesspeople lobbying for environmental policies that help build economic prosperity. E2 is affiliated with the Natural Resources Defense Council. Prior to graduate school, Heather was Director of Corporate Marketing & Business Development at Time Warner and Assistant Director of Development at Stanford University Law School. She currently serves on the Board of Trustees of the Phillips Brooks House Association, the Harvard undergraduate social service organization, and on Secretary Napolitano's Sustainability and Efficiency Task Force, Department of Homeland Security. She holds a B.A. from Tulane University.

MAKING SUSTAINABILITY SUSTAINABLE

by Sarah Boll

To understand the importance of sustainability in today's workplace, it is necessary to define what sustainability really means and to whom it pertains. Does it mean a company's sustainability—the ability to continue to grow and expand its business? Does it mean the sustainability of the workforce—those individuals who rely on their jobs to support families and in turn stimulate the economy? Or does it mean the sustainability of the world supporting both the business and the worker?

As all pervasive as the word sustainability has become, it still means different things to different people, and even those working in the area of sustainability have varying definitions of the word. To me, sustainability means protecting the world, the businesses, and the people, because without a holistic approach there is always a losing side. You cannot tell a mother of 3 children that she can only use the resources of one person. Instead, you have to provide the education and opportunities that enable that mother to slowly step down off society's current over-scheduled, super-convenient cliff and begin to change her behavior as a consumer and citizen of the world. There's no question that it takes patience, solid facts, firm steps, and an incredible amount of persistence to change someone's habits in the jam-packed world that has been built around the idea of convenience.

It also takes some serious candidness. Often, those of us who are working toward a more sustainable planet "sell" sustainable ideas and actions to businesses and workers by making them sound so easy that it would actually be harder not to do them (or at least as easy and convenient as whatever habit we are trying to compete with). In some cases this may be true, such as supplying a recycling bin that is closer to work areas than trash bins. But by using this sales pitch, we are selling ourselves and our goals short. Changing the habits of a community, the nation, and the world is not easy, but even harder is changing the underlying mindsets that created the behaviors in the first place.

Is it good enough to make recycling more convenient only in the workplace? If faced with a more time-consuming process at home, will someone who recycles at work simply throw their can or bottle into the trash can in their kitchen? Perhaps we should be going after the underlying understanding that makes it an action of thought and value rather than convenience. What we need to change is not the isolated behaviors in certain areas but rather the mindset of our society. This means altering the viewpoints of businesses and the people in them that ultimately can make the necessary impact on our world.

Anyone who has run an education campaign on sustainability can tell you that it is much more difficult than simply changing a light bulb. In most communities, trying to increase sustainability is a much harder task. After a basic awareness campaign, handing out recycling bins and recycled content paper, and installing technologies (often completely behind the scenes), the next step is get folks to reduce their water and energy consumption, and, in some cases, to produce less waste.

After these small but important "first-step" habitual changes and with the growing "green" technical revolution, I believe it is time to tackle the harder objectives and go after the fundamental changes required in the mindset of our society. We need to shift away from being consumers and disposers and instead become creators and builders of permanent and lasting things and ideas.

Thanks in a large part to the same societal choices that led to the polluted land, sea, and air all around us, we now find ourselves asking hard questions and seeking major changes in both government and business. I believe it is time for the sustainability professionals to get on the bandwagon. It's time to go after the harder issues, to make a case for intense education and outreach campaigns to promote the underlying ideas of sustainable living, even if one cannot track the results on a spreadsheet.

From my perspective on promoting sustainability in a very dense urban setting, it is clear that there will be different solutions in each social environment. Rural communities have space and more opportunity to build their programs and spaces from the ground up but may experience a lack of service providers and resources, whereas urban communities have a surplus of the latter, but it is much harder to get into spaces and programs at the design stage. Because of these differences, urban communities may have to rely more on education and changing the habits of the people in the social environment, rather than changing the environment around the people. In both critical situations, outreach and education are important to meeting the goal of fundamental change in the way people make their lifestyle choices.

The definition of sustain is to support, hold, or bear up from below or to bear the weight of, as a structure (*Random House Unabridged Dictionary,* 2nd Edition). If we expect our planet to sustain life, including ours, it is time to start making fundamental changes along with the easy and convenient ones we have been making in the area of sustainability. The disposable, super-convenient world we have created needs to be reassessed, values refocused on quality rather than quantity, and priorities pointed toward a life full of lasting rewards rather than materialistic ones. It is time for the professionals in sustainability to start standing out rather than trying to blend into life as we know it.

Sarah Boll has a bachelor's degree in biology from Tulane and a master's degree in environmental protection and management from the University of Edinburgh. For the past two years, she has been a member of the Office of Energy and Sustainability at NYU, working on recycling and energy reduction projects as well as basic education and outreach on all areas of sustainability.

AT A CROSSROADS

by Tony Ash, Director of Operations, and Jennifer Berry,
Public & Strategic Relations, Earth911.com

As professionals in the "green" industry, we've seen a tremendous upswing in companies' interest in providing environmentally conscious products and services—whether it's by creating a more sustainable supply line, taking responsibility for their products at their end of life, or creating eco-friendly initiatives within their business operations. We see this as a rapidly increasing trend that shows no signs of slowing, even considering current economic conditions. Though companies are cutting budgets, they are still investing in environmental initiatives. In fact, a survey by the American Marketing Association and Fleishman-Hillard, Inc., revealed that 58 percent of corporate marketers and communicators believe their organizations will *increase* their involvement in environmental sustainability initiatives during the next two to three years.

We're at a fascinating turning point in the business world, where companies are beginning to realize that investing in environmental efficiency and sustainability initiatives will actually *add* to their bottom line—both through cost savings and by increasing revenue as consumers consciously turn to their eco-friendly products. These changes are a result of the market trend that consumers *expect* companies to be as "green" as possible and will continue to support businesses' sustainability efforts. In fact, according to a study commissioned by Green Seal and EnviroMedia Social Marketing, 4 out of 5 people say they are still buying green products and services, which sometimes cost more, even in the midst of a U.S. recession.

How We Personally Connect

We work to promote recycling and reuse both as an introductory step to helping people understand what they can do on an individual, local level to help the environment and as part of a comprehensive, multifaceted way of life that is environmentally sustainable. Our primary focus in sustainability is connecting people with the products they buy in a meaningful way, which translates into reduced waste, a heightened awareness about the concept of reuse, and increased recycling (or proper disposal of) products at their end of life.

This focus is of particular interest when it applies to "hazardous" waste. For many people, it's easy to recycle a newspaper or aluminum can. But what do you do with an old television or the leftover paint from your last home improvement effort? We know that substances that require proper disposal, such as used motor oil, pesticides, and electronic waste, will always exist. However, we can mitigate the risks associated with these products by ensuring they are not dumped or poured down a drain where they don't belong.

Being involved in nurturing awareness around these issues adds purpose and a personal connection to our work that would be difficult to replicate outside of the sustainability sphere. Knowing that the current and future state of our environment's health depends a great deal on ensuring that products like these are sent where they can be responsibly processed (i.e., *not* the landfill), it's incredibly fulfilling to be involved with these issues directly and know you have an impact. Through our work promoting environmentally sound disposal methods, we are helping to preserve the integrity of our ecosystems; minimize potential contamination from substances like mercury, lead, and other toxins; and take advantage of readily available materials for reuse—reducing our reliance on the virgin materials and excess energy and resources needed to harvest them.

Future Hopes

The transition of the corporate mindset to place more emphasis on green initiatives, along with an increase in consumer demand for eco-oriented products and spending by the government to encourage green jobs, has resulted in a "perfect storm" for sustainability: both a *desire* and a *need* for a workforce that can implement, enhance, and carry out a new wave of environmentally focused products and services.

In this line of thought, the emergence of the "Next Industrial Revolution" (a concept developed by William McDonough and Michael Braungart in their book, *Cradle-to-Cradle*) is creating a wholly new—and required—skill and knowledge set. Involvement in this industry now, while it's still young and growing, will be a key factor in determining employees' future marketability and value.

To put this in perspective, ten to twenty years ago, an understanding of the computer was not required in the workplace. Moving forward, we hope to see experience and skills aligned with sustainability concepts become just as necessary as using a keyboard. Our hope is that, one day, the term "sustainability" is no longer needed, as it becomes a seamless part of the core of future societies—inherent in all aspects of both personal and professional life.

Tony Ash brings a diverse and expansive background to Earth911.com. With a focus on technology issues, Tony has worked with many small businesses and nonprofits in designing and implementing IT systems that promote productivity and bridge the digital divide. Tony is also an artist and creative aspirationist, graduating magna cum laude with a B.F.A. in intermedia video from Arizona State University. He builds interactive software-driven sculpture and has also taught Digital Multimedia for the Film School at Scottsdale Community College. A vegan since 1999, Tony maintains a vibrant vegetable garden and has been engaged with and driven by environmental issues in every aspect of his own life for more than a decade.

Jennifer Berry works in public relations, social media, sales, and editorial for Earth911.com. Joining the team in 2008, she utilizes her love for writing and communication in a number of facets to support the company's growth and reach into new arenas. Outside of work, Jennifer enjoys an active, green lifestyle that includes swimming, cycling, hiking, and being vegan. After completing a double major in psychology and public relations from Baylor University, Jennifer continues to explore the relationship between people and the environment, both at work and at home.

Earth911.com

Earth911.com is an environmental services company that addresses product end-of-life solutions for businesses and consumers.

GREENING THE "QUARTERLIFE" CRISIS

by Rachel Gutter, Director of the Education Sector
U.S. Green Building Council (USGBC)

I graduated from college without a plan. I wasn't ready to go to grad school or make any binding career decisions. I had majored in English because writing seemed like a useful skill for any profession and because I wanted to leave my options open. Like many children of baby boomers, I felt entitled to like my job. I wasn't willing to settle for just any career.

So I decided to wander.

I should point out that the act of wandering is somewhat antithetical to my nature. I'm more of a straightest-distance-between-two-points-is-a-line kind of girl. But I felt certain that if I held out, the right opportunity would come along. Two years out of college I was self-employed as a private tutor and was coaching ice skating and teaching Sunday school. I loved my many jobs, and I especially loved that most days my job didn't start until 3 in the afternoon. My parents found less to love in my hodgepodge work, and, like all loving parents who have just shelled out a small fortune for their child's education, they were getting a little nervous about my lack of direction. What if I wandered forever? What if I never actualized my potential?

Books started showing up in my care packages with titles like *Now What?* and *Conquering Your Quarterlife Crisis.* I took the hint.

I packed my car and drove cross-country to be a magazine editor in California. When that didn't work out, I packed my car and moved to New Mexico to work on a curriculum development project. When that fell through, I stumbled upon a job as the design director for an interior architecture firm in Albuquerque, New Mexico.

My first assignment was to "green" our product library. My passion for recycled aluminum tile, cork flooring, and low VOC paint was ignited. I had always been intrigued by design, but adding the sustainability angle satisfied the part of me that wanted my job to involve doing the right thing.

In 2006, my boss and I made a last-minute decision to attend the U.S. Green Building Council (USGBC) Greenbuild International Conference. We drove through a snowstorm to get to Denver and scored the only remaining hotel room in the city. I noted in my conference program a session on the upcoming launch of the USGBC's LEED for Schools Green Building Rating System. Green buildings for kids? It sounded right up my alley.

After the session, I waited patiently to talk to one of the presenters, Lindsay, who ran the Green Schools program at USGBC.

"My name is Rachel Gutter," I said, shaking her hand, "I want to work for you."

We exchanged business cards, and I hurried out of the room and speed-dialed my parents. "Mom," I said when she picked up the phone, "I figured out what I want to do with my life."

After the third time of "accidentally" running into Lindsay in the 1.2-million square foot convention center, she confided that she was leaving USGBC in six months and heading to grad school.

"Great," I told her, "What do I need to do to get your job?"

The next few months were a resume-cramming blur. I sought out every networking and educational opportunity I could find. I flew to Ohio to take a LEED workshop. Though I could have taken a course closer to home, the Ohio course was being taught by the chair of the LEED for Schools Committee. Guess who I chatted up at lunch?

Instead of taking a winter vacation, I read the *LEED for New Construction Reference Guide* cover to cover. I attended a green schools conference in Arizona, and, when I handed Lindsay my updated resume, she mentioned that USGBC wanted to hire someone who had experience working for a school district.

The next day I called the head of the green building program for a school system in Maryland to offer my services as an unpaid intern. "When can you start?" she asked.

"Give me three weeks."

I said goodbye to my life in Albuquerque, packed up my car one last time, and drove from New Mexico to Maryland in three days flat. In order to be able to take an unpaid internship, I did something I had sworn I would never do: I moved back in with my parents.

Five months, four resumes, two interviews, and my entire life savings later, USGBC called and offered me my dream job.

I have been with USGBC for nearly three years now. The job isn't as good as I dreamed it would be—it's better! As the Director of the Education Sector, I oversee the National Green Schools Campaign and USGBC's green campus initiatives. At USGBC, the pace is fast, the people are incredibly smart, and every day is different. One day I'm helping members of Congress draft green schools legislation, and the next day I'm convincing a room full of facilities managers that greening their universities will save money while improving the health of their students, faculty, and staff members. I have traveled all over the country to meet with representatives of colleges and school districts and to speak at national conferences. I've rubbed elbows with governors and mayors, made

U.S. Green Building Council

The Washington, D.C.-based U.S. Green Building Council is committed to a prosperous and sustainable future for the nation through cost-efficient and energy-saving green buildings. With a community comprising 78 local affiliates, more than 20,000 member companies and organizations, and more than 131,000 LEED Accredited Professionals, USGBC is the driving force of an industry that is projected to soar to $60 billion by 2010.

Buildings in the United States are responsible for 39 percent of CO_2 emissions, 40 percent of energy consumption, 13 percent of water consumption, and 15 percent of GDP per year, making green building a source of significant economic and environmental opportunity. Greater building efficiency can meet 85 percent of future U.S. demand for energy, and a national commitment to green building has the potential to generate 2.5 million American jobs.

presentations to the Department of Education, and have been interviewed by reporters from *The Washington Post* and CNN.

At the ripe old age of 28, I never imagined I would have these sorts of opportunities, but there is so much room for leadership and growth in the field of sustainability. Some days I leave the office and think to myself, "How did I get so lucky?" But I didn't get lucky at all. I got inspired, I got motivated, and I got myself this job.

I guess it turns out my "quarterlife" crisis wasn't a crisis at all—it was just wandering with intention.

As the Director of the Education Sector for the U.S. Green Building Council (USGBC), Rachel Gutter works on a national level to promote and facilitate the design, construction, and operations of high performance, green schools and higher education facilities. She oversees USGBC's National Green Schools Campaign as well as the LEED for Schools Green Building Rating System®, USGBC's market-specific guidelines that recognize the unique nature and educational aspects of the design and construction of K–12 educational facilities. Rachel works closely with colleges and universities to assist them in greening their campuses. Through collaborative efforts with energy service companies, utility companies, foundations, and a variety of other organizations, Rachel is working to create green building incentives to assist the education sector in achieving their green building goals.

About the National Green Schools Campaign

The USGBC is leading the National Green Schools Campaign to put every child in a healthier, green school within a generation. Twenty percent of the nation's population spends their days in a K–12 school, and too many those schools are substandard by any measure. Green schools cost less money to operate and use substantially less energy and water. Those savings add up and put money back into the classroom. On average, green schools save $100,000 per year, which could pay for 2 new teachers, buy 100 new computers, or purchase 5,000 new textbooks.

Better performing school buildings produce better performing students and teachers. Improving indoor air quality, enhancing natural light, and promoting students' overall health and well-being leads to reduced absences and increased test scores.

Seven Steps to Landing Your Dream Job

by Rachel Gutter, U.S. Green Building Council

1. **Be willing to start at the bottom of the totem pole and work your way up.** Figure out where there are gaps in your knowledge base and/or resume and find a position that will allow you to fill them. If you can afford to take an unpaid internship at a place that will give you good access or relevant experience, do it—even if you have to live with your parents.

2. **Zero in on a few organizations or companies that most interest you and haunt their job pages.** Even in this economy, Washington, D.C., is always hiring...eventually.

3. **Find a mentor who has your dream job and wow him or her.** If your mentor is your supervisor or someone else you work with, make yourself indispensable to him/her. If you don't work with him/her, try to do extra research or a side project to show how interested you are in the work he or she does. Shadow him/her for a week.

4. **Be persistent.** Always follow up. Always check back in. Always remind them you are still interested.

5. **Do your homework.** It's not so much about the job itself, it is about the culture of the organization. If you don't like the latter, you probably won't like the former.

6. **In the first few years of your career (not necessarily your first years of work experience, but your first years of work on a career track) you should work harder than you ever have and possibly harder than you ever will.**

7. **There's a lot more to life than work and it's always important to keep that in mind, even in Washington.** There is something to be said for having an employer that values personal sustainability.

HOW TO USE THIS GREEN GUIDE

Peterson's Green Jobs for a New Economy contains a wealth of information for anyone interested in undergraduate, graduate, or training programs leading to a "green" job or career. This section details what you will find in each part of this book.

PART I: PROFESSIONAL AND SKILLED JOBS

In the first part of the book, Chapter 1 focuses on professional jobs and Chapter 2 highlights skilled jobs in ten industries that have a strong focus on environmental, economic, or social sustainability:

Agriculture	Environmental Health
Biotechnology	Natural Resources Management and Conservation
Construction	Parks, Recreation, and Tourism
Design	Policy, Administration, Analysis, and Advocacy
Energy	Transportation

Thirty different jobs, representing a variety of interests, are discussed in each chapter, and many of these jobs can be found across multiple industries.

The job categories included are projected to be in demand over the next decade, according to Career Voyages (www.careervoyages.gov), a joint effort of the U.S. Department of Labor and the U.S. Department of Education. Rankings are based on the U.S. Bureau of Labor Statistics data and projections from 2006 to 2016. In some cases, jobs were selected from the 2008−09 edition of the *Occupational Outlook Handbook,* produced by the U.S. Bureau of Labor Statistics, and publications such as *Fast Company* and the state of California's *Green Jobs Guide.* A few were selected from O*Net OnLine (http://online.onetcenter.org), sponsored by the U.S. Department of Labor/Employment and Training Administration (USDOL/ETA).

Details on industry overview, job trends, nature of the work, career paths, earning potential, education licensure, and contact information follow each job listed. Information on how the information was obtained for each of these sections—and what this data means to you as a student or job seeker—can be found at the start of chapter 1 and chapter 2.

Special Features Throughout This Guide

All of the chapters in this guide also provide full-length features that offer tips on what you can do now to make a difference for the environment, where the greenest places are to live, how to find out if a potential employer is socially responsible, and how to dress fashionably in eco-friendly clothing, including clothes made from bamboo fiber (which is actually softer than rayon!).

In addition, in shaded boxes throughout this guide, you will find useful information called "About . . ." that will help you find out what others are doing to live more eco-friendly lives and how to make your own life greener. Tips include where to recycle your old computer, cell phone, tennis balls, and even your sneakers; what to look for in environmentally sound home furnishings; why you should be careful about how you fertilize your garden and lawn; and what community colleges, colleges, and universities are doing to commit to campus sustainability.

PART II: COLLEGES AND UNION ORGANIZATIONS WITH GREAT GREEN PROGRAMS

Chapters 3 and 4 describe innovative programs in sustainability at both the undergraduate and graduate levels. Four-year institutions are highlighted in Chapter 3. Chapter 4 features two-year schools as well as information on union-training programs for a variety of "green" jobs. The programs were chosen to reflect a broad range of majors related to sustainability, all regions of the country, public and private schools, and large and small schools. The "Fast Facts" feature in each profile underscores on-campus sustainability programs, awards that schools have won, and other notable highlights of the schools' efforts to be good citizens of the local and global communities.

PART III: WORKFORCE TRAINING

Chapter 5 contains a list of the One-Stop Career Centers for training, job search, and career assistance information that are available in each of the fifty states and the District of Columbia. Under each state's name, you will find important

contact information and a brief description of the job-related training services each state offers.

PART IV: PROFILES OF SUSTAINABILITY PROGRAMS

The following is an overview of the various data-driven profiles of *Peterson's Green Jobs for a New Economy,* along with background information on the criteria used for including institutions in this profile section, and explanatory material to help users interpret details presented within the guide.

Sustainability Programs at Two-Year and Four-Year Colleges

Part IV's Profiles of Sustainability Programs contains detailed profiles of schools that responded to *Peterson's Survey of Sustainability Efforts in Higher Education* online survey. This section is organized by school type: two-year schools are listed alphabetically by state and province, followed by four-year schools listed alphabetically by state and province. The profiles contain basic information about the sustainability programs at the colleges and universities.

An outline of the profile follows. The items of information found under each section heading are defined and displayed. Any item discussed below that is omitted from an individual profile either does not apply to that particular college or university or is one for which no information was supplied. Each profile begins with a heading with the name of the institution (the college or university) and the city and state where the institution is located.

Sustainability Initiatives: This section deals with any formal sustainability initiatives the institution currently has in place. The Association for the Advancement of Sustainability in Higher Education (AASHE) is a membership organization focusing on sustainable solutions throughout the higher education community. The Talloires Declaration is an action plan signed by university administrators around the world who have committed to incorporating sustainability and environmental literacy on their campuses. The American College & University Presidents' Climate Commitment is a similar type of plan focused on institutions located within the United States. Green fees are required or optional fees imposed by the institution that are used to further campus sustainability programs.

Academics: This section lists sustainability-focused undergraduate and graduate majors and/or degree programs, courses, and lecture series, as well as nonacademic courses and programs.

Student Services and Green Events: This section includes sustainability-focused leadership roles at the institution; clubs, activities, and events with a sustainability theme; and other types of services available at the institution. On-campus organic gardens or sustainability-themed housing are examples of other types of services. Sustainability-themed housing is defined as one or more residential buildings on campus that have implemented green/sustainable initiatives, such as solar panels, water collection system, low-flow showerheads, etc.

Food: This section describes any sustainable food options that are available at the institution, such as Fair Trade coffee or vegan menu items. Fair Trade guarantees to poor farmers organized in cooperatives around the world a living wage, credit at fair prices, and long-term relationships. These payments are invested in health care, education, environmental stewardship, and economic independence.

Transportation: This section describes other transportation alternatives that may be available to students, such as public transportation and bike- or car-sharing programs.

Buildings and Grounds: This section provides information about enhanced building standards and grounds-care methods that may be employed on campus. Leadership in Energy and Environment Design (LEED) certification for existing buildings (LEED-EB) is based on operations and maintenance, occupant health, and financial return of the

initial investment in sustainability technology and strategies. It's worth noting that although many institutions may build to LEED standards, not all of them go through the formal process of obtaining certification. Water conservation devices may be any device that reduces the use of fresh water. Light pollution is excessive or inefficient light use.

Recycling: This section includes such diverse subjects as events, programs, and campus dining projects that are focused on recycling. Composting, limiting printing of materials, and trayless dining are included in the recycling alternatives found in this section.

Energy: This section deals with alternative energy sources that may be used on campus. Biomass energy comes from plants and plant-based materials; geothermal energy is generated by heat stored beneath the Earth's surface. LED lights are high-efficiency bulbs that have a relatively long, useful life. Energy-related performance contracting involves working with an energy service company that designs and installs a system based on the needs of the facility. The energy service company is paid through reduced energy bills, typically sharing the energy cost savings over a predetermined length of time, after which all of the energy savings revert back to the facility owner.

Purchasing: This section asks institutions to identify sustainable purchasing programs that may be used on campus. Generally, these are programs that have been certified to be conforming to a sustainable standard. Some more recognizable programs include Energy Star and FSC/SFI paper products.

Contact: The contact person listed here is the person at the institution designated as the sustainability communications, outreach, or education coordinator. In instances where there may not be a specific contact person at a particular institution, general contact information for the school is listed.

Data Collection Procedures

The data contained in the majority of the sustainability college profiles were collected through *Peterson's Survey of Sustainability Efforts in Higher Education* online survey from fall 2008 through winter 2009. With minor exceptions, data for those institutions that responded to the questionnaires were submitted by officials at the schools themselves. All usable information received in time for publication has been included. The omission of a particular item from a profile means that it is either not applicable to that institution or was not available or usable. Because of the extensive system of checks performed on the data collected by Peterson's, we believe that the information presented in this guide is accurate. Nonetheless, errors and omissions are possible in a data collection and processing endeavor of this scope. Also, facts and figures can suddenly change. Therefore, students should check with a specific college or university at the time of application to verify all pertinent information.

Criteria for Inclusion in This Book

Peterson's Green Jobs for a New Economy profile data covers accredited institutions in the United States, U.S. territories, and Canada that grant associate, baccalaureate, and graduate degrees. The institutions must be accredited by accrediting agencies approved by the U.S. Department of Education (USDE) or the Council for Higher Education Accreditation (CHEA) or be candidates for accreditation with an agency recognized by the USDE for its pre-accreditation category. Canadian schools may be provincially chartered instead of accredited.

PART V: APPENDIXES

The appendixes provide additional information that can help you in your search for a great green job. Appendix A: Professional Jobs by Industries is a handy tool to help you navigate the professional jobs listed in Chapter 1. Appendix B: Skilled Jobs by Industries can assist you when looking at those skilled jobs listed in Chapter 2. If you want to find out more about what a particular college or university is doing to support the environment, take a look at its environmental center or institute. Appendix C: Environmental and Energy Institutes and Centers provides the additional resource information you need to master your search for the perfect "green" degree program and/or green job or career.

PART I

PROFESSIONAL AND SKILLED JOBS

CHAPTER 1

PROFESSIONAL JOBS IN THE NEW GREEN ECONOMY

The ten industries or job clusters that are represented in this chapter have a strong focus on environmental, economic, or social sustainability. The thirty professional jobs/categories that have been selected represent a cross-section of jobs in the new green economy as represented by these industries. Most of the industries included here are traditional ones that are being transformed by the new emphasis on sustainability. Many of the jobs are also traditional jobs that have been "greened" to promote the factors that produce sustainability: efficient use of energy, renewable energy sources, and preservation and protection of the environment. Jobs also become "green" when they are performed for companies whose ultimate products promote sustainability.

ABOUT THE LISTINGS

Here's what you need to know to navigate this chapter.

How Jobs Were Selected

The jobs in this chapter have been selected to represent a variety of interests, and many of the jobs can be found across multiple industries. Jobs in engineering, science, and technology are the most prevalent in industries that deal with energy and the environment. However, jobs have been included in business, medicine, the arts, and the law to show that you don't need a science, engineering, or technology background to be part of the greening of the U.S. economy. People with many different interests and backgrounds can find meaningful employment in work that is environmentally friendly.

Each job title lists a variety of alternate job titles that come under that category. For example, a person looking for a job as an agricultural engineer might find suitable jobs with titles such as biological systems engineer, bioresource engineer, or environmental engineer.

Demand for Jobs

Job categories have been included that are projected to be in demand over the next decade. This was done by choosing "in-demand" jobs from Career Voyages (www.careervoyages.gov), a joint effort of the U.S. Department of Labor and the U.S. Department of Education. Rankings are based on the U.S. Bureau of Labor Statistics data and projections from 2006 to 2016. The Web site features industries that are projected to have a large number of new job openings or that require new skill sets because technology, sustainability, and economic incentives are changing the nature of the industry. In particular, Career Voyages contains a section on green industries and jobs in those industries. These industries are among those featured in this chapter.

Career Voyages ranks demand in two ways: fastest-growing occupations and occupations with the most openings. As much as possible, jobs for this guide were selected from the in-demand list for each industry. First, those that appear on the list of the top 50 fastest-growing occupations and/or the top 50 occupations with the most openings were selected. After that, jobs were chosen from the list of the top 50 in-demand occupations and then the list of all in-demand occupations. A good job, however, is not just one that is in high demand but one that also matches a person's interests and abilities.

In some cases, jobs were selected from the 2008–09 edition of the *Occupational Outlook Handbook,* produced by the U.S. Bureau of Labor Statistics. A few were selected from O*Net OnLine (online. onetcenter.org). O*Net is sponsored by the U.S. Department of Labor/Employment and Training Administration (USDOL/ETA).

Industry Overview

The Industry Overview section describes overall trends in the entire industry. It also explains how developments in energy and the environment are changing the industry and providing new general job opportunities. Wherever possible, information is taken from the *Career Guide to Industries,* 2008–09 edition, or the *Occupational Outlook Quarterly,* both published by the U.S. Bureau of Labor Statistics. Some information is from professional organizations.

Job Trends

The information on overall job trends is taken from the U.S. Bureau of Labor Statistics projections in the *Occupational Outlook Handbook,* Career Voyages, or the *Occupational Outlook Quarterly.*

In a few cases it comes from O*Net. Occasionally, information from professional organizations is included.

Nature of the Work

This section describes the kind of work that people in each job do. Most of the descriptive information is from the *Occupational Outlook Handbook,* although some comes from O*Net and from trade organizations or other sources. The section contains a description of the general work of the job category and a description of how this job contributes to the green economy. Industries where this job typically occurs are noted.

Career Paths

As much as possible, entry-level jobs were selected for inclusion in this guide. In this section, opportunities for advancement are noted, with a description of potential career paths for each specific job.

Earning Potential

Earning potential is given as mean hourly wage and mean annual wage where possible. Most are from 2008, as reported in the latest available *Occupational Outlook Handbook,* 2008–09 edition. In a few cases, wage data were not available in the *Occupational Outlook Handbook;* in these cases, they were taken either from O*Net, where median (rather than mean) hourly and annual wages are given, or from other sources where only a range is given.

Education/Licensure

The jobs listed in this chapter generally require a minimum bachelor's degree, followed by graduate or professional degrees, certification, or years of experience for career advancement. Information about certifications and licenses, including the names of organizations that grant them, is provided here. These organizations often offer courses or materials to help prepare for the exams as well as professional development opportunities needed to maintain certification.

For More Information

Many of the organizations listed offer accreditation, professional development opportunities, and continuing education. Some offer certifications that are respected by employers and an advantage to job seekers. Most also contain information on their Web sites about careers in the field and many have job banks. Some have links to academic institutions with programs in the discipline.

AGRICULTURE INDUSTRY

With more than 2 million workers, agriculture is one of the largest of the nation's industries in terms of employment. The industry supplies the nation—and much of the world—with food and other agricultural products. The field can be divided into two major areas, crop production and animal production, and into two subsectors, forestry and fishing.

As individual farms continue to be consolidated into agribusinesses, overall employment in agriculture is expected to decline by 8 percent by 2016, especially for small farmers and ranchers and their employees. Advances in technology, including the ability to bioengineer crops that are more resistant to disease and drought and that yield a larger harvest with fewer jobs, are contributing to the decline. On the other hand, the growing trends toward sustainable agriculture and preservation of the environment have brought developments in the industry that promise to slow the declining employment rate.

One area of particular promise is the emerging interest in producing biofuels from agricultural products—especially the conversion of corn to ethanol. The growing interest in organic farming will also provide opportunities for growth in agriculture. Over the past ten years, sales of organic food products have grown about 20 percent, and the demand for organic produce grown without

About Sustainable Agriculture

What is sustainable agriculture exactly? Isn't farming, well, green? A possible definition of sustainable agriculture is that it promotes environmental health while providing economic profitability for its practitioners who farm in a socially responsible manner.

chemicals or pesticides is expected to continue increasing. Moreover, organic products are grown mostly on smaller farms, where the decline in agricultural employment is most prominent.

Agricultural Engineer

Alternate Job Titles:

- Agricultural and Biological Engineer
- Agricultural Engineer
- Biological Systems Engineer
- Bioresource Engineer
- Environmental Engineer
- Food and Process Engineer
- Forest Engineer

The position of agricultural engineer is relatively new, but it carries great potential as new demands are made on the U.S. agriculture industry.

Job Trends

The 2008–09 *Occupational Outlook Handbook* projects employment growth for agricultural engineers at 9 percent by 2016, which is about average for all occupations. Agricultural engineering is a relatively small engineering field at present, so the percentage works out to about 300 new jobs. However, very few students are currently majoring in this specialty, and the potential exists for new applications in new areas of research and production. According to the American Society of Agricultural and Biological Engineers (ASABE), increasing world population will require ever higher yields of agricultural products that use fewer natural resources and avoid environmental harm. New uses for agricultural products, byproducts, and the waste that is generated must be developed. These demands will likely result in new career opportunities for agricultural engineers in bioprocessing, food safety, and renewable energy.

Nature of the Work

Most agricultural engineers are employed in agriculture, of course, but many also work in engineering services and with the federal government. Some conduct research; others work in production and sales. Agricultural engineers are also in demand as professors at colleges and universities.

The profession makes use of science and engineering technologies to solve problems related to the production of food, fiber, wood, and renewable fuel. The ASABE has identified specialties that encompass all the activities in which agricultural engineers are involved:

- agricultural structure design (e.g., animal housing, storage facilities, systems for handling waste products)
- aquaculture (fisheries) engineering
- biological engineering (e.g., processing biomass, remediation, environmental protection)
- food and bioprocess engineering
- forest engineering
- information and electrical technologies (e.g., bioinformatics, global positioning systems, geographic information systems) natural resource conservation and management
- nursery and greenhouse engineering
- power system and machinery design
- renewable energy and alternative energy systems development
- safety and health

Keep in mind that in this field, the development of new technology invariably leads to new specialties.

Career Paths

As agricultural engineers gain experience, they advance into supervisory positions. Some become managers. Some earn a master's in business administration (MBA) degree to prepare for high-level managerial positions.

Earning Potential

2008 mean hourly wage: $35.02; mean annual wage: $72,850

Education/Licensure

A bachelor's degree in engineering from a college or university program that is accredited by the Accreditation Board for Engineering and Technology (ABET) is the minimum requirement for becoming an agricultural engineer. The American Academy of Environmental Engineering (AAEE) partners with ABET in accrediting environmental engineering programs. Your degree may be in environmental engineering or in chemical, civil, or mechanical engineering. Many colleges and universities offer environmental engineering in the civil engineering department. Having a master's degree in environmental engineering provides job candidates with much better opportunities; earning a Ph.D. improves long-range opportunities as well.

The ASABE Web site (www.asabe.org) provides links to colleges and universities that offer programs in agricultural and biological engineering. Many of these programs are offered in the college's School of Agriculture rather than its School of Engineering. Some colleges and universities offer five-year programs culminating in a master's degree; some offer five- or six-year programs that include cooperative experience. In some cases, four-year colleges have arranged with nearby community colleges or liberal arts colleges to allow students to spend two or three years at the initial school before transferring for the last two years to complete their agricultural engineering degree.

All fifty states and the District of Columbia require engineers to be licensed as professional engineers (PE) if they serve the public directly. In most states, licensure requires that a candidate graduate from a four-year engineering program accredited by ABET, obtain four years of experience, and pass the state's exam. Many prospective engineers take the Fundamentals of Engineering portion of the exam upon graduation to become engineers in training (EIT). After obtaining appropriate work experience, they take the Principles and Practice of Engineering portion of the exam to complete their professional licensure. Most states recognize licenses from other states, provided the other state's requirements are the same or more stringent than their own. Some states also have continuing education requirements.

For More Information

Accreditation Board for Engineering and
  Technology (ABET)
111 Market Place, Suite 1050
Baltimore, Maryland 21202
410-347-7700
www.abet.org

American Society of Agricultural and Biological
  Engineers
2950 Niles Road
St. Joseph, Michigan 49085
269-429-0300
www.asabe.org

Agricultural Extension Agent

Also called an agricultural extension specialist, the agricultural extension agent provides a link between new technologies and farmers who use them.

Job Trends

According to the U.S. Bureau of Labor Statistics, the United States had 15,000 extension agents in 2006. Growth of 3–6 percent is expected through 2016, which translates into about 3,000 openings. Extension agents are employed by local, county, state, and federal governments and by universities.

Nature of the Work

The United States has more than 100 land-grant colleges—institutions designated by a state legislature or by Congress to receive the benefits of the Morrill Acts of 1862 and 1890. The original mission of these institutions, according to the first Morrill Act, was to teach agriculture, military tactics, the mechanic arts, and classical studies, so that working-class citizens could obtain a liberal, practical education. The first Act provided grants in the form of federal lands to each state for the establishment of a public institution to fulfill the act's provisions. At different times, money was appropriated through legislation (such as the second Morrill Act), but the funding provisions of these acts are no longer in effect. Each land-grant college now receives annual federal appropriations for research and extension work, provided that those funds are matched by state funds.

Land-grant colleges have a threefold mission: education, research, and extension of expertise and research results to the community. In conjunction with the U.S. Department of Agriculture, these universities support the department's agricultural extension services—a key component of the land-grant system that was originally intended to serve farmers and rural communities. As the country's population has shifted from rural areas, the extension service has spread to urban and suburban areas, but it continues to serve rural communities.

Extension agents educate homeowners and landowners about the responsible use of natural resources through the following types of programs:

- alternative energy
- composting
- lawn waste management
- recycling
- timber management
- water quality preservation

Extension agents also teach farmers and ranchers the latest methods for managing resources, improving productivity, controlling pests, and using fertilizers in environmentally safe ways. They perform the following duties:

- collect and analyze data related to agriculture and help solve problems by applying research findings
- conduct soil testing
- foster youth development through 4-H leadership provide advice on a wide variety of agricultural topics
- recruit and train community volunteers
- teach nutrition and home economics

Career Paths

Experienced extension specialists may become staff supervisors.

Earning Potential

2008 median hourly wage: $19.97; median annual wage: $41,530

Education/Licensure

A bachelor's degree is required for agricultural extension agents; in some instances a master's degree is preferred. Your degree may be in agriculture, family and consumer science, youth and community development, or education. Every state has at least one land-grant college that offers agriculture programs, but other universities offer similar curricula.

For More Information

National FFA Organization (formerly Future
    Farmers of America)
P.O. Box 68960
6060 FFA Drive
Indianapolis, Indiana 46268-0960
317-802-6060
www.ffa.org

United States Department of Agriculture
Cooperative State Research, Education, and
    Extension Service (CSREES)
1400 Independence Avenue SW, Stop 2201
Washington, D.C. 20250-2201
202-720-4423
www.csrees.usda.gov

About Green Farming Practices

The Conservation Technology Information Center and The Fertilizer Institute conducted a survey in 2008 about green farming practices, which include conservation tillage, soil nutrient management, grassed waterways, and integrated pest management. Of the 2,000 farmers who responded, more than 50 percent said they had adopted all of these practices, but the survey's funders stated that full compliance must be the goal.

Agricultural Scientist

Also known as agronomists, professionals in this field work in a variety of applications.

Job Trends

According to the 2008–09 *Occupational Outlook Handbook,* employment for agronomists is expected to increase about 9 percent by 2016, which is about average for all occupations. Job prospects are expected to be good, especially for those with advanced degrees.

Environmental concerns are expected to contribute to growth in this field. For example, agronomists are needed to work on improving soil and water quality. Insects and plant diseases constantly adapt to pesticides, so new, effective but environmentally safe pesticides are in demand. Likewise, the agriculture industry needs new methods for developing crop resistance so that lower amounts of pesticides are required in the first place. The growing interest in producing biofuels from agricultural products might also improve job opportunities in this field.

Nature of the Work

Agricultural scientists usually specialize in animal, crop, or plant science. Many agronomists work in applied research, where they study chemical and biological processes in plants and animals as a means of developing ways to improve quality and production. Some agricultural scientists manage research and development departments; others work for private-sector companies that produce and market agricultural supplies, including chemicals and equipment. Agricultural scientists also act as consultants to government and private corporations. About 14 percent work in state, local, and federal government jobs.

Agricultural scientists develop methods of improving production rates and the quality of farm crops and livestock. Their goal is to improve yield with less labor, conserve water and soil, and effectively control insects, weeds, and fungi in the safest way.

This last goal involves developing environmentally safe pesticides that can be used in lower quantities. It also involves researching ways in which crops can be made more resistant to pests and drought conditions. In cooperation with scientists in related fields, agricultural scientists are also developing agricultural products for alternate-energy production.

Career Paths

Agricultural scientists who have advanced degrees work in education, research, and management.

Earning Potential

2008 mean hourly wage: $30.82; mean annual wage: $64,110

Education/Licensure

A bachelor's degree in agricultural science or a related area such as biology, chemistry, or engineering qualifies a job seeker for some positions in applied research or product development. To conduct or direct basic research in the field, an advanced degree is required. Graduate students usually choose a specialty, such as animal science, crop science, or horticulture; undergraduate students usually do not specialize. In some ways, having general education or experience in the field rather than specializing may broaden job opportunities, since the field continues to change. Land-grant colleges and other institutions offer degrees in agricultural science, although not all offer every specialty.

Certification is voluntary. The American Society of Agronomy offers two certifications: Certified Professional Agronomist (CPAg) and Certified Crop Adviser (CCA). The CPAg requires that you obtain a degree and experience and that you pass an exam. The CCA requires that you pass two exams and gain a specified level of experience or education.

The Soil Science Society of America also offers two certifications: Certified Professional Soil Scientist (CPSS) and Certified Professional Soil Classifier (CPSC). Both require that you have a degree and working experience and that you pass two exams. Continuing education is required to maintain all certifications.

For More Information

American Society of Agronomy*
677 S. Segoe Road
Madison, Wisconsin 53711-1086
608-273-8080
608-273-8085 (certification information)
www.agronomy.org

Crop Science Society of America*
677 S. Segoe Road
Madison, Wisconsin 53711-1086
608-273-8080
608-273-8085 (certification information)
www.crops.org

National FFA Organization (formerly Future Farmers of America)
P.O. Box 68960
6060 FFA Drive
Indianapolis, Indiana 46268-0960
317-802-6060
www.ffa.org

Soil Science Society of America*
677 S. Segoe Road
Madison, Wisconsin 53711-1086
608-273-8080
608-273-8085 (certification information)
www.soils.org

USDA Living Science
Purdue University
1140 Agricultural Administration Building
West Lafayette, Indiana 47907-1140
765-494-8392
www.agriculture.purdue.edu/USDA/careers

---

*The organizations noted with an asterisk are autonomous but work closely together and share headquarters and office staff.

BIOTECHNOLOGY INDUSTRY

The biotechnology industry is an emerging industry with consequent rapid growth. Entrepreneurs are founding biotechnology start-ups and new applications are being developed and rushed to market. New green technologies such as converting ethanol to fuel will increase the number of jobs, and there are often more jobs available than workers. The projected number of jobs exceeds the number of persons currently enrolled in training programs.

Chemical Engineer

Alternate Job Titles:

- Analytical Chemist
- Biochemical Engineer
- Chemical Process Engineer
- Environmental Engineer
- Process Engineer

All engineering specialties project good job opportunities in the green economy.

Job Trends

According to the *Occupational Outlook Handbook,* there are currently about 31,000 chemical engineers, and the number of jobs is projected to grow by 8 percent by 2016. The Career Voyages Web site (www.careervoyages.gov) lists chemical engineering as an in-demand occupation. While employment in chemical manufacturing is expected to decline, growth is expected in energy research and the emerging biotechnology and nanotechnology industries. The best manufacturing opportunities will be in pharmaceuticals.

Nature of the Work

Chemical engineers, individuals trained in chemistry, engineering principles, physics, and mathematics, use these principles to design processes and equipment to manufacture biochemicals and other chemicals on a large scale. Chemical engineers may also work on problems associated with chemical use and treatment of the by-products of production processes. They may specialize in a particular process or a production of a specific product. They must

> **About Biotech in Agriculture**
>
> Arcadia Biosciences is an example of a biotech company working to find solutions to world hunger. It is developing a nitrogen-efficient sorghum and has developed herbicide-tolerant wheat, longer-lasting tomatoes, and a rice crop that will grow well in Africa's drought conditions. Among its partners are the U.S. Agency for International Development, Advanta, DuPont, and ScottsMiracle Gro (for nitrogen-efficient grass).

consider how the manufacturing process affects the environment and the health and safety of workers. In addition to biotechnology and chemical manufacturing, chemical engineers work in industries that produce energy, electronics, paper, and other products.

Career Paths

As chemical engineers gain experience, they become specialists and advance into positions where they supervise a team of engineers and other staff members. Some chemical engineers eventually become managers or move into sales jobs where their technical background is particularly useful. Some go on to earn a master's in business administration (MBA) degree or graduate degrees in engineering to prepare them for high-level managerial and executive positions in industry and government.

Earning Potential

2008 mean hourly wage: $42.67; mean annual wage: $88,760

Education/Licensure

For entry-level positions, a bachelor's degree in engineering from a college or university program that is accredited by the Accreditation Board for Engineering and Technology (ABET) is required. In some cases, engineers with degrees in one type of engineering may qualify for jobs in other areas of engineering.

Some colleges and universities offer five-year programs that culminate in a master's degree. Some offer five- or six-year programs that include coop-erative experience. Some four-year schools have arrangements with community colleges or liberal arts colleges that allow students to spend two or three years at the initial school and transfer for the last two years to the engineering school to com-plete their engineering degree.

All fifty states as well as the District of Columbia require engineers to be licensed as professional engineers (PE) if they serve the public directly. In most states, licensure requires graduation from a four-year engineering program accredited by ABET, four years of experience, and passing the state exam. Many engineers take the Fundamentals of Engineering portion of the exam upon gradu-ation. They are then engineers in training (EIT). After obtaining appropriate work experience, they take the Principles and Practice of Engineering exam to complete their professional license. Most states recognize licenses from other states as long as the requirements are the same or more stringent. Some states have continuing education requirements.

For More Information

Accreditation Board for Engineering and
    Technology (ABET)
111 Market Place, Suite 1050
Baltimore, Maryland 21202
410-347-7700
www.abet.org

American Chemical Society (ACS)
Education Division, Career Publications
1155 16th Street NW
Washington, D.C. 20036
800-227-5558 (toll-free)
http://portal.acs.org/portal/acs/corg/content

About Cleaning Products

Check the cleaning products aisle of the supermarket for environmental friendly products like Green Works by Clorox, Nature's Source by S.C. Johnson & Son, and Seventh Generation by Seventh Generation, Inc.

American Institute of Chemical Engineers
    (AIChE)
3 Park Avenue
New York, NY 10016-5991
800-242-4363 (toll-free)
www.aiche.org

Microbiologist

Alternate Job Titles:

- Bacteriologist
- Bioprocessing Engineer
- Clinical Lab Technician
- Clinical Medical Technician
- Industrial Microbiologist
- Quality Assurance Technician
  Microbiologists have opportunities in a
  variety of job areas.

Job Trends

According to the *Occupational Outlook Handbook*, there are currently 17,000 microbiologists, and the need is expected to increase about 11 percent by 2016. This is about average for all occupations. The Career Voyages Web site lists this as one of the in-demand occupations.

Nature of the Work

About 60 percent of microbiologists work in scien-tific research and development and pharmaceutical manufacturing. Another 30 percent work in federal and state government, and the remainder work in colleges and universities.

Microbiologists may specialize in areas such as agricultural, food, environmental, or indus-trial microbiology. They may also specialize in a number of medically related areas, including public health. Microbiologists carry out analyses of soil, water, air, and other types of samples, and they participate in quality assurance by evaluating analytical and sampling methods, evaluating data, and developing protocols.

Career Paths

After gaining experience, microbiologists have opportunities to administer programs for testing.

> ### About Biotech in Your Garden
> Biotech is not just bioengineered food. That organic fertilizer you use in your garden may have been bioengineered. Check out products like Dr. Earth's line of organic plant fertilizers.

They may also move into scientific managerial positions or other positions such as sales.

Earning Potential

2008 mean hourly wage: $33.73; mean annual wage: $70,150

Education/Licensure

The minimum is a bachelor's degree, which is adequate for jobs in testing, inspection, or sales or as a laboratory technician or research assistant. Most positions in research require a master's or doctoral degree. Clinical laboratory science training is helpful for medically related jobs and jobs in biotech companies. For certain government positions, specialized certifications are required and may be obtained through course work and passing required exams. For example, for the federal government position of Certified Drinking Water Inspector, the Safe Drinking Water Act certification is required.

For More Information

American Institute of Biological Sciences
1444 I Street NW, Suite 200
Washington, D.C. 20005
202-628-1500
www.aibs.org

American Society for Microbiology
1752 N Street NW
Washington, D.C. 20036
202-737-3600
www.asm.org

Biotechnology Institute
2000 North 14th Street, Suite 700
Arlington, Virginia 22201
703-248-8681
www.biotechinstitute.org

Society for Industrial Microbiology
3929 Old See Highway
Suite 92A
Fairfax, Virginia 22030-2421
703-691-3357
www.simhq.org

Technical and Scientific Sales Representative

Alternate Job Titles:

- Account Manager
- Product Line Sales Manager

Sales representatives in technical and scientific sales need knowledge of the field as well as the product.

Job Trends

In 2006, there were about 2 million wholesale sales representatives. Of these, about 21 percent were in scientific and technical product sales, according to the *Occupational Outlook Handbook*. So even though growth in this occupation is projected to be about average, 12 percent by 2016, the increase will result in about 51,000 new jobs in technical sales. The Career Voyages Web site lists this as one of the top 50 in-demand occupations.

Nature of the Work

For scientific and technical sales, knowledge of biology, chemistry, engineering, or electronics is required, depending on the product. Knowledge of marketing principles and customer service is important. Familiarity with computer software, such as customer relationship management software, is also necessary. In addition to a technical background, persons in this occupation must enjoy working with people and have a personality that enables them to interact well with customers. Sales representatives may work inside a company, taking orders and resolving customer problems, or they may work outside, going out to meet prospective customers. Some positions require extensive travel.

Technical and scientific sale representatives sell products for manufacturers or wholesalers.

Products include agricultural products, pharmaceuticals, and mechanical or electrical equipment. Technical sales representatives also work in many other industries, including the advanced manufacturing, aerospace, energy, geospatial technologies, health care, information technology, and nanotechnology industries.

Career Paths

Promotions to sales supervisor or district manager are usually based on sales performance. Some people move on to careers in marketing or advertising.

Earning Potential

2008 mean hourly wage: $38.11; mean annual wage: $79,260

Education/Licensure

The minimum educational requirement for technical sales is two years of postsecondary education. However, about half of those currently in the occupation have bachelor's degrees or higher. A bachelor's degree is especially important in scientific and technical sales. Some manufacturer's representatives who have their own independent companies also hold master's degrees in business administration. On-the-job training is particularly important in this occupation.

Two certifications are available from the Manufacturers' Representatives Education Research Foundation: Certified Professional Manufacturers' Representative (CPMR) and Certified Sales Professional (CSP). Certification requires completing a training program and passing an exam.

For More Information

Manufacturers' Agents National Association (MANA)
16 A Journey, Suite 200
Aliso Viejo, California 92656-3317
949-859-4040
www.manaonline.org

Manufacturers' Representatives Educational Research Foundation (MRERF)
8329 Cole Street
Arvada, Colorado 80005
303-463-1801
www.mrerf.org

CONSTRUCTION INDUSTRY

The *Occupational Outlook Handbook* reports that 7.7 million people were employed in the construction industry in 2006. The number of jobs is predicted to increase 10.2 percent for a total of 8.5 million workers by 2016. Overall, experienced workers should have excellent job opportunities with relatively high wages.

Heavy construction including roads, bridges, and tunnels as well as repairs to existing highways and bridges is expected to generate most of the demand for construction workers. However, green nonresidential and residential building should experience an increase in demand, even though construction of new residential and commercial buildings overall is expected to slow. In an April 2009 summary, the U.S. Green Building Council reported that green building is expected to more than double by 2013. Major growth in nonresidential green building is expected in the education, office, and health-care sectors as well as increased demand in the government, industrial, hospitality, and retail sectors. Government initiatives along with increased interest in residential green building are encouraging energy-efficient, environmentally sustainable green construction. Remodeling of existing structures, especially to retrofit them as green buildings, is expected to generate additional demand for construction workers.

Civil Engineer

Alternate Job Titles:

- Aerospace Engineer
- Architectural Engineer
- Environmental Engineer
- Geotechnical Engineer

- Ocean/Marine Engineer
- Structural Engineer
- Traffic Engineer
- Transportation Engineer

This field will benefit from the 2009 federal stimulus package that includes funding for infrastructure repair and new construction.

Job Trends

The Career Voyages Web site ranks civil engineering as number 21 on the list of the top 50 in-demand occupations requiring at least a bachelor's degree. Almost 12,000 openings are expected by 2016. According to the *Occupational Outlook Handbook,* employment in civil engineering is expected to grow by 18 percent. This is much greater than the average for all occupations. Environmental regulations and considerations increase the demand by requiring more engineers to expand existing transportation systems or to design and build new systems. Engineers are also needed to repair existing roads and bridges and design and build new water supply and wastewater treatment systems.

Nature of the Work

According to the *Occupational Outlook Handbook,* about half of all civil engineers are employed in architectural, engineering, and related services. About a third work in local, state, and federal government, and about 10 percent work in non-residential construction. The remainder works in education, research, and other areas.

Civil engineers have a variety of skills and an extensive knowledge base. They

- plan, design, and oversee the construction of buildings, road, bridges, tunnels, dams, railroads, airports, harbors, channels, water supply systems, sewer systems, power plants, pipelines, and irrigation systems and are involved in repairs and renovations to these structures.
- have to consider in planning and designing these structures potential hazards that may damage the structure, such as earthquakes,

hurricanes, tornadoes, and the force of waves.
- estimate costs and project the lifetime of the project.
- must be aware of government regulations and ensure that the project is in compliance.
- evaluate the impact the project may have on the environment, particularly water runoff and contamination.

Civil engineers often specialize. Some of the major specializations include architectural engineering, structural engineering, construction, and geotechnical engineering. Those who specialize in water resources work on water and wastewater systems. Transportation or traffic engineers work in the transportation industry. Environmental engineers are concerned with preventing pollution and remediation of existing pollution hazards. Some civil engineers specialize in ocean or marine engineering, and others specialize in air and space engineering.

Career Path

As civil engineers gain experience, they become specialists and advance into positions where they supervise a team of engineers and other staff members. Some eventually become managers. Some go on to earn an MBA degree to prepare them for high-level managerial and executive positions.

Earning Potential

2008 mean hourly wage: $37.77; mean annual wage: $78,560

Education/Licensure

For entry-level positions, a bachelor's degree in engineering from a college or university program that is accredited by the Accreditation Board for Engineering and Technology (ABET) is required. In some cases, engineers with degrees in one type of engineering may qualify for jobs in other areas

---

About Green Buildings

The Pittsburgh area has the greatest number of certified green buildings in the nation, according to the U.S. Green Building Council.

---

of engineering. Most colleges and universities offer transportation engineering as a specialty in civil engineering.

Some colleges and universities offer five-year programs that culminate in a master's degree. Some offer five- or six-year programs that include cooperative experience. Some four-year schools have arrangements with community colleges or liberal arts colleges that allow students to spend two or three years at the initial school and transfer for the last two years to complete their engineering degree.

All fifty states as well as the District of Columbia require engineers to be licensed as professional engineers (PE) if they serve the public directly. In most states, licensure requires graduation from a four-year engineering program accredited by ABET, four years of experience, and passing the state exam. Many engineers take the Fundamentals of Engineering portion of the exam upon graduation. They are then engineers in training (EIT). After obtaining appropriate work experience, they take the Principles and Practice of Engineering exam to complete their professional license. Most states recognize licenses from other states as long as the requirements are the same or more stringent. Some states have continuing education requirements.

For More Information

Accreditation Board for Engineering and
Technology (ABET)
111 Market Place, Suite 1050
Baltimore, Maryland 21202
410-347-7700
www.abet.org

American Society of Civil Engineers
Transportation and Development Institute
1801 Alexander Bell Drive
Reston, Virginia 20191-4400
800-548-2723 (toll-free)
www.asce.org

National Society of Professional Engineers
(NSPE)
1420 King Street
Alexandria, Virginia 22314
703-684-2800
www.nspe.org

About the Next Cool Thing

Dark roofs will be a thing of the past if the scientists at Lawrence Berkeley Laboratory and other researchers have their way. They have been experimenting with light-colored roofs for years. According to various studies, air-conditioning use can be reduced by as much as 20 percent with white roofs. Roofs needn't be white to result in energy—and cost—savings, but a lemon-yellow roof won't save as much a white roof.

Construction Manager

All kinds of building projects require construction managers.

Job Trends

The Career Voyages Web site lists construction manager as one of the top 50 in-demand occupations and ranks it number 15 out of the top 50 occupations requiring at least a bachelor's degree with the most openings. According to the *Occupational Outlook Handbook,* employment growth of 16 percent is expected by 2016. This is greater than the average for all occupations. Job opportunities should be excellent because the need is expected to exceed the number of qualified persons entering this profession.

Demand for construction mangers is generated by increasing construction of homes, offices, schools, hospitals, restaurants, and retail spaces as a result of population growth. In addition, the need to replace and repair roads, highways, and bridges will also generate demand. Increasing complexity of projects along with more laws and regulations regarding energy efficiency, environmental protection, worker safety, and environmentally friendly construction processes and materials also contribute to the demand for construction mangers.

Nature of the Work

Construction managers oversee and coordinate the entire construction process from planning and development through the completion of the project. They are responsible for making sure that the work gets done within budget and on schedule. On a very large project, different construction managers may handle different portions of the project. Construction managers schedule all the work and hire the general and trades contractors. They arrange delivery of materials, tools, and equipment; obtain the necessary licenses and permits; and ensure compliance with all regulations.

The majority of construction managers work on residential and nonresidential construction such as homes, apartment buildings, commercial buildings, schools, and hospitals. However, construction managers also work on large industrial complexes, bridges, highways, and wastewater treatment plants.

Career Paths

Experienced construction managers in large companies may become high-level managers or administrators. An additional degree in business administration, finance, or accounting may be necessary for the highest positions. Many construction managers are self-employed in their own small construction or consulting companies.

Earning Potential

2008 mean hourly wage: $43.16; mean annual wage: $89,770

Education/Licensure

Traditionally, trades workers such as carpenters, electricians, and plumbers with significant construction experience could advance to construction managers. According to the Career Voyages Web site, only about 30 percent of currently employed construction managers have college degrees. However, the trend is for employers to hire people with bachelor's degrees or higher in construction

management, construction science, or civil engineering. In addition to education, construction industry experience is critical in getting a job. For those in college and university programs, internships are a good way to gain experience.

The American Council for Construction Education provides links to accredited bachelor's and associate degree programs in construction sciences. The National Center for Construction Education and Research also provides links to accredited programs and sponsors Construction Management Academies that offer professional training and certifications. The American Institute of Constructors offers online continuing education courses through www.RedVector.com. Many are green construction courses.

Certification is voluntary for construction managers but it is a growing trend. Employers value certification because it ensures a certain level of training and experience. The Construction Management Association of America offers the Construction Manager in Training (CMIT) certification for college juniors, seniors, and recent graduates and the Certified Construction Manager (CCM) for those with experience. The CCM requires a combination of education and experience plus passing an exam. The American Institute of Constructors also offers certification for construction managers. LEED (Leadership in Energy and Environmental Design) certification from the U.S. Green Building Council is also available.

For More Information

American Council for Construction Education
1717 North Loop 1604 E, Suite 320
San Antonio, Texas 78232-1570
210-495-6161
www.acce-hq.org

American Institute of Constructors
P.O. Box 26334
Alexandria, Virginia 22314
703-683-4999
www.aicnet.org

Construction Management Association of America
7926 Jones Branch Drive, Suite 800
McLean, Virginia 22102-3303
703-356-2622
www.cmaanet.org

National Center for Construction Education and
    Research
3600 NW 43rd Street, Building G
Gainesville, Florida 32606
888-622-3720 (toll-free)
www.nccer.org

Cost Estimator

Regardless of the field, cost estimators perform the same type of work.

Job Trends

The Career Voyages Web site ranks cost estimators as one of the top 50 in-demand occupations with 86,000 new employees needed by 2016. This occupation is also ranked number 50 among the top 50 fastest-growing occupations and numbers 34 among the top 50 occupations with the most openings requiring at least a bachelor's degree. The *Occupational Outlook Handbook* predicts growth of 19 percent by 2016, which is greater than the average for all occupations. Employment opportunities should be very good, especially for those with bachelor's degrees and industry experience. The most jobs are in the construction and manufacturing industries. According to the *Occupational Outlook Handbook,* approximately 62 percent work in construction and 15 percent work in manufacturing.

Most of the growth in this occupation is expected in the construction sector. The need to repair highways, bridges, water and sewer systems, airports, and subways will generate jobs for cost estimators. An increasing population will generate the need for homes, schools, and offices, while the aging population contributes to the need for hospitals, extended-care facilities, and nursing homes. In addition, the market for home remodeling is currently strong. This is partially driven by economic conditions but also by environmental concerns.

Retrofitting and remodeling to improve energy efficiency is increasing. In addition, retrofitting of industrial plants, government buildings, and schools will provide job opportunities.

Nature of the Work

Cost estimators use mathematics, engineering, technology, economics, and accounting in their work. They estimate the costs, scope, and duration of construction projects and product manufacturing or for services. These estimates are used to prepare bids and to decide if a project will be profitable. Cost estimators must be familiar with spreadsheet software and software for accounting and financials.

Construction estimators must analyze all factors that affect the cost, including location, site, materials, machinery, labor, and length of the project. Estimators may work for the construction company, the architect, or the owner. In large companies, estimators may specialize in the type of work they estimate. For example, some may specialize in estimating only the electrical work or the plumbing.

Estimators in the manufacturing industry work with engineers to determine the processes involved, machinery required, and parts and supplies needed to produce a new product or redesign an existing one. They must consider the cost and availability of raw materials or whether purchasing the components is more cost effective, as well as any computer programming or software development that will be needed. Some estimators specialize in only a certain product.

Career Paths

Cost estimators generally advance by receiving higher pay. However, some become project managers in construction or engineering managers in manufacturing. Some start their own consulting firms to provide services to construction or manufacturing companies or to the government.

Earning Potential

2008 mean hourly wage: $29.00; mean annual wage: $60,320

Education/Licensure

About 40 percent of currently employed cost estimators have some college education but less than a bachelor's degree. However, those with a bachelor's degree have the best job prospects now and in the future. Keep in mind that colleges and universities do not offer degree programs in cost estimating. Instead a bachelor's degree in construction management, construction science, or building science is preferred for the construction industry. Most colleges and universities include cost estimating in the curriculum for civil and industrial engineering and construction management. Associate degree programs in construction engineering technology also include cost estimating. For the manufacturing industry, those with a degree in engineering, mathematics, statistics, business administration, accounting, or economics have the best opportunities.

Experience is critical for job candidates. Students can gain valuable experience through internships and cooperative education experiences while working toward their degrees. Those already working in other areas of the construction industry can gain practical experience and knowledge of costs, materials, and procedures that they can translate into a cost estimation job. On-the-job training is also important because each company has its own methods for cost estimating.

Certification is voluntary but valuable for job candidates, and some employers do require it. The Society of Cost Estimating and Analysis (SCEA) and the Association for the Advancement of Cost Engineering (AACE International) offer certifications that require two to eight years of experience and passing an exam. These organizations also offer training for certification and professional development opportunities. Many community colleges, technical schools, and universities offer specialized courses in cost estimation procedures and techniques.

For More Information

Association for the Advancement of Cost
   Engineering (AACE International)
209 Prairie Avenue, Suite 100
Morgantown, West Virginia 26501-5934
800-858-2678 (toll-free)
www.aacei.org

Society of Cost Estimating and Analysis (SCEA)
527 Maple Avenue East, Suite 301
Vienna, Virginia 22180
703-938-5090
www.sceaonline.net

DESIGN INDUSTRY

Trends for architecture and landscape architecture are related to trends in the construction industry. Even though new construction of residential and commercial buildings is expected to slow, remodeling and retrofitting of existing structures are expected to generate demand. In an April 2009 summary, the U.S. Green Building Council reported that green building is expected to more than double by 2013. Major growth in nonresidential green building is expected in the education, office, and health-care sectors. Additional green building is expected in the government, industrial, hospitality, and retail sectors. Government initiatives, along with increased interest in residential green building, are encouraging energy-efficient, environmentally sustainable green construction. Both architects and landscape architects will find opportunities in green building.

Trends for product designers reflect trends in the manufacturing industry. In all manufacturing sectors, most design jobs remain in the United States and will not be as adversely affected as production jobs. Research and development resulting in rapid changes in technology are characteristic of the computer and electronics manufacturing industry. Electronics are incorporated into automobiles, cell phones, toys, and other products that constantly require updated designs. This translates into demand for commercial and industrial designers, even though overall employment in computer and electronics manufacturing is expected to decline between now and 2016. Overall employment in motor vehicle manufacturing is also expected to decline, but new designs for alternate energy and hybrid vehicles will be needed as the industry focuses more on energy efficiency.

Architect

Alternate Job Titles:

- Architectural Engineer
- Building Contractor
- Building Inspector
- Furniture Designer
- Interior Designer
- Marine Architect
- Surveyor
- Urban Planner

A background in architecture offers a number of varied job opportunities.

Job Trends

Employment for architects is expected to grow by 18 percent by 2016, according to the *Occupational Outlook Handbook,* which is greater than the average for all occupations. It is listed as an in-demand occupation by Career Voyages. Demand for architects will be generated mainly by non-residential construction such as new schools at all levels to meet the educational needs of the expanding population. Green building design is also expected to generate demand for architects as environmental concerns and energy costs increase.

About Environmentally Friendly Floors

Look for flooring and floor coverings that are environmentally friendly. ECOTimbers are exotic hardwoods that are certified by the Forest Stewardship Council as harvested according to sustainable forestry standards. Linoleum, cork, bamboo, and engineered wood products are other types of environmentally friendly floorings. FLOR™ carpet tiles are made from renewable and recyclable materials and can be recycled when you want a change.

Approximately 70 percent of architects currently work for architectural, engineering, and related firms. About 20 percent are self-employed. The remainder work for construction companies and government agencies.

Nature of the Work

Architects design houses, schools, hospitals, office buildings, churches, college buildings, urban centers, and industrial parks. In addition to the structure itself, architects also design the electrical system; heating, air conditioning, and ventilation system; plumbing; and communication system. The structures must be safe, functional, and cost-effective. Architects work with many other professionals, such as engineers, landscape architects, interior designers, and urban planners.

In creating their plans, architects must consider federal, state, and local regulations, building codes, zoning laws, and fire codes. Much of their work is done using building information modeling (BIM) and computer-aided design (CAD). Their work also includes preparing reports, cost estimates, environmental impact studies, land-use studies, models and presentations for clients, and plans for regulatory approvals. During construction, architects monitor the work being done by construction contractors.

Green building and sustainable design require the expertise of architects. The U.S. Green Building Council LEED (Leadership in Energy and Environmental Design) building certification program includes credit for energy-efficient systems for heating and cooling, lighting, and water usage and disposal; clean renewable energy use; natural and sustainably produced materials; indoor air quality; innovative design; educating the people who use the building; location to transportation and services; and a sustainable site. This is a great deal of expertise for architects to master.

Career Paths

Architecture graduates usually begin a three-year intern program, working under the supervision of a licensed architect. After completing that program, they are eligible to take licensing exams. After passing the exams, they become licensed and gain responsibility for projects. With greater experience, they may become managers or partners in an architecture firm. Some work in related areas, such as real estate development and urban planning.

Earning Potential

2008 mean hourly wage: $36.90; mean annual wage: $76,750

Education/Licensure

A bachelor's degree is the minimum required for architects. Bachelor of Arts or Bachelor of Science in architecture, Bachelor of Environmental Design, and Bachelor of Architectural Studies are considered preprofessional degrees. A preprofessional bachelor's degree may qualify a person for licensure in some states, but, in most states, further education is required to get a professional degree. Professional degrees are Bachelor of Architecture (B.Arch.), Master of Architecture (M.Arch.), and Doctor of Architecture (D.Arch.) from an accredited program. The Bachelor of Architecture degree usually requires five years.

All fifty states and the District of Columbia require architects to be licensed. Licensing normally requires a professional degree from an accredited school, completion of a three-year intern program, and passing a national exam. The National Council of Architectural Registration Boards administers the exam. There are some alternate provisions for those who do not have a professional degree. Only Arizona does not require the three-year intern program. Students who complete part of their internship while in school will have an advantage.

The National Council of Architectural Registration Boards offers certification that allows an architect licensed in one state to become licensed in another state through reciprocity.

Most states require continuing education to maintain a license. From 2009 through 2012, the American Institute of Architects requires 4 hours of continuing education in sustainable design every year to maintain membership. The U.S.

Green Building Council offers LEED (Leadership in Energy and Environmental Design) professional accreditation.

For More Information

Association of Collegiate Schools of Architecture
1735 New York Avenue, NW
Washington, D.C. 20006
202-785-2324
www.asca-arch.org

National Council of Architectural Registration Boards
1801 K Street NW, Suite 700K
Washington, D.C. 20006
202-783-6500
www.ncarb.org

The American Institute of Architects
1735 New York Avenue, NW
Washington, D.C. 20006-5292
202-626-7300
www.aia.org

U.S. Green Building Council
2101 L Street, NW, Suite 500
Washington, D.C. 20037
800-795-1747 (toll-free)
www.usgbc.org

Landscape Architect

Alternate Job Titles

- Environmental Landscape Architect
- Landscape Designer

Becoming a landscape architect means learning a great deal more than where to plant a bush.

Job Trends

According to the *Occupational Outlook Handbook,* employment for landscape architects is expected to increase by 16 percent by 2016. This is greater than the average for all occupations. One factor increasing the demand for landscape architects is new construction to meet the needs of the growing population. Increasingly, landscape architects are also needed in planning the remediation and restoration of environmentally sensitive sites, such as wetlands and forests, and in preserving and restoring historic sites. Even the planning of safe bike trails and walkways involves landscape architects.

More than half of all landscape architects work for architectural, engineering, and related services. Almost 20 percent are self-employed. About 6 percent work for state and local governments. Most work in urban and suburban areas, but some who work for the federal government design recreation areas and parks in rural areas.

Nature of the Work

Environmental landscape architects are involved in many types of environmental projects. They design plans for remediating and restoring natural sites such as forested areas, mining sites, stream corridors, and wetlands. They also work in national parks and recreation areas and preserve and restore historic sites and cultural landscapes. In their work, they consult with hydrologists, environmental scientists, and foresters.

Green building and sustainable design also require the expertise of landscape architects. They design green roofs and plan tree coverage. These designs save energy, reduce runoff, and improve water and air quality. The U.S. Green Building Council LEED (Leadership in Energy and Environmental Design) building certification includes credit for a sustainable site that minimizes water use, erosion, light pollution, and other environmental impact.

Landscape architects design a variety of projects: residential developments, college campuses, parks, recreation areas, golf courses, shopping centers, parkways, and airports. In creating their plans, they

- consider the natural elements of the site, such as land contours, drainage, sunlight, and climate.
- consider how the site should function and where to place walkways, roads, gardens, and even buildings.
- work with many other professionals such as civil engineers, architects, and surveyors.
- consider federal, state, and local environmental regulations and zoning laws.

- prepare reports, cost estimates, environmental impact studies, models and presentations for clients, and plans for regulatory approvals.
- monitor the work being done by the landscape contractors on site.

Much of the work of landscape architects is done using computer-aided design (CAD) and, for larger projects, geographic information systems (GIS).

Career Paths

Generally, beginning landscape architects are apprentices or interns for about three years, working under the supervision of a licensed landscape architect. During this time, they do research and prepare drawings, but they are not responsible for the entire project. After becoming licensed, they take on responsibility for their own projects. With more experience, they may become managers or partners in a firm. Some may work as consultants or environmental planners. Many are self-employed.

Earning Potential

2008 mean hourly wage: $30.77; mean annual wage: $64,000

Education/Licensure

A bachelor's degree in landscape architecture from an accredited school is the minimum requirement for a job. The Landscape Architectural Accreditation Board (LAAB), under the auspices of the American Society of Landscape Architects (ASLA), accredits educational programs. Some programs are in specialized schools, such as Boston Architectural College. Most programs include a design-studio experience. Employers also recommend that undergraduates participate in internships.

A master's degree is an advantage. Master's degree programs require two years for students entering with a bachelor's degree in landscape architecture and three years for those entering with a degree in another area. Training in urban planning is an advantage in finding a job in firms that do site planning and landscape design.

According to the ASLA, forty-nine states require licensing because landscape architecture has an impact on the safety, health, and welfare of the public. The Council of Landscape Architectural Registration Boards sponsors the national licensing exam. Before taking the exam, a candidate must have a degree from an accredited school and one to four years of experience (three-year apprenticeship is typical), depending on state laws. In addition, fifteen states require passing a state exam. Continuing education is required in most states to maintain one's license.

The U.S. Green Building Council offers LEED (Leadership in Energy and Environmental Design) Professional Accreditation.

For More Information

American Society of Landscape Architects
636 Eye Street NW
Washington, D.C. 20001-3736
888-999-2752 (toll-free)
www.asla.org

Council of Landscape Architectural Registration
 Boards
3949 Pender Drive, Suite 120
Fairfax, Virginia 22030
571-432-0332
www.clarb.org

U.S. Green Building Council
2101 L Street, NW, Suite 500
Washington, DC 20037
800-795-1747 (toll-free)
www.usgbc.org

Product Designer

Alternate Job Titles:

- Commercial Designer
- Industrial Designer

Within each category, designers can specialize in areas such as furniture design, interior design, and automotive design.

About Furniture Made with Renewable Resources

When you're purchasing furniture, see if the pieces are made with any of the following renewable resources: bamboo, cork, beech wood, reclaimed lumber, recycled wood scraps, hemp, wool, jute, bent plywood, stainless steel, or coconut palm trees.

Job Trends

The outlook for product designers is 7 percent growth by 2016, according to the *Occupational Outlook Handbook*. This is about average for all occupations. The Career Voyages Web site lists commercial and industrial design as an in-demand occupation.

This increase is fueled by the growing demand for new and upgraded consumer products that are environmentally safe and produced in an environmentally friendly way. Most design jobs are contracted out to design firms, rather than staying in manufacturing companies. A trend toward using design firms in other countries causes some decrease in domestic jobs. However, since industrial designers are needed in so many industries, job opportunities and pay are generally good.

Nature of the Work

Sustainable design incorporates energy efficiency and materials that have been recycled and are capable of being recycled. Product designers are involved in the design of everything from alternative energy and hybrid vehicles to yogurt cups and clothing made from organic fibers. They design energy-efficient household appliances and contribute to environmental design for furniture and interiors.

Commercial and industrial designers design the products that people use every day. These include automobiles, furniture, appliances, toys, and computers. Designers are concerned with the function, style, and safety of products. They participate in market research to determine the features consumers want and work with cost estimators, accountants, and engineers as they design products. They prepare reports, cost estimates, models, and presentations for clients. Much of their work is done using computer-aided design (CAD).

Career Paths

Beginning designers usually receive up to three years of on-the-job training. With more experience, they may become supervisors or chief designers. Some open their own studio for consulting, start a design firm, or teach in colleges and universities.

Earning Potential

2008 mean hourly wage: $29.60; mean annual wage: $61,580

Education/Licensure

Most entry-level jobs require a bachelor's degree in industrial design, engineering, or architecture. Many designers earn master's degrees to improve their opportunities. An undergraduate degree in marketing, engineering, or information technology combined with a master's degree in industrial design is one possibility. Another is a master's degree in business administration (MBA) combined with an industrial design degree.

The National Association of Schools of Art and Design provides a list and links to accredited art and design programs. These include colleges, universities, and other institutions. The Industrial Designers Society of America provides a specific list of schools with design programs. Many programs include internships.

For More Information

Industrial Designers Society of America
45195 Business Court, Suite 250
Dulles, Virginia 20166-6717
703-707-6000
www.idsa.org

National Association of Schools of Art and Design
11250 Roger Bacon Drive, Suite 21
Reston, Virginia 20190-5248
703-437-0700
http://nasad.arts-accredit.org

ENERGY INDUSTRY

The energy industry is expected to be a continual source of new jobs for many years. Energy demands continue to grow, but environmental sustainability is forcing the industry to look to renewable and alternative energy sources such as wind, solar, and geothermal power. Development of these relatively new energy sources and improved efficiency of energy use are expected to create many new jobs. Research and development in the energy industry will increase the number of professional and technical jobs, especially in all areas of engineering.

Computer Software Applications Engineers

Alternate Job Titles:

- Computer Consultant
- Information Technologist
- Programmer
- Software Developer

Name any industrial sector today, and you'll find software applications engineers working in it. They are especially important as the nation's population grows and its energy needs multiply.

Job Trends

According to the *Occupational Outlook Handbook*, computer software applications engineering is one of the fastest-growing occupations. Employment is projected to grow by 38 percent by 2016. Over 300,000 new jobs are predicted by 2016, which is among the largest increases of all occupations. The Career Voyages Web site ranks this as one of the top 50 in-demand occupations and ranks it in the top 50 fastest-growing occupations requiring at least a bachelor's degree. It is ranked number 6 on the list of the top 50 occupations requiring at least a

---

About Renting Cars

Whether renting for business or vacation, go green in your rental car. Hertz was the first to introduce fuel-efficient rentals, and Enterprise has the biggest fleet of fuel-efficient cars.

---

bachelor's degree with the most openings. *MONEY Magazine* and Salary.com rated this occupation as number 1 among "The Top 10 Best Jobs."

Nature of the Work

Knowledge of computers, programming languages, electronics, engineering principles, technology, telecommunications, and mathematics are important for computer software engineers. These computer specialists design, develop, or modify computer software for specific applications. They analyze the needs of the user and create software or databases to address those needs and optimize efficiency. The green economy needs software developers to design and build networks and systems such as smart energy grids and systems that analyze and report information on energy use, carbon emissions, and pollutant levels.

Career Paths

Opportunities for advancement are good, but computer professionals must constantly acquire new skills to keep up with emerging technology. Entry-level computer software engineers begin by testing designs. As they gain experience, they work on software design and development. With more experience, they may become project managers. Those with business training have additional opportunities in higher-level management, such as management of information systems. Some become independent consultants.

Earning Potential

2008 mean hourly wage: $42.26; mean annual wage: $87,900

About Mowing the Lawn

Get some exercise while you mow the lawn. Instead of a riding mower with gas fumes trailing you across the lawn, try one of the battery-powered mowers or a reel mower that (gasp!) you push to power. There's even a solar-hybrid robot mower by www.automower.com.

Education/Licensure

The minimum requirement is a bachelor's degree in software engineering, computer engineering, or computer science. Graduate degrees are necessary for some jobs. Degree programs may be offered through the computer science or engineering departments. Completing an internship or co-op as an undergraduate is recommended because it improves chances for a job after graduation. Those with advanced degrees in system design and mathematics have particularly good opportunities in government agencies, consulting firms, and software development companies. In addition to computer training, industry-related knowledge and skills are important.

Continuing education is particularly important in this field since technology evolves rapidly. Colleges and universities, software vendors, professional societies, and employers offer professional development courses. The Institute of Electronics and Electrical Engineers (IEEE) Computer Society offers training through a number of colleges, universities, and technical institutes. Many courses are offered online.

Certifications are also available through software vendors and professional societies. For example, IEEE Computer Society offers Computer Software Development Associate (entry level) and Computer Software Development Professional (experienced) certificates. The Computing Technology Industry Association offers certifications for Information Technologists. The Institute for Certification of Computing Professionals (ICCP) offers certification programs that may qualify for college credit or even a bachelor's degree.

For More Information

Association for Computing Machinery (ACM)
2 Penn Plaza, Suite 701
New York, New York 10121-0701
800-342-6626 (toll-free)
www.acm.org

·Computer Science & Engineering
University of Washington
AC101 Paul G. Allen Center, Box 352350
185 Stevens Way
Seattle, Washington 98195-2350
206-543-1695
www.cs.washington.edu/WhyCSE

Computing Technology Industry Association
 (CompTIA)
1815 S. Meyers Road, Suite 300
Oakbrook Terrace, Illinois 60181-5228
630-678-8300
www.comptia.org

Institute for Certification of Computing
 Professionals (ICCP)
2400 East Devon Avenue, Suite 281
Des Plaines, Illinois 60018
847-299-4227
www.iccp.org

Institute of Electronics and Electrical Engineers
 Computer Society
Headquarters Office
2001 L Street N.W., Suite 700
Washington, D.C. 20036-4910
202-371-0101
www.computer.org

National Workforce Center for Emerging
 Technologies (NWCET)
Bellevue College
3000 Landerholm Circle SE, N258
Bellevue, Washington 98007-6484
425-564-4229
www.nwcet.org/programs/cyberCareers/
 default.asp

Electrical Engineer

Alternate Job Titles:

- Battery Engineer
- Electrical Engineer Project Manager
- Electrical Product Engineer
- Electrical Systems Designer
- Electro-Mechanical Engineer
- Electronics Engineer
- Geothermal Electrical Engineer

- Hydroelectric Electrical Engineer
- Power Electronics Engineer
- Substation Engineer

Every area of the new energy initiatives will need electrical engineers.

Job Trends

In 2006, there were 153,000 electrical engineers. According to the *Occupational Outlook Handbook,* expected growth is about 6 percent by 2016, which amounts to almost 10,000 new jobs. Replacement of engineers reaching retirement age or transferring to sales and management will result in additional job opportunities. The Career Voyages Web site lists electrical engineering as one of the in-demand occupations.

Nature of the Work

Electrical engineers work in a wide variety of industries, including automotive, aerospace, bio-engineering, computers, construction, information technology, manufacturing, nanotechnology, semi-conductors, and telecommunications. Some are even hired by the service, financial, and entertainment industries.

Electrical engineers conduct research to design and develop electric and electronic systems and equipment and also test and oversee manufacturing systems and equipment. Systems include navigational systems and wiring in buildings, aircraft, and automobiles. Equipment includes motors, devices for generating power, controls, and transmission devices. Engineers who work on applications of electric power are also called electronics engineers.

Career Paths

As electrical engineers gain experience, they become specialists and advance into positions where they supervise a team of engineers and other staff members. Some eventually become managers or move into sales jobs where their technical background is particularly useful. Some go on to earn a master's in business administration (MBA) to prepare them for high-level managerial positions.

Earning Potential

2008 mean hourly wage: $41.04; mean annual wage: $85,350

Education/Licensure

For entry-level positions, a bachelor's degree in engineering from a college or university program that is accredited by the Accreditation Board for Engineering and Technology (ABET) is required. In some cases, engineers with degrees in one type of engineering may qualify for jobs in other areas of engineering.

Some colleges and universities offer five-year programs that culminate in a master's degree. Some offer five- or six-year programs that include cooperative experience. Some four-year schools have arrangements with community colleges or liberal arts colleges that allow students to spend two or three years at the initial school and transfer for the last two years to complete their engineering degree.

All fifty states as well as the District of Columbia require engineers to be licensed as professional engineers (PE) if they serve the public directly. In most states, licensure requires graduation from a four-year engineering program accredited by ABET, four years of experience, and passing the state exam. Many engineers take the Fundamentals of Engineering portion of the exam upon graduation. They are then engineers in training (EIT). After obtaining appropriate work experience, they take the Principles and Practice of Engineering exam to complete their professional license. Most states recognize licenses from other states as long as the requirements are the same or more stringent. Some states have continuing education requirements.

For More Information

Accreditation Board for Engineering and
    Technology (ABET)
111 Market Place, Suite 1050
Baltimore, Maryland 21202
410-347-7700
www.abet.org

American Society for Engineering Education
    (ASEE)
1818 N Street NW, Suite 600
Washington, D.C. 20036-2479
202-331-3500
www.asee.org

Institute of Electrical and Electronics Engineers
    (IEEE)
445 Hoes Lane
Piscataway, New Jersey 08854-4141
732-981-0060
www.ieee.org

National Society of Professional Engineers
    (NSPE)
1420 King Street
Alexandria, Virginia 22314
703-684-2800
www.nspe.org

Geoscientist

Alternate Job Titles:

- Atmospheric Scientist
- Economic Geologist
- Engineering Geologist
- Environmental Geologist
- Geochemist
- Geologist Geophysicist
- Glacial Geologist
- Hydrologist
- Oceanographer
- Petroleum Geologist
- Soil Scientist

These are just some of the specialties and titles that can be classified under "geoscience."

Job Trends

There are currently 31,000 geoscientists, and demand for an additional 15,000 is expected by 2016. Projected growth in this occupation is 22 percent, much greater than the average for all occupations according to the *Occupational Outlook Handbook*. The Career Voyages Web site ranks this as number 35 on the list of the top 50 fastest-growing occupations and includes it on the list of in-demand occupations.

Demand for geoscientists will increase as concerns for environmental protection, land management, and energy needs increase. Growth in scientific and technical consulting is expected to provide additional jobs working on government contracts and aiding companies in environmental management. Construction is also a growing area for geoscientists, particularly engineering geologists.

Nature of the Work

Geosciences is actually a broad area that includes scientists working in a variety of specialties, many related to the green economy. All of these specialties study the Earth and its structure, composition, and physical properties. Geoscientists use principles of geology, physics, chemistry, and mathematics. Computer skills are very important because computer modeling is a technique often used in this occupation.

According to the *Occupational Outlook Handbook,* 32 percent of geoscientists work in architectural, engineering, and related services; 24 percent in oil and gas extraction; 23 percent in management, scientific, and technical consulting services; and 21 percent in federal and state government. Some geoscientists are involved in searching for such resources as oil or water. In the energy industry, developing the potential of geothermal energy is a growing area for employment. Some geoscientists work on solutions to other environmental problems such as preserving and cleaning the environment. Still others work in industries like construction or geospatial technologies. All of these industries are expected to experience growth in the next decade.

Career Paths

Geoscientists usually begin their careers as research assistants or technicians. After gaining experience, they may become senior researchers, project leaders, or even managers.

Earning Potential

2008 mean hourly wage: $42.93; mean annual wage: $89,300

Education/Licensure

Most positions require at least a master's degree, although there are some entry-level positions for those with bachelor's degrees. Doctorates are required for high-level research positions and for positions at colleges and universities. Some states require geoscientists, especially geologists, to be licensed if they provide public service. Requirements vary but generally include education, experience, and passing a state exam.

For More Information

American Association of Petroleum Geologists (AAPG)
1444 S. Boulder
Tulsa, Oklahoma 74119
800-364-2274 (toll-free)
www.aapg.org

American Geological Institute (AGI)
4220 King Street
Alexandria, Virginia 22302-1502
703-379-2480
www.agiweb.org

Marine Technology Society (MTS)
5565 Sterrett Place, Suite 108
Columbia, Maryland 21004
410-884-5330
www.mtsociety.org/home.aspx

ENVIRONMENTAL HEALTH

Environmental health itself is not an industry. It is a collection of health-related professions practiced in a number of different industries and in all levels of government. The professions are united in their common goals of preserving the environment, conserving resources, and protecting all living things from injury, disease, and the effects of hazardous materials.

The Agency for Toxic Substances and Disease Registry, the Centers for Disease Control and Prevention, and the National Institutes of Health jointly authored the chapter on environmental health in the U.S. Department of Health and

About Stormwater Pollution

Storm drains are connected to local bodies of water, so limit the use of fertilizers and pesticides, clean up after your dogs, and don't feed wildlife. These all leave harmful residues that rainstorms can wash into stormdrains and pollute streams, lakes, and rivers.

Human Services report "Healthy People 2010: Understanding and Improving Health." The three agencies state that the three main factors affecting human health are the environment (which includes infectious agents), personal behavior, and genetics. The agencies estimate that 25 percent of preventable illness is related to environmental quality and state that the six major environmental issues that can and must be addressed are outdoor air quality, water quality, toxins and waste, healthy homes and healthy communities, infrastructure surveillance, and global environmental health. Although important strides have been made, many issues still must be addressed, and this is the work of environmental health professionals.

Environmental Health Specialist

Alternate Job Titles:

- Environmental Protection Officer
- Health Physicist
- Industrial Hygienist
- Occupational Safety and Health Specialist

These professionals are on the frontline of occupational safety.

Job Trends

Occupational safety and health specialist, another name for environmental health specialist, is one of the in-demand occupations listed by the Career Voyages Web site. According to the *Occupational Outlook Handbook,* employment is expected to grow by 9 percent by 2016, which is about average for all occupations. Increasing public demand for safety and health in the workplace will generate jobs for occupational health and safety specialists in government. Employment in private industry will grow as companies comply with government health and safety policies and regulations.

Nature of the Work

Environmental health specialists evaluate workplaces and monitor the environment for health hazards. Health hazards include biological agents, chemicals, ergonomic factors, noise, temperature extremes, and vibration. Health and safety specialists develop programs and procedures for preventing injury and disease and minimizing exposure to hazards. They also conduct inspections and enforce regulations. About 40 percent of environmental health specialists are employed in federal, state, and local governments where their job is to enforce safety, health, and environmental regulations. Others are employed in private industry.

Occupational health and safety specialists have various job descriptions depending on their area of focus. Environmental protection officers focus on the environment and are concerned with cleaning up contaminated water and soil. They establish procedures for storing, handling, and disposing of hazardous materials and may monitor drinking water and wastewater for contamination. Industrial hygienists are particularly concerned with exposure to workplace hazards such as asbestos, lead, and pesticides. Health physicists develop procedures to prevent exposure to hazardous radiation, protecting both people and the environment.

Career Paths

In government positions, environmental health specialists can advance through the civil service

About Yogurt

Yogurt is good for you, and Stoneyfield Farms, the maker of a variety of yogurt products, is trying to make the world a better place, too. Its motto is "Stoneyfield Farms for a Healthful Planet." It uses organic ingredients and the least amount of packaging possible to maintain the safety of its products, and it creates some of its own energy with solar panels.

career ladder, and some eventually become supervisors. Private industry is similar. Professional organizations offer opportunities to stay up-to-date in the field and broaden areas of expertise, both of which are important for advancement. Obtaining an advanced degree is also an advantage for advancement.

Earning Potential

2008 mean hourly wage: $30.31; mean annual wage: $63,030

Education/Licensure

Most jobs require a bachelor's degree in occupational health and safety, health physics, or industrial hygiene. Degrees in related fields such as biology, chemistry, public health, or toxicology qualify an individual for some positions. Master's degrees are required for some positions. The Accreditation Board for Engineering and Technology (ABET) accredits programs in environmental health and safety, health physics, industrial hygiene, and safety. Its Web site has links to accredited programs. The Board of Certified Safety Professionals also provides a database of programs offering degrees and certificates.

Certification is voluntary, but employers value it. The American Board of Industrial Hygiene offers Certified Industrial Hygienist (CIH) and Certified Associate Industrial Hygienist (CAIH). These require a combination of education, experience, and current practice and passing an exam. The Board of Certified Safety Professionals offers the Certified Safety Professional (CSP) certification, which requires an associate degree or higher, current employment as a safety professional, and passing an exam. Periodic recertification is required. The American Industrial Hygiene Association offers professional development opportunities in continuing education and distance learning.

For More Information

Accreditation Board for Engineering and
    Technology (ABET)
111 Market Place, Suite 1050
Baltimore, Maryland 21202
410-347-7700
www.abet.org

American Board of Industrial Hygiene
6015 West St. Joseph, Suite 102
Lansing, Michigan 48917-3890
517-321-2638
www.abih.org

American Industrial Hygiene Association
2700 Prosperity Avenue, Suite 250
Fairfax, Virginia 22031
703-849-8888
www.aiha.org

Board of Certified Safety Professionals
208 Burwash Avenue
Savoy, Illinois 61874
217-359-9263
www.bcsp.org

Health Physics Society
1313 Dolley Madison Boulevard
Suite 402
McLean, Virginia 22101
703-790-1745
www.hps.org

Public Health Nurse

Alternate Job Title: Community Health Nurse

This nursing field—similar to nursing overall—has more openings than professionals to fill available jobs.

Job Trends

In 2006, there were about 2.5 million registered nurses. About 60 percent worked in hospitals, and about 15 percent worked in community or public health according to the American Nurses Association. *Occupational Outlook Handbook* predicts that employment for registered nurses will grow 23 percent by 2016, which is much greater than the average for all occupations. The Career Voyages Web site ranks registered nursing number 17 out of the top 50 fastest-growing occupations requiring at least an associate degree. It is ranked number 1 of the top 50 occupations with the most openings. More than 1 million openings are projected by 2016.

A critical shortage of registered nurses has existed for some time. This fact combined with increasing emphasis on prevention, technological advances, and an aging population will generate new jobs. The shortage of registered nurses extends to those in public health.

Nature of the Work
Public health nurses work at the interface between the public and policy makers. According to the American Public Health Association, public health nurses

- monitor, anticipate, and respond to public health problems.
- evaluate health trends and risk factors.
- work within the community to develop public health policy and targeted health promotion and disease prevention.
- assess the health needs and experiences of individuals, families, and populations.
- communicate their findings to those who formulate plans and policies.
- communicate strategies for prevention and intervention back to the community.

The Nursing Section of the American Public Health Association identified environmental health as a strategic priority. Public health nurses are involved in tracking and reporting the incidence of diseases that are associated with environmental contaminants. These conditions include childhood asthma, autism spectrum disorders, birth defects, cancer, high levels of lead in blood, and multiple sclerosis, among others. Public health nurses educate the public on ways to prevent exposure to environmental hazards.

Career Paths
Public health nurses have some leadership opportunities. A graduate degree improves job opportunities.

Earning Potential
Registered Nurses:
2008 mean hourly wage: $31.31; mean annual wage: $65,130

Education/Licensure
There are three educational routes to becoming a registered nurse. The first is a Bachelor of Science degree in nursing, which takes about four years. Next is an associate degree in nursing, offered by junior colleges and community colleges, which takes two to three years. Finally, a few hospitals offer diploma programs that usually require three years.

According to the Career Voyages Web site, 56 percent of registered nurses have a bachelor's degree or higher, while 43 percent have some college education. Some registered nurses with associate degrees or diplomas return to college to earn a bachelor's degree in order to improve job opportunities. A bachelor's degree or even a master's degree is required for some specialties and administrative positions.

A bachelor's degree is generally considered the minimum for public health nurses, although only a few states actually require it. Bachelor's degree programs include public health in the curriculum. Master's degree programs allow specialization in public health. The Association of Community Health Nursing Educators provides a list of master's degree programs in public health nursing.

In all fifty states, the District of Columbia, and U.S. territories, nurses must be licensed. Licensing requires passing the NCLEX-RN exam (National Council Licensure Examination for Registered Nurses) developed by the National Council of State Boards of Nursing (NCSBN). Nurses may qualify for an endorsement to become licensed in more than one state, and the NCSBN also sponsors the Nurse Licensure Compact (NLC), which allows a licensed nurse from one member state to practice in another member state.

Public health nurses may become certified to improve job opportunities and pay. The American Nurses Credentialing Center offers the APHN–BC (Advanced Public Health Nurse–Board Certified) for those who have passed the appropriate exams, and the PHCNS–BC credential (Public/Community Health Clinical Nurse Specialist–Board Certified) for those who graduated from an appropriate program.

For More Information

American Nurses Association
8515 Georgia Avenue, Suite 400
Silver Spring, Maryland 20910-3492
301-628-5000
www.nursingworld.org

American Nurses Credentialing Center
8515 Georgia Avenue, Suite 400
Silver Spring, Maryland 20910-3492
800-284-2378 (toll-free)
www.nursecredentialing.org

American Public Health Association
800 I Street, NW
Washington, D.C. 20001-3710
202-777-2742
www.apha.org

American Society of Registered Nurses
1001 Bridgeway, Suite 233
Sausalito, California 94965
415-331-2700
www.asrn.org

Association of Community Health Nursing
  Educators
10200 West 44th Avenue, Suite 304
Wheat Ridge, Colorado 80033
303-422-0769
www.achne.org

Association of State and Territorial Directors of
  Nursing
P.O. Box 4166, Halfmoon Station
Clifton Park, New York 12065
www.astdn.org

National Council of State Boards of Nursing
111 E. Wacker Drive, Suite 2900
Chicago, Illinois 60601-4277
312-525-3600
www.ncsbn.org

Statistician

Alternate Job Titles:
- Analytics Statistician
- Applied Statistician
- Biostatistician
- Clinical Trials Research Analyst
- Research Analyst
- Statistics Analyst

Statisticians work in a variety of fields that require analysis of large amounts of data, such as government, insurance, and finance. Public health is an especially important area that employs statisticians.

Job Trends

According to the *Occupational Outlook Handbook,* employment for statisticians is expected to grow about 9 percent by 2016, which is about average for all occupations. Demand will stem from technological advances that allow statisticians to manipulate more data faster. Biostatisticians are expected to have more job opportunities as the pharmaceutical industry grows.

Nature of the Work

Statisticians design methods for collecting numerical data. These may be experiments, surveys, studies, or questionnaires. Statisticians utilize a variety of mathematical methods for analyzing data, and they must select the most appropriate method for solving the problems they are working on. Finally, they determine the best methods for presenting and interpreting the results, and sometimes they develop risk assessments based on the data.

Statisticians work in almost all areas of business, science, and technology. About 30 percent work in federal government agencies, such as the Environmental Protection Agency or the National Forest Service, where they address environmental and ecological problems. In medicine and health, statisticians work in animal health, biostatistics, epidemiology, and public health. Statisticians also work in industries that have environmental applications, particularly agriculture, computer science, economics, engineering, manufacturing, and quality assurance.

Biostatistics is the practice of using statistical techniques in public health. Biostatisticians study the incidence of disease and try to determine which factors can be modified and effectively controlled. In some cases, these are environmental factors, such as the level of chemicals in drinking water. Biostatisticians in epidemiology study the causes of disease. They may calculate the incidence rates of cancers and relate them to exposure to hazardous materials in the home, workplace, and environment. Another area of study is the relationship between the constituents of air pollution and the incidence of respiratory disease and mortality. Biostatisticians also model interactions between genes and the environment.

Career Paths

Beginning statisticians usually work under the supervision of experienced statisticians. As they gain experience, they may work independently or become supervisors themselves. Those with advanced degrees have the most opportunities for advancement. Some statisticians with extensive experience become consultants.

Earning Potential

2008 mean hourly wage: $35.96; mean annual wage: $74,790

Education/Licensure

A bachelor's degree in statistics, mathematics, operations research, or other fields with significant statistics course work is required for jobs in the federal government. Jobs in industry usually require at least a master's degree, which could be in statistics, biostatistics, or mathematics. A Ph.D. is usually required for research and teaching positions in colleges and universities. A subject-area background is advantageous in the job market.

For example, an undergraduate degree in biology, chemistry, or health science combined with a graduate degree in statistics is good preparation for a job in the agriculture or pharmaceutical industries. A strong background in computer science is also important.

For More Information

American Mathematical Society
201 Charles Street
Providence, Rhode Island 02904
401-455-4000
www.ams.org

American Statistical Association
720 North Washington Street
Alexandria, Virginia 22314-1943
888-231-3473 (toll-free)
www.amstat.org

NATURAL RESOURCES MANAGEMENT AND CONSERVATION

The U.S. Department of Agriculture's natural resources strategic plan for 2005–10, "Productive Lands, Healthy Environment," states:

> We envision a productive, sustainable agricultural sector in balance with a high-quality environment. Productive use of the Nation's cropland, grazing land, and forest land is essential to the Nation's security and the health and well-being of its citizens. These lands form the foundation of a vibrant agricultural economy that provides food, fiber, forest products, and energy for the nation. These lands also produce environmental benefits that people need—clean and abundant water, clean air, and healthy ecosystems.

This vision summarizes the commitment made to managing and conserving natural resources. In 2009, even stronger emphasis was placed on sustainable agriculture and on alternate, renewable forms of energy. The challenges in bringing this vision to fruition require the work of a variety of professionals involved in all aspects of conservation and natural resources management.

Conservation Scientist and Forester

Alternate Job Titles:

- Environmental Educator
- Forestry Carbon Scientist
- Naturalist/Outdoor Educator
- Range Scientist
- Soil Conservationist
- Systems Arborist
- Urban Forester
- Utility Arborist
- Utility Forester
- Water Conservationist
- Water Quality Coordinator
- Water Resource Project Manager

Students interested in the natural resources industry have many different fields from which to choose.

Job Trends

The *Occupational Outlook Handbook* covers conservation science and forestry together because they are closely related. Employment for conservation scientists and foresters is expected to grow 5 percent by 2016, which would result in about 1,700 new jobs. However, retirements among government workers in this occupational group at both the federal and state levels are expected to provide additional jobs. Most job opportunities will be in conservation consulting and private forestry as well as in government. New career areas, such as urban forestry, are also emerging for foresters and conservation scientists.

A number of public policy initiatives will also increase opportunities for this field:

- Federal and state governments are creating incentives for industry to adopt and maintain environmentally responsible forestry practices.
- Stormwater management for the control of runoff and erosion are becoming increasingly important as cities and suburbs grow.

- States are implementing plans to improve water resources and prevent pollution from agricultural and industrial sources.
- Opening federal lands to oil and gas production will require range scientists who work as consultants to prepare environmental impact statements.
- Forestry jobs are concentrated in the western and southeastern areas of the country. Rangeland management is concentrated in the western states, and soil conservationists work in every state.

Nature of the Work

Foresters are scientists who manage the environmental, economic, and recreational aspects of forests. In general, foresters

- take inventory of the amount and location of trees and their economic value.
- develop plans for planting and harvesting trees.
- conserve soil, water, and wildlife habitat.
- are responsible for compliance with environmental regulations.

The Society of American Foresters provides a list of forestry career opportunities. These include biotechnology, environmental technology, forest biology, forest conservation, forest ecology, forest science, and paper and wood science. Two newer areas are conservation education and urban forestry. Urban foresters focus on air quality, stormwater runoff, property value, and aesthetics.

Conservation scientists manage natural resources. The rangelands of the western United States contain extensive natural resources, including wildlife habitat, grasses, minerals, water, and recreational areas. There are two major specialties for

About Weeds and Pests

The National Gardening Association in 2004 released a study that showed that 66 million households use chemical pesticides and fertilizers on their lawns and gardens. Try one of the synthetic or organic fertilizers and pesticides including commercial products to keep deer out of gardens.

conservation scientists: rangeland management and soil conservation. Range scientists advise farmers and ranchers in land-use issues, erosion, and how to improve conditions for livestock grazing and agricultural production. Soil conservationists develop plans to improve ecosystems, preserve soil and vegetation, and use the land for recreation.

Career Paths

Entry-level foresters and conservation scientists begin working under supervision. As they gain experience, they move to positions with more responsibility and may become supervisors themselves. With additional experience, they can move to top-level management positions either in private forestry or in the federal government.

Earning Potential

Conservation scientists:
2008 mean hourly wage: $28.93; mean annual wage: $60,170

Foresters:
2008 mean hourly wage: $26.46; mean annual wage: $55,040

Education/Licensure

A bachelor's degree is required for both foresters and conservation scientists. The degree may be in forestry, rangeland management, natural resources management, environmental science, biology, agriculture, or ecology. Those with extensive experience may qualify for a job in the federal government without a degree.

The Society of American Foresters (SAF) accredits educational programs in forestry, forestry technology, and urban forestry at the associate, bachelor's, and master's degree levels. The Society for Range Management accredits academic programs in rangeland management. At the moment, there are only nine such programs in the country. Check the society's Web site (see below) for links to the programs.

Certification is voluntary. The SAF offers the Certified Forester certification, which requires a degree in forestry or related area, experience, and passing an exam. The Society for Range Management offers Certified Professional in Rangeland Management (CPRM) and Certified Range Management Consultant (CRMC). Both are based on education and experience.

For More Information

Society for Range Management
10030 West 27th Avenue
Wheat Ridge, Colorado 80215-6601
303-986-3309
www.rangelands.org/srm.shtml

Society of American Foresters
5400 Grosvenor Lane
Bethesda, Maryland 20814-2198
866-897-8720 (toll-free)
www.safnet.org

Environmental Engineer

Alternate Job Titles:

- Air Pollution Control Engineer
- Civil/Environmental Engineer
- Environmental Hydrogeologist
- Environmental Scientist
- Piping Engineer
- Quality Engineer
- Remedial Project Engineer
- Water Resources Engineer

The jobs in this industry sector cover a wide range of areas within environmental protection.

Job Trends

According to the *Occupational Outlook Handbook,* environmental engineering, with an estimated growth rate of 25 percent, is projected to have the largest growth of any engineering field through 2016. This is much greater than the average for all occupations. In 2006, there were 54,000 environmental engineers, and by 2016, an additional 14,000 jobs are expected. Environmental engineering is ranked number 19 on the Career Voyages Web site list of the top 50 fastest-growing occupations requiring at least a bachelor's degree. It is also on the list of in-demand occupations. Job opportunities are excellent because for many years there have been more environmental engineering positions than qualified people to fill them.

The increasing demand for environmental engineers is a result of increasing regulatory compliance, efforts to clean up hazards that already exist, increasing public health concerns as the population grows, and an emphasis on preventing further environmental damage.

Nature of the Work

Environmental engineering is a very diverse field. Training in environmental engineering prepares a person to work in any area of environmental protection, including air pollution, hazardous waste, industrial hygiene, public health, land management, radiation control, solid waste disposal, stormwater management, toxic materials, and water and wastewater management. In addition, each of these areas has subspecialties.

Environmental engineers may be employed in planning, design, research, or regulatory work. They can be found in major corporations, consulting firms, research firms, pollution control facilities, universities, and at the local, state, and federal government levels. The biggest employers are engineering services, consulting services, and government. In any type of organization, the work is subject to change as government and public policies change.

Career Paths

As environmental engineers gain experience, they become specialists and advance into positions where they supervise a team of engineers and other staff members. Some eventually become managers. Some choose to earn a master's in business administration (MBA) to prepare for high-level management positions; others obtain a graduate degree in engineering, enabling them to move into executive positions in industry and government.

Earning Potential

2008 mean hourly wage: $37.49; mean annual wage: $77,970

Education/Licensure

A bachelor's degree in engineering from a college or university program that is accredited by the Accreditation Board for Engineering and Technology (ABET) is the minimum requirement. The American Academy of Environmental Engineering (AAEE) partners with ABET in accrediting environmental engineering programs. The degree may be in environmental engineering or in chemical, civil, or mechanical engineering as well. Many colleges and universities offer environmental engineering in the civil engineering department. A master's degree in environmental engineering gives the job candidate much better opportunities, and a Ph.D. improves the long-range job opportunities.

Some colleges and universities offer five-year programs that culminate in a master's degree. Some offer five- or six-year programs that include cooperative experience. Some four-year schools have arrangements with community colleges or liberal arts colleges that allow students to spend two or three years at the initial school and transfer for the last two years to complete their engineering degree.

All fifty states as well as the District of Columbia require engineers to be licensed as professional engineers (PE) if they serve the public directly. In most states, licensure requires graduation from a four-year engineering program accredited by ABET, four years of experience, and passing the state exam. Many engineers take the Fundamentals of Engineering portion of the exam upon graduation. They are then engineers in training (EIT). After obtaining appropriate work experience, they take the Principles and Practice of Engineering exam to complete their professional license. Most states recognize licenses from other states as long as the requirements are the same or more stringent. Some states have continuing education requirements.

The American Academy of Environmental Engineers offers Board Certified Environmental Engineer (BCEE) for PE holders and Board Certified Environmental Engineering Member

(BCEEM) for non-PE holders. Both require a bachelor's degree in engineering or a related field, eight years of professional experience, and successfully passing an exam in the specialty area for which a person is becoming certified. Specialty areas include air pollution control, general environmental engineering, hazardous waste management, industrial hygiene, radiation protection, solid waste management, and water supply/wastewater engineering.

For More Information

Accreditation Board for Engineering and
    Technology (ABET)
111 Market Place, Suite 1050
Baltimore, Maryland 21202
410-347-7700
www.abet.org

American Academy of Environmental Engineers
130 Holiday Court, Suite 100
Annapolis, Maryland 21401
410-266-3311
www.aaee.net

American Society of Civil Engineers
Transportation and Development Institute
1801 Alexander Bell Drive
Reston, Virginia 20191-4400
800-548-2723 (toll-free)
www.asce.org

Geographic Information Specialist

Alternate Job Titles:

- Cartographer
- Computer Programmer
- Computer Systems Analyst
- Database Administrator
- Database Design Analyst
- Geospatial Information Specialist
- Information Scientist
- Information Systems Management Specialist
- Photogrammetrist

Many jobs for geographic information specialists are related to the design, development, and use of computer databases of geographic information.

Job Trends

Employment for this field is expected to increase by 21 percent by 2016. This is much greater than the average for all occupations. Career Voyages ranks cartographers and photogrammetrists number 41 on the list of the top 50 fastest-growing occupations requiring at least a bachelor's degree. They are also on the list of in-demand occupations. Rapid growth is generated by development of the many types of applications for which geographic information is being used. It is applied to problems in all types of organizations, including government, private firms, and nonprofit advocacy organizations.

Nature of the Work

Most geographical information specialists are employed in architectural, engineering, and related services. Local government employs many others. Other opportunities exist in environmental consulting, transportation, environmental organizations, and state departments of natural resources.

Geographic information specialists manipulate and interpret data using geographic information systems (GIS). GIS are composed of a database, a system to analyze or model the data, and a graphical display. Cartographers map the surface of the Earth by using data collected from surveys, geographical research, and remote sensing systems such as aerial cameras, lasers, and satellites. By combining the digital information generated from these systems with research and location information, geographical information specialists generate databases. Photogrammetrists perform the same functions using data from photographs. Using GIS, geographic information specialists can display and interpret data, deciding how best to display or model the information for a specific user or problem.

GIS is being applied to a wide variety of problems in almost all environmental areas. Natural resource management is using it to manage forests and rangelands, preserve wetlands and wildlife habitats, model migration of toxic chemicals, and assess groundwater contamination and air quality. Urban and regional planners model urban growth using the technology. Public health officials are using it to track the incidence of certain diseases in relation to natural and environmental factors.

Career Path

At the entry level, geographic information specialists with bachelor's degrees work in groups producing maps. As these specialists gain experience, they may become project managers. Those with master's degrees, however, may begin by managing projects.

Earning Potential

2008 mean hourly wage: $27.87; mean annual wage: $57,980

Education/Licensure

Most cartographers and photogrammetrists have a bachelors' degree in geography, cartography, engineering, forestry, surveying, or computer science. Degrees in geographic information are often offered in the geography department. The American Congress on Surveying and Mapping provides links to accredited college and university programs.

In some states, cartographers and photogrammetrists must be licensed as surveyors. Some states have licenses specifically for photogrammetrists.

The Imaging and Geospatial Information Society offers three certifications based on experience and passing an exam: Certified Photogrammetrist; Certified Mapping Scientist, Remote Sensing; and Certified Mapping Scientist, GIS/LIS (geographic information systems/land information systems).

For More Information

American Congress on Surveying and Mapping
6 Montgomery Village Avenue
Suite 403
Gaithersburg, Maryland 20879
240-632-9716
www.acsm.net

ASPRS: Imaging and Geospatial Information
Society
5410 Grosvenor Lane
Suite 210
Bethesda, Maryland 20814-2160
301-493-0290
www.asprs.org

PARKS, RECREATION, AND TOURISM

Trends for parks, recreation, and tourism reflect trends in the leisure and hospitality industry. The *Occupational Outlook Handbook* includes an overview of this industry and breaks it down into three categories: arts, entertainment, and recreation; food and drink; and hotels. Employment in arts, entertainment, and recreation was predicted to increase 31 percent by 2016. Employment in hotels was expected to increase 14 percent. Museums are expanding; however, this industry sector has been affected by the economy, and the outlook is currently not as good as it had been. New jobs in these areas are not as plentiful as predicted, but the situation will likely improve as the economy recovers.

The American Recovery and Reinvestment Act (ARRA) passed in 2009 invested funding in these areas to bring about recovery and create jobs. As a result of ARRA, the National Park Service had $750 million to invest in projects to preserve historic landscapes and national icons, remediate mine sites, improve trails, increase use of renewable energy, and increase energy efficiency. The funding for the Federal Highway Administration included money to improve park roads. Under ARRA, the National Endowment for the Arts received funding for theaters and art projects across the country.

About Eco-Travel

Like to travel, but feel guilty about the carbon footprint you leave behind? Find out how to travel responsibly at www.independenttraveler.com and at www.ecotourism.org, the Web site for the International Ecotourism Society.

These projects and others funded by ARRA will improve job opportunities.

Curator and Conservator

Alternate Job Titles:

- Conservation Administrator
- Conservation Scientist
- Conservation Technician
- Museum Director
- Museum Technician
- Preservation Specialist

If you have an interest in historic preservation, material culture, and the environment, this is one field where you can combine these interests.

Job Trends

According to the *Occupational Outlook Handbook,* employment for curators and conservators is expected to increase 18 percent, or 2,400 jobs, by 2016. This is greater than the average for all occupations. The Career Voyages Web site ranks curators number 29 of the top 50 fastest-growing occupations; however, current economic conditions should be taken into account when evaluating this position.

In 2006, about 38 percent of curators and conservators worked in museums and at historical sites. About 18 percent worked in colleges and universities, mainly in libraries. About 31 percent worked in local, state, and federal government. Local and state governments employ curators in historical museums, parks, and zoos. The federal government employs them in the Smithsonian museum system and in the National Park Service at historic parks and sites.

Nature of the Work

Curators and conservators work in museums, historic sites, nature centers, botanical gardens, arboretums, zoos, aquariums, and science and technology centers. They specialize in fields such as art, history, or botany. They may further specialize in one aspect of their field. Conservators usually specialize in materials such as textiles, paintings, or biological materials.

Curators

- preserve objects with historical, cultural, and biological significance, such as historic objects, art objects, living plants and animals, preserved specimens of animals and plants, photographs, and documents.
- direct the exhibition, acquisition, cataloging, and storage of items in collections.
- are involved in research to evaluate and authenticate artifacts and catalog them.
- provide, when involved in the natural sciences, educational outreach to the public to give them an understanding and appreciation of the natural world and its diversity, current and past.

Conservators

- examine objects using a variety of methods, including chemical, X-ray, and microscopic analyses.
- determine the best ways to restore or preserve objects.
- conduct research and publish scholarly articles.

Career Paths

Those entering the field with a bachelor's degree begin as technicians. In small museums, they may have some opportunity to advance to curator, but a master's degree is usually required for curators. With experience, a curator can advance in responsibility, eventually becoming a museum director. One form of advancement for both conservators and curators is to move to a larger institution. Research and scholarly publications are important for advancement.

Earning Potential

Curators:
2008 mean hourly wage: $24.78; mean annual wage: $51,540

Museum technicians and conservators:
2008 mean hourly wage: $19.59; mean annual wage: $40,750

Education/Licensure

A bachelor's degree qualifies a person to work as a museum technician. The degree may be in any area of a museum specialty, such as history, art, archae-ology, or botany. Very few schools offer bachelor's degree programs in museum studies.

To be qualified as a curator or conservator, a master's degree is required. Many schools offer master's degrees in museum studies. However, a degree in the museum specialty along with experience in the form of a museum internship is another route.

For More Information

American Association of Museums
1575 Eye Street NW, Suite 400
Washington, D.C. 20005
202-289-1818
www.aam-us.org

Parks and Recreation Specialist

Alternate Job Titles:

- Education Specialist
- Environmental Education Specialist
- Interpretive Naturalist
- Outdoor Education Naturalist
- Park Activities Coordinator
- Park Interpretive Specialist
- Park Manager
- Park Naturalist
- Park Ranger
- Program Manager

This field combines outdoor work, a background in the natural sciences, and contact with the public.

Job Trends

The *Occupational Outlook Handbook* predicts growth in employment of park naturalists between 3 and 6 percent by 2016, which amounts to 7,000 new job openings. According to the National Recreation and Park Association, over 400,000 people are employed providing services and programs in state and local parks and recreation, so retirements will also provide job openings.

Nature of the Work

Parks and recreational activities contribute to the public health. Parks also have a mission for environmental stewardship and conservation. Parklands, protected from development, contribute

About Green Movies

Even the makers of Hollywood movies are going green. Fox Pictures has the "Fox Green Guide" that recommends ways to cut down on a film's carbon footprint as it's being made. On one of Focus Features' movie productions, actors and crew members were given metal refillable water bottles, which saved 15,000 plastic water bottles from ending up in a landfill.

to overall environmental quality in terms of soil and water conservation and improved air quality. Educating the public regarding the natural and historical resources of an area, state, or the nation and teaching people how to enjoy the features without damaging them are two primary functions of park and recreation specialists.

The job of park naturalists is varied. They

- plan and conduct programs for the public at local, state, and national parks.
- provide services to visitors, explaining park regulations and answering questions.
- conduct tours and field trips where they explain the natural, scientific, and historical features of the park.
- present interpretive talks and prepare displays at nature centers and historical and scientific visitor centers.
- respond to emergencies and perform maintenance.

The job of recreation specialist is varied, and safety is a major responsibility. Recreation specialists

- plan and conduct activities and programs, particularly in local and state parks, which may include sports activities, educational programs, and cultural programs.
- organize outdoor activities such as hikes, rock climbing, or canoe trips.
- may be responsible for facilities such as playgrounds, swimming pools, ice skating rinks, and trails.

Career Paths

As naturalists and recreation specialists gain experience, they may become supervisors or managers.

They may move to larger parks or oversee systems of parks.

Earning Potential

2008 median hourly wage: $28.23; median annual wage: $58,720

Education/Licensure

A bachelor's degree in environmental science, ecology, education, biology, or botany is required for most positions. Experience with pioneering skills, nature crafts, Native American lifestyles, colonial history, ropes courses, rock climbing, backpacking, and similar activities is also an advantage.

Certification is voluntary. The National Recreation and Park Association offers several certifications. The Certified Park and Recreation Professional (CPRP) requires a combination of education, experience, and passing an exam. The Aquatic Facility Operator (AFO) and Certified Playground Safety Inspector (CPSI) require passing an exam. Lifeguarding and CPR certifications are sometimes beneficial.

For More Information

Association for Environmental and Outdoor
  Education (AEOE)
P.O. Box 187
Angelus Oaks, California 92305
www.aeoe.org

Association of Outdoor and Recreation Education
  (AORE)
National Office
6511 Buckshore Drive
Whitmore Lake, Michigan 48189
810-299-2782
www.aore.org

National Recreation and Park Association
22377 Belmont Ridge Road
Ashburn, Virginia 20148-4501
800-626-6772 (toll-free)
www.nrpa.org

Turfgrass Manager

Alternate Job Titles:
- Athletic Fields Superintendent
- Buildings and Grounds Supervisor
- Golf Course Superintendent
- Grounds Crew Supervisor
- Grounds Foreman
- Groundskeeper Supervisor
- Grounds Maintenance Supervisor
- Grounds Supervisor
- Landscape Manager
- Landscape Supervisor
- Sod Farm Manager
- Sports Turf Manager

This is an interesting field for someone who likes sports and working outdoors.

Job Trends

The *Occupational Outlook Handbook* groups turfgrass managers and golf course managers with grounds maintenance workers. Employment in this occupation is expected to grow by 18 percent by 2016, which is greater than the average for all occupations. Career Voyages lists first-line supervisors and managers of landscaping, lawn service, and groundskeeping as an in-demand occupation.

According to the Department of Plant Sciences at North Dakota State University, there is a demand nationwide for turfgrass managers. The University's Sports and Urban Turfgrass Management program reports that between 200 and 300 new golf courses are built in this country each year, and the cost for lawn care in this country totals more than $17 billion annually. The School of Environmental and Biological Sciences at Rutgers University notes that the industry has grown steadily and continues to generate a need for turfgrass professionals.

Turfgrass
The Michigan Turfgrass Stewardship Initiative of the Michigan Turfgrass Foundation has information on how turfgrass can mitigate environmental problems and create good jobs in urban areas.

Nature of the Work

Turfgrass managers are responsible for the maintenance of golf courses, football fields, baseball fields, soccer fields, college and university athletic fields, fields for professional sports, parks, corporate parks, and home lawns. Their work includes overseeing personnel, grounds work, and budgets. They must have a thorough understanding of plant and soil science, pest control, irrigation, and environmental science in addition to business management. Turfgrass managers may also work in sales, research, or consulting for environmental groups.

Turfgrass provides numerous benefits to people and the environment. In addition to providing an aesthetically pleasing surface for sports and recreation, it improves air quality and reduces effects of global warming by absorbing carbon dioxide from the atmosphere and releasing oxygen. It also reduces erosion and conserves soil. Like other green plants, turfgrass has a cooling effect in urban areas. Care of turfgrass, however, can be detrimental to the environment when pesticides and chemical fertilizers are used and when excessive watering is needed. The challenge for turfgrass managers is to use natural fertilizers and grass varieties that require less water and are resistant to pests.

Career Paths

Turfgrass graduates usually begin as assistants. After several years, they may become superintendents of a golf course or an athletic field. Moving to larger courses or private courses or a larger sports complex is one form of advancement. Some golf course superintendents may eventually become managers of an entire resort facility. Entrepreneurial opportunities exist in the lawncare business.

Earning Potential

First-Line Supervisors/Managers of Landscaping, Lawn Service, and Groundskeeping:
2008 median hourly wage: $19.19; median annual wage: $39,920

Golf Course Superintendent:
Average annual salary: $57,000–$105,000

Starting salary (assistant with no experience): $28,000–$35,000

Sports Turf Manager:
Annual salary: $44,000

Education/Licensure

A bachelor's degree is required for jobs such as golf course superintendent or sports turf manager. A number of colleges and universities now offer specific degree programs or certificate programs in turfgrass management. A degree in agronomy or horticulture also qualifies a person to work in this area. Those with bachelor's degrees in other subjects may be able to enter the field by obtaining a certificate or associate degree in turfgrass management. Internship programs are good preparation. Some jobs may be available to those with an associate degree or other postsecondary training, but the best opportunities are for those who hold at least a bachelor's degree. Those with master's degrees may work in research or as agricultural extension agents.

Certification is voluntary. The Golf Course Superintendents Association offers the Certified Golf Course Superintendent (CGCS) certification. The Professional Grounds Management Society offers the Certified Grounds Manager (CGM) certification, which requires a combination of education, experience, and passing an exam. The Professional Landcare Network offers the Certified Turfgrass Professional (CTP) certification program through the University of Georgia. Completion of the self-study program and passing two exams are required.

For More Information

Golf Course Superintendents Association of
    America
1421 Research Park Drive
Lawrence, Kansas 66049
800-472-7878 (toll-free)
www.gcsaa.org

Michigan Turfgrass Foundation
3225 West St. Joseph
Lansing, Michigan 48917
517-327-9207
www.michiganturfgrass.org

Professional Grounds Management Society
720 Light Street
Baltimore, Maryland 21230
410-223-2861
www.pgms.org

Professional Landcare Network
950 Herndon Parkway, Suite 450
Herndon, Virginia 20170-5528
703-736-9666
www.landcarenetwork.org

Turfgrass Producers International
2 East Main Street
East Dundee, Illinois 60118
847-649-5555
www.turfgrasssod.org

POLICY, ADMINISTRATION, ANALYSIS, AND ADVOCACY

The area of policy, administration, analysis, and advocacy is not an industry in itself but a broad and diverse collection of jobs. The purpose of these jobs is to examine all aspects of the condition of the environment—social, economic, justice, and political—and propose and implement solutions. The people employed in these jobs develop and implement policies, regulations, laws, standards, procedures, and guidelines. They study industries and technology and propose modifications that will be sustainable, create jobs, stimulate the economy, conserve resources, and protect the environment.

Many of the jobs in this area are in federal, state, and local government agencies. Others are in advocacy organizations or special interest groups that influence government and the public. Some jobs are in private companies, consulting firms, and industry groups. Job opportunities abound in the green economy for people with diverse interests and backgrounds.

Environmental Economist
Alternate Job Title: Resources Economist

Environmental economists work in a variety of fields.

Job Trends
According to the *Occupational Outlook Handbook,* employment for economists is expected to grow about 7 percent through 2016. This is about average growth compared to all occupations. Of the 15,000 economists employed in 2006, 32 percent worked in the federal government and 20 percent in state governments. Others worked in private industry, particularly in management, scientific, and technical consulting services. Most of the jobs expected during the next decade are as consultants in private industry because many corporations prefer to hire consultants to address increasingly complex global economic issues. Economists' jobs in state government are also expected to show growth. Teaching economics is another area of growth.

Nature of the Work
Environmental economists specialize in natural resources and the environment and may work for government agencies at all levels of government, companies, or industry groups. Jobs include the following:

- researching the economic impact of environmental standards and regulation
- developing models to predict the consequences of activities
- analyzing the economic impact of conservation, ecological, climate control, and pollution control strategies

About Lighting Standards

In 2009, U.S. efficiency standards were increased for general service fluorescent lamps, the kind in overhead lighting, and incandescent reflector lamps often used in track lighting. Together, the changes should amount to a 15 to 25 percent reduction in energy use and $1 billion to $4 billion in energy bill savings.

- studying how the quality of natural resources and science policy affect agricultural productivity

Economists use sampling, statistical, and analytical techniques to research economic issues. They collect, analyze, and model data to determine how resources are distributed to produce services or products. Resources include such things as land, natural resources, and human resources. Economists also analyze historical trends and develop models to make forecasts of future trends. They may specialize in a variety of areas, for example, agriculture, education, energy, the environment, health, or urban and regional economic issues. In all cases, quantitative and computer skills are essential for a career in economics.

Career Path

Individuals holding a bachelor's degree in economics qualify for some entry-level positions, particularly in the federal government. They also qualify for some industry positions in sales or as research assistants. However, a master's degree or even a Ph.D. is required for many positions in private industry and for advancement opportunities in any setting.

Economists may initially work as research assistants, and, after gaining experience, they may be given their own projects. Some experienced economists move into administration. A background in economics opens pathways to other jobs such as public policy consultant or purchasing manager. Economists with advanced degrees may become college or university professors, and some with bachelor's degrees may acquire teaching credentials to teach high school economics.

Earning Potential

2008 mean hourly wage: $43.67; mean annual wage: $90,830

Education/Licensure

Economics students at both the undergraduate and graduate levels may choose from a variety of specializations, but quantitative courses, including mathematics, statistics, and computer science, are most valuable. There is no licensure required for the field of environmental economics.

For More Information

National Association for Business Economics
1233 20th Street NW, Suite 505
Washington, D.C. 20036
202-463-6223
www.nabe.com

Environmental Scientist

Environmental scientists may have a major in environmental science or in another field such as earth science, hydrology, or chemistry.

Job Trends

According to the Career Voyages Web site, environmental scientists and specialists, including those with a health background, rank number 20 in the top 50 fastest-growing occupations requiring at least a bachelor's degree and are in-demand occupations. There are currently more than 80,000 environmental scientists, and the demand is expected to be over 100,000 by 2016. The *Occupational Outlook Handbook* predicts growth in employment of 25 percent through 2016, which is much greater than the average for all occupations. The most demand is expected in private-sector consulting. Those with field experience will have the most opportunities.

About the EPA

Consider a job with the Environmental Protection Agency. In addition to the federal EPA, states have similar agencies charged with the same mission. The federal EPA site has the following description of jobs with its Office of Enforcement and Compliance Assurance: the office "maximizes compliance with the nation's environmental laws and reduces threats to public health and the environment through an integrated approach of compliance assistance, compliance incentives, and innovative civil and criminal enforcement."

Growth in this occupation is due in large part to the increasing demands that population growth places on water supplies and on the environment. Growth is also due to increasing environmental regulations regarding clean air and decontamination of groundwater. New strategies for restoring ecosystems and continual monitoring of the human impact on the environment will also contribute to job growth. New jobs will be created by the shift in focus from investigation to remediation and prevention. This means that environmental scientists will have more roles as consultants in business and development processes.

Nature of the Work

State government is the biggest employer of environmental scientists followed in decreasing order by consulting services, engineering services, local government, and the federal government. About 45 percent of environmental scientists work for the government on the federal, state, and local levels. Some environmental scientists work for nonprofit advocacy groups as policy analysts or policy specialists. In addition to making policy recommendations, they may be involved in community relations, fundraising, budget proposals, and scientific research.

Environmental scientists attempt to solve a variety of environmental problems, such as reducing carbon dioxide emissions, monitoring waste disposal, and preventing habitat loss. Their goal is to identify, eliminate, and prevent environmental hazards that affect humans, wildlife, and the planet overall. They conduct research by collecting samples of air, water, soil, and food and analyzing them, using the results of their analysis to assess environmental problems and develop solutions.

Career Paths

Environmental scientists often begin their careers with fieldwork or as a laboratory technician or research assistant. After gaining experience, they may become project leaders. Eventually they may become managers. Many will become consultants.

Earning Potential

2008 mean hourly wage: $31.39; mean annual wage: $65,280

Education/Licensure

A bachelor's degree is the minimum requirement for a job as an environmental scientist. However, most positions in federal and state government and in private industry now require a master's degree. Colleges and universities offer multidisciplinary programs in environmental sciences at the undergraduate and graduate levels. Programs are often in the earth sciences or geosciences department; however, a degree in environmental science is not essential. Many people working in this field have degrees in other sciences, such as atmospheric science, chemistry, geology, geophysics, life science, or physics. Colleges and universities often offer internships or research opportunities to undergraduate students in environmental sciences, which is valuable experience in the job market.

Computer skills are essential for environmental scientists. Data are often collected with remote sensing, global positioning systems, and digital mapping, and computer data analysis and computer models are often used to develop solutions. Knowledge of environmental legislation and regulations is also valuable.

For More Information

American Geological Institute (AGI)
4220 King Street
Alexandria, Virginia 22302-1502
703-379-2480
www.agiweb.org

Environmental Technical Writer

Alternate Job Titles:

- Environmental Journalist
- Environmental Reporter

Technical writing is one way to support conservation and the environment if you have an interest in the subject but don't want a lab or field job.

Job Trends

Technical writing is ranked by the Career Voyages Web site as number 47 of the top 50 fastest-growing occupations requiring at least a bachelor's degree. It is also listed as one of the in-demand occupations. Almost 59,000 new openings are expected by 2016. The *Occupational Outlook Handbook* projects a 10-percent growth in employment by 2016, which is about average for all occupations. Competition will be strong because many qualified people enter this field.

Demand is expected to result from increased publishing on the Internet by companies and organizations. Editors and writers with multimedia experience will be needed. Opportunities will be best for writers who have knowledge of a subject area, such as science, medicine, law, economics, or technology. Environmental writing is one such specialty.

Nature of the Work

Many technical writers are freelance writers who are contracted to deliver a written product. In addition to text, writers may be responsible for developing graphics, including diagrams, charts, photographs, and illustrations.

Some environmental technical writers work in architectural, engineering, and related services or in scientific and technical consulting services. In consulting firms, knowledge of an industry and the environmental regulations that pertain to it is necessary.

Working for nonprofit environmental advocacy groups, technical writers may prepare fact sheets, brochures, newsletters, special features, and fundraising materials. They may also develop scripts for video materials. Writing for an advocacy group requires an understanding of the issues and the concerns of the various constituency groups, and it requires collaboration with experts in these areas. Writers must be able to address a variety of audiences.

Environmental journalism is another job area for environmental writers. The Society of Environmental Journalists promotes accurate and responsible reporting on environmental issues in all types of media.

Career Path

If employed in smaller companies, writers may be given writing assignments immediately. In larger companies, they may begin as assistants, researching and checking facts for other writers before getting their own assignments. Advancement usually means working on bigger or more important projects. Writing for nonprofit organizations and small companies is often contracted out to freelance writers who set up their own businesses.

Earning Potential

2008 mean hourly wage: $30.87; mean annual wage: $64,210

Education/Licensure

A college degree is required for most technical writing positions. Degrees in English, journalism, and communications are common, although liberal arts degrees are also acceptable for many positions. A degree in a technical subject area is an advantage for a technical writer. Experience in computer graphics and Web design is also an advantage.

The Society for Technical Communication provides a database of academic institutions with programs in technical communications.

For More Information

Association of Earth Science Editors (AESE)
554 Chess Street
Pittsburgh, Pennsylvania 15205-3212
www.aese.org

Society of Environmental Journalists
P.O. Box 2492
Jenkintown, Pennsylvania 19046
215-884-8174
www.sej.org

Society for Technical Communication
9401 Lee Highway, Suite 300
Fairfax, Virginia 22031
703-522-4114
www.stc.org

TRANSPORTATION INDUSTRY

Growing transportation needs and environmental concerns will generate job opportunities for professionals who plan, design, and build transportation systems and new energy-efficient cars, trucks, buses, trains, ships, and airplanes. New and more stringent environmental regulations place increasing demands on transportation systems. Existing vehicles and fleets must be upgraded to be more energy efficient and meet stricter emissions standards. Vehicles must be designed and built to use alternative fuels.

In addition, new openings are expected in areas of transportation that are less energy intensive, such as rail and water. The Federal Highway Administration has already authorized nearly 6,000 projects in response to the American Recovery and Reinvestment Act of 2009 (ARRA). A portion of the ARRA funding is earmarked for On-the-Job Training/Support Services projects. According to the National Railway Labor Conference, the industry is hiring thousands of new employees to meet the growing needs of railway traffic.

Mechanical Engineer

Alternate Job Titles:

- HVAC Engineer
- Lead Mechanical Engineer
- Lead Process Engineer
- Mechanical Handling Engineer
- Mechanical Packaging Engineer
- Piping Inspector
- Process Design Engineer
- Projects Control Manager
- Structural and Piping Designer
- Subsea Pipeline Engineer
- Valve Engineer
- Wells Project Services Engineer

In addition to manufacturing, a number of jobs in the field of mechanical engineering are in oil and natural gas development, an important area for environmental impacts.

About Airline Emissions

The European Union has adopted a standard that requires air carriers to cut emissions from their planes or begin buying carbon permits in 2012 as part of the EU's cap-and-trade program to reduce greenhouse gases.

Job Trends

An emerging trend in the new green economy is to retool U.S. manufacturing. For example, manufacturing plants that previously made auto components can be modified to make wind turbine components. Plants that built gasoline-powered cars and trucks can be modified to produce hybrid vehicles. These modifications require mechanical engineers to design the products and the processes and equipment to manufacture them.

The *Occupational Outlook Handbook* predicts that growth in mechanical engineering will be 4 percent through 2016, which is less than the average for all occupations but still amounts to 58,000 new openings. This slow growth is tied to declines in the manufacturing industry. Nevertheless, because there were about 226,000 mechanical engineering jobs in 2006, the Career Voyages Web site ranks mechanical engineering as one of the top 50 occupations, requiring at least a bachelor's degree, with the most openings. It is also on the list of in-demand occupations.

Nature of the Work

Mechanical engineering is a broad discipline concerned with power and energy and how these are transmitted, converted, controlled, and utilized effectively in mechanical devices. Mechanical engineers design, develop, and manufacture all types of mechanical devices including tools, engines, turbines, generators, and robots. They design and manufacture heating, ventilation, and cooling systems used in residential and commercial buildings, and they also design biomedical devices such as artificial joints. In designing a product, engineers must consider a wide variety of factors such as cost, safety, performance, appearance, reliability, ergonomics, ability to be recycled, energy efficiency, and environmental impact. Computer simulation and modeling are important tools in the design process.

Mechanical engineers are an important part of the transportation industry. Existing forms of transportation must be continuously improved or replaced. Mechanical engineers design and manufacture all types of vehicles, including the powertrains and components for hybrid and alternative fuel automobiles and trucks. They also develop the software that controls electromechanical systems in vehicles and design energy-efficient engines for buses and trains. Fuel efficiency, by-products of fuel consumption, and environmental impact are critical factors that mechanical engineers address in their work.

Mechanical engineers also work in many other industries that affect the environment, including advanced manufacturing, aerospace, agricultural production, biomedical, construction, energy, geospatial technology, and nanotechnology. In all these industries, energy efficiency and environmental impact are factors.

Career Paths

As mechanical engineers gain experience, they may become specialists or advance into positions where they supervise a team of engineers and other staff members. Some eventually become managers. Some go on to earn a master's in business administration (MBA) degree to prepare them for high-level managerial positions. Some move into technical sales.

Earning Potential

2008 mean hourly wage: $37.59; mean annual wage: $78,200

About Infrastructure Management

One key to reducing energy use and greenhouse gases is smart infrastructure. This is a system of wireless sensors and analytic and visualization software that can result in the more efficient management of everything from commuter traffic to the nation's electric grid.

Education/Licensure

For entry-level positions, a bachelor's degree in engineering from a college or university program that is accredited by the Accreditation Board for Engineering and Technology (ABET) is required. In some cases, engineers with degrees in one type of engineering may qualify for jobs in other areas of engineering. Most colleges and universities offer transportation engineering as a specialty in civil engineering.

Some colleges and universities offer five-year programs that culminate in a master's degree. Some offer five- or six-year programs that include cooperative experience. Some four-year schools have arrangements with community colleges or liberal arts colleges that allow students to spend two or three years at the initial school and transfer for the last two years to complete their engineering degree.

All fifty states as well as the District of Columbia require engineers to be licensed as professional engineers (PE) if they serve the public directly. In most states, licensure requires graduation from a four-year engineering program accredited by ABET, four years of experience, and passing the state exam. Many engineers take the Fundamentals of Engineering portion of the exam upon graduation. They are then engineers in training (EIT). After obtaining appropriate work experience, they take the Principles and Practice of Engineering exam to complete their professional license. Most states recognize licenses from other states as long as the requirements are the same or more stringent. Some states have continuing education requirements.

The American Society of Heating, Refrigerating, and Air-Conditioning Engineers (ASHRAE) offers certification and online training courses. The American Society of Mechanical Engineers (ASME) offers a number of specialized certifications, short courses, Internet seminars, and online courses. The Society of Automotive Engineers (SAE) offers professional development courses in classrooms and via Webcasts and online courses.

Continually updating skills is important to keep up with developments in technology.

For More Information

Accreditation Board for Engineering and
Technology (ABET)
111 Market Place, Suite 1050
Baltimore, Maryland 21202
410-347-7700
www.abet.org

American Society of Heating, Refrigerating, and
Air-Conditioning Engineers (ASHRAE)
1791 Tullie Circle NE
Atlanta, Georgia 30329
404-636-8400
www.ashrae.org

American Society of Mechanical Engineers
(ASME)
3 Park Avenue
New York, New York 10016-5990
800-843-2763 (toll-free)
www.asme.org

National Society of Professional Engineers
(NSPE)
1420 King Street
Alexandria, Virginia 22314
703-684-2800
www.nspe.org

Society of Automotive Engineers (SAE)
400 Commonwealth Drive
Warrendale, Pennsylvania 15096-0001
724-776-4841
www.sae.org

Transportation Engineer

Alternate Job Titles:
- Highway Engineer
- Traffic Engineer
- Transportation Planning Engineer

Job Trends

According to the *Occupational Outlook Handbook,* employment in civil engineering, which includes transportation engineering, is expected to grow by 18 percent. This is much greater than the average for all occupations. The Career Voyages Web site ranks civil engineering as one of the top 50 in-demand occupations. It is ranked number 21 on the list of the top 50 occupations, requiring at least a bachelor's degree, with the most openings through 2016.

Environmental regulations and considerations increase the demand by requiring more engineers to expand existing transportation systems or to design and build new systems. Engineers are also needed to repair existing roads and bridges.

Nature of the Work

Transportation engineering is a specialty of civil engineering that deals with all aspects of transportation. This includes planning, safety, education, traffic, freight, and mass transit. Transportation engineers

- design railway systems, mass transit systems, bridges, and highways.
- analyze traffic patterns and determine the need for signals and other controls.
- analyze the environmental impact of different modes of transportation.
- design pedestrian walkways and bicycle lanes.

Knowledge and understanding of the National Environmental Policy Act (NEPA) and context sensitive solutions (CSS) and how they are applied in the transportation sector are beneficial to job seekers.

Career Paths

As transportation engineers gain experience, they become specialists and advance into positions where they supervise a team of engineers and other staff members. Some eventually become managers. Some go on to earn a master's in business administration (MBA) degree to prepare them for high-level managerial positions. Some transportation engineers continue their education by obtaining graduate degrees in engineering that enable them to move into executive positions in industry and government.

Earning Potential

Civil engineers:
2008 mean hourly wage: $37.77; mean annual wage: $78,560

Education/Licensure

For entry-level positions, a bachelor's degree in engineering from a college or university program that is accredited by the Accreditation Board for Engineering and Technology (ABET) is required. In some cases, engineers with degrees in one type of engineering may qualify for jobs in other areas of engineering. Most colleges and universities offer transportation engineering as a specialty in civil engineering.

Some colleges and universities offer five-year programs that culminate in a master's degree. Some offer five- or six-year programs that include cooperative experience. Some four-year schools have arrangements with community colleges or liberal arts colleges that allow students to spend two or three years at the initial school and transfer for the last two years to complete their engineering degree.

All fifty states as well as the District of Columbia require engineers to be licensed as professional engineers (PE) if they serve the public directly. In most states, licensure requires graduation from a four-year engineering program accredited by ABET, four years of experience, and passing the state exam. Many engineers take the Fundamentals of Engineering portion of the exam upon graduation. They are then engineers in training (EIT). After obtaining appropriate work experience, they take the Principles and Practice of Engineering exam to complete their professional license. Most states recognize licenses from other states as long as the requirements are the same or more stringent. Some states have continuing education requirements.

The Transportation Professional Certification Board (TPCB) of the Institute of Transportation Engineers (ITE) offers certifications in planning and traffic control.

For More Information

Accreditation Board for Engineering and
    Technology (ABET)
111 Market Place, Suite 1050
Baltimore, Maryland 21202
410-347-7700
www.abet.org

American Society of Civil Engineers
Transportation and Development Institute
1801 Alexander Bell Drive
Reston, Virginia 20191-4400
800-548-2723 (toll-free)
www.asce.org

Institute of Transportation Engineers
1099 14th Street NW, Suite 300 West
Washington, D.C. 20005-3438
202-289-0222
www.ite.org

National Society of Professional Engineers
    (NSPE)
1420 King Street
Alexandria, Virginia 22314
703-684-2800
www.nspe.org

Transportation Environmental Planner

Alternate Job Titles:

- Aviation Planner
- Campus Transportation Planner
- Environmental Planner
- Transportation Planner
- Urban and Regional Planner
- Urban Planner This category has one of the highest growth rates according to the U.S. Department of Commerce.

Job Trends

The Career Voyages Web site lists urban and regional planners as one of the in-demand occupations. The *Occupational Outlook Handbook* projects 15 percent growth in this field by 2016, which is greater than the average for all occupations. Planners with master's degrees and good computer skills, including modeling and

- consider economic and social factors such as where population is concentrated and how people get to their jobs.
- draft policy and legislation.
- study current land use, collect and analyze data, and prepare forecasts of future needs and cost estimates.
- write zoning codes and environmental regulations.

Urban and regional planners must coordinate all the stakeholders, including the public, planning boards, civic leaders, and land developers. Planners often work with elected officials in their communities and with state and federal officials.

Specifically, transportation environmental planners develop systems that balance a variety of transportation modes, including private cars, bicycles, pedestrians, and public transportation. Some transportation planners work for universities, where they are responsible for the university's vehicle fleet and may have to develop plans for alternate transportation such as carpools or bicycle sharing. On campus, pedestrian traffic and safety are extremely important considerations. Aviation planners develop master plans for airports and conduct assessments of noise and environmental impact.

In all cases, transportation planners must consider the environmental implications of transportation systems. Knowledge and understanding of the National Environmental Policy Act (NEPA) and context sensitive solutions (CSS) and how they are applied in the transportation sector are beneficial to job seekers.

Career Path

As planners gain experience, they advance to more independent assignments and gain greater responsibility in areas such as policy and budget planning. They may become senior planners or community-planning directors, where they meet with officials and supervise a staff. Often, advancement is to a larger jurisdiction with greater responsibilities and more difficult problems. In larger jurisdictions,

geographic information systems (GIS) skills, will have the best opportunities in all sectors of transportation environmental planning.

Growth for urban and regional planners results from population increases, particularly in rapidly expanding communities that need streets and other services. Currently, 68 percent of planners are employed in local governments. Only 21 percent are employed in private companies that provide architectural, engineering, and related services. However, employment in this sector is expected to increase faster than government employment, especially in firms that provide technical services. Transportation planners also work in construction and emerging geospatial industries.

Nature of the Work

Transportation environmental planners are urban and regional planners who specialize in the environmental aspects of transportation planning. According to a salary survey by the American Planning Association, 26 percent specialize in transportation and 25 percent in environmental and natural resources. Because transportation systems affect the environment in numerous ways, the two areas are often part of the same job.

Urban and regional planners develop short-term and long-range plans to optimize the use of land and resources. They

- are involved in public outreach, modeling systems, and explaining the needs and impacts of proposed plans.

they may advance to bureau chief or community development director.

Earning Potential

2008 mean hourly wage: $30.00; mean annual wage: $62,400

Education/Licensure

Generally a master's degree in urban and regional planning from an accredited program is required. The Association of Collegiate Schools of Planning accredits college and university programs. Their Web site includes links to schools with accredited planning programs. Master's degrees in related fields, such as geography, urban design, urban studies, economics, or business, may be acceptable for many planning jobs. For transportation environmental planning, a bachelor's or master's degree in civil or environmental engineering may also be acceptable.

A few schools offer the bachelor's degree in urban and regional planning. Graduates of these programs qualify for some entry-level jobs, but they may have limited opportunities for advancement.

Only two states currently have requirements for licensing planners. New Jersey requires that planners pass two exams to qualify for a license. One exam tests general planning knowledge and the other tests knowledge of New Jersey laws. Michigan requires community planners to register, and the registration is based on passing state and national exams and on professional experience.

Even though most states do not have requirements for certification, many communities do. The preferred certification is from the American Institute of Certified Planners (AICP), the professional institute of the American Planning Association. The AICP certification is based on education, experience, and passing an exam. Maintaining certification requires professional development on a two-year cycle.

For More Information

American Planning Association
1776 Massachusetts Avenue NW, Suite 400
Washington, D.C. 20036-1904
202-872-0611
www.planning.org

Association of Collegiate Schools of Planning
6311 Mallard Trace
Tallahassee, Florida 32312
850-385-2054
www.acsp.org

How Green Is a Prospective Employer?

Today, just about any company that you interview with will say it is eco-conscious, but how do you know for sure? Here are some things to look for as you do your due diligence on prospective employers. Remember to look at the "small" picture—the daily culture of the company—not just the big picture.

1. **Does the company have a social responsibility officer?** Does the company issue a social responsibility report?

2. **Does the company show up in the news as eco-friendly?**

3. **Depending on the type of company, what is its policy on carbon neutrality?** How is it moving toward becoming carbon neutral?

4. **If it has separate offices or manufacturing plants, what is the company's environmental policy toward new construction and/or toward retrofitting older sites?**

5. **If the company leases autos for employees, does it lease fuel-efficient ones?**

6. **If the company is in a suburban setting, does it encourage carpooling by setting aside special parking close to the building?** Does it reimburse drivers of carpools for part of the mileage or tolls?

7. **If the company is in a suburban setting with nearby train service, does it run a van or bus to meet trains to pick up and drop off employees?**

8. **What is the company's policy on telecommuting?** What is its policy on flextime? Both cut down on auto emissions.

9. **If there's a cafeteria, does it serve locally grown foods?** Does it use paper, plastic, or ceramic dishes? Does it use metal or plastic utensils? What kind of take-out containers does it use?

10. **What is the policy on printing e-mail?** What is the policy on copying: single-sided or double-sided?

11. **Does it have recycle bins for paper and plastic goods in convenient places for employees to use?**

12. **If the company is in retail sales, does it use paper or plastic bags?** Does it encourage customers to use recyclable bags? How?

13. **If it's a manufacturing company, what is its policy on the amount of packaging it uses for its products?**

14. **Does the company support green causes in its locations like the Great American Clean Up?** Does it have a foundation that makes grants to local environmental efforts?

CHAPTER 2

SKILLED JOBS IN THE NEW GREEN ECONOMY

The ten industries or job clusters that are represented in this chapter have a strong focus on environmental, economic, or social sustainability. The thirty skilled jobs/categories that have been selected represent a cross-section of jobs in the new green economy as represented by these industries. Most of the industries included here are traditional ones that are being transformed by the new emphasis on sustainability. Many of the jobs are also traditional jobs that have been "greened" to promote the factors that produce sustainability: efficient use of energy, renewable energy sources, and preservation and protection of the environment. Jobs also become "green" when they are performed for companies whose ultimate products promote sustainability.

ABOUT THE LISTINGS

Here's what you need to know to navigate this chapter.

How Jobs Were Selected

The jobs in this chapter have been selected to represent a variety of interests, and many of the jobs, such as electrical engineering technician, can be found across multiple industries. Jobs in engineering, science, and technology are the most prevalent in industries that deal with energy and the environment. However, jobs have been included in business, medicine, the arts, and law to show that you don't need a science, engineering, or technology background to be part of the greening of the U.S. economy. People with many different interests and backgrounds can find meaningful employment in work that is environmentally friendly.

The jobs included allow people to use different sets of skills in interacting with others, with concrete things, with the planet, or with ideas. Each job title/category lists a variety of alternate job titles that come under that category. For example, a person looking for a job as an agricultural technician might find appropriate jobs with titles such as agricultural research technologist, seed analyst, and county extension agent technician.

Demand for Jobs

The job categories that have been included are projected to be in demand over the next decade. This was done by choosing "in-demand" jobs from Career Voyages (www.careervoyages.gov), a joint effort of the U.S. Department of Labor and the U.S. Department of Education. Rankings are based on the U.S.

Bureau of Labor Statistics data and projections from 2006 to 2016. The Web site features industries that are projected to have a large number of new job openings or that require new skill sets because technology, sustainability, and economic incentives are changing the nature of the industry. In particular, Career Voyages contains a section on green industries and jobs in those industries. These industries are among those featured in this chapter.

Career Voyages ranks demand in two ways: fastest-growing occupations and occupations with the most openings. As much as possible, jobs for this guide were selected from the in-demand list for each industry. First, those that appear on the list of the top 50 fastest-growing occupations and/or the top 50 occupations with the most openings were selected. After that, jobs were chosen from the list of the top 50 in-demand occupations and then the list of all in-demand occupations. Many science, technology, and engineering jobs are in demand, but jobs less in demand, such as paralegal and green travel agent, have been included to appeal to a broad range of interests. A good job is not just one that is in high demand but also one that matches a person's interests and abilities.

In some cases, jobs were selected from the 2008–09 edition of the *Occupational Outlook Handbook,* produced by the U.S. Bureau of Labor Statistics. A few were selected from O*Net OnLine (http://online.onetcenter.org). O*Net is sponsored by the U.S. Department of Labor/Employment and Training Administration (USDOL/ETA).

Industry Overview

The Industry Overview sections describe overall trends in the entire industry. They also explain how developments in energy and the environment are changing the industry and providing new general job opportunities. Wherever possible, information is taken from the *Career Guide to Industries,* 2008–09 edition, or the *Occupational Outlook Quarterly,* both published by the U.S. Bureau of Labor Statistics. Some information comes from trade and professional organizations.

Job Trends

The information on overall job trends is taken from the U.S. Bureau of Labor Statistics projections in the *Occupational Outlook Handbook,* Career Voyages, or the *Occupational Outlook Quarterly.* In a few cases it comes from O*Net. Occasionally information from professional organizations is included.

Nature of the Work

This section describes the kind of work that people in each job do. Most of the descriptive information is from the *Occupational Outlook Handbook,* although some comes from O*Net and from trade organizations or other sources. The section contains a description of the general work of the job category and a description of how this job contributes to the green economy. Industries where this job typically occurs are noted.

Career Paths

As much as possible, entry-level jobs were selected for inclusion in this guide. Jobs that always require a bachelor's degree or higher were not included. However, individuals with bachelor's degrees do have an advantage in some of these jobs, and people working in some technical areas do eventually earn bachelor's degrees in order to advance.

Earning Potential

Earning potential is given as mean hourly wage and mean annual wage where possible. Most are from 2008, as reported in the latest available *Occupational Outlook Handbook,* 2008–09 edition. In a few cases, wage data were not available in the *Occupational Outlook Handbook;* in these cases, they were taken either from O*Net, where median (rather than mean) hourly and annual wages are given, or from other sources where only a range is given.

Education/Licensure

These jobs all generally require some education beyond high school. Most require an associate degree, completion of a vocational or technical program, or completion of an apprenticeship program. General information about programs is included in this section. For a listing of community colleges offering innovative programs and degrees in specific disciplines, as well as union training programs, see Chapter 4.

For some skilled jobs, states require certification or licensing. For many jobs, certification is voluntary. In either case, this section gives information about certifications and licenses, including names of organizations that grant them. These organizations often offer courses or materials to help prepare for the exams as well as professional development opportunities needed to maintain certification.

For some jobs, apprenticeships are available. The Registered Apprenticeship Program is sponsored by the U.S. Department of Labor Employment and Training Administration and provides training opportunities through apprenticeships. These programs provide paid on-the-job training combined with classroom education. To find apprenticeships relevant to your job interests, search the Web site www.doleta.gov/OA/eta_default.cfm. Apprenticeship programs may also be located through the Career Voyages Web site.

For More Information

Many of the organizations listed are trade associations. Most offer professional development opportunities and continuing education. Some offer certifications that are respected by employers and an advantage to job seekers. Most also contain information on their Web sites about careers in the field and many have job banks. Some have links to academic institutions with programs in the discipline, which is a good way to find programs. Some organizations accredit community college and technical institute programs, and the organizations' Web sites usually contain links to accredited programs.

AGRICULTURE INDUSTRY

Agriculture plays an important role in the nation's economy. With more than 2 million workers, it is one of the largest industries in terms of employment. U.S. agriculture supplies the nation and much of the world with food and other agricultural products. The two major areas of agriculture are crop production and animal production, and the two subsectors are forestry and fishing.

Trends toward sustainable agriculture and preservation of the environment have led to developments that look promising to slow the overall decline in agricultural workers that is forecast. As farms are consolidated into agribusinesses, overall employment in agriculture is expected to decline by 8 percent by 2016, especially for small farmers and ranchers and the workers they employ. Advances in technology such as bioengineered crops that are more resistant to disease and drought and yield a larger harvest with fewer jobs are contributing to the decline in these kinds of jobs.

A development that provides opportunities for employment growth is organic farming. Sales of organic food products have grown about 20 percent over the past ten years. Demand for these organic products, grown without chemicals or pesticides, is expected to continue to increase. Organic products are grown mostly on smaller farms. Another area of promise is the emerging interest in producing biofuels from agricultural products, particularly converting corn to ethanol.

About Buying Locally
Buying locally grown food is not the same as buying organically grown food. "Organic" indicates the way food is grown and is a process certified by the U.S. Department of Agriculture (USDA). Buying locally means buying food products that are raised within a 100-mile radius of your home. For more information on what locally grown means, check www.sustainabletable.org.

Agricultural Inspector

Alternate Job Titles:

- Food Regulatory Field Supervisor
- Grain Inspector
- Meat and Poultry Inspector
- Plant Pest Inspector
- Plant Protection Specialist
- Quality Control Specialist
- Seed and Fertilizer Specialist

Agricultural inspectors are the people charged with keeping our food supply safe at the source.

Job Trends

The *Occupational Outlook Handbook* predicts little change in the employment rate for agricultural inspectors through 2016. However, about 4,000 openings are expected, mostly to replace inspectors who leave or retire.

Nature of the Work

Agricultural inspectors inspect agricultural products and the equipment and facilities used to process them to ensure that they comply with regulations and laws that govern food quality, health, and safety. Depending on their jobs, inspectors may do the following:

- advise farmers
- close facilities if contamination is found
- collect samples of meat and other products and send them for laboratory tests
- inspect facilities for cleanliness and compliance
- inspect food labels and packaging
- inspect livestock and horticulture products for disease, infestations, or chemical residues
- inspect meat, milk, and other food products for bacteria
- install and inspect devices for measuring weight and volume
- monitor safety regulations at fishing and logging sites
- prepare for legal action
- work at import and export stations to inspect agricultural products entering and leaving the country
- write reports

Most agricultural inspectors work for federal or state governments. In addition, there are jobs in the U.S. Department of Agriculture (USDA) for accredited certifiers and qualified inspectors who certify and inspect organic farms and products to ensure they meet USDA standards.

Career Paths

Agricultural inspectors who work for the federal government as well as many state and local governments advance on a civil service career ladder. At some point on the ladder, they become supervisors. At the higher levels, advancement is competitive.

Earning Potential

2008 mean hourly wage: $19.87; mean annual wage: $41,330

Education/Licensure

Generally, college courses or an associate degree in agricultural science, biology, or a related field are required. Relevant job experience or vocational training may also be acceptable. Some positions require a bachelor's degree. Training in laws and regulations is necessary to carry out this job.

There are two recognized "apprenticeable" specialties associated with this occupation: Farmer, General and Farmer, Beekeeper.

For More Information

USAJOBS (official job site of the federal government)
703-724-1850
www.usajobs.opm.gov

Agricultural Technician

Alternate Job Titles:

- Agricultural Extension Associate
- Agricultural Research Associate
- Agricultural Research Technician
- Agricultural Research Technologist
- Agricultural Resources Technician
- County Extension Agent Technician
- Precision Agriculture Technician
- Seed Analyst

There are a variety of jobs for people who are interested in agriculture but lack the resources to buy and operate a farm or ranch.

Job Trends

According to the *Occupational Outlook Handbook,* employment for agricultural and food science technicians is expected to grow about average. The Career Voyages Web site reports that this is an in-demand occupation. Technicians who graduate from applied technology programs with training in the use of laboratory equipment will have the best prospects.

Several factors are generating demand for agricultural technicians. One is the growth in biotechnology research. As agricultural production increases, it must be balanced with protecting ecosystems and soil and water quality. This requires both research in pesticides and fertilizers and application of new methods on farms. Another field for agricultural technicians is biotechnology where they work in bioprocessing. Precision agriculture, also called precision farming, is another way to boost production while minimizing environmental impact and is a fast-growing sector of agriculture. Precision agriculture tailors farming methods to each section of a farmer's fields because conditions vary across fields.

Nature of the Work

The duties of agricultural technicians depend on the specific job. Agricultural extension technicians work with extension agents to collect farm data and plan and carry out extension activities with a county's farmers, including advising individual farmers and farm cooperatives. The extension technicians may supervise application of chemicals or train operators who do the applications. Agricultural resource technicians work with agricultural resource officers to collect data and map a region's natural resources, using computerized tools such as geographic information systems (GIS). Those involved in research work either with agricultural researchers on projects or conduct their own research once they have a certain amount of experience. Research may include collecting and analyzing soil, seed, crop, and water samples.

Precision agricultural technicians use technology to determine the best practices to maximize crop production, minimize costs, and reduce environmental impact. Among their tools are computerized maps, GIS, and global positioning technology (GPS). Precision agricultural technicians use computerized maps of crop yield, pests, weather, soil conditions, and drainage patterns to determine where and when to apply agricultural chemicals. Because plants respond to localized conditions, different sections of large fields must be treated differently. Applying just the right amount of pesticide, herbicide, or fertilizer under the right conditions reduces the amount of chemicals that enter the environment.

Other job opportunities for agricultural technicians include working for companies that sell equipment, seeds, livestock, and other farm items as well as services such as grain elevator storage and food processing. In time, some agricultural technicians become consultants working on their own.

Career Paths

Entry-level technicians begin working and training under the supervision of more experienced technicians or scientists. As they gain experience, they gain more responsibility and may work independently. Some eventually become supervisors. Others go on to earn a bachelor's degree and qualify for a more advanced position.

Earning Potential

2008 mean hourly wage: $17.53; mean annual wage: $36,470

Education/Licensure

An associate degree in agricultural technology is generally required for agricultural technicians. A certificate in applied science or a related area of technology may also be acceptable. Some positions require a bachelor's degree.

Many community colleges and technical schools offer associate degrees in agricultural technology.

Some have degree or certificate programs specifically for precision agriculture technology.

For More Information

National Cooperative Business Association
1401 New York Ave., NW, Suite 1100
Washington, D.C. 20005-2160
202-638-6222
www.nba.coop

National FFA Organization (formerly Future
 Farmers of America)
ATTN: Career Information Requests
P.O. Box 68690
Indianapolis, Indiana 46268-0960
www.ffa.org

National Grain and Feed Association
1250 I Street, NW, Suite 1003
Washington, D.C. 20005
202-289-0873
www.ngfa.org

Organic Farmer

Alternate Job Titles:

- Organic Dairy Farmer
- Organic Livestock Farmer/Rancher
- Organic Poultry Farmer

Before farmers may call their food products "organic," products have to be certified according to rules set down by the U.S. Department of Agriculture.

Job Trends

According to the *Occupational Outlook Handbook,* job prospects for farmers will be favorable for the next decade. Few additional people are entering this field, but those who retire or leave farming will need to be replaced, so about 95,000 job openings are expected through 2016.

Organic food production is the fastest-growing area of agriculture. Organic farms are typically small, so there are more opportunities for farmers shifting to organic farming as this segment of the market grows. Some organic farmers sell directly to the public through farmers markets, Internet sales, community-supported agriculture programs, and cooperatives that process products and sell them. Farmers who grow products organically for biofuel production will also see new market opportunities.

Nature of the Work

Instead of using traditional irrigation and chemical pesticides, herbicides, and fertilizers, organic farming, which is also called sustainable agriculture, uses environmentally safe, natural methods. These methods include fertilizing with animal waste, rotating crops to minimize the need for fertilizing, minimizing erosion, mechanically removing weeds, and using predatory insects to eliminate the need for pesticides. Animals that are raised for organic poultry and meat are not fed hormones, antibiotics, or pesticides. They are also raised in healthier natural environments where they are allowed access to the outdoors and pastureland.

Organic farmers must understand environmental regulations and regulations regarding the production, processing, labeling, and sale of organic products. Understanding the environmental impact of farming and the social and community aspects are also critical.

There are a number of career options in organic farming. These include jobs in crop production and management of natural resources and in government and nonprofit organizations. Production and sale of niche products such as "gourmet" dried bean varieties create opportunities for entrepreneurs. Involvement in the entire process, including production, processing, marketing, and sales, is critical to ensure and maintain the "organic" brand.

Career Paths

Organic farmers have opportunities in crop and animal production, processing, marketing, and sales. Advancement could take the form of managing a larger operation with more land or more animals. It could also mean moving into another segment of the industry.

Earning Potential

Farmers and Ranchers:

2008 mean hourly wage: $23.62; mean annual wage: $49,140

Education/Licensure

In general, some postsecondary education or an associate degree is needed to be an organic farmer. The National Sustainable Agriculture Information Service (NSAIS) provides links to educational and training programs in sustainable agriculture. There are two recognized apprentice specialties associated with this occupation: Farmer, General and Farmer, Beekeeper.

Organic farmers must be certified according to the U.S. Department of Agriculture (USDA) National Organic Standards. This involves contracting the services of an organic certifier. Many factors are considered, such as the history of the land's use, source of seeds, and measures to prevent contamination. An inspection is required, and the certifier even reviews the labels for products. The NSAIS provides a description of the certification process.

For More Information

ATTRA—National Sustainable Agriculture
   Information Service
P.O. Box 3657
Fayetteville, Arkansas 72702
800-346-9140 (toll-free)
http://attra.ncat.org

Department of Agronomy and Horticulture
University of Nebraska–Lincoln
279 Plant Science Hall
Lincoln, Nebraska 68583-0915
402-472-2811
www.agronomy.unl.edu/organicfarming.html

National Center for Appropriate Technology
P.O. Box 3838
Butte, Montana 59702
406-494-4572
www.ncat.org

BIOTECHNOLOGY INDUSTRY

The biotechnology industry is an emerging industry with consequent rapid growth. Entrepreneurs are founding biotechnology start-ups, and new applications are being developed and rushed to market. New green technologies, such as converting ethanol to fuel, will increase the number of jobs, and there are often more jobs available than workers. The projected number of jobs exceeds the number of people currently enrolled in training programs. Many skilled jobs exist in quality control and in manufacturing and production.

Biological Technician

Alternate Job Titles:

- Biologist Aide
- Biological Science Technician
- Biological Technologist
- Environmental Technician
- Medical Lab Technician
- Medical Technologist
- Resource Biologist/Fisheries
- Wildlife Technician

The area of work determines the job title.

Job Trends

The *Occupational Outlook Handbook* indicates that there are currently 79,000 biological technicians, and the projected need is 91,000 by 2016. This represents a growth of 16 percent, which is

---

About the Biotechnology Industry

Compared to such industries as auto manufacturing and construction, biotechnology is a new industry. The so-called Age of Biotechnology began in 1977 when Genentech, Inc., produced the first human protein. Currently, there are more than a thousand biotechnology companies in the United States. While experiments like sheep or mice cloning grab big headlines, pharmaceutical and biotechnology companies are also researching cures for a number of cancers and other currently incurable diseases.

---

greater than the average for all occupations. Career Voyages lists this as an in-demand occupation.

The most job growth is expected in scientific research and development settings where about 30 percent of biological technicians currently work, although demand is expected to increase in the pharmaceutical industry. Another 30 percent work in colleges and universities, while about 15 percent work in federal, state, and local government. The rest are in other industries, including agriculture.

Nature of the Work

Biological technicians work in laboratories assisting biologists and other medical scientists. Their jobs include the following:

- analyzing various organic substances
- conducting experiments
- recording results of experiments
- setting up, maintaining, and operating laboratory instruments and equipment

Biological technicians may assist microbiologists in the study of microscopic organisms. In the bio-technology industry, they apply techniques and knowledge from basic research to product development. Biological technicians also work in other industries, including manufacturing, health care, and environmentally related fields such as wildlife management.

Career Paths

Entry-level biological technicians usually begin working under supervision. As they gain more experience, they become involved in more difficult projects with less supervision. Some will eventually become supervisors themselves. Those in universities have more job uncertainty because they typically work for a certain professor whose own job depends on gaining tenure and whose research depends on winning competitive grants. Many jobs now require a bachelor's degree in biology or a related area.

Earning Potential

2008 mean hourly wage: $19.67; mean annual wage: $40,900

Education/Licensure

Requirements vary, but an associate degree or two years of specialized training is typically the minimum. Technical and community colleges offer associate degree programs in specific technologies. Technical institutes offer certificate programs and associate degrees, but these institutions offer less general education and less theory than community or technical colleges.

Some states have apprenticeship programs for biological technicians that enable them to specialize in bio-manufacturing (upstream or downstream) or as dairy technologists.

For More Information

American Institute of Biological Sciences (AIBS)
1444 I Street NW, Suite 200
Washington, D.C. 20005
202-628-1500
www.aibs.org/core/index.html

American Society for Microbiology (ASM)
Education Department
1752 N Street NW
Washington, D.C. 20036-2804
202-737-3600
www.asm.org

Botanical Society of America (BSA)
P.O. Box 299
St. Louis, Missouri 63166-0299
314-577-9566
www.botany.org

Federation of American Societies for
   Experimental Biology (FASEB)
9650 Rockville Pike
Bethesda, Maryland 20814
301-634-7000
www.faseb.org

Industrial Engineering Technician

Alternate Job Titles:

- Broadcast and Sound Engineer Technician
- Engineering Technician
- Industrial Engineering Analyst
- Manufacturing Engineer

- Manufacturing Technician
- Process Documentation and Methods Analyst
- Radio Operator
- Quality Control Engineering Technician
- Quality Control Technician
- Quality Process Engineer

Many different kinds of industries require this job specialty.

Job Trends

According to Career Voyages, industrial engineering technician is number 39 out of the top 50 occupations with the most openings projected by 2016. It is also listed as one of the in-demand occupations. There are currently about 75,000 industrial engineering technicians, and the number is expected to increase 10 percent by 2016 according to the *Occupational Outlook Handbook*. This is about the average rate of growth.

Several reasons are leading to the expected increase. First, companies are continually striving to reduce costs and improve production, which is the major work of industrial engineering technicians. Second, the biotechnology industry is growing rapidly, so job growth is expected in this industry. Third, other rapidly expanding green industries will need industrial engineering technicians, including advanced manufacturing, aerospace, information technology, geospatial technology, and nanotechnology.

Nature of the Work

Industrial engineering technicians plan the efficient use of resources, including materials, equipment, and personnel. They

- analyze costs.
- carry out statistical studies to determine efficiency.
- observe operations and make recommendations for improved efficiency and work production.
- plan the flow of work.

Knowledge of production and processing, engineering, technology, and mathematics is essential for this occupation.

Career Paths

Industrial engineering technicians usually begin work as trainees under supervision. As they gain more experience, they become involved in more difficult projects with less supervision. Some will eventually become supervisors themselves.

Earning Potential

2008 mean hourly wage: $24.07; mean annual wage: $50,070

Education/Licensure

A two-year associate degree in engineering technology is preferred. The Technology Accreditation Commission of the Accreditation Board for Engineering and Technology (ABET) accredits two-year associate degree programs in engineering technology. Graduates of these programs are considered to have an acceptable level of competence. Programs are offered at community colleges, public and private technical institutes, and vocational technical schools and in the armed forces. Some four-year colleges offer bachelor's degrees in engineering technology, but graduates of these programs usually work as applied engineers or technologists.

There are two recognized apprenticeable specialties associated with this occupation: Industrial Engineering Technician and Quality Control Technician.

For More Information

Accreditation Board for Engineering Technology (ABET)
111 Market Place, Suite 1050
Baltimore, Maryland 21202
410-347-7700
www.abet.org

CONSTRUCTION INDUSTRY

The *Occupational Outlook Handbook* reports that 7.7 million people were employed in the construction industry in 2006. The number of jobs is predicted to increase 10.2 percent for a total of 8.5 million workers by 2016. Most of the new jobs are expected for specialty trade workers, including apprentice, journey, and master craft workers. Specialty trades account for about 64 percent of all construction workers and include electricians, carpenters, plumbers, pipe fitters, and heating and air conditioning installers and mechanics. Overall, experienced workers should have excellent job opportunities with relatively high wages.

Heavy construction, including roads, bridges, and tunnels, as well as repairs to existing highways and bridges, is expected to generate most of the demand for construction workers. However, green nonresidential and residential building should experience an increase in demand, even though construction of new residential and commercial buildings overall is expected to slow. In an April 2009 summary, the U.S. Green Building Council reported that green building is expected to more than double by 2013. Major growth in nonresidential green building is expected in the education, office, and health-care sectors, as well as in the government, industrial, hospitality, and retail sectors. Government initiatives along with increased interest in residential green building are encouraging energy-efficient, environmentally sustainable green construction. Remodeling of existing structures, especially to retrofit them as green buildings, is expected to generate additional demand for construction workers.

About Green Building Materials

The Green Guard Institute tests and certifies building products and materials that are low in harmful emissions. You can find listings of these products and materials, a number of which are used in school construction, on the institute's Web site at www.greenguard.org.

Carpenter

Carpentry crosses a number of industries in addition to building construction.

Job Trends

Carpentry is the largest building trade occupation. According to the *Occupational Outlook Handbook,* there were about 1.5 million jobs in 2006. That number is expected to increase about 10 percent by 2016, which is about average for all occupations. Career Voyages lists this as an in-demand occupation. In 2006, about 32 percent of carpenters worked in building construction, about 23 for specialty contractors, and the rest in manufacturing, government, retail, and other industries. Approximately 32 percent were self-employed.

The market for home remodeling is currently strong and will be for some time. This is partially driven by economic conditions but also by environmental concerns. Retrofitting and remodeling homes to improve energy efficiency is increasing. In addition, retrofitting of industrial plants, schools, and government buildings for energy efficiency will also provide job opportunities.

Nature of the Work

Carpenters need knowledge of tools, materials, blueprints, and basic mathematics. They have to be able to estimate materials, time, and cost to complete a job.

In addition to building structures, carpenters install windows and doors and may install wood flooring. They also do repair work and remodeling in homes, office buildings, stores, and industrial plants. Carpenters must be able to read blueprints and other instructions and be familiar with local building codes and how their trade relates to other building trades when they are working on a building site. Today, carpenters must also be aware of the latest in energy-efficient doors, windows, and sealants as well as renewable and environmentally friendly wood products.

About Construction and the Environment

One reason to renovate rather than tear down buildings and start over is the environment. Construction creates more carbon dioxide than any other industry.

Career Paths

Experienced carpenters may become carpentry supervisors. Because they are involved in all aspects of the construction process, they also have opportunities to advance to general construction supervisor. Some may become building inspectors or sales representatives or purchasing agents for building products. Others become teachers in vocational or technical schools. With additional education and experience, there are opportunities for carpenters in management, including becoming self-employed contractors. Speaking both English and Spanish can be an advantage for those who wish to advance.

Earning Potential

2008 mean hourly wage: $20.64; mean annual wage: $42,940

Education/Licensure

Carpenters may begin as carpenter's helpers working with experienced carpenters, but they also need some type of formal instruction to become skilled. There are two main options for formal instruction: attending a trade or vocational school or a community college or enrolling in an apprenticeship program. Apprenticeship programs are offered by some employers and by trade associations and unions as well as some trade and vocational schools. These programs may last three to five years and include both classroom and on-the-job training. Upon completing an apprenticeship program, a person becomes a journey worker and, over time, with additional training and experience, a master carpenter.

Some carpenters get certifications in specialized construction techniques such as building scaffolds. These certifications may enable them to earn additional responsibilities and money. The Green Building Certification Institute, affiliated with the U.S. Green Building Council, offers LEED (Leadership in Energy and Environmental Design) certifications in green building methods.

For More Information

Home Builders Institute
1201 15th Street, NW
Washington, D.C. 20005
202-266-8927
www.buildingcareers.org

National Association of Home Builders
1201 15th Street, NW
Washington, D.C. 20005
800-368-5242 (toll-free)
www.nahb.org

United Brotherhood of Carpenters and Joiners of America
International Training Center
6801 Placid Street
Las Vegas, Nevada 89119
702-938-1111
www.carpenters.org

U.S. Green Building Council
2101 L Street, NW, Suite 500
Washington, D.C. 20037
800-795-1747 (toll-free)
www.usgbc.org

Construction and Building Inspector

Alternate Job Titles:

- Electrical Inspector
- Green Building Inspector
- Home Inspector
- Mechanical Inspector
- Plan Examiner
- Plumbing Inspector
- Public Works Inspector
- Specification Inspector
- Structural Inspector

A public works inspector inspects highways, roads, bridges, tunnels, dams, and water systems. The job of construction and building inspector, like so many others, is being affected by new technologies. In this case, new modeling technology is increasing the resources available to construction and building inspectors to do their work.

Job Trends

In the *Occupational Outlook Handbook,* the U.S. Bureau of Labor Statistics predicts that employment for construction and building inspectors will grow by 18 percent by 2016, which is greater than average for all occupations. According to the *Occupational Outlook Handbook,* local governments employed about 41 percent of inspectors in 2006. Architectural and engineering services companies employed another 26 percent who conducted audits for fee, mostly home audits for potential buyers. Approximately 10 percent of building inspectors were self-employed, many of these as home inspectors.

Career Voyages lists this as an in-demand occupation. Concerns for public safety in light of potential disasters arising from natural or human causes and increasing emphasis on high-quality construction are driving the demand. Emerging emphasis on sustainable and green building will also stimulate employment opportunities for building inspectors. First, buildings may now be certified as green. The U.S. Green Building Council offers several levels of certification called Leadership in Energy and Environmental Design (LEED). Inspectors who are trained to conduct LEED audits will have new job opportunities. Second, new opportunities exist in local government to develop Green Building Programs and local codes for sustainable building. Once codes are in place, inspecting for compliance will continue to provide jobs.

Home inspection also is an area with potential for good job opportunities. This is partly because of economic conditions but also because of environmental concerns. The market for home remodeling is currently strong, and retrofitting and remodeling work to improve energy efficiency is on the rise. In addition, retrofitting industrial plants, office buildings, government buildings, and schools for energy efficiency will also provide job opportunities. New residential construction as well as commercial construction and building and repair of bridges and roads all contribute to employment for construction and building inspectors.

Nature of the Work

Building inspectors must know the federal, state, and local codes that regulate construction. The International Code Council (ICC) publishes national construction and building codes, but there are also many local codes. Many localities also have new green building codes that may be voluntary or mandatory. A new specialty called green building inspectors evaluates buildings for energy efficiency, indoor air quality, and use of natural materials.

Construction and building inspectors are responsible for monitoring work during all phases of construction. They make necessary measurements and observations to ensure that the work follows plans, meets specifications, and complies with all construction and safety codes. In addition to monitoring new construction, inspectors also monitor repairs, remodeling, and maintenance work.

Career Paths

Certification improves job opportunities and opportunities for advancement. A degree in engineering or architecture may be required in order to advance to a supervisory position.

Earning Potential

2008 mean hourly wage: $25.08; mean annual wage: $52,160

Education/Licensure

A high school diploma or GED is generally the minimum educational requirement. Currently, 31 percent of building and construction inspectors have no more than that. About 40 percent have some postsecondary training or an associate degree. Only 28 percent have a bachelor's degree or higher. Substantial construction experience qualifies a person for many jobs. However, employers are increasingly hiring those who have experience and an associate degree from a community college or who have at least studied engineering, architecture, construction technology, building inspection, or home inspection. There are also apprenticeship programs for a variety of inspection specialties.

Many states and municipalities require certification, and those who hold certifications have the best job opportunities. Certification generally requires passing an exam but may also include a specified amount of experience or a minimum level of training and education. There are many ways to become certified. Some states have licensing programs, whereas some require specialized certification from an association such as the National Fire Protection Association. Community colleges often offer certificate programs. The Green Building Certification Institute, affiliated with the U.S. Green Building Council, offers green certifications.

For More Information

American Society of Home Inspectors
932 Lee Street, Suite 101
Des Plaines, Illinois 60016
800-743-2744 (toll-free)
www.ashi.org

Green Building Certification Institute
2101 L Street NW, Suite 650
Washington, D.C. 20037
800-795-1746 (toll-free)
www.gbci.org

International Code Council
500 New Jersey Avenue, NW, 6th Floor
Washington, D.C. 20001-2070
888-422-7233 (toll-free)
www.iccsafe.org

National Association of Home Inspectors
4248 Park Glen Road
Minneapolis, Minnesota 55416
800-448-3942 (toll-free)
www.nahi.org

National Fire Protection Association
1 Batterymarch Park
Quincy, Massachusetts 02169-7471
617-770-3000
www.nfpa.org

U.S. Green Building Council
2101 L Street, NW, Suite 500
Washington, D.C. 20037
800-795-1747 (toll-free)
www.usgbc.org

Electrician

Alternate Job Titles:
- Construction and Building Inspector
- Electrical Drafter
- Electrical Engineering Technician
- Lineman
- Motor Repairer

Electricians are found in many industries, including electronics and automotive manufacturing.

Job Trends

According to the *Occupational Outlook Handbook,* there were over 700,000 electricians in 2006. Of those, 68 percent were employed in the construction industry. Others work in manufacturing, the motion picture and video industry, and power generation. Approximately 80 percent of electricians working in construction are self-employed.

Employment is expected to increase 7 percent by 2016, which is about average for all occupations. However, job prospects are very good. The Career Voyages Web site ranks this among the top 50 in-demand occupations. By 2016, more than 230,000 new jobs are projected. New residential and commercial construction, power plant construction to meet increasing energy demands, computers, telecommunications, and manufacturing automation are all expected to create new jobs during the coming decade. Remodeling homes and retrofitting buildings—public and private—to meet increasing concerns about the environment are also driving demand for construction workers, including electricians.

Nature of the Work

Electricians install, test, and maintain wiring and electrical systems in residential and commercial buildings. Systems may include lighting, security, climate control, communications, or other control systems. They also install electrical equipment and fixtures such as circuit breakers, switches, and fuses. Knowledge of tools, blueprints, materials, and basic math is required. Electricians must also know the National Electrical Code as well as state and local codes and be able to estimate materials, time, and cost to complete a job.

Some electricians install other types of wiring, such as low-voltage wiring used for voice, data, and video transmission. Others install fiber optic and coaxial cables. In factories, electricians wire and maintain more complex equipment, including generators, transformers, motors, and robots.

Career Paths

Experienced electricians may become supervisors, and they also have opportunities to advance to construction managers. Many become electrical inspectors, and many start their own businesses as electrical contractors. Speaking both English and Spanish is an advantage for those who wish to advance.

Earning Potential

2008 mean hourly wage: $23.98; mean annual wage: $49,890

Education/Licensure

Most electricians get training and skills through apprenticeship programs that take between four and five years to complete. These programs consist of classroom instruction and supervised training on the job with pay. The Independent Electrical Contractors group offers apprenticeship programs, continuing education, and online courses. The National Electrical Contractors Association and the International Brotherhood of Electrical Workers jointly sponsor apprenticeship programs. Technical and vocational schools and training academies also offer training programs. All programs require a high school diploma or GED.

Continuing education is important for electricians so they can keep up with changes to the National Electrical Code. Many electricians also take courses on contracting and management in preparation for starting their own businesses or for advancing within a company.

Most states require electricians to be licensed. Obtaining a license requires passing an exam about the National Electrical Code as well as local building and electric codes and electrical theory. Most states also require electricians who do public work to hold a special license. In some cases, this requires that a person be certified as a master electrician. This process requires seven years or more experience in most states. Some states require a bachelor's degree in electrical engineering. The Green Building Certification Institute offers Leadership in Energy and Environmental Design (LEED) certification.

For More Information

Green Building Certification Institute
2101 L Street NW, Suite 650
Washington, D.C. 20037
800-795-1746 (toll-free)
www.gbci.org

Independent Electrical Contractors (IEC)
4401 Ford Avenue, Suite 1100
Alexandria, Virginia 22302
703-549-7351
www.ieci.org

International Brotherhood of Electrical Workers
   (IBEW)
900 Seventh Street, NW
Washington, D.C. 20001
202-833-7000
www.ibew.org

National Association of Home Builders
1201 15th Street, NW
Washington, D.C. 20005
800-368-5242 (toll-free)
www.nahb.org

National Electrical Contractors Association
   (NECA)
3 Bethesda Metro Center, Suite 1100
Bethesda, Maryland 20814
301-657-3110
www.necanet.org

U.S. Green Building Council
2101 L Street, NW, Suite 500
Washington, D.C. 20037
800-795-1747 (toll-free)
www.usgbc.org

Heating, Ventilation, Air Conditioning, and Refrigeration (HVAC/R) Technician

Alternate Job Titles:

- Air Conditioning Technician (AC Tech)
- Commercial Service Technician
- Field Service Technician
- HVAC Installer Mechanic
- HVAC Specialist
- HVAC Technician
- HVAC/R Service Technician
- Refrigeration Mechanic
- Refrigeration Operator
- Refrigeration Technician
- Service Manager
- Service Technician
- VRT (Variable Retention Time) Mechanic

This job, like a number of construction and building occupations, requires a personable manner in dealing with the public because much of the job involves face-to-face contact with customers.

Job Trends

According to the *Occupational Outlook Handbook,* employment for heating, ventilation, air conditioning, and refrigeration (HVAC/R) mechanics and installers is expected to increase 9 percent by 2016. This is about average for all occupations. However, numerous workers are expected to retire and the number of people entering the occupation is low, so job prospects are expected to be excellent for this trade. By 2016, some 77,000 new employees will be needed. Career Voyages lists it as one of the in-demand occupations.

One area in particular that is driving the demand for HVAC/R mechanics and technicians is home remodeling and retrofitting public and private buildings as the population becomes more energy conscious. The need for people who are able to install new, efficient climate-control systems will increase demand for HVAC/R technicians with knowledge of the latest in HVAC/R technology. New residential and commercial construction also requires skilled HVAC/R technicians and installers.

Retrofitting the HVAC systems in residential, commercial, and industrial buildings can result in significant reduction in energy use. HVAC systems can account for as much as half the energy use in homes and 40 percent of electricity use in commercial buildings. Replacing units that are over 10 years old can reduce energy costs between 20 and 50 percent.

Nature of the Work

Heating and air conditioning technicians install and service heating and air conditioning systems in residential and commercial buildings. They test and inspect systems to verify that they comply with specifications and to detect malfunctions if they don't comply. They test all components of a system, including electrical circuits and pressure testing pipes and joints, to ensure that the system meets all standards and that it follows manufacturer's procedures and safety precautions while working.

Refrigeration technicians build refrigeration systems that are often used for air conditioning in commercial buildings and are now beginning to be used in residences. They connect pipes, install the refrigerant, test for leaks, connect the electric power source, and check to ensure that the system meets specifications. Reclaiming and recycling the refrigerant is critical because it is harmful to the environment.

Career Paths

For most HVAC/R technicians, advancement is in the form of higher pay. Some technicians will become supervisors or managers. Others will advance by moving into other positions in the industry, such as sales representative, building supervisor, or contractor.

Earning Potential

2008 mean hourly wage: $20.31; mean annual wage: $42,240

Education/Licensure

Heating, ventilation, air conditioning, and refrigeration technicians may still be able to learn this trade on the job, but those who have completed a formal apprenticeship or postsecondary training program have better opportunities. Community colleges, junior colleges, vocational and trade schools, and the armed forces offer programs, some of which lead to an associate degree. The programs take from six months to two years to complete.

Some states and municipalities require HVAC/R technicians to be licensed. Requirements vary, but all include passing an exam. Some require an apprenticeship.

Apprenticeship programs are another way to be trained. Formal apprenticeship programs last from three to five years. They are often given by local chapters of trade organizations.

There are five apprenticeships for heating and air conditioning technicians:

- Air and Hydronic Balancing Technician
- Furnace Installer
- Furnace Installer-and-Repairer, Hot Air
- Heating-and-Air-Conditioning Installer-Servicer
- Oil-Burner-Servicer-and-Installer

There are two apprenticeships for refrigeration technicians:

- Refrigeration Mechanic
- Refrigeration Unit Repairer

Under Section 608 of the Clean Air Act, the U.S. Environmental Protection Agency (EPA) requires anyone who handles ozone-depleting refrigerants to be properly trained. This includes technicians who work on refrigeration systems and stationary air conditioners. Air-Conditioning Contractors of America offers training.

The North American Technician Excellence (NATE) certification program for HVAC/R technicians is recognized nationwide. HVAC Excellence offers a number of technician certifications at the professional and master level. The U.S. Green Building Council offers the LEED (Leadership in Energy and Environmental Design) Associate and LEED AP certifications that may be appropriate for some HVAC/R technicians.

For More Information

Air-Conditioning, Heating and Refrigeration Institute
2111 Wilson Blvd, Suite 500
Arlington, Virginia 22201
703-524-8800
www.ari.org

HVAC Excellence
1701 Pennsylvania Avenue NW
Washington, D.C. 20006
800-394-5268 (toll-free)
www.hvacexcellence.org

North American Technician Excellence
2111 Wilson Blvd. #510
Arlington, Virginia 22201
703-276-7247
www.natex.org

Refrigeration Service Engineers Society
1666 Rand Road
Des Plaines, Illinois 60016
847-759-4051
www.rses.org

Sheet Metal and Air Conditioning Contractors' National Association
4201 Lafayette Center Drive
Chantilly, Virginia 20151-1209
703-803-2980
www.smacna.org

U.S. Green Building Council
2101 L Street, NW, Suite 500
Washington, D.C. 20037
800-795-1747 (toll-free)
www.usgbc.org

The following organizations sponsor apprenticeships:

Air-Conditioning Contractors of America
2800 Shirlington Road, Suite 300
Arlington, Virginia 22206
703-575-4477
www.acca.org

Associated Builders and Contractors
Workforce Development Department
4250 North Fairfax Drive, 9th Floor
Arlington, Virginia 22203
703-812-2000
www.abc.org

Home Builders Institute
National Association of Home Builders
1201 15th Street NW, 6th Floor
Washington, D.C. 20005
800-795-7955 (toll-free)
www.hbi.org

Mechanical Contractors Association of America
Mechanical Service Contractors of America
1385 Piccard Drive
Rockville, Maryland 20850
301-869-5800
www.mcaa.org/msca

Plumbing-Heating-Cooling Contractors
180 S. Washington Street
P.O. Box 6808
Falls Church, Virginia 22046
703-237-8100
www.phccweb.org

United Association of Journeymen and
   Apprentices of the Plumbing and Pipefitting
   Industry
United Association Building
Three Park Place
Annapolis, Maryland 21401
410-269-2000
www.ua.org

DESIGN INDUSTRY

Trends for architecture, interior design, and landscaping are related to trends in the construction industry. Even though new construction of residential and commercial buildings is expected to slow, remodeling and retrofitting of existing structures are expected to generate demand.

In an April 2009 summary, the U.S. Green Building Council reported that green building is expected to more than double by 2013. Major growth in nonresidential green building is expected in the education, office, and health-care sectors. Additional green building is expected in the government, industrial, hospitality, and retail sectors. Government initiatives, along with increased interest in residential green building, are encouraging energy-efficient, environmentally sustainable green construction. Architectural drafters, interior designers, and landscape designers will find opportunities in green building.

Architectural and Civil Drafter

Alternate Job Titles:

- Architectural Assistant
- CAD Operator
- Designer
- Digital Artist
- Digital Technician
- Drafter
- Engineering Technician
- Facilities Planner
- Technical Illustrator

Knowledge of computer design tools is a basic requirement of this occupation.

Job Trends

According to the *Occupational Outlook Handbook,* employment growth of 6 percent is expected for architectural and civil drafters by 2016, which amounts to 40,000 new employees. Career Voyages lists architectural drafters as an in-demand occupation and ranks it as number 23 of the top 50 occupations with the most openings requiring postsecondary education. Employment opportunities will be best for those with two years of postsecondary training, strong technical skills, and computer-aided design (CAD) experience. The majority of architectural and civil drafters are currently employed by architecture and engineering services.

Demand for architectural drafters will be mainly in nonresidential construction. Construction of new schools at all levels is expected in order to meet the educational needs of the expanding population. Green building design is also expected to generate demand as environmental concerns and energy costs increase.

Nature of the Work

Green building and sustainable design require the expertise of architectural drafters to prepare the drawings for approvals and construction. The U.S. Green Building Council LEED (Leadership in Energy and Environmental Design) building certification encourages innovative designs for energy-efficient systems. It also encourages use of natural and sustainably produced materials. These design considerations add new challenges for architectural drafters.

Architectural drafters prepare drawings of structural and architectural specifications for all types of structures. Drafters may specialize in residential or commercial buildings or other types of structures, and they may specialize in the type of material used, such as concrete or steel. Using computer-aided design and drafting (CADD) systems, they prepare drawings that contain all of the details and specifications for the project, such as dimensions and materials. To do their jobs, architectural drafters must understand standard building techniques.

Career Paths

The entry-level position of junior drafter is closely supervised. As junior drafters gain experience, they become intermediate drafters and are expected to make more calculations and judgments. Eventually, they become senior drafters and may become designers or supervisors. Some continue their education, which may be paid for by their employer, and become engineers, engineering technicians, or architects.

Earning Potential

2008 mean hourly wage: $22.30; mean annual wage: $46,390

Education/Licensure

Although drafting is offered in some high schools, individuals who complete an associate degree or postsecondary technical program have much better job opportunities. Programs are offered at community colleges, technical institutes, and some four-year colleges and universities.

The Accrediting Commission of Career Schools and Colleges of Technology (ACCSCT) accredits drafting programs. Its Web site provides links to accredited programs. The American Design Drafting Association (ADDA) also accredits and certifies schools with drafting programs and provides a list on its Web site; some of them are high schools. There are seven recognized apprenticeable specialties associated with this occupation: Drafter, Architectural; Drafter, Commercial; Drafter, Heating and Ventilating; Drafter, Landscape; Drafter, Marine; Drafter, Plumbing; and Drafter, Structural.

Certification is voluntary but may be an asset in getting a job. The ADDA offers certification as a Certified Drafter, which requires passing an exam. There are different exams for different specializations. Certification must be renewed every five years.

For More Information

Accrediting Commission of Career Schools and
    Colleges of Technology
2101 Wilson Blvd., Suite 302
Arlington, Virginia 22201
703-247-4212
www.accsct.org

American Design Drafting Association
105 East Main Street
Newbern, Tennessee 38059
731-627-0802
www.adda.org

U.S. Green Building Council
2101 L Street, NW, Suite 500
Washington, D.C. 20037
800-795-1747 (toll-free)
www.usgbc.org

Interior Designer

Alternate Job Titles:

- Certified Kitchen Designer
- Color and Materials Designer
- Commercial Interior Designer
- Decorating Consultant
- Director of Interiors
- Interior Decorator
- Interior Design Consultant
- Interior Design Coordinator

Both commercial and residential designers can choose from a wide variety of new products that are environmentally friendly.

Job Trends

Career Voyages lists interior design as number 23 on the list of the top 50 fastest-growing occupations and number 28 on the list of the top 50 occupations with the most openings through 2016. It is also listed as an in-demand occupation. The *Occupational Outlook Handbook* predicts a 19-percent growth in employment, which is greater than the average for all occupations. Competition is expected, however, because many people enter this profession. Most designers work for design services or architectural services. Some are in-store designers in furniture, home, or garden stores. Others are self-employed.

Increased interest in the environment and health concerns and the increasing interest in sustainable green design are driving some of the growth in this occupation. Increased awareness of ergonomics should also generate need for interior designers. People have become interested in home improvement and remodeling kitchens and bathrooms with a view to using more energy-efficient appliances and more environmentally safe and friendly buildings materials.

The hospitality industry is expected to create additional demand for design services for hotels and

About Environmentally Friendly Paint

Painting a room doesn't have to result in releasing clouds of toxic fumes into the atmosphere. The fumes come from VOCs (volatile organic compounds) in paint. Check VOC levels in the Natura brand from Benjamin Moore; Glidden™, This Old House Paint™, and other brands from ICI paints; as well as Harmony® and Progreen™ and other brands from Sherwin-Williams.

restaurants as it expands along with tourism. The health-care sector will also generate demand for new facilities for the aging population.

Nature of the Work

Green design is becoming increasingly popular as people become more aware of environmental and health issues related to indoor air quality. People entering this field need to be aware of what green design is and which products and materials are environmentally safe and do not damage the environment through harvesting or manufacturing.

Interior designers design the interiors of homes, office buildings, hotels, restaurants, stores, schools, and hospitals. They also design outdoor living spaces such as patios and outdoor kitchens. Their objective is to plan spaces that are functional, safe, and attractive for the people who live and work in them. Some designers specialize in residential or commercial interiors, whereas others specialize in kitchens and baths. The job includes

- meeting with the client and usually visiting the space to be designed.
- planning the overall space design.
- planning architectural details such as moldings, built-in components, and sometimes positions of walls or other features.
- knowing the building codes and construction requirements of the locality.
- preparing plans using computer-aided design (CAD) software.
- estimating costs.
- coordinating contractors and supervising the work for some clients.

About New Environmentally Friendly Design Products

The National Kitchen and Bath Association (www.nkba.org) promotes sustainable kitchen and bath design by providing information and resources about energy-efficient, water-efficient, and environmentally friendly products and methods.

Career Paths

Entry-level interior designers spend one to three years in on-the-job training under the supervision of an experienced designer. After they gain experience, interior designers are given responsibility for independent projects and may eventually become supervisors or chief designers. Some open their own design businesses.

Earning Potential

2008 mean hourly wage: $24.53; mean annual wage: $51,020

Education/Licensure

Postsecondary education is necessary for interior designers. An associate degree is the minimum. Some design schools offer programs that take two or three years and grant a certificate or associate degree. This generally qualifies a person to work as an assistant designer. A bachelor's degree is an advantage in a competitive job market and qualifies a person for an apprenticeship program leading to a license.

The Council for Interior Design Accreditation (CIDA) accredits interior design programs that grant bachelor's degrees. Its Web site and the Web site of the American Society of Interior Designers (ASID) provide lists with links to accredited interior design programs. The National Association of Schools of Art and Design (NASAD) accredits schools of art and design, and its Web site provides a list of accredited programs. There is also a recognized apprenticeship program for interior designers.

Twenty-three states, Puerto Rico, and the District of Columbia require registration, certification, or licensing for interior designers. In all cases, a combination of education, experience, and passing an exam is necessary. The National Council for Interior Design Qualification (NCIDQ) administers the nationally recognized licensing exam for interior designers. To qualify to take the exam, a designer must have a combination of six years of education and experience, at least two years of which must be formal education. The exam consists of six sections that cover all areas of interior design. The NCIDQ Web site contains links to the states requiring this exam.

The Green Building Certification Institute offers LEED Professional Accreditation for interior designers. The National Kitchen and Bath Association offers optional certifications for kitchen and bath design.

For More Information

American Society of Interior Designers
608 Massachusetts Avenue, NE
Washington, D.C. 20002-6006
202-546-3480
www.asid.org

Council for Interior Design Accreditation
206 Grandville Avenue, Suite 350
Grand Rapids, Michigan 49503
616-458-0400
www.accredit-id.org

National Association of Schools of Art and Design
11250 Roger Bacon Drive, Suite 21
Reston, Virginia 20190-5248
703-437-0700
http://nasad.arts-accredit.org

National Council for Interior Design Qualification
1602 L Street, NW, Suite 200
Washington, D.C. 20036-5681
202-721-0220
www.ncidq.org

National Kitchen and Bath Association
687 Willow Grove Street
Hackettstown, New Jersey 07840
800-843-6522 (toll-free)
www.nkba.org/student

U.S. Green Building Council
2101 L Street, NW, Suite 500
Washington, D.C. 20037
800-795-1747 (toll-free)
www.usgbc.org

Landscape Designer

Alternate Job Titles:

- Garden Center Salesperson
- Garden Designer
- Landscape Salesperson
- Ornamental Garden Designer

Landscape designers need to know how to manage people because they hire and oversee the workers who implement their designs.

Job Trends

The *Occupational Outlook Handbook* classifies landscape designers with grounds maintenance workers, a category for which an 18-percent growth in employment is expected by 2016. This is greater than the average for all occupations. Landscape designers work for landscape firms, garden centers, nurseries, and greenhouses. Some work with landscape architects and some own their own design businesses.

According to Bakersfield College's program description, environmental horticulture is among the fastest-growing areas in the agricultural industry. In California alone, where some of the largest greenhouses and nurseries are located, this is a multibillion-dollar business.

Nature of the Work

Landscape designers develop plans for residential and commercial landscapes, which include homes, businesses, business parks, campuses, parks, gardens, and golf courses. Designs may include flowers, shrubs, and trees as well as walkways, fountains, and other features. Landscape designers must be familiar with plant sciences, horticulture, ecology, soil and water conditions, design, materials, and computer-aided design (CAD) software.

Landscape designers interview the customer, analyze the site, develop the design, provide the plants and other materials, and implement the design project.

Landscape design is considered environmental landscaping when preservation of ecosystems and the natural environment are considered in the design. The Association of Professional Landscape Designers (APLD) provides a list of considerations for sustainable landscaping. Some items included on the list use recycled materials, local natural or fabricated materials, and biodegradable materials or materials that can be recycled. Other items include designing to reduce maintenance, using renewable energy (in outdoor lighting, for example), eliminating toxic materials, and reducing long-term input.

Career Paths

Landscape designers in a large firm may begin working with more experienced designers. They may be assigned smaller accounts in the beginning and work toward larger accounts as they gain experience. Experienced landscape designers may start their own business.

Earning Potential*

2009 average hourly salary: $30.88; average annual salary: $64,237

This is the average of average annual salaries from thirty-five major cities representing all areas of the country (Economic Research Institute). Salaries may be lower in smaller cities. Average hourly salary calculated based on 2,080 hours per year (U.S. Bureau of Labor Statistics).

About LEED Certification and Landscape Design

The U.S. Green Building Council LEED building certification includes credit for using regionally appropriate landscaping that minimizes water use, prevents erosion, and reduces energy use (e.g., outdoor lighting). For more information, check the USGBC's Web site, www.usgbc.org.

Education/Licensure

Landscape designers need some formal education, such as an associate degree in disciplines such as landscape, landscape design, horticulture, ornamental horticulture, environmental horticulture, or plant sciences. Many landscape designers have bachelor's degrees in similar disciplines.

The APLD Web site provides links to community colleges, junior colleges, colleges, universities, and private schools that offer programs in landscape design and horticulture, including online programs.

Certification is voluntary, but it is an asset to job seekers. The APLD offers certification, which requires one year of formal education, four years of experience, and submission of a portfolio of three completed projects for review. Recertification based on continuing education is required every three years. The Professional Landcare Network offers a number of certifications, including Certified Landscape Professional and Certified Ornamental Landscape Professional. These are based on passing an exam.

For More Information

Association of Professional Landscape Designers
4305 North Sixth Street, Suite A
Harrisburg, Pennsylvania 17110
717-238-9780
www.apld.com

Professional Landcare Network
950 Herndon Parkway, Suite 450
Herndon, Virginia 20170
703-736-9666
www.landcarenetwork.org

U.S. Green Building Council
2101 L Street, NW, Suite 500
Washington, D.C. 20037
800-795-1747 (toll-free)
www.usgbc.org

ENERGY INDUSTRY

The energy industry is expected to be a continual source of new jobs for many years. Energy demands continue to grow, but environmental sustainability is forcing the industry to look to renewable and alternative energy sources such as wind, solar power, and geothermal power. Development of these relatively new energy sources and improved efficiency of energy use are expected to create many new jobs. Application of new energy technologies will create thousands of new jobs for technicians.

Electrical and Electronics Engineering Technician

Alternate Job Titles:

- Electrical Field Technician
- Electrical-Instrument Repairer
- Electrical Technician
- Electric Substation Technician—Wind
- Electronics Field Technician
- Electronics Technician
- High Voltage Relay Technician
- Instrumentation Technician
- Instrument Technician (Utilities)
- Quality Systems Analyst
- Quality Systems Technician
- Relay Test Technician

A variety of specialties exist for electrical and electronics technicians depending on the field.

About Cutting the Nation's Energy Use

Two 2009 reports estimated that the nation could cut energy use by 15–23 percent by 2020 by instituting such energy efficiencies as sealing air ducts and replacing energy inefficient electrical appliances—potentially eliminating $1.2 trillion in waste and reducing 1.1 gigatons of greenhouse gas emissions—the same as taking the entire U.S. fleet of passenger vehicles and light trucks off the roads.*

*Unlocking Energy Efficiency in the U.S. Economy, McKinsey & Company, 2009

An allied occupation, for example, is automotive technician.

Job Trends

The Career Voyages Web site ranks electrical and electronics engineering technician occupation number 24 of the top 50 occupations with the most job openings predicted through 2016. It is also an in-demand occupation. There are currently 170,400 technicians, and about 4,000 new jobs are projected by 2016. This does not include replacements for technicians retiring or moving up to engineer or to other fields.

According to the *Occupational Outlook Handbook,* electrical and electronics engineering technician is one of the highest-paid engineering technician specialties. Only aerospace engineering technicians, which account for 33 percent of engineering technicians, are better paid.

Nature of the Work

Electrical and electronics engineering technicians work in power plants, private companies, and government positions. They assist in designing, developing, manufacturing, and testing equipment, including communication and navigational equipment, control devices, medical and industrial monitoring equipment, and computers. They may also be called ICE (instrumentation/controls/electrical systems) technicians. As part of their job duties, they may also test, diagnose, and repair equipment. In a solar-power or wind-power generating facility, electrical and electronics engineering technicians monitor and repair controls, electrical systems, and instrumentation.

Career Paths

Electrical and electronics engineering technicians usually begin work in training under supervision. As they gain more experience, they become involved in more difficult projects with less supervision. They may also gain greater responsibility for troubleshooting. Some will eventually become supervisors themselves.

Earning Potential

2008 mean hourly wage: $25.96; mean annual wage: $53,990

Education/Licensure

A two-year associate degree in engineering technology is preferred. The Technology Accreditation Commission of the Accreditation Board for Engineering and Technology (ABET) accredits two-year associate programs in engineering technology. Graduates of these programs are considered to have an acceptable level of competence. Other training programs vary widely. Engineering technology programs are available at community colleges, public and private technical institutes, and vocational technical schools and in the armed forces. Some four-year colleges offer bachelor's degrees in engineering technology, but graduates of these programs usually work as applied engineers or technologists.

Apprenticeship specialties associated with this occupation include Electrical Technician, Electrical-Instrument Repairer, Electronics Technician, Instrument Technician (Utilities), and Instrumentation Technician.

Certification through the National Institute for Certification in Engineering Technologies gives job seekers a competitive edge.

For More Information

Accreditation Board for Engineering Technology (ABET)
111 Market Place, Suite 1050
Baltimore, Maryland 21202
410-347-7700
www.abet.org

National Institute for Certification in Engineering Technologies
1420 King Street
Alexandria, Virginia 22314-2794
888-476-4238 (toll-free)
www.nicet.org

Solar Power Installer

Alternate Job Titles:

- Rooftop Solar Installer
- Solar Installer
- Solar Photovoltaic Installer
- Solar Project Manager
- Solar Thermal Installer

A related job is solar sales consultant or sales representative.

Job Trends

As the demand for renewable domestic energy increases, the solar power industry is expected to experience continued growth and to create many job opportunities. A 2008 study by Navigant Consulting, reported by www.RenewableEnergyWorld.com, predicted that growth in the solar power industry will create 440,000 new jobs by 2016. Many of these jobs will be in construction and domestic manufacturing. One such construction job is solar power installer.

Nature of the Work

Solar power installers install the parts of the solar energy system, including the panels, mounting, and electrical wiring. Therefore, construction and wiring knowledge and skills are required. Most of the work requires climbing to and working on rooftops.

About the Solar Tax Credit

In 2008, Congress passed an investment tax credit for residential solar electric systems. The tax credit is in effect until 2016 and will credit homeowners with a full 30 percent of the cost to purchase and install solar electric systems. For example, a home system that produces 4 kilowatts and costs $36,000 would receive a tax credit of $10,800.

Career Paths

A person with experience may lead an installation team or become a project coordinator. Knowledge of building codes is helpful in gaining more job responsibility.

Earning Potential

Hourly wage (2009): $14–$20

Education/Licensure

Job candidates need a combination of training and experience. An individual who has no experience in construction or electrical wiring should begin with a training program, such as a two-year associate degree offered by a community college or trade school. Completion of a training program accredited by the Institute for Sustainable Power Quality (ISPQ) is desirable; however, having at least a year of experience in installation is important for the job candidate.

The Interstate Renewable Energy Council (IREC) maintains a listing of renewable energy training programs, including solar- and wind-energy programs. It also administers the ISPQ accreditation program developed by the Institute for Sustainable Power (ISP) to ensure the quality of training programs, including those online.

Certification is voluntary but gives a person a competitive advantage. The North American Board of Certified Energy Practitioners (NABCEP) is the national organization that certifies renewable energy installers. It offers an Entry Level Certificate of Knowledge, Solar PV (photovoltaic) Installer Certification, and Solar Thermal Installer

Certification. These are voluntary certifications that demonstrate that installers have met a set of national standards of skills and experience.

For More Information

Interstate Renewable Energy Council (IREC)
P.O. Box 1156
Latham, New York 12110-1156
518-458-6059
www.irecusa.org

North American Board of Certified Energy
    Practitioners (NABCEP)
Saratoga Technology + Energy Park
10 Hermes Road, Suite 400
Malta, New York 12020
800-654-0021 (toll-free)
www.nabcep.org

Solar Energy Industry Association (SEIA)
575 7th Street, NW, Suite 400
Washington D.C. 20004
202-682-0556
www.seia.org

Wind Turbine Fabricator

Alternate Job Titles:

- Machinist
- Sheet Metal Worker
- Wind Turbine Machinist

Much of the equipment for wind power, including huge wind turbines, has been manufactured abroad and imported into the United States. However, with a government-backed push to increase the use of wind power, this is changing as U.S. companies see the potential profits to be made in wind power.

Job Trends

Wind turbine fabrication combines the work of several skilled trades. Therefore, this occupation provides an opportunity for workers trained in other manufacturing sectors, such as automobile manufacture, to apply their existing skills in a new industry. Two of the skills needed for wind turbine manufacture are machinist and sheet metal

worker. Sheet metal workers also manufacture hydroelectric power components.

According to the American Wind Energy Association, wind power accounted for 42 percent of new energy generation in 2008. This created 35,000 new jobs in 2008, many of them in manufacturing components such as wind turbines. Over seventy manufacturing facilities were built or expanded in 2007–08 to produce the equipment for wind power generation. According to its *Green Jobs Guidebook,* the California Economic Development Department predicts the need for over 5,000 new jobs in California alone for wind turbine machinists and sheet metal workers.

According to the *Occupational Outlook Handbook,* job opportunities for machinists are expected to be good through the next decade even though the number of jobs is declining slightly because of the overall decline in U.S. manufacturing. The number of persons in training programs, however, is less than the number of machinists expected to retire. Employment for sheet metal workers is expected to increase by 7 percent by 2016. Career Voyages lists sheet metal worker as an in-demand occupation. In addition to jobs in wind energy, the push to install more energy-efficient heating and air conditioning systems will contribute jobs to this category.

Nature of the Work

Machinists make precision metal parts using a variety of machine tools such as milling machines, drill presses, and lathes. They may also machine parts from other materials, like plastic. Machinists must be able to read the specifications and diagrams, determine what cuts will be made, select tools, and plan the sequence of operations. Machinists determine the speed of the machine, the feed rate, and how much material to remove. Precision is critical. Many machines are computer numerically controlled (CNC), so the machinist may work with a programmer to develop the instructions for the computer and then monitor the computer-controlled machining.

Sheet metal workers make, install, and maintain many sheet metal components of wind turbines. They also work in other industries, for example, making duct work for heating and air conditioning systems, siding, and roofing. Sheet metal workers may work either in the mass production of parts or in construction. They measure, cut, bend, and fasten metal pieces according to a plan and specifications. Their equipment includes drills, saws, shears, lasers, and presses, and much of it may be computerized. Like machinists, sheet metal workers must be very accurate in their work.

Career Path

Experienced machinists may become supervisors or administrators in their company. They may become CNC programmers or make tools and equipment. Some may open their own machine shop.

Sheet metal workers may also advance to supervisors. Some move into quality control or building inspection. Some begin their own contractor business.

Earning Potential

Machinist:
2008 mean hourly wage: $18.03; mean annual wage: $37,490

Sheet metal worker:
2008 mean hourly wage: $21.30; mean annual wage: $44,310

Education/Licensure

Machinists generally learn the trade through apprenticeship programs. These consist of classes and paid shop work under supervision lasting as long as four years. Some apprenticeship programs are offered in cooperation with technical schools or community colleges. Manufacturers and unions also run apprenticeship programs. Some community colleges and technical schools have two-year associate degree programs, but on-the-job experience is still needed. In all cases, a high school diploma or GED is required. Training in CNC is essential. High school math classes in algebra and trigonometry, drafting, and metalworking are good preparation.

The National Institute of Metalworking Skills (NIMS) has developed national standards for metalworking skills. Many state apprenticeship boards, training programs, and community colleges are now incorporating these standards into the curriculum. Persons who complete these programs and pass an exam receive a NIMS credential, which is an advantage in obtaining a job. State apprenticeship boards grant journey worker certification to persons who have completed an apprenticeship.

Sheet metal workers must have a high school diploma or GED, including classes in algebra, geometry, physics, and mechanical drawing. A combination of classroom and on-the-job training lasting four to five years is needed to become an experienced sheet metal worker. They may begin in the trade by getting on-the-job training from a contractor or manufacturer. Employers may also send them for courses at technical schools or community colleges. Some employers offer apprenticeship programs that take four to five years and combine classes and paid training on the job. The Sheet Metal Workers' International Association and the Sheet Metal and Air-Conditioning Contractors National Association administer some apprenticeship programs.

A number of organizations offer certifications in sheet metal work specialties. These certifications are helpful in the job market. Individuals who complete registered apprenticeship programs are certified as journey workers.

For More Information

American Wind Energy Association
1501 M Street, NW, Suite 1000
Washington, D.C. 20005
202-383-2500
www.awea.org

International Training Institute for the Sheet Metal and Air-Conditioning Industry
601 N. Fairfax Street, Suite 240
Alexandria, Virginia 22314
703-739-7200
www.sheetmetal-iti.org

National Center for Construction Education and
    Research
3600 NW 43rd Street, Bldg. G
Gainesville, Florida 32606
352-334-0911
www.nccer.org

National Institute for Metalworking Skills
10565 Fairfax Boulevard, Suite 203
Fairfax, Virginia 22030
703-352-4971
www.nims-skills.org/web/nims/home

Sheet Metal and Air-Conditioning Contractors'
    National Association
4201 Lafayette Center Drive
Chantilly, Virginia 20151-1209
703-803-2980
www.smacna.org

Sheet Metal Workers International Association
1750 New York Avenue, NW, 6th Floor
Washington, D.C. 20006
202-783-5880
www.smwia.org

ENVIRONMENTAL HEALTH

Environmental health itself is not an industry. It is
a collection of health-related professions practiced
in a number of different industries and in all levels
of government. The professions are united in their
common goals of preserving the environment, conserving resources, and protecting all living things
from injury, disease, and the effects of hazardous
materials.

The Agency for Toxic Substances and Disease
Registry, the Centers for Disease Control and
Prevention, and the National Institutes of Health
jointly authored the chapter on environmental
health in the U.S. Department of Health and
Human Services report "Healthy People 2010:
Understanding and Improving Health." The three
agencies state that the three main factors affecting
human health are the environment (including
infectious agents), personal behavior, and genetic
factors. The agencies estimate that 25 percent of

preventable illnesses are related to environmental
quality, and the six major environmental issues that
can and must be addressed are

- outdoor air quality
- water quality
- toxics and waste
- healthy homes and healthy communities
- infrastructure surveillance
- global environmental health

Although important strides have been made, many
issues still remain to be addressed, and this is the
work of environmental health professionals.

Environmental Science and Protection Technician

Alternate Job Titles:

- Associate Environmental Professional
- Environmental Health Specialist
- Environmental Specialist
- Environmental Technician
- Indoor Air Quality Manager
- Industrial Environmental Toxicologist
- Industrial Pretreatment Program (IPP)
  Specialist
- Laboratory Specialist
- Laboratory Technician
- Process Laboratory Specialist
- Public Health Sanitarian
- Registered Environmental Laboratory
  Technologist
- Sanitarian
- Sanitarian Specialist

This is one of the occupations getting a real boost
from the growing interest in the environment and
health concerns.

The Service Employees International Union
The Service Employees International Union (SEIU) represents health-care providers and child-care providers
as well as property service and public service workers.
In 2008, the SEIU adopted a resolution for its 2 million
members to advocate for environmental change "to
address the global climate crisis, including supporting
emission reduction targets based on sound science."

About the Brownfields and Land Revitalization Program

The Environmental Protection Agency's Brownfields Program is cleaning up all types of contaminated land for productive reuse. The agency estimates that there are 450,000 brownfields in the United States. For more information, check out http://epa.gov/brownfields/.

Job Trends

According to the *Occupational Outlook Handbook,* employment for environmental science and protection technicians is predicted to grow 28 percent by 2016, which is much greater than average for all occupations. The Career Voyages Web site reports that this in-demand occupation is number 6 out of the top 50 fastest-growing occupations. It is listed as number 37 in the list of the top 50 occupations with the most openings. Increasing environmental management, monitoring, and compliance are expected to generate over 80 percent of the new jobs. These jobs will be in scientific and technical consulting services.

In 2006, most environmental science and protection technicians worked for state and local governments and private consulting firms, according to the *Occupational Outlook Handbook.* They often work under the supervision of environmental scientists to monitor pollutant levels, regulate wastes, clean up contamination, and monitor environmental regulatory compliance.

Nature of the Work

Environmental pollutants and contaminants are detrimental to human health and the environment. Environmental science and protection technicians

- conduct field and laboratory tests to measure contamination and determine sources of environmental pollution.
- set up equipment and collect samples of air, water, soil, gases, and other materials for analysis.
- analyze these samples using a variety of laboratory instrumentation.
- may design and implement monitoring programs.

- may be involved in controlling sources of pollution, remediation, waste management, hazardous materials management, or regulator compliance.
- prepare reports.
- maintain databases.
- interact with customers.

Career Paths

Environmental technicians begin work under the supervision of environmental scientists or more experienced technicians. After gaining experience, they get more responsibility and work more independently. Some may become supervisors.

Earning Potential

Environmental science and protection technicians, including health:

2008 mean hourly wage: $20.76; mean annual wage: $43,180

Education/Licensure

Requirements vary, but an associate degree or two years of specialized training is typically the minimum. Many jobs now require a bachelor's degree in environmental science, biology, chemistry, or a related area. Technical and community colleges offer associate degree programs in specific technologies. Technical institutes offer certificate programs and associate degrees, but these programs typically offer less general education and less theory than programs in community or technical colleges. Opportunities will be best for those who graduate from an applied science technology program that includes hands-on experience with laboratory equipment.

The American Chemical Society Web site provides a list of approved chemical technology programs. Some colleges and universities also offer certificate programs.

Some states have apprenticeship programs for laboratory assistants. The apprenticeships offer paid on-the-job training.

Certification is not required but may be beneficial. The National Registry of Environmental

Professionals offers a number of certifications, including Associate Environmental Professional (AEP), Certified Indoor Air Quality Manager (CIAQM), Registered Environmental Laboratory Technologist (RELT), and Certified Industrial Environmental Toxicologist (CIET). All require passing an exam and some combination of education and experience. In some cases, experience may be substituted for education.

For More Information

American Chemical Society, Education Division
1155 16th Street, NW
Washington, D.C. 20036
800-227-5558 (toll-free)
www.acs.org

National Environmental Health Association
720 S. Colorado Blvd., Suite 1000-N
Denver, Colorado 80246
866-956-2258 (toll-free)
www.neha.org

National Registry of Environmental Professionals
P. O. Box 2099
Glenview, Illinois 60025-6099
847-724-6631
www.nrep.org

Hazardous Materials (HAZMAT) Specialist

Alternate Job Titles:

- Asbestos Abatement Worker
- Decontamination/Decommissioning Operator (D & D Operator)
- Field Technician
- Hazardous Materials (HAZMAT) Technician
- Hazardous Waste Operations and Emergency Response (HAZWOPER) Technician
- Nuclear Waste Handler
- Radiation Safety Technician
- Radiological Control and Safety Technician
- Sampler
- Site Worker
- Waste Handling Technician

The threat of terrorist attacks has made this occupation very visible since 9/11.

Job Trends

Employment for hazardous materials removal workers is expected to increase by 11 percent by 2016, according to the *Occupational Outlook Handbook*. This is about average. Job opportunities are expected to be good, and Career Voyages lists this as an in-demand occupation.

Clean up of hazardous waste sites will continue to create jobs for hazardous materials removal workers. Removal of lead and asbestos from historic structures and federal buildings will continue. However, the most growth is expected for radiation safety technicians who decontaminate and decommission electric power plants and nuclear facilities.

Nature of the Work

Hazardous materials specialists manage HAZMAT (hazardous materials) programs and projects. HAZMAT specialists are involved in every phase of dealing with hazardous materials, including identification, removal, packaging, storage, transport, and disposal. Hazardous materials include such things as lead-based paint, asbestos, radioactive materials, and waste fuel and oil.

HAZMAT specialists investigate possible contaminated sites and develop remediation plans for clean up. HAZMAT workers are among the first responders to emergencies involving hazardous materials, so they also plan and run drills for HAZMAT emergencies. They must follow strict safety procedures and comply with all laws and regulations regarding the materials with which they work. This includes precise recordkeeping and accurate labeling of hazardous materials that are removed from sites.

Career Paths

Additional education and training are necessary for a removal worker to work in hazardous materials management.

Earning Potential

2008 mean hourly wage: $19.37; mean annual wage: $40,290

Average pay is higher in scientific research and development services, aerospace manufacturing, electric power generation and transmission, and the federal government. However, there are significantly fewer positions in these industries than in remediation services where most workers are employed.

Education/Licensure

To remove hazardous materials, no formal education is required beyond high school. However, local, state, and federal regulations require specific on-the-job training. Generally, 40 hours of training are required, and the training must meet standards. Training in handling materials and entering confined spaces is usually required. Workers who remove lead and asbestos must complete a training program that complies with Occupational Safety and Health Administration (OSHA) standards. A federal license requiring OSHA-approved training is also necessary for responding to emergencies. Those who decommission or decontaminate nuclear facilities must complete the standard 40-hour OSHA training in addition to courses covering nuclear and radiation regulations.

To work in a management job, an associate degree in hazardous materials management or environmental science or technology is required. Some jobs may require a bachelor's degree.

The Institute of Hazardous Materials Management (IHMM) offers the Certified Hazardous Materials Practitioner (CHMP) credential. This credential requires an associate of science degree in hazardous materials management, environmental technology, environmental science, or environmental management. It must be from an accredited college or university program. Three years' experience and passing an exam are also required. For seniors in college or those who have recently completed a bachelor's degree but have fewer than three years' experience, IHMM offers the Hazardous Materials

Manager-in-Training (HMMT) program. This requires passing an exam. It is good for five years until a person qualifies to take the exam for the Certified Hazardous Materials Manager (CHMM) credential.

The National Registry of Environmental Professionals offers the Registered Hazardous and Chemical Materials Manager (RHCMM) credential. A bachelor's degree, five years of experience, and passing an exam are required. However, three years of experience may be substituted for each academic year.

For More Information

Institute of Hazardous Materials Management
11900 Parklawn Drive, Suite 450
Rockville, Maryland 20852
301-984-8969
www.ihmm.org

National Environmental Health Association
720 S. Colorado Blvd., Suite 1000-N
Denver, Colorado 80246
866-956-2258 (toll-free)
www.neha.org

National Registry of Environmental Professionals
P.O. Box 2099
Glenview, Illinois 60025-6099
847-724-6631
www.nrep.org

North American Hazardous Materials
   Management Association
3030 W. 81st Avenue
Westminster, Colorado 80031-4111
877-292-1403 (toll-free)
www.nahmma.org

Water and Wastewater Treatment Operator

Alternate Job Titles:

- Backflow Prevention Assembly Tester
- Biosolids Land Applier
- Industrial Waste Operator
- Plant Maintenance Technologist
- Process Operator

- Supervisory Control and Data Acquisition (SCADA) Operator
- Wastewater Operator
- Wastewater Treatment Plant Operator
- Water and Wastewater Laboratory Analyst
- Water System Operator
- Water Treatment Plant Operator

Technicians in this field can be certified in several specialties: water treatment, distribution, collection, and wastewater treatment.

Job Trends

The *Occupational Outlook Handbook* predicts employment growth of 14 percent by 2016 for water and liquid waste treatment plant and system operators. This is greater than the average for all occupations. Job opportunities are expected to be excellent. Demand for operators will increase as the population grows and water demand increases. In its "State of the Industry Report 2008," the American Water Works Association cites workforce issues as a major concern. Many professionals are retiring, and there are few people qualified to replace them.

Local governments employ about 80 percent of water and wastewater treatment operators. However, utilities are starting to rely more on private firms to manage facilities.

Nature of the Work

Water treatment operators treat water to meet safe drinking water standards. Wastewater treatment or liquid waste treatment operators treat industrial and domestic wastewater to remove pollutants and make it safe for the environment. These workers control the entire process either for purifying water or treating and disposing of liquid waste. They

- coordinate workers and operations.
- monitor the equipment to make sure it is working properly.
- add treatment chemicals as needed.
- repair and maintain the equipment, including cleaning tanks and filters.
- collect water samples and analyze them for chemicals or microorganisms.

- must know all the state and federal regulations regarding water quality.

In a small plant, an operator might carry out all these functions, whereas in a large plant, operators may be specialized in certain parts of the system. Recordkeeping is an important part of the job.

Career Paths

At the entry level, people usually begin as operators-in-training. They work under direct supervision of an experienced operator and assist with routine work. Operators are licensed initially at the lowest level. As they gain experience, they may be licensed at a higher level and become responsible for more complex processes. Advancement may be to a supervisory position, to superintendent, or to a larger facility. Superintendents of larger plants need a bachelor's degree, usually in science or engineering.

Some operators may become technicians working in state agencies that control drinking water and wastewater. Community college or technical school training is usually necessary for this advancement. Experienced operators may get jobs in industrial waste treatment plants or in consulting companies.

Earning Potential

2008 mean hourly wage: $19.21; mean annual wage: $39,950

The average annual salary for treatment plant operators increases with increasing population served. It ranges from $38,168 (serving fewer than 10,000 people) to $49,964 (serving over 250,000 people), according to the American Water Works Association.

Education/Licensure

A high school diploma or GED is the minimum requirement for water and wastewater treatment operators. Training takes place on the job, and at a certain level, the person becomes eligible for a license. However, an associate degree or completion of a water quality and treatment certificate program improves job and promotion opportunities. Programs are often run by trade associations, and some are offered at community colleges. The American Water Works Association Web site provides links to colleges and universities, including community colleges, and offers good career resources.

During the training period, new employees may take classroom or self-study instruction offered by the employer. State agencies that regulate drinking water and wastewater usually offer courses covering processes, procedures, laboratory analyses, maintenance, and management. Some employers pay tuition for college courses in related subjects. This occupational area has four specializations for which there may be apprenticeship programs: Water-Treatment-Plant Operator, Waste-Treatment Operator, Wastewater-Treatment-Plant Operator, and Clarifying-Plant Operator.

The U.S. Environmental Protection Agency establishes the minimum guidelines for public water system operator certifications. The states implement these guidelines (there are variations from state to state) with mandatory licensing or certification. Certified operators are critical for compliance with the Safe Drinking Water Act.

The Association of Boards of Certification offers four voluntary certification programs with different classes, or categories, of requirements. The Operator Certification has four classes of certification plus a certification for very small water system operators, the Lab Analyst Certification has four classes, the Biosolids Land Appliers Certification has two classes, and the Plant Maintenance Technologist Certification has four classes. The requirements for each higher class of certification are progressively more demanding, from a high school diploma or GED and one year of experience for the lowest class to 1,800 hours of postsecondary education and four years' experience for the highest class.

The National Environmental Health Association offers a national credential for Certified Installer of Onsite Wastewater Treatment Systems. It is offered at a basic and an advanced level.

For More Information

American Water Works Association
6666 West Quincy Avenue
Denver, Colorado 80235
303-794-7711
www.awwa.org

Association of Boards of Certification
208 Fifth Street, Suite 201
Ames, Iowa 50010-6259
515-232-3623
www.abccert.org

National Environmental Health Association
720 S. Colorado Blvd., Suite 1000-N
Denver, Colorado 80246
866-956-2258 (toll-free)
www.neha.org

National Rural Water Association
2915 S. 13th Street
Duncan, Oklahoma 73533
580-252-0629
www.nrwa.org

Water Environment Federation
601 Wythe Street
Alexandria, Virginia 22314-1994
800-666-0206 (toll-free)
www.wef.org

NATURAL RESOURCES MANAGEMENT AND CONSERVATION

In "Productive Lands, Healthy Environment," its natural resources strategic plan for 2005–10, the U.S. Department of Agriculture states:

We envision a productive, sustainable agricultural sector in balance with a high-quality environment. Productive use of the Nation's cropland, grazing land, and forest land is essential to the Nation's security and the health and well-being of its citizens. These lands form the foundation of a vibrant agricultural economy that provides food, fiber, forest products, and energy for the nation. These lands also produce environmental benefits that people need—clean and abundant water, clean air, and healthy ecosystems.

This vision summarizes the commitment made to managing and conserving natural resources. Even stronger emphasis is currently being placed on sustainable agriculture and on alternate, renewable forms of energy. The challenges in bringing this vision to fruition require the work of a variety of skilled workers involved in all aspects of conservation and natural resources management.

Conservation and Forest Technician

Alternate Job Titles:

- Conservationist
- Forest Technician
- Forestry Aide
- Forestry Technician
- Natural Resources Technician
- Resource Manager
- Resource Technician
- Wildlife Technician

This occupational area is one that is gaining attention as Americans place more emphasis on preserving the nation's natural resources.

Job Trends

The *Occupational Outlook Handbook* covers conservation and forest technicians together because the occupations are closely related. Career Voyages ranks this occupation number 47 out of the top 50 occupations with the most openings. Even though the number of jobs will remain fairly constant through 2016, an estimated 13,000 technicians will be needed to replace those who retire or leave the industry. The majority of conservation and forest technicians work for the federal government. Most of the rest work for state and local government. A few work in colleges and universities or consulting firms.

New opportunities such as urban forestry are emerging and may provide new job opportunities in state and local government to offset projected

About Federal Mapping Projects

One example of how the federal government uses the new technology is the Coastal Barrier Resources Digital Mapping Pilot Project. The project is intended to help preserve the nation's. It is designed to address "the inaccuracies of the outdated maps, correct errors that adversely affect private property owners, increase efficiencies and accessibility by allowing the integration of the Coastal Barrier Resource System (CBRS) information into digital planning tools, conserve natural resources, and preserve the integrity of the CBRS for the long-term."

declines in federal government forestry and conservation jobs. Increasing emphasis on protecting the environment and preserving water resources should provide some new jobs. Emerging concerns such as controlling invasive plants and pests may also create opportunities.

Nature of the Work

Conservation technicians assist conservation scientists to manage and protect wildlife habitats and rangelands. They may also provide technical advice to the public about soil and water conservation, insect and disease control, and other natural resource issues.

Forest technicians work under the supervision of foresters. Most of the work is in forests, but some forest technicians now work in the emerging area of urban forestry. Forest technicians may do some or all of the following:

- collect data about the size of forest land, tree populations, damage from insects and disease, seedling health, and potential fire hazards
- measure timberlands
- supervise harvesting
- monitor logging operations
- assist in building roads
- survey and map access roads and other features
- train and supervise seasonal workers who maintain recreational facilities, plant trees, and fight fires

- conduct public education programs
- patrol forests and parks and enforce environmental regulations and fire safety

Career Paths

Conservation and forest technicians usually begin working under supervision. As they gain more experience, they become involved in more difficult projects with less supervision. Some will eventually become supervisors themselves.

Earning Potential

2008 mean hourly wage: $16.98; mean annual wage: $35,320

Education/Licensure

Requirements vary, but an associate degree or two years of specialized training is typically the minimum. Many jobs now require a bachelor's degree in biology or a related area. Technical and community colleges offer associate degree programs in specific technologies. Technical institutes offer certificate programs and associate degrees, but they offer less general education and less theory than courses in community or technical colleges.

The Society of American Foresters accredits more than twenty associate degree programs in forestry and conservation. The Society for Range Management accredits degree programs in range management. Its Web site provides a list of and links to colleges and universities that offer range management courses and degrees.

The Society of American Foresters offers the Certified Forester certification. Generally, a bachelor's degree or higher in forestry is required. However, one option for certification is an associate degree in forestry and a bachelor's degree in ecology, environmental studies, range management, wildlife management, or a related field.

For More Information

Society for Range Management
10030 West 27th Avenue
Wheat Ridge, Colorado 80215-6601
303-986-3309
www.rangelands.org/srm.shtml

Society of American Foresters
5400 Grosvenor Lane
Bethesda, Maryland 20814-2198
866-897-8720
www.safnet.org

Environmental Engineering Technician

Alternate Job Titles:

- Engineer Technician
- Environmental Engineering Assistant
- Environmental Field Technician
- Environmental Specialist
- Environmental Technician

A variety of issues related to the environment are driving growth in this occupation.

Job Trends

According to the *Occupational Outlook Handbook*, environmental engineering technology is projected to have the highest growth of any engineering technology field through 2016. The projected growth is 25 percent, much greater than the average of all occupations. In 2006, there were 21,000 environmental engineering technicians, and by 2016, an additional 5,200 jobs are projected. Environmental engineering is ranked number 12 on the Career Voyages list of the top 50 fastest-growing occupations requiring postsecondary education.

Although the demand for environmental engineering technicians will be generated by the need to clean up environmental hazards that already exist, the focus is shifting to prevention as public health and safety concerns increase. More technicians will be needed to ensure compliance with regulations as environmental regulations are becoming more complex. The growing population will also contribute to increasing environmental issues that must be addressed.

Nature of the Work

Environmental engineering technicians work with environmental scientists and engineers in almost any area of environmental protection. Environmental engineering technicians operate, test, maintain, and modify devices and equipment used to prevent or remediate environmental problems and control pollution. Depending on their area of work, environmental engineering technicians

- assist engineers or scientists in developing methods for prevention and remediation.
- collect and analyze air, water, and soil samples.
- conduct inspections to monitor regulatory compliance regarding hazardous substances such as asbestos and lead.
- inspect recycling facilities.
- inspect water and wastewater treatment facilities to ensure compliance with pollution control regulations.
- oversee packaging and disposal of hazardous materials.

Career Paths

Environmental engineering technicians usually begin working under supervision. As they gain more experience, they become involved in more difficult projects with less supervision. Some will eventually become supervisors themselves. Some will continue their education to earn a bachelor's degree in environmental engineering. Note that an engineering technology program is different from a pre-engineering program, so not all course work for an associate degree will be applicable.

Earning Potential

2008 mean hourly wage: $21.36; mean annual wage: $44,440

Education/Licensure

A two-year associate degree in environmental engineering technology is preferred. The Technology Accreditation Commission of the Accreditation Board for Engineering and Technology (ABET) accredits two-year associate degree programs in engineering technology. Graduates of these programs are considered to have an acceptable level of competence. Training programs, which may vary widely in terms of course work, are offered at community colleges, public and private technical institutes, and vocational technical schools and in the armed forces. Some four-year colleges offer bachelor's degrees in engineering technology, but graduates of these programs usually work as applied engineers or technologists.

For More Information

Accreditation Board for Engineering Technology (ABET)
111 Market Place, Suite 1050
Baltimore, Maryland 21202
410-347-7700
www.abet.org

Surveying and Mapping Technician

Alternate Job Titles:

- Computer-Aided Design (CAD) Technician
- Drafter
- Field Crew Chief
- Geographical Information System (GIS) Analyst
- Geographical Information System (GIS) Specialist
- Geographical Information System (GIS) Technician
- Hydrographic Surveyor
- Mapping Technician
- Photogrammetric Compilation Specialist
- Photogrammetric Technician
- Stereoplotter Operator
- Survey Crew Chief
- Survey Party Chief
- Survey Technician

There are also a variety of jobs on a survey team, such as chainman, rodman, and instrument man.

Job Trends

According to the *Occupational Outlook Handbook,* employment for surveying and mapping technicians is expected to increase by 19 percent by 2016, which is greater than the average for all occupations. Career Voyages lists surveying and mapping technician as one of the in-demand occupations. Most surveying and mapping technicians work for engineering services firms. Some work for local governments, and fewer work for federal and state governments.

Rapid growth in the geographic information systems (GIS) industry is generated by the development of the many types of applications for which the technology is being used. It is applied to problems in environmental, conservation, and urban planning areas and in all types of organizations, including government, private firms, and nonprofit advocacy organizations.

In natural resource management, GIS technology is being used to manage forests and rangelands, preserve wetlands and wildlife habitats, model migration of toxic chemicals, and assess groundwater contamination and air quality. Urban and regional planners use GIS to model urban growth. Public health officials use it to track the incidence of certain diseases in relation to natural and environmental factors.

Nature of the Work

Surveying and mapping technicians assist geographic information specialists with data collection, calculations, and computer-aided drafting. Much of their work is used in geographic information systems (GIS) to construct digital maps that can be manipulated in many ways.

Surveying technicians assist in conducting field surveys to determine locations of the Earth's natural features and constructed features on the surface as well as underground and underwater. They also

- measure distances, angles, and directions.
- may use electronic distance-measuring equipment for some measurements.
- operate and adjust instruments.
- perform calculations and corrections.
- collect data.
- compare computations to standards.

Mapping technicians

- produce new maps or update maps.
- verify the accuracy of maps.
- use field notes to make calculations, match sequences of aerial photographs, and compare topographical features in aerial photographs and old maps.
- research legal documents to determine the location of property lines.

- compile databases and create maps using computer software.

Mapping technicians use these tools to create various types of maps to serve various purposes, such as photomosaics, overlay maps, and contour maps.

Career Paths

Surveying and mapping technicians usually begin working under supervision. As they gain more experience, they become involved in more difficult projects with less supervision. Some will eventually become supervisors themselves. Some will continue their education and earn bachelor's degrees. Because technology is advancing rapidly, those with bachelor's degrees will have the best opportunities.

Earning Potential

2008 mean hourly wage: $18.03; mean annual wage: $37,500

Education/Licensure

An associate degree or training program is generally required to become a surveying or mapping technician. Many vocational and technical schools and community colleges have programs in surveying and surveying technology. These may take from one to three years to complete. Some offer an associate degree. Some colleges and universities offer bachelor's degree programs.

The Accreditation Board for Engineering and Technology (ABET) accredits surveying and mapping technology programs. The American Congress on Surveying and Mapping Web site provides a list of and links to junior colleges, community colleges, colleges, and universities that have programs in surveying technology, surveying engineering technology, and geomatics technology. They have lists for both ABET-accredited and non-accredited programs.

Certification is voluntary. The ASPRS: Imaging and Geospatial Information Society offers the following certifications based on experience and/or education: Certified Photogrammetric

Technologist, Certified Remote Sensing Technologist, and Certified GIS/LIS Technologist. The National Society of Professional Surveyors offers the Certified Survey Technician (CST) certification program. This program is part of the National Apprenticeship Program sponsored by the U.S. Department of Labor. Apprenticeship specialties for surveying and mapping technicians are Geodetic Computator, Photogrammetric Technician, and Surveyor Assistant (Instruments).

For More Information

Accreditation Board for Engineering and
    Technology (ABET)
111 Market Place, Suite 1050
Baltimore, Maryland 21202
410-347-7700
www.abet.org

American Congress on Surveying and Mapping
6 Montgomery Village Avenue, Suite 403
Gaithersburg, Maryland 20879
240-632-9716
www.acsm.net

ASPRS: Imaging and Geospatial Information
    Society
5410 Grosvenor Lane, Suite 210
Bethesda, Maryland 20814-2160
301-493-0290
www.asprs.org

National Society of Professional
    Surveyors—NSPS
6 Montgomery Village Avenue, Suite 403
Gaithersburg, Maryland 20879
240-632-9716
www.nspsmo.org

Veterinary Technologist

Alternate Job Titles:

- Certified Veterinary Technician
- Licensed Veterinary Technician
- Registered Veterinary Technician
- Veterinary Assistant
- Veterinary Laboratory Technician
- Veterinary Technician

In the new economy, veterinary technicians are more than assistants to veterinarians.

Job Trends

According to Career Voyages, veterinary technologist and technician is the fastest-growing occupation requiring postsecondary training or an associate degree. It ranks number 20 out of the top 50 occupations with the most openings and is listed as one of the in-demand occupations. There are currently about 71,000 veterinary technicians and technologists, and the projected need will be around 100,000 by 2016, for a 41 percent increase as projected by the *Occupational Outlook Handbook*. The demand is expected to exceed the number of qualified technicians.

A growing specialization for veterinary technicians is in restoring wildlife to natural ecosystems. The increasing attention to wildlife preservation and protection of endangered species creates a need for trained veterinary technicians with an interest in working in this niche occupation.

Nature of the Work

Veterinary technologists or technicians may work in a variety of environments, including private veterinary practice, animal shelters, zoos, pharmaceutical sales, or biomedical research facilities. Veterinary technologists are also found in livestock management and food safety.

As concerns over biodiversity escalate, more veterinary technicians are needed to preserve endangered species and restore species to their natural ecosystems. Technicians work in conservation centers and wildlife centers, where their work is focused on restoring natural wildlife populations. This may mean conducting breeding programs in wildlife centers or zoos to increase populations. A major project of the U.S. Fish and Wildlife Service was to reintroduce gray wolves to Yellowstone National Park. Other species that have been reintroduced into their natural habitats are big horn sheep, foxes, coyotes, and a variety of bird species.

Technicians work with conservation biologists to protect the young of endangered species from predators and tourists, for example, by relocating nests.

Veterinary technicians also treat individual animals in wildlife centers where they are rehabilitated and returned to their natural environments. A function of veterinary technicians in the laboratory is to analyze biological samples from wildlife. These analyses provide indicators of ecological health and the effects of disease, pollution, and environmental degradation on populations in the wild.

Career Paths

Veterinary technicians and technologists usually begin working under supervision. As they gain more experience, they become involved in more difficult projects with less supervision. Some will eventually become supervisors themselves.

Earning Potential

2008 mean hourly wage: $14.35; mean annual wage: $29,850

Education/Licensure

Generally, a two-year associate degree in veterinary technology from a community college accredited by the American Veterinary Medical Association (AVMA) is required for veterinary technicians. Technologists generally complete a four-year program.

Each state regulates veterinary technologists and technicians, and all states require passing a credentialing exam determined by the state board of veterinary examiners. Most states use the National Veterinary Technician (NVT) exam and credentials can usually be transferred among states that use this exam. For employment in research facilities, certification through the American Association for Laboratory Animal Science (AALAS) is recommended. There are three levels of AALAS certification. A combination of education and experience is required as well as passing an exam for each level.

For More Information

American Association for Laboratory Animal Science
9190 Crestwyn Hills Drive
Memphis, Tennessee 38125
901-754-8620
www.aalas.org

American Veterinary Medical Association
1931 North Meacham Road, Suite 100
Schaumburg, Illinois 60173-4360
800-248-2862 (toll-free)
www.avma.org

PARKS, RECREATION, AND TOURISM

Trends for parks, recreation, and tourism reflect trends in the leisure and hospitality industry. The *Occupational Outlook Handbook* includes an overview of this industry and breaks it down into three categories: arts, entertainment, and recreation; food and drink; and hotels. Employment in arts, entertainment, and recreation was predicted to increase 31 percent by 2016. Employment in hotels was expected to increase 14 percent. Museums were expanding. However, this industry sector is affected by the economy, and the outlook is not as good as it had been. New jobs in these areas are not currently as plentiful as predicted, but the situation will improve as the economy recovers.

The American Recovery and Reinvestment Act (ARRA) passed in 2009 invested funding in these areas to bring about recovery and create jobs. As a result of ARRA, the National Park Service had $750 million to invest in projects to preserve historic landscapes and national icons, remediate mine sites, improve trails, increase use of renewable energy, and increase energy efficiency. The funding for the Federal Highway Administration included money to improve park roads. Under ARRA, the National Endowment for the Arts received funding for theaters and art projects across the country. These projects and others funded by ARRA will improve job opportunities.

About the National Park Service

In addition to maintaining the nation's almost 400 national parks, recreation sites, historic monuments, and historic parks, the National Park Service (NPS) provides technical assistance to local communities to preserve their own history and create close-to-home recreation sites. The NPS has provided $5 billion in preservation and outdoor recreation grants and $48 billion in historic preservation tax incentives.

Green Travel Agent

Alternate Job Titles:

- Travel Agent
- Travel Consultant
- Travel Counselor

Becoming a green travel agent means knowing a lot more than where to find the best hotel deals.

Job Trends

Employment for travel agents is expected to increase 1 percent by 2016, according to the *Occupational Outlook Handbook*. While many travelers now prefer to book their own trips online, the increase in travelers taking more customized trips will generate demand for travel agents who offer specialized services, such as ecotourism.

Sustainable tourism is a specialized area that is increasing in popularity as a result of concerns over global warming, energy use, and general degradation of the environment. Ecotourism embraces economic and social justice and respect for local peoples and cultures. Volunteering on a project to build a school in a remote area of the Himalayas or to work on a farm in Austria are just two examples of the new kind of vacation.

Nature of the Work

Sustainable tourism is also called green travel, ecotourism, or environmentally responsible travel. Two factors have led to the emergence of this niche area for travel. First, travelers are becoming increasingly aware of the environmental impact of travel, particularly the amount of greenhouse gases emitted by various modes of transportation and the amount of energy resources they use. Second, people are also concerned with the impact of travel on ecosystems and are beginning to understand the social and economic aspects of travel on destinations.

Ecotourism seeks to improve the economic well-being of travel destinations and to support conservation. Efforts are made to make transportation and accommodations in these areas as environmentally responsible as possible. Many destinations include education about conservation and preservation. Some destinations gaining in popularity are natural ecosystems and animal habitats.

Travel agents work with their customers to plan trips or tours. They

- make reservations for accommodations, cruises, tours, and special attractions.
- make transportation reservations and obtain the tickets.
- plan itineraries, put tour packages together, and may even lead tours.
- provide customers with advice about what to see and do in each destination.

Career Path

Some travel companies may train their receptionists or reservation clerks to become travel agents. Travel agents may advance by moving to an office with more travel business or by becoming a manager. Some may go to work in travel departments in large corporations. Ultimately, some experienced travel agents begin their own businesses.

Earning Potential

2008 mean hourly wage: $15.61; mean annual wage: $32,470

Education/Licensure

Although there is no formal educational requirement beyond a high school diploma, an associate degree or equivalent training is generally the minimum. Training is available at community colleges and vocational schools, online, and through adult education programs. Many employers prefer to hire those with bachelor's degrees. A few colleges and universities offer bachelor's and master's degrees in tourism and travel.

The Travel Institute offers Certified Travel Associate (CTA), Certified Travel Counselor (CTC), and Certified Travel Industry Executive (CTIE). All three require passing an exam.

For More Information

American Society of Travel Agents
Education Department
1101 King Street, Suite 200
Alexandria, Virginia 22314
703-739-278
www.asta.org

The Travel Institute
148 Linden Street, Suite 305
Wellesley, Massachusetts 02482
800-542-4282 (toll-free)
www.thetravelinstitute.com

Outdoor Recreation Specialist

Alternate Job Titles:

- Activities Assistant
- Activities Coordinator
- Activities Director
- Activity Specialist
- Certified Therapeutic Recreation Specialist (CTRS)
- Recreation Supervisor
- Recreation Therapist
- Therapeutic Recreation Assistant
- Therapeutic Recreation Director
- Therapeutic Recreation Leader

If you like working outdoors and with people, especially children, this occupation could be a good fit.

Job Trends

The *Occupational Outlook Handbook* predicts employment for recreation workers to increase about 13 percent by 2016, which is about average for all occupations. Career Voyages ranks this as one of the in-demand occupations. Approximately 100,000 new employees will be needed by 2016. Currently local governments, particularly park and recreation departments, employ about 32 percent

About the Benefits of Outdoor Activity for Children

"Outdoor environmental education programming may offer one solution for improving academic and social performance and could start children on the road to becoming more healthy and active adults." –Sierra Club

of recreation workers. Residential care and nursing facilities employ about 16 percent. Social or/and civic organizations, such as scouting, employ about 10 percent.

Concern for fitness and health, along with more leisure time, will generate demand for outdoor recreation specialists. This will be balanced somewhat by budget cuts at the state and local levels. However, opportunities are expected to be good overall, but there will be competition for full-time career positions.

Nature of the Work

Outdoor recreation specialists work in places where people come in contact with the environment. This is an opportunity to teach appreciation of the natural environment and how to enjoy it while at the same time preserving it.

Outdoor recreation specialists organize and conduct recreational activities in parks, playgrounds, campgrounds, community centers, and other outdoor facilities. They act as guides for hikes, cycling trips, mountain biking, rock climbing, canoeing, and kayaking and include educational experiences relating to the environment, proper use of equipment, and safety. Camp counselors conduct activities in day and residential camps where they teach and supervise campers, usually children.

Career Paths

After outdoor recreation specialists gain experience, they may become supervisors. Eventually some will become park and recreation directors.

Earning Potential

2008 mean hourly wage: $11.81; mean annual wage: $24,570

Education/Licensure

Different recreation jobs have different education and training requirements. Many positions are seasonal or part-time, and some of these may require only a high school diploma. However, for most full-time positions, an associate degree in a recreation field is the minimum requirement. Many positions require a bachelor's degree in parks and recreation. An administrative position in a large park system may require an advanced degree.

Many colleges and universities offer associate or bachelor's degree programs in parks and recreation or similar concentrations. The National Recreation and Park Association accredits bachelor's degree programs.

Certification is voluntary. The National Recreation and Park Association offers several certifications. The Certified Park and Recreation Professional (CPRP) requires a combination of education, experience, and passing an exam. The Aquatic Facility Operator (AFO) and Certified Playground Safety Inspector (CPSI) require passing an exam. Lifeguarding and CPR certifications are sometimes beneficial when looking for a job.

For More Information

American Camp Association
5000 State Road 67 North
Martinsville, Indiana 46151-7902
765-342-8456
www.acacamps.org

Association for Environmental and Outdoor
    Education (AEOE)
P.O. Box 187
Angelus Oaks, California 92305
www.aeoe.org

Association of Outdoor and Recreation Education
    (AORE) National Office
6511 Buckshore Drive
Whitmore Lake, Michigan 48189
810-299-2782
www.aore.org

National Recreation and Park Association
22377 Belmont Ridge Road
Ashburn, Virginia 20148-4501
800-626-6772 (toll-free)
www.nrpa.org

Restoration Horticulture Specialist

Alternate Job Titles:

- Ecological Restoration Manager
- Environmental Horticulture Specialist

This is just one of the many fields that have emerged in the last few years driven by the increasing interest in preserving the natural environment.

Job Trends

The *Occupational Outlook Handbook* groups horticulture specialists with farmers and ranchers, for which an 8 percent increase in employment is expected. It is noted, however, that job opportunities will be best in horticulture. There is growing interest in restoring natural ecosystems and habitats as concerns over biodiversity increase. There is also interest in developing urban forests. Both areas will provide opportunities for the restoration horticulture specialist.

Restoration horticulture specialists may work for city, county, or state agencies and also for landscaping, environmental services, and consulting firms.

Nature of the Work

Restoration horticulture, also called restoration ecology, is the art and science of restoring ecosystems and habitats using native plant species. This emerging field combines ecology, horticulture, landscape design, plant and soil science, hydrology, forestry, and wildlife management. For any particular area, it requires an understanding of native plants, climate, soil and water conditions, native wildlife, and conservation as well as a history of how the land has been used and degraded.

Restoration horticulture specialists often work in settings where people spend recreational time such as parks, nature centers, zoos, urban forests, trail systems, and wetlands. They also develop urban green spaces such as urban forests, greenbelts, green roofs, and rain gardens. In restoring these damaged land areas to their natural conditions, restoration horticulture specialists provide spaces for people to appreciate and learn about nature and the environment.

Career Paths

Horticulture specialists may supervise workers or coordinate volunteers.

Earning Potential

According to the College of Agricultural and Environmental Sciences at the University of Georgia, typical annual starting salaries for horticulture graduates (bachelor's degree) are from $28,000 to $40,000. The University of Tennessee reports that starting salaries for public horticulturists are $30,000 to $45,000, depending on the region. The average annual starting salary for graduates with a bachelor's degree in plant sciences was $31,291 in 2007, according to the National Association of Colleges and Employers. Salaries for graduates with associate degrees would be somewhat lower.

Education/Licensure

An associate degree in horticulture or a related area is required. Some jobs may require a bachelor's degree. A number of community colleges, colleges, and universities offer associate and bachelor's degrees in restoration horticulture or environmental horticultural science. Many schools offer associate and bachelor's degrees in horticulture.

For More Information

American Horticultural Society
7931 East Boulevard Drive
Alexandria Virginia 22308
800-777-7931 (toll-free)
www.ahs.org

Society for Ecological Restoration International
285 W.18th Street, Suite 1
Tucson, Arizona 85701
520-622-5485
www.ser.org

POLICY, ADMINISTRATION, ANALYSIS, AND ADVOCACY

The area of policy, administration, analysis, and advocacy is not an industry in itself but a broad and diverse collection of jobs. The purpose of these jobs is to examine all aspects of the condition of the environment—social, economic, justice, and political—and propose and implement solutions. The people employed in these jobs develop and implement policies, regulations, laws, standards, procedures, and guidelines. They study industries and technology and propose modifications that will be sustainable, create jobs, stimulate the economy, conserve resources, and protect the environment.

Many of the jobs in this area are in federal, state, and local government agencies. Others are in advocacy organizations or special-interest groups that influence government and the public. Some jobs are in private companies, consulting firms, and industry groups. Job opportunities abound in the green economy for people with diverse interests and backgrounds.

Paralegal

Alternate Job Titles:

- Judicial Assistant
- Legal Assistant

If you're interested in environmental issues but have no inclination for a science career, working as a paralegal in a law firm that litigates on behalf of environmental and related issues is one way to support the movement for a sustainable future.

Job Trends

The demand for paralegals will increase with the growing population and the issues associated with it such as health care and elder issues. Those paralegals who specialize will be in demand. Environmental law is one of the areas of specialization where paralegal services are expected to expand. The *Occupational Outlook Handbook* predicts that employment for paralegals and legal assistants will increase 22 percent by 2016, much greater than the average for all occupations. Competition for jobs is expected because so many people enter this field, but those who have formal training will have the best opportunities. Career Voyages ranks this occupation number 19 out of the top 50 fastest-growing occupations and number 12 out of the top 50 occupations with the most openings.

Law firms employ about 70 percent of paralegals. Government agencies and corporate legal departments employ most of the rest. However, paralegals work in almost any type of organization.

Nature of the Work

Paralegals are also called legal assistants. In a law firm or a corporate legal department, their duties may include the following:

- preparing the background documentation that lawyers need for a case by researching facts and legal precedents such as relevant laws, court decisions, and legal articles
- searching legal databases to find the information they need
- preparing summaries and briefs for lawyers
- organizing documentation for a case

Paralegals are allowed to prepare some types of documents such as wills, estate plans, contracts, and real estate closings.

In corporate law departments, paralegals monitor environmental laws, regulations, and statutes that may be relevant to the business of the corporation and review health and safety regulations. They must be aware of existing requirements and any new requirements to make sure that the corporation is in compliance. Paralegals who work for government agencies may prepare materials that explain the agency's policies, laws, and regulations. These materials inform the public about the requirements of laws and regulations.

Career Paths

At the beginning of their careers, paralegals handle routine tasks. After gaining some experience, they also gain responsibility. Paralegals may supervise other employees or lead project teams.

Earning Potential

2008 mean hourly wage: $23.46; mean annual wage: $48,790

Education/Licensure

There are a variety of ways to become a paralegal. The most common way is to earn an associate degree in paralegal studies from a community college. A person with a bachelor's degree can complete a paralegal certificate program. A few colleges offer a bachelor's degree in paralegal studies. Other ways include apprenticeships and employer on-the-job training. Some programs include an internship, which will also be an advantage in getting a job.

Many colleges, universities, and law schools offer formal programs to train paralegals. About 260 of these are approved by the American Bar Association (ABA). A list of and links to those programs are available on the ABA's Web site. While it is not necessary to be trained in an ABA-approved program, it may improve job opportunities. About 350 members of the American Association for Paralegal Education also provide paralegal training programs, and these are listed on the association's Web site.

Certification is voluntary, but it is an advantage for getting a job. The National Association of Legal Assistants offers the Certified Legal Assistant/ Certified Paralegal (CLA/CP) credential. It requires education, experience, and passing an exam. The Advanced Paralegal Certification (APC) is for experienced paralegals. The American Alliance of Paralegals offers the American Alliance Certified Paralegal (AACP) certification, which is based on experience and education. The National Federation of Paralegal Associations offers the Paralegal Advanced Competency Exam (PACE) Registered Paralegal certification based on experience, education, and passing the exam. NALS offers the Professional Paralegal (PP) certification based on experience and passing an exam.

For More Information

American Alliance of Paralegals, Inc.
4001 Kennett Pike, Suite 134-146
Wilmington, Delaware 19807
www.aapipara.org

American Association for Paralegal Education
19 Mantua Road
Mt. Royal, New Jersey 08061
856-423-2829
www.aafpe.org

American Bar Association
Standing Committee on Paralegals
321 North Clark Street
Chicago, Illinois 60610
312-988-5000
www.abanet.org/legalservices/paralegals

National Association of Legal Assistants, Inc.
1516 South Boston Street, Suite 200
Tulsa, Oklahoma 74119
918-587-6828
www.nala.org

National Federation of Paralegal Associations
P.O. Box 2016
Edmonds, Washington 98020
425-967-0045
www.paralegals.org

Planning Technician

Alternate Job Titles:

- Code Enforcement Technician
- Development Technician
- Engineering Technician
- GIS (Geographic Information Systems) Technician
- Planning Aide
- Planning Assistant
- Transportation Planning Assistant
- Zoning Technician

This occupation fills a need in a wide variety of fields.

Job Trends

According to the U.S. Bureau of Labor Statistics, as reported on O*NET OnLine, between 7- and 13-percent growth—about 9,000 additional openings—is expected for city and regional planning aides by 2016. This is about average. The factors that create demand for these professionals also create demand for the planning technicians who work with them. Job opportunities will arise from meeting the housing and infrastructure needs of the increasing population, particularly in rapidly expanding communities that need streets and other services.

Currently, 68 percent of planners are employed in local governments. Only 21 percent are employed in private companies such as those that provide architectural, engineering, and related services. However, employment in the private sector is expected to increase faster than government openings, especially in firms that provide technical services. Planning technicians with good computer skills, including competence with geographic information systems (GIS), should have many opportunities.

Nature of the Work

Planning technicians, also known as city and regional planning aides, assist urban and regional planners by compiling information used to create short- and long-term plans for the use of land and resources. Depending on the job, planning technicians

- compile data from field investigations, reports, maps, and other sources.
- conduct interviews, site inspections, and surveys to collect data.
- analyze the data and prepare reports that include graphs and charts of statistics on population, zoning, land use, traffic flow, and other factors.
- develop and maintain databases of information, tracking systems, and records.
- review zoning permit applications or building plans.
- investigate violations of regulations.

Some technicians specialize. For example, some will be GIS (geographic information system) technicians who provide support to planners by creating specialized maps that may show a variety of factors such as land use, population distribution, location of natural resources, or air pollution sources.

Career Paths

Planning technicians work under the supervision of planners. As they gain experience, they move to positions with greater responsibility and more independence. Some may continue their education to become planners.

Earning Potential

2008 median hourly wage: $17.14; median annual wage: $35,650

Education/Licensure

Generally, an associate degree in urban planning, construction management, architecture, or a related field plus two years of experience in building codes, zoning, or plans review are required. However, many employers prefer a bachelor's degree, and that may be substituted for experience.

A few schools offer the bachelor's degree in urban and regional planning. Graduates of these programs qualify for some entry-level jobs, but they may have limited opportunities for advancement. The Association of Collegiate Schools of Planning Web site provides a list of accredited programs starting at the bachelor's degree level.

Even though most states do not have requirements for certification, many communities do. The preferred certification is from the American Institute of Certified Planners (AICP), the professional institute of the American Planning Association. The AICP certification is based on education, experience, and passing an exam. For those who do not have at least a bachelor's degree, eight years of experience is required. Maintaining certification requires professional development on a two-year cycle.

For More Information

American Planning Association
1776 Massachusetts Avenue NW, Suite 400
Washington, D.C. 20036-1904
202-872-0611
www.planning.org

Association of Collegiate Schools of Planning
6311 Mallard Trace
Tallahassee, Florida 32312
850-385-2054
www.acsp.org

TRANSPORTATION INDUSTRY

Growing transportation needs and environmental concerns will generate job opportunities for professionals who plan, design, and build transportation systems and new energy-efficient cars, trucks, buses, trains, ships, and airplanes. New and more stringent environmental regulations place increasing demands on transportation systems. Existing vehicles and fleets must be upgraded to be more energy efficient and meet stricter emissions standards. Vehicles must be designed and built to use alternative fuels.

In addition, new openings are expected in areas of transportation that are less energy intensive such as rail and water. The Federal Highway Administration has already authorized nearly 6,000 projects in response to the American Recovery and Reinvestment Act of 2009 (ARRA). A portion of the ARRA funding is earmarked for on-the-job training/support services projects. According to the National Railway Labor Conference, the industry is hiring thousands of new employees to meet the growing needs of railway traffic.

Growing transportation needs and environmental concerns will generate job opportunities for skilled workers who work to convert vehicles for greater fuel efficiency and for those who work to build and expand public transportation systems. It will also generate jobs in the area of public transportation systems.

Bus and Truck Mechanics and Diesel Engine Specialist

Alternate Job Titles:

- Aircraft and Avionics Equipment Mechanic
- Aircraft and Avionics Equipment Service Technician
- Commercial Transport Mechanic
- Heavy Duty Mechanic
- Heavy Equipment Service Mechanic
- Heavy Equipment Service Technician
- Mobile Equipment Mechanic

There are as many specialties as there are kinds of vehicles powered by diesel engines.

Job Trends

The combined occupation of bus and truck mechanics and diesel engine specialists is ranked number 46 among the top 50 fastest-growing occupations through 2016, according to Career Voyages. It is also ranked number 11 among the occupations with the most job openings. According to the *Occupational Outlook Handbook,* employment opportunities for diesel services technicians and mechanics are expected to increase 11 percent by 2016, about average for all occupations. However, because there are about 275,000 people working in this trade, the number of projected openings is significant.

The need to retrofit existing engines to meet new environmental emissions standards and pollution regulations is a source of the growth. Job candidates who have completed formal training programs should have very good opportunities. The California Economic Development Department predicts nearly 4,000 new jobs just in California by 2016.

About UPS

Early in 2009, UPS began testing a hydraulic hybrid truck. The project, in cooperation with the Environmental Protection Agency, could cut UPS's per-lifetime cost of a truck by $50,000 and cut carbon dioxide emissions by 30 percent or more. The truck uses a diesel engine in combination with a hydraulic fluid pump.

Nature of the Work

Diesel service technicians and mechanics adjust, diagnose, repair, and overhaul buses, trucks, locomotives, automobiles, and heavy equipment that have diesel engines. Diesel technicians usually specialize in either light vehicles like automobiles or heavy vehicles like trucks and buses. Because diesel engines often outlast gasoline engines, retrofitting these engines with filters and controls to comply with environmental and pollution standards is often part of the job. Increasing use of microprocessor controls requires mechanics to use computers to diagnose and solve engine problems.

Career Paths

Experienced diesel service mechanics and technicians specialize by acquiring additional certifications. Some may become supervisors or service managers. Some become sales representatives, and others may open their own shops.

Earning Potential

2008 mean hourly wage: $19.57; mean annual wage: $40,710

Education/Licensure

Job opportunities are best for those who have completed formal training programs. Many community colleges and vocational or trade schools offer training programs in diesel engine repair. These programs may lead to a two-year associate degree or to certification. Some mechanics learn the trade on the job. After three or four years of experience, they advance to the journey level. Employers often send technicians and mechanics to classes offered by manufacturers to learn the latest technology.

Certification is not required. However, national certification is the standard and improves opportunities to get a job and to advance. The National Institute for Automotive Service Excellence (ASE) offers certification for ASE Master Technician (automotive, bus, medium/heavy truck) and ASE Master Medium/Heavy Vehicle Technician. These require a combination of education, experience, and passing a series of tests. Technicians and mechanics must recertify every five years by taking the appropriate tests.

The National Automotive Technicians Education Foundation (NATEF) evaluates training programs and certifies the programs for ASE certification training. Their Web site is a good place to find a training program. The Association of Diesel Specialists provides hands-on training seminars at the entry and continuing education levels.

For More Information

Accrediting Commission of Career Schools and
  Colleges of Technology (ACCSCT)
2101 Wilson Boulevard, Suite 302
Arlington, Virginia 22201
703-247-4212
www.accsct.org

Association of Diesel Specialists
400 Admiral Boulevard
Kansas City, Missouri 64106
816-285-0810
www.diesel.org

National Automotive Technicians Education
  Foundation (NATEF)
101 Blue Seal Drive SE, Suite 101
Leesburg, Virginia 20175
703-669-6650
www.natef.org

National Institute for Automotive Service
  Excellence (ASE)
101 Blue Seal Drive SE, Suite 101
Leesburg, Virginia 20175
703-669-6600
www.asecert.org

Dispatcher and Telecommunicator

Alternate Job Titles:

- Aircraft Flight Dispatcher
- Airline Flight Dispatcher
- Bus Dispatcher
- Public Safety Dispatcher
- Train Dispatcher
- Truck Dispatcher

Public safety dispatchers are known more familiarly as 911 operators.

Job Trends

According to the *Occupational Outlook Handbook,* employment for dispatchers (not including fire, police, and ambulance) is expected to grow by 6 percent by 2016, which is less than average for all occupations. However, as more people switch from driving cars to using public transportation and mass transit, the need for dispatchers to manage schedules for trains and buses is expected to increase. Depending on the job, one of a dispatcher's duties is to plan the most efficient routes. In 2006, 28 percent of dispatchers worked in transportation and warehousing. The rest worked for state and local governments in fire and police departments and for various service industries.

Nature of the Work

Dispatchers (also called telecommunicators) schedule and dispatch vehicles, equipment, and workers. Most use computer-assisted systems. They maintain records and logs of activities and are responsible for all communications within their assigned area.

Dispatchers can specialize in different types of vehicles or jobs.

Aircraft flight dispatchers, also known as airline flight dispatchers, work for airlines and are responsible for all flights, both passenger and cargo. Their duties include planning the most efficient flight route, monitoring the plane while it's in the air, and ensuring that the aircraft and crew meet federal qualifications and regulations.

Bus dispatchers work for local or long-distance bus companies and are responsible for scheduling, arranging repairs, and maintaining service.

Public safety dispatchers may work for police or fire departments and are also responsible for sending ambulances to respond to emergencies.

Train dispatchers are responsible for train schedules, locations of trains on tracks, and positions of switches.

Truck dispatchers work for trucking companies and plan routes, schedule pickups and deliveries of freight, and schedule drivers.

Career Path

Dispatchers who work for large companies such as an airline or urban bus company may become a shift supervisor or, in time, a manager. Those who work for small companies will find little advancement. Public safety dispatchers may work their way up to become a shift or divisional supervisor or into senior management as chief of communications.

Earning Potential

(Not including fire, police, and ambulance dispatchers)

2008 mean hourly wage: $17.58; mean annual wage: $36,560

Education/Licensure

Dispatchers and telecommunicators generally learn the skills they need on the job working under the supervision of an experienced person. A high school diploma or GED is required. Persons with more experience and computer skills will have better job opportunities. The major rail companies train employees at the Railroad Education and Development Institute in Atlanta, Georgia, and the National Academy of Railroad Sciences (NARS) in Overland Park, Kansas. Partnerships have been established with community colleges to provide training. Some training programs lead to certification.

The Federal Aviation Administration licenses and certifies aircraft flight dispatchers.

Many states require specific certifications or training. This usually involves training in the latest technology and using computers to aid in dispatching. The International Municipal Signal Association offers programs that lead to two levels of public safety dispatcher certification. The Association of Public Safety Communications Officials offers certifications that are primarily for police, fire, and ambulance dispatchers.

For More Information

Association of Public Safety Communications
  Officials, International
351 N. Williamson Boulevard
Daytona Beach, Florida 32114-1112
386-322-2500
www.apco911.org

International Municipal Signal Association
P.O. Box 539
165 E. Union Street
Newark, New York 14513-0539
315-331-2182
www.IMSAsafety.org

National Railway Labor Conference
1901 L Street, NW, Suite 500
Washington, D.C. 20036
202-862-7200
www.raillaborfacts.org

Welder

Alternate Job Titles:

- Underwater Welder
- Welder/Brazier
- Welder/Cutter
- Welding Inspector
- Welder/Solderer
- Welding Supervisor

There are 100 methods of welding, but the most common uses an electric current and is called arc welding.

Job Trends

According to the *Occupational Outlook Handbook,* employment is expected to grow by 5 percent by 2016, which is less than average for all occupations. However, employment opportunities should be excellent because there are not enough qualified applicants. Career Voyages ranks this as the ninth-highest in-demand occupation with the most openings through 2016. Over 10,000 openings are predicted. Welding, soldering, and brazing machine setters, operators, and tenders category is ranked number 48 among the top 50 occupations with the most openings.

Nature of the Work

Welding, soldering, and brazing are all methods of joining two pieces of metal using extreme heat. Welding may be done manually, or it may be automated using machines. In either case, the experience of the welder is critical to achieving a joint of sufficient strength. These processes are used in the manufacturing and construction industries. About two thirds of jobs are in manufacturing. Transportation equipment manufacturing is a major industry segment. The rest are mostly in construction.

Career Paths

Experienced welders can advance to welding engineers, supervisors, sales representative, educator, or welding inspectors.

Earning Potential

Welders, solderers, cutters, braziers:
2008 mean hourly wage: $17.01; mean annual wage: $35,370

Welding, soldering, and brazing machine setters, operators, and tenders:
2008 mean hourly wage: $16.20; mean annual wage: $33,700

Education/Licensure

Training for welders, solderers, and braziers depends on the skill level of the position. The lowest levels may require on-the-job training or a few weeks in school. Highly skilled positions may require several years of school and experience. High schools, vocational and technical schools, community colleges, the armed forces, and private welding schools offer formal training. Computer knowledge is becoming more important as more processes are done by computerized machines or robots. The American Welding Society has a welding school locator on its Web site.

Some positions require certifications. These may be a general welding certification or a specialization. The American Welding Society offers a variety of certifications, including Certified Welder, Certified Welding Supervisor, 9-Year Re-Certification, Certified Welding Inspector, and some specialized certifications, such as robotics.

For More Information

American Welding Society
550 NW LeJeune Road
Miami, Florida 33126
800-443-9353 (toll-free)
www.aws.org

International Union, United Automobile,
    Aerospace, and Agricultural Implement
    Workers of America
8000 E. Jefferson Avenue
Detroit, Michigan 48214
313-926-5007
www.uaw.org

Welding Research Council
P.O. Box 1942
New York, New York 10156
212-658-3847
http://www.forengineers.org/wrc

Ten Greenest Places to Live and Work in the United States

Every year a number of magazines and Web sites report on the top 10, 25, or 50 greenest places to live in the United States. The criteria for what makes a city "green" vary somewhat from source to source, but, in general, criteria include factors such as the following:

- air and water quality
- amount of mass transit
- green initiatives
- level of alternative energy use
- number of green-certified buildings
- recycling and waste reduction programs

No two sources assign the same ratings to criteria, but there are similarities in the listings of green cities, as you can see from the following three lists of green "big" cities:

From *Popular Science*

1. Portland, Oregon
2. San Francisco, California
3. Boston, Massachusetts
4. Oakland, California
5. Eugene, Oregon
6. Cambridge, Massachusetts
7. Berkeley, California
8. Seattle, Washington
9. Chicago, Illinois
10. Austin, Texas

From *National Geographic*'s www.thegreenguide.com:

1. Eugene, Oregon
2. Austin, Texas
3. Portland, Oregon
4. St. Paul, Minnesota
5. Santa Rosa, California
6. Oakland, California
7. Berkeley, California
8. Honolulu, Hawaii
9. Huntsville, Alabama
10. Denver, Colorado

From the National Resources Defense Council:

1. Seattle, Washington
2. San Francisco, California
3. Portland, Oregon
4. Oakland, California
5. San Jose, California
6. Austin, Texas
7. Sacramento, California
8. Boston, Massachusetts
9. Denver, Colorado
10. Chicago, Illinois

PART II

COLLEGES AND UNION ORGANIZATIONS WITH GREAT GREEN PROGRAMS

CHAPTER 3

50 FOUR-YEAR SCHOOLS WITH GREAT GREEN PROGRAMS

The fifty colleges and universities profiled in this chapter support innovative programs in environmental or sustainability studies. They also have vibrant on-campus sustainability programs and organizations. Each of the schools listed here includes inventive programs in its curricula, and all have made a commitment to making their campus communities sustainable.

FOUR-YEAR COLLEGES AND UNIVERSITIES

The undergraduate programs listed here are generally interdisciplinary and draw on the strengths of the faculty in many areas. Most of them include research opportunities or internships for undergraduates. Degree programs in other departments also include an environmental focus. Most of the universities on this list also have graduate programs that lead to advanced degrees or certificates in disciplines related to the environment, including engineering, business, policy planning, and public administration. Some of these schools offer online degrees and courses, and almost all have centers or institutes that specialize in some aspect of environmental research. The information presented here has been culled not only from college Web sites, but also from *Peterson's Survey of Sustainability Efforts in Higher Education*, sent to two-year and four-year schools in the United States and Canada and completed by representatives of the schools themselves.

In addition to strong academics, each college or university on this list has a strong commitment to sustainability. More than 50 percent have signed the American College & University Presidents' Climate Commitment, pledging to eliminate global-warming emissions through policy and curriculum. Ten are signatories to the Talloires Declaration, an internationally recognized commitment among college administrators to incorporate sustainability in curriculum and operations. These schools have sustainability policy committees and active student groups promoting the environment through advocacy, action, awareness, and activities. Some offer green residence halls and are building LEED (Leadership in Energy and Environmental Design)-certified buildings.

The colleges and universities listed in this chapter represent a broad cross-section of schools in the United States: public and private institutions, large and small schools, schools in urban and rural settings, state universities, liberal arts colleges, and schools specializing in a single discipline.

Keep in mind that this is a list of highlights: Many other colleges and universities not listed here also offer environmental studies programs. Check out *Peterson's Four-Year Colleges* to find other schools offering similar programs.

ABOUT THE LISTINGS

Here's what you need to know to navigate this chapter.

Contact Info

The first paragraph of each school profile lists the school name, address, phone number, e-mail address, and Web site info.

Fast Facts

The Fast Facts gives an insight into the school's commitment to sustainability and the environment.

Green Campus Organizations

This section gives a sampling of green extracurricular activities that students may participate in. The colleges and universities included in this guide have substantial sustainability efforts and, thus, a variety of ways students may become involved and take leadership roles.

Undergraduate Degrees

This section includes majors and minors in environmental studies or sciences and any other degree program that has an environmental focus. Inclusion of other majors depends on how the college or university describes its program and whether it has an environmentally related component. So a certain program may be included for one school but not for another, even if that school offers the degree. For example, chemistry is included for some schools, but only if the program includes an environmental chemistry option, offers courses in environmental chemistry, or has faculty research interests in this area.

Many schools offer a number of options, concentrations, or specializations within a degree program. This information has been included to show the wide variety of possible study areas.

Undergraduate Distance Learning

A number of schools offer courses online, some of which may meet requirements of the degrees listed in this guide. Some schools offer online degrees, but very few are at the undergraduate level; they are more often at the master's level. However, many offer certificates online at the undergraduate level.

Graduate Degrees

This guide focuses on undergraduate programs, but graduate programs are listed here for several reasons. First, graduate programs combined with the undergraduate degree offerings show the depth and breadth of the programs available at these colleges and universities.

Second, the graduate programs give you an idea of the possibilities for junior or senior research projects. Most of the schools included in this guide encourage or require undergraduates to participate in research projects or internships during their upper-class years. Even though as a prospective freshman, you may not be thinking about graduate school, these programs show you possibilities and give you something to consider as you choose your school and major and map your education.

Third, if you already hold a bachelor's degree, you may be interested in becoming "green" by pursuing an advanced degree, certificate, or training. The graduate programs and certificates listed in this guide show you the myriad possibilities.

Graduate Distance Learning

A number of schools offer courses online, some of which may meet requirements of the degrees listed in this guide. Some schools offer online degrees, often at the master's level. Many offer certificates online at the graduate level.

About Your Old Tech Equipment

Check your campus for a recycling drop-off location. Many local communities also run drop-off locations for recycling used computers, printers, DVD players, and similar equipment. Staples and Best Buy will take most electronics for free, but will charge $10 for computers. Also check out www.ban.org/pledge/Locations.html for other sites.

ARIZONA STATE UNIVERSITY

University Drive and Mill Avenue
Tempe, Arizona 85287
480-965-9011
E-mail: campus.asu.edu/tempe
www.asu.edu

Fast Facts

The Global Institute of Sustainability, which includes the School of Sustainability, conducts research, problem solving, and education with an emphasis on urban sustainability. The institute grew out of the Arizona State University Center for Environmental Studies that conducted research for more than thirty years. Phoenix, because it is among the fastest growing urban areas in the country, is a prime laboratory for the institute's studies. For more information, check out http://sustainability.asu.edu.

Green Campus Organizations

Recycling Club of ASU: Promotes recycling on and off campus by collecting and disposing of recyclable items and holds activities to raise awareness. E-mail: alissa.fiset@asu.edu.

Sustainability Jedi: Enhances students' educational experience through involvement in real-world sustainability projects that improve rural and underprivileged communities worldwide. E-mail: sustjedi@asu.edu.

ASU EGB: For students interested in the green building movement. Offers students opportunities to be involved with the USGBC (U.S. Green Building Council) and other organizations to create a network of green building leaders. E-mail: asu.egb@gmail.com.

EcoAid on Campus: Provides scholarship and internship opportunities, mentoring, and training to students in green industries.
E-mail: ecoaidcampus@gmail.com.

Students of Arizona Network for Sustainability: A network of student organizations and community groups to promote sustainability in Arizona. Activities include education, outreach, and action. Web site: http://azsans.com/.

Undergraduate Degrees

All degrees are offered at the Tempe campus unless otherwise noted.

Applied Biological Sciences (Urban Horticulture, Wildlife and Restoration Ecology), Polytechnic campus
Architectural Studies
Bioengineering
Biological Sciences (Biology and Society, Conservation Biology and Ecological Sustainability, Ecology and Evolution)
Business (Sustainability), Tempe and West campuses
Environmental Chemistry
Civil Engineering (Construction Engineering, Environmental Engineering)
Earth and Space Exploration
Electrical Engineering (Electric Power and Energy Systems)
Electronics Engineering Technology (Alternative Energy Technologies), Polytechnic campus
Environmental Technology Management, Polytechnic campus
Industrial Design
Mechanical Engineering (Energy and Environment)
Molecular Bioscience/Biotechnology
Sustainability
Urban Planning

Graduate Degrees

Alternative Energy Technologies (MSTech)
Applied Biological Sciences (MS)
Biochemistry (MS, PhD)
Biological Design (PhD)
Chemical Engineering (MS, MSE, PhD)
Chemistry (MS, PhD)
Chemistry/Natural Science (MNS)
Civil/Environmental Engineering (MS, MSE, PhD)
Environmental Design/Planning (PhD)
Environmental Life Sciences (PhD)
Environmental Social Science (PhD)
Environmental Technology Management (MSTech)
Geographical Sciences (Urbanism) (PhD)
Landscape Architecture (MLA)
Law: Biotechnology and Genomics (LLM)
Plant Biology (MS, PhD)
Recreation and Tourism Studies (MS)
Science and Technology Policy (MS)
Social Justice and Human Rights (MA)
Sustainability (MA, MS, PhD)
Urban and Environmental Planning (MUEP)
Urban Design (MUD)

Certificates:

Atmospheric Science
Law, Science, and Technology
Transportation Systems

Graduate Distance Learning

Environmental Technology Management (MSTech)

BATES COLLEGE

2 Andrews Road
Lewiston, Maine 04240-6028
207-786-6255
E-mail: www.lists@bates.edu
www.bates.edu

Fast Facts

Students are required to complete a thesis and 200 hours of an environmentally oriented off-campus internship.

Green Campus Organizations

Sustainability Theme Housing: Two dorms that serve as pilots for sustainable campus living and a center for environmental leadership.

Bates College EcoReps: Students work with the Environmental Coordinator to bring a social peer-to-peer dimension to sustainability.

Bates Energy Action Movement (BEAM): A movement organized to achieve carbon neutrality at Bates. Hosted the 5th Annual Maine State Climate Summit.

Committee on Environmental Responsibility: A working group composed of faculty, staff, and students who strive for sustainability and climate neutrality at Bates.

Environmental Coalition: Works to improve environmental responsibility at Bates, in the community, and around the nation through student education, campaigns to change Bates' policies, and focus on issues outside the college.

Undergraduate Degrees

Environmental Studies with a major concentration in one of the following:

Ecology
Environmental Chemistry
Environmental Economics
Environmental Geology
Environmental Health
The Environment and Human Culture
Global Environment and Social Change
Nature in the Literary and Visual Arts
Regional Perspectives on Environment and Society

BEREA COLLEGE

Berea, Kentucky 40404
859-985-3000
E-mail: www.berea.edu/contactus
www.berea.edu

Fast Facts

The 3-2 Dual Degree Engineering Program allows students to earn a BA or BS from Berea and an engineering degree from a partner university in five years. Partner universities are University of Kentucky (Lexington) and Washington University (St. Louis).

Washington University offers a minor in Environmental Engineering.

The University of Kentucky offers Bioenvironmental Engineering and Thermal Environmental Engineering, as well as an Environmental Certificate to students in Agricultural, Chemical, Civil, and Mining Engineering programs.

Green Campus Organizations

Ecovillage: Fifty apartments that provide ecologically sustainable housing for student families and a learning complex for students to explore concepts of sustainable living. Includes a Commons House, Child Development Laboratory, a demonstration house for the Sustainability and Environmental Studies department, forest, wetlands, and gardens. Also includes Jackson L. Oldham Ecological Machine, a sustainable wastewater treatment system that uses fish, snails, plants, and bacteria to purify industrial wastewater and sewage to reusable water standards.

Margaret A. Austin SENS (Sustainability and Environmental Studies) House: A residence in Ecovillage that is self-reliant for water, energy, and waste. It utilizes technologies for energy production and conservation, water treatment and conservation, waste treatment, and is built of local construction materials. Used as a demonstration and teaching facility, as well as housing for 4 students.

Berea College Campus Environmental Policy Committee (CEPC): Composed of faculty members, staff members, and students, CEPC monitors progress and recommends policies to achieve ecological sustainability at Berea.

Share Session on Sustainable and Cooperative Living: A program hosted by the Sustainable and Environmental Studies department to allow students to network with students from Oberlin and Middlebury Colleges regarding sustainable campus living.

Undergraduate Degrees

Agriculture and Natural Resources

Independent Majors:

Ecological Design or Sustainable Environmental Studies

Pre-Professional Programs:

Pre-Engineering with focus in Environmental Engineering (see Fast Facts)
Sustainability and Environmental Studies (minor)

BOSTON ARCHITECTURAL COLLEGE

320 Newbury Street
Boston, Massachusetts 02115
617-262-5000
E-mail: www.the-bac.edu/x231.xml
www.the-bac.edu

Fast Facts

Most students work during the day in the design profession and take classes at night. Students may also take courses at any of five art and design schools in the Boston area. During the last two semesters of the program, students are required to complete a degree project that synthesizes their general and professional education. Through the program, students are able to meet most, if not all, of the intern requirements for licensing by the National Council of Architectural Registration

Boards, or certification by the National Council for Interior Design Qualification.

Green Campus Organizations

Student Sustainable Design Committee

Undergraduate Degrees

Design Studies with concentration in Sustainable Design
Landscape Architecture

Undergraduate Distance Learning

Sustainable Design Courses (8-week courses taught online by green building experts)
Sustainable Design Certificate at undergraduate and graduate levels (the only accredited college in the United States to offer this program completely online)

Graduate Degree

Interior Design (MID)

Graduate Distance Learning

Architecture (MArch)

BOWDOIN COLLEGE

Brunswick, Maine 04011
207-725-3000
E-mail: www.bowdoin.edu/about/contact
www.bowdoin.edu

Fast Facts

The Coastal Studies Center on Orrs Island, Maine, offers student research opportunities and multidisciplinary and interdisciplinary courses, including the humanities, related to all aspects of the coastal environment. It collaborates with the Environmental Studies Program in the Merrymeeting Bay Kennebec Estuary Research Program to study Maine's mid-coast region.

Bowdoin Scientific Station, located on Kent Island, New Brunswick, is the college's biological field station. It includes a sanctuary for seabirds and research facility.

Green Campus Organizations

Climate Commitment Advisory Committee: Composed of the President, trustees, faculty members, staff members, and students, to carry out the agreements of the American College & University Presidents' Climate Commitment.

Green Global Initiative: A student group oriented toward careers in the interdisciplinary environmental area.

Organic Garden Club: Students participate in all aspects of organic farming to produce fruits, vegetables, herbs, and flowers for campus dining halls.

The Evergreens: Promotes awareness of environmental issues on campus, in the local community, and nationwide.

Undergraduate Degrees

Environmental Studies

Coordinate Majors:

Biology/Environmental Studies
Economics/Environmental Studies
Government/Environmental Studies
History/Environmental Studies
Philosophy/Environmental Studies
Spanish/Environmental Studies
Women's Studies/Environmental Studies
Concentration in Arctic Studies (Department of Geology, Department of Sociology and Anthropology, Arctic Studies Center, The Peary-MacMillan Arctic Museum)

BRANDEIS UNIVERSITY

415 South Street
Waltham, Massachusetts 02453
781-736-2000
E-mail: www.brandeis.edu/about/contact.html
www.brandeis.edu

Fast Facts

The Semester in Environmental Science Program offers students the opportunity to study and conduct research at the Marine Biology

Laboratories Ecosystems Center in Woods Hole, Massachusetts. Students receive a full semester credit for participating.

The School for Field Studies allows students to practice environmental problem solving in host communities worldwide.

Environmental Studies Internship Program is part of the curriculum that gives students real environmental challenges in a variety of settings beyond the campus.

The Arava Institute, located in Southern Israel, give students a chance to work on contemporary environmental issues in the Middle East.

SIT Study Abroad Programs with Environmental Themes are located around the world.

Green Campus Organizations

Eco-Reps: Student representatives in each quad act as resources for recycling, energy reduction, and suggestions for improving sustainability.

Brandeis Students for Environmental Action (SEA): An interest group involved in education, outreach, policy, and events connected to environmental issues.

Campus Sustainability Initiative: Collaboration between academic departments, office, and student groups to create a sustainable campus by linking social justice with academic theory.

Brandeis Environmental Sustainability Team (BEST): A working group composed of faculty members, staff members, and students with the mission to discuss the climate action plan for participation in the American College & University Presidents' Climate Commitment.

Undergraduate Degrees

Environmental Studies
International and Global Studies

Graduate Degrees

The Heller School for Social Policy and
    Management Degrees

*Programs in Sustainable International
    Development (http://heller.brandeis.edu/sid):*

International Health Policy and Management
    (MS)
Sustainable International Development (MA,
    MA/MBA, MA/JD)
Sustainable International Development (SID)/
    Coexistence and Conflict (COEX) Dual
    Degree

Graduate School of Arts and Sciences Degrees:

Global Studies (MA)

CALIFORNIA INSTITUTE OF TECHNOLOGY

1200 East California Boulevard
Pasadena, California 91125
626-395-6811
E-mail: www.caltech.edu/contacts
www.caltech.edu

Fast Facts

The mission of the Caltech Center for Sustainable Energy Research is to promote the use of solar energy through innovations in science and engineering. The Center conducts education outreach programs for undergraduates and for schools in the community.

Green Campus Organizations

Caltech Electric Vehicle Club: Mission to utilize personal experience to educate the community about the use of electric vehicles.

Caltech Environmental Task Force: Promotes environmental responsibility on campus and in southern California.

Caltech Vegetarian Club: Sponsors activities to promote the benefits of the vegetarian diet for health and the environment.

Engineers for a Sustainable World: Caltech chapter of the national organization to raise awareness of social responsibility for scientists and engineers;

coordinates forums, workshops, and research opportunities.

NRG 0.1 Lecture Series: Weekly lectures on topics related to the global energy challenge.

Undergraduate Degrees

Chemistry
Environmental Science and Engineering
Geobiology
Mechanical Engineering

Graduate Degrees

Chemistry (PhD)
Environmental Science and Engineering (PhD)
Geobiology (PhD)

CARLETON COLLEGE

1 N. College Street
Northfield, Minnesota 55057
507-222 4000
E-mail: apps.carleton.edu/about/contact
www.carleton.edu

Fast Facts

The Cowling Arboretum is an upland forest adjacent to the campus. It serves as an outdoor classroom for field studies, experiments, research programs, conservation, and ecological restoration. As a State Game Refuge, it is home to some rare plant and animal species and habitat to diverse communities.

Green Campus Organizations

Green House: A campus house dedicated to green living and environmental activism.

Green Network: Affiliation of individuals and organizations promoting environmental advocacy; maintains a listserv with postings of events and information regarding environmental advocacy at Carleton.

Kids for Conservation: Volunteer students teaching environmental education in elementary schools in the Northfield community.

About Your Old Athletic Shoes

Don't trash your old athletic shoes. Recycle them for reuse. Check out:

- www.oneworldrunning.com that sends wearable shoes to athletes in Africa, Latin America, and Haiti
- www.nikereuseashoe.com that recycles old shoes into playground and athletic flooring

Student Organization for the Protection of the Environment (SOPE): Students who promote sustainability and environmental stewardship on campus and in the community. Organization conducts various projects such as Green Bikes, Earth Week, and Adopt-a-River.

Environmental Advocacy Committee (EAC): Committee composed of faculty members, staff members, and students to advise the president on environmental quality on campus.

Undergraduate Degrees

All majors: Environmental and Technology Studies Concentration (ENTS)

CARNEGIE MELLON UNIVERSITY

5000 Forbes Avenue
Pittsburgh, Pennsylvania 15213
412-268–2000
E-mail: www.cmu.edu/contact/index.shtml
www.cmu.edu

Fast Facts

The Green Design Institute is an interdisciplinary effort to improve product and environmental quality and enhance economic development through partnerships with companies, foundations, and government agencies. The institute participates in education and research and offers educational opportunities to students in a variety of degree programs at Carnegie Mellon.

Green Campus Organizations

Eco-Reps: Students who promote peer environmental awareness within their housing units.
Engineers for a Sustainable World
Sustainable Earth

Undergraduate Degrees

Chemistry (Environmental Chemistry option)
Civil and Environmental Engineering
Engineering and Public Policy
Environmental Policy (open to all students as an additional major)
Global Politics
International Relations
Materials Science and Engineering
Mechanical Engineering with minor in Environmental Engineering
Environmental Engineering (minor)
Environmental Science (minor)
Environmental Studies (minor)

Graduate Degrees

Environmental Engineering (MS)
Environmental Engineering, Science and Management (MS, PhD)
Sustainable Design (Architecture) (MS)

Programs through the Green Design Institute and Academic Departments or Tepper School of Business:

Business (including Economics) (PhD)
Green MBA (MBA/MS in Environmental Engineering)
Civil and Environmental Engineering (PhD)
Civil and Environmental Engineering with concentration in Green Design (MS)
Engineering and Public Policy (PhD)
Engineering and Technology Innovation Management (MS)
Mechanical Engineering (PhD)

COLLEGE OF THE ATLANTIC
105 Eden Street
Bar Harbor, Maine 04609
207-288-5015
E-mail: inquiry@coa.edu
www.coa.edu

Fast Facts

College of the Atlantic was the first college to pledge to carbon neutrality and achieved it in 2007.

Green Campus Organizations

Allied Whale: Research and conservation focused on marine mammals and their habitats.

Beech Hill Farm: A hands-on organic farm and educational resource for the campus and the community.

Center for Applied Human Ecology: An interdisciplinary center that brings together educational resources, public issues, and partnerships to understand ecology in the real world.

Island Research Center: Conservation projects and research carried out on the school's Great Duck Island as well as other islands.

Undergraduate Degree

Human Ecology

Graduate Degree

Human Ecology (MPhil)

CORNELL UNIVERSITY
Campus Information and Visitor Relations
Day Hall Lobby
Ithaca, New York 14853
607-254-4636
E-mail: info@cornell.edu
www.cornell.edu

Fast Facts

Weill Hall, home of the Department of Biomedical Engineering and the Weill Institute for Cell and Molecular Biology, was dedicated in 2008 as Cornell's first LEED-certified green building.

Green Campus Organizations

Design, Education, Engineering and Development (DEED): Students discuss, design, plan, and act on sustainable and environmental solutions for developing communities.

Engineers for a Sustainable World: Engineering students working for global sustainability through engagement, education, and mobilization.

Environmental Law Society: Students interested in environmental legal issues.

Farm to Cornell: Students promoting sustainable agriculture by discussing the benefits of eating locally for the environment, the economy, and society.

Sustainability Hub: Carries on research; connects other organizations related to sustainability and environmental issues through events such as Earth Day and Campus Sustainability Day.

Undergraduate Degrees

Applied Economics and Management with double major in Environmental Sciences
Atmospheric Sciences
Biological and Environmental Engineering
Biological Sciences with concentration in Ecology and Evolutionary Biology
Biology and Society
Design and Environmental Analysis
Development Sociology
Entomology
Environmental Engineering
Environmental Engineering Technology
International Agriculture and Rural Development
Landscape Architecture
Materials Science and Engineering
Natural Resources
Science and Technology Studies
Science of Earth Systems
Science of Natural and Environmental Systems

Undergraduate Distance Learning

Some courses and certificate programs are offered online: www.sce.cornell.edu/dl/index.php.

Graduate Degrees

Applied Economics and Management (MS, MPS, PhD)
Atmospheric Sciences (MS, PhD)
Biological and Environmental Engineering (MS, MEng, MPS, PhD)
Design (MA)
Development Sociology (MS/PhD, PhD)
Geological Science (MEng, MS/PhD)
Human Behavior and Design (PhD)
Human Environment Relations (MS)
International Agriculture and Rural Development (MPS)
Landscape Architecture (MLA, MPS)
Materials Science and Engineering (MEng, MS, PhD)
Natural Resources (MS, MPS, PhD)
Science and Technology Studies (PhD)

HUNTER COLLEGE OF CITY UNIVERSITY OF NEW YORK

695 Park Avenue
New York, New York 10065
212-772-4000
E-mail: welcomecenter@hunter.cuny.edu
www.hunter.cuny.edu

Fast Facts

Hunter College Sustainability Council sponsors a Green Ideas contest in which student organizations compete. The organization selected with the best ideas receives $1000 to implement the ideas.

Green Campus Organizations

Campus Sustainability Organization
Hunter Urban Sustainability Collective (Graduate)

Undergraduate Degrees

Biological Sciences/Environmental and Occupational Health Sciences
Environmental Studies: Environmental Earth Science

Environmental Studies: Environmental
  Management and Policy
Urban Studies

Graduate Degrees

Biological Sciences/Environmental and
  Occupational Health Sciences (five-year BA/
  MS)
Earth and Environmental Science (PhD)
Geography (MA)
Master of Urban Planning (MUP)
Polymer and Environmental Chemistry (PhD)
Teachers of Earth Sciences (MA)
Urban Affairs (MS)
Urban Planning (MUP/JD)

DARTMOUTH COLLEGE

Hanover, New Hampshire 03755
603-646-1110
E-mail: contact@dartmouth.ede
www.dartmouth.edu

Fast Facts

One student each serves as a Sustainability
Intern and a Greek Sustainability Intern. The
Sustainability Intern is responsible for coordinating all the green campus organizations, whereas
the Greek Sustainability Intern acts as a liaison to
the sororities and fraternities.

Green Campus Organizations

Big Green Bus: Literally a big green bus that
runs on vegetable oil. Twelve students spend the
summer touring the country to raise awareness of
the impact of consumer choices.

Ecovores: Group that raises awareness of the
social, environmental, and economic implications
of various types of agriculture; that work with
local farmers to create a sustainable food supply,
and that plan to work with campus dining facilities in the future to provide responsible choices
to students.

Environmental Conservation Organization (ECO):
Student group that was influential in starting

recycling in the dorms. The group now works on
energy and climate issues and hosts Earth Week
events such as Carry Your Trash Week.

Sustainable Living Center: Campus residence for
18 students to learn about and teach sustainable
lifestyles; it is based on the principles of residential experience, academics, and outreach to the
community.

The Sustainable Move-Out/In: Sustainable Dartmouth students collect items that students plan
to discard at the end of the spring term, store the
items over the summer, and sell them to students
returning in the fall.

Undergraduate Degrees

Biology with concentration in Ecology
Engineering Sciences modified with
  Environmental Sciences
Environmental Earth Sciences
Environmental Engineering (AB/BE)
Environmental Studies
Geography/Environmental Studies

Graduate Degrees

Biomedical, Biochemical, Chemical &
  Environmental Engineering (MS, PhD)
Earth, Ecosystem, and Ecological Sciences (PhD)
Earth Science (MS, PhD)
IGERT (Integrative Graduate Education and
  Research Traineeship) in Polar Environmental
  Change (PhD)

DICKINSON COLLEGE

P. O. Box 1773
Carlisle, Pennsylvania 17013
717-243-5121
E-mail: www.dickinson.edu/contact.cfm
www.dickinson.edu

Fast Facts

Dickinson, like many other colleges and universities, is committed to carbon neutrality through
the American College & University Presidents'
Climate Commitment.

Green Campus Organizations

Dickinson College Farm: Campus farm that partners with the College Dining Services to provide produce. It also has a mission of education and outreach to the community, and it provides student internships.

Dickinson SAVES (Society Advocating Environmental Sustainability) worked to conduct a greenhouse gas inventory.

Earth Issues: Weekly seminars on environmental topics offered by the Environmental Studies Department.

Green Devil Challenge: Weekly campus challenge for sustainable living, such as replacing incandescent bulbs with compact fluorescents.

The Treehouse (Center for Sustainable Living): A LEED Gold-certified residence for 14 students who are committed to sustainable living, including many energy-saving features.

Undergraduate Degrees

Environmental Science
Environmental Studies

DREXEL UNIVERSITY

3141 Chestnut Street
Philadelphia, Pennsylvania 19104
215-895-2000
E-mail: www.drexel.edu/guide/overview.aspx
www.drexel.edu

Fast Facts

Drexel uses biodiesel fuel in its shuttle buses, has six hybrid vehicles in its fleet, and uses bikes and battery-powered vehicles for patrolling the campus.

Green Campus Organizations

Energy Club: Students interested in energy conservation technologies on campus and in the community; goals are to promote environmental and societal awareness as well as support professional development of members.

Engineers Without Borders: Drexel chapter of EWB-USA; works on sustainable development projects worldwide.

Environmental and Occupational Health Public Health Group

Sustainability Task Force: Composed of faculty, staff, and students to guide university committees in achieving the goals of the Drexel Green Initiative.

Sustainability University-Wide Committees: Students co-chair university committees for academics, buildings, communications, operations, planning/special events, and community outreach.

Undergraduate Degrees

Environmental Engineering
Environmental Science
Urban Environmental Studies

Undergraduate Distance Learning

Certificate in Toxicology and Industrial Hygiene

Graduate Degrees

Chemistry (interdisciplinary with Environmental Engineering; MS, PhD)
Environmental Engineering (MS, PhD)
Environmental Policy (MS)
Environmental Science (MS, five-year BS/MS, PhD)
Geotechnical, Geoenvironmental and Geosynthetics Engineering (MS, PhD)
Hydraulics, Hydrology and Water Resources Engineering (MS, PhD)

DUKE UNIVERSITY

Nicholas School of the Environment and Earth Sciences
Box 90328
Durham, North Carolina 27708-0328
919-613-8004
E-mail: environment@nicholas.duke.edu
www.nicholas.duke.edu

Fast Facts

Duke University offers bachelor's and master's degrees in civil and environmental engineering through the Pratt School of Engineering.

Green Campus Organizations

Environmental Alliance: Promotes sustainable practices and environmental stewardship on campus through advocacy and outreach.

EOS/ENV Majors Union: Support group for undergraduate students who are majors or minors in Environmental Science and Policy or Earth and Ocean Sciences; other interested students also welcome.

Farmhand: Nicholas School volunteers who work with local farmers who produce crops using sustainable agriculture methods.

Smart Home: A green campus residence hall for 10 students that has achieved the U.S. Green Building Council Platinum LEED rating (designed by students and their advisers).

Undergraduate Degrees

Earth and Ocean Sciences
Environmental Sciences
Environmental Sciences and Policy

Certificates:

Marine Science and Conservation Leadership Certificate
Energy and the Environment Certificate for students in Trinity College or Pratt School of Engineering

Graduate Degrees

Marine Science (MA, MS, PhD)
Master of Environmental Management
Master of Environmental Management–Coastal Environmental Management
Master of Forestry

Continuing Education Certificates:

Certificate in the National Environmental Policy Act (NEPA)

Certificate Program in Land Management for Conservation

Graduate Distance Learning

Online Environmental Leadership Master of Environmental Management

DUQUESNE UNIVERSITY

600 Forbes Ave.
Pittsburgh, Pennsylvania 15282
412-396-6000
E-mail: admissions@duq.edu
www.duq.edu

Fast Fact

In a study conducted by the Aspen Institute, Duquesne's MBA Sustainability was ranked No. 8 among the top 100 business schools worldwide for integrating environmental and social concerns into its MBA program. The program requires one year of full-time study.

Green Campus Organizations

Evergreen (Environmental Organization): Student organization protecting the environment and thereby promoting justice and peace, and sponsoring social and educational events, a spring clean-up day, and community clean-up.

Undergraduate Degrees

Environmental Chemistry
Environmental Science
Political Science

Combined Degrees:

Five-year BS Biology/MS Environmental Science and Management

Five-year BS Chemistry/MS Environmental Science and Management

Graduate Degrees

Biological Sciences (MS, PhD)

Environmental Management (MS)

Environmental Management Concentration (MBA)

Environmental Science and Management (MS, MBA/MS, JD/MS)

Environmental Science and Management (MS)/ Certificate in Health & Safety Management

Sustainability (MBA)

Certificates:

Environmental Science

Environmental Management

Graduate Distance Learning

Environmental Management (MS)

Global Leadership (MS)

GEORGETOWN UNIVERSITY

37th and O Streets, NW
Washington, D.C. 20057
202-687-0100
E-mail: contacts.georgetown.edu
www.georgetown.edu

Fast Facts

The student-produced video *Sam's Wasted Semester* is shown to all new students to demonstrate what students can do to help achieve sustainability.

Green Campus Organizations

Campus Climate Challenge: Their goal is to reduce greenhouse gases and energy consumption.

Eco-Action: University environmental group whose goals are sustainability education and improving the environment.

Energia: Student-run club promoting understanding of all aspects of energy; publishes bimonthly journal, runs discussion groups, and a campus working group.

Energy Action Coalition: Student group working to implement efficient energy technology, clean energy, and socially responsible investments.

Green Corp Initiative: Part of Students of Georgetown, Inc., whose goal is to demonstrate how the university and its organizations and individuals can move toward sustainability.

Undergraduate Degrees

Environmental Biology

Environmental Studies Minor

Political Economy

Science, Technology and International Affairs with concentration in Environmental Studies, including Energy

Science, Technology and International Affairs with concentration in Technology, Growth and Development

Graduate Degree

Master of Public Policy (MPP)

GRAND VALLEY STATE UNIVERSITY

1 Campus Drive
Allendale, Michigan 49401-9401
(616) 331-5000
www.gvsu.edu

Fast Facts

The GVSU Sustainable Community Development Initiative provides resources, skills, and tools to address sustainability at the local, regional, national, and global levels. These include multidisciplinary programs, projects, courses, internships, and activities.

Green Campus Organizations and Projects

Campus Sustainability Week: A week of activities for students, faculty members, and staff members;

About "Green" Help for Teachers

Know someone who teaches or is an education major? They might be interested in Grand Valley's distance learning programs, such as Education: Incorporating 'Renewable Energy' into Your Science and Social Studies Curriculum and Education: The Science and Social Studies of "Local Foods."

includes special days for health and wellness, sustainable careers, greening your space, and making a difference.

Recycling Advocacy Club: Promotes recycling on campus; student volunteer projects and a variety of green activities.

Soil and Water Conservation Society: Provides activities for Natural Resources Management students and others interested in the environment; includes community volunteer projects such as restoring streams and cleaning up highways.

Student Environmental Coalition: Sponsors events to promote environmental awareness.

Students for GVSU Sustainability on Facebook: Requires ID and password for access.

Undergraduate Degrees

Chemistry (Environmental Emphasis)
Geography and Planning (with focus in
  Environmental Geography/Environmental
  Studies)
Natural Resources Management

Graduate Degrees

Biology (Aquatic Sciences Emphasis) (MS)
Biology (Natural Resources Emphasis) (MS)

HARVARD UNIVERSITY

Massachusetts Hall
Cambridge, Massachusetts 02138
617-495-1000
www.harvard.edu

Fast Facts

The Harvard Green Campus Initiative Student Internship Program offers summer internships in sustainability by matching students, sponsors, and university research projects.

Green Campus Organizations

Environmental Action Committee Environmental Education Program: Undergraduate students work with middle school students in local schools to raise environmental awareness.

Green Living Program (GLP): Sponsors programs such as "Turn Me Off" (students turn off things that consume electricity while they are away on break), green parties, greening tailgates, and eco-study breaks.

Harvard College Vegetarian Society: Provides education and outreach related to the health, environmental, social, and political implications of plant-based diets.

Harvard Environmental Action Committee: Advocacy to raise student awareness of environmental responsibility, while working for sustainability on campus, in the community, and beyond.

Resource Efficiency Program Student REPs: Students encouraging their residential peers to reduce, conserve, and recycle.

Undergraduate Degrees

Earth and Planetary Sciences
Engineering Sciences: Environmental Science
  and Engineering
Environmental Science and Public Policy
Marine Biology and Biological Oceanography

About the EPA's P3 Program

The Environmental Protection Agency sponsors six grants for college students under its People, Prosperity, and the Planet Program. The goal is to develop programs that use technology to "tackle global environmental challenges." For more information, check out http://epa.gov/ncer/p3.

Undergraduate Distance Learning

Organizational Change Management for
  Sustainability
Sustainable Buildings: Design, Construction, and
  Operations

Many courses are offered online. Check the Harvard University Extension School Web site: www.extension.harvard.edu/distanceed.

Graduate Degrees

Applied Physics: Oceans, Atmospheres, and Geophysics (SM, ME, PhD)
Architecture, Landscape Architecture, and Urban Planning (PhD)
Earth and Planetary Sciences (PhD)
Environmental Science and Engineering (Atmospheric Sciences, Environmental Microbiology and Geochemistry, Energy and Technology, Engineering and Economic Development, Geomechanics, Risk Analysis and Public Health)
Graduate Consortium on Energy and Environment
Master in Public Policy and Urban Planning (MPP/UP)
Organismic and Evolutionary Biology (PhD)
Political Economy and Government (PhD)
Public Policy (PhD)

Graduate Distance Learning

Environmental Management (ALM, Graduate Certificate)

LEWIS UNIVERSITY

One University Parkway
Romeoville, Illinois 60446-2200
815-838-0500 or 800-897-9000 (toll-free)
E-mail: www.lewisu.edu/portals/contactus.htm
www.lewisu.edu

Fast Facts

Lewis University Adult Accelerated Program offers options for degree completion at both the undergraduate and graduate levels for adults who work full-time. Courses are offered evenings, weekends, during the day, and online.

Green Campus Organizations

Recycling and Environment Committee: Composed of faculty members, staff members, and students; developed the recycling initiative on campus; sponsors environmental events such as the Earth Day Celebration and a campus clean-up.

Undergraduate Degrees

Chemistry with Environmental Chemistry course
  work
Contemporary Global Studies
Environmental Science
Environmental Studies with concentration in
  Chemistry
Public Administration

Undergraduate Distance Learning

Many courses are offered online each semester. Although some environmental science courses are offered online, none of the above degree programs is offered completely online.

MASSACHUSETTS INSTITUTE OF TECHNOLOGY

77 Massachusetts Avenue
Cambridge, Massachusetts 02139-4307
617-253-1000
E-mail: web.mit.edu/comment-form.html
http://web.mit.edu

Fast Facts

Two MIT doctoral students won 2009 grants from the Environmental Protection Agency's People, Prosperity, and the Planet (P3) program for their work to replace diesel generators with solar-powered alternatives in Lesotho.

Green Campus Organizations

Impact2009: A career expo featuring businesses that are environmentally and socially responsible.

MIT Electric Vehicle Team: Students from various disciplines who design, build, and test electric vehicles.

MIT Energy Club: Student and faculty group dedicated to all issues related to energy; sponsors events such as Wind Week (seminars, networking, field trips related to wind energy).

MIT Society for Ocean Conservation: Solar Electric Vehicle Team: Students design, build, and race solar electric vehicles; participate in environmental and ecological events where they promote vehicles powered by alternative energy.

Undergraduate Degrees

Atmospheres, Oceans, and Climate
Chemical Engineering
Chemistry with environmental chemistry research opportunity
Civil and Environmental Engineering (minor)
Civil and Environmental Engineering Science
Environmental Engineering
Environmental Science
Geoscience
Materials Science and Engineering
Science, Technology, and Society
Urban Studies and Planning

Graduate Degrees

Atmospheres, Oceans and Climate (SM, ScD, PhD)
Chemistry (with environmental research) (PhD)
Engineering Systems (PhD) Environmental and Water Quality Engineering (MEng)
Environmental Chemistry (MS, PhD)

Environmental Fluid Mechanics and Coastal Engineering (MS, PhD)
Environmental Microbiology (MS, PhD)
Geology, Geochemistry, and Geobiology (SM, ScD, PhD)
Geophysics (SM, ScD, PhD)
Geotechnical Engineering and Geomechanics (MS, PhD)
Geotechnology (MEng)
History, Anthropology and Science, Technology, and Society (PhD)
Hydrology and Hydroclimatology (MS, PhD)
Materials Science and Engineering (MEng, SM, ScD, PhD)
Mechanics of Materials and Structures (MEng, MS, PhD)
Oceanography (joint program with Woods Hole Oceanographic Institution) (SM, ScD, PhD)
Transportation (MS, PhD)
Technology and Policy (SM)
Technology, Management and Policy (PhD)
Urban Studies and Planning (PhD)

MIDDLEBURY COLLEGE

Middlebury, Vermont 05753
802-443-5000
E-mail: midd@middlebury.edu
www.middlebury.edu

Fast Facts

Middlebury College has received the Sustainable Endowments Institute's Campus Sustainability Report Card, grade A–. Middlebury was ranked

No. 6 in "10 That Get It," in *Sierra Magazine* and No. 2 in the "15 Green Colleges and Universities" Grist listing. Middlebury's programs have also been highlighted in a number of articles in publications such as *Newsweek,* the *New York Times,* and the *Wall Street Journal.*

Green Campus Organizations

The Environmental Council: A standing committee composed of students, faculty members, and staff members with the goal of reducing the environmental impact of the college.

Environmental Quality (EQ): Goal to provide information and activate the Middlebury College community on matters of environmental interest.

Middlebury Mountain Club (MMC): Offers outings throughout the year and also sponsors symposia and presentations on environmental topics.

Slow the Plow: An organic garden run by students using sustainable techniques; sells produce to the dining services and donates produce to a local food shelter.

Undergraduate Degrees

Environmental Studies
Environmental Studies (international concentration)
Environmental Studies and Chemistry joint major
International Studies
Political Science

NEW YORK SCHOOL OF INTERIOR DESIGN

170 East 70th St
New York, New York 10021
212-472-1500
E-mail: www.nysid.edu/contact
www.nysid.edu

Fast Facts

2009 Earth Day Lecture on Green Design: Respect for the Future (reconsidering materials and methods for sustainable design).

Undergraduate Degrees

Associate in Applied Science in Interior Design
Bachelor of Fine Arts in Interior Design
Basic Interior Design Certificate
Courses in Environmental Science and
    Environmental Psychology

Graduate Degree

Master of Fine Arts in Interior Design

OBERLIN COLLEGE

College of Arts & Sciences
101 N. Professor St.
Oberlin, Ohio 44074
440-775-8121
http://new.oberlin.edu/

Fast Facts

The college's Andrew Joseph Lewis Center for Environmental Studies was designed to be an educational center and also a research and demonstration project for sustainable building and landscape design.

Green Campus Organizations

Ecolympics 2009: A month-long sustainability fair with activities, contests, lectures, and representatives from various environmental groups.

Green EDGE Fund: Ecological Design and General Efficiency Fund. Students initiated this fund to support the college's sustainability efforts. Students are charged a fee of $10 per semester to provide funding (waiver is available for those who do not wish to participate).

Ohio Public Interest Research Group: Oberlin chapter of the state group that focuses on problems such as global warming, carbon neutrality, and other issues in the public interest.

Sustainability and Entrepreneurship Symposium: Symposium to discuss careers, development, alternate energy, and sustainable enterprise particular to northeastern Ohio.

Undergraduate Degrees

Biochemistry
Chemistry
Environmental Studies (major and minor)
Geology

OREGON STATE UNIVERSITY
Corvallis, Oregon 97331-4501
541-737-1000
E-mail: oregonstate.edu; choose "Contact us"
http://oregonstate.edu

Fast Facts

Oregon State was ranked No. 17 in Environmental Science research and development expenditures among U.S. universities in a study conducted by the National Science Foundation.

Green Campus Organizations

Bug Zoo: Organization that educates the public about arthropods and their role in biodiversity and ecosystems; maintains a live collection.

Environmental Consortium of Sustainable Technology: Students from all majors who work on sustainable technology projects.

Hydrophiles: Group concerned with water and all its aspects.

Renewable Energy Action: People committed to renewable energy; education, outreach and action.

Solar Vehicle Team: Students, faculty, and staff designing and building solar-powered vehicles.

Student Sustainability Initiative: Student group whose goal is to make the university as environmentally responsible as possible through education, community outreach, volunteering, and investment; maintains the Student Sustainability Center, maintains a house being converted into a green building that will utilize renewable energy

and have a composting system and organic garden, and serves as a place for people interested in environmental issues to interact.

Undergraduate Degrees

Agricultural and Resource Economics
Bioengineering
Biology
Bioresource Research Interdisciplinary Science
Chemical Engineering
Chemistry
Civil Engineering (Environmental Engineering Option)
Crop Management
Earth Science
Ecological Engineering
Environmental and Molecular Toxicology (minor)
Environmental Economics, Policy and Management
Environmental Engineering
Environmental Geosciences (minor)
Environmental Safety and Health (minor)
Environmental Sciences
Fisheries and Wildlife Science
Forest Engineering
Forest Engineering–Civil Engineering
Forest Management
Geography
Geology
Horticulture (Ecological and Sustainable Horticulture Production option)
Horticulture (Environmental Landscape option)
Housing Studies
Marine Biology/Marine Science
Mechanical Engineering
Natural Resources
Oceanography (minor)
Recreation Resource Management
Soil Resource Management
Statistics (Environmental Statistics options)
Zoology

Undergraduate Distance Learning

Bachelor's Degrees:

Environmental Sciences
Environmental Sciences Applied Ecology &
    Resource Management Option
Environmental Sciences Business &
    Entrepreneurship (minor)
Environmental Sciences Environmental
    Conservation and Sustainability Option
Environmental Sciences Environmental Policy
    Option
Environmental Sciences Fisheries & Wildlife
    (minor)
Natural Resource and Environmental Law and
    Policy (minor)
Natural Resources
Political Science
Rangeland Ecology and Management
Tourism and Outdoor Leadership (International
    Ecotourism option)
Tourism and Outdoor Leadership (Outdoor and
    Experiential Education)

Certificates:

Geographic Information Science Certificate
Master Gardener Basic Training
Classes for high school students for college credit
    are also offered online.

Graduate Degrees

Agricultural and Resource Economics (MS, PhD)
Biological and Ecological Engineering (MS,
    MEng, PhD)
Chemical Engineering (MS, MEng, PhD)
Civil Engineering (MS, PhD)
Ecosystem Informatics (PhD)
Engineering (Coast and Ocean, Geotechnical,
    Water Resources Options) (MEng)
Environmental Engineering (MS, MEng, PhD)
Environmental Sciences (MS, Professional
    Science Master's, PhD)
Fisheries and Wildlife (MAg)
Fisheries Science (MS, PhD)
Forest Resources (MF, MS, PhD)
Horticulture (MAg, MS, PhD)

Natural Resources Management (MAIS)
Ocean Engineering (MS)
Public Policy (Environmental Policy concen-
    tration) (MPP)
Rangeland Ecology and Management (MAg, MS,
    PhD)
Statistics (Environmental Statistics options) (MA,
    MS, PhD)
Water Resources (MS, PhD)
Wildlife Science (MS, PhD)

Certificates:

Fisheries Management Graduate Certificate
Sustainable Natural Resources Graduate
    Certificate
Water Conflict Management Graduate Certificate

PARSONS THE NEW SCHOOL FOR DESIGN

66 5th Avenue
New York, New York 10011
212-229-8900
E-mail: www.newschool.edu/contactus/default.
    aspx
www.parsons.newschool.edu

Fast Facts

The Environmental Studies program brings
together urban ecology, natural science, social
science, and urban policy and management with
the School of Design for a unique approach.

Green Campus Organizations

Global Issues in Design and Visuality: Lecture
series dealing with sustainable design.

Student Sustainability Committee: Students
working toward a sustainable campus.

Sustainable Design Review: Mission to raise
student awareness of sustainable solutions.

Undergraduate Degrees

Architectural Design
Environmental Studies

Interior Design
Interior Design (AAS)

Undergraduate Distance Learning

The New School offers bachelor's degrees online.

Graduate Degrees

Architecture (MArch)
Interior Design (MFA)
Lighting Design (MFA)

PENN STATE UNIVERSITY PARK

201 Old Main
University Park, Pennsylvania 16802
814-865-4700
E-mail: ask.psu.edu/psu.html
www.psu.edu

Fast Facts

On April 22, 2009, Penn State became the first member of the Environmental Protection Agency's Sustainability Partnership Program (SPP) for the Mid-Atlantic region. The SPP, a pilot project of the EPA, enlists large organizations like Penn State to reduce energy and water use, waste generation, and impact on climate.

Green Campus Organizations

Eco Action: Organizes environmental activities to educate the public about conservation and environmental issues; conducts long-term projects.

Environmental Society: Raises awareness of environmental issues by hosting discussions, speakers, and events.

About Online Courses at Penn State

Penn State offers a number of environmentally related courses online. For listings, go to the Penn State World Campus Web site: www.worldcampus.psu.edu.

Penn State Solar Decathlon Team: Interdisciplinary project to design and build a solar home on campus, the MorningStar Solar Home; over 900 faculty and student participants; project stimulated curriculum related to sustainability.

Students Taking Action to Encourage Recycling (Staters): Students promoting campus recycling.

Sustainability Coalition: Coordinates relationships among students, staff members, faculty members, clubs, and the community to provide outreach, education, and support regarding sustainability issues.

Undergraduate Degrees

Associate (Two-Year) Degrees offered at various Penn State campuses:

Agricultural Business
Forest Technology
Mining Technology
Wildlife Technology

Some degrees are completed at other campuses in the Penn State system:

Agricultural and Extension Education
    (Environmental Science option)
Agricultural Science
Agricultural Systems Management
Agribusiness Management
Agroecology
Architecture
Biological Engineering
Biology (Ecology option)
Chemical Engineering (Energy and Fuels option)
Civil Engineering
Community, Environment and Development
Earth Sciences
Energy, Business and Finance
Energy Engineering
Environmental Engineering
Environmental Resource Management
Environmental Soil Science
Environmental Studies
Environmental Systems Engineering
Forest Science
Geography

Geosciences
Landscape Architecture
Mining Engineering.
Nuclear Engineering
Public Policy
Recreation, Park and Tourism Management
(Outdoor Recreation option)
Turfgrass Science
Wildlife and Fisheries Science

Certificates:

Community and Economic Development
Policy Analysis and Evaluation (Environmental
Policy)

Undergraduate Distance Learning

Turfgrass Science (BS) is offered online.

Graduate Degrees

Agricultural and Biological Engineering (MS,
PhD)
Agricultural, Environmental and Regional
Economics (MS, PhD)
Agronomy (MS, PhD)
Architectural Engineering (MS, MAE, MEng,
PhD)
Biogeochemistry (PhD)
Chemical Engineering (MS, PhD)
Chemistry (MS, PhD)
Civil Engineering (MS, MEng, PhD)
Community and Economic Development (MS,
MPS)
Earth Sciences (MEd)
Ecology (MS, PhD)
Energy and Geo-Environmental Engineering
(MS, PhD)
Energy and Mineral Engineering (MS, PhD)
Environmental Engineering (MS, MEng, PhD)
Environmental Pollution Control (MS, MEPC)
Forest Resources (MS, MAg, MFR, PhD)
Geography (MS, PhD)
Geosciences (MS, PhD)
Horticulture (MS, MAg, PhD)
Landscape Architecture (Community and Urban
Design, Watershed Steward options) (MLA)
Mineral Processing (MS, PhD)

About Portland State's Green Programs

Check Portland State's EcoWiki for all things green on campus. The site lists information about upcoming sustainability events, green jobs, fellowships, grants, scholarships, courses, and campus projects. Check out www.ecowiki.pdx.edu.

Mining Engineering (MS, MEng, PhD)
Nuclear Engineering (MS, MEng, PhD)
Petroleum and Mineral Engineering (MS, PhD)
Petroleum and Natural Gas Engineering (MS,
PhD)
Recreation, Park and Tourism Management (MS,
PhD)
Soil Science (MS, PhD)
Wildlife and Fisheries Science (MS, MAg, MFR,
PhD)

PORTLAND STATE UNIVERSITY

PO Box 751
Portland, Oregon 97207
503-725-3000 or 800-547-8887 (toll-free)
E-mail: www.pdx.edu/contact-us
www.pdx.edu

Fast Facts

In its commitment to sustainability, Portland State has six green buildings, which have either been designed or retrofitted according to green building guidelines. Three of them meet the U.S. Green Building Council's Silver or Gold LEED certification criteria. In addition, the campus has several buildings that are constructed with renewable natural materials.

Green Campus Organizations

Environmental Club: Students interested in environmental issues; connection within the university and the wider community.

Food for Thought: Organization promotes and offers food choices that support sustainability in its environmental, cultural, and economic aspects, including composting and recycling.

PSU Recycles: Team committed to recycling and reducing waste; welcomes student participation.

Sustainability Group: Volunteer and intern opportunities for students.

Undergraduate Degrees

Architecture
Biology
Environmental Engineering (major or minor)
Environmental Science
Environmental Studies
Geology
Mechanical Engineering
Environmental Geology (minor)
Environmental Sciences (minor)
Environmental Sustainability (minor)
Sustainable Urban Development (minor)

Undergraduate Distance Learning

Several undergraduate courses in geology, as well as English, history, and mathematics, are offered online for credit.

Graduate Degrees

Biology (MA, MS, MST, PhD)
Chemistry (Environmental Chemistry concentration) (MA, MS)
Civil and Environmental Engineering (MS, MEng, PhD)
Civil and Environmental Engineering Management (MEng)
Community Development (major or minor)
Environmental Management (MEM)
Environmental Science (MS, PhD)
Environmental Sciences and Resources/Biology (PhD)
Environmental Sciences and Resources/ Chemistry (PhD)
Environmental Sciences and Resources/Civil Engineering (PhD)

Environmental Sciences and Resources/Geology (PhD)
Environmental Sciences and Resources/ Geography (PhD)
Environmental Sciences and Resources/Physics (PhD)
Geography (MA, MS)
Geology-Hydrogeology (MA, MS)
Urban and Regional Planning (MURP)
Urban Studies (MUS, PhD)

Certificates:

Engineering Geology
Environmental Geology
Geographic Information Systems
Hydrogeology
Sustainability
Transportation
Transportation Studies
Urban Design

PRINCETON UNIVERSITY

Princeton, New Jersey
609-258-3000
E-mail (Admissions): uaoffice@princeton.edu
www.princeton.edu

Fast Facts

Princeton's Dining Services buys about 43 percent of its food within 200 miles of the campus. In 2008, this amounted to 40,000 pounds of local produce as well as milk, beef, cheese, pork, poultry, and eggs.

Green Campus Organizations

Greening Princeton: Students work with the university administration to promote sustainability on campus; projects in areas such as energy, construction, recycling, and dining.

Princeton Conservation Society: Goal to raise awareness regarding environmental and conservation issues.

Princeton Environmental Action: Student group concerned with the environment.

About Partnering for the Environment

Princeton University, Columbia University, and the New York Public Library collaborated on the building of a new solar system to heat, cool, and light the Research Collections and Preservation Consortium (ReCAP) building on the Forrestal Campus of Princeton University. The building houses collections from all three institutions. The Solar Renewable Energy Certificate (SREC) program, established by the state of New Jersey, provided support for the project along with Pennsylvania Power and Light, which will sell or trade extra power generated by ReCAP.

Students United for a Responsible Global Environment: Student initiative to raise awareness about greenhouse gas emissions and to campaign for policy changes to reduce emissions.

Water Watch: Student environmental group sponsoring education and activities related to water quality.

Undergraduate Degrees

Chemical Engineering
Chemistry
Ecology and Evolutionary Biology
Environmental Engineering
Geosciences

Undergraduate Certificate Programs: Students from various majors may add these specializations to their major program.

Architecture and Engineering
Environmental Biology
Environmental Studies (available to all majors)
Geological Engineering
Sustainable Energy
Urban Studies

Graduate Degrees

Atmospheric and Ocean Science (PhD)
Chemical Engineering (MS, MSE, PhD)

Chemistry (MS, PhD)
Ecology and Evolutionary Biology (PhD)
Environmental Engineering and Water Resources (MS, MSE, PhD)
Geosciences (PhD)
Mechanical and Aerospace Engineering (MSE, MEng, PhD)
Public Affairs (PhD)
Public Policy (PhD)

Certificates:

Health and Health Policy
Science, Technology and Environmental Policy

PURDUE UNIVERSITY

West Lafayette, Indiana 47907
765-494-4600
E-mail: www.purdue.edu/purdue/about/contact.html
www.purdue.edu

Fast Facts

Purdue Climate Change Research Center, a multidisciplinary research center, was chartered in 2004 to study all aspects of climate change. Course offerings include Engineering Environmental Sustainability, Environmental and Natural Resource Economics, Environmental Conservation and Biology, Terrestrial Ecosystem Ecology, Organizational Leadership and Supervision, and Environmental Data Handling, among others. Graduate fellowships and PhD program are also offered. Check out www.purdue.edu/climate.

Green Campus Organizations

Boiler Green Initiative: Multidisciplinary student organization that raises awareness of sustainability issues at Purdue and in the community with a particular focus on green building. The organization is leading the way in installing the first green roof on campus. Check out www.boilergreen.com/index.html.

Carbon Neutrality at Purdue University: Student organization whose goals are to reduce energy consumption on campus and raise awareness of carbon neutrality in the community; part of Boiler Green Initiative. Check out www.housing.purdue.edu/universityresgreen/.

GreenBuild: A student/faculty/staff organization promoting green building practices; provides students with green career opportunities through industry partners and sponsors. For more information, e-mail mrebbec@purdue.edu.

Purdue Green Week: A week of campus activities to bring awareness to sustainability issues; check out www.purdue.edu/dp/energy/events/green_week_2008.

Purdue Sustainability Council: Composed of members from various departments and offices; the council identifies issues and options, educates the campus community, and makes recommendations. Check out www.purdue.edu/sustainability/council.htm.

Undergraduate Degrees

Architectural Engineering
Biological Sciences
Building Construction and Management
Chemical Engineering
Chemistry/Atmospheric Chemistry
Chemistry/Chemical Engineering
Chemistry/Environmental Chemistry
Construction Engineering and Management
Earth and Atmospheric Science
Ecology, Evolution and Environmental Biology
Environmental and Ecological Engineering
Environmental Chemistry
Environmental Engineering
Environmental Geosciences
Environmental Health Science
Environmental Plant Studies
Environmental Science
Environmental Soil Science
Forestry
Geomatics Engineering
Hydraulics and Hydrology Engineering (Water Resources Engineering)
Landscape Architecture

Natural Resources and Environmental Science
Political Science
Pre-environmental Studies
Transportation Engineering
Wildlife Science
Wood Products Manufacturing Technology
Global Engineering (minor)

Undergraduate Distance Learning

Geomatics (MS)
Geomatics Engineering (MSE)
Technology (weekend with distance learning MS)

Graduate Degrees

Agricultural & Biological Engineering (MS, PhD)
Agronomy (MS, PhD)
Biological Sciences (PhD)
Chemical Engineering (PhD)
Chemistry (MS, PhD)
Earth and Atmospheric Science (MS, PhD)
Ecological Sciences and Engineering (MS, PhD)
Environmental Engineering (MS, PhD)
Fisheries and Aquatic Sciences (MS, PhD)
Forest Biology (MS, MSF, PhD)
Forest Management and Assessment/GIS (MS, MSF, PhD)
Horticulture (MS, MAg, PhD)
Hydraulics and Hydrology Engineering (Water Resources Engineering)
Natural Resource and Social Sciences (MS, PhD)
Political Science/Public Policy/Public Administration (MA, PhD)
Technology/Sustainable Energy Systems (MS, PhD)
Transportation Engineering
Wildlife Science (MS, PhD)
Wood Products and Wood Products Manufacturing (MS, PhD)

RUTGERS, THE STATE UNIVERSITY OF NEW JERSEY

New Brunswick, New Jersey 08901
732-445-4636
E-mail: colonelhenry.rutgers.edu
www.rutgers.edu

Fast Facts

The Rutgers Environmental Stewards Program was created to educate the public about the importance of preserving the environment in New Jersey. It is a cooperative effort between the Rutgers Cooperative Extension and Duke Farms. Students earn an Environmental Stewardship Certificate after 60 hours of classwork and 60 hours of service in a volunteer internship. Details can be found on the Environmental Stewards Web site: enviro-stewards.rutgers.edu.

Green Campus Organizations

Anime and Japanese Environmental Society: Provides a connection between the environment and Japanese animation and clubs.

Ecological Change Coalition: Considers environmental issues, especially global warming.

Green Print: Rutgers' environmental newspaper.

Outdoors Club: Promotes responsible conservation in addition to sponsoring outdoor activities.

Students for Environmental Awareness: Education and action on environmental issues.

Undergraduate Degrees

Agricultural Science (Agroecology)
Applied Environmental Science
Biological Sciences
Biological Sciences and Environmental Science (double major, planned program)
Biology
Biotechnology (Bioscience Policy and Management)
Chemical Engineering
Chemistry (Environmental Option)
Civil and Environmental Engineering
Ecology and Natural Resources
Environmental and Business Economics (Environmental and Natural Resource Economics)
Environmental Geology
Environmental Planning and Design (Environmental Geomatics Option)
Environmental Planning and Design (Environmental Planning Option)
Environmental Planning and Design (Landscape Architecture Option)
Environmental Planning and Design (Landscape Industry Option)
Environmental Policy, Institutions and Behavior (Health and Environmental Policy Option)
Environmental Policy, Institutions and Behavior (Individual Option)
Environmental Policy, Institutions and Behavior (International Environmental and Resource Policy Option)
Environmental Policy, Institutions and Behavior (U.S. Environmental and Resource Policy Option)
Environmental Policy, Institutions and Behavior (minor)
Environmental Science (major or minor)
Geography
Geoscience Engineering
Marine Sciences (major or minor)
Mechanical Engineering
Meteorology
Planning and Public Policy
Plant Science
Urban Studies (Urban and Regional Planning Option)
Zoology

Certificate:

Social Strategies for Environmental Protection

Undergraduate Distance Learning

Selected courses for the majors listed above are available online each term. See the Rutgers Online Course Schedule: soc.ess.rutgers.edu/soc.

Graduate Degrees

Atmospheric Science (MS, PhD)
Biological Sciences (MS)
Biological Sciences/Ecology and Evolutionary
    Biology Track (PhD)
Biology (MS)
City and Regional Planning (MCRP)
City and Regional Planning/Agricultural
    Economics (MCRP/MS)
City and Regional Studies (MCRS)
Civil and Environmental Engineering (MS, PhD)
Construction and Regional Planning/MBA
    (MCRP/MBA)
Ecology and Evolution (MS, PhD)
Geography (MS, PhD)
Geological Science (Environmental Geosciences
    Option) (MS)
Geological Sciences (MS, PhD)
Landscape Architecture (MLA)
Oceanography (MS, PhD)
Operational Oceanography (MS)
Planning and Public Policy (PhD)
Public Affairs (MPA)
Public Policy (BS/MPP)
Public Policy (MPP)
Public Policy/MBA (MPP/MBA)
Public Policy/City and Regional Planning (MPP/
    MCRP)
Science, Technology and Management (PhD)
Transportation
Urban Planning and Policy Development (PhD)

Certificates:

Geospatial Information Science
Human Dimensions of Environmental Change
Transportation Studies

SANTA CLARA UNIVERSITY

500 El Camino Real
Santa Clara, California 95053
408-554-4000
E-mail: www.scu.edu/utility/feedback.cfm
www.scu.edu

Fast Facts

Since 2007, Santa Clara University has hosted a Sustainability Decathlon. The competition is open to area schools and involves ten events related to social, economic, and environmental sustainability. Undergraduate students in the Sustainability Outreach course serve as mentors for the school teams.

Green Campus Organizations

Annual Move-Out Event: Each year, tons of waste are generated when students move out at the end of the spring term. This event facilitates recycling and reuse in the residence halls to reduce the waste.

Bottom Line and Beyond: Student organization committed to social justice with a business perspective.

Bronco Urban Garden (BUG): Community garden, which promotes environmental awareness.

Green Club: The student sustainability organization that sponsors education, advocacy, and events related to sustainability.

SCU Global Water Brigade: Committed to making clean water and sanitation available worldwide.

Undergraduate Degrees

Biology (Ecology and Evolution)
Chemistry
Civil Engineering
Environmental Science
Environmental Studies (companion major or
    minor)
Mechanical Engineering
Science, Technology and Society (minor)

Undergraduate Distance Learning

Some Business, Technology and Society courses, as well as others, are offered online during the summer session.

Graduate Degree

Mechanical Engineering (five-year BS/MS)

SOUTHERN METHODIST UNIVERSITY

6425 Boaz Lane
Dallas, Texas 75205
214-768-2000
E-mail: www.smu.edu/AboutSMU/ContactSMU.
   aspx
www.smu.edu

Fast Facts

Greening the Way Awards are presented by SMU's Dedman College (Arts and Sciences). The awards of $3000 each are given to students, faculty members, or staff members of Dedman College for innovative ideas to improve sustainability and reduce the environmental impact of the College.

Green Campus Organizations

Earth Week: Annual week-long series of events to raise environmental awareness, particularly recycling.

Environmental Society: Student chapter of the Air and Waste Management Association and the Water Environment Association of Texas; provides resources and tips for recycling and other types of environmental responsibility.

SPARC (Students Promoting Awareness, Responsibility and Citizenship): Recreation and Environmental Committee organizes student volunteer activities with community organizations dealing with environment and recreation such as parks, recycling initiatives, and Earth Day events.

Undergraduate Degrees

Biology
Civil Engineering (major or minor)
Environmental Chemistry
Environmental Engineering (major or minor)
Environmental Geology
Environmental Science
Public Policy/Political Economy
Public Policy/Law and Social Policy
Statistical Science

Graduate Degrees

Civil Engineering (MS)
Civil Engineering (Air Pollution Control and
   Atmospheric Sciences Track) (PhD)
Civil Engineering (Water and Wastewater
   Engineering Track) (PhD)
Environmental Engineering (MS)
Environmental Science (MS)
Environmental Science (Environmental Systems
   Management) (MS)
Environmental Science (Hazardous and Waste
   Materials Management) (MS)
Facilities Management (MS)

Certificates:

Air Quality Engineering
Environmental Management and Compliance
Facilities Management
Hazardous and Waste Materials Management
Occupational Health and Industrial Hygiene
Pollution Control and Prevention
Sustainability
Water Quality Engineering

Graduate Distance Learning

All master's degrees in engineering are offered online, including Environmental Science.

About Your Unused Cell Phone

Donate old cell phones, batteries, chargers, and PDAs to help. Check out these Web site for more information:

- Protect victims of domestic violence:
   www.donateaphone.com
- Soldiers call home: www.cellphonesforsoldiers.com
- People in developing nations buy phones:
   www.collectivegood.tradeups.com

STANFORD UNIVERSITY

450 Serra Mall
Stanford, California 94305
650-723-230
E-mail: www.stanford.edu/contact
www.stanford.edu

Fast Facts

Sustain.edu–A Guide for Sustainable Living at Stanford provides information on how students, faculty members, and staff members can have a positive impact on sustainability in three areas on campus: transportation, dining choices, and residence halls. Check out the guide at http://ssu. stanford.edu/sites/sem.stanford.edu/files/documents/sustain.edu.pdf.

Green Campus Organizations

Energy Crossroads: Coalition for clean energy.

Engineers for a Sustainable World, Stanford Chapter: Engineering students and students from other majors working to provide sustainable solutions to developing communities in the U.S. and abroad by networking within Stanford and with outside organizations.

Green Living Council: Green Living Coordinators work in residence halls to promote sustainability in campus living.

Science and Environmental Education: Stanford students teaching science in a local elementary school.

Students for a Sustainable Stanford: Undergraduate and graduate students seeking to raise campus awareness about sustainability issues, including environmental practices and green building, economics, and business.

Undergraduate Degrees

Biology (major or minor)
Chemical Engineering
Civil Engineering (Environment and Water Studies track)
Earth Systems (Tracks: Anthrosphere, Biosphere, Geosphere, Energy Science & Technology, Oceans, Land Management)
Energy Resources Engineering (major or minor)
Engineering (Architectural Design specialization)
Engineering Geology and Hydrogeology
Environmental Engineering (Atmosphere/Energy designation)
Environmental Engineering (Atmosphere/Energy individually designed major)
Geological and Environmental Sciences (major or minor)
Geophysics (major or minor)
Mechanical Engineering
Public Policy (Environment, Resources, and Population concentration)
Public Policy (Urban and Regional Policy concentration)
Science, Technology and Society

Graduate Degrees

Bioengineering (BS/MS, MS, PhD)
Biology (BS/MS, MS, PhD)
Chemical Engineering (MS, PhD)
Civil and Environmental Engineering (Atmosphere/Energy designation) (MS, PhD)
Civil and Environmental Engineering (Structural Engineering and Geomechanics) (MS Eng, PhD)
Computational and Mathematical Engineering (MS, PhD, PhD minor)
Earth, Energy and Environmental Sciences (MS, PhD)
Earth Systems (BS/MS)
Energy Resources Engineering (Other major BS/MS, MS Eng, PhD)
Environment and Resources (MS, MBA/MS, JD/MS, MOM (Master of Medicine)/MS, PhD)
Environmental Earth System Science (MS Eng, PhD)
Environmental Engineering and Science (MS Eng, PhD)
Environmental Fluid Mechanics and Hydrology (MS Eng, PhD)

Geological and Environmental Sciences (MS Eng, PhD, PhD minor)

Geophysics (MS, PhD)

Law/Business (JD/MBA)

Mechanical Engineering (MS Eng, PhD)

Petroleum Engineering (MS, PhD, PhD minor)

Public Health/Medicine (Environmental Health specialization) (MD-MPH)

Public Policy (MPP, MAPP, MBA/MPP)

Urban Studies (Urban Society and Social Change concentration)

Certificate:

Environmental and Water Studies Summer Program

Graduate Distance Learning

Master's degrees offered completely or partially online:

Chemical Engineering

Civil and Environmental Engineering

SYRACUSE UNIVERSITY

Syracuse, New York 13244

315-443-1870

E-mail: www.syr.edu/contact.html

www.syr.edu

Fast Facts

In September 2009, the Syracuse Center on Excellence in Environmental and Energy Innovations (SyracuseCoE) opened its new headquarters, a LEED Platinum-certified building, the highest LEED rating given by the U.S. Green Building Council. The building has many energy conserving and environmental features and houses research space for SyracuseCoE's three focus areas: clean and renewable energy, indoor environmental quality, and water resources.

Green Campus Organizations

Campus Sustainability Committee: Students, staff, and faculty committee; develops policies and guidelines for the university sustainability program.

Irish Today, Green Forever: Joint project between the Residence Hall Association, the university residence hall office, and the university sustainability program to increase recycling in residence halls and decrease consumption of bottled water.

SU Sustainability Showcase: Event held the day before Earth Day 2009, featuring student sustainable design projects.

University Sustainability Action Coalition: Committed to improving sustainability, energy use, and recycling on campus; sponsors campus events to educate and raise awareness.

Undergraduate Degrees

Anthropology (major or minor)

Architecture

Biology (major or minor)

Biology (Ecology and Evolution)

Biology (Environmental Science)

Chemical Engineering

Civil Engineering

Environmental Engineering

Environmental Science

Geography (major or minor)

Geography (Culture, Justice and Urban Space)

Geography (Environmental Systems and Landscape Dynamics)

Geography (Geographic Information Science: Analysis, Modeling and Applications)

Geography (Globalization, Development and Citizenship)

About the U.S. Green Building Council

The U.S. Green Building Council is a nonprofit trade organization founded in 1993 to advocate for sustainability in the design and construction of buildings. It developed a rating system for buildings and is dedicated to making "green buildings available to everyone within a generation."

Geography (Nature, Society, Sustainability)
Geology
Geology (Environmental Science) (major or
    minor)
Geology (Policy Studies)
Mechanical Engineering
Policy Studies (Environment)
Political Science (Public Policy)
Sociology (major or minor)
Earth Sciences (minor)
Science, Technology and Society (minor)

Graduate Degrees

Architecture (MArch)
Biology (MS, PhD)
Business Administration (MBA)
Chemical Engineering (MS)
Civil Engineering (MS, PhD)
Earth Sciences (MS, PhD)
Earth Sciences (Paleoclimate/Environmental
    Studies) (MS, PhD)
Environmental Engineering (MS)
Environmental Engineering (Administration)
    (MS)
Environmental Engineering Science (MS)
Executive MPA (EMPA)
Geography (MA, PhD)
Geography/Public Administration (MA)
Law/Engineering and Computer Science (JD/MS)
Law/Forest and Natural Resource Management
    (JD/MPS)
Law/Public Administration (JD/MPA)
Mechanical and Aerospace Engineering (MS,
    PhD)
Public Administration (MPA, PhD)
Public Administration (Environmental Policy and
    Administration) (MPA)
Science Education (Earth Science) (MS)
Structural Biology, Biochemistry and Biophysics
    (offered jointly with SUNY College of
    Environmental Science and Forestry and
    SUNY Upstate Medical University) (PhD)

Certificates:

Environmental Decision Making (offered through
    SUNY College of Environmental Science and
    Forestry)
Public Administration

TEXAS A&M UNIVERSITY

College Station, Texas 77843
979-845-3211
E-mail: services.tamu.edu/directory-search
www.tamu.edu

Fast Facts

Texas A&M has begun a pilot project to use solar
energy to power trash compactors. Five units,
knows as "Big Belly," have been placed around
the campus.

Green Campus Organizations

Aggies Cleaning the Environment: Promotes leadership and service regarding environmental issues.

Emerging Green Builders: Student chapter of
the U.S. Green Building Council; for students
and others getting started in the green building
industry.

Environmental Issues Committee: Committee of
the Student Government Association providing
environmental awareness and education and promoting environmental legislation.

Texas A&M Ducks Unlimited: Educates students
about how they can help preserve and restore
North American wetlands; promotes good hunting
ethics.

Texas Environmental Action Coalition: Students
and community members work to improve the
environment and increase awareness of environmental issues.

Undergraduate Degrees

Agricultural Economics (Policy and Economic
    Analysis option) (major or minor)
Agronomy and Environmental Crop and Soil
    Science

Bioenvironmental Sciences
Biological and Agricultural Engineering
Chemical Engineering
Civil Engineering (Coastal and Ocean emphasis)
Community Development
Ecological Restoration
Entomology (major or minor)
Environmental Design (Architecture)
Environmental Engineering
Environmental Geosciences
Environmental Studies
Forestry (major or minor)
Geography (major or minor)
Geology (Environmental Geology track)
Geophysics
Geotechnical Engineering
General Civil Engineering
Horticulture (major or minor)
Landscape Architecture
Marine Biology
Marine Environmental Law and Policy
Marine Fisheries
Marine Sciences
Mechanical Engineering
Meteorology
Ocean and Coastal Resources
Ocean Engineering
Rangeland Ecology and Management (major or minor)
Recreation, Park and Tourism Sciences (major or minor)
Renewable Natural Resources
Spatial Sciences
Transportation Engineering
Urban and Regional Sciences
Water Resources Engineering
Wildlife and Fisheries Sciences (major or minor)
Geoinformatics (minor)
Oceanography (minor)
Soil and Crop Sciences (minor)
Urban Planning (minor)

Certificate:

Energy Engineering

Undergraduate Distance Learning

Many courses are available online. Some meet requirements of the degrees listed above.

For complete listing of all ELearning courses, degrees, certificates, and programs, check out http://distance.tamu.edu/futureaggies/distance-degrees.

Online Certificate:

Geoscientists

Graduate Degrees

Agricultural Economics (MS, MAgr, PhD)
Agronomy (MS, PhD)
Architecture (MS, MArch, 4+2 BArch/MArch, PhD)
Atmospheric Sciences (MS, PhD)
Bioenvironmental Sciences/Public Health 4+1 Program (BESC/MPH)
Biological and Agricultural Engineering (MS, MAgr, MEng, PhD, DEng)
Biology (PhD)
Chemical Engineering (MS, MEng, PhD, DEng)
Chemistry (PhD)
Entomology (MS, PhD)
Environmental Engineering (MS, MEng, PhD)
Fisheries and Wildlife Science (MAgr)
Fisheries Science (MAgr)
Forestry (MS, PhD)
Geography (MS, PhD)
Geology (MS, PhD)
Geophysics (MS, PhD)
Geoscience (MGsc)
Geotechnical Engineering (MS, MEng, PhD)
Horticulture (MS, MAgr, PhD)
Landscape Architecture (MS)
Land Development (MSLD)
Marine Biology (MS, PhD)
Marine Resources Management (MARM)
Maritime Systems Engineering (MASE)
Mechanical Engineering (MS, MEng, PhD, DEng)
Molecular and Environmental Plant Sciences (MS, PhD)
Natural Resources Development (MAgr)

Ocean Engineering (MS, MEng, PhD)
Oceanography (MS, PhD)
Public Service Administration (Public Management track) (MPSA)
Public Service Administration (Public Policy track) (MPSA)
Rangeland Ecology and Management (MS, MAgr, PhD)
Recreation and Resources Development (MRRD)
Recreation, Park and Tourism Sciences (MS, PhD)
Science and Technology Journalism (MS)
Soil Science (MS, PhD)
Toxicology (MS, PhD)
Transportation Engineering (MS, MEng, PhD)
Urban and Regional Science (PhD)
Urban Planning (MUP)
Urban Planning and Land Development (MUP/MSLD)
Water Management (MS)
Water Management and Hydrological Science (MS, PhD)
Water Resources Engineering (MS, MEng, PhD)
Wildlife and Fisheries Sciences (MS, PhD)
Wildlife Science (MAgr)

Certificates:

Community Development
Environmental Hazard Management
Geographic Information Systems (GIS)
International Agriculture and Resource Development (IARM)
Ocean Observing Systems
Remote Sensing (RS)
Sustainable Urbanism
Transportation Planning

Graduate Distance Learning

Online Degrees:

Agriculture (MAgr)
Fisheries Science (MFS)
Natural Resource Development (MNRD)
Petroleum Engineering (MEng)
Wildlife Science (MWS)

Online Professional Development Programs:

Ecology and Society
Urban Wildlife Management

TUFTS UNIVERSITY

Medford, Massachusetts 02155
617-628-5000
E-mail: www.tufts.edu/home/contact
www.tufts.edu

Fast Facts

One of Tufts' Points of Pride is that it has taken the lead among universities in climate change. It was the first to become part of the Chicago Climate Exchange and also the first to adopt the climate change goals set forth in the Kyoto Protocol. Through its Climate Change, Climate Justice Initiative, it seeks to link the social justice and environmental movements.

Green Campus Organizations

Climate Fest: October event that features speakers, exhibits, and food to raise awareness about climate change.

Climate Solutions Coalition: Undergraduate students reaching out to the campus and community with education about climate change.

Eco-Reps: Students helping peers to develop environmentally friendly practices.

Environmental Consciousness Outreach (ECO): Raises environmental awareness by sponsoring programs related to recycling, reducing electricity use, alternative energy, green buildings, and similar issues.

Get Clean! Power Your Room Green!: Program sponsored by the Office of Sustainability for students, faculty members, staff members, and community members to pool contributions to purchase wind energy.

Undergraduate Degrees

Architectural Studies (major or minor)
Biology

Engineering (Environmental Health program)

Environmental Engineering

Environmental Studies (Environmental Science track) (second major only)

Environmental Studies (Environment and Society track) (second major only)

Environmental Studies (Environment and Technology track) (second major only)

Geology (major or minor)

Geosciences (major or minor)

Peace and Justice Studies (major or certificate)

Postbaccalaureate Degrees:

Civil and Environmental Engineering

Graduate Degrees

Agriculture, Food and Environment (MS, PhD)

Biology (Conservation and the Environment concentration) (MS, PhD)

Biology (Ecology, Behavior and Evolution concentration) (MS, PhD)

Chemical and Biological Engineering (MS, PhD)

Chemistry (MS, PhD)

Environmental and Water Resources Engineering (MS, MEng, PhD)

Environmental Health (MS, PhD)

Geotechnical and Geoenvironmental Engineering (MS, MEng, PhD)

Public Policy (MPP)

Urban and Environmental Policy and Planning (MA)

Urban and Environmental Policy and Planning/ Biology (Joint Master's)

Urban and Environmental Policy and Planning/ Environmental and Water Resources Engineering (Joint Master's)

Urban and Environmental Policy and Planning/ Environmental Engineering (Joint Master's)

Urban and Environmental Policy and Planning/ Environmental Health (Joint Master's)

Urban and Environmental Policy and Planning/ Law and Diplomacy (MA/MALD Dual Degree)

Urban and Environmental Policy and Planning/ Nutrition (MA/MS Dual Degree)

Urban and Environmental Policy and Planning/ Water Resources Engineering (Joint Master's)

Certificates:

Civil and Environmental Engineering

Community Environmental Studies

Energy and Sustainability

Environmental Management

Environmental Restoration

Environmental Systems Engineering

Environmental and Water Resources Engineering

Geotechnical and Geoenvironmental Engineering

Humanitarian Engineering

Water: Systems, Science and Society (WSSS)

UNIVERSITY OF ALASKA, FAIRBANKS

PO Box 757500

Fairbanks, Alaska 99775

907-474-7211

E-mail: www.uaf.edu/uaf/contact

www.uaf.edu

Fast Facts

The University of Alaska, Fairbanks, has been participating in the International Polar Year (IPY), 2007–09, along with more than 300 institutions around the world. Researchers at the university have taken leading roles in the many research and educational projects in polar science.

Green Campus Organizations

Alternative Spring Break 2009—Fairbanks: Volunteers for a variety of community organizations and agencies that address issues in Alaska such as sustainable living and conservation.

SpringFest Service: Volunteers for community projects, including conservation and community clean-up.

Sustainable Campus Task Force (SCTF): Students working for a sustainable campus and community while also considering global implications.

Undergraduate Degrees

Associate (Two-Year) Degrees:

Environmental Technology (Associate AS)
Renewable Resources (Associate AS)

Bachelor's (Four-Year) Degrees:

Biological Sciences
Chemistry (Environmental Chemistry)
Civil Engineering
Earth Science
Environmental Politics (minor)
Forestry
Geography (Environmental Studies)
Geological Engineering
Geology (major or minor)
Mechanical Engineering
Mining Engineering
Plant, Animal and Soil Sciences
Resources
Rural Development (Resources and
   Environmental Management)
Wildlife Biology

Certificates:

Fisheries Technology (Fish Culture)
Fisheries Technology (Fisheries Management)
High Latitude Range Management
Mining Applications and Technologies (Mineral
   Processing Operations)
Residential Building Science
Safety, Health and Environmental Awareness

About Used Sports Equipment

Check www.sportsgift.org for information on how to recycle used athletic equipment such as baseballs, basketballs, soccer balls, volleyballs, cleats, and shin guards. Sports Gifts donates the equipment to some 40,000 children worldwide. Play on a team? Team uniforms and coaching equipment are also welcomed.

Undergraduate Distance Learning

Environmental Technology (two-year Associate
   AS; certificate available)
Rural Development (Resources and
   Environmental Management) (BA)

Graduate Degrees

Arctic Engineering (MS)
Atmospheric Sciences (MS, PhD)
Biological Sciences (PhD)
Biology (MS)
Civil Engineering (MS, MCE, PhD)
Engineering (Arctic, Civil, Environmental, or
   Geological) (PhD)
Environmental Chemistry (Aquatic Chemistry/
   Aqueous Geochemistry) (MS, PhD)
Environmental Chemistry (Atmospheric
   Chemistry) (MS, PhD)
Environmental Engineering (Contaminants in the
   Natural Environment) (MS)
Environmental Engineering (Environmental
   Science and Management) (MS)
Environmental Chemistry (Environmental
   Toxicology and Contaminants) (MS, PhD)
Environmental Engineering (Water Supply,
   Wastewater and Waste Treatment) (MS)
Environmental Quality Science (PhD)
Environmental Quality Science (Contaminants in
   the Natural Environment) (MS)
Environmental Quality Science (Environmental
   Science and Management) (MS)
Environmental Quality Science (Water Supply,
   Wastewater and Waste Treatment) (MS)
Fisheries (MS, PhD)
Geological Engineering (MS)
Geology (MS, PhD)
Geophysics (Remote Sensing Geophysics) (MS,
   PhD)
Global Studies (Science Policy and the
   Environment) (minor)
Interdisciplinary (PhD)
Marine Biology (MS, PhD)
Mechanical Engineering (MS)
Mineral Preparation Engineering (MS)
Mining Engineering (MS)

Natural Resources and Sustainability (PhD)
Natural Resources Management (MS, MNRMG)
Northern Studies—Global Environmental Policy
  (MA)
Oceanography (MS, PhD)
Regional Resilience and Adaptation (MS, PhD)
Resource and Applied Economics (MS)
Rural Development (MA)
Wildlife Biology (MS)

Graduate Distance Learning

Arctic Engineering (MA)
Public Administration (MPA)
Rural Development (MA)

UNIVERSITY OF GEORGIA

Athens, Georgia 30602
706-542-3000
E-mail: www.uga.edu/inside/contact.html
www.uga.edu

Fast Facts

The College of Environment & Design offers an interdisciplinary program of research, education, and outreach with a design vision for communities, cities, and global landscapes. Its activities focus on environmental and urban design, natural resources, land use, design for recreation, and historical landscapes.

In 2009, the Bachelor of Landscape Architecture program was ranked number 1 and the Master of Landscape Architecture program was ranked number 2 on the list of America's Best Architecture and Design Schools published by *DesignIntelligence,* the publication of the Design Futures Council, an interdisciplinary network of design, product, and construction practitioners.

Green Campus Organizations

Clean Out Your Files Day: Recycling day for the entire campus held as part of RecycleMania.

Go Green Alliance: Educates the university community and the Athens community on sustainability and environmental issues; promotes

conservation of energy and other resources as well as recycling and interacts with the administration, faculty members, and staff members.

Green Giraffe: Encourages students and faculty to adopt environmentally sound practices.

Students for Environmental Awareness: Activist group promoting environmental responsibility on campus, in the community, and worldwide through programs and involvement in politics.

Sustainapalooza: A fair sponsored by the Physical Plant and the Go Green Alliance as part of the Go Green Initiative.

Undergraduates Degrees

Agribusiness (also offered at Griffin campus)
Agriculture and Applied Economics
Agricultural Communication
Agricultural Engineering
Agriscience and Environmental Systems
Biochemical Engineering
Biological Engineering
Biological Science (also offered at Griffin)
Biology
Ecology
Environmental Chemistry
Environmental Economics and Management
Environmental Engineering
Environmental Health
Environmental Resource Science (also offered at
  Griffin)
Fisheries and Aquaculture
Forestry
Geography
Geology
Horticulture
Landscape Architecture
Natural Resource Recreation and Tourism
Plant Biology
Statistics
Turfgrass Management
Water and Soil Resources
Wildlife
Public Administration (minor)
Public Policy (minor)

Certificates:

Atmospheric Sciences
Community Forestry
Environmental Ethics
Geographic Information Science
Water Resources

Undergraduate Distance Learning

Courses are offered in the following areas, some of which lead to degrees:

Agricultural and Applied Economics
Biological Sciences
Chemistry
Crop and Soil Sciences
Engineering
Entomology
Environmental Chemistry
Forest Resources
Geography
Geology
Horticulture
Political Science
Public Administration
Natural Resources, Recreation, and Tourism

Online Degrees:

Biology (Associate of Science)
Forestry (Associate of Science)
Political Science (Associate)

Offered through University System of Georgia: Georgia ONmyLINE at www.georgiaonmyline.org.

Graduate Degrees

Agricultural Engineering (MS)
Agriculture and Applied Economics (MS, PhD)
Biochemical Engineering (MS)
Biological and Agricultural Engineering (PhD)
Biological Engineering (MS)
Conservation Ecology and Sustainable Development (MS)
Crop and Soil Sciences (MS, MCSS, PhD)
Ecology (MS, PhD)
Entomology (MS, PhD)
Environmental Economics (MS)

Environmental Engineering (MS
Environmental Health (MS)
Environmental Planning and Design (MEPD)
Forest Resources (MFR, MS, PhD)
Geography (MA, MS, PhD)
Geology (MS, PhD)
Historic Preservation (includes natural resources) (MHP)
Horticulture (MS, PhD)
Landscape Architecture (MLA)
Marine Sciences (MS, PhD)
Plant Biology (MS, PhD)
Plant Protection and Pest Management (MPPM)
Political Science (MA, PhD)
Public Administration and Policy (MPA, PhD)
Toxicology (MS, PhD)

Professional Certificates:

Green Supply-Chain Professional
Sustainability Professional

Graduate Distance Learning

Environmental Engineering (MS)
Public Administration (MS, PhD)

UNIVERSITY OF ILLINOIS AT CHICAGO

601 S. Morgan St.
Chicago, Illinois 60607-7128
312-996-7000
E-mail: www.uic.edu/index.html/contactus.shtml
www.uic.edu

Fast Facts

Earth Month 2009 was a month-long celebration of sustainability throughout April sponsored by the university's Office of Sustainability.

Green Campus Organizations

Agape House: Christian campus ministry devoted to environmental stewardship and justice.

College of Cycling: Students working with faculty and administration to create an urban community of cyclists; provides support to cycling commuters, education, and problem solving.

EcoCampus: Students committed to environmental issues on campus, in the community, in the nation, and globally.

Real Estate Group: Students, alumni, and others interested in real estate; issues related to Green Building and other trends.

Undergraduate Degrees

Architecture
Bioengineering (major or minor)
Biological Sciences (major or minor)
Chemical Engineering (major or minor)
Chemistry (major or minor)
Civil Engineering (major or minor)
Earth and Environmental Sciences (Earth
    Sciences concentration)
Earth and Environmental Sciences
    (Environmental Earth Sciences concentration)
Mechanical Engineering (major or minor)
Urban and Public Affairs
Earth and Environmental Science (minor)
Environmental Engineering (minor)

Undergraduate Certificate

Geospatial Analysis and Visualization

Undergraduate Distance Learning

Offered through the University of Illinois Global Campus

Online Degree:

Environmental Sustainability (BS-completion
    program)

Online Certificate:

Environmental Health Informatics

Graduate Degrees

Architecture (MS, MArch)
Bioengineering (MS, PhD)
Biological Sciences (MS, PhD)
Chemical Engineering (MS, PhD)
Chemistry (MS, PhD)
Civil Engineering (MS, PhD)

Earth and Environmental Science (MS, PhD)
Energy Engineering (MEE)
Environmental and Urban Geography (MA)
Mechanical Engineering (MS, PhD)
Public Administration (MPA, PhD)
Public Health (MS, MPH, PhD, DrPH)
Urban Planning and Policy (MUPP, PhD)

Graduate Distance Learning

Offered through the University of Illinois Global Campus

Online Degrees:

Environmental Studies (Sustainable Development
    and Policy) (MA)
Natural Resources and Environmental Sciences
    (MS)
Public Health (Environmental Health concentration) (MPH)
Recreation, Sport and Tourism (MS)

Online Certificate:

Environmental and Water Resources Engineering
    (graduate)

UNIVERSITY OF MARYLAND, COLLEGE PARK

College Park, Maryland 20742
301-405-1000
E-mail: www.umd.edu/contactus
www.umd.edu

Fast Facts

The Chesapeake Project: Integrating Sustainability Across the Curriculum encourages University of Maryland faculty to incorporate sustainability into all disciplines. During a two-day faculty workshop, participants learn about major environmental and sustainability concepts and how to modify courses to include these concepts. Participants who revise at least one course for the following semester are awarded a stipend.

Green Campus Organizations

Clean Energy for UMD: Promotes energy efficiency and clean energy on campus and in the community.

College Park Environmental Group: Environmental action service organization.

Emerging Green Builders: Promotes sustainability awareness and green building practices on campus and in the community.

"Earth to College Park" Earth Month: During April, student groups and departments host activities to promote green practices. Events include a green career exhibition, speakers, service opportunities, concerts, and performances.

Society for Green Business: Promotes sustainable business practices and environmental awareness; advocates for green initiatives on campus; and performs community service.

Undergraduate Degrees

Agribusiness Economics (minor)
Agricultural and Resource Economics (Environmental and Resource Policy)
Agricultural and Resource Economics (Political Process)
Agricultural Education
Agricultural Science and Technology
Animal and Avian Sciences (Animal Biotechnology)
Applied Agriculture (Landscape Management)
Applied Agriculture (Golf Course Management)
Applied Agriculture (Sports Turf Management)
Applied Agriculture (Turfgrass Management)
Architecture
Atmospheric Chemistry
Atmospheric Sciences
Biochemistry
Biological Resources Engineering
Biological Sciences (Ecology and Evolution)
Biological Sciences (General Biology)
Biological Sciences (Microbiology)
Chemical and Biomolecular Engineering
Chemistry

Civil and Environmental Engineering (Environmental and Water Resources)
Community Health
Earth History (minor)
Earth Material Properties (minor)
Environmental Economics and Policy (minor)
Environmental Science and Policy (Biodiversity and Conservation Biology)
Environmental Science and Policy (Earth Surface Processes)
Environmental Science and Policy (Environment and Agriculture)
Environmental Science and Policy (Environmental Economics)
Environmental Science and Policy (Environmental Restoration and Management)
Environmental Science and Policy (Global Environmental Change)
Environmental Science and Policy (Land Use)
Environmental Science and Policy (Mapping and Data Management)
Environmental Science and Policy (Marine and Coastal Management)
Environmental Science and Policy (Politics and Policy)
Environmental Science and Policy (Society and Environmental Issues)
Environmental Science and Policy (Soil, Water and Land Resources)
Environmental Science and Policy (Wildlife Ecology and Management)
Environmental Science and Technology (Ecological Technology Design)
Environmental Science and Technology (Environmental Health)
Environmental Science and Technology (Natural Resources Management)
Environmental Science and Technology (Soil and Watershed Science)
Geographic Information Science (minor)
Geography
Geography (Geographic Information Science and Computer Cartography)
Geology
Hydrology (minor)

Landscape Architecture
Landscape Management (minor)
Mechanical Engineering
Natural Resource Sciences
Natural Resources Management
Physical Sciences (Meteorology)
Physical Sciences (Science Journalism)
Plant Sciences (Horticulture and Crop
    Production)
Plant Sciences (Landscape Management)
Plant Sciences (Plant Science)
Plant Sciences (Turf and Golf Course
    Management)
Plant Sciences (Urban Forestry)
Resource and Agricultural Policy in Economic
    Development (minor)
Soil Science (minor)
Surficial Geology

Certificates:

Applied Agriculture (Golf Course Management)
    (two-year certificate)
Applied Agriculture (Landscape Management)
    (two-year certificate)
Applied Agriculture (Sports Turf Management)
    (two-year certificate)
Applied Agriculture (Turfgrass Management)
    (two-year certificate)
International Agriculture and Natural Resources
Science, Technology and Society

Graduate Degrees

Agriculture and Resource Economics (MS, PhD)
Animal Sciences (Biometrics) (MS, PhD)
Architecture (MS, MArch)
Architecture/Community Planning (MArch/MCP)
Architecture/Historic Preservation (MArch/MHP)
Atmospheric and Oceanic Science (MS, PhD)
Behavior, Ecology, Evolution and Systematics
    (PhD)
Biochemistry (MS, PhD)
Biological Resources Engineering (MS, PhD)
Biology (MS, PhD)
Chemical and Biomolecular Engineering (MS,
    PhD)
Chemical Engineering (MEng)

Chemical Physics (MS, PhD)
Chemistry (MS, PhD)
Civil Engineering (MEng)
Community Planning (MCP)
Energetic Concepts (MEng)
Engineering and Public Policy (MEPP)
Environmental Engineering (MS, MEng, PhD)
Environmental Science and Policy/Public Policy
    (five-year BA/MPP)
Environmental Science and Technology
    (Ecological Technology Design) (MS, PhD)
Environmental Science and Technology (Soil and
    Watershed Sciences) (MS, PhD)
Environmental Science and Technology (Wetland
    Science) (MS, PhD)
Geographic Information Sciences (MPS)
Geography (MA)
Geography (Environmental and Biological
    Aspects of Earth Systems Science) (PhD)
Geography (Human Dimensions of Global
    Change) (PhD)
Geography (Geographic Information Sciences)
    (PhD)
Geology (MS, PhD)
Geospatial Information Systems (MPGS)
Government and Politics (PhD)
Historic Preservation (MHP)
Landscape Architecture (MLA)
Marine-Estuarine Environmental Sciences
    (Ecology) (MS, PhD)
Marine-Estuarine Environmental Sciences
    (Environmental Chemistry) (MS, PhD)
Marine-Estuarine Environmental Sciences
    (Environmental Molecular Biology/
    Biotechnology) (MS, PhD)
Marine-Estuarine Environmental Sciences
    (Environmental Science) (MS, PhD)
Marine-Estuarine Environmental Sciences
    (Fisheries) (MS, PhD)
Marine-Estuarine Environmental Sciences
    (Oceanography) (MS, PhD)
Mechanical Engineering (MS, MEng, PhD)
Natural Resource Science (Plant Science) (MS,
    PhD)

Natural Resource Science (Soil Science) (MS, PhD)
Plant Science (MS, PhD)
Policy Studies (PhD)
Public and Community Health (PhD)
Public Health (Environmental Health Sciences) (MPH)
Public Health (Epidemiology) (MPH, PhD)
Public Policy (MPP)
Public Policy/Business Administration (MPP/MBA)
Public Policy/Conservation Biology (MPP/MS)
Sustainable Development and Conservation Biology (MS)
Sustainable Development and Conservation Biology/(MS)/Peace Corp Master's International
Sustainable Development and Conservation Biology/Public Policy (MS/MPP)
Urban and Regional Planning and Design (PhD)
Water Resources Engineering (MS, PhD)

Certificates:

Ecological Economics
Environmental Engineering
Mechanical Engineering
Historic Preservation
Population Studies
Urban Design

Graduate Distance Learning

Master of Chemical and Life Sciences (Biology) (for high school science teachers)
Master of Chemical and Life Sciences (Chemistry) (for high school science teachers)

UNIVERSITY OF MASSACHUSETTS AMHERST

Amherst, Massachusetts 01003
413-545-0111
E-mail: www.umass.edu/umhome/contact.php
www.umass.edu

Fast Facts

UMass Dining Services participates in Seafood Watch, a program that educates the public about the importance of purchasing seafood from sustainable sources.

Green Campus Organizations

Eco-Reps: Students who coordinate environmental awareness and promote environmentally responsible lifestyles in residence halls.

Students for Environmental Awareness and Action: Students working to educate one another and the campus about the environment.

Undergraduate Degrees

Arboriculture and Community Forest Management (two-year AS)
Biology
Building Materials and Wood Technology (major or minor)
Chemical Engineering
Civil Engineering
Earth Systems
Environmental Design (Built Environment concentration)
Environmental Design (Horticultural Studies concentration)
Environmental Design (Landscape Studies concentration)
Environmental Design (minor)
Environmental Design (Urban concentration)
Environmental Sciences (Environmental Biology concentration)
Environmental Sciences (Environmental Policy concentration)
Environmental Sciences (Environmental Toxicology and Chemistry concentration)
Environmental Sciences (minor)
Forestry (minor)
Geology
Geography
Landscape Architecture (Built Environment concentration)
Landscape Architecture (Horticultural Studies concentration)

Landscape Architecture (Landscape Studies
  concentration)
Landscape Architecture (minor)
Landscape Architecture (Urban Studies
  concentration)
Mechanical Engineering
Microbiology (major or minor)
Natural Resource Studies
Natural Resources Conservation (Forest Ecology
  and Conservation concentration, Forestry
  Conservation track)
Natural Resources Conservation (Forest Ecology
  and Conservation concentration, Urban
  Forestry/Arboriculture track)
Plant and Soil Sciences (minor)
Plant Pathology (minor)
Plant Soil and Insect Sciences (General Studies)
Plant Soil and Insect Sciences (Ornamental
  Horticulture concentration)
Plant Soil and Insect Sciences (Soil Science
  concentration)
Plant Soil and Insect Sciences (Sustainable
  Agriculture-Crop Production concentration)
Plant Soil and Insect Sciences (Sustainable
  Agriculture-Food Systems concentration)
Plant Soil and Insect Sciences (Turf Management
  concentration)
Resource Economics (Natural Resource
  Economics option)
Turfgrass Management (two-year AS)
Wildlife and Fisheries Conservation (Fisheries
  option)
Wildlife and Fisheries Conservation (Wildlife
  option)
Wildlife and Fisheries (minor)

Certificates and Professional Development:

Conservation Law Enforcement Officer Training
International Winter School for Turf Managers
Marine and Coastal Sciences
New England Regional Soil Science
Population Studies
Public Policy

Undergraduate Distance Learning

Undergraduate online classes in geoscience; plant
and soil science; and plant, soil, and insect science.
See UMassOnline at www.umassonline.net.

Online Degree:

Sustainable Entrepreneurship (BA)

Online Certificates:

Environmental Policy Postbaccalaureate
  Certificate
Sustainability Studies
Urban Landscape and Garden Development
University Without Walls Programs:
Environmental Education (some courses may be
  offered online, most are on campus)

Graduate Degrees

Environmental and Water Resources Engineering
  (MS, PhD)
Forest Resources (MS, PhD)
Geography (MS)
Geosciences (MS, PhD)
Geotechnical Engineering (MS, PhD)
Landscape Architecture (Design and Management
  of Cultural Landscapes concentration) (MLA)
Landscape Architecture (Ecological Landscape
  Planning and Design concentration) (MLA)
Landscape Architecture (Information Technology
  in Planning and Design concentration) (MLA)
Landscape Architecture (Urban Planning, Policy
  and Design concentration) (MLA)
Landscape Architecture/Regional Planning dual
  degree (MLA/MRP)
Mechanical Engineering (MS, PhD)
Microbiology (fifth-year MS, MS, PhD)
Natural Resource and Environmental Economics
  (MS, PhD)
Organismic and Evolutionary Biology (Ecology)
  (MS, PhD)
Planning and Law (dual degree) (MRP/JD)
Plant and Soil Sciences (MS, PhD)
Plant Biology (Environmental, Ecological and
  Integrative) (MS, five-year MS, PhD)
Public Policy and Administration (MPPA, MPPA/
  MBA)

Regional Planning (MRP, PhD)

Wildlife and Fisheries Conservation (MS, PhD)

Wildlife and Fisheries Conservation (Conservation Biology and Planning) (Professional MS)

Wildlife and Fisheries Conservation (Spatial Data Analysis) (Professional MS)

Wildlife and Fisheries Conservation (Watershed Science and Management) (Professional MS)

Wildlife and Fisheries Conservation (Wetlands Conservation) (Professional MS)

Graduate Distance Learning

Graduate online classes in plant and soil science. See UMassOnline at www.umassonline.net.

Online Degree:

Plant and Soil Sciences (MS)

UNIVERSITY OF MICHIGAN

Ann Arbor, Michigan 48109
734-764-1817
E-mail: www.umich.edu/contact_us.php
www.umich.edu

Fast Facts

The Graham Scholars Program, offered through the Graham Environmental Sustainability Institute at the University of Michigan, gives students hands-on education in all aspects of environmental sustainability. It includes political, economic, engineering, scientific, and social course work to provide an interdisciplinary approach. The program includes an undergraduate component as well as graduate fellowships.

Green Campus Organizations

BLUElab: Student group that focuses on engineering solutions to sustainability issue

Environment Action (EnAct): Student group that organizes the annual Earth Week events, lobbies for environmental responsibility, and provides educational outreach to the campus and community.

Environmental Issues Commission: Commission of the Michigan Student Assembly.

Michigan Students Advocating Recycling: Student group that promotes recycling by utilizing resources on and off campus.

Undergraduate Degrees

Architecture

Biology (Ecology and Evolutionary Biology concentration or minor)

Chemical Engineering

Civil Engineering

Climate Physics

Environment (minor or concentration)

Geological Sciences

Geological Sciences (Earth Sciences concentration)

Geological Sciences (Earth Systems Science concentration)

Geological Sciences (Environmental Geoscience concentration)

Geological Sciences (Oceanography)

Mechanical Engineering (Energy concentration)

Meteorology

Nuclear Engineering and Radiological Sciences

Public Policy

Earth Sciences (minor)

Environmental Geology (minor)

Geochemistry (minor)

Global Change (minor)

Oceanography (minor)

Graduate Degrees

Architecture (MS, MArch, PhD)

Architecture/Business Administration (MArch/ MBA)

Architecture/Engineering (MArch/MEng)

Architecture/Urban Design (MArch/MUD)

Architecture/Urban Planning (MArch/MUP)

Atmospheric and Space Sciences (MS)

Atmospheric, Ocean and Space Sciences (PhD)

Atmospheric/Space Sciences (Sequential Graduate/Undergraduate Studies BSE/MS)

Chemical Engineering (BSE/MSE)

Chemical Engineering (MSE/PhD)

Civil Engineering (BSE)/Environmental Engineering (MSE) (Sequential Graduate/ Undergraduate Studies)

Civil Engineering (MSE)/Natural Resources and Environment (MS) Dual degree specializing in Engineering Sustainable Systems: Specialization in Sustainable Water Resources

Concentration in Environmental Sustainability may be combined with MSE degrees in Atmospheric, Oceanic and Space Sciences; Civil and Environmental Engineering; Chemical Engineering; Mechanical Engineering; or Naval Architecture and Marine Engineering

Engineering Sustainable Systems: Natural Resources and the Environment (MS)/ Engineering (MSE)

Environmental and Water Resources Engineering (BSE Chemical Engineering/MSE)

Environmental Engineering (MSE, PhD)

Environmental Engineering (MSE)/Natural Resources and Environment (MS) Dual degree specializing in Engineering Sustainable Systems: Specialization in Sustainable Water Resources

Geological Sciences (MS, PhD)

Landscape Architecture (MLA, PhD)

Mechanical Engineering (BSE/MSE Sequential Graduate/Undergraduate Studies)

Mechanical Engineering (MSE, PhD)

Natural Resources and the Environment (MS, PhD)

Natural Resources and the Environment (Aquatic Sciences: Research and Management) (MS)

Natural Resources and the Environment (Behavior, Education and Communication) (MS)

Natural Resources and the Environment (Conservation Biology) (MS)

Natural Resources and the Environment (Environmental Informatics: GIS and Modeling) (MS)

Natural Resources and the Environment (Environmental Justice) (MS)

Natural Resources and the Environment (Environmental Policy and Planning) (MS)

Natural Resources and the Environment (Sustainable Systems) (MS)

Natural Resources and the Environment (Terrestrial Ecosystems) (MS)

Natural Resources and the Environment/Business Administration (MS/MBA)

Natural Resources and the Environment/Public Policy (MS/MPP)

Natural Resources and the Environment/Urban Planning (MS/MUP)

Nuclear Engineering and Radiological Sciences (MS, PhD)

Oceanography (MS, PhD)

Political Science and Public Policy (PhD)

Public Policy (MPP, PhD))

Public Policy/Business Administration (MPP/ MBA)

Public Policy/Public Affairs (MPP/MPA)

Urban and Regional Planning (PhD)

Urban Design (MUD)

Urban Planning (MUP)

Urban Planning/Business Administration (MUP/ MBA)

Urban Planning/Law (MUP/JD)

Certificates:

Industrial Ecology
Real Estate Development
Spatial Analysis

Graduate Distance Learning

College of Engineering Off-Campus Education
Programs: Master's of Engineering

UNIVERSITY OF MINNESOTA, TWIN CITIES CAMPUS

Minneapolis, Minnesota 55455
612-625-5000
E-mail: www.directory.umn.edu/twincities.cfm
www1.umn.edu/twincities/index.php

Fast Facts

The University of Minnesota chapter of the student organization Engineers Without Borders recently received grants of $50,000 to be used for projects in Haiti and Uganda. The grants were made by the University of Minnesota Institute on the Environment and its Initiative for Renewable Energy and the Environment. The mission of the student organization is to help underprivileged communities through environmentally and economically sustainable engineering projects.

Green Campus Organizations

Active Energy Club: Students working to raise awareness and promote energy conservation and alternative energy technology.

EcoWatch: Student group raising awareness about environmental issues by hosting an energy forum each fall, hosting speakers, and working with the university and other student groups for more sustainability on campus.

Greenlight: Student group that uses design creativity to raise environmental and social awareness.

Minnesota Environmental Studies Club: Student group that sponsors events, discussions, speakers, and fundraisers to promote interaction among groups and individuals committed to preserving the environment.

Recreation Resource Management: Students, faculty members, and staff members interested in managing natural resources, the environment, tourism, and recreation; sponsors outings, river clean-up, and children's educational opportunities.

Undergraduate Degrees

Agricultural Education (Natural and Managed Environmental Education)
Applied Economics (Environmental and Resource Economics)
Applied Plant Science (Agroecology)
Applied Plant Science (Plant Utilization)
Architecture (major or minor)
Bio-Based Products (Bio-based Products Marketing and Management)
Bio-Based Products (Residential Building Science and Technology)
Biochemistry
Biology
Biology, Society and the Environment
Bioproducts and Biosystems Engineering (Bioprocessing and Food Engineering)
Bioproducts and Biosystems Engineering (Bioproducts Engineering)
Bioproducts and Biosystems Engineering (Environmental and Ecological Engineering)
Chemical Engineering
Chemistry (major or minor)
Civil Engineering
Design in Architecture
Ecology, Evolution and Behavior
Environmental Design (major or minor)
Environmental Horticulture (Organic Horticulture)
Environmental Horticulture (Restoration Ecology)
Environmental Horticulture (Turfgrass Science)
Environmental Sciences, Policy and Management (Conservation and Resource Management)
Environmental Sciences, Policy and Management (Corporate Environmental Management)
Environmental Sciences, Policy and Management (Environmental Education and Communication)
Environmental Sciences, Policy and Management (Environmental Science)

Environmental Sciences, Policy and Management (Policy, Planning, Law and Society)

Environmental Sciences, Policy and Management (minor)

Fisheries and Wildlife (Conservation Biology)

Fisheries and Wildlife (Fisheries)

Fisheries and Wildlife (Wildlife)

Forest Resources (Forest Conservation and Ecosystem Management)

Forest Resources (Forest Management and Planning)

Forest Resources (Urban and Community Forestry)

Geography (major or minor)

Geological Engineering

Geology (major or minor)

Housing Studies (major or minor)

Mechanical Engineering

Microbiology

Plant Biology

Recreation Resource Management

Recreation Resource Management (Resource-Based Tourism)

Scientific and Technical Communication

Urban Studies (major or minor)

Agricultural Public Health (minor)

Agronomy (minor)

Applied Economics (minor)

Bio-Based Products Engineering (minor)

Climatology (minor)

Corporate Environmental Management (minor)

Environmental Geosciences (minor)

Fisheries and Wildlife (minor)

Food Systems and the Environment (minor)

Forest Resources (minor)

Geographic Information Science (minor)

Horticulture (minor)

Integrated Pest Management in Cropping Systems (minor)

Land, Nature and Environmental Values (minor)

Recreation Resource Management (minor)

Soil Science (minor)

Sustainability Studies (minor)

Sustainable Agriculture (minor)

Technical Communication (minor)

Urban and Community Forestry (minor)

Water Science (minor)

Undergraduate Distance Learning

Online Degrees:

Applied Studies (student-tailored degree completion)

Multidisciplinary Studies (student-tailored degree completion)

Online Courses:

Many courses fulfilling requirements for the degrees listed above are offered online for credit. See the Digital Campus Web site for information: http://digitalcampus.umn.edu.

Graduate Degrees

Agricultural Education (MS, MEd, PhD, EdD)

Applied Economics (Environmental and Resource Economics) (MS, PhD)

Applied Plant Sciences (Agronomy/Agroecology) (MS, PhD)

Applied Plant Sciences (Horticulture) (MS, PhD)

Biochemistry (Microbial Biochemistry and Biotechnology) (PhD)

Biological Sciences (MS)

Bioproducts and Biosystems Science, Engineering and Management (Bioproducts Marketing and Management) (MS, PhD)

Bioproducts and Biosystems Science, Engineering and Management (Bioproducts Science and Engineering) (MS, PhD)

Bioproducts and Biosystems Science, Engineering and Management (Biosystems Science and Engineering) (MS, PhD)

Business/Public Policy (MBA/MPP)

Chemical Engineering (MS, MChE, PhD)

Civil Engineering (MS, MCE, PhD)

Civil Engineering (Environmental Planning and Engineering)/Urban and Regional Planning (MSCE/MURP)

Civil Engineering (Transportation Planning and Engineering)/Urban and Regional Planning (MSCE/MURP)

Conservation Biology (MS, PhD)

Conservation Biology/Law (MS/JD, PhD/JD)

Ecology, Evolution and Behavior (MS, PhD)

Environmental and Occupational Epidemiology (MS, MPH, PhD)

Environmental Chemistry (MS, PhD)

Environmental Education (MEd)

Environmental Engineering (MS, PhD)

Environmental Health (MS, MPH, PhD)

Environmental Health/Journalism (MPH/MA)

Environmental Health/Law (MS/JD, MPH/JD, PhD/JD)

Environmental Health Policy (MS, MPH, PhD)

Environmental Infectious Diseases (MS, MPH, PhD)

Environmental Psychology (PhD)

Exposure Sciences (MS)

Fisheries and Aquatic Biology (MS, PhD)

Geographic Information Science (MGIS)

Geography (MA, PhD)

Geology (MS, PhD)

Geomechanical Engineering (MS, MGeoE, PhD)

Global Environmental Health (MS, MPH)

Health Journalism (MA)

Horticulture (MAg)

Housing Studies (MA, PhD)

Industrial Hygiene (MS, MPH, PhD)

Landscape Architecture (MLA, MSLA)

Landscape Architecture/Urban and Regional Planning (MLA/MURP)

Law/Conservation Biology (JD/MS, JD/PhD)

Law/Ecology, Evolution and Behavior (JD/MS, JD/PhD)

Law/Natural Resource Science and Management (JD/MS, JD/PhD)

Law/Public Policy (JD/MPP)

Law/Science, Technology and Environmental Policy (JD/MS)

Law/Urban and Regional Planning (JD/MURP)

Mechanical Engineering (five-year BME/MS, MSME, PhD)

Microbial Engineering (MS)

Microbiology

Natural Resources Science and Management (Assessment, Monitoring, and Geospatial Analysis) (MS, PhD)

Natural Resources Science and Management (Economics, Policy, Management, and Society) (MS, PhD)

Natural Resources Science and Management (Forest Hydrology and Watershed Management) (MS, PhD)

Natural Resources Science and Management (Forest Products) (MS, PhD)

Natural Resources Science and Management (Forests: Biology, Ecology, Conservation and Management (MS, PhD)

Natural Resources Science and Management (Paper Science and Engineering) (MS, PhD)

Natural Resources Science and Management (Recreation Resources, Tourism, and Environmental Education) (MS, PhD)

Natural Resources Science and Management (Wildlife Ecology and Management) (MS, PhD)

Occupational and Environmental Health Nursing (MS, MPH, PhD)

Occupational Health Services Research and Policy (PhD)

Plant Biological Sciences (MS, PhD)

Policy Management/Public Policy (MS/MPP)

Public Administration and Policy/Journalism (MPH/MA)

Public Administration and Policy/Law (MPH/JD)

Regulatory Toxicology and Risk Assessment (MPH)

Rhetoric and Scientific and Technical Communication (MA, PhD)

Scientific and Technical Communication (MS)

Statistics (MS, PhD)

Transportation Engineering (MS, PhD)

Water Resources Engineering (MS, PhD)

Water Resources Science (MS, PhD)

Certificates:

Housing Studies

Metropolitan Design

Technical Communication

Continuing Education:

Hazardous Waste Worker Training

Graduate Distance Learning

Natural Resources Learning Modules

UNIVERSITY OF NEW HAMPSHIRE

Durham, New Hampshire 03824
603-862-1234
E-mail: www.unh.edu/unhedutop/directories.html
www.unh.edu

Fast Facts

The Sustainability Internship Program provides students with opportunities to work with companies, agencies, and organizations that are striving to create sustainable communities, primarily in New Hampshire. Students receive mentoring on how sustainability can be part of their lives in professional and personal situations, which enables them to take what they have learned in the classroom and apply it to identify solutions to real-world problems.

Green Campus Organizations

Ecological Advocates: Student group to raise awareness about sustainable living on campus.

Organic Garden Club: Maintains a USDA sustainable farm for the campus and community; strives to create an environmentally, socially, and economically sustainable community; provides locally produced food to the UNH Dining Services.

Student Energy Waste Watch Challenge: Competition each fall semester for students in residence halls and apartments to reduce their water and energy use relative to previous years.

Sustainable YouNH: Student group helping students to make the university into a sustainable community.

Undergraduate Degrees

Biology (Ecology, Evolution and Behavior)
Biology (Marine and Freshwater Biology option)
Chemistry (major or minor)

Civil Engineering
Civil Technology (two-year Associate)
Community and Environmental Planning
Earth Sciences
EcoGastronomy (dual major combined with
  another major)
Economics (Public Policy Economics option)
Environmental and Resource Economics
Environmental Conservation Studies
Environmental Education
Environmental Engineering
Environmental Horticulture (major, minor, or
  two-year Associate)
Environmental Sciences (Ecology option)
Environmental Sciences (Hydrology option)
  (major or minor)
Environmental Sciences (Soil and Watershed
  Management option)
Environmental Sciences (Water Resources
  option) (minor)
Environmental Sciences (Wetland Ecology
  option) (minor)
Forestry
Geography
Geology
Marine Biology (minor)
Mechanical Engineering
Microbiology
Ocean Engineering (minor)
Oceanography
Plant Biology (major or minor)
Tourism Planning and Development
Wetland Ecology (minor)
Wildlife Ecology
Zoology

Undergraduate Distance Learning

Far View Distance Learning makes select engineering and science courses available online, including the Energy and Environment course.

Graduate Degrees

Biochemistry (MS, PhD)
Chemical Engineering (MS, PhD)
Civil Engineering (Environmental Engineering
  specialization) (MS, PhD)

Civil Engineering (Water Resources specialization) (MS, PhD)
Earth Science (MS)
Economics (MA, PhD)
Environmental Conservation (MS)
Environmental Education (MA)
Forestry (MS)
Geochemical Systems (MS)
Geology (MS)
Hydrology (MS)
Mechanical Engineering (MS, PhD)
Microbiology (MS, PhD)
Natural Resources (MS)
Natural Resources and Earth Systems Sciences (PhD)
Natural Resources: Environmental Conservation (MS)
Natural Resources: Forestry (MS)
Natural Resources: Water Resources (MS)
Natural Resources: Wildlife (MS)
Ocean Engineering (MS, PhD)
Ocean Mapping (MS)
Oceanography (MS)
Plant Biology (MS, PhD)
Public Administration (MPA)
Resource Administration and Management (MS)
Resource Economics (MS)
Soil Science (MS)
Water Resources (MS)
Wildlife (MS)
Zoology (MS, PhD)

Certificates:

Ocean Mapping (Advanced)
Ocean Mapping (Basic)

UNIVERSITY OF NORTH CAROLINA AT CHAPEL HILL

Chapel Hill, North Carolina 27599
919-962-2211
E-mail: www.unc.edu/atn/
   uncweb/#otherquestions
www.unc.edu

Fast Facts

In April 2009, UNC-CH was awarded a $17.5 million grant by the U.S. Department of Energy and the American Recovery and Reinvestment Act to fund development of "solar fuels from next-generation photovoltaic technology." The research will be conducted through the University's Energy Frontier Research Center, one of only forty-six in the nation.

Green Campus Organizations

Carolina Environmental Student Alliance: Brings campus and community together to consider environmental issues through education, service, and events.

FLO-Food: Students working with Carolina Dining Services to develop a sustainable food supply utilizing fair, local, organic foods.

Student Environmental Action Coalition: Students working to improve the environment.

UNC-CH Chapter of the Culinary Arts and Beverage Association: Students promoting sustainable food production and clean water development through education and fundraising to support nonprofit organizations involved in these causes.

UNC-CH Collegians for a Constructive Tomorrow: Student group promoting entrepreneurship to solve environmental problems.

Undergraduate Degrees

Anthropology (Ecology and Evolution)
Applied Science and Engineering (Materials Science)
Biology (major or minor)
Environmental Geology
Environmental Science
Environmental Studies
Geochemistry
Geography (Earth Environmental Systems)
Geography (Geographic Information Sciences)
Geography (Human Activity)
Geology (major or minor)
Geophysics

PaleoBiology
Public Health (with environmental sciences and
    engineering emphasis)
Public Policy (major or minor)
Environmental (minor)
Marine Science (minor)
Sustainability (minor)
Urban Studies and Planning (minor)

Undergraduate Distance Learning

Some courses are offered each semester online
for credit for part-time students in areas such as
biology, geography, geological sciences, and
public policy. Check the Carolina Courses Online
Web site for offerings: http://fridaycenter.unc.edu/
cp/cco/index.htm.

Graduate Degrees

Anthropology (Archaeology, Ecology and
Evolution) (MA)
Biochemistry (Environmental Pathology) (PhD)
Biology (Evolution, Ecology and Organismal
    Biology) (MA, MS, PhD)
Business (Sustainable Enterprise) (MBA)
City and Regional Planning (Design and
    Preservation of the Built Environment)
    (MCRP)
City and Regional Planning (Economic
    Development) (MCRP)
City and Regional Planning (Housing, Real Estate
    and Community Development) (MCRP)
City and Regional Planning (Land Use and
    Environmental Planning) (MCRP)
City and Regional Planning (Transportation
    Planning) (MCRP)
City and Regional Planning/Public
    Administration (MCRP/MPA)
Ecology (MA, MS, PhD)
Environmental Engineering (MSEE)
Environmental Sciences and Engineering (MS,
    PhD)
Environmental Sciences and Engineering/City
    and Regional Planning (MS/MCRP)
Geography (Biophysical Geography and Earth
    Systems Science) (MA, PhD)

Geography (Culture, Society and Space) (MA,
    PhD)
Geography (Geographic Information Science)
    (MA, PhD)
Geography (Globalization and Development)
    (MA, PhD)
Geography (Nature-Society Studies and Human-
    Environment Interactions) (MA, PhD)
Geological Sciences (MS, PhD)
Landscape Architecture/Planning (MLA/MCRP)
Law/City and Regional Planning (JD/MCRP)
Marine Sciences (MS, PhD)
Materials Science (MS, PhD)
Planning (Land Use, Transportation and
    Environmental Planning) (PhD)
Public Health (MPH, MS)
Public Policy (Environmental and Energy Policy)
    (PhD)
Toxicology (PhD)

Certificates:

Geographic Information Sciences
Public Policy

Other Graduate Courses:

Environmental Communication and the Public
Sphere
Environmental Law
Government and the Environment
Human Ecology
Mathematical Modeling
Resource and Environmental Economics

UNIVERSITY OF VERMONT

Burlington, Vermont 05405
802-656-3131
E-mail: www.uvm.edu/talk_to_us
www.uvm.edu

Fast Facts

In 2007, the Sustainable Endowments Institute
ranked the University of Vermont among the six
top colleges and universities in the nation for
green policies and practices.

Green Campus Organizations

SEEDS (Student Environmental Educators Doing Service): Student volunteers teach environmental lessons in after-school programs in Burlington-area elementary schools.

Sprouting Possibilities: Environmental education group; works with elementary and middle school girls to give them an appreciation of the outdoors.

Students for Peace and Global Justice: Supports several advocacy and activist projects that strive for environmental and economic justice.

University of Vermont Campus Energy Group: Advocates for renewable energy.

Vermont Student Environmental Program: Coordinates campus environmental activities to increase awareness and promote sustainable university policies.

Undergraduate Degrees

Business Administration (Management and the Environment)

Chemistry (Environmental)

Civil Engineering (Urban and Community Planning)

Civil Engineering (Water Resources Engineering)

Community and International Development (major or minor)

Community Entrepreneurship (major or minor)

Ecological Agriculture (major or minor)

Environmental Engineering (Air Quality and Air Pollution Control)

Environmental Engineering (Groundwater Quality and Remediation)

Environmental Engineering (Hazardous Materials Management)

Environmental Engineering (Hydrology and Water Resources)

Environmental Engineering (Restoration of Environmental Systems)

Environmental Engineering (Sustainable Approaches and Technologies)

Environmental Engineering (Water and Wastewater Treatment)

Environmental Science (Agriculture and Environment)

Environmental Science (Conservation Biology and Biodiversity)

Environmental Science (Ecological Design)

Environmental Science (Environmental Analysis and Assessment)

Environmental Science (Environmental Biology)

Environmental Science (Environmental Chemistry)

Environmental Science (Environmental Geology)

Environmental Science (Environmental Resources)

Environmental Science (Water Resources)

Environmental Sciences (Biology) (minor)

Environmental Studies (major or minor)

Food Systems (minor)

Forestry (major or minor)

Geography (major or minor)

Geology (major or minor)

Geospatial Technologies (minor)

Green Building and Community Design (minor)

Integrated Biological Science

Mathematics (Statistics) (major or minor)

Mechanical Engineering

Microbiology (major or minor)

Natural Resources (Integrated Natural Resources)

Natural Resources (Resource Ecology)

Natural Resources (Resource Planning)

Plant Biology (Ecology and Evolutionary Biology of Plants)

Plant Biology (minor)

Public Communication (major or minor)

Recreation Management (minor)

Recreation Management (Private Outdoor Recreation and Tourism)

Recreation Management (Public Outdoor Recreation)

Soil Science (minor)

Sustainable Landscape Horticulture (major or minor)

Wildlife and Fisheries Biology (Fisheries Biology)

Wildlife and Fisheries Biology (Wildlife Biology)

Wildlife Biology (minor)
Zoology

Undergraduate Distance Learning

Introduction to Ecological Economics
Introduction to Simulation Modeling

Various courses are offered online each term. See the Web site for course listing: www.uvm. edu/~learn/online.

Graduate Degrees

Biology (five-year BS/MS, MS, PhD)
Biostatistics (MS)
Botany (MS, PhD)
Business Administration (MBA)
Civil and Environmental Engineering
(Sustainable Systems) (MS, PhD)
Community Development and Applied
Economics (MS)
Field Naturalist (MS)
Geology (MS, PhD)
Historic Preservation (MS)
Mechanical Engineering (Sustainable Systems)
(MS, PhD)
Microbiology and Molecular Genetics (five-year
BS/MS, PhD)
Natural Resources (PhD)
Natural Resources (Aquatic Ecology and
Watershed Science) (MS)
Natural Resources (Environmental Thought and
Culture) (MS)
Natural Resources (Environment, Society and
Public Affairs) (MS)
Natural Resources (Forestry) (MS)
Natural Resources (Recreation Management)
(MS)
Natural Resources (Wildlife Biology) (MS)
Plant and Soil Science (MS, PhD)
Plant Biology (MS, PhD)
Public Administration (MPA)
Statistics (MS)

Certificates and Programs:

AgroEcology Training (graduate and
undergraduate)
Ecological Design
Ecological Economics
Permaculture Design
Sustainable Business

UNIVERSITY OF WASHINGTON

Seattle, Washington 98195
206-543-2100
E-mail: www.washington.edu/home/siteinfo/form
www.washington.edu

Fast Facts

In May 2009, the UW Law School hosted a two-day event called "The Law of Climate Change and Human Rights Conference." The purpose was to look at climate change from the human perspective and consider the human consequences of climate change and the ethical role of the law in shaping responses.

Green Campus Organizations

Bourgeois Environmental Stewardship Street Team: Utilizes street team model to promote environmental change through individual actions.

Earth Club, UW Chapter: Sponsors projects that promote environmental stewardship on campus as well as in the community.

Go Green: Educates the Greek community on environmental sustainability and focuses on water and energy conservation.

About Committing to Climate Change

. . . Colleges and universities must exercise their leadership in their communities and throughout society by modeling ways to eliminate global warming emissions, and by providing the knowledge and the educated graduates to achieve climate neutrality. . . .

—The Signatories of the American College & University Presidents' Climate Commitment

---

Students Expressing Environmental Dedication (SEED): Promotes environmental responsibility in residence halls.

Urban Farmers UW Chapter: Promotes sustainability on campus and supports urban agriculture.

Undergraduate Degrees

Anthropology (major or minor)
Applied and Computational Mathematical
    Sciences (Biological and Life Sciences)
Aquatic and Fishery Sciences (major or minor)
Architecture
Atmospheric Sciences (Atmospheric Chemistry
    and Air Quality)
Atmospheric Sciences (Climate)
Atmospheric Sciences (Meteorology)
Atmospheric Sciences (minor)
Biocultural Anthropology
Biology Teacher Preparation
Chemical Engineering (Environmental
    Engineering)
Civil and Environmental Engineering
Community, Environment and Planning
Earth and Space Sciences (major or minor)
Earth and Space Sciences (Biology)
Earth and Space Sciences (Environmental)
Earth and Space Sciences (Physics)
Ecology, Evolution, and Conservation Biology
Economics
Environmental Health
Environmental Science and Resource
    Management (major or minor)
Environmental Studies (major or minor)
Geography (Economic Geography)
Geography (Geographic Information Systems)
Geography (Regional Geography and
    International Development)
Geography (Society and Environment)
Geography (Urban, Social and Political
    Processes)
Geological Sciences
General Biology
Landscape Architecture
Landscape Studies (minor)
Marine Biology (minor)

Materials Science and Engineering
Mechanical Engineering
Oceanography (Biological Oceanography)
Oceanography (Chemical Oceanography)
Oceanography (Marine Geology and Geophysics)
Oceanography (minor)
Oceanography (Physical Oceanography)
Paper Science and Engineering
Plant Biology
Quantitative Science (minor)
Sociocultural Anthropology
Streamside Studies (minor)
Values in Society (minor)

Certificates:

Environmental and Natural Resource Economics
Restoration Ecology

Undergraduate Distance Learning

Online Certificates:

Decision-Making for Climate Change
The Practice and Policy of Composting,
    Recycling and Waste Prevention
Public Health
Sustainable Transportation

Online Courses:

Atmospheric Sciences
Geographic Information Systems Fundamentals
Survey of Oceanography

Graduate Degrees

Aquatic and Fishery Sciences (MS, PhD)
Archeology (PhD)
Architecture (MArch, MS)
Atmospheric Sciences (MS, PhD)
Biocultural Anthropology (PhD)
Biology (Ecology and Conservation Biology)
    (PhD)
Biology (Plant Biology) (PhD)
Biology Teaching (MS)
Biology (Zoology) (PhD)
Built Environments (Sustainable Systems and
    Prototypes) (PhD)
Business Administration (MBA, MSBA, PhD)

Chemical Engineering (Living Systems and Biological Processes) (MSE, MSChE, PhD)

Chemical Engineering (Molecular Energy Processes) (MSE, MSChE, PhD)

Chemistry (MS, PhD)

Civil Engineering (Environmental Engineering) (MS, MSCE, MSE, PhD)

Civil Engineering (Geotechnical Engineering) (MS, MSCE, MSE, PhD)

Civil Engineering (Hydrology, Water Resources, and Environmental Fluid Mechanics) (MS, MSCE, MSE, PhD)

Civil Engineering (Transportation Engineering) (MS, MSCE, MSE, PhD)

Earth and Space Sciences (MS, PhD)

Economics (MA, PhD)

Environmental Anthropology (PhD)

Environmental Health (MS)

Environmental Horticulture (MEH)

Environmental and Occupational Health (MPH)

Environmental and Occupational Hygiene (PhD)

Occupational and Environmental Exposure Sciences (MS)

Occupational and Environmental Medicine (MPH)

Oceanography (Biological Oceanography) (MS, PhD)

Oceanography (Chemical Oceanography) (MS, PhD)

Oceanography (Marine Geology and Geophysics) (MS, PhD)

Oceanography (Physical Oceanography) (MS, PhD)

Epidemiology (MPH)

Forest Resources (Bioresource Science and Engineering) (MS, PhD)

Forest Resources (Forest Ecology) (MS, PhD)

Forest Resources (Forest Soils) (MS, PhD)

Forest Resources (Forest Systems and Bioenergy) (MS, PhD)

Forest Resources (Restoration Ecology and Environmental Horticulture) (MS, PhD)

Forest Resources (Social Sciences) (MS, PhD)

Forest Resources (Sustainable Resource Management) (MS, PhD)

Forest Resources (Wildlife Science) (MS, PhD)

Forest Resources/Forest Management (MFR)

Forest Resources/Public Affairs (MS/MPA)

Geography (Access) (MA, PhD)

Geography (The City) (MA, PhD)

Geography (Health) (MA, PhD)

Geography (Nature-Society) (MA, PhD)

Geography (Social Justice) (MA, PhD)

Geography (Sustainability) (MA, PhD)

Landscape Architecture (MLA)

Law (Environmental Law) (JD)

Law (Sustainable International Development) (LLM)

Marine Affairs (MMA)

Materials Science and Engineering (five-year BS/MS, MS, PhD)

Mechanical Engineering (MSE, MSME, PhD)

Microbiology (PhD)

Occupational and Environmental Exposure Sciences (MS)

Peace Corps Master's International Program (PCMI)

Psychology (Animal Behavior) (PhD)

Public Affairs (Environmental Policy) (MPA)

Public Affairs/Environmental and Occupational Health (MPA/MPH)

Public Affairs/Environmental Health (MPA/MS)

Public Affairs/Exposure Sciences (MPA/MS)

Public Affairs and Forestry (MPA/MS)

Public Affairs and Urban Planning (MPA/MUP)

Public Affairs/Toxicology (MPA/MS)

Public Policy and Management (PhD)

Real Estate (MSRE)

Quantitative Ecology and Resource Management (MS, PhD)

Sociocultural Anthropology (PhD)

Toxicology (MS, PhD)

Urban Design and Planning (PhD)

Urban Planning (MUP)

Certificates:

Advanced Practice Environmental Health

Astrobiology

Climate Science

Education for Environment and Community

Environmental Law and Regulation
Environmental Management
Geographic Information Systems
Historical Preservation
Interdisciplinary and Policy Dimensions of the
    Earth Sciences
Lighting Design
Low Impact Development
The Practice and Policy of Composting,
    Recycling and Waste Prevention
Urban Design
Values in Society
Wetland Science and Management

Graduate Distance Learning

Mechanical Engineering (MSME)
Public Health (MPH)
Strategic Planning for Critical Infrastructures
    (MSPCI)

WASHINGTON STATE UNIVERSITY

Pullman, Washington 99164
509-335-3564
E-mail: about.wsu.edu/contact
www.wsu.edu

Fast Facts

The newest residence hall on campus, which was
opened in 2009 and houses 230 students, was
designed to meet LEED Silver rating requirements. It has a number of green features, including
natural lighting and geothermal cooling and
heating. Certified wood and recycled or regional
materials have been used in construction.

Green Campus Organizations

Environmental Science Club: Supports university
sustainability program and promotes environmental education and awareness.

Environmental Task Force: Supports the university sustainability programs and sponsors environmental awareness activities and education.

About the Tallories Declaration
In 1990, 35 university presidents met to discuss the universities' role in environmental education and stewardship. The result was the Tallories Declaration, a commitment by higher education institutions from around the world to promote awareness of environmental issues and to establish policies and programs to counter environmental problems.

Raptor Club at WSU: Nonprofit organization that
rehabilitates raptors and gives students the opportunity to learn about raptors, their role in the environment, and conservation.

Solar Splash at WSU: Students design and build
a solar-powered boat to compete in international
competition.

Sustainable Agriculture Club: Works to improve
sustainability of the university and community
through interdisciplinary interactions, educational
opportunities, and activities.

Undergraduate Degrees

Agricultural Business and Technology Systems
Agricultural Business and Technology Systems
    (Agricultural Communication)
Agricultural Business and Technology Systems
    (Agricultural Technology)
Agricultural Business and Technology Systems
    (Agri-Food Production Management)
Agricultural Education
Architecture
Biology (major or minor)
Biology (Botany)
Biology (Ecology/Evolutionary Biology)
Biotechnology
Chemical Engineering (Environmental
    Engineering)
Chemistry (Environmental Chemistry) (major or
    minor)
Civil Engineering (Environmental Engineering)
Civil Engineering (Hydraulic Engineering)
Civil Engineering (Transportation Engineering)
Crop Science (major or minor)

Crop Science (Biotechnology)
Crop Science (Business and Industry)
Crop Science (Turf Management)
Earth Science Teaching
Environmental and Resource Economics and
    Management (major or minor)
Environmental Science (major or minor)
Geology (major or minor)
Horticulture
Horticulture (Environmental Horticulture)
Landscape Architecture
Mathematics (Mathematical Modeling)
Mechanical Engineering (major or minor)
Microbiology (major or minor)
Natural Resource Sciences (major or minor)
Natural Resource Sciences (Forest Management)
Natural Resource Sciences (Policy/Pre-Law)
Natural Resource Sciences (Wetland/Aquatic
    Resources)
Natural Resource Sciences (Wildlife Ecology)
Organic Agriculture Systems
Pest Management Systems
Physics (Environmental Physics)
Plant and Soil Systems
Plant and Soil Systems (Cropping Systems)
Plant and Soil Systems (Horticulture Systems)
Plant and Soil Systems (Soil Management)
Plant Pathology
Sociology (Society, Environment, and
    Technology)
Soil Science (major or minor)
Soil Science (Environmental Soil Science)
Soil Science (Sustainable Agriculture)
Wildlife Ecology (major or minor)
Zoology (major or minor)

Certificate:

Sustainable Small Acreage Farming and Ranching

Undergraduate Distance Learning

A variety of courses that apply to the degrees
listed above are offered online. See the Center for
Distance and Professional Education Web page:
http://online.wsu.edu/future_students.

Graduate Degrees

Agricultural Economics (Environmental & Natural
Resource Economics) (PhD)
Agriculture (MS)
Animal Science (MS, PhD)
Archeology (Environmental Archeology) (MA,
    PhD)
Architecture (MArch)
Biological and Agricultural Engineering (MS,
    PhD)
Biology (MS)
Biotechnology (MS)
Botany (MS, PhD)
Chemical Engineering (MS, PhD)
Chemistry (Environmental Chemistry) (MA, MS,
    PhD)
Civil Engineering (MS, PhD)
Clean Technologies (combined with various PhD
    programs)
Crop Science (MS, PhD)
Design
Entomology (MS, PhD)
Environmental and Natural Resource Sciences
    (PhD)
Environmental Anthropology (Master's
    International)
Environmental Engineering (MS)
Environmental Research (combined with various
    PhD programs)
Environmental Science (MS)
Environmental Science and Regional Planning
    (MS, PhD)
Geology (MS, PhD)
Horticulture (MS, PhD)
Landscape Architecture (MSLA)
Law/Business Administration (MBA/JD)
Mathematics (Applied Mathematics) (MS, PhD)
Mechanical Engineering (MS, PhD)
Microbiology (MS, PhD)
Molecular Biosciences (MS, PhD)
Molecular Plant Sciences (MS, PhD)
Natural Resource Sciences (MS)
Plant Pathology (MS, PhD)
Sociology (Environment, Technology, and
    Community) (MA, PhD)

Green Jobs for a New Economy

Soil Science (MS, PhD)
Statistics (MS)
Wildlife Ecology (MS, PhD)
Zoology (MS, PhD)

Certificates:

Interdisciplinary Environmental Biogeochemistry
Sustainable Agriculture

Continuing Education:

Sustainable Small Acreage Farming and
    Ranching Certificate

Graduate Distance Learning

Online Degrees:

Agriculture (MS)
Business Administration (MBA)

Online Certificate:

Organic Agriculture

RecycleMania

RecycleMania began in 2001 with a competition between Miami University of Ohio and Ohio University to see which school could recycle the most campus waste. By 2009, the ten-week competition had grown to 510 schools, 4.7 million students, 1.1 million faculty and staff members, and eight categories of awards. Participating colleges and universities in all fifty states, the District of Columbia, and Canada recycled or composted 69.4 million pounds of waste. The list below names the 2009 participating schools profiled in this chapter.

Arizona State University
Berea College
Bowdoin College
Brandeis University
Carnegie Mellon University
Cornell University
Dartmouth College
Dickinson College
Drexel University
Duke University
Georgetown University
Grand Valley State University
Harvard University
Massachusetts Institute of Technology
Middlebury College
Oregon State University
Portland State University
Princeton University

Purdue University
Rutgers University*
Santa Clara University
Southern Methodist University
Stanford University
Texas A&M University
Tufts University
University of Alaska, Fairbanks
University of Georgia
University of Illinois at Chicago
University of Maryland, College Park
University of Massachusetts Amherst
University of Michigan
University of Minnesota, Twin Cities Campus
University of New Hampshire
University of North Carolina at Chapel Hill
Washington State University

Won the 2009 Gorilla Prize for the greatest overall tonnage.

Green Jobs for a New Economy

Keep America Beautiful: Great American Cleanup™

In addition to RecycleMania, students can join the Keep America Beautiful: Great American Cleanup™. It happens every spring from March 1 through May 31. More than 3 million people participate each year. In 2008, Americans gave more than 6.7 million hours in 17,000 communities to work on 30,000 specific events. Communities in all fifty states took part.

Projects ranged from cleaning up parks and recreation centers to conducting educational programs and litter-free events. Litter was removed from waterways and beaches, trees and flowers were planted to enhance urban areas, and recycling events were held.

In 2009, national sponsors such as GLAD™ Trash Bags, Pepsi-Cola Company, The Scotts Miracle-Gro Company, Solo Cup Company, and Waste Management, Inc., provided a variety of support, including in-kind donations for local initiatives as well as encouraging their employees to volunteer.

To see how you can become involved, visit www.kab.org.

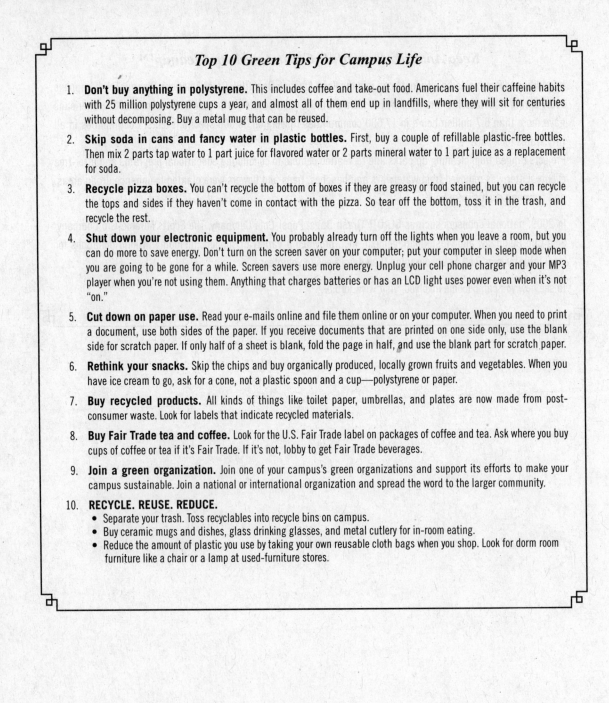

Top 10 Green Tips for Campus Life

1. **Don't buy anything in polystyrene.** This includes coffee and take-out food. Americans fuel their caffeine habits with 25 million polystyrene cups a year, and almost all of them end up in landfills, where they will sit for centuries without decomposing. Buy a metal mug that can be reused.

2. **Skip soda in cans and fancy water in plastic bottles.** First, buy a couple of refillable plastic-free bottles. Then mix 2 parts tap water to 1 part juice for flavored water or 2 parts mineral water to 1 part juice as a replacement for soda.

3. **Recycle pizza boxes.** You can't recycle the bottom of boxes if they are greasy or food stained, but you can recycle the tops and sides if they haven't come in contact with the pizza. So tear off the bottom, toss it in the trash, and recycle the rest.

4. **Shut down your electronic equipment.** You probably already turn off the lights when you leave a room, but you can do more to save energy. Don't turn on the screen saver on your computer; put your computer in sleep mode when you are going to be gone for a while. Screen savers use more energy. Unplug your cell phone charger and your MP3 player when you're not using them. Anything that charges batteries or has an LCD light uses power even when it's not "on."

5. **Cut down on paper use.** Read your e-mails online and file them online or on your computer. When you need to print a document, use both sides of the paper. If you receive documents that are printed on one side only, use the blank side for scratch paper. If only half of a sheet is blank, fold the page in half, and use the blank part for scratch paper.

6. **Rethink your snacks.** Skip the chips and buy organically produced, locally grown fruits and vegetables. When you have ice cream to go, ask for a cone, not a plastic spoon and a cup—polystyrene or paper.

7. **Buy recycled products.** All kinds of things like toilet paper, umbrellas, and plates are now made from post-consumer waste. Look for labels that indicate recycled materials.

8. **Buy Fair Trade tea and coffee.** Look for the U.S. Fair Trade label on packages of coffee and tea. Ask where you buy cups of coffee or tea if it's Fair Trade. If it's not, lobby to get Fair Trade beverages.

9. **Join a green organization.** Join one of your campus's green organizations and support its efforts to make your campus sustainable. Join a national or international organization and spread the word to the larger community.

10. **RECYCLE. REUSE. REDUCE.**
    - Separate your trash. Toss recyclables into recycle bins on campus.
    - Buy ceramic mugs and dishes, glass drinking glasses, and metal cutlery for in-room eating.
    - Reduce the amount of plastic you use by taking your own reusable cloth bags when you shop. Look for dorm room furniture like a chair or a lamp at used-furniture stores.

CHAPTER 4

TWO-YEAR COLLEGES AND UNION ORGANIZATIONS WITH GREAT GREEN PROGRAMS

This chapter is divided into two parts. The first part contains profiles of twenty-two community colleges that confer "green" degrees and certificates. The second part contains profiles of seven labor unions, which offer apprenticeship and training programs to upgrade members' skills for the green economy, and the National Labor College, which grants undergraduate degrees and certificates to AFL-CIO members.

TWO-YEAR COLLEGES

The twenty-two community colleges were chosen to represent a cross-section of types of programs, different areas of the country, and innovative programs. All have their own campus sustainability programs, and many have green student organizations that sponsor a variety of education and community service projects. Some of the colleges offer online courses, and some also have environmental research facilities or energy demonstration projects that involve students as part of their course work.

If you are interested in retraining for the new economy, degree and certificate programs at local community colleges are a good way to learn new skills. Community colleges welcome older students and career-changers.

ABOUT THE TWO-YEAR COLLEGE LISTINGS

Here's what you need to know to navigate the two-year college profiles.

Contact Info

The first paragraph of each school profile lists the school name, address, phone number, e-mail address, and Web site info.

Fast Facts

The Fast Facts gives an insight into the school's commitment to sustainability and the environment.

Green Campus Organizations

This section gives a sampling of green activities that students may participate in. The schools included in this guide have substantial sustainability efforts and, thus, a variety of ways students may become involved and take leadership roles.

Undergraduate Degrees

This section includes associate degrees and certificates in environmental studies or sciences and any other program that has an environmental focus, such as landscape technician. Some degrees allow a student to concentrate in a particular aspect of a science, such as a Coastal Zone Management concentration in Environmental Technology at Cape Cod Community College.

While this section focuses solely on "green" degree programs and certificates, many degree programs may offer courses that are relevant to green industries. For example, green lodging has been introduced into the Hospitality Associate Science degree, and sustainability has been introduced in the Parks and Leisure Services program, both at St. Petersburg College. If you have an interest in "going green," but don't want to learn about operating a wind turbine, check out how green your career interest could be.

Undergraduate Distance Learning

A number of two-year schools offer courses online, some of which may meet requirements of the degrees listed in this guide.

UNION RESOURCES

Because of the move away from manufacturing to new green industries and the greening of older industries, unions are working aggressively to train current members and recruit new members for jobs in these industries. The goal is not only to provide a well-trained union membership to fill these "green jobs," but to gain new members for the labor movement and to ensure that all members have access to "family-sustaining careers" in the words of John Sweeney, president of the AFL-CIO.

Apprenticeship programs are available through union locals. To join a union, a person has to contact the local and see if there are any openings for apprentices. Unions try not to hire more apprentices than they think they will need in the

foreseeable future, so there may be a wait, especially if the work is seasonal like construction. A potential union member must meet certain requirements and often has to pass an interview with a committee of the local. Training costs are negotiated as part of contracts with employers, and, as a result, apprenticeships are earn-while-you-learn programs.

ABOUT THE LISTINGS OF UNION ORGANIZATIONS

Here's what you need to know to navigate the union training and apprentice program profiles.

Contact Info

The first paragraph of each union profile lists the union's name, address, phone number, e-mail address, and Web site info.

About the Union

This section details important information about the union. It may include union goals or the history of the organization, as well as any relevant data about available apprenticeships. This section is noted as About the College for the National Labor College profile.

Programs and Training

The final paragraph of the profile includes a description of the program or apprenticeship. In some cases, more than one may be listed. This section will also explain the training process and the necessary program skills and requirements.

ABOUT PARTNERSHIPS FOR GREEN JOBS

In this section, two alliances are discussed: Apollo Alliance and Blue Green Alliance. These national-level partnerships bring together union leaders with environmentalists and business leaders.

Two-Year Colleges with Great Green Programs

CAPE COD COMMUNITY COLLEGE

2240 Iyannough Road
West Barnstable, Massachusetts 02668
877-846-3672
E-mail: info@capecod.edu
www.capecod.mass.edu

Fast Facts

The Lorusso Applied Technology Center, completed in 2006, was the first state-owned building in Massachusetts to receive LEED certification. This "green" building uses alternative energy sources, such as solar panels, was built with recycled materials, was designed for water conservation, and has low-impact environmentally appropriate landscaping.

The Wilkens Library is powered by a 200-kilowatt fuel cell.

CCCC is constructing a 750-kilowatt wind turbine that will provide power to the campus and to low-income families in the community.

Green Campus Organizations

Students for Sustainability: Promotes awareness among students, faculty members, staff members, and the Cape Cod community about sustainability issues; it encourages community involvement.

Undergraduate Degrees

Environmental Studies (AS)
Environmental Technology (AS)

Certificates:

Environmental Technology:
Coastal Zone Management
Geographic Information Systems
Photovoltaic Technology
Site Assessment
Small Wind Technology
Solar Thermal Technology

About Being Car-Less

Need a car for a couple of hours? Try Zipcar, the car-sharing company. More than seventy campuses now have Zipcars. You can rent a car for a couple of hours or a day for $10 an hour or less.

Wastewater Management
Water Supply

Undergraduate Distance Learning

Some courses are available as e-courses. Class lectures are accessed via the Web; assignments are submitted by fax, mail, or over the Internet; and testing is scheduled on a flexible basis. Some materials for online courses or online components may be available from the Web via Blackboard, the college's Learning Management System. For more information, contact the Office of Online and Learning Technologies at 503-375-4040.

CLEVELAND STATE COMMUNITY COLLEGE

PO Box 3570
Cleveland, Tennessee 37320
423-472-7141
800-604-2722 (toll-free)
E-mail: clscc_info@clevelandstatecc.edu
www.clevelandstatecc.edu

Fast Facts

CSCC was the only community college in the state to receive a stimulus grant totaling approximately $328,000. The grant enabled the Technology Department to enhance the Energy Efficient Construction program.

CSCC was awarded $5000 from Tennessee Valley Authority (TVA) for solar-powered sun tracking equipment, which will be used by students to monitor the local weather conditions in order to track the energy production of the solar panel. This innovative program teaches students how to install and maintain solar paneling on residential and commercial structures.

Green Jobs for a New Economy

A 1-kilowatt solar panel array is installed outside the Technology Building. The array, including its controlling electronics, is an educational aid for Cleveland State tech classes and was installed to tie directly to the Cleveland Utilities electric grid to help CU and TVA generate "green power."

Green Campus Organizations

Sustainability Committee: Formed in fall 2008; set up recycling program.

It'$ All About the Green!: One-day campus event celebrating environmental awareness on Earth Day 2009; presentations and exhibits by local vendors and college departments on ways to improve the environment as well as own lives and the community.

Arbor Day Celebration: Held in March at the state-certified arboretum on campus; includes walk led by Cleveland's city forester.

Undergraduate Degrees

Associate of Applied Science degree with
    Construction Technology Concentration
Biology (includes courses in Environmental
    Science) (AAS)
Wildlife Management (AAS)

Certificates:

Climate Control Technology
Construction Technology
Workforce Preparedness Technology
Zero Energy Housing

CROWDER COLLEGE

601 Laclede
Neosho, Missouri 64850
417-451-3223
E-mail: admissions@crowder.edu
www.crowder.edu

Fast Facts

In 1984, Crowder students designed and built the first solar-powered vehicle to successfully complete a coast-to-coast journey across the United States.

Crowder's Solar House entry in the Solar Decathlon in Washington, DC, was selected as the "People's Choice" and placed 6th overall in the competition.

Green Campus Organizations

Sustainable Practices Club
Solar Vehicle Club

Undergraduate Degrees

Alternative Energy (AA)
Environmental Science (AA)
Pre-Engineering, Alternative Energy Option (AS)

Certificate:

Environmental Health Technology

CUYAHOGA COMMUNITY COLLEGE

700 Carnegie Avenue
Cleveland, Ohio 44115
800-954-8742 (toll-free)
E-mail: CustomerService@tri-c.edu
www.tri-c.edu

Fast Facts

Tri-C is Ohio's oldest and largest public community college, opening in 1963.

Green Campus Organizations

The Green Academy and Center for Sustainability @ Tri-C trains individuals in the principles of sustainability, green construction, green interior design, green business development, sustainable investing, and more. Classes, seminars, and certifications are offered. Campus initiatives include CFL light bulb exchange, Eco-Lounge, waste audit, green newsletter, and green office audit.

Undergraduate Degrees

Environmental Health and Safety Technology (AAS)
Plant Science and Landscape Technology (AAS)

Certificates:

Environmental Health & Safety Technology
Landscape Technician

EDMONDS COMMUNITY COLLEGE

20000 68th Ave West
Lynnwood, Washington 98036
425-640-1459
E-mail: info@edcc.edu
www.edcc.edu

Fast Facts

Alternative Transportation Contest: Held in April/May; weekly prize awarded to students trying something that lessens their impact on the planet.

April Is Earth/Sustainability Month: Variety of activities: speakers, Sustainability Curriculum Showcase, Earth Day Fair, Bike to Work/School Day.

Campus Tree Walk: Over seventy species of trees have been identified on the 50-acre campus, and the horticulture department has developed a map to help students and the community learn about and understand how trees benefit the environment and improve the quality of life. The walk was developed with a Community Forestry Assistance Grant provided by the Washington State Department of Natural Resources with support from the U.S. Department of Agriculture Forest Service.

Green Campus Organizations

The Learn-and-Serve Environmental Anthropology Field (LEAF) School provides an opportunity for students to earn academic credit and an AmeriCorps scholarship while working collaboratively with local tribes, governments, nonprofits, and businesses to help make fishing, farming, and forestry more sustainable. Financial aid for this program is available through AmeriCorps awards or from the Edmonds Community College Foundation.

About IKEA

Looking for a job with an environmentally responsible company? Check out IKEA. It buys wood products only from responsibly managed forests and bans harmful substances from its merchandise. Beginning in 2009, it will sell only solar-powered outdoor electric lights.

S.A.V.E. the Earth Club (Student Association for a Viable Environment).

Sustainability Council: Composed of faculty members, administrators, staff members, and students.

Recycling Program: Headed by grounds department with student assistance.

Undergraduate Degrees

Energy Management (AS)
Environmental Science (AS)
Geology (AS)
Occupational Safety and Health (Transfer, AAS)
Restoration Horticulture (ATA)

FOX VALLEY TECHNICAL COLLEGE

P.O. Box 2277
Appleton, Wisconsin 54912-2277
www.fvtc.edu

Fast Facts

FVTC is a member of the Association for Advancement of Sustainability in Higher Education to promote the message of sustainability among its campus communities.

As part of the sixteen-member Wisconsin Technical College System, FVTC is part of the newly launched Regional Industry Skills Education (RISE) program, financed with economic stimulus money. The program's goal is "to connect worker education to student and employer needs" in a career pathways model.

Green Campus Organizations

Natural Resources Club: Provides educational experiences to Natural Resources majors and outreach to the community and school district to promote the conservation ethic and the principles of ecology/natural resources.

Undergraduate Degree

Natural Resources Technician (AS)

GREAT BASIN COLLEGE

1500 College Parkway
Elko, Nevada 89801
775-738-8493
E-mail: stdsvc@gbcnv.edu
www.gbcnv.edu

Fast Facts

The new AAS degree program in industrial energy efficiency is a distance learning program and combines courses from existing HVAC, construction technology, and electrical systems and millwright technology programs.

Green Campus Organizations

Electrical Systems Technology program has constructed an electric car that is solar-power rechargeable.

Undergraduate Degrees

Agriculture (AAS)
Agriculture (AS)
Industrial Energy Efficiency (AAS)

GBC also grants a limited number of bachelor's degrees. Those related to "green industries" include a BA in Integrative Studies with a Resource Management concentration, a BAS in Agriculture Management, and a BAS in Land Surveying/Geomatics.

HUDSON VALLEY COMMUNITY COLLEGE

80 Vandenburgh Avenue
Troy, New York 12180
518-629-HVCC
877-325-HVCC (toll-free)
E-mail: input@hvcc.edu
www.hvcc.edu

Fast Facts

Hudson Valley Community College's Workforce Development Institute was one of the hosts and led the educational sessions for the first Northeast Green Building Conference, the leading "green" building educational event in upstate New York. New York State is the first state to register for LEED certification for the governor's residence as part of the "Greening the Executive Mansion" initiative.

HVCC's Workforce Development Institute includes the Center for Energy Efficiency & Building Science, which provides ongoing training on incorporating energy efficiency methods into the building trades.

Green Campus Organizations

Adventure Club: Involved in outdoor activities.

Air Conditioning Club: Student branch of the American Society of Heating, Refrigeration and Air Conditioning Engineers (ASHRAE).

Animal Outreach Club: Fund-raising efforts include "Empties for Animals" that collects empty bottles and cans and donates the proceeds to the local Humane Society.

Environmental Club: Promotes and practices responsible use of the Earth's natural resources on campus and in the community; educates and encourages participation in conserving, improving, and enjoying the natural world.

Hudson Valley Community College Builders Club: Student chapter of the National Association of Home Builders (NAHB).

Undergraduate Degrees

Architectural Technology (AAS)

Environmental Science (AS)

Certificates:

Photovoltaic Installation Certificate

Refrigeration and Air Conditioning Certificate

IOWA LAKES COMMUNITY COLLEGE

3200 College Drive

Emmetsburg, Iowa 50536

712-362-2604

800-521-5054 (toll-free)

E-mail: info@iowalakes.edu

www.iowalakes.edu

Fast Facts

Students in the Land and Turfgrass Technology program get hands-on experience on the college-owned, irrigated 330-yard fairway with PGA specification green, a native green, and a 300-yard driving range.

The Wind Energy and Turbine Technology program is the first in Iowa and has been in existence since 2004. The college owns and operates a V-82 turbine located about a half-mile south of the campus in Estherville. Power generated there is sold to the city of Estherville with proceeds used to offset the energy consumed by the college. Students learn maintenance activities as well as equipment operation and safety practices.

Green Campus Organizations

Landscape and Turfgrass Club: Community projects to promote and educate; money-making projects such as aerating yards, laying sod, and landscaping.

Wind Energy Club: Promotes to and educates public about wind energy and the ILCC program.

Conservation Club: Projects include an extensive prairie restoration project at Fort Defiance State Park, participation in the Iowa Adopt-A-Highway program, tree-planting project for the Estherville city park system, various projects for local county conservation boards and the Iowa Department of Natural Resources.

Undergraduate Degrees

Biorenewable Fuels Technology (AAS)

Environmental Studies (AS)

Land and Turfgrass Technician (AAS)

Sustainable Energy Resource Management (AS)

Wind Energy and Turbine Technology (AAS)

Certificates and Diplomas:

Biorenewable Fuels Technology Certificate

Land and Turfgrass Technology Diploma

Sustainable Energy Resource Management
    Certificate

Wind Energy and Turbine Technology Diploma

KANKAKEE COMMUNITY COLLEGE

100 College Drive

Kankakee, Illinois 60901

815-802-8100

E-mail: www.kcc.edu/Pages/ContactUs.aspx

www.kcc.edu

Fast Facts

As part of Sustainability Week, the Solar Globe Art Project was featured. The globe uses light and dark orange to depict energy use throughout the world. Solar panels mounted on the globe collect solar energy, which is stored and used at night to power the lights that represent the energy use of major cities.

Green Campus Organizations

Campus Sustainability Committee: Projects include campus recycling, auditing energy consumption, curriculum and course development, Sustainability Week, dissemination of information.

Undergraduate Degrees

Agriculture (AS)

Biological Sciences (AS)

Horticulture (AAS)
Renewable Energy Technology (AAS)

LAKESHORE TECHNICAL COLLEGE

1290 North Avenue
Cleveland, Wisconsin 53015
920-693-1000
888-468-6582 (toll-free)
E-mail: info@gotoltc.edu
www.gotoltc.edu

Fast Facts

LTC constructed a grid-tied small commercial wind turbine on campus in 2004. It takes advantage of the campus' location along the windy shoreline of Lake Michigan and supplies nearly 3 percent of the campus' electrical energy. The turbine is used for technical training, workshops, seminars, and courses on renewable energy resources. LTC received a grant from Focus on Energy to help construct the wind turbine.

LTC received the 2005 Innovation Award from the Interstate Renewable Energy Council for its Wind Energy Demonstration Site.

Green Campus Organizations

RecycleMania: Participated in the benchmarking division for 2009 competition.

Undergraduate Degrees

Nuclear Technology (AAS)
Wind Energy Technology (AAS)

Undergraduate Distance Learning

Nuclear Technology with Radiation Safety
   Concentration (AAS)

Online Certificate:

Radiation Safety Technician

LANE COMMUNITY COLLEGE

4000 East 30th Avenue
Eugene, Oregon 97405
541-463-3100
E-mail: haywardj@lanecc.edu
www.lanecc.edu

Fast Facts

Lane received a $100,000 grant from EWEB to build a solar-powered electric vehicle charging station for use by students and community.

In 2008, Lane hosted the first Conference on Sustainability for Community Colleges. Forty-seven colleges and organizations from sixteen states attended.

Lane has set a goal of becoming carbon-neutral by 2050 and has established benchmarks and mechanisms for tracking progress and impact of efforts.

Northwest Energy Education Institute is located at Lane and provides energy- and building-related continuing education across the United States.

Green Campus Organizations

RecycleMania: Thirteenth place in the Waste Minimization Category in 2009; second year of competition and improved by 37 percent over previous year's cumulative waste-per-person figure.

Green Chemistry Club: Currently building a biodiesel processor that will be used to turn waste grease from the campus kitchen into fuel for campus boilers and vehicles.

Oregon Student Public Interest Research Group (OSPIRG) chapter.

Learning Garden Club: Oversees all aspects of Lane's organic learning garden; provides practical hands-on experience in sustainable local food production.

Sustainability Group: Committee of Lane staff and student volunteers who work together on sustainability issues; initiatives include recycling, reuse, composting, using organic and local foods, energy conservation, water conservation.

Undergraduate Degrees

Energy Management Technician (AAS)
Renewable Energy Technology (AAS)
Water Conservation Technician (AAS)

Sustainability Continuing Education Classes include Introduction to Permaculture and Gardening and Organic Gardening Principles and Practice.

LANSING COMMUNITY COLLEGE

P.O. Box 40010
Lansing, Michigan 48901
517-483-1957
800-644-4522 (toll-free)
E-mail: wilso23@lcc.edu
www.lcc.edu

Fast Facts

LCC is one of the nation's first colleges to incorporate alternative energy into its curricula and its sustainable practices on campus.

LCC's West Campus is heated and cooled by a geothermal system, which is seeking LEED certification. The college also has a small solar array and wind turbine on campus.

Automotive technology students work on hybrid vehicles and are building an internal combustion engine powered by a fuel cell.

Green Campus Organizations

Sustainability Committee

"Spring Fling Goes Green" annual event: Sponsors a dumpster-diving competition.

Undergraduate Degrees

Advanced Technology Vehicles (AAS)
Alternative Energy Technology (AAS)
Energy Management Technology (AAS)
Geographic Information Systems and Geospatial Technology (AAS)
Heating and Air Conditioning (AAS)

Horticulture (AAS)
Precision Agriculture (AAS)

Certificates:

Advanced Technology Vehicles
Alternative Energy Engineering Technology
Energy Efficiency Technician
Geographic Information Systems
Geothermal Technician
Precision Agriculture
Solar Energy Technician
Sustainability
Wind Turbine Technician

LONG BEACH CITY COLLEGE

Long Beach, California 90808-1706
www.lbcc.edu

Fast Facts

LBCC's Advanced Transportation Technology Center provides courses in alternate fuels, such as compressed natural gas, liquefied natural gas, and propane, and in automotive technologies, such as hydrogen fuel cells, hybrids, and electric vehicles.

Green Campus Organizations

Eco-Terra: Promotes environmental issues, participates in political action campaigns, and runs outdoor field trips.

Undergraduate Degrees

Advanced Transportation Technology, Alternate Fuels (AS)
Advanced Transportation Technology, Electric Vehicles (AS)

Certificates:

Advanced Transportation Technology, Alternate Fuels
Advanced Transportation Technology, Electric Vehicles

About Air Quality Standards

In 2007, California became the first state to require that the construction industry retrofit heavy equipment to cut down on toxic fumes from diesel engines.

LOS ANGELES TRADE-TECHNICAL COLLEGE

400 West Washington Boulevard
Los Angeles, California 90015-4108
213-763-7000
E-mail: McintoMF@lattc.edu
www.lattc.edu

Fast Facts

In May 2008, the college established the Sustainable Energy Center, a dedicated lab for courses, activities, and programs related to renewable energy and energy efficiency technologies.

Diesel instructor and students in the alternative fuels course were featured in the ABC news feature story "Going Green to Make Green" aired on the show *Focus Earth* with Bob Woodward.

Green Campus Organizations

Culinary Arts Department: Recycling of used vegetable oil for biodiesel fuel.

Electronics Department: Computer recycling program.

Building Green/Building Healthy: As part of commitment to sustainable principles, four major building initiatives underway to obtain LEED certification.

Green Business Certification Project: The automotive and technology department is operating a pilot program to bring its practices into compliance with the standards of a certified green business. Plans are in place to implement the program in all departments.

Undergraduate Degrees

Chemical Technology (AAS)
Supply Water Technology (AAS)
Wastewater Technology (AAS)

Certificates:

Chemical Technology
Process Technology Skills Certificate
Solid Waste Management Technology

MESALANDS COMMUNITY COLLEGE

911 South Tenth Street
Tucumcari, New Mexico 88401
575-461-4413
E-mail: jarredp@mesalands.edu
www.mesalands.edu

Fast Facts

Mesalands is home to the North American Wind Research and Training Center.

Mesalands installed a GE 1.5-megawatt wind turbine in 2008. It is the latest cutting-edge ESS model.

Undergraduate Degree

Wind Energy Technology (AAS)

Certificate:

Wind Energy Technology

MOUNT WACHUSETT COMMUNITY COLLEGE

444 Green Street
Gardner, Massachusetts 01440
978-632-6600
E-mail: admissions@mwcc.mass.edu
www.mwcc.edu

Fast Facts

In 2007, Mount Wachusett Community College was named the winner of the National Wildlife Federation's Campus Ecology Chill-Out Contest. The competition recognizes institutions of higher education that are implementing innovative programs to reduce the impacts of global warming.

Mount Wachusett converted its all-electric main campus to a biomass heating system, using wood chips as fuel. The system saves the college an estimated $300,000 a year.

Undergraduate Degrees

Energy Management (A)
Natural Resources Degree (A)

Certificate:

Energy Management

RED ROCKS COMMUNITY COLLEGE

13300 West Sixth Avenue
Lakewood, Colorado 80228
303-914-6600
E-mail: admissions@rrcc.edu
www.rrcc.edu

Fast Facts

RRCC was honored with the 2008 Governor's Excellence in Renewable Energy Award. RRCC's Energy Technology Program grew from 10 students in fall 2007 to 231 students by spring 2009.

The Environmental Training Center at RRCC is one of only twelve centers in the country where students can acquire the knowledge and skills needed to develop a career in environmental technology. The center is also the home of the only Water Quality Management Technology degree program in Colorado.

Green Campus Organizations

RRCC Campus Green Initiative Club: Reduce, reuse, recycle.

Undergraduate Degrees

Electro-Mechanical Industrial Maintenance (AAS)
Environmental Technology (AAS)
Industrial Maintenance Technology, Electrical (AAS)
Industrial Maintenance Technology, Mechanical (AAS)
Process Technology, Energy Operations (AAS)
Renewable Energy Technology: Solar Photovoltaic Specialty (AAS)
Renewable Energy Technology: Solar PV Business Owner Specialty (AAS)
Renewable Energy Technology: Solar Thermal Business Owner Specialty (AAS)
Renewable Energy Technology: Solar Thermal Specialty (AAS)
Wind Energy Technology (AAS)

Certificates:

Advanced PV Installation
Codes and Standards
Commercial and Industrial Heating and Cooling
Electro-Mechanical Technician
Energy Efficiency–Energy Auditing
Environmental Compliance Operations
Environmental Pre-Engineering
Environmental Safety Systems
Grid Tie, Entry Level
Industrial Electrical Technician
Industrial Maintenance Technology
Introduction to Air Compliance
Introduction to Process Equipment
Introduction to Process Plant Instrumentation
Introduction to Process Plant Operations
Introduction to Process Plant Quality Management
Introduction to Process Plant Safety
Introduction to Soil Compliance
Introduction to Water Compliance
Introduction to Wind Energy Technology
Low-Voltage Technician
Post EIC Degree Solar Photovoltaic Specialty
Post HVA Degree Solar Thermal Specialty
Solar PV Designer
Solar Thermal Designer
Solar Thermal Entry Level
Solar Thermal Installer
Wind Energy, Advanced Electrical
Wind Energy, Advanced Mechanical
Wind Energy, Basic Electro-Mechanical
Wind Energy Safety

SANTA FE COMMUNITY COLLEGE

6401 Richards Avenue
Santa Fe, New Mexico 87508-4887
505-428-1000
E-mail: info@sfccnm.edu
www.sfccnm.edu

Fast Facts

The new Health and Sciences Building, begun in early 2009, is expected to meet or exceed LEED Silver standards.

The SFCC Technologies Sustainability Center incorporates twenty-first-century trades with advanced technologies and "green" curricula to promote a sustainable economy. A new facility is slated for construction in 2010 and will provide space for credit and noncredit courses as well as for workforce development programs.

Campus electricity is being generated by a grid-tied solar photovoltaic system. Solar thermal collectors heat the campus swimming pool.

Students in the Principles of Accounting classes completed a campuswide survey and calculations for a profile of campus energy usage and carbon footprint as benchmarks for efforts at energy efficiency and reduction of carbon emissions.

SFCC was awarded over $500,000 in grant money for the 2009–10 academic year for its green initiatives. The money is targeted to scholarships, curriculum development, a bio-fuels program, and training at-risk youth in green technologies.

Green Campus Organizations

Student Environmental Education Development (SEED): Campuswide recycling program, low-consumption lighting, recycling wastewater for campus irrigation, filtered water available to reduce plastic bottle usage, use of recycled copier paper.

Undergraduate Degrees

Environmental Technologies, Solar Energy (AAS)
Environmental Technologies, Water Conservation (AAS)

Certificates:

Environmental Technology
Green Building Systems
Solar Energy

About Recycling Clothes

In 2005, Patagonia launched Common Threads Garment Recycling for its used Capilene® Performance Baselayers, Patagonia® fleece clothing, Polartec® fleece clothing, Patagonia cotton T-shirts, and other Patagonia clothing with the Common Threads tag. The goal is to reduce the use of new polyester fabrics and, thus, use less oil each year. To learn more, check out www.patagonia.com.

ST PETERSBURG COLLEGE

P.O. Box 13489
St. Petersburg, Florida 33733-3489
727-341-4772
E-mail: information@spcollege.edu
www.spcollege.edu

Fast Facts

SPC is developing a Natural Habitat Park and Environmental Center on the Seminole Campus that will serve as an educational, environmental, and passive recreational "green zone" for use by SPC students, faculty and staff members, and the larger community.

The Biology AS degree includes course work in tropical ecology.

Green Campus Organizations

Sustainability Club: Coordinates the recycle program as well as participates in community events; plans and coordinates educational environmental activities on campus.

Adopt a Highway: SPC chapter of Phi Theta Kappa; adopted a portion of 113th Street North and periodically removes litter and debris.

Adopt a Shore: Sustainability Club project.

Undergraduate Degrees

Architectural Design (AS)
Construction Technology (AS)
Environmental Science Technology, Environmental Resources/Energy Management (AS)
Environmental Science Technology, Sustainability (AS)

Environmental Science Technology, Water
   Resource Management (AS)
Sustainability Management (BAS)

TIDEWATER COMMUNITY COLLEGE

P.O. Box 9000
Norfolk, Virginia 23509
757-822-1122
800-371-0898 (toll-free)
E-mail: tccinfo@tcc.edu
www.tcc.edu

Fast Facts

The 23rd highest producer of associate degrees in the nation, and the 35th largest community college, TCC is among the twenty fastest-growing, large, two-year institutions in the United States.

TCC celebrates Earth Day Week with its "Living Green Expo" to help educate the community on opportunities to incorporate green into daily work and life.

The Chesapeake Campus received status as an Audubon Sanctuary, the only school to hold that status in the state. The Sanctuary is used as an outdoor classroom for many disciplines at the college.

TCC owns a reconditioned Navy Swift boat, the research vessel *Matthew F. Maury,* which is used by the college for its Coastal Studies program and to do community outreach to surrounding K–12 schools.

Green Campus Organizations

Engineering Club: In 1999 and 2000, placed first in the American Society for Engineering Education (ASEE) Battery-Powered Car Competition; involved since 1997 in the CANstruction design/build competition with cans of food that are then contributed to food banks.

Geology Club and Oceanography Club: Draws members from the Coastal Studies Program; there are educational activities and field trips.

Undergraduate Degrees

Engineering (Environmental Engineering focus) (AS)
Interior Design (AAS)
Science, Geophysical concentration (AS)

Certificate:

Green Design

WAKE TECHNICAL COMMUNITY COLLEGE

9101 Fayetteville Road
Raleigh, North Carolina 27603
919-866-5500
E-mail: admissions.waketech.edu/
   askanadvisor.php
www.waketech.edu

Fast Facts

Wake Tech's Northern Wake Campus, opened in 2007, is the first campus in North Carolina and one of the first in the nation to be completely LEED certified.

Wake Tech developed a Long-Term Water Efficiency Plan in 2006. It recognizes utility conservation, water conservation, water quality management, resource management, and sustainability efforts as the responsibility of everyone at Wake Tech—faculty members, staff members, and students.

Green Campus Organizations

Architecture Club
Design and Garden Club
Students for Environmental Education Club

Undergraduate Degrees

Architectural Technology (AAS)
Environmental Science Technology (AAS)
Landscape Architecture Technology (AAS)

Union Organizations with Great Green Programs

INTERNATIONAL ASSOCIATION OF BRIDGE, STRUCTURAL, ORNAMENTAL AND REINFORCING IRON WORKERS (IRON WORKERS)

1750 New York Avenue, NW, Suite 400
Washington, DC 20006
202-383-480
E-mail: iwmagazine@iwintl.org
www.ironworkers.org

About the Union

The union's Department of Apprenticeship and Training and the National Training Fund oversee, coordinate, and manage the education and training programs that range from the basic to the very advanced. The goal is to ensure that members receive comprehensive and effective education and training that will enable them to carry out their work safely and efficiently and with the highest standards of quality.

Programs and Training

Apprenticeship Programs

Apprentices are required to sign an indenture agreement with their Joint Apprenticeship Committee/Trade Improvement Committee that spells out the requirements and expectations of an apprentice ironworker. Most ironworker apprenticeships last three or four years depending on the requirements of the local union. An ideal schedule provides equal training in structural, reinforcing, ornamental, welding, and rigging. The actual length of training for each subject may vary depending on the predominant type of work available in the local area.

Apprentices are required to receive at least 204 hours of classroom and shop instruction during each year of training. The subjects taken in the

About Green Initiatives

The Iron Workers are an affiliate of the Building and Construction Trades Department (BCTD) of the AFL-CIO. The BCTD is partnering with the Green Jobs Center of the AFL-CIO to help the more than 1,100 affiliate training programs incorporate the skills needed for the new green economy.

shop and classroom components complement the hands-on training received in the field. Subjects include blueprint reading, care and safe use of tools, mathematics, safety issues, welding, and oxy-acetylene flame cutting.

Apprentices receive an evaluation about every six months to determine if they are learning the craft. If the on-the-job or school work is not satisfactory, they may be dropped from the program or sent back to repeat that segment. If, however, their work is satisfactory, they will receive a pay raise.

Additional Training Options

Beyond the apprenticeship program, additional training options exist. Apprenticeship training in the ironworking trade can be applied toward college credit. A worker can earn as many as 65 credits toward a college degree. An associate degree can be completed online through Ivy Tech Community College of Indiana. A bachelor's degree can be completed online through the National Labor College.

Journeyman upgrade classes (available through the local union and contractors) provide opportunities to continually increase skills and keep up with the new technologies being introduced into the industry.

INTERNATIONAL BROTHERHOOD OF ELECTRICAL WORKERS (IBEW)

900 Seventh Street, NW
Washington, DC 20001
202-833-7000
www.ibew.org

About the Union

The National Joint Apprenticeship and Training Committee (NJATC) of the National Electrical Contractors Association (NECA) and the International Brotherhood of Electrical Workers (IBEW) operate programs for apprentice and journeyman electricians. The programs are privately funded, and most apprenticeship programs last five years. The NJATC developed uniform standards that have been adopted and used nationwide to select and train thousands of qualified men and women annually.

Programs and Training

Through the NJATC, the IBEW and NECA sponsor hundreds of local programs offering apprenticeship and training in the following areas:

Journeyman Tree Trimmer

Residential Wireman: Specializes in installing the electrical systems in single-family and multi-family homes.

Outside Lineman: Installs the distribution and transmission lines that move power from power plants to buildings and homes.

Inside Wireman: Installs the power, lighting, controls, and other electrical equipment in commercial and industrial buildings.

Telecommunication VDV Installer-Technician: Installs circuits and equipment for telephones, computer networks, video distribution systems, security and access control systems, and other low-voltage systems.

INTERNATIONAL UNION OF OPERATING ENGINEERS (IUOE)

1125 17th Street, NW
Washington, DC 20036
202-429-9100
www.iuoe.org

About the Union

The union consists of two broad job classifications: operating engineers and stationary engineers. Operating engineers do the heavy lifting and are often referred to as hoisting and portable engineers because the equipment they control lifts and/or moves. Stationary engineers operate, maintain, renovate, and repair mechanical systems in a facility. For example, in the wind-turbine industry, operating engineers run the cranes that put the turbines and towers in place. Stationary engineers are in charge of continuing operations, maintenance, and repair.

Programs and Training

Operating Engineer

IUOE locals provide training programs nationwide, and most are registered with the state or federal apprenticeship agency. Apprentices are paid while they work and learn. Apprentices work with skilled journey-level operators on actual job sites as well as attend related classroom instruction and field training. The average length of an operating engineer apprenticeship is three to four years.

After completing an apprenticeship, many journey workers take additional classes offered by their locals. Continued training upgrades skills, making union members more employable, and also helps them move into management and supervisory jobs. Certification is conducted by outside groups. For example, crane operators are tested by the

---

About the IBEW's Commitment to Going Green

In May 2009, the IBEW's apprenticeship and training committee launched a new green jobs training curriculum. According to the IBEW, the program is being "woven into the . . . apprenticeship training and will serve as a resource of journeymen looking to upgrade their skills in the growing green market." The seventy-five program lessons include topics such as green building fundamentals and automated building operation.

About Green Jobs for Operating Engineers

Operating Engineers are essential in the construction of wind farms. This is a major growth initiative, especially in the corridor of the Texas–Oklahoma Panhandle, western Oklahoma, and along the corridor north to the Canadian border.

National Commission for the Certification of Crane Operators (NCCCO).

Stationary Engineer

IUOE stationary local unions provide skill-development training programs for apprentices and journey-level engineers. The programs are jointly sponsored by IUOE local unions and the employers who hire stationary engineers.

The average length of an apprenticeship is four years. During this period, apprentices learn their craft by working with skilled stationary engineers at an actual workplace and also attend related classroom instruction. Apprentice training may also be supplemented by course work at trade or technical schools. Training is critical for preparing apprentices to take the test for the stationary engineer license, which is required by most states.

Employers often encourage journey-level stationary engineers to continue their education. Many IUOE locals offer free training to members to help them broaden and update their skills and improve their employability. Because of the increasing complexity of the equipment, many stationary engineers also take college courses.

LABORERS' INTERNATIONAL UNION OF NORTH AMERICA (LIUNA)

905 16th Street, NW
Washington, DC 20006
202-737-8320

About the Union

LIUNA members build and repair roads, highways, bridges, and tunnels; construct residential and commercial buildings; clean up hazardous waste sites; drill and blast sites; build scaffolds; prepare and clean up job sites; lay pipe underground; pour concrete; flag and control traffic on highways; and remove asbestos and lead from buildings.

Programs and Training

LIUNA training is available in every state in the United States and every province in Canada. Among the fifty courses that are offered are hazardous materials remediation, remote tunneling, concrete work, and a variety of building construction skills. Apprenticeship training consists of a minimum of 288 hours of classroom training. These skills are practiced with a skilled journey worker for 4,000 hours of on-the-job training.

SERVICE EMPLOYEES INTERNATIONAL UNION (SEIU)

1800 Massachusetts Ave, NW
Washington, DC 20036
202-730-7000
800-424-8592 (toll-free)
www.seiu.org

About the Union

The Service Employees International Union is the largest and the fastest-growing union in the nation, reflecting the changing nature of the U.S. economy from manufacturing to service. The union represents workers in three key service sectors: health-care, public service, and property services. Health-care union members include registered

About a Green Jobs Pilot and LIUNA

A green-collar job initiative between LIUNA and the state of New Jersey was launched in January 2009. Its first training class of 22 graduated in April 2009 in Newark. They had previously been unemployed or underemployed. The program trained them to work in green construction and in retrofitting existing buildings. A similar program was launched in June 2009 in Trenton.

nurses, licensed practical nurses, doctors, lab technicians, nursing home workers, and home health-care workers. Union members in the public service sector include local and state government workers, public school employees, bus drivers, and child-care providers. Workers who protect and clean commercial and residential office buildings, private security officers, and public safety personnel make up the membership of the property services sector. Membership depends on whether a job site is organized.

Programs and Training

Environmental Labor-Management Committees are involved in many green initiatives. Green initiatives, which are part of contract negotiations, include the use of green cleaning products, healthier health-care practices, and recycling.

SEIU Green Training Initiative

The following summary is provided by James Barry, Manager of Program Development, Building Service 32BJ, Thomas Shortman Training Program.

SEIU Local 32BJ in New York City is the largest building service workers union in the country, representing more than 100,000 cleaners, doormen, porters, maintenance workers, superintendents, resident managers, window cleaners, and security guards. The Building Service 32BJ Thomas Shortman Training Program (TSTP), founded in 1971, is a nonprofit education fund supported primarily by contributions from participating employers. Every year, the program provides industry,

academic, and computer courses to thousands of Local 32BJ building service workers at over twenty locations in New York, New Jersey, Connecticut, Pennsylvania, the District of Columbia, and Maryland.

Since 2005, the Shortman program has worked with the New York State Energy Research and Development Authority (NYSERDA) and other partners to offer a wide range of training focusing on existing buildings. The major program is an eleven-session green building review that includes basic instruction on green building concepts, energy and water efficiency, building controls, and green cleaning supplies as well as two building tours: an energy audit of a typical residential building and a tour of a LEED-certified green building.

The Shortman program has also launched a lighting retrofitting workshop, provided a recycling seminar, hosted a LEED-Existing Building (EB) Technical Review and worked with The Center for Sustainable Energy to prepare several 32BJ instructors for the Building Performance Institute's (BPI) Building Analyst Certification.

During the next year, 32BJ plans to expand its training to give workers a deeper understanding of the connection between their jobs and the environment. The local will offer a second green building course, prepare students for a series of new trades-oriented U.S. Green Building Council certifications, and launch a Green Diploma Program. This diploma program will offer an educational track for those who wish to work in green buildings or make improvements in the buildings where they currently work. Workers will learn how to run a building efficiently, use cleaning supplies and materials that have a low impact on indoor air quality, reduce waste, and recycle effectively in their buildings.

UNITED ASSOCIATION OF JOURNEYMEN AND APPRENTICES OF THE PLUMBING AND PIPEFITTING INDUSTRY OF THE UNITED STATES AND CANADA (UA)

Three Park Place
Annapolis, Maryland 21401
410-269-2000
E-mail: http://www.ua.org/contact.asp
www.ua.org

About the Union

The UA has a variety of apprenticeship and training programs, as well as delivery methods, which are coordinated through its Sustainable Technologies Department. This department is responsible for all the activities, training, and outreach for sustainable technologies in the plumbing and pipefitting industry.

Programs and Training

5-Star Service Training Program

This apprenticeship program teaches the core skills of plumbing, pipefitting, sprinkler fitting, or HVAC/R services along with basic mathematics, safety, and customer service skills. On-the-job training is combined with classroom training in this five-year program. Apprentices earn while learning.

At the completion of the program, the apprentice has 32 college credits toward an Associate in Applied Science (AAS) degree and is a UA STAR certified technician. The college credits can be transferred to a local community college or the UA's College On Demand Degree program in partnership with Washtenaw Community College in Ann Arbor, Michigan. College On Demand is a distance-learning program that delivers text, Web-based materials, and classroom lectures on DVD for self-paced study. Graduates earn an AAS degree in Sustainable Technology with a choice of majoring in HVAC/R, plumbing, sprinkler fitting, or construction supervision.

Green Systems Awareness Certificate

The UA offers a Green Systems Awareness Certificate. It requires a 16- to 20-hour course and a written exam, administered by a third-party certification group. The U.S. Green Building Council recognizes the UA as a certified training provider.

Partnership in Environmental Leadership

The Partnership in Environmental Leadership provides less formal training in sustainable mechanical service and construction, and "new building system technologies that promote greater energy efficiency, use fewer natural resources, have minimal impact on the environment, and use materials that can be reused or recycled." The program is a collaboration of the UA, Mechanical Contractors Association of America (MCAA), Mechanical Service Contractors of America (MSCA), Plumbing Contractors of America (PCA), United States Green Building Council (USGBC), and Green Mechanical Council.

Training is delivered through the Green Trailer and the Sustainable Technology Demonstration Trailer. Both are mobile units that travel from local to local. The Green Trailer provides trainers and simulators. The trailer drives to a site, the sides go up, the chairs come out, and the training begins. Topics include the latest environmental systems: fuel cell technologies, wind power generation, solar heating system, solar photovoltaic system, grey water toilet flushing system, anaerobic treatment process, infiltration demonstrator, geothermal system trainer, gas-fired warm air heating demonstrator, 1/8 GPF urinal, high-efficiency toilet, and water-saving toilet.

The Sustainable Technology Demonstration Trailer is the newest mobile unit used for outreach and training. While the Green Trailer provides simulators, the Sustainable Technology Demonstration Trailer contains working systems in the latest green technologies, including, among other items, a geothermal heat pump that feeds the radiant heating and cooling systems used in the trailer.

UNITED STEEL, PAPER AND FORESTRY, RUBBER, MANUFACTURING, ENERGY, ALLIED INDUSTRIAL & SERVICE WORKERS INTERNATIONAL UNION (USW) (STEELWORKERS)

Five Gateway Center
Pittsburgh, Pennsylvania 15222
412-562-2400
www.usw.org

About the Union

The Institute for Career Development (ICD), headquartered in Merrillville, Indiana, develops and offers workforce training programs for the United Steelworkers Union. The ICD was created in 1989 as a result of contract negotiations between the USW and major steel companies. Since then, ICD has expanded to include training programs for the employees of rubber companies.

Programs and Training

ICD is a joint initiative between labor and management. The emphasis is on teaching "portable" skills that workers can use in their current careers or take with them to new careers. Most classes are taught in learning centers in or near the plants or in the union halls and are offered before and after shift changes.

Union members may also take other courses, such as those offered by community colleges, through a tuition assistance program. Each worker may receive up to $1800 annually for tuition, books, and fees at accredited institutions. The program is paid for by a fund created as a result of contract negotiations in 1989 between the USW and participating companies. Companies pay a certain

> **About Manufacturing for the Green Economy**
>
> Spain's Gamesa Corporation has located its first U.S. manufacturing plant for wind turbines in Pennsylvania. Gamesa is one of the largest makers of wind turbines in the world and is the only major wind turbine manufacturer that produces its blades, nacelles, and towers in the United States. Tax incentives and the adoption of a Renewable Portfolio Standard (RPS), coordinated efforts by Governor Edward Rendell, Pennsylvania's Environmental Secretary Kathleen McGinty, the State Legislature, the Apollo Alliance, and the USW, made possible Gamesa's investment in new manufacturing jobs in Pennsylvania.

amount into the fund for each hour worked by a steelworker.

NATIONAL LABOR COLLEGE (NLC)

10000 New Hampshire Avenue
Silver Spring, Maryland 20903
301-431-6400
800-462-4237 (toll-free)
www.nlc.edu

About the College

The National Labor College was originally founded in 1969 by the AFL-CIO as a labor studies center. In 1974, the center moved to its present site and began offering undergraduate degrees through a partnership with Antioch College. In 1997, the center was granted the authority to confer undergraduate degrees and was renamed the National Labor College. It offers certificate programs as well as degree programs and is "the nation's only accredited higher education institution devoted exclusively to educating union leaders, members, and activists."

Programs and Training

The NLC offers a green workplace representative certificate program, which is part of the

AFL-CIO's Center for Green Jobs (CGJ) initiative. "This certificate program will provide education that empowers workers to become change agents, working to advance sustainability values and practices that meet the mutual interests of worker and managers, as well as enhance the competitiveness of American firms in the global economy," said Tom Kriger, NLC provost, when the program was announced. "The NLC is also exploring other curricula related to labor and climate change."

PARTNERSHIPS FOR GREEN JOBS

In addition to providing training and apprenticeship programs, labor unions have been active in lobbying for and supporting the growth of green jobs. Their influence was evident in passage of the economic stimulus package in 2009. While working to help their members adapt to the changing economy, union leaders also recognize their responsibility to the environment. The following two alliances, which bring together union leaders with environmentalists and business leaders, are examples on the national level of these partnerships.

Apollo Alliance

The slogan of the Apollo Association is "Clean Energy, Good Jobs." According to its mission statement, the Apollo Alliance is "a coalition of labor, business, environmental, and community leaders working to catalyze a clean energy revolution that will put millions of Americans to work in a new generation of high-quality, green-collar jobs. Inspired by the Apollo space program, we promote investments in energy efficiency, clean power, mass transit, next-generation vehicles, and emerging technology, as well as in education and training. Working together, we will reduce carbon emissions and oil imports, spur domestic job growth, and position America to thrive in the twenty-first-century economy."

About the Center for Green Jobs

In February 2009, the AFL-CIO created the Center for Green Jobs to partner with affiliated unions to, according to AFL-CIO President John Sweeney, "make progressive energy and climate change a first order priority" and "... to help our labor unions implement real green jobs initiatives—initiatives that retain and create good union jobs, provide pathways to those jobs, and assist with the design and implementation of training programs to prepare incumbent workers as well as job seekers for these family-sustaining careers."

The Board of Apollo Alliance includes the president of United Steelworkers Union, the executive vice president of Service Employees International Union, the general president of Laborers International Union of North America, and business, environmental, and community leaders. Among union supporters are the national AFL-CIO and various state affiliates. The Alliance has published numerous reports and research on environmental issues and is active in lobbying efforts to promote increasing the number of well-paying, career-track, green-collar jobs.

For more information, check the Web site http://apolloalliance.org.

Blue Green Alliance

The Blue Green Alliance is a national partnership of labor unions (blue) and environmental organizations (green) dedicated to expanding the number and quality of jobs in the green economy. The alliance, now numbering more than 6 million people, was launched in 2006 by the Sierra Club and United Steelworkers. Today, it includes the Communications Workers of America (CWA), National Resource Defense Council (NRDC), Laborers' International Union of North America (LIUNA), and Service Employees International Union (SEIU).

Among its goals, the Blue Green Alliance seeks to educate the public about solutions that "reduce global warming in the timeframe necessary to avoid the effects of climate change" and "curb the use of toxic chemicals in order to enhance public health and promote safer alternatives." The Alliance also advocates for fair "labor, environmental, and human rights standards in trade policies."

To achieve these goals, the Alliance works in partnership with the Good Jobs, Green Jobs National Conference; the Green Jobs for America campaign,

including additional partners such as Working America, the community affiliate of the AFL-CIO; Green for All; the Center for American Progress; and the Labor-Climate Project, a partnership with Al Gore's Alliance for Climate Protection. The Blue Green Alliance also publishes groundbreaking research reports focused on renewable energy and green chemistry.

For more information, check the Web site www.bluegreenalliance.org.

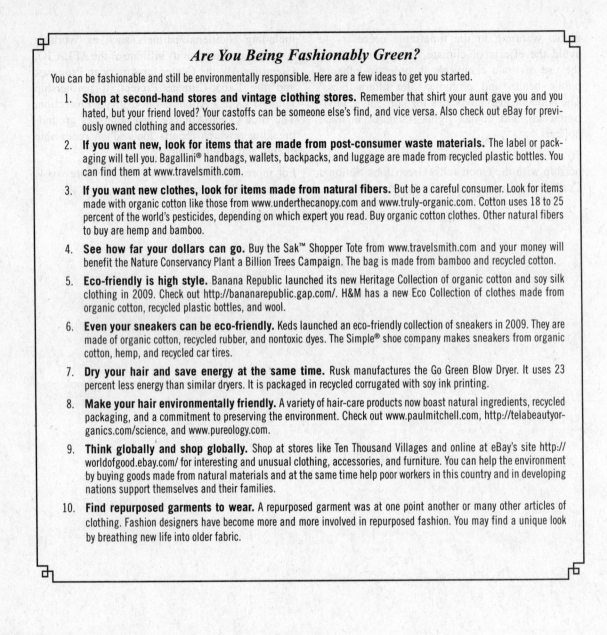

Are You Being Fashionably Green?

You can be fashionable and still be environmentally responsible. Here are a few ideas to get you started.

1. **Shop at second-hand stores and vintage clothing stores.** Remember that shirt your aunt gave you and you hated, but your friend loved? Your castoffs can be someone else's find, and vice versa. Also check out eBay for previously owned clothing and accessories.

2. **If you want new, look for items that are made from post-consumer waste materials.** The label or packaging will tell you. Bagallini® handbags, wallets, backpacks, and luggage are made from recycled plastic bottles. You can find them at www.travelsmith.com.

3. **If you want new clothes, look for items made from natural fibers.** But be a careful consumer. Look for items made with organic cotton like those from www.underthecanopy.com and www.truly-organic.com. Cotton uses 18 to 25 percent of the world's pesticides, depending on which expert you read. Buy organic cotton clothes. Other natural fibers to buy are hemp and bamboo.

4. **See how far your dollars can go.** Buy the Sak™ Shopper Tote from www.travelsmith.com and your money will benefit the Nature Conservancy Plant a Billion Trees Campaign. The bag is made from bamboo and recycled cotton.

5. **Eco-friendly is high style.** Banana Republic launched its new Heritage Collection of organic cotton and soy silk clothing in 2009. Check out http://bananarepublic.gap.com/. H&M has a new Eco Collection of clothes made from organic cotton, recycled plastic bottles, and wool.

6. **Even your sneakers can be eco-friendly.** Keds launched an eco-friendly collection of sneakers in 2009. They are made of organic cotton, recycled rubber, and nontoxic dyes. The Simple® shoe company makes sneakers from organic cotton, hemp, and recycled car tires.

7. **Dry your hair and save energy at the same time.** Rusk manufactures the Go Green Blow Dryer. It uses 23 percent less energy than similar dryers. It is packaged in recycled corrugated with soy ink printing.

8. **Make your hair environmentally friendly.** A variety of hair-care products now boast natural ingredients, recycled packaging, and a commitment to preserving the environment. Check out www.paulmitchell.com, http://telabeautyorganics.com/science, and www.pureology.com.

9. **Think globally and shop globally.** Shop at stores like Ten Thousand Villages and online at eBay's site http://worldofgood.ebay.com/ for interesting and unusual clothing, accessories, and furniture. You can help the environment by buying goods made from natural materials and at the same time help poor workers in this country and in developing nations support themselves and their families.

10. **Find repurposed garments to wear.** A repurposed garment was at one point another or many other articles of clothing. Fashion designers have become more and more involved in repurposed fashion. You may find a unique look by breathing new life into older fabric.

PART III

WORKFORCE TRAINING

CHAPTER 5

STATE AND FEDERAL WORKFORCE TRAINING

The Web site for the state of Arkansas defines "workforce development" as follows:

> [E]ducation and/or training beyond high school which leads to a GED, certificate, two- to four-year degree; and/or other short-term, customized training designed to meet the needs of employers to upgrade the skills of existing, emerging, transitional, and entrepreneurial workforces.

The other forty-nine states and the District of Columbia view workforce development similarly: In every case, the emphasis is on *employer* needs and attracting new employers to the state. Training and apprenticeship programs are also geared to a state's major employers, who often receive tax incentives and access to free services for hiring employees or for implementing existing training resources. What does this mean for you, the job seeker? Workforce development emphasizes the provision of resources for finding jobs, writing resumes, and developing interview skills.

USING THE INTERNET

Every state has an Internet portal through which job seekers can post resumes, search for job openings, or apply for unemployment benefits—and where state employers can post job openings and review resumes of prospective employees. The quality and thoroughness of these portals vary by state: Some are more user-friendly than others; some are more comprehensive than others. To access these resources, one usually needs to establish an online user ID and password, so you'll have at least a minimum level of security for the information you post.

FINDING A ONE-STOP CAREER CENTER

The Workforce Investment Act (WIA) of 1998, which took effect in 2000, was enacted to replace the Job Training Partnership Act and other federal job-training laws. The WIA aims to encourage businesses to participate in local Workforce Development Services through Workforce Investment Boards. These boards are chaired by community members in the private sector. The WIA established a national workforce preparation and employment system—called America's Workforce Network—to meet the needs of businesses, job seekers, and citizens who are interested in furthering their careers.

A main feature of Title I of the WIA is the creation of One-Stop Career Center system, which provides easy access to information and services through which job seekers can access a broad range of employment-related and training services at a single point of entry. Each year, nearly 16 million Americans find job placement assistance through One-Stop Career Centers. The following programs are required by federal law to deliver their services through this system:

- Title I of WIA (adults, youth, and dislocated workers)
- Job Corps
- Native American job programs
- Wagner-Peyser (employment service)
- Unemployment Insurance
- Trade Adjustment Assistance
- North American Free Trade Association (NAFTA) Transitional Adjustment Assistance
- Welfare-to-Work
- Senior Community Service Employment
- Veterans Employment and Training
- Vocational Rehabilitation
- Adult Education
- Postsecondary Vocational Education
- Community Services Block Grant
- Employment and Training Activities
- Housing and Urban Development
- Migrant and Seasonal Farm Worker Programs

You'll find One-Stop Career Centers in each state and in the District of Columbia; all are funded with federal money, and users are not charged for services. The number and locations of One-Stop Centers throughout each state are largely based on population density (for example, rural states will have fewer resources in outlying areas). These centers play several roles: They operate as career centers, workforce centers, job centers, unemployment benefit centers, and state or regional government services centers all at once.

Veterans are also served through One-Stop Career Centers. For example, Helmets to Hardhats is a national program that connects National Guard, Reserve, and transitioning active-duty military members with high-quality career training and employment opportunities in the construction industry. The program is administered by the Center for Military Recruitment, Assessment, and Veterans Employment and is headquartered in Washington, DC.

In many states, Workforce Development is a separate department or agency within the state government. In other states, it is part of the Department of Labor, Commerce, or Employment. Each state is required to have a specific entity to administer the services required under the WIA, to certify providers of services, and to report regularly to the federal government.

The list in this chapter provides main contact information for One-Stop Centers in all fifty states and the District of Columbia, as well as a general description of the individual programs and other relevant workforce development information provided in each center. Use your state's workforce home page to find the location of the center nearest to you. Not all centers or states have green training or retraining programs, but this is the place to start your search.

Note that the American Recovery and Reinvestment Act of 2009, which was signed into law to stimulate the economy, included $4 billion for workforce investment initiatives in retraining and education. Your state, in partnership with local colleges and training providers, may have accessed this money to increase its workforce training programs.

ALABAMA

Office of Workforce Development
P.O. Box 302130
Montgomery, Alabama 36130-2130
334-353-1686
https://joblink.alabama.gov/ada

Alabama Joblink is a portal to services offered through the Alabama Career Center system, which administers the state's One-Stop Centers. The CareerLink centers are administered by three area centers: Central Alabama Skills Center at Southern Union State Community College, North Alabama Skills Center, and South Alabama Skills Center. Career Centers are located in each county.

ALASKA

Alaska Workforce Investment Board
1016 West 6th Avenue, Suite 105
Anchorage, Alaska 99501
907-269-7485
www.jobs.state.ak.us/jt

Job-related training services are available to eligible youth, adults, and dislocated workers through the Alaska Job Center Network (AJCN) and select training providers and partners across the state. Funding for these training services is available primarily through the WIA, the State Training Employment Program (STEP), the Trade Assistance Act (TAA), and the High Growth Job Training Initiative (HGJTI). These funds may be leveraged with federal Pell grants and/or the Alaska State Student Loan program. For Alaska Native Americans, other funding for training is available through recognized tribal organizations throughout the state. Job training resources are available for a limited number of residents of select rural locations through the Denali Training Fund via the Denali Commission.

ARIZONA

Department of Commerce: Workforce
  Development
1700 W. Washington, Suite 600
Phoenix, Arizona 85007
602-771-1100
www.arizonaworkforceconnection.com

Arizona Workforce Connection is a statewide system of workforce development partners who provide free services to employers seeking access to skilled new hires or to existing worker training resources. Through a network of One-Stop Centers and online services, Arizona Workforce Connection provides access to employee recruitment, labor market information, job training and hiring tax credits, customized training and skills upgrading, and pre-layoff assistance.

ARKANSAS

Arkansas Workforce Centers
Department of Workforce Services
#2 Capitol Mall

About Veterans' Services

Go online to www.careeronestop.org/militarytransition/ and click on "Find State Resources for Veterans" under "Hot Topics." Here you can search by state for veteran-specific job and educational resources. Some are provided by the One-Stop Centers; others by other agencies and institutions.

Little Rock, Arkansas 72201
501-371-1020
E-mail: arkansaswib@arkansas.gov
www.arworks.org/index.html

Arkansas Workforce Centers provide locally developed and operated services, including training and linking employers and job seekers through a statewide delivery system. Convenient one-stop centers are designed to eliminate the need to visit different locations.

CALIFORNIA

Employment Development Department
800 Capitol Mall, MIC 83
Sacramento, California 95814
916-654-7799
www.edd.ca.gov/Jobs_and_Training

California's Employment Development Department (EDD) provides a comprehensive range of employment and training services in partnership with state and local agencies and organizations. These services are provided statewide through the state's One-Stop Career Center system or EDD Workforce Services Offices. Each county has at least one One-Stop Career Center.

COLORADO

Department of Labor and Employment
633 17th Street, Suite 201
Denver, Colorado 80202-3660
303-318-8000
www.coworkforce.com/emp/WFCs.asp

In nearly all of Colorado's nine federally recognized workforce regions, program administration and service delivery of WIA and Wagner-Peyser

Act programs are consolidated, providing local businesses and job seekers with easy access to a broader range of workforce center services. The centers provide an array of employment and training services at no charge to employers or job seekers.

About Resource Areas in One-Stop Career Centers

Many One-Stop Career Centers have resource rooms or separate areas where job seekers can access the Internet and use the printers, phones, copiers, and fax machines in their job search. Employment professionals in these resource rooms are happy to help job seekers find what they need. Some centers may have child-care areas as well, but call your local center to be sure.

CONNECTICUT

Department of Labor
200 Folly Brook Boulevard
Wethersfield, Connecticut 06109
860-263-6000
www.ctdol.state.ct.us/ContactInfo

The One-Stop Career Center system in Connecticut is called CTWorks. The system helps more than 80,000 state residents annually with resume writing, interview skills, job training, and much more. Most training results in certification and job placement.

DELAWARE

Department of Labor: Workforce Investment
   Board (WIB)
4425 N. Market Street
Fox Valley
Wilmington, Delaware 19802
302-761-8160
www.delawareworks.com/wib

The WIB oversees Delaware's One-Stop Centers to ensure that the state's citizens are provided with occupational training and employment service opportunities to help them gain employment that will sustain them and their families. One-Stop Centers are located within each of Delaware's Department of Labor locations: Wilmington, Pencader, Dover, and Georgetown.

DISTRICT OF COLUMBIA

Department of Employment Services (DOES)
Government of the District of Columbia
64 New York Avenue NE, Suite 3000
Washington, D.C. 20002
202-724-7000
E-mail: does@dc.gov
http://does.dc.gov/does/cwp/
   view,a,1233,q,538261.asp

The Department of Employment Services administers One-Stop Career Centers in the District of Columbia. Each DOES center provides a range of services, including career counseling, career planning, resume assistance, direct job placement, classroom and on-the-job training, online and phone access to America's Job Bank, information about local and national labor markets, and unemployment compensation.

FLORIDA

Agency for Workforce Innovation
107 East Madison Street
Caldwell Building
Tallahassee, Florida 32399-4120
850-245-7105
www.floridajobs.org/onestop/onestopdir

Florida's Office of Workforce Services (WFS) provides one-stop program support services to the Regional Workforce Boards that administer the One-Stop Centers. Florida's state-of-the-art Web site, "Employ Florida Marketplace," helps match Florida's job seekers and employers. The site offers assistance in selecting a new career, finding a new job, or locating suitable education or training.

GEORGIA

Department of Labor
404-232-3540
www.dol.state.ga.us/find_one_stop_centers.htm

Most of the direct services of Georgia's Department of Labor are provided through the Internet or by staff in fifty-three local Career Centers, more than fifty local Vocational Rehabilitation Offices, and twenty Workforce Areas, offering a wide range of services to both job seekers and employers. Each county has multiple One-Stop Centers that provide individuals who seek employment with the most up-to-date tools to find and keep jobs, including resource areas, education and training services, local and national job listings, and job search and financial management workshops.

HAWAII

Department of Labor and Industrial Relations:
    Workforce Development Division
830 Punchbowl Street #329
Honolulu, Hawaii 96813
808-586-8877
http://dlir.workforce.develop@hawaii.gov
http://hawaii.gov/labor/wdd/onestops

Hawaii's One-Stop Centers provide free services to job seekers and employers, including job-search assistance; personal career-planning services; training opportunities; support for HireNet Hawaii, the online employment site; and a resource area. Centers are located on Oahu, Maui, Hila, Kona, and Kauai.

IDAHO

Department of Labor
317 W. Main Street
Boise, Idaho 83735
208-332-3570
www.idahoworks.org/IW_career.shtml

The IdahoWorks Career Center is the primary point of access to a full range of labor market and education services. More than seventeen programs have been assembled under the One-Stop system to meet the needs of workers, students, and businesses. Six centers throughout the state offer a variety of self-service options, a comprehensive resource center, and highly trained staff. For those seeking employment or education, the Career Centers provide one-stop access to national, state, and local job listings; career guidance; specialized

workshops; and education and training services and resources in the community.

ILLINOIS

Illinois Department of Employment Security
    (IDES)
33 South State Street
Chicago, Illinois 60603
312-793-5700

850 East Madison Street
Springfield, Illinois 62702-5603
217-785-5069
www.ides.state.il.us/

IDES helps job seekers find jobs and employers find workers. With nearly sixty locations throughout the state, local IDES offices and Illinois workNet Centers are the primary one-stop sources for the state's workforce development services.

INDIANA

Department of Workforce Development
Indiana Government Center South
10 North Senate Avenue
Indianapolis, Indiana 46204
800-891-6499 (toll-free)
www.in.gov/dwd/WorkOne/

Indiana's WorkOne portal provides valuable information about WorkOne and its programs. The WorkOne Center is the heart of Indiana's workforce development system and helps people find a new or better job, choose a career, find a good employee, or find training. Indiana has eleven WorkOne Regions, with centers located throughout the state.

IOWA

Iowa Workforce Development
1000 East Grand Avenue
Des Moines, Iowa 50319-0209
515-281-5387
800-JOB-IOWA (toll-free)
www.iowaworkforce.org/centers/
    regionalsites.htm

Fifteen regions make up the Iowa Workforce Development network. The network provides complete one-stop services for job search, unemployment information, career guidance, and training.

KANSAS

Department of Commerce: Workforce Services Division
Workforce Center Support Services
1000 S.W. Jackson Street, Suite 100
Topeka, Kansas 66612-1354
785-296-0607
E-mail: workforcesvcs@kansasworks.com
https://www.kansasworks.com/ada

The Kansas Department of Commerce administers the KansasWorks system, which links businesses, job seekers, and educational institutions to ensure that the state's employers can find skilled workers. The system operates workforce centers throughout the state to help connect Kansas businesses with skilled job seekers in their area.

KENTUCKY

Office of Employment and Training
275 East Main Street, 2nd Floor
Frankfort, Kentucky 40601
502-564-7456
www.oet.ky.gov/des/

The Kentucky Office of Employment and Training (OET) is part of the Department for Workforce Investment. OET staff members provide job services, unemployment insurance services, labor market information, and training opportunities.

LOUISIANA

Louisiana Workforce Commission
1001 N. 23rd Street
Baton Rouge, Louisiana 70802
225-342-3111
www.laworks.net/servicelocator.asp

The Louisiana Workforce Commission, under the LaWorks network, provides an online portal to services such as resume posting, career options, education, and training. It also provides access to youth services information and administers One-Stop Career Centers throughout the state.

MAINE

Department of Labor
54 State House Station
Augusta, Maine 04333
207-623-7981
E-mail: mdol@maine.gov
www.mainecareercenter.com/

Maine's CareerCenter, the state's online workforce portal, offers a variety of job-related information, including links to One-Stop Centers located throughout the state.

MARYLAND

Department of Labor, Licensing and Regulation
500 North Calvert Street, #401
Baltimore, Maryland 21202
410-230-6001
E-mail: det@dllr.state.md.us
https://mwe.dllr.state.md.us

Workforce Exchange is a virtual one-stop network aimed at improving access to information about jobs, training, and workforce support throughout Maryland. The exchange connects agencies, programs, and services electronically to assist employers and individuals in making the right career decisions. The heart of Maryland's workforce system is its more than forty workforce service centers, which provide locally designed and operated services to meet local labor market needs.

Get Funding for Training or Retraining

If you need financial help, ask your local One-Stop employment professionals about the possibility of funding while training. Some states and programs may also provide supportive funding.

MASSACHUSETTS

Labor and Workforce Development, Division of
  Career Services
Charles F. Hurley Building
19 Staniford Street
Boston, Massachusetts 02114
617-626-5300
E-mail: DCSCustomerfeedback@detma.org
https://web.detma.org/Jobseeker/CM1.ASP

The state's online portal, JobQuest, provides access to job-search and training programs available online. Thirty-seven One-Stop Career Centers form the foundation of the state's delivery system for employment and training services.

MICHIGAN

Department of Labor and Economic Growth
201 N. Washington Square
Victor Office Center, 7th Floor
Lansing, Michigan 48913
888-253-6855 (toll-free)
E-mail: careerhelp@michigan.gov
www.michiganworks.org

Michigan's Employment Service program provides services to job seekers online through the Michigan Talent Bank portal and more than 100 Michigan Works! Service Centers statewide. Local Michigan Works! Agencies oversee a wide variety of programs designed to help employers find skilled workers and help job seekers find satisfying careers. The programs are also designed to prepare youth and unskilled adults for entry into the labor force and to aid individuals who face serious barriers to employment to obtain the assistance necessary to get and keep a job.

MINNESOTA

Department of Employment and Economic
  Development
Minnesota Workforce Center System
888-GET-JOBS (438-5627) (toll-free)
www.mnwfc.org/field/index.htm

Fifty-three One-Stop Centers serve Minnesota residents in every area of the state. Workforce Centers provide comprehensive services to job seekers, including training programs. They also provide youth services. An online portal, MinnesotaWorks, provides Internet-based services for connecting job seekers and registered employers.

MISSISSIPPI

Department of Employment Security
Office of the Governor
1235 Echelon Parkway
P.O. Box 1699
Jackson, Mississippi 39215-1699
601-321-6000
www.mdes.ms.gov/wps/portal

Workforce Investment Network (WIN) Job Centers, located throughout Mississippi, provide convenient, one-stop employment and training services to employers and job seekers.

MISSOURI

Department of Economic Development
Division of Workforce Development
888-728-JOBS (toll-free)
E-mail: wfd@ded.mo.gov
www.missouricareersource.com/mcs/mcs/
  default.seek

WorkSmart Missouri is the portal to Internet resources available to job seekers and employers in Missouri. Missouri Career Centers provide training development services to workers and employers through the coordination of a variety of partner agencies. Career Centers are located throughout the state.

MONTANA

Department of Labor: Workforce Services
  Division
P.O. Box 1728
Helena, Montana 59624-1728
406-444-4100
http://wsd.dli.mt.gov/service/officelist.asp

Montana's Workforce Services Division (WSD) is a gateway to government services in employment and training. The WSD consists of twenty-four Job Service Workforce Center sites located throughout Montana along with a team of experts who are located in a central support office. The focus is on developing and maintaining a high-quality workforce in the state.

NEBRASKA

Department of Labor: Nebraska Workforce
    Development
http://www.dol.state.ne.us/
http://nejoblink.nebraska.gov/

Joblink is Nebraska's Internet portal providing job searches, resume services, and assistance to job seekers. Sixteen Workforce Development Career Centers are located statewide, offering comprehensive services, including training programs, to job seekers.

NEVADA

Department of Employment, Training and
    Rehabilitation
500 East Third Street
Carson City, Nevada 89713-0021
E-mail: detrinfo@nvdetr.org
http://detr.state.nv.us/es/es_office.htm

Nevada's JobConnect Career Centers provide businesses and job seekers with personalized attention and a variety of services, including access to job listings and placement; work registration; labor market information; career information, guidance, and assessment; information about education and training opportunities; unemployment insurance information; resume preparation; referrals to other partner agency services; and more.

NEW HAMPSHIRE

New Hampshire Employment Security (NHES)
32 South Main Street
Concord, New Hampshire 03301
603-224-3311
800-852-3400 (toll-free)
http://www.nh.gov/nhes/locations/index.htm

New Hampshire Employment Security offers free services, resources, and tools to help the job seeker with the entire job-search process. NH WORKS Resource Centers, located within each of the thirteen local offices, provide services, information, resources, and tools for job seekers in a one-stop setting. The NH WORKS System is a partnership of a number of government agencies and community organizations to provide services, resources, and information to job seekers and employers.

NEW JERSEY

Department of Labor and Workforce
    Development
1 John Fitch Way
P.O. Box 110
Trenton, New Jersey 08625-0110
http://lwd.dol.state.nj.us/labor/wnjpin/findjob/
    onestop/services.html

Located county-wide throughout New Jersey, One-Stop Career Centers assist with obtaining employment and training at their sites. The One-Stop Career Centers also offer educational training programs at vocational and trade schools or on-site at the One-Stop, including on-the-job training with employers and apprenticeships in many fields.

NEW MEXICO

Department of Workforce Solutions
401 Broadway NE
Albuquerque, New Mexico 87102
E-mail: infodws@state.nm.us
www.dws.state.nm.us/index.html

The One-Stop System is intended to meet the needs of job seekers and workers through services such as access to job listings, career-planning resources, soft skills training, and training and education for high-growth industries. One-Stop Centers are located throughout New Mexico.

NEW YORK

Department of Labor
W. Averell Harriman State Office Campus
Building 12
Albany, New York 12240
518-457-9000
888-4-NYSDOL (toll-free)
E-mail: nysdol@labor.state.ny.us
www.labor.state.ny.us/workforcenypartners/
    osview.asp

At New York's One-Stop Career Centers, job seekers can learn resume writing and successful interviewing techniques, access apprenticeship training and training grants, search online job listings, and attend a job fair. Job seekers can research occupations on the Career Zone site and post customized resumes on Job Zone, part of Job Portfolio.

NORTH CAROLINA

Employment Security Commission of North
  Carolina
P.O. Box 25903
Raleigh, North Carolina 27611-5903
919-733-6745
E-mail: esc.employmentservice@ncmail.net
www.ncesc.com/locator/locatormain.
  asp?init=true

Employment Security Commission offices are located in every county in North Carolina. Most Commission offices are also JobLink Centers, where resources are available for job search and worker training.

NORTH DAKOTA

Job Service North Dakota
P.O. Box 5507
Bismarck, North Dakota 58506-5507
701-328-2825
www.jobsnd.com/

Job Service's online labor exchange system provides individuals with maximum flexibility in their job searches. Customers may use the online services exclusively, or they may consult with a Job Service employment professional who can assist them in a variety of ways. Job seekers may attend workshops to learn about resume writing, interviewing, and other job search techniques. They may work through an assessment of their interests and abilities to find an appropriate career path. If job seekers do not have the necessary skills to pursue their desired occupations, Job Service employment professionals offer guidance on ways to access funds for training. Fourteen full-service offices and two part-time offices are located in the state.

OHIO

Department of Jobs and Family Services (JFS)
Office of Workforce Development
P.O. Box 1618
Columbus, Ohio 43216-1618
614-644-0677
E-mail: Workforce@jfs.ohio.gov
http://jfs.ohio.gov/workforce/
http://jfs.ohio.gov/workforce/jobseekers/
  onestopmap.stm

In Ohio, there are thirty-one comprehensive, full-service One-Stop sites and fifty-nine satellite sites throughout twenty local workforce development areas, with at least one site in every Ohio county. The local workforce development areas are based on population, economic development, educational resources, and labor markets, and the One-Stops tailor their services to meet local customer needs. Job-seeking customers can expect services such as resource rooms, job-related workshops, supportive services, individual training accounts, and other activities that match job seekers to employment.

OKLAHOMA

Department of Commerce
900 North Stiles Avenue
Oklahoma City, Oklahoma 73104-3234
405-557-7100
www.workforceok.org/locator.htm

Under the umbrella of Workforce Oklahoma, business leaders, educators, training providers, and employment professionals are working together to achieve job growth, employee productivity, and employer satisfaction within the workforce system. A network of statewide offices integrates employment, education, and training to assist employers in finding qualified employees and helps workers find jobs, make career decisions, and access training opportunities.

OREGON

Employment Department
875 Union Street, NE
Salem, Oregon 97311
800-237-3710 (toll-free)
http://findit.emp.state.or.us/locations/index.cfm

Through forty-seven WorkSource Center offices across the state, the department serves job seekers and employers by helping workers find suitable employment, providing qualified applicants for employers, supplying statewide and local labor market information, and offering unemployment insurance benefits to workers temporarily unemployed through no fault of their own. The department helps job seekers find jobs that match their skills and employers' needs, provides up-to-date information about trends in occupations and skills needed for success in the job market, and works with other agencies to direct workers to appropriate training programs and job experiences.

PENNSYLVANIA

Department of Labor and Industry
Room 1700
651 Boas Street
Harrisburg, Pennsylvania 17121
717-787-5279
www.dli.state.pa.us/

The department prepares job seekers for the global workforce through employment and job-training services for adult, youth, older workers, and dislocated workers. The Commonwealth Workforce Development System (CWDS) is an Internet-based system of services for use by customers and potential customers of the PA CareerLink offices. CWDS provides online access to job openings; information about employers; services and training opportunities for job seekers; and labor market information. The department administers a network of PA CareerLink centers around the state.

RHODE ISLAND

RI Department of Labor and Training
Center General Complex
1511 Pontiac Avenue
Cranston, Rhode Island 02920
401-462-8000
www.networkri.org/

Rhode Island's One-Stop Career Center System, netWORKri, is a partnership of professional labor, training, and education organizations. The net-WORKri Centers, located throughout the state, match job seekers and employers through high-quality employment programs and services.

SOUTH CAROLINA

Department of Commerce: Workforce
  Development
1201 Main Street, Suite 1600
Columbia, South Carolina 29201-3200
803-737-0400
800-868-7232 (toll-free)
www.sces.org/Individual/locations/1stoploc.htm

Matching the needs of businesses for skilled workers and training with the needs of individuals for education and employment, the Workforce Division seeks to provide customers timely information and services. Through its One-Stop system, South Carolina's Workforce Division assists in finding appropriate training for adults and enables smooth coordination with industries, education, and economic development.

SOUTH DAKOTA

Department of Labor: Workforce Training
700 Governors Drive
Pierre, South Dakota 57501-2291
605-773-5017
http://dol.sd.gov/workforce_training/clcs.aspx

The South Dakota Department of Labor (DOL) offers a variety of training and education programs to help ensure that employers have the skilled workforce they need and to help individuals realize their potential as employees. Some of these programs are geared toward helping target groups successfully overcome unique employment challenges, such as those for whom English is a second language or those who do not possess a high school diploma. The department also helps individuals assess their training and educational needs and

Green Jobs for a New Economy

identify options. Career Learning Centers (CLCs) work closely with the DOL to provide education and employment training services that meet the needs of local job seekers and businesses.

TENNESSEE

Department of Labor and Workforce
   Development
220 French Landing Drive
Nashville, Tennessee 37243
615-741-6642
E-mail: TDLWD@tn.gov
http://state.tn.us/labor-wfd/cc/

Tennessee has a network of Career Centers across the state where employers can go to find the workers they need and job seekers can get assistance and career information. In addition to job placement, recruitment, and training referrals, each center offers computerized labor market information, Internet access, workshops, and an online talent bank.

TEXAS

Employment and Labor
Texas Workforce Commission
101 E. 15th Street
Austin, Texas 78778-0001
www.twc.state.tx.us/dirs/wdas/wdamap.html

The Texas Workforce Commission (TWC) is part of a local/state network dedicated to developing the workforce. It oversees and provides workforce development services to employers and job seekers. For job seekers, TWC offers career-development information, job-search resources, training programs, and, as appropriate, unemployment benefits. Customers can access local workforce solutions and statewide services in a single location, the Texas Workforce Centers.

UTAH

Department of Workforce Services
P.O. Box 45249
Salt Lake City, Utah 84145-0249
801-526-WORK (9675)
E-mail: dwscontactus@utah.gov
http://jobs.utah.gov/regions/ec.asp

Utah's one-stop Employment Centers provide training information and job-search assistance. Job seekers receive assistance in determining their interests, abilities, and current skill levels; develop individual employment plans; and explore potential training options.

VERMONT

Department of Labor
5 Green Mountain Drive
P.O. Box 488
Montpelier, Vermont 05601-0488
802-828-4000
http://labor.vermont.gov/Default.aspx?tabid=285

Vermont's fourteen Resource Centers provide interview space for employers, assistance in posting jobs, and help with human resources issues. A Resource Room in each center provides job seekers with services and resources such as personal computers and access to the Internet. The centers are equipped with assistive technology for individuals with disabilities. Staff members are also available to provide specific resources for veterans.

VIRGINIA

The Virginia Employment Commission
703 East Main Street
Richmond, Virginia 23219
804-786-1485
http://www.vec.virginia.gov/vecportal/field/
   field_offices.cfm

The Virginia Workforce Centers provide one-stop access to workforce, employment, and training services of various programs and partner organizations. Each Virginia Workforce Center provides services required by federal legislation plus services designed to meet the needs of the local community. The Virginia Workforce Connection is an online job-seeker service that provides job search and career information, training opportunities, skill requirements, and labor market information, including wage data and industry and occupational trends.

WASHINGTON

Employment Security Department (ESD)

P.O. Box 9046

Olympia, Washington 98507

360-438-4123

E-mail: work@esd.wa.gov

https://fortress.wa.gov/esd/
worksource/StaticContent.
aspx?Context=WSDirectorySeeker

WorkSource is a partnership of Washington State's businesses, government agencies, community and technical colleges, and nonprofit organizations. It has become the cornerstone for improving access to employment and training services via one-stop career centers in the state. WorkSource services are delivered to customers in a variety of ways that include self-directed efforts, such as kiosks or via the Internet; group programs and activities, such as workshops; one-on-one discussions; training programs; and business consultations.

WEST VIRGINIA

Department of Commerce

WORKFORCE West Virginia

Capitol Complex Building 6, Room 525

1900 Kanawha Boulevard E

Charleston, West Virginia 25305

304-558-7024

www.wvbep.org/scripts/bep/jobs/locals/

WORKFORCE West Virginia, a consortium of partners, assists workers in finding suitable employment and employers in finding qualified workers. It seeks to match job seekers with employers in an efficient manner, help those in need become job ready, and to analyze and disseminate labor market information. The one-stop Workforce Centers are located throughout the state.

WISCONSIN

Department of Workforce Development (DWD)

P.O. Box 7946

Madison, Wisconsin 53707-7946

608-266-3131

www.wisconsinjobcenter.org/directory/
default.htm/

The Department of Workforce Development's responsibilities include providing training and employment assistance to job seekers and working with employers to find appropriate job candidates. The Wisconsin Job Center system has more than seventy Job Centers located throughout the state.

WYOMING

Department of Workforce Services

122 W. 25th Street

Herschler Building 2E

Cheyenne, Wyoming 82002

307-777-8728

http://wyomingworkforce.org/contact/offices.aspx

Wyoming's Department of Workforce Services (DWS) has a number of programs available for individuals seeking jobs throughout the state—whether laid off, disabled, otherwise unemployed, or simply wanting to change career direction. The DWS administers numerous education and training programs to meet a variety of needs and groups through its local Workforce Centers.

About the Energy Star Program

For information on the Energy Star program of the U.S. Department of Energy, go to www.energystar.gov or call 888-782-7937 (toll-free). For information on available Energy Star tax credits for energy-efficient home improvements, check out www.energystar.gov/taxcredits.

Ten Eco-Friendly Actions You Can Take Now

1. **Buy a couple of refillable water bottles and fill them with tap water.** If you don't like the taste of your local water, buy a water filter that fits on the faucet. Depending on the filter, the cost of twenty bottles of water will quickly pay for it. Remember to wash refillable bottles so they don't breed bacteria.

2. **Reuse shopping bags.** The debate rages over whether paper or plastic bags are worse for the environment. If you have your groceries packed in either, reuse the bags as many times as possible. Better yet, buy and use eco-friendly reusable bags that many supermarkets sell. These stores reduce your bill by a few cents for each bag you bring and use.

3. **Replace incandescent light bulbs with compact fluorescent light bulbs (CFLs).** CFLs are more expensive than regular light bulbs but last ten times longer—if they are not turned on and off frequently. CFLs need to be used in fixtures that you regularly leave on for at least 15 minutes. Also, CFLs have mercury in them, so you can't throw them in the trash when they burn out—in about seven years. BUT, changing just 25 percent of your light bulbs to CFLs will save 50 percent on what you spend to light your house. CFLs save you about $30 in electricity costs over the life of a bulb.

4. **Repair leaky faucets.** A slow drip can fill five 10-gallon containers in a month.

5. **Install a water-saving showerhead.** Depending on what you buy, you will use one-third to one-half the water of a regular showerhead. For a family of 4, that translates into 20,000 fewer gallons of water a year.

6. **Caulk windows and doors to keep air out.** Tightly sealed windows and doors will keep out heat in the summer and cold in the winter, thus saving money on your energy bills.

7. **Look for the Energy Star label and Energy Guide when you buy appliances such as air conditioners and washers.** The guide shows you how much it costs to run the appliance and the range of costs for similar machines.

8. **Install a programmable thermostat to operate your heating and air conditioning systems.** Set it to a high of 68° in the winter and 72° in the summer. Also set it to turn down automatically at night in the winter or when you are out of the house. In the summer, set it to turn up automatically when you are out during the day so you aren't wasting energy cooling an empty house.

9. **Don't turn the car on to idle on cold mornings.** It takes only 30 seconds for the engine to warm up. It may take you longer to warm up, but consider the fewer carbon emissions your car will generate and the money you'll save on gas.

10. **Check your car's owner manual for the proper pressure for your tires.** Keep your tires inflated to the correct pressure and save money on gas.

PART IV

PROFILES OF SUSTAINABILITY PROGRAMS

TWO-YEAR COLLEGES

UNITED STATES

Arizona

Rio Salado College
Tempe, Arizona

Sustainability Initiatives Rio Salado College's president has signed the American College & University Presidents Climate Commitment.

Academics *Sustainability courses and programs:* sustainability-focused course(s) or lecture series, noncredit sustainability course(s).

Student Services and Green Events *Sustainability leadership:* sustainability coordinator/director, sustainability committee/advisory council, energy manager. *Student clubs and activities:* Campus Climate Challenge, student club(s)/group(s) focused on sustainability. *Major sustainability events:* Campus Sustainability Day, Focus the Nation, National Teach-In, Food Drives.

Food Sustainable, organic, and/or locally produced foods available in on-campus dining facilities. Fair Trade coffee is used. Vegan and vegetarian dining options are available for every meal.

Transportation Provides public transportation access to local destinations and incentives to carpool or use public transportation.

Buildings and Grounds *Renovation and maintenance:* registered for LEED certification for new construction and/or renovation; uses a Green Seal certified cleaning service. *Campus grounds care:* uses water conservation devices; employs strategies to reduce light pollution; landscapes with native plant species; protects, restores, and/or creates habitat on campus.

Recycling *Events and organizations:* RecycleMania. *Programs and activities:* sustains a computer/technology recycling program; maintains an on-campus recycling center; reuses surplus department/office supplies; replaces paper materials with online alternatives; limits free printing in computer labs and libraries. *Campus dining operations:* offers discounts for reusable mugs; uses bulk condiment dispensers and decreased packaging for to-go food service purchases.

Energy Currently uses or plans to use alternative sources of power; motion, infrared, and/or light sensors to reduce energy uses for lighting; LED lighting; and energy-related performance contracting.

Purchasing Sustainability criteria used in purchasing include Energy Star (EPA), Green Cleaning Products (Green Seal/Environmental Choice certified), and Forest Stewardship Council (FSC) or American Forest and Paper Association's Sustainable Forestry Initiative (SFI) paper.

Contact Sustainability Coordinator, Rio Salado College, 2323 West 14th Street, Tempe, AZ 85281. *Phone:* 480-517-8534. *E-mail:* danielle.tomerlin@riosalado.edu. *Web site:* www.rio.maricopa.edu/.

Arkansas

North Arkansas College
Harrison, Arkansas

Sustainability Initiatives North Arkansas College's president has signed the American College & University Presidents Climate Commitment.

Student Services and Green Events *Sustainability leadership:* sustainability coordinator/director, sustainability committee/advisory council, recycling manager. *Student clubs and activities:* outreach materials available about on-campus sustainability efforts.

Transportation Provides public transportation access to local destinations.

Recycling *Programs and activities:* maintains an on-campus recycling center; composts yard waste; replaces paper materials with online alternatives.

Energy Currently uses or plans to use timers to regulate temperatures based on occupancy hours; motion, infrared, and/or light sensors to reduce energy uses for lighting; LED lighting; and energy-related performance contracting.

Contact North Arkansas College, 1515 Pioneer Drive, Harrison, AR 72601. *Phone:* 870-743-3000. *Web site:* www.northark.edu/.

California

Cabrillo College
Aptos, California

Sustainability Initiatives Cabrillo College's president has signed the American College & University Presidents Climate Commitment.

Academics *Sustainability courses and programs:* sustainability-focused course(s) or lecture series, noncredit sustainability course(s).

Student Services and Green Events *Sustainability leadership:* sustainability committee/advisory council, recycling manager. *Student clubs and activities:* student club(s)/group(s) focused on sustainability. *Major sustainability events:* Earth Week "Turn it Off".

Food Fair Trade coffee is used. Vegan and vegetarian dining options are available for every meal.

Transportation Provides public transportation access to local destinations, a bike loan/rental program, a car sharing program, and incentives to carpool or use public transportation.

Buildings and Grounds *Renovation and maintenance:* registered for LEED certification for new construction and/or renovation. *Campus grounds care:* uses water conservation devices; employs strategies to reduce light pollution; landscapes with native plant species; protects, restores, and/or creates habitat on campus.

Recycling *Programs and activities:* sustains a computer/technology recycling program; maintains an on-campus recycling center; sustains a pre-consumer food waste composting program; sustains a post-consumer food waste composting program; composts yard waste; reuses surplus department/office supplies; reuses chemicals; replaces paper materials with online alternatives; limits free printing in computer labs and libraries. *Campus dining operations:* operates without trays; offers discounts for reusable mugs; uses bulk condiment dispensers and decreased packaging for to-go food service purchases.

Energy Currently uses or plans to use alternative sources of power; timers to regulate temperatures based on occupancy hours; motion, infrared, and/or light sensors to reduce energy uses for lighting; LED lighting; vending machine motion sensors; and energy-related performance contracting.

Purchasing Sustainability criteria used in purchasing include Energy Star (EPA) and Green Cleaning Products (Green Seal/Environmental Choice certified).

Contact Cabrillo College, 6500 Soquel Drive, Aptos, CA 95003-3194. *Phone:* 831-479-6100. *Web site:* www.cabrillo.edu/.

Citrus College
Glendora, California

Student Services and Green Events *Sustainability leadership:* recycling manager.

Food Vegan and vegetarian dining options are available for every meal.

Transportation Provides public transportation access to local destinations.

Buildings and Grounds *Renovation and maintenance:* registered for LEED certification for new construction and/or renovation. *Campus grounds care:* landscapes with native plant species.

Recycling *Programs and activities:* sustains a computer/technology recycling program; maintains an on-campus recycling center; sustains a post-consumer food waste composting program; reuses surplus department/office supplies; reuses chemicals; replaces paper materials with online alternatives; limits free printing in computer labs and libraries. *Campus dining operations:* uses bulk condiment dispensers and decreased packaging for to-go food service purchases.

Energy Currently uses or plans to use timers to regulate temperatures based on occupancy hours; motion, infrared, and/or light sensors to reduce energy uses for lighting; and energy-related performance contracting.

Contact Citrus College, 1000 West Foothill Boulevard, Glendora, CA 91741-1899. *Phone:* 626-963-0323. *Web site:* www.citruscollege.edu/.

Los Angeles Trade-Technical College
Los Angeles, California

Sustainability Initiatives Los Angeles Trade-Technical College's president has signed the American College & University Presidents Climate Commitment.

Academics *Sustainability-focused undergraduate major(s):* Chemical Technology (AS), Wastewater Technology (AS). *Sustainability courses and programs:* sustainability-focused course(s) or lecture series.

Student Services and Green Events *Sustainability leadership:* sustainability coordinator/director, sustainability committee/advisory council, recycling manager, energy manager. *Student clubs and activities:* Campus Climate Challenge, student club(s)/group(s) focused on sustainability, outreach materials available about on-campus sustainability efforts. *Major sustainability events:* Two-day Green Industry and Educators Forum.

Food Sustainable, organic, and/or locally produced foods available in on-campus dining facilities. Fair Trade coffee is used. Vegan and vegetarian dining options are available for every meal.

Transportation Provides incentives to carpool or use public transportation.

Buildings and Grounds *Renovation and maintenance:* registered for LEED certification for new construction and/or renovation. *Campus grounds care:* uses water conservation devices; landscapes with native plant species.

Recycling *Programs and activities:* maintains an on-campus recycling center; reuses surplus department/office supplies; reuses chemicals; limits free printing in computer labs and libraries. *Campus dining operations:* operates without trays.

Energy Currently uses or plans to use alternative sources of power; timers to regulate temperatures based on occupancy hours; motion, infrared, and/or light sensors to reduce energy uses for lighting; LED lighting; and energy-related performance contracting.

Purchasing Sustainability criteria used in purchasing include Energy Star (EPA) and Green Cleaning Products (Green Seal/Environmental Choice certified).

Contact Director, Los Angeles Trade-Technical College, 400 West Washington Boulevard, Los Angeles, CA 90015. *Phone:* 213-763-7385. *E-mail:* wilsonmr@lattc.edu. *Web site:* www.lattc.edu/.

San Joaquin Delta College
Stockton, California

Sustainability Initiatives San Joaquin Delta College's president has signed the American College & University Presidents Climate Commitment.

Student Services and Green Events *Sustainability leadership:* sustainability committee/advisory council, energy manager. *Housing and facilities:* student-run café that serves environmentally or socially preferable foods, on-campus organic garden for students.

Food Sustainable, organic, and/or locally produced foods available in on-campus dining facilities. Fair Trade coffee is used. Vegan and vegetarian dining options are available for every meal.

Transportation Provides public transportation access to local destinations.

Buildings and Grounds *Campus grounds care:* uses water conservation devices; employs strategies to reduce light pollution; landscapes with native plant species; protects, restores, and/or creates habitat on campus.

Recycling *Programs and activities:* sustains a computer/technology recycling program; maintains an on-campus recycling center; reuses surplus department/office supplies; replaces paper materials with online alternatives. *Campus dining operations:* uses bulk condiment dispensers and decreased packaging for to-go food service purchases.

Energy Currently uses or plans to use alternative sources of power; timers to regulate temperatures based on occupancy hours; motion, infrared, and/or light sensors to reduce energy uses for lighting; and vending machine motion sensors.

Purchasing Sustainability criteria used in purchasing include Green Cleaning Products (Green Seal/Environmental Choice certified).

Contact Dean of Planning, Research, and Institutional Effectiveness, San Joaquin Delta College, 5151 Pacific Avenue, Stockton, CA 95207. *Phone:* 209-954-5039. *E-mail:* mwetstein@deltacollege.edu. *Web site:* www.deltacollege.edu/.

Santa Rosa Junior College
Santa Rosa, California

Academics *Sustainability courses and programs:* sustainability-focused course(s) or lecture series, noncredit sustainability course(s), sustainability-focused nonacademic certificate program(s).

Student Services and Green Events *Sustainability leadership:* recycling manager, sustainability-focused student government. *Student clubs and activities:* student club(s)/group(s) focused on sustainability. *Housing and facilities:* on-campus organic garden for students.

Food Sustainable, organic, and/or locally produced foods available in on-campus dining facilities. Vegan and vegetarian dining options are available for every meal.

Transportation Provides public transportation access to local destinations and incentives to carpool or use public transportation.

Buildings and Grounds *Campus grounds care:* uses water conservation devices; employs strategies to reduce light pollution; landscapes with native plant species; protects, restores, and/or creates habitat on campus; applies to its grounds only pesticides and fertilizers allowable under the U.S. Department of Agriculture's standards for crop production.

Recycling *Programs and activities:* sustains a computer/technology recycling program; composts yard waste; reuses surplus department/office supplies; replaces paper materials with online alternatives; limits free printing in computer labs and libraries. *Campus dining operations:* operates without trays; uses bulk condiment dispensers and decreased packaging for to-go food service purchases.

Energy Currently uses or plans to use alternative sources of power (solar energy); timers to regulate temperatures based on occupancy hours; motion, infrared, and/or light sensors to reduce energy uses for lighting; LED lighting; vending machine motion sensors; and energy-related performance contracting.

Purchasing Sustainability criteria used in purchasing include Energy Star (EPA), WaterSense (EPA), and Green Cleaning Products (Green Seal/Environmental Choice certified).

Contact Santa Rosa Junior College, 1501 Mendocino Avenue, Santa Rosa, CA 95401-4395. *Phone:* 707-527-4011. *Web site:* www.santarosa.edu/.

Shasta College
Redding, California

Sustainability Initiatives Shasta College is a signatory to the Talloires Declaration. This institution's president has signed the American College & University Presidents Climate Commitment.

Academics *Sustainability courses and programs:* sustainability-focused course(s) or lecture series, noncredit sustainability course(s), sustainability-focused nonacademic certificate program(s).

Student Services and Green Events *Sustainability leadership:* sustainability coordinator/director, sustainability committee/advisory council, recycling manager, energy manager. *Student clubs and activities:* student club(s)/group(s) focused on sustainability, outreach materials available about on-campus sustainability efforts. *Major sustainability events:* Shasta College Sustainability Conference.

Food Fair Trade coffee is used. Vegan and vegetarian dining options are available for every meal.

Transportation Provides free on-campus transportation (bus or other) and public transportation access to local destinations.

Buildings and Grounds *Campus grounds care:* uses water conservation devices; landscapes with native plant species; protects, restores, and/or creates habitat on campus.

Recycling *Programs and activities:* sustains a computer/technology recycling program; maintains an on-campus recycling center; sustains a post-consumer food waste composting program; composts yard waste; reuses surplus department/office supplies; replaces paper materials with online alternatives; limits free printing in computer labs and libraries. *Campus dining operations:* uses reusable dishware.

Energy Currently uses or plans to use alternative sources of power (solar energy); timers to regulate temperatures based on occupancy hours; motion, infrared, and/or light sensors to reduce energy uses for lighting; LED lighting; and energy-related performance contracting.

Purchasing Sustainability criteria used in purchasing include Energy Star (EPA).

Contact Dean, Economic and Workforce Development Division, Shasta College, 1504 Market Street, Suite 200, PO Box 496006, Redding, CA 96001. *Phone:* 530-225-4835. *Fax:* 530-225-3904. *E-mail:* bbanghart@shastacollege.edu. *Web site:* www.shastacollege.edu/.

Colorado

Institute of Business & Medical Careers
Fort Collins, Colorado

Student Services and Green Events *Sustainability leadership:* recycling manager. *Student clubs and activities:* student club(s)/group(s) focused on sustainability. *Major sustainability events:* Chamber and BBB meetings.

Transportation Provides public transportation access to local destinations, a car sharing program, and incentives to carpool or use public transportation.

Buildings and Grounds *Percentage of institution's eligible buildings as of September 2008 meeting LEED and/or*

LEED-EB certification criteria: 50%. *Campus grounds care:* uses water conservation devices; employs strategies to reduce light pollution; landscapes with native plant species; applies to its grounds only pesticides and fertilizers allowable under the U.S. Department of Agriculture's standards for crop production.

Recycling *Events and organizations:* RecycleMania. *Programs and activities:* sustains a computer/technology recycling program; maintains an on-campus recycling center.

Energy Currently uses or plans to use timers to regulate temperatures based on occupancy hours.

Purchasing Sustainability criteria used in purchasing include Energy Star (EPA), WaterSense (EPA), Green Electronics Council (GEC) Electronic Product Environmental Assessment Tool (EPEAT) Silver or Gold, and Green Cleaning Products (Green Seal/Environmental Choice certified).

Contact President, Institute of Business & Medical Careers, 3842 South Mason Street, Fort Collins, CO 80525. *Phone:* 970-223-2669. *Fax:* 970-223-2796. *E-mail:* ssteele@ibmc.edu. *Web site:* www.ibmcedu.com/.

Florida

Chipola College
Marianna, Florida

Academics *Sustainability-focused undergraduate major(s):* Business Management (BAS), Education (BS), Nursing (BS). *Sustainability courses and programs:* sustainability-focused course(s) or lecture series.

Student Services and Green Events *Sustainability leadership:* sustainability coordinator/director, sustainability committee/advisory council, sustainability-focused student government. *Student clubs and activities:* outreach materials available about on-campus sustainability efforts.

Buildings and Grounds *Campus grounds care:* uses water conservation devices; landscapes with native plant species.

Recycling *Programs and activities:* reuses surplus department/office supplies; replaces paper materials with online alternatives; limits free printing in computer labs and libraries.

Energy Currently uses or plans to use timers to regulate temperatures based on occupancy hours and motion, infra-red, and/or light sensors to reduce energy uses for lighting.

Contact Recruitment Coordinator, Chipola College, 3235 Kynesville Road, Marianna, FL 32446. *Phone:* 850-718-2314. *E-mail:* johnsonn@chipola.edu. *Web site:* www.chipola.edu/.

St. Petersburg College
St. Petersburg, Florida

Academics *Sustainability-focused undergraduate major(s):* Environmental Science Technology (AS), Management and Organizational Leadership (BAS), Sustainability Management (BAS). *Sustainability courses and programs:* sustainability-focused course(s) or lecture series, noncredit sustainability course(s), sustainability-focused nonacademic certificate program(s).

Student Services and Green Events *Sustainability leadership:* sustainability coordinator/director, sustainability committee/advisory council, energy manager. *Student clubs and activities:* student club(s)/group(s) focused on sustainability, outreach materials available about on-campus sustainability efforts. *Major sustainability events:* Applying Sustainable Management Seminar, Green Cleaning Seminar.

Food Sustainable, organic, and/or locally produced foods available in on-campus dining facilities. Vegan and vegetarian dining options are available for every meal.

Transportation Provides public transportation access to local destinations and a car sharing program.

Buildings and Grounds *Renovation and maintenance:* registered for LEED certification for new construction and/or renovation; uses a Green Seal certified cleaning service. *Campus grounds care:* uses water conservation devices; employs strategies to reduce light pollution; landscapes with native plant species; protects, restores, and/or creates habitat on campus.

Recycling *Programs and activities:* sustains a computer/technology recycling program; maintains an on-campus recycling center; reuses surplus department/office supplies; replaces paper materials with online alternatives. *Campus dining operations:* operates without trays.

Energy Currently uses or plans to use timers to regulate temperatures based on occupancy hours; motion, infrared, and/or light sensors to reduce energy uses for lighting; LED lighting; vending machine motion sensors; and energy-related performance contracting.

Purchasing Sustainability criteria used in purchasing include Energy Star (EPA) and Green Cleaning Products (Green Seal/Environmental Choice certified).

Contact Sustainability Coordinator, St. Petersburg College, PO Box 13489, St. Petersburg, FL 33733. *Phone:* 727-341-3283. *Fax:* 727-341-3777. *E-mail:* green.jason@spcollege.edu. *Web site:* www.spjc.edu/.

Southwest Florida College
Fort Myers, Florida

Academics *Sustainability courses and programs:* sustainability-focused course(s) or lecture series.

Transportation Provides public transportation access to local destinations.

Recycling *Programs and activities:* maintains an on-campus recycling center.

Contact Southwest Florida College, 1685 Medical Lane, Fort Myers, FL 33907. *Phone:* 239-939-4766. *Web site:* www.swfc.edu/.

Georgia

Emory University, Oxford College
Oxford, Georgia

Academics *Sustainability courses and programs:* sustainability-focused course(s) or lecture series.

Student Services and Green Events *Sustainability leadership:* sustainability coordinator/director, sustainability committee/advisory council, recycling manager, energy manager. *Student clubs and activities:* student club(s)/group(s) focused on sustainability, outreach materials available about on-campus sustainability efforts. *Major sustainability events:* The Piedmont Project, annual celebration of Earth Day; films, lectures, and guest speakers. *Housing and facilities:* on-campus organic garden for students.

Food Sustainable, organic, and/or locally produced foods available in on-campus dining facilities. Vegan and vegetarian dining options are available for every meal.

Transportation Provides free on-campus transportation (bus or other), a bike loan/rental program, a car sharing program, and incentives to carpool or use public transportation.

Buildings and Grounds *Percentage of institution's eligible buildings as of September 2008 meeting LEED and/or LEED-EB certification criteria:* 5%. *Renovation and maintenance:* registered for LEED certification for new construction and/or renovation. *Campus grounds care:* uses water conservation devices; employs strategies to reduce light pollution; landscapes with native plant species; protects, restores, and/or creates habitat on campus.

Recycling *Events and organizations:* RecycleMania. *Programs and activities:* sustains a computer/technology recycling program; maintains an on-campus recycling center; composts yard waste; reuses surplus department/office supplies; limits free printing in computer labs and libraries. *Campus dining operations:* uses reusable dishware; offers discounts for reusable mugs.

Energy Currently uses or plans to use timers to regulate temperatures based on occupancy hours; motion, infrared, and/or light sensors to reduce energy uses for lighting; LED lighting; and energy-related performance contracting.

Contact Special Assistant to the Dean for Strategic Initiatives, Emory University, Oxford College, 100 Hamill Street, Oxford, GA 30054. *Phone:* 770-784-4692. *E-mail:* erik.oliver@emory.edu. *Web site:* http://oxford.emory.edu.

Young Harris College
Young Harris, Georgia

Sustainability Initiatives Young Harris College has Green Fees (optional/required) dedicated to sustainability initiatives.

Academics *Sustainability courses and programs:* sustainability-focused course(s) or lecture series.

Student Services and Green Events *Sustainability leadership:* sustainability coordinator/director, sustainability committee/advisory council, recycling manager. *Student clubs and activities:* Campus Climate Challenge. *Housing and facilities:* on-campus organic garden for students.

Food Vegan and vegetarian dining options are available for every meal.

Buildings and Grounds *Renovation and maintenance:* registered for LEED certification for new construction and/or renovation. *Campus grounds care:* uses water conservation devices; landscapes with native plant species; protects, restores, and/or creates habitat on campus.

Recycling *Programs and activities:* sustains a computer/technology recycling program; maintains an on-campus recycling center; composts yard waste; limits free printing in computer labs and libraries. *Campus dining operations:* uses reusable dishware; operates without trays; offers discounts for reusable mugs; uses bulk condiment dispensers and decreased packaging for to-go food service purchases.

Energy Currently uses or plans to use alternative sources of power (geothermal energy); timers to regulate temperatures based on occupancy hours; and motion, infrared, and/or light sensors to reduce energy uses for lighting.

Contact Sustainability Coordinator, Young Harris College, PO Box 68, 1 College Street, Young Harris, GA 30582. *Phone:* 706-379-5153. *E-mail:* bkhull@yhc.edu. *Web site:* www.yhc.edu/.

Illinois

City Colleges of Chicago, Wilbur Wright College
Chicago, Illinois

Sustainability Initiatives City Colleges of Chicago, Wilbur Wright College's president has signed the American College & University Presidents Climate Commitment.

Academics *Sustainability-focused undergraduate major(s):* Building Energy Technology. *Sustainability courses and programs:* sustainability-focused course(s) or lecture series.

Student Services and Green Events *Sustainability leadership:* sustainability coordinator/director, recycling manager. *Student clubs and activities:* outreach materials available about on-campus sustainability efforts. *Housing and facilities:* student-run café that serves environmentally or socially preferable foods.

Food Fair Trade coffee is used. Vegan and vegetarian dining options are available for every meal.

Buildings and Grounds *Campus grounds care:* landscapes with native plant species; protects, restores, and/or creates habitat on campus.

Recycling *Programs and activities:* sustains a computer/technology recycling program; maintains an on-campus recycling center.

Purchasing Sustainability criteria used in purchasing include Energy Star (EPA) and Green Cleaning Products (Green Seal/Environmental Choice certified).

Contact Director, Sustainability Program, City Colleges of Chicago, Wilbur Wright College, 4300 North Narragansett Avenue, Chicago, IL 60634. *Phone:* 773-777-7900. *E-mail:* dinman@ccc.edu. *Web site:* http://wright.ccc.edu/.

College of Lake County
Grayslake, Illinois

Sustainability Initiatives College of Lake County's president has signed the American College & University Presidents Climate Commitment.

Academics *Sustainability courses and programs:* sustainability-focused course(s) or lecture series, noncredit sustainability course(s).

Student Services and Green Events *Sustainability leadership:* sustainability committee/advisory council, recycling manager, energy manager, sustainability-focused student government. *Student clubs and activities:* Campus Climate Challenge. *Housing and facilities:* on-campus organic garden for students.

Food Vegan and vegetarian dining options are available for every meal.

Transportation Provides public transportation access to local destinations and incentives to carpool or use public transportation.

Buildings and Grounds *Renovation and maintenance:* registered for LEED certification for new construction and/or renovation. *Campus grounds care:* landscapes with native plant species; protects, restores, and/or creates habitat on campus; applies to its grounds only pesticides and fertilizers allowable under the U.S. Department of Agriculture's standards for crop production.

Recycling *Programs and activities:* replaces paper materials with online alternatives; limits free printing in computer labs and libraries. *Campus dining operations:* offers discounts for reusable mugs; uses bulk condiment dispensers and decreased packaging for to-go food service purchases.

Energy Currently uses or plans to use timers to regulate temperatures based on occupancy hours; motion, infrared, and/or light sensors to reduce energy uses for lighting; LED lighting; and energy-related performance contracting.

Purchasing Sustainability criteria used in purchasing include Green Cleaning Products (Green Seal/ Environmental Choice certified).

Contact Acting Vice President for Administrative Affairs, College of Lake County, 19351 West Washington Street, Grayslake, IL 60030. *Phone:* 847-543-2631. *Fax:* 847-223-1639. *E-mail:* nmcnerney@clcillinois.edu. *Web site:* www.clcillinois.edu/.

Heartland Community College
Normal, Illinois

Sustainability Initiatives Heartland Community College's president has signed the American College & University Presidents Climate Commitment. Heartland Community College has Green Fees (optional/required) dedicated to sustainability initiatives.

Academics *Sustainability courses and programs:* sustainability-focused course(s) or lecture series, noncredit sustainability course(s), sustainability-focused nonacademic certificate program(s).

Student Services and Green Events *Sustainability leadership:* sustainability coordinator/director, sustainability committee/advisory council. *Student clubs and activities:* student club(s)/group(s) focused on sustainability, outreach materials available about on-campus sustainability efforts. *Major sustainability events:* Green Team Symposium, Illinois Energy Expo.

Food Sustainable, organic, and/or locally produced foods available in on-campus dining facilities. Fair Trade coffee is used. Vegan and vegetarian dining options are available for every meal.

Transportation Provides public transportation access to local destinations.

Buildings and Grounds *Percentage of institution's eligible buildings as of September 2008 meeting LEED and/or LEED-EB certification criteria:* 30%. *Renovation and maintenance:* registered for LEED certification for new construction and/or renovation. *Campus grounds care:* uses water conservation devices; employs strategies to reduce light pollution; landscapes with native plant species; protects, restores, and/or creates habitat on campus.

Recycling *Programs and activities:* sustains a computer/technology recycling program; maintains an on-campus recycling center; composts yard waste; reuses surplus department/office supplies; replaces paper materials with online alternatives. *Campus dining operations:* operates without trays.

Energy Currently uses or plans to use alternative sources of power (geothermal energy); timers to regulate temperatures based on occupancy hours; motion, infrared, and/or light sensors to reduce energy uses for lighting; LED lighting; and energy-related performance contracting.

Purchasing Sustainability criteria used in purchasing include Energy Star (EPA) and Green Cleaning Products (Green Seal/Environmental Choice certified).

Contact Coordinator of the Green Institute, Heartland Community College, 1500 West Raab Road, WDC Suite 2400, Normal, IL 61761. *Phone:* 309-268-8166. *Fax:* 309-268-7882. *E-mail:* julie.elzanati@heartland.edu. *Web site:* www.heartland.edu/.

Kankakee Community College
Kankakee, Illinois

Sustainability Initiatives Kankakee Community College is a member of the Association for the Advancement of Sustainability in Higher Education (AASHE). This institution's president has signed the American College & University Presidents Climate Commitment.

Academics *Sustainability-focused undergraduate major(s):* Small Wind Technician (AAS), Solar Photovoltaic technician (AAS), Solar Thermal technician (AAS), Survey of Renewable Energy (AAS). *Sustainability courses and programs:* sustainability-focused course(s) or lecture series, noncredit sustainability course(s), sustainability-focused nonacademic certificate program(s).

Student Services and Green Events *Sustainability leadership:* sustainability coordinator/director, sustainability committee/advisory council. *Student clubs and activities:* student club(s)/group(s) focused on sustainability, outreach materials available about on-campus sustainability efforts. *Major sustainability events:* Taste of Sustainability, Suburban/Urban Permaculture Design Course (with Midwest Permaculture), The Great Recycling Weigh-in, Women in Business, Solar Tour.

Food Vegan and vegetarian dining options are available for every meal.

Transportation Provides public transportation access to local destinations and incentives to carpool or use public transportation.

Buildings and Grounds *Percentage of institution's eligible buildings as of September 2008 meeting LEED and/or LEED-EB certification criteria:* 10%. *Renovation and maintenance:* uses a Green Seal certified cleaning service. *Campus grounds care:* uses water conservation devices; employs strategies to reduce light pollution; landscapes with native plant species; protects, restores, and/or creates habitat on campus; applies to its grounds only pesticides and fertilizers allowable under the U.S. Department of Agriculture's standards for crop production.

Recycling *Events and organizations:* RecycleMania. *Programs and activities:* sustains a computer/technology recycling program; maintains an on-campus recycling center; reuses surplus department/office supplies; replaces paper materials with online alternatives. *Campus dining operations:* uses bulk condiment dispensers and decreased packaging for to-go food service purchases.

Energy Currently uses or plans to use alternative sources of power (solar energy); motion, infrared, and/or light sensors to reduce energy uses for lighting; and LED lighting.

Purchasing Sustainability criteria used in purchasing include Energy Star (EPA), Green Cleaning Products (Green Seal/Environmental Choice certified), and Forest Stewardship Council (FSC) or American Forest and Paper Association's Sustainable Forestry Initiative (SFI) paper.

Contact Dean of Sustainability and Planning, Kankakee Community College, 100 College Drive, Kankakee, IL 60901. *Phone:* 815-802-8242. *E-mail:* bjacobson@kcc.edu. *Web site:* www.kcc.cc.il.us/.

Indiana

Ancilla College
Donaldson, Indiana

Sustainability Initiatives Ancilla College is a signatory to the Talloires Declaration. This institution's president has signed the American College & University Presidents Climate Commitment.

Student Services and Green Events *Sustainability leadership:* sustainability committee/advisory council. *Student clubs and activities:* Campus Climate Challenge.

Food Vegan and vegetarian dining options are available for every meal.

Transportation Provides a car sharing program.

Buildings and Grounds *Renovation and maintenance:* uses a Green Seal certified cleaning service. *Campus grounds care:* uses water conservation devices; employs strategies to reduce light pollution; landscapes with native plant species; protects, restores, and/or creates habitat on campus; applies to its grounds only pesticides and fertilizers allowable under the U.S. Department of Agriculture's standards for crop production.

Recycling *Programs and activities:* sustains a computer/technology recycling program; maintains an on-campus recycling center; composts yard waste; reuses surplus department/office supplies.

Energy Currently uses or plans to use alternative sources of power (geothermal energy) and timers to regulate temperatures based on occupancy hours.

Purchasing Sustainability criteria used in purchasing include Energy Star (EPA) and Green Cleaning Products (Green Seal/Environmental Choice certified).

Contact Ancilla College, Union Road, PO Box 1, Donaldson, IN 46513. *Phone:* 574-936-8898. *Web site:* www.ancilla.edu/.

Kansas

Johnson County Community College
Overland Park, Kansas

Sustainability Initiatives Johnson County Community College's president has signed the American College & University Presidents Climate Commitment.

Academics *Sustainability courses and programs:* sustainability-focused course(s) or lecture series, noncredit sustainability course(s), sustainability-focused nonacademic certificate program(s).

Student Services and Green Events *Sustainability leadership:* sustainability coordinator/director, sustainability committee/advisory council, energy manager. *Student clubs and activities:* student club(s)/group(s) focused on sustainability. *Major sustainability events:* American Wind Energy Association Kansas Tour, Earth Day events, sustainability dinners with local foods. *Housing and facilities:* on-campus organic garden for students.

Food Sustainable, organic, and/or locally produced foods available in on-campus dining facilities. Fair Trade coffee is used. Vegan and vegetarian dining options are available for every meal.

Transportation Provides public transportation access to local destinations.

Buildings and Grounds *Renovation and maintenance:* registered for LEED certification for new construction and/or renovation; uses a Green Seal certified cleaning service. *Campus grounds care:* uses water conservation devices; landscapes with native plant species; protects, restores, and/or creates habitat on campus.

Recycling *Events and organizations:* RecycleMania. *Programs and activities:* sustains a computer/technology recycling program; reuses surplus department/office supplies; replaces paper materials with online alternatives. *Campus dining operations:* uses reusable dishware; offers discounts for reusable mugs.

Energy Currently uses or plans to use alternative sources of power and motion, infrared, and/or light sensors to reduce energy uses for lighting.

Purchasing Sustainability criteria used in purchasing include Energy Star (EPA).

Contact Executive Director, JCCC Sustainability Center, Johnson County Community College, 12345 College Boulevard, Overland Park, KS 66210. *Phone:* 913-469-8500 Ext. 4245. *E-mail:* jantle@jccc.edu. *Web site:* www.johnco.cc.ks.us/.

Pratt Community College
Pratt, Kansas

Transportation Provides public transportation access to local destinations.

Recycling *Programs and activities:* sustains a computer/technology recycling program; sustains a post-consumer food waste composting program; reuses surplus department/office supplies; reuses chemicals; replaces paper materials with online alternatives; limits free printing in computer labs and libraries. *Campus dining operations:* uses reusable dishware; uses bulk condiment dispensers and decreased packaging for to-go food service purchases.

Energy Currently uses or plans to use alternative sources of power (wind energy); timers to regulate temperatures based on occupancy hours; motion, infrared, and/or light sensors to reduce energy uses for lighting; LED lighting; and energy-related performance contracting.

Contact Vice President, Finance and Operations, Pratt Community College, 348 NE SR 61, Pratt, KS 67124. *Phone:* 620-450-2250. *E-mail:* kenta@prattcc.edu. *Web site:* www.prattcc.edu/.

Maryland

Anne Arundel Community College
Arnold, Maryland

Academics *Sustainability-focused undergraduate major(s):* Architecture, Biology, Environmental Science, Interior Design, Landscape Architecture, Plant Science. *Sustainability courses and programs:* sustainability-focused course(s) or lecture series, noncredit sustainability course(s).

Student Services and Green Events *Sustainability leadership:* sustainability committee/advisory council, recycling manager. *Student clubs and activities:* outreach materials available about on-campus sustainability efforts.

Food Sustainable, organic, and/or locally produced foods available in on-campus dining facilities. Fair Trade coffee is used. Vegan and vegetarian dining options are available for every meal.

Transportation Provides incentives to carpool or use public transportation.

Buildings and Grounds *Percentage of institution's eligible buildings as of September 2008 meeting LEED and/or LEED-EB certification criteria:* 10%. *Renovation and maintenance:* uses a Green Seal certified cleaning service. *Campus grounds care:* uses water conservation devices; employs strategies to reduce light pollution; landscapes with native plant species; protects, restores, and/or creates habitat on campus.

Recycling *Programs and activities:* sustains a computer/technology recycling program; maintains an on-campus recycling center; reuses surplus department/office supplies; replaces paper materials with online alternatives. *Campus *dining operations:* operates without trays; offers discounts for reusable mugs; uses bulk condiment dispensers and decreased packaging for to-go food service purchases.

Energy Currently uses or plans to use alternative sources of power and motion, infrared, and/or light sensors to reduce energy uses for lighting.

Purchasing Sustainability criteria used in purchasing include Energy Star (EPA), Green Cleaning Products (Green Seal/Environmental Choice certified), and Forest Stewardship Council (FSC) or American Forest and Paper Association's Sustainable Forestry Initiative (SFI) paper.

Contact Anne Arundel Community College, 101 College Parkway, Arnold, MD 21012-1895. *Phone:* 410-647-7100. *Web site:* www.aacc.edu/.

Howard Community College
Columbia, Maryland

Sustainability Initiatives Howard Community College's president has signed the American College & University Presidents Climate Commitment.

Academics *Sustainability-focused undergraduate major(s):* Environmental Science (AA). *Sustainability courses and programs:* sustainability-focused course(s) or lecture series, noncredit sustainability course(s), sustainability-focused nonacademic certificate program(s).

Student Services and Green Events *Sustainability leadership:* sustainability coordinator/director, sustainability committee/advisory council. *Student clubs and activities:* Campus Climate Challenge.

Food Sustainable, organic, and/or locally produced foods available in on-campus dining facilities. Fair Trade coffee is used. Vegan and vegetarian dining options are available for every meal.

Transportation Provides public transportation access to local destinations.

Buildings and Grounds *Percentage of institution's eligible buildings as of September 2008 meeting LEED and/or LEED-EB certification criteria:* 25%. *Campus grounds care:* employs strategies to reduce light pollution; landscapes with native plant species; protects, restores, and/or creates habitat on campus.

Recycling *Events and organizations:* RecycleMania. *Programs and activities:* sustains a computer/technology recycling program; composts yard waste; reuses surplus department/office supplies; limits free printing in computer labs and libraries. *Campus dining operations:* offers discounts for reusable mugs.

Energy Currently uses or plans to use timers to regulate temperatures based on occupancy hours; motion, infrared, and/or light sensors to reduce energy uses for lighting; and LED lighting.

Purchasing Sustainability criteria used in purchasing include Energy Star (EPA), Green Cleaning Products (Green Seal/Environmental Choice certified), and Forest Stewardship Council (FSC) or American Forest and Paper Association's Sustainable Forestry Initiative (SFI) paper.

Contact Sustainability Manager, Howard Community College, 10901 Little Patuxent Parkway, Columbia, MD 21044. *Phone:* 410-772-4962. *Fax:* 410-772-4909. *E-mail:* rmarietta@howardcc.edu. *Web site:* www.howardcc.edu/.

Massachusetts

Bunker Hill Community College
Boston, Massachusetts

Sustainability Initiatives Bunker Hill Community College is a member of the Association for the Advancement of Sustainability in Higher Education (AASHE). This institution's president has signed the American College & University Presidents Climate Commitment.

Academics *Sustainability courses and programs:* sustainability-focused course(s) or lecture series.

Student Services and Green Events *Sustainability leadership:* sustainability committee/advisory council, recycling manager. *Student clubs and activities:* student club(s)/group(s) focused on sustainability. *Major sustainability events:* CANstruction, mini expo for businesses and vendors, Project Green.

Food Sustainable, organic, and/or locally produced foods available in on-campus dining facilities. Fair Trade coffee is used. Vegan and vegetarian dining options are available for every meal.

Transportation Provides free on-campus transportation (bus or other), public transportation access to local destinations, and incentives to carpool or use public transportation.

Buildings and Grounds *Renovation and maintenance:* registered for LEED certification for new construction and/or renovation; uses a Green Seal certified cleaning service. *Campus grounds care:* uses water conservation devices; landscapes with native plant species.

Recycling *Events and organizations:* RecycleMania. *Programs and activities:* sustains a computer/technology recycling program; maintains an on-campus recycling center; reuses surplus department/office supplies.

Energy Currently uses or plans to use alternative sources of power; timers to regulate temperatures based on occupancy hours; motion, infrared, and/or light sensors to reduce energy uses for lighting; LED lighting; and energy-related performance contracting.

Purchasing Sustainability criteria used in purchasing include Energy Star (EPA) and Green Cleaning Products (Green Seal/Environmental Choice certified).

Contact Manager of Buildings and Grounds, Bunker Hill Community College, 250 New Rutherford Avenue, Boston, MA 02129. *Phone:* 617-228-3474. *E-mail:* prighi@bhcc.mass.edu. *Web site:* www.bhcc.mass.edu/.

Cape Cod Community College
West Barnstable, Massachusetts

Sustainability Initiatives Cape Cod Community College's president has signed the American College & University Presidents Climate Commitment.

Academics *Sustainability-focused undergraduate major(s):* Environmental Technology (AA), Environmental Technology (AS). *Sustainability courses and programs:* sustainability-focused course(s) or lecture series, noncredit sustainability course(s), sustainability-focused nonacademic certificate program(s).

Student Services and Green Events *Sustainability leadership:* sustainability coordinator/director, sustainability committee/advisory council, recycling manager, energy manager. *Student clubs and activities:* Campus Climate Challenge, student club(s)/group(s) focused on sustainability, outreach materials available about on-campus sustainability efforts. *Major sustainability events:* Annual Cape Cod

Sustainability Festival. *Housing and facilities:* student-run café that serves environmentally or socially preferable foods.

Food Sustainable, organic, and/or locally produced foods available in on-campus dining facilities. Vegan and vegetarian dining options are available for every meal.

Transportation Provides public transportation access to local destinations, a car sharing program, and incentives to carpool or use public transportation.

Buildings and Grounds *Percentage of institution's eligible buildings as of September 2008 meeting LEED and/or LEED-EB certification criteria:* 10%. *Renovation and maintenance:* registered for LEED certification for new construction and/or renovation; uses a Green Seal certified cleaning service. *Campus grounds care:* uses water conservation devices; employs strategies to reduce light pollution; landscapes with native plant species; protects, restores, and/or creates habitat on campus; applies to its grounds only pesticides and fertilizers allowable under the U.S. Department of Agriculture's standards for crop production.

Recycling *Programs and activities:* sustains a computer/technology recycling program; maintains an on-campus recycling center; sustains a pre-consumer food waste composting program; sustains a post-consumer food waste composting program; composts yard waste; reuses surplus department/office supplies; reuses chemicals; limits free printing in computer labs and libraries. *Campus dining operations:* uses reusable dishware; uses bulk condiment dispensers and decreased packaging for to-go food service purchases.

Energy Currently uses or plans to use alternative sources of power (solar energy); timers to regulate temperatures based on occupancy hours; motion, infrared, and/or light sensors to reduce energy uses for lighting; LED lighting; vending machine motion sensors; and energy-related performance contracting.

Purchasing Sustainability criteria used in purchasing include Energy Star (EPA), WaterSense (EPA), and Green Cleaning Products (Green Seal/Environmental Choice certified).

Contact Director of College Communications, Cape Cod Community College, 2240 Iyannough Road, West Barnstable, MA 02668-1599. *Phone:* 508-362-2131 Ext. 4714. *Fax:* 508-375-4057. *E-mail:* mgross@capecod.edu. *Web site:* www.capecod.mass.edu/.

Greenfield Community College
Greenfield, Massachusetts

Sustainability Initiatives Greenfield Community College's president has signed the American College & University Presidents Climate Commitment. Greenfield Community College has Green Fees (optional/required) dedicated to sustainability initiatives.

Academics *Sustainability-focused undergraduate major(s):* Renewable Energy/Efficiency (AS). *Sustainability courses and programs:* sustainability-focused course(s) or lecture series, noncredit sustainability course(s), sustainability-focused nonacademic certificate program(s).

Student Services and Green Events *Sustainability leadership:* sustainability coordinator/director, sustainability committee/advisory council, recycling manager, energy manager. *Student clubs and activities:* Campus Climate Challenge, Public Interest Research Group (PIRG) chapter on campus, student club(s)/group(s) focused on sustainability, outreach materials available about on-campus sustainability efforts.

Food Fair Trade coffee is used.

Transportation Provides free on-campus transportation (bus or other), public transportation access to local destinations, a car sharing program, and incentives to carpool or use public transportation.

Buildings and Grounds *Renovation and maintenance:* registered for LEED certification for new construction and/or renovation. *Campus grounds care:* uses water conservation devices; employs strategies to reduce light pollution; landscapes with native plant species; protects, restores, and/or creates habitat on campus.

Recycling *Programs and activities:* sustains a computer/technology recycling program; composts yard waste; reuses surplus department/office supplies; reuses chemicals; replaces paper materials with online alternatives. *Campus dining operations:* uses reusable dishware; operates without trays; offers discounts for reusable mugs; uses bulk condiment dispensers and decreased packaging for to-go food service purchases.

Energy Currently uses or plans to use alternative sources of power (solar energy); timers to regulate temperatures based on occupancy hours; motion, infrared, and/or light sensors to reduce energy uses for lighting; LED lighting; and energy-related performance contracting.

Purchasing Sustainability criteria used in purchasing include Energy Star (EPA), WaterSense (EPA), and Forest Stewardship Council (FSC) or American Forest and Paper Association's Sustainable Forestry Initiative (SFI) paper.

Contact Green Committee Chair and Coordinator, Greenfield Community College, One College Drive, Greenfield, MA 01301. *Phone:* 413-755-1331. *E-mail:* archbald@gcc.mass.edu. *Web site:* www.gcc.mass.edu/.

Quinsigamond Community College
Worcester, Massachusetts

Sustainability Initiatives Quinsigamond Community College's president has signed the American College & University Presidents Climate Commitment.

Academics *Sustainability courses and programs:* sustainability-focused course(s) or lecture series, noncredit sustainability course(s).

Student Services and Green Events *Sustainability leadership:* sustainability coordinator/director, sustainability committee/advisory council, recycling manager.

Transportation Provides public transportation access to local destinations, a car sharing program, and incentives to carpool or use public transportation.

Buildings and Grounds *Renovation and maintenance:* registered for LEED certification for new construction and/or renovation; uses a Green Seal certified cleaning service. *Campus grounds care:* uses water conservation devices; employs strategies to reduce light pollution; landscapes with native plant species.

Recycling *Programs and activities:* sustains a computer/technology recycling program; maintains an on-campus recycling center; sustains a post-consumer food waste composting program; reuses surplus department/office supplies; replaces paper materials with online alternatives; limits free printing in computer labs and libraries.

Energy Currently uses or plans to use timers to regulate temperatures based on occupancy hours; motion, infrared, and/or light sensors to reduce energy uses for lighting; LED lighting; and vending machine motion sensors.

Purchasing Sustainability criteria used in purchasing include Energy Star (EPA) and Green Cleaning Products (Green Seal/Environmental Choice certified).

Contact Assistant Director of Facilities, Quinsigamond Community College, 670 West Boylston Street, Worcester, MA 01606. *Phone:* 508-854-4523. *E-mail:* sgauthier@qcc.mass.edu. *Web site:* www.qcc.mass.edu/.

Michigan

Grand Rapids Community College

Grand Rapids, Michigan

Sustainability Initiatives Grand Rapids Community College is a signatory to the Talloires Declaration. This institution's president has signed the American College & University Presidents Climate Commitment.

Academics *Sustainability courses and programs:* sustainability-focused course(s) or lecture series, noncredit sustainability course(s), sustainability-focused nonacademic certificate program(s).

Student Services and Green Events *Sustainability leadership:* sustainability coordinator/director, sustainability committee/advisory council, recycling manager, energy manager, sustainability-focused student government. *Student clubs and activities:* Campus Climate Challenge, student club(s)/group(s) focused on sustainability, outreach materials available about on-campus sustainability efforts. *Major sustainability events:* Multiple Sustainability Conferences, Earth Week Activities.

Food Fair Trade coffee is used. Vegan and vegetarian dining options are available for every meal.

Transportation Provides public transportation access to local destinations.

Buildings and Grounds *Percentage of institution's eligible buildings as of September 2008 meeting LEED and/or LEED-EB certification criteria:* 5%. *Renovation and maintenance:* registered for LEED certification for new construction and/or renovation. *Campus grounds care:* uses water conservation devices; employs strategies to reduce light pollution; landscapes with native plant species; applies to its grounds only pesticides and fertilizers allowable under the U.S. Department of Agriculture's standards for crop production.

Recycling *Programs and activities:* sustains a computer/technology recycling program; maintains an on-campus recycling center; reuses surplus department/office supplies; replaces paper materials with online alternatives; limits free printing in computer labs and libraries. *Campus dining operations:* operates without trays; offers discounts for reusable mugs; uses bulk condiment dispensers and decreased packaging for to-go food service purchases.

Energy Currently uses or plans to use alternative sources of power (hydroelectricity/water power); timers to regulate temperatures based on occupancy hours; motion, infrared, and/or light sensors to reduce energy uses for lighting; and energy-related performance contracting. Participates in College & University Green Power Challenge activities.

Purchasing Sustainability criteria used in purchasing include Energy Star (EPA) and Green Cleaning Products (Green Seal/Environmental Choice certified).

Contact Director of Sustainability, Grand Rapids Community College, G2 Main Building, 143 Bostwick Avenue NW, Grand Rapids, MI 49503. *Phone:* 616-234-4284. *E-mail:* gburbrid@grcc.edu. *Web site:* www.grcc.edu/.

Jackson Community College

Jackson, Michigan

Sustainability Initiatives Jackson Community College is a member of the Association for the Advancement of Sustain-

ability in Higher Education (AASHE). This institution's president has signed the American College & University Presidents Climate Commitment.

Academics *Sustainability courses and programs:* sustainability-focused course(s) or lecture series, noncredit sustainability course(s).

Student Services and Green Events *Sustainability leadership:* sustainability coordinator/director, sustainability committee/advisory council.

Food Vegan and vegetarian dining options are available for every meal.

Transportation Provides public transportation access to local destinations and incentives to carpool or use public transportation.

Recycling *Campus dining operations:* operates without trays.

Energy Currently uses or plans to use alternative sources of power.

Purchasing Sustainability criteria used in purchasing include Energy Star (EPA).

Contact Sustainability Coordinator, Jackson Community College, 1362 Marlborough Drive, Ann Arbor, MI 48104. *Phone:* 617-872-8651. *E-mail:* rabinskmarkj@jccmi.edu. *Web site:* www.jccmi.edu/.

Lake Michigan College

Benton Harbor, Michigan

Sustainability Initiatives Lake Michigan College's president has signed the American College & University Presidents Climate Commitment.

Student Services and Green Events *Sustainability leadership:* sustainability coordinator/director, sustainability committee/advisory council.

Food Vegan and vegetarian dining options are available for every meal.

Transportation Provides public transportation access to local destinations.

Buildings and Grounds *Renovation and maintenance:* registered for LEED certification for new construction and/or renovation. *Campus grounds care:* uses water conservation devices; landscapes with native plant species; protects, restores, and/or creates habitat on campus.

Recycling *Programs and activities:* sustains a computer/technology recycling program; replaces paper materials with online alternatives. *Campus dining operations:* uses bulk condiment dispensers and decreased packaging for to-go food service purchases.

Energy Currently uses or plans to use motion, infrared, and/or light sensors to reduce energy uses for lighting and LED lighting.

Purchasing Sustainability criteria used in purchasing include Energy Star (EPA) and Green Cleaning Products (Green Seal/Environmental Choice certified).

Contact Executive Director, Facilities Management, Lake Michigan College, 2755 East Napier Avenue, Benton Harbor, MI 49022. *Phone:* 269-927-8611. *Fax:* 269-927-6658. *E-mail:* vanginhoven@lakemichigancollege.edu. *Web site:* www.lmc.cc.mi.us/.

Minnesota

Century College

White Bear Lake, Minnesota

Sustainability Initiatives Century College's president has signed the American College & University Presidents Climate Commitment.

Academics *Sustainability courses and programs:* sustainability-focused course(s) or lecture series.

Student Services and Green Events *Sustainability leadership:* sustainability committee/advisory council. *Student clubs and activities:* student club(s)/group(s) focused on sustainability. *Major sustainability events:* Focus the Nation National Teach-In, Century College Campus Conferences.

Buildings and Grounds *Percentage of institution's eligible buildings as of September 2008 meeting LEED and/or LEED-EB certification criteria:* 20%. *Campus grounds care:* landscapes with native plant species; protects, restores, and/or creates habitat on campus.

Recycling *Events and organizations:* RecycleMania. *Programs and activities:* composts yard waste.

Energy Currently uses or plans to use alternative sources of power and motion, infrared, and/or light sensors to reduce energy uses for lighting.

Contact Co-Chair, President's Climate Committee and Biology Faculty, Century College, Science Department, 3300 Century Avenue North, White Bear Lake, MN 55110. *Phone:* 651-779-3476. *E-mail:* pamela.thinesen@century.edu. *Web site:* www.century.edu/.

Lake Superior College
Duluth, Minnesota

Sustainability Initiatives Lake Superior College's president has signed the American College & University Presidents Climate Commitment.

Academics *Sustainability courses and programs:* sustainability-focused course(s) or lecture series.

Student Services and Green Events *Sustainability leadership:* sustainability committee/advisory council. *Student clubs and activities:* outreach materials available about on-campus sustainability efforts.

Food Vegan and vegetarian dining options are available for every meal.

Transportation Provides free on-campus transportation (bus or other), public transportation access to local destinations, and incentives to carpool or use public transportation.

Buildings and Grounds *Percentage of institution's eligible buildings as of September 2008 meeting LEED and/or LEED-EB certification criteria:* 15%. *Renovation and maintenance:* registered for LEED certification for new construction and/or renovation; uses a Green Seal certified cleaning service. *Campus grounds care:* uses water conservation devices; employs strategies to reduce light pollution; protects, restores, and/or creates habitat on campus.

Recycling *Events and organizations:* WasteWise (EPA). *Programs and activities:* sustains a computer/technology recycling program; maintains an on-campus recycling center; sustains a post-consumer food waste composting program; replaces paper materials with online alternatives; limits free printing in computer labs and libraries. *Campus dining operations:* uses reusable dishware; uses bulk condiment dispensers and decreased packaging for to-go food service purchases.

Energy Currently uses or plans to use timers to regulate temperatures based on occupancy hours; motion, infrared, and/or light sensors to reduce energy uses for lighting; and vending machine motion sensors.

Purchasing Sustainability criteria used in purchasing include Energy Star (EPA) and Green Cleaning Products (Green Seal/Environmental Choice certified).

Contact Vice President, Finance and Administration, Lake Superior College, 2101 Trinity Road, Duluth, MN 55811. *Phone:* 218-733-7613. *E-mail:* m.winson@lsc.edu. *Web site:* www.lsc.edu/.

Mesabi Range Community and Technical College
Virginia, Minnesota

Academics *Sustainability courses and programs:* sustainability-focused course(s) or lecture series.

Student Services and Green Events *Sustainability leadership:* sustainability committee/advisory council. *Student clubs and activities:* student club(s)/group(s) focused on sustainability. *Major sustainability events:* Northeast Higher Education District Sustainability Conference.

Recycling *Programs and activities:* sustains a computer/technology recycling program; maintains an on-campus recycling center; replaces paper materials with online alternatives.

Energy Currently uses or plans to use alternative sources of power; timers to regulate temperatures based on occupancy hours; motion, infrared, and/or light sensors to reduce energy uses for lighting; and LED lighting.

Purchasing Sustainability criteria used in purchasing include Green Cleaning Products (Green Seal/Environmental Choice certified).

Contact Executive Assistant, Mesabi Range Community and Technical College, 1001 Chestnut Street West, Virginia, MN 55792. *Phone:* 218-749-7786. *Fax:* 218-748-2419. *E-mail:* a.deloria@mr.mnscu.edu. *Web site:* www.mr.mnscu.edu/.

Rochester Community and Technical College
Rochester, Minnesota

Sustainability Initiatives Rochester Community and Technical College's president has signed the American College & University Presidents Climate Commitment.

Academics *Sustainability-focused undergraduate major(s):* Environmental Science. *Sustainability courses and programs:* sustainability-focused course(s) or lecture series.

Student Services and Green Events *Sustainability leadership:* sustainability committee/advisory council. *Student clubs and activities:* student club(s)/group(s) focused on sustainability. *Major sustainability events:* College Common Book with nationally known speaker.

Food Vegan and vegetarian dining options are available for every meal.

Transportation Provides public transportation access to local destinations.

Buildings and Grounds *Campus grounds care:* landscapes with native plant species; protects, restores, and/or creates habitat on campus.

Recycling *Programs and activities:* sustains a computer/technology recycling program; reuses surplus department/office supplies; replaces paper materials with online alternatives. *Campus dining operations:* operates without trays; offers discounts for reusable mugs.

Energy Currently uses or plans to use alternative sources of power (biomass energy); motion, infrared, and/or light sensors to reduce energy uses for lighting; and vending machine motion sensors.

Purchasing Sustainability criteria used in purchasing include Energy Star (EPA) and Green Cleaning Products (Green Seal/Environmental Choice certified).

Contact Rochester Community and Technical College, 851 30th Avenue, SE, Rochester, MN 55904-4999. *Phone:* 507-285-7210. *Web site:* www.rctc.edu/.

Missouri

Crowder College
Neosho, Missouri

Academics *Sustainability-focused undergraduate major(s):* Alternative Energy—Biofuels (AA, AAS), Alternative Energy—Solar (AA, AAS), Alternative Energy—Wind (AA, AAS), Pre-Engineering—Alternative Energy (AS). *Sustainability courses and programs:* sustainability-focused course(s) or lecture series, noncredit sustainability course(s), sustainability-focused nonacademic certificate program(s).

Student Services and Green Events *Sustainability leadership:* sustainability coordinator/director, sustainability committee/advisory council, recycling manager, energy manager, sustainability-focused student government. *Student clubs and activities:* student club(s)/group(s) focused on sustainability. *Major sustainability events:* annual "E-Conference". *Housing and facilities:* sustainability-themed housing.

Food Vegan and vegetarian dining options are available for every meal.

Transportation Provides a car sharing program.

Buildings and Grounds *Renovation and maintenance:* registered for LEED certification for new construction and/or renovation. *Campus grounds care:* employs strategies to reduce light pollution; landscapes with native plant species; protects, restores, and/or creates habitat on campus; applies to its grounds only pesticides and fertilizers allowable under the U.S. Department of Agriculture's standards for crop production.

Recycling *Programs and activities:* sustains a computer/technology recycling program; maintains an on-campus recycling center; reuses surplus department/office supplies; reuses chemicals; replaces paper materials with online alternatives. *Campus dining operations:* uses reusable dishware; uses bulk condiment dispensers and decreased packaging for to-go food service purchases.

Energy Currently uses or plans to use alternative sources of power (biomass energy, geothermal energy, solar energy, and wind energy) and LED lighting.

Purchasing Sustainability criteria used in purchasing include Energy Star (EPA) and Green Cleaning Products (Green Seal/Environmental Choice certified).

Contact Director, Crowder College, 601 Laclede Ave, Neosho, MO 64850. *Phone:* 417-455-5666. *Fax:* 417-455-5669. *E-mail:* eberle@crowder.edu. *Web site:* www.crowder.edu/.

Saint Charles Community College
St. Peters, Missouri

Food Sustainable, organic, and/or locally produced foods available in on-campus dining facilities. Fair Trade coffee is used. Vegan and vegetarian dining options are available for every meal.

Buildings and Grounds *Campus grounds care:* landscapes with native plant species; applies to its grounds only pesticides and fertilizers allowable under the U.S. Department of Agriculture's standards for crop production.

Recycling *Programs and activities:* sustains a computer/technology recycling program; reuses surplus department/office supplies; replaces paper materials with online alternatives. *Campus dining operations:* offers discounts for reusable mugs; uses bulk condiment dispensers and decreased packaging for to-go food service purchases.

Energy Currently uses or plans to use timers to regulate temperatures based on occupancy hours; motion, infrared, and/or light sensors to reduce energy uses for lighting; and LED lighting.

Purchasing Sustainability criteria used in purchasing include Forest Stewardship Council (FSC) or American Forest and Paper Association's Sustainable Forestry Initiative (SFI) paper.

Contact Saint Charles Community College, 4601 Mid Rivers Mall Drive, St. Peters, MO 63376-0975. *Phone:* 636-922-8000. *Web site:* www.stchas.edu/.

New Jersey

Atlantic Cape Community College
Mays Landing, New Jersey

Academics *Sustainability courses and programs:* noncredit sustainability course(s), sustainability-focused nonacademic certificate program(s).

Student Services and Green Events *Sustainability leadership:* sustainability coordinator/director, sustainability committee/advisory council.

Transportation Provides public transportation access to local destinations.

Buildings and Grounds *Percentage of institution's eligible buildings as of September 2008 meeting LEED and/or LEED-EB certification criteria:* 20%. *Renovation and maintenance:* uses a Green Seal certified cleaning service. *Campus grounds care:* employs strategies to reduce light pollution; landscapes with native plant species; protects, restores, and/or creates habitat on campus.

Recycling *Programs and activities:* reuses surplus department/office supplies; replaces paper materials with online alternatives; limits free printing in computer labs and libraries.

Energy Currently uses or plans to use alternative sources of power (geothermal energy); timers to regulate temperatures based on occupancy hours; and motion, infrared, and/or light sensors to reduce energy uses for lighting.

Purchasing Sustainability criteria used in purchasing include Energy Star (EPA), WaterSense (EPA), and Green Cleaning Products (Green Seal/Environmental Choice certified).

Contact Dean, Facilities, Planning and Research, Atlantic Cape Community College, 5100 Black Horse Pike, Mays Landing, NJ 08232. *Phone:* 609-343-5670. *E-mail:* rpernici@atlantic.edu. *Web site:* www.atlantic.edu/.

New Mexico

Santa Fe Community College
Santa Fe, New Mexico

Sustainability Initiatives Santa Fe Community College's president has signed the American College & University Presidents Climate Commitment.

Academics *Sustainability-focused undergraduate major(s):* Environmental Technologies (AAS). *Sustainability courses and programs:* sustainability-focused course(s) or lecture series, noncredit sustainability course(s), sustainability-focused nonacademic certificate program(s).

Student Services and Green Events *Sustainability leadership:* sustainability coordinator/director, sustainability committee/advisory council, recycling manager. *Student clubs and activities:* student club(s)/group(s) focused on sustainability, outreach materials available about on-campus sustainability efforts. *Major sustainability events:* Sustainability Day in October, workshops and speakers at Faculty Development Day.

Food Vegan and vegetarian dining options are available for every meal.

Transportation Provides public transportation access to local destinations.

Buildings and Grounds *Renovation and maintenance:* registered for LEED certification for new construction and/or renovation; uses a Green Seal certified cleaning service. *Campus grounds care:* uses water conservation devices; employs strategies to reduce light pollution; landscapes with native plant species; protects, restores, and/or creates habitat on campus; applies to its grounds only pesticides and fertilizers allowable under the U.S. Department of Agriculture's standards for crop production.

Recycling *Programs and activities:* sustains a computer/technology recycling program; maintains an on-campus recycling center; reuses surplus department/office supplies; reuses chemicals; replaces paper materials with online alternatives; limits free printing in computer labs and libraries. *Campus dining operations:* uses reusable dishware; offers discounts for reusable mugs.

Energy Currently uses or plans to use timers to regulate temperatures based on occupancy hours; motion, infrared, and/or light sensors to reduce energy uses for lighting; and energy-related performance contracting.

Purchasing Sustainability criteria used in purchasing include Energy Star (EPA) and Green Cleaning Products (Green Seal/Environmental Choice certified).

Contact Director of Workforce Development, Santa Fe Community College, 6401 Richards Avenue, Santa Fe, NM 87501. *Phone:* 505-428-1617. *Fax:* 505-428-1302. *E-mail:* lschreiber@sfccnm.edu. *Web site:* www.sfccnm.edu/.

New York

Fiorello H. LaGuardia Community College of the City University of New York
Long Island City, New York

Academics *Sustainability courses and programs:* sustainability-focused course(s) or lecture series, noncredit sustainability course(s), sustainability-focused nonacademic certificate program(s).

Student Services and Green Events *Sustainability leadership:* sustainability coordinator/director, sustainability committee/advisory council, recycling manager, energy manager. *Student clubs and activities:* student club(s)/group(s) focused on sustainability, outreach materials available about on-campus sustainability efforts. *Major sustainability events:* Annual Earth Day event.

Food Sustainable, organic, and/or locally produced foods available in on-campus dining facilities. Vegan and vegetarian dining options are available for every meal.

Transportation Provides public transportation access to local destinations.

Buildings and Grounds *Campus grounds care:* uses water conservation devices; employs strategies to reduce light pollution.

Recycling *Programs and activities:* sustains a computer/technology recycling program; replaces paper materials with online alternatives. *Campus dining operations:* operates without trays; offers discounts for reusable mugs; uses bulk condiment dispensers and decreased packaging for to-go food service purchases.

Energy Currently uses or plans to use timers to regulate temperatures based on occupancy hours; motion, infrared, and/or light sensors to reduce energy uses for lighting; and LED lighting.

Purchasing Sustainability criteria used in purchasing include Energy Star (EPA) and Green Cleaning Products (Green Seal/Environmental Choice certified).

Contact Executive Director of Facilities Management and Planning, Fiorello H. LaGuardia Community College of the City University of New York, 31-10 Thomson Avenue, Room E 409, Long Island City, NY 11101. *Phone:* 718-482-5502. *Fax:* 718-482-5495. *E-mail:* serfan@lagcc.cuny.edu. *Web site:* www.lagcc.cuny.edu/.

Kingsborough Community College of the City University of New York
Brooklyn, New York

Student Services and Green Events *Sustainability leadership:* sustainability coordinator/director, sustainability committee/advisory council, recycling manager, energy manager, sustainability-focused student government. *Student clubs and activities:* student club(s)/group(s) focused on sustainability, outreach materials available about on-campus sustainability efforts. *Major sustainability events:* Bi-Annual Campus Cleanup, Eco-Festival, Sustainability Summit, Annual NOAA Conference on Maritime Environment.

Food Fair Trade coffee is used. Vegan and vegetarian dining options are available for every meal.

Transportation Provides public transportation access to local destinations.

Buildings and Grounds *Renovation and maintenance:* uses a Green Seal certified cleaning service. *Campus grounds care:* uses water conservation devices; employs strategies to reduce light pollution; landscapes with native plant species; protects, restores, and/or creates habitat on campus.

Recycling *Events and organizations:* RecycleMania. *Programs and activities:* sustains a computer/technology recycling program; composts yard waste; reuses surplus department/office supplies; replaces paper materials with online alternatives; limits free printing in computer labs and libraries. *Campus dining operations:* operates without trays; offers discounts for reusable mugs; uses bulk condiment dispensers and decreased packaging for to-go food service purchases.

Energy Currently uses or plans to use alternative sources of power (solar energy); timers to regulate temperatures based on occupancy hours; motion, infrared, and/or light sensors to reduce energy uses for lighting; and energy-related performance contracting.

Purchasing Sustainability criteria used in purchasing include Energy Star (EPA), Green Cleaning Products (Green Seal/Environmental Choice certified), and Forest Stewardship Council (FSC) or American Forest and Paper Association's Sustainable Forestry Initiative (SFI) paper.

Contact Public Relations Director, Kingsborough Community College of the City University of New York, 2001 Oriental Boulevard, Brooklyn, NY 11235. *Phone:* 718-368-5543. *Fax:* 718-368-4705. *E-mail:* rryles@kbcc.cuny.edu. *Web site:* www.kbcc.cuny.edu/.

Onondaga Community College
Syracuse, New York

Sustainability Initiatives Onondaga Community College's president has signed the American College & University Presidents Climate Commitment.

Academics *Sustainability-focused undergraduate major(s):* Architectural Technology (AAS), Environmental Technology (AAS). *Sustainability courses and programs:* sustainability-focused course(s) or lecture series, noncredit sustainability course(s).

Student Services and Green Events *Sustainability leadership:* sustainability coordinator/director, sustainability committee/advisory council, recycling manager, energy manager. *Student clubs and activities:* student club(s)/group(s) focused on sustainability. *Major sustainability events:* Focus the Nation events, National Teach-In Days, Earth Week.

Food Vegan and vegetarian dining options are available for every meal.

Transportation Provides public transportation access to local destinations and incentives to carpool or use public transportation.

Buildings and Grounds *Percentage of institution's eligible buildings as of September 2008 meeting LEED and/or LEED-EB certification criteria:* 10%. *Renovation and maintenance:* registered for LEED certification for new construction and/or renovation. *Campus grounds care:* uses water conservation devices; landscapes with native plant species; protects, restores, and/or creates habitat on campus.

Recycling *Events and organizations:* RecycleMania. *Programs and activities:* sustains a computer/technology recycling program; sustains a pre-consumer food waste composting program; sustains a post-consumer food waste composting program; composts yard waste; reuses surplus department/office supplies; replaces paper materials with online alternatives. *Campus dining operations:* uses reusable dishware; offers discounts for reusable mugs; uses bulk condiment dispensers and decreased packaging for to-go food service purchases.

Energy Currently uses or plans to use alternative sources of power; timers to regulate temperatures based on occupancy hours; motion, infrared, and/or light sensors to reduce energy uses for lighting; LED lighting; and energy-related performance contracting.

Purchasing Sustainability criteria used in purchasing include Energy Star (EPA) and Green Cleaning Products (Green Seal/Environmental Choice certified).

Contact Director of Corporate and Public Partnerships, Onondaga Community College, 4585 West Seneca Turnpike, Syracuse, NY 13215-4585. *Phone:* 315-498-2543. *E-mail:* walld@sunyocc.edu. *Web site:* www.sunyocc.edu/.

Tompkins Cortland Community College
Dryden, New York

Sustainability Initiatives Tompkins Cortland Community College's president has signed the American College & University Presidents Climate Commitment.

Academics *Sustainability-focused undergraduate major(s):* Environmental Studies. *Sustainability courses and programs:* sustainability-focused course(s) or lecture series.

Student Services and Green Events *Sustainability leadership:* sustainability committee/advisory council, energy manager. *Student clubs and activities:* student club(s)/group(s) focused on sustainability. *Major sustainability events:* Earth Day events, Dinner and a Movie.

Transportation Provides public transportation access to local destinations.

Buildings and Grounds *Campus grounds care:* uses water conservation devices; landscapes with native plant species; protects, restores, and/or creates habitat on campus.

Recycling *Events and organizations:* RecycleMania. *Programs and activities:* sustains a computer/technology recycling program; sustains a pre-consumer food waste composting program; limits free printing in computer labs and libraries. *Campus dining operations:* operates without trays; uses bulk condiment dispensers and decreased packaging for to-go food service purchases.

Energy Currently uses or plans to use alternative sources of power and motion, infrared, and/or light sensors to reduce energy uses for lighting.

Purchasing Sustainability criteria used in purchasing include Energy Star (EPA).

Contact Assistant Professor of Biology, Tompkins Cortland Community College, 170 North Street, Dryden, NY 13053. *Phone:* 607-844-8211. *E-mail:* wesselk@TC3.edu. *Web site:* www.TC3.edu/.

Westchester Community College
Valhalla, New York

Sustainability Initiatives Westchester Community College's president has signed the American College & University Presidents Climate Commitment.

Academics *Sustainability courses and programs:* sustainability-focused course(s) or lecture series.

Student Services and Green Events *Sustainability leadership:* sustainability committee/advisory council. *Student clubs and activities:* student club(s)/group(s) focused on sustainability. *Major sustainability events:* Focus the Nation Teach-In on Global Warming Solutions, Earth Day.

Food Vegan and vegetarian dining options are available for every meal.

Transportation Provides public transportation access to local destinations.

Buildings and Grounds *Renovation and maintenance:* registered for LEED certification for new construction and/or renovation. *Campus grounds care:* uses water conservation devices; landscapes with native plant species; protects, restores, and/or creates habitat on campus.

Recycling *Events and organizations:* WasteWise (EPA). *Programs and activities:* maintains an on-campus recycling center; composts yard waste; reuses chemicals. *Campus dining operations:* uses bulk condiment dispensers and decreased packaging for to-go food service purchases.

Energy Currently uses or plans to use timers to regulate temperatures based on occupancy hours; motion, infrared, and/or light sensors to reduce energy uses for lighting; and LED lighting.

Purchasing Sustainability criteria used in purchasing include Energy Star (EPA) and Green Cleaning Products (Green Seal/Environmental Choice certified).

Contact Director, Physical Plant, Westchester Community College, 75 Grasslands Road, Valhalla, NY 10595. *Phone:* 914-606-6940. *E-mail:* kevin.garvey@sunywcc.edu. *Web site:* www.sunywcc.edu/.

North Carolina

Wilson Community College
Wilson, North Carolina

Sustainability Initiatives Wilson Community College's president has signed the American College & University Presidents Climate Commitment.

Academics *Sustainability courses and programs:* noncredit sustainability course(s).

Student Services and Green Events *Sustainability leadership:* sustainability coordinator/director, sustainability committee/advisory council, recycling manager. *Student clubs and activities:* Campus Climate Challenge.

Buildings and Grounds *Renovation and maintenance:* registered for LEED certification for new construction and/or renovation. *Campus grounds care:* uses water conservation devices; landscapes with native plant species.

Recycling *Events and organizations:* RecycleMania. *Programs and activities:* sustains a computer/technology recycling program; maintains an on-campus recycling center; reuses surplus department/office supplies; replaces paper materials with online alternatives.

Energy Currently uses or plans to use alternative sources of power (geothermal energy and solar energy) and motion, infrared, and/or light sensors to reduce energy uses for lighting.

Purchasing Sustainability criteria used in purchasing include Energy Star (EPA), Green Cleaning Products (Green Seal/Environmental Choice certified), and Forest Stewardship Council (FSC) or American Forest and Paper Association's Sustainable Forestry Initiative (SFI) paper.

Contact Dean of Continuing Education and Sustainability, Wilson Community College, 902 Herring Avenue, Wilson, NC 27893. *Phone:* 252-246-1254. *E-mail:* rholsten@wilsoncc.edu. *Web site:* www.wilsoncc.edu/.

North Dakota

United Tribes Technical College
Bismarck, North Dakota

Academics *Sustainability-focused undergraduate major(s):* Tribal Environmental Science. *Sustainability courses and programs:* sustainability-focused course(s) or lecture series.

Student Services and Green Events *Sustainability leadership:* sustainability committee/advisory council, recycling manager. *Student clubs and activities:* Campus Climate Challenge, student club(s)/group(s) focused on sustainability, outreach materials available about on-campus sustainability efforts. *Housing and facilities:* sustainability-themed housing, on-campus organic garden for students.

Transportation Provides free on-campus transportation (bus or other) and public transportation access to local destinations.

Buildings and Grounds *Campus grounds care:* employs strategies to reduce light pollution; landscapes with native plant species; protects, restores, and/or creates habitat on campus.

Recycling *Programs and activities:* maintains an on-campus recycling center; reuses surplus department/office supplies; replaces paper materials with online alternatives.

Contact United Tribes Technical College, 3315 University Drive, Bismarck, ND 58504-7596. *Phone:* 701-255-3285. *Web site:* www.uttc.edu/.

Oregon

Lane Community College
Eugene, Oregon

Sustainability Initiatives Lane Community College is a signatory to the Talloires Declaration. This institution's president has signed the American College & University Presidents Climate Commitment.

Academics *Sustainability-focused undergraduate major(s):* Energy Management Technician (AAS), Renewable Energy Technician (AAS), Water Conservation Technician (AAS). *Sustainability courses and programs:* sustainability-focused course(s) or lecture series, noncredit sustainability course(s), sustainability-focused nonacademic certificate program(s).

Student Services and Green Events *Sustainability leadership:* sustainability coordinator/director, sustainability committee/advisory council, recycling manager, energy manager. *Student clubs and activities:* Campus Climate Challenge, Public Interest Research Group (PIRG) chapter on campus, student club(s)/group(s) focused on sustainability, outreach materials available about on-campus sustainability efforts. *Major sustainability events:* National Conference on Sustainability for Community Colleges, Peace Conference, Local Food Network. *Housing and facilities:* on-campus organic garden for students.

Food Sustainable, organic, and/or locally produced foods available in on-campus dining facilities. Fair Trade coffee is used. Vegan and vegetarian dining options are available for every meal.

Transportation Provides free on-campus transportation (bus or other), public transportation access to local destinations, a car sharing program, and incentives to carpool or use public transportation.

Buildings and Grounds *Renovation and maintenance:* registered for LEED certification for new construction and/or renovation; uses a Green Seal certified cleaning service. *Campus grounds care:* uses water conservation devices; employs strategies to reduce light pollution; landscapes with native plant species; protects, restores, and/or creates habitat on campus; applies to its grounds only pesticides and fertilizers allowable under the U.S. Department of Agriculture's standards for crop production.

Recycling *Events and organizations:* RecycleMania, WasteWise (EPA). *Programs and activities:* sustains a computer/technology recycling program; maintains an on-campus recycling center; sustains a pre-consumer food waste composting program; sustains a post-consumer food waste composting program; composts yard waste; reuses surplus department/office supplies; replaces paper materials with online alternatives. *Campus dining operations:* uses reusable dishware; offers discounts for reusable mugs.

Energy Currently uses or plans to use alternative sources of power (biomass energy, geothermal energy, hydroelectricity/water power, solar energy, and wind energy); timers to regulate temperatures based on occupancy hours; motion, infrared, and/or light sensors to reduce energy uses for lighting; and vending machine motion sensors.

Purchasing Sustainability criteria used in purchasing include Energy Star (EPA) and Green Cleaning Products (Green Seal/Environmental Choice certified).

Contact Sustainability Coordinator, Lane Community College, 4000 East 30th Avenue, Eugene, OR 97405. *Phone:* 541-463-5594. *Fax:* 541-463-4199. *E-mail:* haywardj@lanecc.edu. *Web site:* www.lanecc.edu/.

Pennsylvania

Montgomery County Community College
Blue Bell, Pennsylvania

Sustainability Initiatives Montgomery County Community College's president has signed the American College & University Presidents Climate Commitment.

Academics *Sustainability courses and programs:* sustainability-focused course(s) or lecture series, noncredit sustainability course(s).

Student Services and Green Events *Sustainability leadership:* sustainability committee/advisory council. *Student clubs and activities:* Campus Climate Challenge, student club(s)/group(s) focused on sustainability, outreach materials available about on-campus sustainability efforts. *Major sustainability events:* Community Day.

Food Sustainable, organic, and/or locally produced foods available in on-campus dining facilities. Vegan and vegetarian dining options are available for every meal.

Transportation Provides public transportation access to local destinations and a bike loan/rental program.

Buildings and Grounds *Renovation and maintenance:* registered for LEED certification for new construction and/or renovation; uses a Green Seal certified cleaning service. *Campus grounds care:* uses water conservation devices; employs strategies to reduce light pollution; landscapes with native plant species; protects, restores, and/or creates habitat on campus; applies to its grounds only pesticides and fertilizers allowable under the U.S. Department of Agriculture's standards for crop production.

Recycling *Events and organizations:* RecycleMania. *Programs and activities:* sustains a computer/technology recycling program; composts yard waste; reuses chemicals; replaces paper materials with online alternatives. *Campus dining operations:* uses reusable dishware; offers discounts for reusable mugs; uses bulk condiment dispensers and decreased packaging for to-go food service purchases.

Energy Currently uses or plans to use timers to regulate temperatures based on occupancy hours and motion, infrared, and/or light sensors to reduce energy uses for lighting.

Purchasing Sustainability criteria used in purchasing include Energy Star (EPA), Green Electronics Council (GEC) Electronic Product Environmental Assessment Tool (EPEAT) Silver or Gold, Green Cleaning Products (Green Seal/Environmental Choice certified), and Forest Stewardship Council (FSC) or American Forest and Paper Association's Sustainable Forestry Initiative (SFI) paper.

Contact Director, College Services, Montgomery County Community College, 340 DeKalb Pike, Blue Bell, PA 19422. *Phone:* 215-619-7353. *E-mail:* gshal@mc3.edu. *Web site:* www.mc3.edu/.

South Carolina

Trident Technical College
Charleston, South Carolina

Student Services and Green Events *Sustainability leadership:* recycling manager, energy manager.

Transportation Provides public transportation access to local destinations and incentives to carpool or use public transportation.

Buildings and Grounds *Renovation and maintenance:* registered for LEED certification for new construction and/or renovation. *Campus grounds care:* landscapes with native plant species.

Recycling *Programs and activities:* sustains a computer/technology recycling program; reuses surplus department/office supplies; reuses chemicals; replaces paper materials with online alternatives.

Energy Currently uses or plans to use timers to regulate temperatures based on occupancy hours and motion, infrared, and/or light sensors to reduce energy uses for lighting.

Purchasing Sustainability criteria used in purchasing include Energy Star (EPA).

Contact Trident Technical College, PO Box 118067, Charleston, SC 29423-8067. *Phone:* 843-574-6111. *Web site:* www.tridenttech.edu/.

Tennessee

Cleveland State Community College
Cleveland, Tennessee

Academics *Sustainability-focused undergraduate major(s):* Agriculture (AS), Construction (AAS), Natural Science (AS), Wildlife Management (AS). *Sustainability courses and programs:* sustainability-focused course(s) or lecture series, noncredit sustainability course(s), sustainability-focused nonacademic certificate program(s).

Student Services and Green Events *Sustainability leadership:* sustainability committee/advisory council. *Student clubs and activities:* student club(s)/group(s) focused on sustainability. *Major sustainability events:* Arbor Day Celebration, The Green Festival. *Housing and facilities:* on-campus organic garden for students.

Buildings and Grounds *Campus grounds care:* landscapes with native plant species; protects, restores, and/or creates habitat on campus.

Recycling *Programs and activities:* maintains an on-campus recycling center; composts yard waste.

Energy Currently uses or plans to use alternative sources of power (geothermal energy and solar energy); timers to regulate temperatures based on occupancy hours; motion, infrared, and/or light sensors to reduce energy uses for lighting; and LED lighting.

Contact Cleveland State Community College, PO Box 3570, Cleveland, TN 37320-3570. *Phone:* 423-472-7141. *Web site:* www.clevelandstatecc.edu/.

Texas

McLennan Community College
Waco, Texas

Sustainability Initiatives McLennan Community College's president has signed the American College & University Presidents Climate Commitment.

Student Services and Green Events *Sustainability leadership:* sustainability coordinator/director, sustainability committee/advisory council, recycling manager, energy manager.

Transportation Provides free on-campus transportation (bus or other), public transportation access to local destinations, a bike loan/rental program, and incentives to carpool or use public transportation.

Buildings and Grounds *Renovation and maintenance:* registered for LEED certification for new construction and/or renovation. *Campus grounds care:* uses water conservation devices; employs strategies to reduce light pollution; applies to its grounds only pesticides and fertilizers allowable under the U.S. Department of Agriculture's standards for crop production.

Recycling *Events and organizations:* RecycleMania. *Programs and activities:* sustains a computer/technology recycling program; maintains an on-campus recycling center; limits free printing in computer labs and libraries. *Campus dining operations:* uses bulk condiment dispensers and decreased packaging for to-go food service purchases.

Energy Currently uses or plans to use alternative sources of power (geothermal energy and solar energy); motion, infrared, and/or light sensors to reduce energy uses for lighting; and LED lighting.

Purchasing Sustainability criteria used in purchasing include Energy Star (EPA).

Contact Director, Facilities Planning and Scheduling, McLennan Community College, 1400 College Drive, Waco, TX 76708. *Phone:* 254-299-8849. *E-mail:* sross@mclennan. edu. *Web site:* www.mclennan.edu/.

Odessa College
Odessa, Texas

Food Vegan and vegetarian dining options are available for every meal.

Transportation Provides public transportation access to local destinations.

Buildings and Grounds *Percentage of institution's eligible buildings as of September 2008 meeting LEED and/or LEED-EB certification criteria:* 40%. *Renovation and maintenance:* uses a Green Seal certified cleaning service. *Campus grounds care:* uses water conservation devices; employs strategies to reduce light pollution; landscapes with native plant species; applies to its grounds only pesticides and fertilizers allowable under the U.S. Department of Agriculture's standards for crop production.

Recycling *Events and organizations:* RecycleMania. *Programs and activities:* sustains a computer/technology recycling program; composts yard waste; reuses surplus department/office supplies; reuses chemicals; replaces paper materials with online alternatives; limits free printing in computer labs and libraries. *Campus dining operations:* uses reusable dishware; offers discounts for reusable mugs; uses bulk condiment dispensers and decreased packaging for to-go food service purchases.

Energy Currently uses or plans to use alternative sources of power; timers to regulate temperatures based on occupancy hours; motion, infrared, and/or light sensors to reduce energy uses for lighting; LED lighting; vending machine motion sensors; and energy-related performance contracting.

Purchasing Sustainability criteria used in purchasing include Energy Star (EPA), WaterSense (EPA), and Green Cleaning Products (Green Seal/Environmental Choice certified).

Contact Odessa College, 201 West University Avenue, Odessa, TX 79764-7127. *Phone:* 432-335-6400. *Web site:* www.odessa.edu/.

Vermont

Landmark College
Putney, Vermont

Student Services and Green Events *Sustainability leadership:* sustainability coordinator/director, recycling manager,

energy manager. *Student clubs and activities:* Campus Climate Challenge. *Housing and facilities:* sustainability-themed housing, model dorm room that demonstrates sustainable living principles.

Food Fair Trade coffee is used. Vegan and vegetarian dining options are available for every meal.

Transportation Provides public transportation access to local destinations, a bike loan/rental program, and a car sharing program.

Buildings and Grounds *Percentage of institution's eligible buildings as of September 2008 meeting LEED and/or LEED-EB certification criteria:* 20%. *Renovation and maintenance:* uses a Green Seal certified cleaning service. *Campus grounds care:* uses water conservation devices; employs strategies to reduce light pollution; landscapes with native plant species; protects, restores, and/or creates habitat on campus.

Recycling *Programs and activities:* sustains a computer/technology recycling program; maintains an on-campus recycling center; replaces paper materials with online alternatives. *Campus dining operations:* operates without trays; offers discounts for reusable mugs; uses bulk condiment dispensers and decreased packaging for to-go food service purchases.

Energy Currently uses or plans to use timers to regulate temperatures based on occupancy hours; motion, infrared, and/or light sensors to reduce energy uses for lighting; and energy-related performance contracting. Participates in College & University Green Power Challenge activities.

Purchasing Sustainability criteria used in purchasing include Energy Star (EPA), WaterSense (EPA), Green Cleaning Products (Green Seal/Environmental Choice certified), and Forest Stewardship Council (FSC) or American Forest and Paper Association's Sustainable Forestry Initiative (SFI) paper.

Contact Director of Facilities Planning and Operations, Landmark College, PO Box 820, Putney, VT 05346. *Phone:* 802-387-1611. *Fax:* 802-387-6796. *E-mail:* cparamithiotti@ landmark.edu. *Web site:* www.landmark.edu/.

Virginia

Southside Virginia Community College
Alberta, Virginia

Transportation Provides public transportation access to local destinations.

Buildings and Grounds *Campus grounds care:* uses water conservation devices; landscapes with native plant species; protects, restores, and/or creates habitat on campus; applies to its grounds only pesticides and fertilizers allowable under the U.S. Department of Agriculture's standards for crop production.

Recycling *Programs and activities:* maintains an on-campus recycling center; replaces paper materials with online alternatives; limits free printing in computer labs and libraries. *Campus dining operations:* operates without trays.

Energy Currently uses or plans to use alternative sources of power (geothermal energy); timers to regulate temperatures based on occupancy hours; and motion, infrared, and/or light sensors to reduce energy uses for lighting.

Contact Southside Virginia Community College, 109 Campus Drive, Alberta, VA 23821-9719. *Phone:* 434-949-1000. *Web site:* www.sv.vccs.edu/.

Southwest Virginia Community College
Richlands, Virginia

Student Services and Green Events *Sustainability leadership:* sustainability coordinator/director, sustainability committee/advisory council.

Transportation Provides free on-campus transportation (bus or other) and public transportation access to local destinations.

Buildings and Grounds *Campus grounds care:* uses water conservation devices.

Recycling *Programs and activities:* maintains an on-campus recycling center; composts yard waste; reuses surplus department/office supplies; replaces paper materials with online alternatives; limits free printing in computer labs and libraries.

Energy Currently uses or plans to use alternative sources of power; timers to regulate temperatures based on occupancy hours; and energy-related performance contracting.

Purchasing Sustainability criteria used in purchasing include Energy Star (EPA).

Contact Director, Southwest Virginia Community College, PO Box SVCC, Richlands, VA 24641. *Phone:* 276-964-7558. *Fax:* 276-935-2165. *E-mail:* eddie.hannah@sw.edu. *Web site:* www.sw.edu/.

Washington

Edmonds Community College
Lynnwood, Washington

Sustainability Initiatives Edmonds Community College is a member of the Association for the Advancement of Sustainability in Higher Education (AASHE). This institution's president has signed the American College & University Presidents Climate Commitment.

Academics *Sustainability-focused undergraduate major(s):* Environmental Science, Geology, Earth Sciences (AS); Occupational Safety and Health (AAS); Restoration Horticulture (ATA); Energy Management (ATA) in development. *Sustainability courses and programs:* sustainability-focused course(s) or lecture series, noncredit sustainability course(s).

Student Services and Green Events *Sustainability leadership:* sustainability coordinator/director, sustainability committee/advisory council, recycling manager, energy manager. *Student clubs and activities:* student club(s)/group(s) focused on sustainability, outreach materials available about on-campus sustainability efforts. *Major sustainability events:* Earth Month, Campus Sustainability Day, lecture speakers throughout the year, planning energy campaign, Alternative Transportation Contest during Earth Month.

Food Sustainable, organic, and/or locally produced foods available in on-campus dining facilities. Vegan and vegetarian dining options are available for every meal.

Transportation Provides free on-campus transportation (bus or other), public transportation access to local destinations, and incentives to carpool or use public transportation.

Buildings and Grounds *Percentage of institution's eligible buildings as of September 2008 meeting LEED and/or LEED-EB certification criteria:* 6%. *Renovation and maintenance:* registered for LEED certification for new construction and/or renovation; uses a Green Seal certified cleaning service. *Campus grounds care:* uses water conservation

devices; employs strategies to reduce light pollution; landscapes with native plant species; protects, restores, and/or creates habitat on campus; applies to its grounds only pesticides and fertilizers allowable under the U.S. Department of Agriculture's standards for crop production.

Recycling *Programs and activities:* sustains a computer/technology recycling program; maintains an on-campus recycling center; sustains a pre-consumer food waste composting program; composts yard waste; reuses surplus department/office supplies; replaces paper materials with online alternatives; limits free printing in computer labs and libraries. *Campus dining operations:* uses reusable dishware.

Energy Currently uses or plans to use alternative sources of power (hydroelectricity/water power and wind energy); timers to regulate temperatures based on occupancy hours; motion, infrared, and/or light sensors to reduce energy uses for lighting; and energy-related performance contracting.

Purchasing Sustainability criteria used in purchasing include Energy Star (EPA) and Green Cleaning Products (Green Seal/Environmental Choice certified).

Contact Sustainability Researcher, Edmonds Community College, 20000 68th Avenue West, Lynnwood, WA 98036. *Phone:* 425-640-1509. *Fax:* 425-640-1532. *E-mail:* alison.pugh@edcc.edu. *Web site:* www.edcc.edu/.

Olympic College
Bremerton, Washington

Sustainability Initiatives Olympic College's president has signed the American College & University Presidents Climate Commitment.

Academics *Sustainability-focused undergraduate major(s):* Environmental Studies (ATA). *Sustainability courses and programs:* sustainability-focused course(s) or lecture series, noncredit sustainability course(s).

Student Services and Green Events *Sustainability leadership:* sustainability committee/advisory council, recycling manager, energy manager. *Student clubs and activities:* student club(s)/group(s) focused on sustainability. *Major sustainability events:* Earth Week, community environmental agency showcase, National Teach-In. *Housing and facilities:* student-run café that serves environmentally or socially preferable foods.

Food Sustainable, organic, and/or locally produced foods available in on-campus dining facilities. Vegan and vegetarian dining options are available for every meal.

Transportation Provides public transportation access to local destinations and incentives to carpool or use public transportation.

Buildings and Grounds *Renovation and maintenance:* registered for LEED certification for new construction and/or renovation. *Campus grounds care:* uses water conservation devices; employs strategies to reduce light pollution; landscapes with native plant species; protects, restores, and/or creates habitat on campus.

Recycling *Programs and activities:* sustains a computer/technology recycling program; maintains an on-campus recycling center; reuses surplus department/office supplies; limits free printing in computer labs and libraries. *Campus dining operations:* uses bulk condiment dispensers and decreased packaging for to-go food service purchases.

Energy Currently uses or plans to use alternative sources of power (geothermal energy and hydroelectricity/water power); timers to regulate temperatures based on occupancy hours; motion, infrared, and/or light sensors to reduce energy uses for lighting; LED lighting; and energy-related performance contracting.

Purchasing Sustainability criteria used in purchasing include Energy Star (EPA), Green Cleaning Products (Green Seal/Environmental Choice certified), and Forest Stewardship Council (FSC) or American Forest and Paper Association's Sustainable Forestry Initiative (SFI) paper.

Contact Director, Shelton Campus, Olympic College, 1600 Chester Avenue, Bremerton, WA 98337. *Phone:* 360-432-5404. *Fax:* 360-432-5412. *E-mail:* kmcnamara@oc.ctc.edu. *Web site:* www.olympic.edu/.

Peninsula College
Port Angeles, Washington

Sustainability Initiatives Peninsula College's president has signed the American College & University Presidents Climate Commitment.

Academics *Sustainability-focused undergraduate major(s):* Energy Efficiency (AAS). *Sustainability courses and programs:* sustainability-focused course(s) or lecture series, noncredit sustainability course(s).

Student Services and Green Events *Sustainability leadership:* sustainability coordinator/director, sustainability committee/advisory council. *Student clubs and activities:* student club(s)/group(s) focused on sustainability, outreach materials available about on-campus sustainability efforts. *Major sustainability events:* Annual campus sustainability event (October). *Housing and facilities:* student-run café that serves environmentally or socially preferable foods.

Food Sustainable, organic, and/or locally produced foods available in on-campus dining facilities. Fair Trade coffee is used. Vegan and vegetarian dining options are available for every meal.

Transportation Provides public transportation access to local destinations.

Buildings and Grounds *Renovation and maintenance:* registered for LEED certification for new construction and/or renovation. *Campus grounds care:* uses water conservation devices; employs strategies to reduce light pollution; landscapes with native plant species; protects, restores, and/or creates habitat on campus; applies to its grounds only pesticides and fertilizers allowable under the U.S. Department of Agriculture's standards for crop production.

Recycling *Programs and activities:* sustains a computer/technology recycling program; sustains a pre-consumer food waste composting program; sustains a post-consumer food waste composting program; composts yard waste; reuses surplus department/office supplies; replaces paper materials with online alternatives. *Campus dining operations:* operates without trays; offers discounts for reusable mugs; uses bulk condiment dispensers and decreased packaging for to-go food service purchases.

Energy Currently uses or plans to use alternative sources of power (geothermal energy); timers to regulate temperatures based on occupancy hours; motion, infrared, and/or light sensors to reduce energy uses for lighting; and energy-related performance contracting.

Purchasing Sustainability criteria used in purchasing include Energy Star (EPA).

Contact Sustainability Coordinator, Peninsula College, 1502 East Lauridsen Boulevard, Port Angeles, WA 98362. *Phone:* 360-417-6237. *Fax:* 360-417-6438. *E-mail:* almac@pcadmin.ctc.edu. *Web site:* www.pc.ctc.edu/.

Wisconsin

Lakeshore Technical College
Cleveland, Wisconsin

Sustainability Initiatives Lakeshore Technical College's president has signed the American College & University Presidents Climate Commitment.

Academics *Sustainability-focused undergraduate major(s):* Wind Energy Technology. *Sustainability courses and programs:* sustainability-focused course(s) or lecture series, sustainability-focused nonacademic certificate program(s).

Student Services and Green Events *Sustainability leadership:* sustainability committee/advisory council. *Student clubs and activities:* student club(s)/group(s) focused on sustainability, outreach materials available about on-campus sustainability efforts. *Major sustainability events:* Power of Green, Wind, Solar.

Transportation Provides a car sharing program and incentives to carpool or use public transportation.

Buildings and Grounds *Campus grounds care:* protects, restores, and/or creates habitat on campus.

Recycling *Events and organizations:* RecycleMania. *Programs and activities:* reuses surplus department/office supplies; replaces paper materials with online alternatives. *Campus dining operations:* offers discounts for reusable mugs; uses bulk condiment dispensers and decreased packaging for to-go food service purchases.

Energy Currently uses or plans to use alternative sources of power (solar energy and wind energy); motion, infrared, and/or light sensors to reduce energy uses for lighting; and energy-related performance contracting.

Purchasing Sustainability criteria used in purchasing include Energy Star (EPA).

Contact Lakeshore Technical College, 1290 North Avenue, Cleveland, WI 53015-1414. *Phone:* 920-693-1000. *Web site:* www.gotoltc.com/.

Northeast Wisconsin Technical College
Green Bay, Wisconsin

Academics *Sustainability courses and programs:* sustainability-focused course(s) or lecture series, noncredit sustainability course(s), sustainability-focused nonacademic certificate program(s).

Student Services and Green Events *Sustainability leadership:* sustainability coordinator/director, recycling manager, energy manager. *Student clubs and activities:* student club(s)/group(s) focused on sustainability, outreach materials available about on-campus sustainability efforts. *Major sustainability events:* Wisconsin Electrathon Series, Renewable Energy Summit, Focus the Nation, Earth Day, Skills USA.

Transportation Provides public transportation access to local destinations.

Buildings and Grounds *Percentage of institution's eligible buildings as of September 2008 meeting LEED and/or LEED-EB certification criteria:* 25%. *Campus grounds care:* uses water conservation devices; employs strategies to reduce light pollution; landscapes with native plant species; protects, restores, and/or creates habitat on campus.

Recycling *Programs and activities:* sustains a computer/technology recycling program; maintains an on-campus recycling center; reuses surplus department/office supplies; reuses chemicals; replaces paper materials with online alternatives; limits free printing in computer labs and libraries. *Campus dining operations:* uses reusable dishware; offers discounts for reusable mugs; uses bulk condiment dispensers and decreased packaging for to-go food service purchases.

Energy Currently uses or plans to use alternative sources of power (solar energy); timers to regulate temperatures based on occupancy hours; motion, infrared, and/or light sensors to reduce energy uses for lighting; LED lighting; vending machine motion sensors; and energy-related performance contracting.

Purchasing Sustainability criteria used in purchasing include Energy Star (EPA) and WaterSense (EPA).

Contact Sustainable Programs Manager, Northeast Wisconsin Technical College, 2740 West Mason, PO Box 19042, Green Bay, WI 54307-9042. *Phone:* 920-498-6908. *Fax:* 920-498-6315. *E-mail:* amy.kox@nwtc.edu. *Web site:* www.nwtc.edu/.

FOUR-YEAR COLLEGES

UNITED STATES

Alabama

Auburn University
Auburn University, Alabama

Sustainability Initiatives Auburn University's president has signed the American College & University Presidents Climate Commitment.

Academics *Sustainability courses and programs:* sustainability-focused course(s) or lecture series.

Student Services and Green Events *Sustainability leadership:* sustainability coordinator/director, sustainability committee/advisory council, recycling manager, energy manager, sustainability-focused student government. *Student clubs and activities:* student club(s)/group(s) focused on sustainability, outreach materials available about on-campus sustainability efforts. *Major sustainability events:* National Teach-In on Climate Change, RecycleMania, Sustainability in the Curriculum Workshop Sustain-a-Bowl. *Housing and facilities:* on-campus organic garden for students.

Food Fair Trade coffee is used. Vegan and vegetarian dining options are available for every meal.

Transportation Provides free on-campus transportation (bus or other) and public transportation access to local destinations.

Buildings and Grounds *Percentage of institution's eligible buildings as of September 2008 meeting LEED and/or LEED-EB certification criteria:* 1%. *Renovation and maintenance:* registered for LEED certification for new construction and/or renovation. *Campus grounds care:* uses water conservation devices; landscapes with native plant species; protects, restores, and/or creates habitat on campus.

Recycling *Events and organizations:* RecycleMania. *Programs and activities:* sustains a computer/technology recycling program; maintains an on-campus recycling center; composts yard waste; reuses chemicals; replaces paper materials with online alternatives; limits free printing in computer labs and libraries. *Campus dining operations:* offers discounts for reusable mugs; uses bulk condiment dispensers and decreased packaging for to-go food service purchases.

Energy Currently uses or plans to use timers to regulate temperatures based on occupancy hours; motion, infrared, and/or light sensors to reduce energy uses for lighting; and LED lighting.

Contact Director, Office of Sustainability, Auburn University, 200 Langdon Annex, Auburn University, AL 36849. *Phone:* 334-844-7777. *E-mail:* biggslb@auburn.edu. *Web site:* www.auburn.edu/.

Auburn University Montgomery
Montgomery, Alabama

Student Services and Green Events *Sustainability leadership:* sustainability committee/advisory council, sustainability-focused student government.

Food Sustainable, organic, and/or locally produced foods available in on-campus dining facilities. Vegan and vegetarian dining options are available for every meal.

Transportation Provides public transportation access to local destinations.

Buildings and Grounds *Renovation and maintenance:* registered for LEED certification for new construction and/or renovation. *Campus grounds care:* landscapes with native plant species.

Recycling *Programs and activities:* reuses surplus department/office supplies; replaces paper materials with online alternatives; limits free printing in computer labs and libraries. *Campus dining operations:* operates without trays; uses bulk condiment dispensers and decreased packaging for to-go food service purchases.

Energy Currently uses or plans to use energy-related performance contracting.

Contact Senior Director, Special Projects, Auburn University Montgomery, PO Box 244023, Montgomery, AL 36124-4023. *Phone:* 334-244-3625. *Fax:* 334-244-3986. *E-mail:* jroberts@aum.edu. *Web site:* www.aum.edu/.

Samford University
Birmingham, Alabama

Sustainability Initiatives Samford University is a member of the Association for the Advancement of Sustainability in Higher Education (AASHE).

Academics *Sustainability-focused graduate degree program(s):* Environmental Science (MS). *Sustainability courses and programs:* sustainability-focused course(s) or lecture series, noncredit sustainability course(s).

Student Services and Green Events *Sustainability leadership:* sustainability coordinator/director, sustainability committee/advisory council, recycling manager, energy manager. *Student clubs and activities:* student club(s)/

group(s) focused on sustainability, outreach materials available about on-campus sustainability efforts. *Major sustainability events:* Earth Week, Commutesmart Day, Campus Sustainability Day.

Food Sustainable, organic, and/or locally produced foods available in on-campus dining facilities. Fair Trade coffee is used. Vegan and vegetarian dining options are available for every meal.

Transportation Provides free on-campus transportation (bus or other), public transportation access to local destinations, and incentives to carpool or use public transportation.

Buildings and Grounds *Campus grounds care:* employs strategies to reduce light pollution; landscapes with native plant species.

Recycling *Programs and activities:* sustains a computer/technology recycling program; maintains an on-campus recycling center; reuses surplus department/office supplies; replaces paper materials with online alternatives. *Campus dining operations:* uses reusable dishware; operates without trays; offers discounts for reusable mugs; uses bulk condiment dispensers and decreased packaging for to-go food service purchases.

Energy Currently uses or plans to use timers to regulate temperatures based on occupancy hours; motion, infrared, and/or light sensors to reduce energy uses for lighting; and LED lighting.

Contact Vice President for Operations and Planning, Samford University, 800 Lakeshore Drive, Birmingham, AL 35229. *Phone:* 205-726-4502. *E-mail:* sclatham@samford.edu. *Web site:* www.samford.edu/.

University of Montevallo
Montevallo, Alabama

Academics *Sustainability courses and programs:* sustainability-focused course(s) or lecture series.

Student Services and Green Events *Sustainability leadership:* recycling manager, energy manager.

Food Fair Trade coffee is used. Vegan and vegetarian dining options are available for every meal.

Transportation Provides free on-campus transportation (bus or other).

Buildings and Grounds *Campus grounds care:* uses water conservation devices; employs strategies to reduce light pollution; protects, restores, and/or creates habitat on campus.

Recycling *Programs and activities:* maintains an on-campus recycling center; composts yard waste; reuses surplus department/office supplies; reuses chemicals; replaces paper materials with online alternatives. *Campus dining operations:* uses reusable dishware; operates without trays; offers discounts for reusable mugs.

Energy Currently uses or plans to use timers to regulate temperatures based on occupancy hours; motion, infrared, and/or light sensors to reduce energy uses for lighting; LED lighting; and energy-related performance contracting.

Purchasing Sustainability criteria used in purchasing include Energy Star (EPA) and Green Cleaning Products (Green Seal/Environmental Choice certified).

Contact University of Montevallo, Station 6001, Montevallo, AL 35115. *Phone:* 205-665-6000. *Web site:* www.montevallo.edu/.

Alaska

Alaska Pacific University
Anchorage, Alaska

Sustainability Initiatives Alaska Pacific University is a signatory to the Talloires Declaration. This institution's president has signed the American College & University Presidents Climate Commitment.

Academics *Sustainability-focused undergraduate major(s):* Earth Science (BA), Earth Science (BS), Environmental Science (BA), Environmental Science (BS), Environmental Studies (BA). *Sustainability-focused graduate degree program(s):* Environmental Science (MS). *Sustainability courses and programs:* sustainability-focused course(s) or lecture series.

Student Services and Green Events *Sustainability leadership:* sustainability committee/advisory council. *Student clubs and activities:* Campus Climate Challenge. *Housing and facilities:* on-campus organic garden for students.

Food Sustainable, organic, and/or locally produced foods available in on-campus dining facilities. Vegan and vegetarian dining options are available for every meal.

Transportation Provides public transportation access to local destinations and a bike loan/rental program.

Buildings and Grounds *Campus grounds care:* landscapes with native plant species.

Recycling *Programs and activities:* maintains an on-campus recycling center; reuses chemicals; replaces paper materials with online alternatives. *Campus dining operations:* uses reusable dishware; uses bulk condiment dispensers and decreased packaging for to-go food service purchases.

Energy Currently uses or plans to use motion, infrared, and/or light sensors to reduce energy uses for lighting; LED lighting; and energy-related performance contracting.

Purchasing Sustainability criteria used in purchasing include Energy Star (EPA).

Contact Alaska Pacific University, 4101 University Drive, Anchorage, AK 99508. *Phone:* 907-564-8257. *E-mail:* rmyers@alaskapacific.edu. *Web site:* www.alaskapacific.edu/.

Arizona

Arizona State University
Tempe, Arizona

Sustainability Initiatives Arizona State University is a member of the Association for the Advancement of Sustainability in Higher Education (AASHE). This institution's president has signed the American College & University Presidents Climate Commitment.

Academics *Sustainability-focused undergraduate major(s):* Sustainability (BA), Sustainability (BS). *Sustainability-focused graduate degree program(s):* Sustainability (MA), Sustainability (MS), Sustainability (PhD). *Sustainability courses and programs:* sustainability-focused course(s) or lecture series, noncredit sustainability course(s).

Student Services and Green Events *Sustainability leadership:* sustainability coordinator/director, sustainability committee/advisory council, recycling manager, energy manager, sustainability-focused student government. *Student clubs and activities:* Campus Climate Challenge, Public Interest Research Group (PIRG) chapter on campus, student club(s)/group(s) focused on sustainability, outreach materials available about on-campus sustainability efforts. *Major sustainability events:* Campus Sustainability Day, Wrigley Lecture Series, Sustainability Month. *Housing and facilities:* sustainability-themed housing, on-campus organic garden for students.

Food Sustainable, organic, and/or locally produced foods available in on-campus dining facilities. Fair Trade coffee is used. Vegan and vegetarian dining options are available for every meal.

Transportation Provides free on-campus transportation (bus or other), public transportation access to local destinations, a bike loan/rental program, a car sharing program, and incentives to carpool or use public transportation.

Buildings and Grounds *Percentage of institution's eligible buildings as of September 2008 meeting LEED and/or LEED-EB certification criteria: 5%. Renovation and maintenance:* registered for LEED certification for new construction and/or renovation. *Campus grounds care:* uses water conservation devices; employs strategies to reduce light pollution; landscapes with native plant species; applies to its grounds only pesticides and fertilizers allowable under the U.S. Department of Agriculture's standards for crop production.

Recycling *Events and organizations:* RecycleMania. *Programs and activities:* sustains a computer/technology recycling program; composts yard waste; reuses surplus department/office supplies; reuses chemicals; replaces paper materials with online alternatives; limits free printing in computer labs and libraries. *Campus dining operations:* uses reusable dishware; operates without trays; offers discounts for reusable mugs; uses bulk condiment dispensers and decreased packaging for to-go food service purchases.

Energy Currently uses or plans to use alternative sources of power (hydroelectricity/water power, solar energy, and wind energy); timers to regulate temperatures based on occupancy hours; motion, infrared, and/or light sensors to reduce energy uses for lighting; LED lighting; and energy-related performance contracting.

Purchasing Sustainability criteria used in purchasing include Energy Star (EPA), WaterSense (EPA), Green Electronics Council (GEC) Electronic Product Environmental Assessment Tool (EPEAT) Silver or Gold, Green Cleaning Products (Green Seal/Environmental Choice certified), and Forest Stewardship Council (FSC) or American Forest and Paper Association's Sustainable Forestry Initiative (SFI) paper.

Contact Director, Communications and Marketing, Arizona State University, PO Box 877205, Tempe, AZ 85287-7205. *Phone:* 480-965-0013. *E-mail:* karen.leland@asu.edu. *Web site:* www.asu.edu/.

Prescott College
Prescott, Arizona

Sustainability Initiatives Prescott College is a member of the Association for the Advancement of Sustainability in Higher Education (AASHE). This institution's president has signed the American College & University Presidents Climate Commitment. Prescott College has Green Fees (optional/required) dedicated to sustainability initiatives.

Academics *Sustainability-focused undergraduate major(s):* Environmental Studies (BA), Sustainable Community Development (BA). *Sustainability-focused graduate degree program(s):* Sustainability Education (PhD), Sustainability Science and Practice (MA). *Sustainability courses and programs:* sustainability-focused course(s) or lecture series, noncredit sustainability course(s).

Student Services and Green Events *Sustainability leadership:* sustainability coordinator/director, sustainability committee/advisory council, recycling manager, energy manager. *Student clubs and activities:* student club(s)/group(s) focused on sustainability. *Major sustainability events:* First Annual Sustainability Education Symposium held in 2009, Green to Gold Sustainable Cities Conference. *Housing and facilities:* student-run café that serves environmentally or socially preferable foods, on-campus organic garden for students.

Food Sustainable, organic, and/or locally produced foods available in on-campus dining facilities. Fair Trade coffee is used. Vegan and vegetarian dining options are available for every meal.

Transportation Provides a bike loan/rental program.

Buildings and Grounds *Campus grounds care:* uses water conservation devices; employs strategies to reduce light pollution; landscapes with native plant species; protects, restores, and/or creates habitat on campus; applies to its grounds only pesticides and fertilizers allowable under the U.S. Department of Agriculture's standards for crop production.

Recycling *Programs and activities:* maintains an on-campus recycling center; sustains a pre-consumer food waste composting program; composts yard waste; reuses surplus department/office supplies; replaces paper materials with online alternatives; limits free printing in computer labs and libraries. *Campus dining operations:* uses reusable dishware; uses bulk condiment dispensers and decreased packaging for to-go food service purchases.

Energy Currently uses or plans to use alternative sources of power; timers to regulate temperatures based on occupancy hours; motion, infrared, and/or light sensors to reduce energy uses for lighting; and LED lighting.

Purchasing Sustainability criteria used in purchasing include Green Cleaning Products (Green Seal/Environmental Choice certified) and Forest Stewardship Council (FSC) or American Forest and Paper Association's Sustainable Forestry Initiative (SFI) paper.

Contact Sustainability Coordinator, Prescott College, 220 Grove Avenue, Prescott, AZ 86301. *Phone:* 928-350-3217. *E-mail:* lwalmsley@prescott.edu. *Web site:* www.prescott.edu/.

Western International University
Phoenix, Arizona

Student Services and Green Events *Sustainability leadership:* recycling manager.

Transportation Provides public transportation access to local destinations and incentives to carpool or use public transportation.

Buildings and Grounds *Renovation and maintenance:* uses a Green Seal certified cleaning service. *Campus grounds care:* landscapes with native plant species.

Recycling *Programs and activities:* sustains a computer/technology recycling program; reuses surplus department/office supplies; replaces paper materials with online alternatives; limits free printing in computer labs and libraries.

Energy Currently uses or plans to use alternative sources of power and LED lighting.

Purchasing Sustainability criteria used in purchasing include Energy Star (EPA) and Green Cleaning Products (Green Seal/Environmental Choice certified).

Contact Campus Manager, Western International University, 14100 North 83rd Avenue, Suite 100, Peoria, AZ 85381. *Phone:* 602-429-1404. *E-mail:* tracy.oconnell@wintu.edu. *Web site:* www.wintu.edu/.

Arkansas

Harding University
Searcy, Arkansas

Academics *Sustainability courses and programs:* sustainability-focused course(s) or lecture series.

Student Services and Green Events *Sustainability leadership:* sustainability coordinator/director, sustainability committee/advisory council, recycling manager, energy manager, sustainability-focused student government. *Student clubs and activities:* student club(s)/group(s) focused on sustainability, outreach materials available about on-campus sustainability efforts. *Housing and facilities:* student-run café that serves environmentally or socially preferable foods, on-campus organic garden for students.

Food Sustainable, organic, and/or locally produced foods available in on-campus dining facilities. Fair Trade coffee is used. Vegan and vegetarian dining options are available for every meal.

Buildings and Grounds *Renovation and maintenance:* uses a Green Seal certified cleaning service. *Campus grounds care:* employs strategies to reduce light pollution; landscapes with native plant species; protects, restores, and/or creates habitat on campus; applies to its grounds only pesticides and fertilizers allowable under the U.S. Department of Agriculture's standards for crop production.

Recycling *Programs and activities:* sustains a computer/technology recycling program; maintains an on-campus recycling center; sustains a post-consumer food waste composting program; composts yard waste; reuses surplus department/office supplies; replaces paper materials with online alternatives; limits free printing in computer labs and libraries. *Campus dining operations:* uses reusable dishware; operates without trays; uses bulk condiment dispensers and decreased packaging for to-go food service purchases.

Energy Currently uses or plans to use timers to regulate temperatures based on occupancy hours; motion, infrared, and/or light sensors to reduce energy uses for lighting; LED lighting; and energy-related performance contracting.

Purchasing Sustainability criteria used in purchasing include Energy Star (EPA) and Forest Stewardship Council (FSC) or American Forest and Paper Association's Sustainable Forestry Initiative (SFI) paper.

Contact Harding University, 915 East Market Avenue, Searcy, AR 72149-0001. *Phone:* 501-279-4000. *Web site:* www.harding.edu/.

University of Arkansas
Fayetteville, Arkansas

Sustainability Initiatives University of Arkansas is a member of the Association for the Advancement of Sustainability in Higher Education (AASHE). This institution's president has signed the American College & University Presidents Climate Commitment.

Academics *Sustainability-focused graduate degree program(s):* Environmental dynamics (PhD). *Sustainability courses and programs:* sustainability-focused course(s) or lecture series.

Student Services and Green Events *Sustainability leadership:* sustainability coordinator/director, recycling manager. *Student clubs and activities:* student club(s)/group(s) focused on sustainability, outreach materials available about on-campus sustainability efforts. *Major sustainability events:* Focus the Nation Teach-In.

Food Sustainable, organic, and/or locally produced foods available in on-campus dining facilities. Fair Trade coffee is used. Vegan and vegetarian dining options are available for every meal.

Transportation Provides free on-campus transportation (bus or other), public transportation access to local destinations, a bike loan/rental program, and a car sharing program.

Buildings and Grounds *Percentage of institution's eligible buildings as of September 2008 meeting LEED and/or LEED-EB certification criteria:* 10%. *Renovation and maintenance:* registered for LEED certification for new construction and/or renovation; uses a Green Seal certified cleaning service. *Campus grounds care:* uses water conservation devices; employs strategies to reduce light pollution.

Recycling *Events and organizations:* RecycleMania. *Programs and activities:* sustains a computer/technology recycling program; maintains an on-campus recycling center; sustains a pre-consumer food waste composting program; composts yard waste; reuses surplus department/office supplies; replaces paper materials with online alternatives. *Campus dining operations:* uses reusable dishware; operates without trays; offers discounts for reusable mugs; uses bulk condiment dispensers and decreased packaging for to-go food service purchases.

Energy Currently uses or plans to use alternative sources of power; timers to regulate temperatures based on occupancy hours; motion, infrared, and/or light sensors to reduce energy uses for lighting; LED lighting; vending machine motion sensors; and energy-related performance contracting.

Purchasing Sustainability criteria used in purchasing include Energy Star (EPA) and Green Cleaning Products (Green Seal/Environmental Choice certified).

Contact Executive Assistant for Sustainability, University of Arkansas, 521 South Razorback Road, Fayetteville, AR 72701. *Phone:* 479-575-3591. *E-mail:* nick.brown@uark.edu. *Web site:* www.uark.edu/.

California

Antioch University Santa Barbara
Santa Barbara, California

Sustainability Initiatives Antioch University Santa Barbara's president has signed the American College & University Presidents Climate Commitment.

Student Services and Green Events *Sustainability leadership:* recycling manager. *Student clubs and activities:* outreach materials available about on-campus sustainability efforts.

Transportation Provides public transportation access to local destinations and incentives to carpool or use public transportation.

Recycling *Programs and activities:* sustains a computer/technology recycling program; maintains an on-campus recycling center; replaces paper materials with online alternatives; limits free printing in computer labs and libraries.

Contact Antioch University Santa Barbara, 801 Garden Street, Santa Barbara, CA 93101-1581. *Phone:* 805-962-8179. *Web site:* www.antiochsb.edu/.

California College of the Arts
San Francisco, California

Academics *Sustainability courses and programs:* sustainability-focused course(s) or lecture series, noncredit sustainability course(s).

Student Services and Green Events *Student clubs and activities:* student club(s)/group(s) focused on sustainability. *Major sustainability events:* Solar decathalon, Rising Tide: The Arts and Environmental Ethics conference.

Food Sustainable, organic, and/or locally produced foods available in on-campus dining facilities. Fair Trade coffee is used. Vegan and vegetarian dining options are available for every meal.

Transportation Provides free on-campus transportation (bus or other), a bike loan/rental program, and incentives to carpool or use public transportation.

Buildings and Grounds *Percentage of institution's eligible buildings as of September 2008 meeting LEED and/or LEED-EB certification criteria:* 50%. *Renovation and maintenance:* uses a Green Seal certified cleaning service. *Campus grounds care:* uses water conservation devices; employs strategies to reduce light pollution; landscapes with native plant species; protects, restores, and/or creates habitat on campus; applies to its grounds only pesticides and fertilizers allowable under the U.S. Department of Agriculture's standards for crop production.

Recycling *Programs and activities:* sustains a computer/technology recycling program; composts yard waste; reuses surplus department/office supplies; reuses chemicals; replaces paper materials with online alternatives; limits free printing in computer labs and libraries. *Campus dining operations:* operates without trays; offers discounts for reusable mugs; uses bulk condiment dispensers and decreased packaging for to-go food service purchases.

Energy Currently uses or plans to use alternative sources of power (biomass energy and solar energy); timers to regulate temperatures based on occupancy hours; motion, infrared, and/or light sensors to reduce energy uses for lighting; and energy-related performance contracting.

Purchasing Sustainability criteria used in purchasing include Energy Star (EPA), Green Cleaning Products (Green Seal/Environmental Choice certified), and Forest Stewardship Council (FSC) or American Forest and Paper Association's Sustainable Forestry Initiative (SFI) paper.

Contact California College of the Arts, 1111 Eighth Street, San Francisco, CA 94107. *Phone:* 415-703-9500. *Web site:* www.cca.edu/.

California Institute of Technology
Pasadena, California

Academics *Sustainability-focused undergraduate major(s):* Engineering and Applied Science (BS), Geobiology (BS), Geochemistry (BS). *Sustainability-focused graduate degree program(s):* Applied Physics (MS, PhD), Biochemistry (MS, PhD), Chemical Engineering (MS, PhD), Environmental Science and Engineering (MS, PhD), Materials Science (MS, PhD). *Sustainability courses and programs:* sustainability-focused course(s) or lecture series.

Student Services and Green Events *Sustainability leadership:* sustainability coordinator/director, sustainability committee/advisory council, recycling manager, energy manager, sustainability-focused student government. *Student clubs and activities:* student club(s)/group(s) focused on sustainability, outreach materials available about on-campus sustainability efforts. *Major sustainability events:*

Olive Harvest, Alternative Transportation Festival, Earth Day, Sustainability Lecture Series. *Housing and facilities:* on-campus organic garden for students.

Food Sustainable, organic, and/or locally produced foods available in on-campus dining facilities. Fair Trade coffee is used. Vegan and vegetarian dining options are available for every meal.

Transportation Provides public transportation access to local destinations and incentives to carpool or use public transportation.

Buildings and Grounds *Renovation and maintenance:* registered for LEED certification for new construction and/or renovation; uses a Green Seal certified cleaning service. *Campus grounds care:* uses water conservation devices; landscapes with native plant species; protects, restores, and/or creates habitat on campus.

Recycling *Programs and activities:* sustains a computer/technology recycling program; maintains an on-campus recycling center; composts yard waste; reuses surplus department/office supplies; replaces paper materials with online alternatives. *Campus dining operations:* uses reusable dishware; offers discounts for reusable mugs; uses bulk condiment dispensers and decreased packaging for to-go food service purchases.

Energy Currently uses or plans to use alternative sources of power (solar energy and wind energy); motion, infrared, and/or light sensors to reduce energy uses for lighting; LED lighting; and energy-related performance contracting.

Purchasing Sustainability criteria used in purchasing include Energy Star (EPA), Green Cleaning Products (Green Seal/Environmental Choice certified), and Forest Stewardship Council (FSC) or American Forest and Paper Association's Sustainable Forestry Initiative (SFI) paper.

Contact Manager for Sustainability Programs, California Institute of Technology, 1200 East California Boulevard, Pasadena, CA 91125. *Phone:* 626-395-4724. *Fax:* 626-577-7543. *E-mail:* john.onderdonk@caltech.edu. *Web site:* www.caltech.edu/.

California Polytechnic State University, San Luis Obispo
San Luis Obispo, California

Sustainability Initiatives California Polytechnic State University, San Luis Obispo is a member of the Association for the Advancement of Sustainability in Higher Education (AASHE) and a signatory to the Talloires Declaration. California Polytechnic State University, San Luis Obispo has Green Fees (optional/required) dedicated to sustainability initiatives.

Academics *Sustainability-focused undergraduate major(s):* Environmental Engineering (BS). *Sustainability-focused graduate degree program(s):* Engineering (MS). *Sustainability courses and programs:* sustainability-focused course(s) or lecture series.

Student Services and Green Events *Sustainability leadership:* sustainability coordinator/director, sustainability committee/advisory council, recycling manager, energy manager, sustainability-focused student government. *Student clubs and activities:* Campus Climate Challenge, student club(s)/group(s) focused on sustainability, outreach materials available about on-campus sustainability efforts. *Major sustainability events:* CSU/UC/CCC Sustainability Conference, Focus the Nation, The Business of Green Media Conference, Sustainability by Design Retreat, Sea Change—Regional Energy Conference, Engineers Without

Borders Western Regional. *Housing and facilities:* sustainability-themed housing, on-campus organic garden for students.

Food Sustainable, organic, and/or locally produced foods available in on-campus dining facilities. Fair Trade coffee is used. Vegan and vegetarian dining options are available for every meal.

Transportation Provides free on-campus transportation (bus or other), public transportation access to local destinations, a car sharing program, and incentives to carpool or use public transportation.

Buildings and Grounds *Percentage of institution's eligible buildings as of September 2008 meeting LEED and/or LEED-EB certification criteria:* 1%. *Renovation and maintenance:* registered for LEED certification for new construction and/or renovation; uses a Green Seal certified cleaning service. *Campus grounds care:* uses water conservation devices; employs strategies to reduce light pollution; landscapes with native plant species; protects, restores, and/or creates habitat on campus.

Recycling *Programs and activities:* sustains a computer/technology recycling program; maintains an on-campus recycling center; sustains a pre-consumer food waste composting program; sustains a post-consumer food waste composting program; composts yard waste; reuses surplus department/office supplies; reuses chemicals; replaces paper materials with online alternatives. *Campus dining operations:* offers discounts for reusable mugs.

Energy Currently uses or plans to use alternative sources of power (biomass energy, geothermal energy, hydroelectricity/water power, solar energy, and wind energy); timers to regulate temperatures based on occupancy hours; motion, infrared, and/or light sensors to reduce energy uses for lighting; LED lighting; vending machine motion sensors; and energy-related performance contracting.

Purchasing Sustainability criteria used in purchasing include Energy Star (EPA), Green Electronics Council (GEC) Electronic Product Environmental Assessment Tool (EPEAT) Silver or Gold, Green Cleaning Products (Green Seal/Environmental Choice certified), and Forest Stewardship Council (FSC) or American Forest and Paper Association's Sustainable Forestry Initiative (SFI) paper.

Contact Sustainability Manager, California Polytechnic State University, San Luis Obispo, Facility Services, Building 70, 1 Grand Avenue, San Luis Obispo, CA 93407-0130. *Phone:* 805-756-2090. *Fax:* 805-756-6114. *E-mail:* delliot@calpoly.edu. *Web site:* www.calpoly.edu/.

California State University, Chico
Chico, California

Sustainability Initiatives California State University, Chico is a member of the Association for the Advancement of Sustainability in Higher Education (AASHE) and a signatory to the Talloires Declaration. This institution's president has signed the American College & University Presidents Climate Commitment. California State University, Chico has Green Fees (optional/required) dedicated to sustainability initiatives.

Academics *Sustainability-focused undergraduate major(s):* Environmental Science (BS). *Sustainability-focused graduate degree program(s):* Environmental Science (MS). *Sustainability courses and programs:* sustainability-focused course(s) or lecture series, noncredit sustainability course(s).

Student Services and Green Events *Sustainability leadership:* sustainability coordinator/director, recycling manager,

energy manager, sustainability-focused student government. *Student clubs and activities:* Campus Climate Challenge, student club(s)/group(s) focused on sustainability, outreach materials available about on-campus sustainability efforts. *Major sustainability events:* This Way to Sustainability IV, Greendance Film Festival. *Housing and facilities:* sustainability-themed housing, model dorm room that demonstrates sustainable living principles, student-run café that serves environmentally or socially preferable foods.

Food Sustainable, organic, and/or locally produced foods available in on-campus dining facilities. Fair Trade coffee is used. Vegan and vegetarian dining options are available for every meal.

Transportation Provides public transportation access to local destinations and incentives to carpool or use public transportation.

Buildings and Grounds *Renovation and maintenance:* registered for LEED certification for new construction and/or renovation; uses a Green Seal certified cleaning service. *Campus grounds care:* uses water conservation devices; landscapes with native plant species; protects, restores, and/or creates habitat on campus.

Recycling *Events and organizations:* RecycleMania. *Programs and activities:* sustains a computer/technology recycling program; maintains an on-campus recycling center; sustains a pre-consumer food waste composting program; sustains a post-consumer food waste composting program; reuses surplus department/office supplies; reuses chemicals; replaces paper materials with online alternatives; limits free printing in computer labs and libraries. *Campus dining operations:* uses reusable dishware; offers discounts for reusable mugs; uses bulk condiment dispensers and decreased packaging for to-go food service purchases.

Energy Currently uses or plans to use alternative sources of power (solar energy); timers to regulate temperatures based on occupancy hours; motion, infrared, or light sensors to reduce energy uses for lighting; LED lighting; and energy-related performance contracting. Participates in College & University Green Power Challenge activities.

Purchasing Sustainability criteria used in purchasing include Energy Star (EPA) and Green Cleaning Products (Green Seal/Environmental Choice certified).

Contact Sustainability Coordinator, California State University, Chico, 633 Brice Avenue, Chico, CA 95926. *Phone:* 530-898-3333. *Fax:* 530-898-3336. *Web site:* www.csuchico.edu/.

California State University, Long Beach
Long Beach, California

Academics *Sustainability-focused undergraduate major(s):* Earth Science (BS), Environmental Science and Policy (BA, BS). *Sustainability courses and programs:* sustainability-focused course(s) or lecture series, sustainability-focused nonacademic certificate program(s).

Student Services and Green Events *Sustainability leadership:* sustainability coordinator/director, recycling manager, energy manager. *Student clubs and activities:* student club(s)/group(s) focused on sustainability. *Major sustainability events:* UC/CSU/CCC Annual Sustainability Conference.

Food Fair Trade coffee is used. Vegan and vegetarian dining options are available for every meal.

Transportation Provides free on-campus transportation (bus or other), public transportation access to local destinations, and incentives to carpool or use public transportation.

Buildings and Grounds *Renovation and maintenance:* registered for LEED certification for new construction and/or

renovation. *Campus grounds care:* uses water conservation devices; employs strategies to reduce light pollution; landscapes with native plant species.

Recycling *Programs and activities:* sustains a computer/technology recycling program; maintains an on-campus recycling center; composts yard waste; reuses surplus department/office supplies; reuses chemicals; replaces paper materials with online alternatives. *Campus dining operations:* uses reusable dishware; uses bulk condiment dispensers and decreased packaging for to-go food service purchases.

Energy Currently uses or plans to use alternative sources of power (solar energy); timers to regulate temperatures based on occupancy hours; motion, infrared, and/or light sensors to reduce energy uses for lighting; LED lighting; and energy-related performance contracting.

Purchasing Sustainability criteria used in purchasing include Energy Star (EPA) and Green Cleaning Products (Green Seal/Environmental Choice certified).

Contact Energy and Sustainability Manager, California State University, Long Beach, 1250 Bellflower Boulevard, Attn: Facilities Management, Long Beach, CA 90840. *Phone:* 562-985-8167. *Fax:* 562-985-8723. *E-mail:* pwingco@csulb.edu. *Web site:* www.csulb.edu/.

California State University, Northridge
Northridge, California

Sustainability Initiatives California State University, Northridge has Green Fees (optional/required) dedicated to sustainability initiatives.

Academics *Sustainability courses and programs:* sustainability-focused course(s) or lecture series, noncredit sustainability course(s).

Student Services and Green Events *Sustainability leadership:* sustainability coordinator/director, sustainability committee/advisory council, recycling manager, energy manager. *Student clubs and activities:* student club(s)/group(s) focused on sustainability. *Major sustainability events:* Focus the Nation Climate Change Teach-In, Envisioning California.

Food Fair Trade coffee is used.

Transportation Provides free on-campus transportation (bus or other) and public transportation access to local destinations.

Buildings and Grounds *Percentage of institution's eligible buildings as of September 2008 meeting LEED and/or LEED-EB certification criteria:* 2%. *Renovation and maintenance:* registered for LEED certification for new construction and/or renovation. *Campus grounds care:* landscapes with native plant species.

Recycling *Programs and activities:* maintains an on-campus recycling center; replaces paper materials with online alternatives; limits free printing in computer labs and libraries.

Energy Currently uses or plans to use alternative sources of power (solar energy and wind energy) and motion, infrared, and/or light sensors to reduce energy uses for lighting.

Purchasing Sustainability criteria used in purchasing include Energy Star (EPA).

Contact Director, Institute for Sustainability, California State University, Northridge, 18111 Nordhoff Street, SH 208, Northridge, CA 91330. *Phone:* 818-677-6137. *E-mail:* vasishth@csun.edu. *Web site:* www.csun.edu/.

California State University, San Bernardino
San Bernardino, California

Academics *Sustainability-focused undergraduate major(s):* Biology, Ecology and Evolution option (BS); Environmental Studies (BA); Geology, Environmental Geology option (BS); Health Science, Environmental Health Science concentration (BS). *Sustainability-focused graduate degree program(s):* Environmental Sciences (MS). *Sustainability courses and programs:* sustainability-focused course(s) or lecture series.

Student Services and Green Events *Sustainability leadership:* sustainability committee/advisory council, recycling manager, energy manager, sustainability-focused student government. *Student clubs and activities:* student club(s)/group(s) focused on sustainability, outreach materials available about on-campus sustainability efforts. *Major sustainability events:* Energy Summit.

Food Sustainable, organic, and/or locally produced foods available in on-campus dining facilities. Fair Trade coffee is used. Vegan and vegetarian dining options are available for every meal.

Transportation Provides public transportation access to local destinations, a car sharing program, and incentives to carpool or use public transportation.

Buildings and Grounds *Renovation and maintenance:* registered for LEED certification for new construction and/or renovation. *Campus grounds care:* uses water conservation devices; employs strategies to reduce light pollution; landscapes with native plant species; protects, restores, and/or creates habitat on campus.

Recycling *Programs and activities:* sustains a computer/technology recycling program; maintains an on-campus recycling center; composts yard waste; reuses surplus department/office supplies; reuses chemicals; replaces paper materials with online alternatives; limits free printing in computer labs and libraries. *Campus dining operations:* uses reusable dishware; operates without trays; offers discounts for reusable mugs; uses bulk condiment dispensers and decreased packaging for to-go food service purchases.

Energy Currently uses or plans to use alternative sources of power (solar energy); timers to regulate temperatures based on occupancy hours; motion, infrared, and/or light sensors to reduce energy uses for lighting; LED lighting; and energy-related performance contracting.

Purchasing Sustainability criteria used in purchasing include Energy Star (EPA), WaterSense (EPA), and Green Cleaning Products (Green Seal/Environmental Choice certified).

Contact Senior Director of Facilities Services, California State University, San Bernardino, 5500 University Parkway, San Bernardino, CA 92407-2393. *Phone:* 909-537-5166. *Fax:* 909-537-7256. *E-mail:* tsimpson@csusb.edu. *Web site:* www.csusb.edu/.

California State University, Stanislaus
Turlock, California

Academics *Sustainability-focused graduate degree program(s):* Ecology—Sustainability (MA). *Sustainability courses and programs:* sustainability-focused course(s) or lecture series.

Student Services and Green Events *Sustainability leadership:* recycling manager, energy manager, sustainability-focused student government. *Student clubs and activities:* student club(s)/group(s) focused on sustainability. *Major sustainability events:* Great Central Valley Beaming Bion-

PART IV: PROFILES OF SUSTAINABILITY PROGRAMS
California

eers Conference, Council for Sustainability Futures, Save the Air Day, Sustainability speaker series. *Housing and facilities:* on-campus organic garden for students.

Food Sustainable, organic, and/or locally produced foods available in on-campus dining facilities. Fair Trade coffee is used.

Transportation Provides public transportation access to local destinations and a car sharing program.

Buildings and Grounds *Percentage of institution's eligible buildings as of September 2008 meeting LEED and/or LEED-EB certification criteria:* 12%. *Renovation and maintenance:* registered for LEED certification for new construction and/or renovation; uses a Green Seal certified cleaning service. *Campus grounds care:* uses water conservation devices; landscapes with native plant species; protects, restores, and/or creates habitat on campus.

Recycling *Programs and activities:* sustains a computer/technology recycling program; maintains an on-campus recycling center; sustains a pre-consumer food waste composting program; composts yard waste; reuses chemicals; replaces paper materials with online alternatives; limits free printing in computer labs and libraries. *Campus dining operations:* offers discounts for reusable mugs.

Energy Currently uses or plans to use alternative sources of power (solar energy); timers to regulate temperatures based on occupancy hours; motion, infrared, and/or light sensors to reduce energy uses for lighting; and LED lighting.

Purchasing Sustainability criteria used in purchasing include Energy Star (EPA), Green Electronics Council (GEC) Electronic Product Environmental Assessment Tool (EPEAT) Silver or Gold, and Green Cleaning Products (Green Seal/Environmental Choice certified).

Contact California State University, Stanislaus, One University Circle, Turlock, CA 95382. *Phone:* 209-667-3122. *Web site:* www.csustan.edu/.

Chapman University
Orange, California

Student Services and Green Events *Sustainability leadership:* sustainability committee/advisory council, sustainability-focused student government. *Student clubs and activities:* student club(s)/group(s) focused on sustainability. *Major sustainability events:* Environmental Leadership Academy, Sustainability Learning Living Community, Earth Week/Peace and Earth Fair. *Housing and facilities:* sustainability-themed housing.

Food Sustainable, organic, and/or locally produced foods available in on-campus dining facilities. Fair Trade coffee is used. Vegan and vegetarian dining options are available for every meal.

Transportation Provides incentives to carpool or use public transportation.

Buildings and Grounds *Campus grounds care:* uses water conservation devices; employs strategies to reduce light pollution; landscapes with native plant species.

Recycling *Programs and activities:* sustains a computer/technology recycling program; replaces paper materials with online alternatives; limits free printing in computer labs and libraries. *Campus dining operations:* uses reusable dishware; operates without trays; offers discounts for reusable mugs; uses bulk condiment dispensers and decreased packaging for to-go food service purchases.

Energy Currently uses or plans to use alternative sources of power (solar energy); timers to regulate temperatures based on occupancy hours; motion, infrared, and/or light sensors to reduce energy uses for lighting; and LED lighting.

Purchasing Sustainability criteria used in purchasing include Energy Star (EPA), Green Electronics Council (GEC) Electronic Product Environmental Assessment Tool (EPEAT) Silver or Gold, and Forest Stewardship Council (FSC) or American Forest and Paper Association's Sustainable Forestry Initiative (SFI) paper.

Contact Chapman University, One University Drive, Orange, CA 92866. *Phone:* 714-997-6815. *Web site:* www.chapman.edu/.

Claremont McKenna College
Claremont, California

Sustainability Initiatives Claremont McKenna College's president has signed the American College & University Presidents Climate Commitment.

Academics *Sustainability-focused undergraduate major(s):* Environment, Economics, and Politics (EEP); Environmental Studies. *Sustainability courses and programs:* sustainability-focused course(s) or lecture series.

Student Services and Green Events *Sustainability leadership:* sustainability committee/advisory council, energy manager.

Food Sustainable, organic, and/or locally produced foods available in on-campus dining facilities. Fair Trade coffee is used. Vegan and vegetarian dining options are available for every meal.

Transportation Provides public transportation access to local destinations, a car sharing program, and incentives to carpool or use public transportation.

Buildings and Grounds *Renovation and maintenance:* registered for LEED certification for new construction and/or renovation. *Campus grounds care:* uses water conservation devices; landscapes with native plant species.

Recycling *Programs and activities:* sustains a computer/technology recycling program; composts yard waste; reuses chemicals; replaces paper materials with online alternatives; limits free printing in computer labs and libraries. *Campus dining operations:* uses reusable dishware; uses bulk condiment dispensers and decreased packaging for to-go food service purchases.

Energy Currently uses or plans to use alternative sources of power (hydroelectricity/water power); motion, infrared, and/or light sensors to reduce energy uses for lighting; and vending machine motion sensors.

Purchasing Sustainability criteria used in purchasing include Energy Star (EPA) and Green Cleaning Products (Green Seal/Environmental Choice certified).

Contact Director of Facilities and Campus Services, Claremont McKenna College, 742 North Amherst Avenue, Claremont, CA 91711. *Phone:* 909-607-1637. *Fax:* 909-621-8542. *E-mail:* bworley@cmc.edu. *Web site:* www.claremontmckenna.edu/.

Cogswell Polytechnical College
Sunnyvale, California

Student Services and Green Events *Sustainability leadership:* recycling manager.

Transportation Provides public transportation access to local destinations.

Buildings and Grounds *Campus grounds care:* uses water conservation devices; employs strategies to reduce light pollution; landscapes with native plant species; applies to its grounds only pesticides and fertilizers allowable under the U.S. Department of Agriculture's standards for crop production.

Recycling *Programs and activities:* sustains a computer/technology recycling program; maintains an on-campus recycling center; reuses surplus department/office supplies; limits free printing in computer labs and libraries.

Energy Currently uses or plans to use timers to regulate temperatures based on occupancy hours; motion, infrared, and/or light sensors to reduce energy uses for lighting; and LED lighting.

Purchasing Sustainability criteria used in purchasing include Energy Star (EPA) and Green Cleaning Products (Green Seal/Environmental Choice certified).

Contact Cogswell Polytechnical College, 1175 Bordeaux Drive, Sunnyvale, CA 94089-1299. *Phone:* 408-541-0100. *Web site:* www.cogswell.edu/.

Hope International University
Fullerton, California

Academics *Sustainability-focused graduate degree program(s):* International Development Concentration (MSM).

Student Services and Green Events *Sustainability leadership:* recycling manager, energy manager. *Housing and facilities:* student-run café that serves environmentally or socially preferable foods.

Food Sustainable, organic, and/or locally produced foods available in on-campus dining facilities. Fair Trade coffee is used. Vegan and vegetarian dining options are available for every meal.

Transportation Provides public transportation access to local destinations.

Buildings and Grounds *Percentage of institution's eligible buildings as of September 2008 meeting LEED and/or LEED-EB certification criteria: 25%. Campus grounds care:* applies to its grounds only pesticides and fertilizers allowable under the U.S. Department of Agriculture's standards for crop production.

Recycling *Programs and activities:* sustains a computer/technology recycling program; maintains an on-campus recycling center; reuses surplus department/office supplies; replaces paper materials with online alternatives; limits free printing in computer labs and libraries. *Campus dining operations:* uses reusable dishware; uses bulk condiment dispensers and decreased packaging for to-go food service purchases.

Energy Currently uses or plans to use timers to regulate temperatures based on occupancy hours; motion, infrared, and/or light sensors to reduce energy uses for lighting; and energy-related performance contracting.

Contact Hope International University, 2500 East Nutwood Avenue, Fullerton, CA 92831-3138. *Phone:* 714-879-3901. *Web site:* www.hiu.edu/.

Loyola Marymount University
Los Angeles, California

Sustainability Initiatives Loyola Marymount University's president has signed the American College & University Presidents Climate Commitment.

Student Services and Green Events *Sustainability leadership:* sustainability committee/advisory council, recycling manager, energy manager, sustainability-focused student government. *Student clubs and activities:* student club(s)/group(s) focused on sustainability. *Major sustainability events:* Bellarmine Forum, Peace Jam, Water and Politics in Southern California.

Food Sustainable, organic, and/or locally produced foods available in on-campus dining facilities. Fair Trade coffee is used. Vegan and vegetarian dining options are available for every meal.

Transportation Provides public transportation access to local destinations and a bike loan/rental program.

Buildings and Grounds *Percentage of institution's eligible buildings as of September 2008 meeting LEED and/or LEED-EB certification criteria: 7%. Renovation and maintenance:* registered for LEED certification for new construction and/or renovation. *Campus grounds care:* uses water conservation devices; landscapes with native plant species; protects, restores, and/or creates habitat on campus; applies to its grounds only pesticides and fertilizers allowable under the U.S. Department of Agriculture's standards for crop production.

Recycling *Events and organizations:* RecycleMania. *Programs and activities:* sustains a computer/technology recycling program; maintains an on-campus recycling center; composts yard waste; replaces paper materials with online alternatives. *Campus dining operations:* uses reusable dishware; operates without trays; offers discounts for reusable mugs; uses bulk condiment dispensers and decreased packaging for to-go food service purchases.

Energy Currently uses or plans to use alternative sources of power (solar energy); timers to regulate temperatures based on occupancy hours; motion, infrared, and/or light sensors to reduce energy uses for lighting; and LED lighting.

Purchasing Sustainability criteria used in purchasing include Energy Star (EPA), WaterSense (EPA), Green Cleaning Products (Green Seal/Environmental Choice certified), and Forest Stewardship Council (FSC) or American Forest and Paper Association's Sustainable Forestry Initiative (SFI) paper.

Contact Director of Plant Operations, Loyola Marymount University, 1 LMU Drive, MS 8120, Los Angeles, CA 90045-2659. *Phone:* 310-568-6670. *E-mail:* mlotito@lmu.edu. *Web site:* www.lmu.edu/.

Mills College
Oakland, California

Sustainability Initiatives Mills College is a member of the Association for the Advancement of Sustainability in Higher Education (AASHE). This institution's president has signed the American College & University Presidents Climate Commitment.

Academics *Sustainability-focused undergraduate major(s):* Environmental Science (BA, BS), Environmental Studies (BA). *Sustainability courses and programs:* sustainability-focused course(s) or lecture series.

Student Services and Green Events *Sustainability leadership:* sustainability coordinator/director, sustainability committee/advisory council, recycling manager, sustainability-focused student government. *Student clubs and activities:* student club(s)/group(s) focused on sustainability, outreach materials available about on-campus sustainability efforts. *Major sustainability events:* Earth Week, The Food Forum, Socially Responsible Business lecture series. *Housing and facilities:* sustainability-themed housing, model dorm room that demonstrates sustainable living principles, on-campus organic garden for students.

Food Sustainable, organic, and/or locally produced foods available in on-campus dining facilities. Fair Trade coffee is used. Vegan and vegetarian dining options are available for every meal.

Transportation Provides free on-campus transportation (bus or other) and public transportation access to local destinations.

Buildings and Grounds *Percentage of institution's eligible buildings as of September 2008 meeting LEED and/or*

LEED-EB certification criteria: .3%. *Renovation and maintenance:* registered for LEED certification for new construction and/or renovation; uses a Green Seal certified cleaning service. *Campus grounds care:* uses water conservation devices; employs strategies to reduce light pollution; landscapes with native plant species; protects, restores, and/or creates habitat on campus.

Recycling *Events and organizations:* RecycleMania. *Programs and activities:* sustains a computer/technology recycling program; maintains an on-campus recycling center; sustains a pre-consumer food waste composting program; sustains a post-consumer food waste composting program; composts yard waste; reuses surplus department/office supplies; replaces paper materials with online alternatives. *Campus dining operations:* uses reusable dishware; operates without trays; uses bulk condiment dispensers and decreased packaging for to-go food service purchases.

Energy Currently uses or plans to use alternative sources of power (solar energy); timers to regulate temperatures based on occupancy hours; and motion, infrared, and/or light sensors to reduce energy uses for lighting.

Purchasing Sustainability criteria used in purchasing include Energy Star (EPA) and Green Cleaning Products (Green Seal/Environmental Choice certified).

Contact Sustainability Coordinator, Mills College, 5000 MacArthur Boulevard, Oakland, CA 94613. *Phone:* 510-430-3224. *E-mail:* recycmgr@mills.edu. *Web site:* www.mills.edu/.

Occidental College
Los Angeles, California

Sustainability Initiatives Occidental College is a signatory to the Talloires Declaration. Occidental College has Green Fees (optional/required) dedicated to sustainability initiatives.

Academics *Sustainability-focused undergraduate major(s):* Urban and Environmental Policy (AB). *Sustainability courses and programs:* sustainability-focused course(s) or lecture series.

Student Services and Green Events *Sustainability leadership:* sustainability committee/advisory council, recycling manager, energy manager. *Student clubs and activities:* student club(s)/group(s) focused on sustainability. *Major sustainability events:* Solar Cup Technical Workshop 2009.

Food Sustainable, organic, and/or locally produced foods available in on-campus dining facilities. Fair Trade coffee is used. Vegan and vegetarian dining options are available for every meal.

Transportation Provides public transportation access to local destinations and incentives to carpool or use public transportation.

Buildings and Grounds *Campus grounds care:* uses water conservation devices; landscapes with native plant species; protects, restores, and/or creates habitat on campus.

Recycling *Programs and activities:* sustains a computer/technology recycling program; maintains an on-campus recycling center; composts yard waste; reuses surplus department/office supplies; replaces paper materials with online alternatives; limits free printing in computer labs and libraries. *Campus dining operations:* uses reusable dishware; offers discounts for reusable mugs.

Energy Currently uses or plans to use alternative sources of power; timers to regulate temperatures based on occupancy hours; motion, infrared, and/or light sensors to reduce energy uses for lighting; and LED lighting.

Purchasing Sustainability criteria used in purchasing include Energy Star (EPA) and Green Cleaning Products (Green Seal/Environmental Choice certified).

Contact Director of Communications, Occidental College, 1600 Campus Road, Los Angeles, CA 90041-3314. *Phone:* 323-259-2990. *E-mail:* jtranqua@oxy.edu. *Web site:* www.oxy.edu/.

Pitzer College
Claremont, California

Sustainability Initiatives Pitzer College is a signatory to the Talloires Declaration. This institution's president has signed the American College & University Presidents Climate Commitment.

Academics *Sustainability-focused undergraduate major(s):* Environmental Science, Environmental Studies, Human Biology, Self-designed Majors. *Sustainability courses and programs:* sustainability-focused course(s) or lecture series.

Student Services and Green Events *Sustainability leadership:* sustainability committee/advisory council, recycling manager, sustainability-focused student government. *Housing and facilities:* sustainability-themed housing, model dorm room that demonstrates sustainable living principles, student-run café that serves environmentally or socially preferable foods, on-campus organic garden for students.

Food Sustainable, organic, and/or locally produced foods available in on-campus dining facilities. Fair Trade coffee is used. Vegan and vegetarian dining options are available for every meal.

Transportation Provides public transportation access to local destinations, a bike loan/rental program, a car sharing program, and incentives to carpool or use public transportation.

Buildings and Grounds *Percentage of institution's eligible buildings as of September 2008 meeting LEED and/or LEED-EB certification criteria:* 25%. *Renovation and maintenance:* registered for LEED certification for new construction and/or renovation; uses a Green Seal certified cleaning service. *Campus grounds care:* uses water conservation devices; employs strategies to reduce light pollution; landscapes with native plant species; protects, restores, and/or creates habitat on campus.

Recycling *Programs and activities:* sustains a computer/technology recycling program; sustains a pre-consumer food waste composting program; sustains a post-consumer food waste composting program; composts yard waste; reuses surplus department/office supplies; replaces paper materials with online alternatives; limits free printing in computer labs and libraries. *Campus dining operations:* uses reusable dishware; operates without trays; uses bulk condiment dispensers and decreased packaging for to-go food service purchases.

Energy Currently uses or plans to use alternative sources of power (solar energy); timers to regulate temperatures based on occupancy hours; motion, infrared, and/or light sensors to reduce energy uses for lighting; and LED lighting.

Purchasing Sustainability criteria used in purchasing include Energy Star (EPA), Green Cleaning Products (Green Seal/Environmental Choice certified), and Forest Stewardship Council (FSC) or American Forest and Paper Association's Sustainable Forestry Initiative (SFI) paper.

Contact Pitzer College, 1050 North Mills Avenue, Claremont, CA 91711-6101. *Phone:* 909-621-8000. *Web site:* www.pitzer.edu/.

Pomona College
Claremont, California

Sustainability Initiatives Pomona College is a member of the Association for the Advancement of Sustainability in Higher Education (AASHE). This institution's president has signed the American College & University Presidents Climate Commitment. Pomona College has Green Fees (optional/required) dedicated to sustainability initiatives.

Academics *Sustainability-focused undergraduate major(s):* Environmental Analysis in Geology; Environmental Biology; Environmental Chemistry; Environmental Ethics; Environmental Policy; Race, Class, Gender, and the Environment. *Sustainability courses and programs:* sustainability-focused course(s) or lecture series, noncredit sustainability course(s).

Student Services and Green Events *Sustainability leadership:* sustainability coordinator/director, sustainability committee/advisory council, sustainability-focused student government. *Student clubs and activities:* Campus Climate Challenge, student club(s)/group(s) focused on sustainability, outreach materials available about on-campus sustainability efforts. *Major sustainability events:* Sustainability speakers/lectures/events. *Housing and facilities:* student-run café that serves environmentally or socially preferable foods, on-campus organic garden for students.

Food Sustainable, organic, and/or locally produced foods available in on-campus dining facilities. Fair Trade coffee is used. Vegan and vegetarian dining options are available for every meal.

Transportation Provides public transportation access to local destinations, a bike loan/rental program, a car sharing program, and incentives to carpool or use public transportation.

Buildings and Grounds *Renovation and maintenance:* registered for LEED certification for new construction and/or renovation; uses a Green Seal certified cleaning service. *Campus grounds care:* uses water conservation devices; employs strategies to reduce light pollution; landscapes with native plant species; protects, restores, and/or creates habitat on campus.

Recycling *Programs and activities:* sustains a computer/technology recycling program; sustains a pre-consumer food waste composting program; composts yard waste; replaces paper materials with online alternatives; limits free printing in computer labs and libraries. *Campus dining operations:* uses reusable dishware; offers discounts for reusable mugs; uses bulk condiment dispensers and decreased packaging for to-go food service purchases.

Energy Currently uses or plans to use alternative sources of power (solar energy); timers to regulate temperatures based on occupancy hours; motion, infrared, and/or light sensors to reduce energy uses for lighting; LED lighting; and energy-related performance contracting.

Purchasing Sustainability criteria used in purchasing include Energy Star (EPA), WaterSense (EPA), Green Cleaning Products (Green Seal/Environmental Choice certified), and Forest Stewardship Council (FSC) or American Forest and Paper Association's Sustainable Forestry Initiative (SFI) paper.

Contact Sustainability Coordinator, Pomona College, 101 North College Way, Claremont, CA 91711. *Phone:* 909-607-1765. *Fax:* 909-621-8656. *E-mail:* bowen.patterson@pomona.edu. *Web site:* www.pomona.edu/.

San Diego State University
San Diego, California

Sustainability Initiatives San Diego State University has Green Fees (optional/required) dedicated to sustainability initiatives.

Academics *Sustainability-focused undergraduate major(s):* Sustainability and Environmental Studies major (BA). *Sustainability courses and programs:* sustainability-focused course(s) or lecture series, noncredit sustainability course(s), sustainability-focused nonacademic certificate program(s).

Student Services and Green Events *Sustainability leadership:* sustainability committee/advisory council, recycling manager, energy manager, sustainability-focused student government. *Student clubs and activities:* student club(s)/group(s) focused on sustainability. *Major sustainability events:* Student Research Symposium with Sustainability focus, Common Experience Program.

Food Sustainable, organic, and/or locally produced foods available in on-campus dining facilities. Fair Trade coffee is used. Vegan and vegetarian dining options are available for every meal.

Transportation Provides free on-campus transportation (bus or other), public transportation access to local destinations, and incentives to carpool or use public transportation.

Buildings and Grounds *Renovation and maintenance:* registered for LEED certification for new construction and/or renovation. *Campus grounds care:* uses water conservation devices; employs strategies to reduce light pollution; landscapes with native plant species; protects, restores, and/or creates habitat on campus; applies to its grounds only pesticides and fertilizers allowable under the U.S. Department of Agriculture's standards for crop production.

Recycling *Events and organizations:* RecycleMania. *Programs and activities:* sustains a computer/technology recycling program; maintains an on-campus recycling center; sustains a pre-consumer food waste composting program; sustains a post-consumer food waste composting program; composts yard waste; reuses surplus department/office supplies; replaces paper materials with online alternatives; limits free printing in computer labs and libraries. *Campus dining operations:* uses reusable dishware; operates without trays; offers discounts for reusable mugs; uses bulk condiment dispensers and decreased packaging for to-go food service purchases.

Energy Currently uses or plans to use alternative sources of power; timers to regulate temperatures based on occupancy hours; motion, infrared, and/or light sensors to reduce energy uses for lighting; LED lighting; vending machine motion sensors; and energy-related performance contracting. Participates in College & University Green Power Challenge activities.

Purchasing Sustainability criteria used in purchasing include Energy Star (EPA) and Green Cleaning Products (Green Seal/Environmental Choice certified).

Contact Dean of Undergraduate Studies, San Diego State University, 5500 Campanile Drive, Administration Building, Room 101, San Diego, CA 92182. *Phone:* 619-594-5842. *E-mail:* gchase@mail.sdsu.edu. *Web site:* www.sdsu.edu/.

Santa Clara University
Santa Clara, California

Sustainability Initiatives Santa Clara University is a member of the Association for the Advancement of Sustainability in Higher Education (AASHE). This institution's president has signed the American College & University Presidents Climate Commitment.

Academics *Sustainability-focused undergraduate major(s):* Environmental Science (BS), Environmental Studies (BS). *Sustainability courses and programs:* sustainability-focused course(s) or lecture series.

Student Services and Green Events *Sustainability leadership:* sustainability coordinator/director, sustainability committee/advisory council, recycling manager, energy manager. *Student clubs and activities:* student club(s)/group(s) focused on sustainability, outreach materials available about on-campus sustainability efforts. *Major sustainability events:* Campus Sustainability Day, Clean and Green Silicon Valley Projections. *Housing and facilities:* sustainability-themed housing, on-campus organic garden for students.

Food Sustainable, organic, and/or locally produced foods available in on-campus dining facilities. Fair Trade coffee is used. Vegan and vegetarian dining options are available for every meal.

Transportation Provides public transportation access to local destinations and incentives to carpool or use public transportation.

Buildings and Grounds *Percentage of institution's eligible buildings as of September 2008 meeting LEED and/or LEED-EB certification criteria:* 4%. *Campus grounds care:* uses water conservation devices; employs strategies to reduce light pollution; landscapes with native plant species; protects, restores, and/or creates habitat on campus.

Recycling *Events and organizations:* RecycleMania. *Programs and activities:* sustains a computer/technology recycling program; maintains an on-campus recycling center; composts yard waste; reuses surplus department/office supplies; limits free printing in computer labs and libraries. *Campus dining operations:* uses reusable dishware; offers discounts for reusable mugs; uses bulk condiment dispensers and decreased packaging for to-go food service purchases.

Energy Currently uses or plans to use alternative sources of power (solar energy and wind energy); timers to regulate temperatures based on occupancy hours; motion, infrared, and/or light sensors to reduce energy uses for lighting; LED lighting; and energy-related performance contracting.

Purchasing Sustainability criteria used in purchasing include Energy Star (EPA), Green Cleaning Products (Green Seal/Environmental Choice certified), and Forest Stewardship Council (FSC) or American Forest and Paper Association's Sustainable Forestry Initiative (SFI) paper.

Contact Sustainability Coordinator, Santa Clara University, Office of Sustainability, Environmental Studies Institute, 500 El Camino Real, Santa Clara, CA 95053. *Phone:* 408-554-2369. *E-mail:* lcromwell@scu.edu. *Web site:* www.scu.edu/.

Stanford University
Stanford, California

Academics *Sustainability-focused undergraduate major(s):* Civil and Environmental Engineering, Earth Systems, Ecology and Evolution, Environmental Earth Systems Science, Geological and Environmental Engineering, Interdisciplinary Program in Environment and Resources, Environmental and Natural Resources. *Sustainability-focused graduate degree program(s):* Civil and Environmental Engineering (MS Eng, PhD), Ecology and Evolution (PhD), Environmental and Natural Resources Law (JD), Environmental Earth Systems Science (MS Eng, PhD), Geological and Environmental Engineering (MS Eng, PhD), Interdisciplinary Program in

Environment and Resources (MS, PhD), Earth Systems (MS). *Sustainability courses and programs:* sustainability-focused course(s) or lecture series, noncredit sustainability course(s).

Student Services and Green Events *Sustainability leadership:* sustainability coordinator/director, sustainability committee/advisory council, recycling manager, energy manager, sustainability-focused student government. *Student clubs and activities:* Campus Climate Challenge, Public Interest Research Group (PIRG) chapter on campus, student club(s)/group(s) focused on sustainability, outreach materials available about on-campus sustainability efforts. *Major sustainability events:* Woods Institute Environmental Series (weekly), Students for Sustainable Stanford Series (weekly), Earth Week Celebration, Energy Crossroads, Ethics and Food Lecture Series, Department of PM sponsored green building events. *Housing and facilities:* sustainability-themed housing, model dorm room that demonstrates sustainable living principles, on-campus organic garden for students.

Food Sustainable, organic, and/or locally produced foods available in on-campus dining facilities. Fair Trade coffee is used. Vegan and vegetarian dining options are available for every meal.

Transportation Provides free on-campus transportation (bus or other), public transportation access to local destinations, a bike loan/rental program, a car sharing program, and incentives to carpool or use public transportation.

Buildings and Grounds *Renovation and maintenance:* registered for LEED certification for new construction and/or renovation; uses a Green Seal certified cleaning service. *Campus grounds care:* uses water conservation devices; employs strategies to reduce light pollution; landscapes with native plant species; protects, restores, and/or creates habitat on campus.

Recycling *Events and organizations:* RecycleMania. *Programs and activities:* sustains a computer/technology recycling program; maintains an on-campus recycling center; sustains a pre-consumer food waste composting program; sustains a post-consumer food waste composting program; composts yard waste; reuses surplus department/office supplies; reuses chemicals; replaces paper materials with online alternatives; limits free printing in computer labs and libraries. *Campus dining operations:* uses reusable dishware; operates without trays; offers discounts for reusable mugs; uses bulk condiment dispensers and decreased packaging for to-go food service purchases.

Energy Currently uses or plans to use alternative sources of power (solar energy); timers to regulate temperatures based on occupancy hours; motion, infrared, and/or light sensors to reduce energy uses for lighting; LED lighting; and vending machine motion sensors. Participates in College & University Green Power Challenge activities.

Purchasing Sustainability criteria used in purchasing include Energy Star (EPA), WaterSense (EPA), Green Electronics Council (GEC) Electronic Product Environmental Assessment Tool (EPEAT) Silver or Gold, Green Cleaning Products (Green Seal/Environmental Choice certified), and Forest Stewardship Council (FSC) or American Forest and Paper Association's Sustainable Forestry Initiative (SFI) paper.

Contact Manager, Sustainability Programs, Stanford University, 340 Bonair Siding, Stanford, CA 94305. *Phone:* 650-721-1518. *E-mail:* fahmida@stanford.edu. *Web site:* www.stanford.edu/.

University of California, Berkeley
Berkeley, California

Sustainability Initiatives University of California, Berkeley's president has signed the American College & University Presidents Climate Commitment. University of California, Berkeley has Green Fees (optional/required) dedicated to sustainability initiatives.

Academics *Sustainability-focused undergraduate major(s):* Conservation and Resource Studies (BS), Environmental Economics (BS), Environmental Engineering (BS), Environmental Planning (BS), Environmental Science (BS), Forestry and Natural Resources (BS). *Sustainability-focused graduate degree program(s):* Agricultural and Environmental Chemistry (MA, PhD), Agricultural and Resource Economics (PhD), Energy Resources Group (MA, MS, PhD), Environmental and Science Journalism (MJ), Environmental Law (JD, PhD), Society and Environment (MS, PhD). *Sustainability courses and programs:* sustainability-focused course(s) or lecture series.

Student Services and Green Events *Sustainability leadership:* sustainability coordinator/director, sustainability committee/advisory council, recycling manager, energy manager, sustainability-focused student government. *Student clubs and activities:* Campus Climate Challenge, Public Interest Research Group (PIRG) chapter on campus, student club(s)/group(s) focused on sustainability. *Major sustainability events:* CACS Summit, BERC Energy Symposium, Green Week. *Housing and facilities:* sustainability-themed housing, model dorm room that demonstrates sustainable living principles, on-campus organic garden for students.

Food Sustainable, organic, and/or locally produced foods available in on-campus dining facilities. Fair Trade coffee is used. Vegan and vegetarian dining options are available for every meal.

Transportation Provides free on-campus transportation (bus or other), public transportation access to local destinations, a bike loan/rental program, a car sharing program, and incentives to carpool or use public transportation.

Buildings and Grounds *Renovation and maintenance:* registered for LEED certification for new construction and/or renovation. *Campus grounds care:* uses water conservation devices; employs strategies to reduce light pollution; landscapes with native plant species; protects, restores, and/or creates habitat on campus.

Recycling *Programs and activities:* sustains a computer/technology recycling program; maintains an on-campus recycling center; sustains a pre-consumer food waste composting program; sustains a post-consumer food waste composting program; composts yard waste; reuses surplus department/office supplies; replaces paper materials with online alternatives. *Campus dining operations:* uses reusable dishware; uses bulk condiment dispensers and decreased packaging for to-go food service purchases.

Energy Currently uses or plans to use alternative sources of power (solar energy); timers to regulate temperatures based on occupancy hours; motion, infrared, and/or light sensors to reduce energy uses for lighting; and vending machine motion sensors.

Purchasing Sustainability criteria used in purchasing include Energy Star (EPA), Green Electronics Council (GEC) Electronic Product Environmental Assessment Tool (EPEAT) Silver or Gold, Green Cleaning Products (Green Seal/Environmental Choice certified), and Forest Stewardship Council (FSC) or American Forest and Paper Association's Sustainable Forestry Initiative (SFI) paper.

Contact Director of Sustainability, University of California, Berkeley, 381 University Hall, MC 1150, Berkeley, CA 94720. *Phone:* 510-643-5907. *E-mail:* lmcneilly@berkeley. edu. *Web site:* www.berkeley.edu/.

University of California, Davis
Davis, California

Sustainability Initiatives University of California, Davis's president has signed the American College & University Presidents Climate Commitment.

Academics *Sustainability-focused undergraduate major(s):* Atmospheric Sciences, Avian Sciences, Ecological and Management Restoration, Entomology, Environmental Science and Management, Plant Sciences, Agricultural Sustainability Institute (Student Farm), Science & Society, Environmental Horticulture & Urban Forestry, Environmental Policy Analysis & Planning, Environmental Toxicology. *Sustainability-focused graduate degree program(s):* Biological Systems Engineering (MS, MEngr, PhD, DEngr), Civil and Environmental Engineering (MS, MEngr, PhD, DEngr), Ecology (MS, PhD), Geography (MA, PhD), International Agricultural Development (MS), Transportation Technology and Policy (MS, PhD). *Sustainability courses and programs:* sustainability-focused course(s) or lecture series, noncredit sustainability course(s), sustainability-focused nonacademic certificate program(s).

Student Services and Green Events *Sustainability leadership:* sustainability coordinator/director, sustainability committee/advisory council, recycling manager, energy manager, sustainability-focused student government. *Student clubs and activities:* Public Interest Research Group (PIRG) chapter on campus, student club(s)/group(s) focused on sustainability. *Major sustainability events:* California Student Sustainability Coalition Summit. *Housing and facilities:* student-run café that serves environmentally or socially preferable foods, on-campus organic garden for students.

Food Sustainable, organic, and/or locally produced foods available in on-campus dining facilities. Fair Trade coffee is used. Vegan and vegetarian dining options are available for every meal.

Transportation Provides free on-campus transportation (bus or other), public transportation access to local destinations, a bike loan/rental program, a car sharing program, and incentives to carpool or use public transportation.

Buildings and Grounds *Renovation and maintenance:* registered for LEED certification for new construction and/or renovation; uses a Green Seal certified cleaning service. *Campus grounds care:* uses water conservation devices; employs strategies to reduce light pollution; landscapes with native plant species; protects, restores, and/or creates habitat on campus.

Recycling *Events and organizations:* RecycleMania. *Programs and activities:* sustains a computer/technology recycling program; maintains an on-campus recycling center; sustains a post-consumer food waste composting program; composts yard waste; reuses surplus department/office supplies; replaces paper materials with online alternatives; limits free printing in computer labs and libraries. *Campus dining operations:* uses reusable dishware; operates without trays; offers discounts for reusable mugs; uses bulk condiment dispensers and decreased packaging for to-go food service purchases.

Energy Currently uses or plans to use alternative sources of power (biomass energy, geothermal energy, hydroelectricity/water power, and solar energy); timers to regulate temperatures based on occupancy hours; motion, infrared, and/or light sensors to reduce energy uses for lighting; and LED lighting.

Purchasing Sustainability criteria used in purchasing include Energy Star (EPA), Green Electronics Council (GEC) Electronic Product Environmental Assessment Tool (EPEAT) Silver or Gold, Green Cleaning Products (Green Seal/Environmental Choice certified), and Forest Steward-ship Council (FSC) or American Forest and Paper Association's Sustainable Forestry Initiative (SFI) paper.

Contact Assistant Vice Chancellor for Environmental Stewardship and Sustainability, University of California, Davis, Office of Resource Management and Planning, One Shields Avenue, Davis, CA 95616. *Phone:* 530-752-2432. *Fax:* 530-752-5808. *E-mail:* asengland@ucdavis.edu. *Web site:* www.ucdavis.edu/.

University of California, Santa Barbara
Santa Barbara, California

Sustainability Initiatives University of California, Santa Barbara is a signatory to the Talloires Declaration. This institution's president has signed the American College & University Presidents Climate Commitment. University of California, Santa Barbara has Green Fees (optional/required) dedicated to sustainability initiatives.

Academics *Sustainability-focused undergraduate major(s):* Earth Science (BA, BS); Ecology, Evolution, Marine Biology (BA, BS); English—Literature and the Environment (BA); Environmental Studies (BA, BS); Geography (BA, BS); Global and International Studies (BA). *Sustainability-focused graduate degree program(s):* Earth Science (MA, PhD); Ecology, Evolution, Marine Biology (MA, PhD); Environmental Science and Management (MESM; PhD); Geography (MA, PhD). *Sustainability courses and programs:* sustainability-focused course(s) or lecture series.

Student Services and Green Events *Sustainability leadership:* sustainability coordinator/director, sustainability committee/advisory council, recycling manager, energy manager. *Student clubs and activities:* Public Interest Research Group (PIRG) chapter on campus, student club(s)/group(s) focused on sustainability, outreach materials available about on-campus sustainability efforts. *Major sustainability events:* UC/CSU/CCC Sustainability Conference, Bren School Colloquia Series, Sustainable Foods Vendor Fair, Sustainable Office Products Vendor Fair. *Housing and facilities:* sustainability-themed housing, model dorm room that demonstrates sustainable living principles, on-campus organic garden for students.

Food Sustainable, organic, and/or locally produced foods available in on-campus dining facilities. Fair Trade coffee is used. Vegan and vegetarian dining options are available for every meal.

Transportation Provides public transportation access to local destinations, a car sharing program, and incentives to carpool or use public transportation.

Buildings and Grounds *Percentage of institution's eligible buildings as of September 2008 meeting LEED and/or LEED-EB certification criteria:* 40%. *Renovation and maintenance:* registered for LEED certification for new construction and/or renovation. *Campus grounds care:* uses water conservation devices; employs strategies to reduce light pollution; landscapes with native plant species; protects, restores, and/or creates habitat on campus; applies to its grounds only pesticides and fertilizers allowable under the U.S. Department of Agriculture's standards for crop production.

Recycling *Events and organizations:* RecycleMania. *Programs and activities:* sustains a computer/technology recycling program; maintains an on-campus recycling center; sustains a pre-consumer food waste composting program; composts yard waste; reuses surplus department/office supplies; reuses chemicals; replaces paper materials with online alternatives. *Campus dining operations:* uses reusable dishware; offers discounts for reusable mugs; uses bulk condiment dispensers and decreased packaging for to-go food service purchases.

Energy Currently uses or plans to use alternative sources of power (solar energy); motion, infrared, and/or light sensors to reduce energy uses for lighting; LED lighting; and energy-related performance contracting.

Purchasing Sustainability criteria used in purchasing include Energy Star (EPA), Green Electronics Council (GEC) Electronic Product Environmental Assessment Tool (EPEAT) Silver or Gold, Green Cleaning Products (Green Seal/Environmental Choice certified), and Forest Steward-ship Council (FSC) or American Forest and Paper Association's Sustainable Forestry Initiative (SFI) paper.

Contact Campus Sustainability Coordinator, University of California, Santa Barbara, Office of Vice Chancellor, Administrative Services, Santa Barbara, CA 93106-2033. *Phone:* 805-893-8367. *E-mail:* jill.richardson@vcadmin.ucsb.edu. *Web site:* www.ucsb.edu/.

University of California, Santa Cruz
Santa Cruz, California

Sustainability Initiatives University of California, Santa Cruz is a member of the Association for the Advancement of Sustainability in Higher Education (AASHE). This institution's president has signed the American College & University Presidents Climate Commitment. University of California, Santa Cruz has Green Fees (optional/required) dedicated to sustainability initiatives.

Academics *Sustainability-focused undergraduate major(s):* Ecology and Evolution (BS), Environmental Studies (BA, BS). *Sustainability-focused graduate degree program(s):* Environmental Studies (PhD), Environmental Toxicology (MS, PhD), Ocean Sciences (MS, PhD). *Sustainability courses and programs:* sustainability-focused course(s) or lecture series, noncredit sustainability course(s).

Student Services and Green Events *Sustainability leadership:* sustainability coordinator/director, sustainability committee/advisory council, recycling manager, energy manager, sustainability-focused student government. *Student clubs and activities:* Campus Climate Challenge, Public Interest Research Group (PIRG) chapter on campus, student club(s)/group(s) focused on sustainability, outreach materials available about on-campus sustainability efforts. *Major sustainability events:* Annual Campus Earth Summit, Annual Campus Earth Festival/Earth Day, Annual Harvest Festival, Annual Fred Keeley Lecture in Environmental Policy. *Housing and facilities:* sustainability-themed housing, on-campus organic garden for students.

Food Sustainable, organic, and/or locally produced foods available in on-campus dining facilities. Fair Trade coffee is used. Vegan and vegetarian dining options are available for every meal.

Transportation Provides free on-campus transportation (bus or other), public transportation access to local destinations, a bike loan/rental program, a car sharing program, and incentives to carpool or use public transportation.

Buildings and Grounds *Percentage of institution's eligible buildings as of September 2008 meeting LEED and/or*

LEED-EB certification criteria: 10%. Renovation and maintenance: registered for LEED certification for new construction and/or renovation. Campus grounds care: uses water conservation devices; employs strategies to reduce light pollution; landscapes with native plant species; protects, restores, and/or creates habitat on campus.

Recycling Events and organizations: RecycleMania. Programs and activities: sustains a computer/technology recycling program; maintains an on-campus recycling center; sustains a pre-consumer food waste composting program; composts yard waste; reuses surplus department/office supplies; limits free printing in computer labs and libraries. Campus dining operations: uses reusable dishware; operates without trays; uses bulk condiment dispensers and decreased packaging for to-go food service purchases.

Energy Currently uses or plans to use alternative sources of power; timers to regulate temperatures based on occupancy hours; motion, infrared, and/or light sensors to reduce energy uses for lighting; and vending machine motion sensors. Participates in College & University Green Power Challenge activities.

Purchasing Sustainability criteria used in purchasing include Energy Star (EPA), Green Electronics Council (GEC) Electronic Product Environmental Assessment Tool (EPEAT) Silver or Gold, and Green Cleaning Products (Green Seal/Environmental Choice certified).

Contact Sustainability Coordinator, University of California, Santa Cruz, 1156 High Street, Santa Cruz, CA 95064. Phone: 831-459-3011. Fax: 831-459-5121. E-mail: sustain@ucsc.edu. Web site: www.ucsc.edu/.

University of Redlands
Redlands, California

Sustainability Initiatives University of Redlands is a member of the Association for the Advancement of Sustainability in Higher Education (AASHE). This institution's president has signed the American College & University Presidents Climate Commitment.

Academics Sustainability-focused undergraduate major(s): Environmental Studies (BA, BS). Sustainability courses and programs: sustainability-focused course(s) or lecture series.

Student Services and Green Events Sustainability leadership: sustainability coordinator/director, sustainability committee/advisory council, recycling manager, energy manager. Student clubs and activities: student club(s)/group(s) focused on sustainability, outreach materials available about on-campus sustainability efforts. Major sustainability events: Series of faculty and student workshops and project "studios". Housing and facilities: sustainability-themed housing, model dorm room that demonstrates sustainable living principles, on-campus organic garden for students.

Food Sustainable, organic, and/or locally produced foods available in on-campus dining facilities. Fair Trade coffee is used. Vegan and vegetarian dining options are available for every meal.

Transportation Provides public transportation access to local destinations, a bike loan/rental program, and incentives to carpool or use public transportation.

Buildings and Grounds Renovation and maintenance: registered for LEED certification for new construction and/or renovation. Campus grounds care: uses water conservation devices; employs strategies to reduce light pollution; landscapes with native plant species.

Recycling Programs and activities: sustains a computer/technology recycling program.

Energy Currently uses or plans to use alternative sources of power (solar energy); timers to regulate temperatures based on occupancy hours; motion, infrared, and/or light sensors to reduce energy uses for lighting; and vending machine motion sensors.

Purchasing Sustainability criteria used in purchasing include Energy Star (EPA).

Contact University of Redlands, 1200 East Colton Avenue, PO Box 3080, Redlands, CA 92373-0999. Phone: 909-793-2121. Web site: www.redlands.edu/.

University of the Pacific
Stockton, California

Academics Sustainability courses and programs: sustainability-focused course(s) or lecture series, sustainability-focused nonacademic certificate program(s).

Student Services and Green Events Sustainability leadership: sustainability coordinator/director, sustainability committee/advisory council, sustainability-focused student government. Student clubs and activities: Campus Climate Challenge. Housing and facilities: sustainability-themed housing.

Food Sustainable, organic, and/or locally produced foods available in on-campus dining facilities. Fair Trade coffee is used. Vegan and vegetarian dining options are available for every meal.

Transportation Provides public transportation access to local destinations and a bike loan/rental program.

Buildings and Grounds Percentage of institution's eligible buildings as of September 2008 meeting LEED and/or LEED-EB certification criteria: 1%. Renovation and maintenance: registered for LEED certification for new construction and/or renovation. Campus grounds care: uses water conservation devices; landscapes with native plant species.

Recycling Programs and activities: sustains a computer/technology recycling program; reuses surplus department/office supplies; replaces paper materials with online alternatives. Campus dining operations: uses reusable dishware; offers discounts for reusable mugs; uses bulk condiment dispensers and decreased packaging for to-go food service purchases.

Energy Currently uses or plans to use motion, infrared, and/or light sensors to reduce energy uses for lighting and LED lighting.

Purchasing Sustainability criteria used in purchasing include Energy Star (EPA) and Green Cleaning Products (Green Seal/Environmental Choice certified).

Contact Research Manager/Part-Time Sustainability Coordinator, University of the Pacific, 3601 Pacific Avenue, Stockton, CA 95211. Phone: 209-946-7367. Fax: 209-946-2014. E-mail: cbrodie@pacific.edu. Web site: www.pacific.edu/.

Colorado

The Colorado College
Colorado Springs, Colorado

Sustainability Initiatives The Colorado College is a member of the Association for the Advancement of Sustainability in Higher Education (AASHE).

Academics Sustainability-focused undergraduate major(s): Environmental Chemistry (BA), Environmental Physics (BA), Environmental Policy (BA), Environmental Science (BA).

Sustainability courses and programs: sustainability-focused course(s) or lecture series, noncredit sustainability course(s).

Student Services and Green Events *Sustainability leadership:* sustainability coordinator/director, sustainability committee/advisory council, recycling manager, energy manager, sustainability-focused student government. *Student clubs and activities:* Campus Climate Challenge, student club(s)/group(s) focused on sustainability, outreach materials available about on-campus sustainability efforts. *Major sustainability events:* State of the Rockies Lecture Series and Conference, Food Chained Lecture Series, Linneman Lecture Series, Earth Week. *Housing and facilities:* sustainability-themed housing, on-campus organic garden for students.

Food Sustainable, organic, and/or locally produced foods available in on-campus dining facilities. Fair Trade coffee is used. Vegan and vegetarian dining options are available for every meal.

Transportation Provides public transportation access to local destinations and a bike loan/rental program.

Buildings and Grounds *Percentage of institution's eligible buildings as of September 2008 meeting LEED and/or LEED-EB certification criteria:* 2%. *Renovation and maintenance:* registered for LEED certification for new construction and/or renovation; uses a Green Seal certified cleaning service. *Campus grounds care:* uses water conservation devices; employs strategies to reduce light pollution; landscapes with native plant species; protects, restores, and/or creates habitat on campus.

Recycling *Events and organizations:* RecycleMania. *Programs and activities:* sustains a computer/technology recycling program; sustains a pre-consumer food waste composting program; sustains a post-consumer food waste composting program; composts yard waste; reuses surplus department/office supplies; reuses chemicals; replaces paper materials with online alternatives. *Campus dining operations:* uses reusable dishware; operates without trays; offers discounts for reusable mugs; uses bulk condiment dispensers and decreased packaging for to-go food service purchases.

Energy Currently uses or plans to use alternative sources of power (solar energy); timers to regulate temperatures based on occupancy hours; motion, infrared, and/or light sensors to reduce energy uses for lighting; and LED lighting.

Purchasing Sustainability criteria used in purchasing include Energy Star (EPA) and Green Cleaning Products (Green Seal/Environmental Choice certified).

Contact Sustainability Coordinator/Co-Chair, Campus Sustainability Council/Chaplain, The Colorado College, 14 East Cache La Poudre, Colorado Springs, CO 80903. *Phone:* 719-389-6638. *E-mail:* bcoriell@coloradocollege.edu. *Web site:* www.coloradocollege.edu/.

Colorado State University–Pueblo
Pueblo, Colorado

Student Services and Green Events *Sustainability leadership:* sustainability committee/advisory council, recycling manager. *Student clubs and activities:* student club(s)/group(s) focused on sustainability. *Major sustainability events:* Environmental Awareness Conferences.

Food Fair Trade coffee is used. Vegan and vegetarian dining options are available for every meal.

Transportation Provides public transportation access to local destinations, a bike loan/rental program, and incentives to carpool or use public transportation.

Buildings and Grounds *Renovation and maintenance:* registered for LEED certification for new construction and/or renovation. *Campus grounds care:* uses water conservation devices; landscapes with native plant species; applies to its grounds only pesticides and fertilizers allowable under the U.S. Department of Agriculture's standards for crop production.

Recycling *Programs and activities:* sustains a computer/technology recycling program; limits free printing in computer labs and libraries. *Campus dining operations:* uses reusable dishware; uses bulk condiment dispensers and decreased packaging for to-go food service purchases.

Energy Currently uses or plans to use alternative sources of power (solar energy); timers to regulate temperatures based on occupancy hours; motion, infrared, and/or light sensors to reduce energy uses for lighting; LED lighting; vending machine motion sensors; and energy-related performance contracting.

Purchasing Sustainability criteria used in purchasing include Green Cleaning Products (Green Seal/Environmental Choice certified) and Forest Stewardship Council (FSC) or American Forest and Paper Association's Sustainable Forestry Initiative (SFI) paper.

Contact Colorado State University–Pueblo, 2200 Bonforte Boulevard, Pueblo, CO 81001-4901. *Phone:* 719-549-2100. *Web site:* www.colostate-pueblo.edu/.

Fort Lewis College
Durango, Colorado

Sustainability Initiatives Fort Lewis College's president has signed the American College & University Presidents Climate Commitment.

Academics *Sustainability-focused undergraduate major(s):* Environmental Studies (BA). *Sustainability courses and programs:* sustainability-focused course(s) or lecture series.

Student Services and Green Events *Sustainability leadership:* sustainability committee/advisory council, recycling manager. *Student clubs and activities:* student club(s)/group(s) focused on sustainability. *Major sustainability events:* Earth Week, Homegrown Local Food Festival. *Housing and facilities:* sustainability-themed housing, on-campus organic garden for students.

Food Sustainable, organic, and/or locally produced foods available in on-campus dining facilities. Fair Trade coffee is used. Vegan and vegetarian dining options are available for every meal.

Transportation Provides public transportation access to local destinations, a bike loan/rental program, and incentives to carpool or use public transportation.

Buildings and Grounds *Renovation and maintenance:* registered for LEED certification for new construction and/or renovation. *Campus grounds care:* uses water conservation devices; employs strategies to reduce light pollution; landscapes with native plant species; protects, restores, and/or creates habitat on campus.

Recycling *Programs and activities:* sustains a computer/technology recycling program; sustains a pre-consumer food waste composting program; sustains a post-consumer food waste composting program; replaces paper materials with online alternatives; limits free printing in computer labs and libraries. *Campus dining operations:* uses reusable dishware; offers discounts for reusable mugs.

Energy Currently uses or plans to use timers to regulate temperatures based on occupancy hours; motion, infrared, and/or light sensors to reduce energy uses for lighting; and vending machine motion sensors.

Purchasing Sustainability criteria used in purchasing include Energy Star (EPA) and Green Cleaning Products (Green Seal/Environmental Choice certified).

Contact Environmental Center Coordinator, Fort Lewis College, 1000 Rim Drive, Durango, CO 81301. *Phone:* 970-247-7091. *Fax:* 970-247-7487. *E-mail:* renner_m@fortlewis.edu. *Web site:* www.fortlewis.edu/.

Naropa University
Boulder, Colorado

Sustainability Initiatives Naropa University's president has signed the American College & University Presidents Climate Commitment.

Academics *Sustainability-focused undergraduate major(s):* Environmental Studies (BA). *Sustainability-focused graduate degree program(s):* Environmental Leadership (MA). *Sustainability courses and programs:* sustainability-focused course(s) or lecture series.

Student Services and Green Events *Sustainability leadership:* recycling manager. *Student clubs and activities:* student club(s)/group(s) focused on sustainability, outreach materials available about on-campus sustainability efforts. *Major sustainability events:* Annual Sustainability Fair. *Housing and facilities:* on-campus organic garden for students.

Food Sustainable, organic, and/or locally produced foods available in on-campus dining facilities. Vegan and vegetarian dining options are available for every meal.

Transportation Provides free on-campus transportation (bus or other), public transportation access to local destinations, a bike loan/rental program, and a car sharing program.

Buildings and Grounds *Campus grounds care:* uses water conservation devices; employs strategies to reduce light pollution; landscapes with native plant species; applies to its grounds only pesticides and fertilizers allowable under the U.S. Department of Agriculture's standards for crop production.

Recycling *Events and organizations:* RecycleMania. *Programs and activities:* sustains a computer/technology recycling program; maintains an on-campus recycling center; sustains a pre-consumer food waste composting program; sustains a post-consumer food waste composting program; composts yard waste; reuses surplus department/office supplies; replaces paper materials with online alternatives; limits free printing in computer labs and libraries. *Campus dining operations:* uses reusable dishware; operates without trays; offers discounts for reusable mugs; uses bulk condiment dispensers and decreased packaging for to-go food service purchases.

Energy Currently uses or plans to use alternative sources of power (solar energy and wind energy); timers to regulate temperatures based on occupancy hours; and motion, infrared, and/or light sensors to reduce energy uses for lighting.

Purchasing Sustainability criteria used in purchasing include Energy Star (EPA), Green Cleaning Products (Green Seal/Environmental Choice certified), and Forest Stewardship Council (FSC) or American Forest and Paper Association's Sustainable Forestry Initiative (SFI) paper.

Contact Interim Director of Marketing and Communications, Naropa University, 2130 Arapahoe Road, Boulder, CO 80302. *Phone:* 303-546-3566. *E-mail:* pjohnson@naropa.edu. *Web site:* www.naropa.edu/.

Rocky Mountain College of Art + Design
Lakewood, Colorado

Academics *Sustainability-focused undergraduate major(s):* Interior Design Program, Green Design emphasis. *Sustainability courses and programs:* sustainability-focused course(s) or lecture series.

Student Services and Green Events *Sustainability leadership:* sustainability coordinator/director, sustainability committee/advisory council. *Student clubs and activities:* Campus Climate Challenge, student club(s)/group(s) focused on sustainability, outreach materials available about on-campus sustainability efforts. *Major sustainability events:* Campus Sustainability Day. *Housing and facilities:* on-campus organic garden for students.

Food Fair Trade coffee is used.

Transportation Provides free on-campus transportation (bus or other) and a bike loan/rental program.

Buildings and Grounds *Campus grounds care:* employs strategies to reduce light pollution; protects, restores, and/or creates habitat on campus.

Recycling *Programs and activities:* sustains a computer/technology recycling program; maintains an on-campus recycling center; replaces paper materials with online alternatives; limits free printing in computer labs and libraries. *Campus dining operations:* offers discounts for reusable mugs; uses bulk condiment dispensers and decreased packaging for to-go food service purchases.

Energy Currently uses or plans to use timers to regulate temperatures based on occupancy hours and LED lighting.

Purchasing Sustainability criteria used in purchasing include Energy Star (EPA), Green Cleaning Products (Green Seal/Environmental Choice certified), and Forest Stewardship Council (FSC) or American Forest and Paper Association's Sustainable Forestry Initiative (SFI) paper.

Contact Director, Institute for Sustainable Studies/Coordinator, Campus Sustainability, Rocky Mountain College of Art + Design, 1600 Pierce Street, Lakewood, CA 80214. *Phone:* 303-225-8534. *E-mail:* jpollack@rmcad.edu. *Web site:* www.rmcad.edu/.

University of Denver
Denver, Colorado

Sustainability Initiatives University of Denver's president has signed the American College & University Presidents Climate Commitment. University of Denver has Green Fees (optional/required) dedicated to sustainability initiatives.

Academics *Sustainability-focused undergraduate major(s):* Biology (BA), Ecology and Biodiversity (BA), Environmental Policy and Management (MA), Environmental Science (BA), Environmental Science (BS), Geography (BS).

Student Services and Green Events *Sustainability leadership:* sustainability coordinator/director, sustainability committee/advisory council, recycling manager, energy manager, sustainability-focused student government. *Student clubs and activities:* student club(s)/group(s) focused on sustainability, outreach materials available about on-campus sustainability efforts. *Major sustainability events:* Provost's Conference on Sustainability. *Housing and facilities:* sustainability-themed housing.

Food Fair Trade coffee is used. Vegan and vegetarian dining options are available for every meal.

Transportation Provides free on-campus transportation (bus or other), public transportation access to local destinations, and incentives to carpool or use public transportation.

Buildings and Grounds *Percentage of institution's eligible buildings as of September 2008 meeting LEED and/or LEED-EB certification criteria:* 50%. *Renovation and maintenance:* registered for LEED certification for new construction and/or renovation. *Campus grounds care:* uses water conservation devices; employs strategies to reduce light pollution; landscapes with native plant species; protects, restores, and/or creates habitat on campus.

Recycling *Events and organizations:* RecycleMania. *Programs and activities:* sustains a computer/technology recycling program; maintains an on-campus recycling center; reuses surplus department/office supplies; reuses chemicals; replaces paper materials with online alternatives; limits free printing in computer labs and libraries. *Campus dining operations:* uses reusable dishware; uses bulk condiment dispensers and decreased packaging for to-go food service purchases.

Energy Currently uses or plans to use alternative sources of power (wind energy); timers to regulate temperatures based on occupancy hours; motion, infrared, and/or light sensors to reduce energy uses for lighting; LED lighting; and energy-related performance contracting.

Purchasing Sustainability criteria used in purchasing include Energy Star (EPA), Green Cleaning Products (Green Seal/Environmental Choice certified), and Forest Stewardship Council (FSC) or American Forest and Paper Association's Sustainable Forestry Initiative (SFI) paper.

Contact Professor of Law, University of Denver, University Sustainability Council, 2199 South University Boulevard, Denver, CO 80208. *E-mail:* green@du.edu. *Web site:* www.du.edu/.

Connecticut

Central Connecticut State University
New Britain, Connecticut

Sustainability Initiatives Central Connecticut State University's president has signed the American College & University Presidents Climate Commitment.

Academics *Sustainability courses and programs:* sustainability-focused course(s) or lecture series.

Student Services and Green Events *Sustainability leadership:* sustainability committee/advisory council, recycling manager, energy manager. *Student clubs and activities:* student club(s)/group(s) focused on sustainability, outreach materials available about on-campus sustainability efforts. *Major sustainability events:* Global sustainability and climate change symposium, roundtable discussions on sustainability.

Food Sustainable, organic, and/or locally produced foods available in on-campus dining facilities. Fair Trade coffee is used. Vegan and vegetarian dining options are available for every meal.

Transportation Provides free on-campus transportation (bus or other) and public transportation access to local destinations.

Buildings and Grounds *Renovation and maintenance:* registered for LEED certification for new construction and/or renovation; uses a Green Seal certified cleaning service. *Campus grounds care:* uses water conservation devices; employs strategies to reduce light pollution; landscapes with native plant species; protects, restores, and/or creates habitat on campus; applies to its grounds only pesticides and fertilizers allowable under the U.S. Department of Agriculture's standards for crop production.

Recycling *Programs and activities:* sustains a computer/technology recycling program; maintains an on-campus recycling center; reuses surplus department/office supplies; replaces paper materials with online alternatives; limits free printing in computer labs and libraries. *Campus dining operations:* uses reusable dishware; offers discounts for reusable mugs; uses bulk condiment dispensers and decreased packaging for to-go food service purchases.

Energy Currently uses or plans to use timers to regulate temperatures based on occupancy hours; motion, infrared, and/or light sensors to reduce energy uses for lighting; and LED lighting.

Purchasing Sustainability criteria used in purchasing include Energy Star (EPA) and Green Cleaning Products (Green Seal/Environmental Choice certified).

Contact Environmental Health and Safety Officer, Central Connecticut State University, 1615 Stanley Street, New Britain, CT 06050. *Phone:* 860-832-2499. *E-mail:* forcellad@ccsu.edu. *Web site:* www.ccsu.edu/.

Fairfield University
Fairfield, Connecticut

Sustainability Initiatives Fairfield University's president has signed the American College & University Presidents Climate Commitment.

Academics *Sustainability courses and programs:* sustainability-focused course(s) or lecture series, sustainability-focused nonacademic certificate program(s).

Student Services and Green Events *Sustainability leadership:* sustainability committee/advisory council, recycling manager, energy manager, sustainability-focused student government. *Student clubs and activities:* student club(s)/group(s) focused on sustainability, outreach materials available about on-campus sustainability efforts. *Major sustainability events:* Sheri Liao, Beijing Village, Honorary Degree and Public Lecture, Focus the Nation 2009. *Housing and facilities:* sustainability-themed housing, model dorm room that demonstrates sustainable living principles.

Food Sustainable, organic, and/or locally produced foods available in on-campus dining facilities. Fair Trade coffee is used. Vegan and vegetarian dining options are available for every meal.

Transportation Provides free on-campus transportation (bus or other) and public transportation access to local destinations.

Buildings and Grounds *Renovation and maintenance:* uses a Green Seal certified cleaning service. *Campus grounds care:* uses water conservation devices; landscapes with native plant species; protects, restores, and/or creates habitat on campus.

Recycling *Programs and activities:* sustains a computer/technology recycling program; sustains a post-consumer food waste composting program; replaces paper materials with online alternatives. *Campus dining operations:* uses reusable dishware; operates without trays; offers discounts for reusable mugs.

Energy Currently uses or plans to use motion, infrared, and/or light sensors to reduce energy uses for lighting.

Purchasing Sustainability criteria used in purchasing include Energy Star (EPA).

Contact Assistant Vice President and Director of Facilities Management, Fairfield University, 1073 North Benson Road, Fairfield, CT 06824. *Phone:* 203-254-4254. *Fax:* 203-254-4239. *E-mail:* dfrassinelli@mail.fairfield.edu. *Web site:* www.fairfield.edu/.

Quinnipiac University
Hamden, Connecticut

Student Services and Green Events *Sustainability leadership:* sustainability committee/advisory council.

Food Sustainable, organic, and/or locally produced foods available in on-campus dining facilities. Vegan and vegetarian dining options are available for every meal.

Transportation Provides free on-campus transportation (bus or other), public transportation access to local destinations, and incentives to carpool or use public transportation.

Buildings and Grounds *Campus grounds care:* uses water conservation devices.

Recycling *Programs and activities:* sustains a computer/technology recycling program; maintains an on-campus recycling center; replaces paper materials with online alternatives; limits free printing in computer labs and libraries. *Campus dining operations:* uses bulk condiment dispensers and decreased packaging for to-go food service purchases.

Energy Currently uses or plans to use alternative sources of power (solar energy and wind energy); timers to regulate temperatures based on occupancy hours; motion, infrared, and/or light sensors to reduce energy uses for lighting; and LED lighting.

Purchasing Sustainability criteria used in purchasing include Energy Star (EPA).

Contact Quinnipiac University, 275 Mount Carmel Avenue, Hamden, CT 06518-1940. *Phone:* 203-582-8200. *Web site:* www.quinnipiac.edu/.

Trinity College
Hartford, Connecticut

Sustainability Initiatives Trinity College's president has signed the American College & University Presidents Climate Commitment.

Student Services and Green Events *Sustainability leadership:* sustainability coordinator/director, sustainability committee/advisory council. *Student clubs and activities:* Public Interest Research Group (PIRG) chapter on campus. *Housing and facilities:* sustainability-themed housing.

Food Sustainable, organic, and/or locally produced foods available in on-campus dining facilities. Fair Trade coffee is used.

Transportation Provides free on-campus transportation (bus or other), public transportation access to local destinations, a car sharing program, and incentives to carpool or use public transportation.

Buildings and Grounds *Renovation and maintenance:* registered for LEED certification for new construction and/or renovation. *Campus grounds care:* protects, restores, and/or creates habitat on campus.

Recycling *Events and organizations:* RecycleMania. *Programs and activities:* sustains a computer/technology recycling program; sustains a pre-consumer food waste composting program; composts yard waste; reuses chemicals. *Campus dining operations:* uses reusable dishware; operates without trays; offers discounts for reusable mugs; uses bulk condiment dispensers and decreased packaging for to-go food service purchases.

Energy Currently uses or plans to use motion, infrared, and/or light sensors to reduce energy uses for lighting and vending machine motion sensors.

Purchasing Sustainability criteria used in purchasing include Energy Star (EPA).

Contact EH&S Manager and Sustainability Coordinator, Trinity College, 238 New Britain Avenue, Hartford, CT 06106. *Phone:* 860-297-4250. *E-mail:* karen.misbach@trincoll.edu. *Web site:* www.trincoll.edu/.

University of Connecticut
Storrs, Connecticut

Sustainability Initiatives University of Connecticut is a member of the Association for the Advancement of Sustainability in Higher Education (AASHE). This institution's president has signed the American College & University Presidents Climate Commitment.

Student Services and Green Events *Sustainability leadership:* sustainability coordinator/director, sustainability committee/advisory council, recycling manager, energy manager. *Student clubs and activities:* Campus Climate Challenge, Public Interest Research Group (PIRG) chapter on campus, student club(s)/group(s) focused on sustainability, outreach materials available about on-campus sustainability efforts. *Major sustainability events:* Climate Change Conference, Earth Day, EcoMadness, Climate Change Teach-In. *Housing and facilities:* sustainability-themed housing, on-campus organic garden for students.

Food Sustainable, organic, and/or locally produced foods available in on-campus dining facilities. Fair Trade coffee is used. Vegan and vegetarian dining options are available for every meal.

Transportation Provides free on-campus transportation (bus or other) and public transportation access to local destinations.

Buildings and Grounds *Renovation and maintenance:* registered for LEED certification for new construction and/or renovation; uses a Green Seal certified cleaning service. *Campus grounds care:* uses water conservation devices; employs strategies to reduce light pollution; landscapes with native plant species; protects, restores, and/or creates habitat on campus.

Recycling *Events and organizations:* RecycleMania. *Programs and activities:* sustains a computer/technology recycling program; composts yard waste; reuses surplus department/office supplies; replaces paper materials with online alternatives; limits free printing in computer labs and libraries. *Campus dining operations:* uses reusable dishware; operates without trays; offers discounts for reusable mugs.

Energy Currently uses or plans to use alternative sources of power (solar energy); timers to regulate temperatures based on occupancy hours; motion, infrared, and/or light sensors to reduce energy uses for lighting; LED lighting; and vending machine motion sensors.

Purchasing Sustainability criteria used in purchasing include Energy Star (EPA) and Green Cleaning Products (Green Seal/Environmental Choice certified).

Contact Sustainability Coordinator, University of Connecticut, 31 LeDoyt Road, Unit 3055, Storrs, CT 06269. *Phone:* 860-486-5773. *E-mail:* jennifer.sayers@uconn.edu. *Web site:* www.uconn.edu/.

Wesleyan University
Middletown, Connecticut

Sustainability Initiatives Wesleyan University's president has signed the American College & University Presidents Climate Commitment.

Academics *Sustainability courses and programs:* sustainability-focused course(s) or lecture series.

Student Services and Green Events *Sustainability leadership:* sustainability coordinator/director, sustainability committee/advisory council, recycling manager, energy manager, sustainability-focused student government. *Student clubs and activities:* Public Interest Research Group (PIRG) chapter on campus, outreach materials available about on-campus sustainability efforts. *Housing and facilities:* sustainability-themed housing, on-campus organic garden for students.

Food Sustainable, organic, and/or locally produced foods available in on-campus dining facilities. Fair Trade coffee is used. Vegan and vegetarian dining options are available for every meal.

Buildings and Grounds *Renovation and maintenance:* registered for LEED certification for new construction and/or renovation. *Campus grounds care:* uses water conservation devices; employs strategies to reduce light pollution; landscapes with native plant species; protects, restores, and/or creates habitat on campus.

Recycling *Events and organizations:* RecycleMania, WasteWise (EPA). *Programs and activities:* sustains a computer/technology recycling program; maintains an on-campus recycling center; sustains a pre-consumer food waste composting program; composts yard waste; reuses chemicals; limits free printing in computer labs and libraries. *Campus dining operations:* uses reusable dishware; operates without trays; offers discounts for reusable mugs.

Energy Currently uses or plans to use alternative sources of power (geothermal energy, hydroelectricity/water power, and solar energy); timers to regulate temperatures based on occupancy hours; motion, infrared, and/or light sensors to reduce energy uses for lighting; LED lighting; and vending machine motion sensors.

Purchasing Sustainability criteria used in purchasing include Energy Star (EPA), Green Cleaning Products (Green Seal/Environmental Choice certified), and Forest Stewardship Council (FSC) or American Forest and Paper Association's Sustainable Forestry Initiative (SFI) paper.

Contact Director, Environmental Health, Safety, and Sustainability, Wesleyan University, 170 Long Lane, Middletown, CT 06459. *Phone:* 860-685-2771. *E-mail:* wnelligan@wesleyan.edu. *Web site:* www.wesleyan.edu/.

Yale University
New Haven, Connecticut

Sustainability Initiatives Yale University is a member of the Association for the Advancement of Sustainability in Higher Education (AASHE).

Academics *Sustainability courses and programs:* sustainability-focused course(s) or lecture series.

Student Services and Green Events *Sustainability leadership:* sustainability coordinator/director, sustainability committee/advisory council, recycling manager, energy manager, sustainability-focused student government. *Student clubs and activities:* student club(s)/group(s) focused on sustainability. *Housing and facilities:* student-run café that serves environmentally or socially preferable foods, on-campus organic garden for students.

Food Sustainable, organic, and/or locally produced foods available in on-campus dining facilities. Fair Trade coffee is used. Vegan and vegetarian dining options are available for every meal.

Transportation Provides free on-campus transportation (bus or other), public transportation access to local destinations, a car sharing program, and incentives to carpool or use public transportation.

Buildings and Grounds *Renovation and maintenance:* registered for LEED certification for new construction and/or renovation; uses a Green Seal certified cleaning service. *Campus grounds care:* uses water conservation devices; employs strategies to reduce light pollution; landscapes with native plant species; applies to its grounds only pesticides and fertilizers allowable under the U.S. Department of Agriculture's standards for crop production.

Recycling *Events and organizations:* RecycleMania, WasteWise (EPA). *Programs and activities:* sustains a computer/technology recycling program; maintains an on-campus recycling center; composts yard waste; reuses surplus department/office supplies; reuses chemicals; replaces paper materials with online alternatives. *Campus dining operations:* uses reusable dishware; offers discounts for reusable mugs; uses bulk condiment dispensers and decreased packaging for to-go food service purchases.

Energy Currently uses or plans to use alternative sources of power (geothermal energy, solar energy, and wind energy); motion, infrared, and/or light sensors to reduce energy uses for lighting; LED lighting; vending machine motion sensors; and energy-related performance contracting. Participates in College & University Green Power Challenge activities.

Purchasing Sustainability criteria used in purchasing include Energy Star (EPA), Green Electronics Council (GEC) Electronic Product Environmental Assessment Tool (EPEAT) Silver or Gold, Green Cleaning Products (Green Seal/Environmental Choice certified), and Forest Stewardship Council (FSC) or American Forest and Paper Association's Sustainable Forestry Initiative (SFI) paper.

Contact Director, Yale University, Office of Sustainability, 70 Whitney Avenue, PO Box 208275, New Haven, CT 06520-8275. *Phone:* 203-432-2523. *Fax:* 203-436-3578. *E-mail:* julie.newman@yale.edu. *Web site:* www.yale.edu/.

District of Columbia

The George Washington University
Washington, District of Columbia

Sustainability Initiatives The George Washington University's president has signed the American College & University Presidents Climate Commitment.

Academics *Sustainability courses and programs:* sustainability-focused course(s) or lecture series.

Student Services and Green Events *Sustainability leadership:* sustainability coordinator/director, sustainability committee/advisory council.

Recycling *Events and organizations:* RecycleMania.

Purchasing Sustainability criteria used in purchasing include Energy Star (EPA).

Contact The George Washington University, 2121 Eye Street, NW, Washington, DC 20052. *Phone:* 202-99GREEN. *E-mail:* sustaingw@gwu.edu. *Web site:* www.gwu.edu/.

Howard University
Washington, District of Columbia

Academics *Sustainability courses and programs:* sustainability-focused course(s) or lecture series.

Student Services and Green Events *Sustainability leadership:* energy manager.

Transportation Provides free on-campus transportation (bus or other) and public transportation access to local destinations.

Recycling *Programs and activities:* sustains a computer/technology recycling program; replaces paper materials with online alternatives.

Contact Howard University, 2400 Sixth Street, NW, Washington, DC 20059-0002. *Phone:* 202-806-6100. *Web site:* www.howard.edu/.

Florida

Bethune-Cookman University
Daytona Beach, Florida

Academics *Sustainability-focused undergraduate major(s):* Environmental Science. *Sustainability courses and programs:* sustainability-focused course(s) or lecture series.

Student Services and Green Events *Sustainability leadership:* sustainability committee/advisory council, energy manager.

Transportation Provides free on-campus transportation (bus or other) and public transportation access to local destinations.

Buildings and Grounds *Percentage of institution's eligible buildings as of September 2008 meeting LEED and/or LEED-EB certification criteria:* 1%. *Renovation and maintenance:* uses a Green Seal certified cleaning service. *Campus grounds care:* uses water conservation devices; employs strategies to reduce light pollution; landscapes with native plant species; applies to its grounds only pesticides and fertilizers allowable under the U.S. Department of Agriculture's standards for crop production.

Recycling *Events and organizations:* RecycleMania. *Programs and activities:* sustains a computer/technology recycling program; maintains an on-campus recycling center; reuses surplus department/office supplies; replaces paper materials with online alternatives; limits free printing in computer labs and libraries. *Campus dining operations:* uses reusable dishware.

Energy Currently uses or plans to use timers to regulate temperatures based on occupancy hours; LED lighting; and energy-related performance contracting.

Purchasing Sustainability criteria used in purchasing include Energy Star (EPA) and Green Cleaning Products (Green Seal/Environmental Choice certified).

Contact Bethune-Cookman University, 640 Dr Mary McLeod Bethune Blvd, Daytona Beach, FL 32114-3099. *Phone:* 386-481-2000. *Web site:* www.bethune.cookman.edu/.

Eckerd College
St. Petersburg, Florida

Sustainability Initiatives Eckerd College is a signatory to the Talloires Declaration. This institution's president has signed the American College & University Presidents Climate Commitment.

Academics *Sustainability-focused undergraduate major(s):* Environmental Studies (BA). *Sustainability courses and programs:* sustainability-focused course(s) or lecture series.

Student Services and Green Events *Sustainability leadership:* sustainability committee/advisory council, recycling manager, sustainability-focused student government. *Student clubs and activities:* student club(s)/group(s) focused on sustainability. *Major sustainability events:* Earth Fest.

Food Sustainable, organic, and/or locally produced foods available in on-campus dining facilities. Fair Trade coffee is used. Vegan and vegetarian dining options are available for every meal.

Transportation Provides free on-campus transportation (bus or other), public transportation access to local destinations, and a bike loan/rental program.

Buildings and Grounds *Percentage of institution's eligible buildings as of September 2008 meeting LEED and/or LEED-EB certification criteria:* 7%. *Renovation and maintenance:* uses a Green Seal certified cleaning service. *Campus grounds care:* landscapes with native plant species; protects, restores, and/or creates habitat on campus.

Recycling *Events and organizations:* RecycleMania. *Programs and activities:* sustains a computer/technology recycling program; maintains an on-campus recycling center; replaces paper materials with online alternatives. *Campus dining operations:* uses reusable dishware; operates without trays; uses bulk condiment dispensers and decreased packaging for to-go food service purchases.

Energy Currently uses or plans to use motion, infrared, and/or light sensors to reduce energy uses for lighting; LED lighting; and energy-related performance contracting.

Purchasing Sustainability criteria used in purchasing include Energy Star (EPA) and Green Cleaning Products (Green Seal/Environmental Choice certified).

Contact Eckerd College, 4200 54th Avenue South, St. Petersburg, FL 33711. *Phone:* 727-867-1166. *Web site:* www.eckerd.edu/.

Florida Atlantic University
Boca Raton, Florida

Sustainability Initiatives Florida Atlantic University is a signatory to the Talloires Declaration. This institution's president has signed the American College & University Presidents Climate Commitment. Florida Atlantic University has Green Fees (optional/required) dedicated to sustainability initiatives.

Academics *Sustainability courses and programs:* sustainability-focused course(s) or lecture series, sustainability-focused nonacademic certificate program(s).

Student Services and Green Events *Sustainability leadership:* sustainability coordinator/director, sustainability committee/advisory council, recycling manager, energy manager, sustainability-focused student government. *Student clubs and activities:* Campus Climate Challenge, student club(s)/group(s) focused on sustainability, outreach materials available about on-campus sustainability efforts. *Major sustainability events:* Small Steps to a Greener Campus, Campus Sustainability Day. *Housing and facilities:* sustainability-themed housing, student-run café that serves environmentally or socially preferable foods.

Food Vegan and vegetarian dining options are available for every meal.

Transportation Provides public transportation access to local destinations, a car sharing program, and incentives to carpool or use public transportation.

Buildings and Grounds *Renovation and maintenance:* registered for LEED certification for new construction and/or renovation. *Campus grounds care:* landscapes with native plant species; protects, restores, and/or creates habitat on campus.

Recycling *Events and organizations:* RecycleMania. *Programs and activities:* sustains a computer/technology recycling program; maintains an on-campus recycling center; sustains a pre-consumer food waste composting program; reuses surplus department/office supplies; reuses chemicals; replaces paper materials with online alternatives. *Campus dining operations:* uses reusable dishware; operates without trays; uses bulk condiment dispensers and decreased packaging for to-go food service purchases.

Energy Currently uses or plans to use alternative sources of power.

Contact Florida Atlantic University, 777 Glades Road, Boca Raton, FL 33431. *Phone:* 561-297-3450. *Web site:* www.fau.edu/.

Florida Atlantic University, Jupiter Campus
Jupiter, Florida

Sustainability Initiatives Florida Atlantic University, Jupiter Campus's president has signed the American College & University Presidents Climate Commitment.

Academics *Sustainability-focused undergraduate major(s):* Biology—Environmental Science (BA), Civil Engineering (BS), Geography—Human Environmental Systems (BA), Ocean Engineering (BS), Urban and Regional Planning (BA). *Sustainability-focused graduate degree program(s):* Civil Engineering (MS), Environmental Education (MEd), Environmental Sciences (MS), Geography (MA), Ocean Engineering (MS), Urban and Regional Planning (MA). *Sustainability courses and programs:* sustainability-focused course(s) or lecture series.

Student Services and Green Events *Sustainability leadership:* sustainability committee/advisory council. *Student clubs and activities:* student club(s)/group(s) focused on sustainability, outreach materials available about on-campus sustainability efforts. *Major sustainability events:* Campus Sustainability Day, Earth Day, Interdisciplinary and Environmental Sustainability, Breast Cancer and the Environment, Public Lands Acquisition and Management Partnership Conference, Sustaining Florida's Wildlife Heritage Amid 21st Century Challenges. *Housing and facilities:* sustainability-themed housing, model dorm room that demonstrates sustainable living principles.

Food Sustainable, organic, and/or locally produced foods available in on-campus dining facilities. Fair Trade coffee is used. Vegan and vegetarian dining options are available for every meal.

Transportation Provides public transportation access to local destinations, a bike loan/rental program, and incentives to carpool or use public transportation.

Buildings and Grounds *Renovation and maintenance:* registered for LEED certification for new construction and/or renovation; uses a Green Seal certified cleaning service. *Campus grounds care:* uses water conservation devices; landscapes with native plant species; protects, restores, and/or creates habitat on campus.

Recycling *Programs and activities:* sustains a preconsumer food waste composting program; sustains a postconsumer food waste composting program; reuses surplus department/office supplies; reuses chemicals; replaces paper materials with online alternatives; limits free printing in computer labs and libraries. *Campus dining operations:* uses reusable dishware; operates without trays; uses bulk condiment dispensers and decreased packaging for to-go food service purchases.

Energy Currently uses or plans to use alternative sources of power (solar energy); timers to regulate temperatures based on occupancy hours; motion, infrared, and/or light sensors to reduce energy uses for lighting; LED lighting; vending machine motion sensors; and energy-related performance contracting.

Purchasing Sustainability criteria used in purchasing include Energy Star (EPA) and Green Cleaning Products (Green Seal/Environmental Choice certified).

Contact Interim Director, Space Utilization and Analysis, Florida Atlantic University, Jupiter Campus, 777 Glades Road, Building #69, Boca Raton, FL 33431. *Phone:* 561-297-2211. *Fax:* 561-297-0195. *E-mail:* sclounts@fau.edu. *Web site:* www.fau.edu/jupiter/.

Florida Gulf Coast University
Fort Myers, Florida

Sustainability Initiatives Florida Gulf Coast University is a member of the Association for the Advancement of Sustainability in Higher Education (AASHE). This institution's president has signed the American College & University Presidents Climate Commitment.

Academics *Sustainability courses and programs:* noncredit sustainability course(s).

Student Services and Green Events *Sustainability leadership:* sustainability coordinator/director, sustainability committee/advisory council, recycling manager, energy manager, sustainability-focused student government. *Student clubs and activities:* student club(s)/group(s) focused on sustainability. *Major sustainability events:* Focus the Campus.

Food Sustainable, organic, and/or locally produced foods available in on-campus dining facilities. Vegan and vegetarian dining options are available for every meal.

Transportation Provides free on-campus transportation (bus or other) and public transportation access to local destinations.

Buildings and Grounds *Renovation and maintenance:* registered for LEED certification for new construction and/or renovation. *Campus grounds care:* uses water conservation devices; employs strategies to reduce light pollution; landscapes with native plant species; protects, restores, and/or creates habitat on campus.

Recycling *Programs and activities:* sustains a computer/technology recycling program; maintains an on-campus recycling center; composts yard waste; reuses surplus department/office supplies; reuses chemicals; limits free printing in computer labs and libraries. *Campus dining operations:* uses reusable dishware; operates without trays.

Energy Currently uses or plans to use alternative sources of power (geothermal energy); timers to regulate temperatures based on occupancy hours; motion, infrared, and/or light sensors to reduce energy uses for lighting; and energy-related performance contracting.

Purchasing Sustainability criteria used in purchasing include Energy Star (EPA) and Green Electronics Council (GEC) Electronic Product Environmental Assessment Tool (EPEAT) Silver or Gold.

Contact Director, Florida Gulf Coast University, 10501 FGCU Boulevard South, Fort Myers, FL 33965. *Phone:* 239-590-1414. *E-mail:* ljohnson@fgcu.edu. *Web site:* www.fgcu.edu/.

Florida International University
Miami, Florida

Sustainability Initiatives Florida International University's president has signed the American College & University Presidents Climate Commitment.

Academics *Sustainability-focused undergraduate major(s):* Environmental Engineering (BS), Environmental Studies (BS). *Sustainability-focused graduate degree program(s):* Environmental Engineering (MS), Environmental Studies (MS), Landscape Architecture (MLA). *Sustainability courses and programs:* sustainability-focused course(s) or lecture series, noncredit sustainability course(s).

Student Services and Green Events *Sustainability leadership:* sustainability committee/advisory council, recycling manager, energy manager. *Student clubs and activities:* student club(s)/group(s) focused on sustainability. *Major sustainability events:* Energy Conservation Week, Earth Week, Recycle Mania, FIU's Future House USA. *Housing and facilities:* student-run café that serves environmentally or socially preferable foods, on-campus organic garden for students.

Food Sustainable, organic, and/or locally produced foods available in on-campus dining facilities. Vegan and vegetarian dining options are available for every meal.

Transportation Provides free on-campus transportation (bus or other), public transportation access to local destinations, a car sharing program, and incentives to carpool or use public transportation.

Buildings and Grounds *Renovation and maintenance:* registered for LEED certification for new construction and/or renovation. *Campus grounds care:* uses water conservation devices; employs strategies to reduce light pollution; landscapes with native plant species; protects, restores, and/or creates habitat on campus.

Recycling *Events and organizations:* RecycleMania. *Programs and activities:* sustains a computer/technology recycling program; reuses surplus department/office supplies; replaces paper materials with online alternatives; limits free printing in computer labs and libraries. *Campus dining operations:* uses reusable dishware; operates without trays; uses bulk condiment dispensers and decreased packaging for to-go food service purchases.

Energy Currently uses or plans to use alternative sources of power (solar energy); timers to regulate temperatures based on occupancy hours; motion, infrared, and/or light sensors to reduce energy uses for lighting; LED lighting; and energy-related performance contracting.

Purchasing Sustainability criteria used in purchasing include Energy Star (EPA), WaterSense (EPA), and Green Cleaning Products (Green Seal/Environmental Choice certified).

Contact Executive Director/Chair, President's Climate Commitment Task Force, Florida International University, 11200 SW 8th Street, Gold Garage, Miami, FL 33199. *Phone:* 305-348-1655. *E-mail:* bill.foster@fiu.edu. *Web site:* www.fiu.edu/.

Jacksonville University
Jacksonville, Florida

Academics *Sustainability-focused undergraduate major(s):* Biology, Geography and the Environment, Marine Science, Sustainability Major under development. *Sustainability courses and programs:* sustainability-focused course(s) or lecture series.

Student Services and Green Events *Sustainability leadership:* sustainability coordinator/director, sustainability committee/advisory council, recycling manager. *Student clubs and activities:* student club(s)/group(s) focused on sustainability, outreach materials available about on-campus sustainability efforts. *Major sustainability events:* RecycleMania, Weigh-the-Waste, Green Month.

Food Sustainable, organic, and/or locally produced foods available in on-campus dining facilities. Fair Trade coffee is used. Vegan and vegetarian dining options are available for every meal.

Buildings and Grounds *Renovation and maintenance:* registered for LEED certification for new construction and/or renovation; uses a Green Seal certified cleaning service. *Campus grounds care:* uses water conservation devices; employs strategies to reduce light pollution; landscapes with native plant species; protects, restores, and/or creates habitat on campus; applies to its grounds only pesticides and fertilizers allowable under the U.S. Department of Agriculture's standards for crop production.

Recycling *Events and organizations:* RecycleMania. *Programs and activities:* sustains a computer/technology recycling program; reuses surplus department/office supplies; reuses chemicals; replaces paper materials with online alternatives; limits free printing in computer labs and libraries. *Campus dining operations:* uses reusable dishware; operates without trays; offers discounts for reusable mugs; uses bulk condiment dispensers and decreased packaging for to-go food service purchases.

Purchasing Sustainability criteria used in purchasing include Energy Star (EPA) and Green Cleaning Products (Green Seal/Environmental Choice certified).

Contact Executive Director, Marine Science Research Institute, Jacksonville University, 2800 University Boulevard North, Jacksonville, FL 32211. *Phone:* 904-256-7766. *Fax:* 904-256-7960. *E-mail:* qwhite@ju.edu. *Web site:* www.ju.edu/.

Palm Beach Atlantic University
West Palm Beach, Florida

Food Fair Trade coffee is used. Vegan and vegetarian dining options are available for every meal.

Transportation Provides public transportation access to local destinations.

Buildings and Grounds *Renovation and maintenance:* registered for LEED certification for new construction and/or renovation. *Campus grounds care:* uses water conservation devices; employs strategies to reduce light pollution; landscapes with native plant species.

Recycling *Programs and activities:* sustains a computer/technology recycling program; reuses chemicals; replaces paper materials with online alternatives; limits free printing in computer labs and libraries. *Campus dining operations:* uses reusable dishware; operates without trays; uses bulk condiment dispensers and decreased packaging for to-go food service purchases.

Energy Currently uses or plans to use timers to regulate temperatures based on occupancy hours; motion, infrared, and/or light sensors to reduce energy uses for lighting; LED lighting; and energy-related performance contracting.

Contact Palm Beach Atlantic University, 901 South Flagler Drive, PO Box 24708, West Palm Beach, FL 33416-4708. *Phone:* 561-803-2000. *Web site:* www.pba.edu/.

Schiller International University
Largo, Florida

Academics *Sustainability-focused undergraduate major(s):* Sustainable Business Ventures and Development (BBA). *Sustainability-focused graduate degree program(s):* Sustainable Business and Development (MBA). *Sustainability courses and programs:* sustainability-focused course(s) or lecture series.

Student Services and Green Events *Sustainability leadership:* sustainability coordinator/director, sustainability committee/advisory council, recycling manager, sustainability-focused student government.

Transportation Provides public transportation access to local destinations.

Buildings and Grounds *Campus grounds care:* employs strategies to reduce light pollution; landscapes with native plant species.

Recycling *Programs and activities:* sustains a computer/technology recycling program; reuses surplus department/office supplies; replaces paper materials with online alternatives. *Campus dining operations:* uses reusable dishware; operates without trays.

Contact Center of Excellence Coordinator, Schiller International University, 300 East Bay Drive, Largo, FL 33770. *Phone:* 727-738-6345. *E-mail:* watson_ragin@schiller.edu. *Web site:* www.schiller.edu/.

University of Central Florida
Orlando, Florida

Sustainability Initiatives University of Central Florida is a member of the Association for the Advancement of Sustainability in Higher Education (AASHE). This institution's president has signed the American College & University Presidents Climate Commitment.

Academics *Sustainability courses and programs:* sustainability-focused course(s) or lecture series, noncredit sustainability course(s).

Student Services and Green Events *Sustainability leadership:* sustainability coordinator/director, sustainability committee/advisory council, recycling manager, energy manager, sustainability-focused student government. *Student clubs and activities:* Campus Climate Challenge, student club(s)/group(s) focused on sustainability, outreach materials available about on-campus sustainability efforts. *Major sustainability events:* Campus and Community Sustainability Conference for the state of Florida. *Housing and facilities:* on-campus organic garden for students.

Transportation Provides free on-campus transportation (bus or other).

Buildings and Grounds *Renovation and maintenance:* registered for LEED certification for new construction and/or renovation. *Campus grounds care:* uses water conservation devices; employs strategies to reduce light pollution; landscapes with native plant species; protects, restores, and/or creates habitat on campus; applies to its grounds only pesticides and fertilizers allowable under the U.S. Department of Agriculture's standards for crop production.

Recycling *Events and organizations:* RecycleMania. *Programs and activities:* sustains a computer/technology recycling program; maintains an on-campus recycling center; reuses surplus department/office supplies; replaces paper materials with online alternatives. *Campus dining operations:* operates without trays.

Energy Currently uses or plans to use timers to regulate temperatures based on occupancy hours and motion, infrared, and/or light sensors to reduce energy uses for lighting.

Purchasing Sustainability criteria used in purchasing include Energy Star (EPA) and Green Cleaning Products (Green Seal/Environmental Choice certified).

Contact Senior Information Specialist, University of Central Florida, PO Box 163600, Orlando, FL 32816. *Phone:* 407-823-0970. *Fax:* 407-823-5726. *E-mail:* dnorvell@mail.ucf.edu. *Web site:* www.ucf.edu/.

University of South Florida
Tampa, Florida

Sustainability Initiatives University of South Florida's president has signed the American College & University Presidents Climate Commitment.

Academics *Sustainability-focused undergraduate major(s):* Anthropology, Civil and Environmental Engineering, Environmental Science and Policy, Geography. *Sustainability-focused graduate degree program(s):* Anthropology, Civil and Environmental Engineering, Community and Family Health, Environmental and Occupational Health, Environmental Science and Policy, Geography. *Sustainability courses and programs:* sustainability-focused course(s) or lecture series.

Student Services and Green Events *Sustainability leadership:* sustainability committee/advisory council, recycling manager. *Student clubs and activities:* Campus Climate Challenge, Public Interest Research Group (PIRG) chapter on campus, student club(s)/group(s) focused on sustainability. *Major sustainability events:* Going Green Tampa Bay Expo, Conversation on Green Building, Environmental Research Interdisciplinary Colloquium Series. *Housing and facilities:* on-campus organic garden for students.

Food Sustainable, organic, and/or locally produced foods available in on-campus dining facilities. Fair Trade coffee is used. Vegan and vegetarian dining options are available for every meal.

Transportation Provides free on-campus transportation (bus or other), public transportation access to local destinations, and incentives to carpool or use public transportation.

Recycling *Programs and activities:* maintains an on-campus recycling center; composts yard waste; replaces paper materials with online alternatives; limits free printing in computer labs and libraries. *Campus dining operations:* operates without trays.

Energy Currently uses or plans to use alternative sources of power (biomass energy and solar energy); timers to regulate temperatures based on occupancy hours; motion, infrared, and/or light sensors to reduce energy uses for lighting; LED lighting; and vending machine motion sensors.

Contact Associate Vice President for Academic Affairs and Strategic Initiatives, University of South Florida, 4202 East Fowler, ADM 226, Tampa, FL 33620. *Phone:* 813-974-8394. *Fax:* 813-974-5093. *E-mail:* lwhiteford@acad.usf.edu. *Web site:* www.usf.edu/.

Georgia

Agnes Scott College
Decatur, Georgia

Sustainability Initiatives Agnes Scott College is a member of the Association for the Advancement of Sustainability in Higher Education (AASHE). This institution's president has signed the American College & University Presidents Climate Commitment.

Academics *Sustainability courses and programs:* sustainability-focused course(s) or lecture series.

Student Services and Green Events *Sustainability leadership:* sustainability coordinator/director, sustainability committee/advisory council, recycling manager, energy manager, sustainability-focused student government. *Student clubs and activities:* student club(s)/group(s) focused on sustainability, outreach materials available about on-campus sustainability efforts. *Major sustainability events:* Regional Forum on Climate Action, campus charrettes, Georgia Organics Statewide Conference, Earth Hour.

Food Sustainable, organic, and/or locally produced foods available in on-campus dining facilities. Fair Trade coffee is used. Vegan and vegetarian dining options are available for every meal.

Transportation Provides public transportation access to local destinations, a bike loan/rental program, a car sharing program, and incentives to carpool or use public transportation.

Buildings and Grounds *Renovation and maintenance:* registered for LEED certification for new construction and/or renovation. *Campus grounds care:* uses water conservation devices; employs strategies to reduce light pollution; protects, restores, and/or creates habitat on campus.

Recycling *Programs and activities:* sustains a computer/technology recycling program; maintains an on-campus recycling center; reuses surplus department/office supplies; replaces paper materials with online alternatives; limits free printing in computer labs and libraries. *Campus dining operations:* uses reusable dishware; operates without trays; offers discounts for reusable mugs; uses bulk condiment dispensers and decreased packaging for to-go food service purchases.

Energy Currently uses or plans to use alternative sources of power; timers to regulate temperatures based on occupancy hours; motion, infrared, and/or light sensors to reduce energy uses for lighting; and energy-related performance contracting.

Purchasing Sustainability criteria used in purchasing include Energy Star (EPA), WaterSense (EPA), Green Electronics Council (GEC) Electronic Product Environmental Assessment Tool (EPEAT) Silver or Gold, Green Cleaning Products (Green Seal/Environmental Choice certified), and Forest Stewardship Council (FSC) or American Forest and Paper Association's Sustainable Forestry Initiative (SFI) paper.

Contact Director of Sustainability, Agnes Scott College, 141 East College Avenue, Decatur, GA 30030. *Phone:* 404-471-6080. *Fax:* 404-471-6638. *E-mail:* sakidd@agnesscott.edu. *Web site:* www.agnesscott.edu/.

Berry College
Mount Berry, Georgia

Sustainability Initiatives Berry College's president has signed the American College & University Presidents Climate Commitment.

Academics *Sustainability-focused undergraduate major(s):* Environmental Science Major (BS). *Sustainability courses and programs:* sustainability-focused course(s) or lecture series.

Student Services and Green Events *Sustainability leadership:* sustainability coordinator/director, sustainability committee/advisory council, sustainability-focused student government. *Student clubs and activities:* student club(s)/group(s) focused on sustainability. *Major sustainability events:* Green Week. *Housing and facilities:* on-campus organic garden for students.

Food Sustainable, organic, and/or locally produced foods available in on-campus dining facilities. Fair Trade coffee is used. Vegan and vegetarian dining options are available for every meal.

Transportation Provides free on-campus transportation (bus or other).

Buildings and Grounds *Renovation and maintenance:* registered for LEED certification for new construction and/or renovation. *Campus grounds care:* uses water conservation devices; landscapes with native plant species; protects, restores, and/or creates habitat on campus.

Recycling *Events and organizations:* RecycleMania. *Programs and activities:* sustains a computer/technology recy-

cling program; composts yard waste; replaces paper materials with online alternatives; limits free printing in computer labs and libraries. *Campus dining operations:* uses reusable dishware; operates without trays.

Energy Currently uses or plans to use alternative sources of power (geothermal energy); motion, infrared, and/or light sensors to reduce energy uses for lighting; LED lighting; and vending machine motion sensors.

Purchasing Sustainability criteria used in purchasing include Energy Star (EPA), Green Electronics Council (GEC) Electronic Product Environmental Assessment Tool (EPEAT) Silver or Gold, and Green Cleaning Products (Green Seal/Environmental Choice certified).

Contact Associate Professor, Berry College, 2277 Martha Berry Highway NW, Mount Berry, GA 30149. *Phone:* 706-290-2663. *E-mail:* bdavin@berry.edu. *Web site:* www.berry.edu/.

Georgia Southern University
Statesboro, Georgia

Sustainability Initiatives Georgia Southern University's president has signed the American College & University Presidents Climate Commitment.

Academics *Sustainability-focused undergraduate major(s):* Green Building and Sustainability Research. *Sustainability courses and programs:* sustainability-focused course(s) or lecture series.

Student Services and Green Events *Sustainability leadership:* sustainability coordinator/director, energy manager. *Student clubs and activities:* student club(s)/group(s) focused on sustainability, outreach materials available about on-campus sustainability efforts. *Major sustainability events:* Student Sustainability Summit, Living Green 30 Days Challenge. *Housing and facilities:* on-campus organic garden for students.

Food Fair Trade coffee is used. Vegan and vegetarian dining options are available for every meal.

Transportation Provides free on-campus transportation (bus or other), a bike loan/rental program, a car sharing program, and incentives to carpool or use public transportation.

Buildings and Grounds *Percentage of institution's eligible buildings as of September 2008 meeting LEED and/or LEED-EB certification criteria:* .03%. *Renovation and maintenance:* registered for LEED certification for new construction and/or renovation. *Campus grounds care:* uses water conservation devices; employs strategies to reduce light pollution; landscapes with native plant species; protects, restores, and/or creates habitat on campus.

Recycling *Programs and activities:* sustains a computer/technology recycling program; maintains an on-campus recycling center; composts yard waste; reuses surplus department/office supplies; replaces paper materials with online alternatives; limits free printing in computer labs and libraries. *Campus dining operations:* uses reusable dishware; offers discounts for reusable mugs; uses bulk condiment dispensers and decreased packaging for to-go food service purchases.

Energy Currently uses or plans to use alternative sources of power (hydroelectricity/water power); timers to regulate temperatures based on occupancy hours; motion, infrared, and/or light sensors to reduce energy uses for lighting; LED lighting; and vending machine motion sensors.

Purchasing Sustainability criteria used in purchasing include Energy Star (EPA) and Green Cleaning Products (Green Seal/Environmental Choice certified).

Contact Interim Sustainability Coordinator, Georgia Southern University, PO Box 8072-01, Statesboro, GA 30460-8072. *Phone:* 912-478-7225. *Fax:* 912-478-7169. *E-mail:* moniquedipple@georgiasouthern.edu. *Web site:* www.georgiasouthern.edu/.

Kennesaw State University
Kennesaw, Georgia

Sustainability Initiatives Kennesaw State University's president has signed the American College & University Presidents Climate Commitment.

Academics *Sustainability-focused undergraduate major(s):* Interdisciplinary Studies—Environmental Studies (BS). *Sustainability courses and programs:* sustainability-focused course(s) or lecture series.

Student Services and Green Events *Sustainability leadership:* sustainability coordinator/director, sustainability committee/advisory council. *Student clubs and activities:* student club(s)/group(s) focused on sustainability. *Major sustainability events:* Southface workshop: Indoor Air Quality on College Campuses.

Food Vegan and vegetarian dining options are available for every meal.

Transportation Provides public transportation access to local destinations and incentives to carpool or use public transportation.

Buildings and Grounds *Percentage of institution's eligible buildings as of September 2008 meeting LEED and/or LEED-EB certification criteria:* 4%. *Renovation and maintenance:* registered for LEED certification for new construction and/or renovation. *Campus grounds care:* landscapes with native plant species; protects, restores, and/or creates habitat on campus.

Recycling *Events and organizations:* RecycleMania. *Programs and activities:* composts yard waste; reuses surplus department/office supplies; replaces paper materials with online alternatives; limits free printing in computer labs and libraries.

Energy Currently uses or plans to use alternative sources of power; timers to regulate temperatures based on occupancy hours; and motion, infrared, and/or light sensors to reduce energy uses for lighting.

Purchasing Sustainability criteria used in purchasing include Energy Star (EPA) and Green Cleaning Products (Green Seal/Environmental Choice certified).

Contact Director of Sustainability, Kennesaw State University, Department of Biology and Physics, 1000 Chastain Road, Kennesaw, GA 30144. *Phone:* 770-423-6179. *E-mail:* rpaul@kennesaw.edu. *Web site:* www.kennesaw.edu/.

Life University
Marietta, Georgia

Sustainability Initiatives Life University's president has signed the American College & University Presidents Climate Commitment.

Student Services and Green Events *Sustainability leadership:* sustainability coordinator/director, sustainability committee/advisory council, recycling manager, energy manager.

Food Vegan and vegetarian dining options are available for every meal.

Transportation Provides free on-campus transportation (bus or other), public transportation access to local destinations, and incentives to carpool or use public transportation.

Buildings and Grounds *Renovation and maintenance:* registered for LEED certification for new construction and/or renovation. *Campus grounds care:* uses water conservation devices; protects, restores, and/or creates habitat on campus.

Recycling *Programs and activities:* sustains a computer/technology recycling program; maintains an on-campus recycling center; reuses surplus department/office supplies; replaces paper materials with online alternatives. *Campus dining operations:* operates without trays; offers discounts for reusable mugs.

Energy Currently uses or plans to use alternative sources of power; timers to regulate temperatures based on occupancy hours; and motion, infrared, and/or light sensors to reduce energy uses for lighting.

Purchasing Sustainability criteria used in purchasing include Energy Star (EPA) and Green Cleaning Products (Green Seal/Environmental Choice certified).

Contact Project Manager, Life University, 1269 Barclay Circle, Building 1085, Marietta, GA 30060. *Phone:* 770-426-2979. *E-mail:* richard.shaw@life.edu. *Web site:* www.life.edu/.

Savannah State University
Savannah, Georgia

Food Vegan and vegetarian dining options are available for every meal.

Transportation Provides free on-campus transportation (bus or other).

Buildings and Grounds *Campus grounds care:* uses water conservation devices.

Recycling *Programs and activities:* maintains an on-campus recycling center; replaces paper materials with online alternatives; limits free printing in computer labs and libraries. *Campus dining operations:* uses reusable dishware; operates without trays; uses bulk condiment dispensers and decreased packaging for to-go food service purchases.

Energy Currently uses or plans to use motion, infrared, and/or light sensors to reduce energy uses for lighting.

Contact Savannah State University, 3219 College Avenue, Savannah, GA 31404. *Phone:* 912-356-2186. *Web site:* www.savstate.edu/.

Southern Polytechnic State University
Marietta, Georgia

Sustainability Initiatives Southern Polytechnic State University is a member of the Association for the Advancement of Sustainability in Higher Education (AASHE). This institution's president has signed the American College & University Presidents Climate Commitment.

Academics *Sustainability courses and programs:* sustainability-focused nonacademic certificate program(s).

Student Services and Green Events *Sustainability leadership:* sustainability coordinator/director, sustainability committee/advisory council, recycling manager. *Student clubs and activities:* student club(s)/group(s) focused on sustainability. *Major sustainability events:* National Teach-In, Earth Hour Flagship Campus, Earth Day.

Food Vegan and vegetarian dining options are available for every meal.

Transportation Provides public transportation access to local destinations.

Buildings and Grounds *Renovation and maintenance:* registered for LEED certification for new construction and/or renovation.

Recycling *Programs and activities:* sustains a computer/technology recycling program; replaces paper materials with online alternatives; limits free printing in computer labs and libraries. *Campus dining operations:* uses reusable dishware; uses bulk condiment dispensers and decreased packaging for to-go food service purchases.

Energy Currently uses or plans to use timers to regulate temperatures based on occupancy hours and LED lighting.

Purchasing Sustainability criteria used in purchasing include Energy Star (EPA) and Forest Stewardship Council (FSC) or American Forest and Paper Association's Sustainable Forestry Initiative (SFI) paper.

Contact Executive Director of Strategic Marketing and Sustainability Initiatives, Southern Polytechnic State University, 1100 South Marietta Parkway, Marietta, GA 30060. *Phone:* 678-915-4986. *Fax:* 678-915-7483. *E-mail:* green@spsu.edu. *Web site:* www.spsu.edu/.

University of Georgia
Athens, Georgia

Sustainability Initiatives University of Georgia is a member of the Association for the Advancement of Sustainability in Higher Education (AASHE) and a signatory to the Talloires Declaration.

Academics *Sustainability-focused undergraduate major(s):* Ecology (BS). *Sustainability-focused graduate degree program(s):* Ecology (MS), Ecology (PhD). *Sustainability courses and programs:* sustainability-focused course(s) or lecture series, noncredit sustainability course(s), sustainability-focused nonacademic certificate program(s).

Student Services and Green Events *Sustainability leadership:* recycling manager, energy manager. *Student clubs and activities:* student club(s)/group(s) focused on sustainability, outreach materials available about on-campus sustainability efforts. *Major sustainability events:* Academy of the Environment annual symposium, conferences sponsored by Odum School of Ecology. *Housing and facilities:* sustainability-themed housing, on-campus organic garden for students.

Food Sustainable, organic, and/or locally produced foods available in on-campus dining facilities. Vegan and vegetarian dining options are available for every meal.

Transportation Provides free on-campus transportation (bus or other), public transportation access to local destinations, and incentives to carpool or use public transportation.

Buildings and Grounds *Renovation and maintenance:* registered for LEED certification for new construction and/or renovation; uses a Green Seal certified cleaning service. *Campus grounds care:* uses water conservation devices; employs strategies to reduce light pollution; landscapes with native plant species; protects, restores, and/or creates habitat on campus.

Recycling *Events and organizations:* RecycleMania. *Programs and activities:* sustains a computer/technology recycling program; maintains an on-campus recycling center; sustains a pre-consumer food waste composting program; sustains a post-consumer food waste composting program; composts yard waste; reuses surplus department/office supplies; reuses chemicals; replaces paper materials with online alternatives; limits free printing in computer labs and libraries. *Campus dining operations:* uses reusable dishware; uses bulk condiment dispensers and decreased packaging for to-go food service purchases.

Energy Currently uses or plans to use alternative sources of power (solar energy); timers to regulate temperatures based on occupancy hours; motion, infrared, and/or light sensors to reduce energy uses for lighting; LED lighting; and vending machine motion sensors.

Purchasing Sustainability criteria used in purchasing include Energy Star (EPA) and Green Cleaning Products (Green Seal/Environmental Choice certified).

Contact University of Georgia, Athens, GA 30602. *Phone:* 706-542-3000. *Web site:* www.uga.edu/.

Valdosta State University
Valdosta, Georgia

Academics *Sustainability courses and programs:* sustainability-focused course(s) or lecture series.

Student Services and Green Events *Sustainability leadership:* sustainability committee/advisory council, recycling manager. *Student clubs and activities:* student club(s)/group(s) focused on sustainability. *Major sustainability events:* Regional SAVE Conference, hosted LEED Course for local Architects/Engineers.

Food Sustainable, organic, and/or locally produced foods available in on-campus dining facilities. Fair Trade coffee is used. Vegan and vegetarian dining options are available for every meal.

Transportation Provides free on-campus transportation (bus or other).

Buildings and Grounds *Campus grounds care:* uses water conservation devices; employs strategies to reduce light pollution; landscapes with native plant species; protects, restores, and/or creates habitat on campus.

Recycling *Programs and activities:* maintains an on-campus recycling center; composts yard waste; reuses surplus department/office supplies; limits free printing in computer labs and libraries. *Campus dining operations:* uses reusable dishware; offers discounts for reusable mugs.

Energy Currently uses or plans to use alternative sources of power (solar energy); timers to regulate temperatures based on occupancy hours; and motion, infrared, and/or light sensors to reduce energy uses for lighting.

Purchasing Sustainability criteria used in purchasing include Energy Star (EPA) and Green Cleaning Products (Green Seal/Environmental Choice certified).

Contact Director of Facilities, Valdosta State University, 2903 North Ashley Street, Valdosta, GA 31602. *Web site:* www.valdosta.edu/.

Idaho

Boise State University
Boise, Idaho

Sustainability Initiatives Boise State University is a member of the Association for the Advancement of Sustainability in Higher Education (AASHE). This institution's president has signed the American College & University Presidents Climate Commitment. Boise State University has Green Fees (optional/required) dedicated to sustainability initiatives.

Academics *Sustainability-focused undergraduate major(s):* Environmental Studies (BA). *Sustainability-focused graduate degree program(s):* Public Administration (MPA). *Sustainability courses and programs:* sustainability-focused course(s) or lecture series.

Student Services and Green Events *Sustainability leadership:* sustainability coordinator/director, sustainability committee/advisory council, recycling manager, energy manager, sustainability-focused student government. *Student clubs and activities:* student club(s)/group(s) focused on sustainability, outreach materials available about on-campus sustainability efforts. *Major sustainability events:* Focus The Nation, National Teach-In, Campus Sustainability Day, Earth Week.

Food Sustainable, organic, and/or locally produced foods available in on-campus dining facilities. Fair Trade coffee is used. Vegan and vegetarian dining options are available for every meal.

Transportation Provides free on-campus transportation (bus or other), public transportation access to local destinations, a bike loan/rental program, a car sharing program, and incentives to carpool or use public transportation.

Buildings and Grounds *Renovation and maintenance:* uses a Green Seal certified cleaning service. *Campus grounds care:* uses water conservation devices; landscapes with native plant species; protects, restores, and/or creates habitat on campus.

Recycling *Events and organizations:* RecycleMania. *Programs and activities:* sustains a computer/technology recycling program; sustains a pre-consumer food waste composting program; sustains a post-consumer food waste composting program; replaces paper materials with online alternatives; limits free printing in computer labs and libraries. *Campus dining operations:* uses reusable dishware; operates without trays; offers discounts for reusable mugs; uses bulk condiment dispensers and decreased packaging for to-go food service purchases.

Energy Currently uses or plans to use alternative sources of power (hydroelectricity/water power); timers to regulate temperatures based on occupancy hours; motion, infrared, and/or light sensors to reduce energy uses for lighting; vending machine motion sensors; and energy-related performance contracting.

Purchasing Sustainability criteria used in purchasing include Energy Star (EPA) and Green Cleaning Products (Green Seal/Environmental Choice certified).

Contact Associate Vice President for Energy Research, Policy and Campus Sustainability, Boise State University, 1910 University Drive, Mail Stop 1012, Boise, ID 83725. *Phone:* 208-426-4840. *Fax:* 208-426-4834. *E-mail:* jgardner@boisestate.edu. *Web site:* www.boisestate.edu/.

University of Idaho
Moscow, Idaho

Sustainability Initiatives University of Idaho is a member of the Association for the Advancement of Sustainability in Higher Education (AASHE) and a signatory to the Talloires Declaration. This institution's president has signed the American College & University Presidents Climate Commitment. University of Idaho has Green Fees (optional/required) dedicated to sustainability initiatives.

Academics *Sustainability-focused undergraduate major(s):* Ecology and Conservation Biology (BS), Environmental Science (BS), Rangeland Ecology and Management (BS), Resource Recreation and Tourism (BS), Wildlife Resources (BS). *Sustainability-focused graduate degree program(s):* Conservation Social Sciences (MS), Environmental Science (MS, PhD), Natural Resources (PhD), Rangeland Ecology and Management (MS, PhD), Soil and Land Resources (MS, PhD), Wildlife Resources (MS). *Sustainability courses and programs:* sustainability-focused course(s) or lecture series.

Student Services and Green Events *Sustainability leadership:* sustainability coordinator/director, sustainability

committee/advisory council, recycling manager, energy manager, sustainability-focused student government. *Student clubs and activities:* Public Interest Research Group (PIRG) chapter on campus, student club(s)/group(s) focused on sustainability, outreach materials available about on-campus sustainability efforts. *Major sustainability events:* President's Sustainability Symposium, National Teach-In on Global Warming Solutions, Earth Week/Focus the Nation. *Housing and facilities:* model dorm room that demonstrates sustainable living principles, on-campus organic garden for students.

Food Sustainable, organic, and/or locally produced foods available in on-campus dining facilities. Fair Trade coffee is used.

Transportation Provides free on-campus transportation (bus or other), public transportation access to local destinations, and a bike loan/rental program.

Buildings and Grounds *Campus grounds care:* uses water conservation devices; landscapes with native plant species; protects, restores, and/or creates habitat on campus.

Recycling *Events and organizations:* RecycleMania. *Programs and activities:* sustains a computer/technology recycling program; sustains a post-consumer food waste composting program; composts yard waste; reuses surplus department/office supplies; replaces paper materials with online alternatives; limits free printing in computer labs and libraries. *Campus dining operations:* uses reusable dishware; offers discounts for reusable mugs; uses bulk condiment dispensers and decreased packaging for to-go food service purchases.

Energy Currently uses or plans to use alternative sources of power (biomass energy); motion, infrared, and/or light sensors to reduce energy uses for lighting; and energy-related performance contracting.

Contact Communications Coordinator, University of Idaho, UI Sustainability Center, Moscow, ID 83844-2007. *Phone:* 208-885-0127. *Fax:* 208-885-0181. *E-mail:* uisc-communications@uidaho.edu. *Web site:* www.uidaho.edu/.

Illinois

Augustana College
Rock Island, Illinois

Sustainability Initiatives Augustana College is a member of the Association for the Advancement of Sustainability in Higher Education (AASHE).

Academics *Sustainability-focused undergraduate major(s):* Environmental Studies, Geography. *Sustainability courses and programs:* sustainability-focused course(s) or lecture series.

Student Services and Green Events *Sustainability leadership:* sustainability committee/advisory council, recycling manager, energy manager. *Student clubs and activities:* student club(s)/group(s) focused on sustainability, outreach materials available about on-campus sustainability efforts. *Major sustainability events:* Earth Week activities. *Housing and facilities:* sustainability-themed housing.

Food Sustainable, organic, and/or locally produced foods available in on-campus dining facilities. Fair Trade coffee is used. Vegan and vegetarian dining options are available for every meal.

Transportation Provides free on-campus transportation (bus or other), public transportation access to local destinations, a car sharing program, and incentives to carpool or use public transportation.

Buildings and Grounds *Renovation and maintenance:* registered for LEED certification for new construction and/or renovation. *Campus grounds care:* uses water conservation devices; employs strategies to reduce light pollution; landscapes with native plant species; protects, restores, and/or creates habitat on campus.

Recycling *Events and organizations:* RecycleMania. *Programs and activities:* sustains a computer/technology recycling program; maintains an on-campus recycling center; sustains a post-consumer food waste composting program; composts yard waste; reuses surplus department/office supplies; replaces paper materials with online alternatives. *Campus dining operations:* uses reusable dishware; uses bulk condiment dispensers and decreased packaging for to-go food service purchases.

Energy Currently uses or plans to use alternative sources of power (geothermal energy); timers to regulate temperatures based on occupancy hours; motion, infrared, and/or light sensors to reduce energy uses for lighting; LED lighting; vending machine motion sensors; and energy-related performance contracting.

Purchasing Sustainability criteria used in purchasing include Energy Star (EPA), Green Cleaning Products (Green Seal/Environmental Choice certified), and Forest Stewardship Council (FSC) or American Forest and Paper Association's Sustainable Forestry Initiative (SFI) paper.

Contact Augustana College, 639 38th Street, Rock Island, IL 61201-2296. *Web site:* www.augustana.edu/.

Benedictine University
Lisle, Illinois

Academics *Sustainability-focused graduate degree program(s):* Sustainable Business (MBA), Sustainable Leadership Development (MBA). *Sustainability courses and programs:* sustainability-focused course(s) or lecture series.

Student Services and Green Events *Sustainability leadership:* sustainability committee/advisory council, recycling manager, sustainability-focused student government. *Student clubs and activities:* Campus Climate Challenge, student club(s)/group(s) focused on sustainability. *Major sustainability events:* Years for the Environment, DuPage Conservation Foundation Environmental Summit, Faith and Reason: What is Sufficiency?. *Housing and facilities:* on-campus organic garden for students.

Food Fair Trade coffee is used. Vegan and vegetarian dining options are available for every meal.

Transportation Provides free on-campus transportation (bus or other), public transportation access to local destinations, and a bike loan/rental program.

Buildings and Grounds *Campus grounds care:* employs strategies to reduce light pollution; landscapes with native plant species; protects, restores, and/or creates habitat on campus; applies to its grounds only pesticides and fertilizers allowable under the U.S. Department of Agriculture's standards for crop production.

Recycling *Programs and activities:* sustains a computer/technology recycling program; reuses surplus department/office supplies; replaces paper materials with online alternatives; limits free printing in computer labs and libraries. *Campus dining operations:* uses reusable dishware; operates without trays; offers discounts for reusable mugs.

Energy Currently uses or plans to use alternative sources of power; motion, infrared, and/or light sensors to reduce energy uses for lighting; LED lighting; vending machine motion sensors; and energy-related performance contracting.

Purchasing Sustainability criteria used in purchasing include Energy Star (EPA), Green Cleaning Products (Green Seal/Environmental Choice certified), and Forest Stewardship Council (FSC) or American Forest and Paper Association's Sustainable Forestry Initiative (SFI) paper.

Contact Assistant Professor, Benedictine University, 5700 College Road, Lisle, IL 60532. *Phone:* 630-829-6272. *E-mail:* jkauth@ben.edu. *Web site:* www.ben.edu/.

DePaul University
Chicago, Illinois

Academics *Sustainability-focused undergraduate major(s):* Environmental Studies (BA), Environmental Studies (BS), Public Policy Studies with environmental policy track (BA). *Sustainability courses and programs:* sustainability-focused course(s) or lecture series.

Student Services and Green Events *Sustainability leadership:* sustainability coordinator/director, sustainability committee/advisory council, recycling manager, energy manager, sustainability-focused student government. *Student clubs and activities:* student club(s)/group(s) focused on sustainability. *Major sustainability events:* DePaul's Institute for Nature and Culture forum. *Housing and facilities:* student-run café that serves environmentally or socially preferable foods.

Food Sustainable, organic, and/or locally produced foods available in on-campus dining facilities. Fair Trade coffee is used. Vegan and vegetarian dining options are available for every meal.

Transportation Provides public transportation access to local destinations, a car sharing program, and incentives to carpool or use public transportation.

Buildings and Grounds *Percentage of institution's eligible buildings as of September 2008 meeting LEED and/or LEED-EB certification criteria:* 1.67%. *Renovation and maintenance:* registered for LEED certification for new construction and/or renovation; uses a Green Seal certified cleaning service. *Campus grounds care:* uses water conservation devices; employs strategies to reduce light pollution; landscapes with native plant species; protects, restores, and/or creates habitat on campus; applies to its grounds only pesticides and fertilizers allowable under the U.S. Department of Agriculture's standards for crop production.

Recycling *Programs and activities:* sustains a computer/technology recycling program; maintains an on-campus recycling center; reuses surplus department/office supplies; reuses chemicals; replaces paper materials with online alternatives. *Campus dining operations:* uses reusable dishware; operates without trays; offers discounts for reusable mugs; uses bulk condiment dispensers and decreased packaging for to-go food service purchases.

Energy Currently uses or plans to use alternative sources of power (solar energy); timers to regulate temperatures based on occupancy hours; motion, infrared, and/or light sensors to reduce energy uses for lighting; LED lighting; and energy-related performance contracting.

Purchasing Sustainability criteria used in purchasing include Energy Star (EPA), Green Cleaning Products (Green Seal/Environmental Choice certified), and Forest Stewardship Council (FSC) or American Forest and Paper Association's Sustainable Forestry Initiative (SFI) paper.

Contact Vice President for Facility Operations, DePaul University, 14 East Jackson Boulevard, Suite 600, Chicago, IL 60604. *Phone:* 312-362-8762. *Fax:* 312-362-5912. *E-mail:* bjanis@depaul.edu. *Web site:* www.depaul.edu/.

Eastern Illinois University
Charleston, Illinois

Student Services and Green Events *Sustainability leadership:* sustainability coordinator/director, sustainability committee/advisory council, recycling manager, energy manager.

Food Fair Trade coffee is used. Vegan and vegetarian dining options are available for every meal.

Transportation Provides free on-campus transportation (bus or other) and public transportation access to local destinations.

Buildings and Grounds *Renovation and maintenance:* registered for LEED certification for new construction and/or renovation; uses a Green Seal certified cleaning service. *Campus grounds care:* uses water conservation devices; employs strategies to reduce light pollution; protects, restores, and/or creates habitat on campus.

Recycling *Events and organizations:* RecycleMania, WasteWise (EPA). *Programs and activities:* composts yard waste; reuses surplus department/office supplies; replaces paper materials with online alternatives; limits free printing in computer labs and libraries. *Campus dining operations:* uses reusable dishware; offers discounts for reusable mugs; uses bulk condiment dispensers and decreased packaging for to-go food service purchases.

Energy Currently uses or plans to use alternative sources of power; timers to regulate temperatures based on occupancy hours; motion, infrared, and/or light sensors to reduce energy uses for lighting; and energy-related performance contracting.

Contact Campus Energy and Sustainability Coordinator, Eastern Illinois University, 600 Lincoln Avenue, FPM South, Charleston, IL 61920. *Phone:* 217-581-8395. *Fax:* 217-581-5716. *E-mail:* rwsiegel@eiu.edu. *Web site:* www.eiu.edu/.

East-West University
Chicago, Illinois

Academics *Sustainability courses and programs:* sustainability-focused course(s) or lecture series.

Transportation Provides public transportation access to local destinations and incentives to carpool or use public transportation.

Buildings and Grounds *Campus grounds care:* employs strategies to reduce light pollution.

Recycling *Events and organizations:* RecycleMania. *Programs and activities:* sustains a computer/technology recycling program; maintains an on-campus recycling center; sustains a post-consumer food waste composting program; reuses surplus department/office supplies; replaces paper materials with online alternatives; limits free printing in computer labs and libraries. *Campus dining operations:* uses bulk condiment dispensers and decreased packaging for to-go food service purchases.

Energy Currently uses or plans to use timers to regulate temperatures based on occupancy hours and LED lighting.

Contact Director of Public Relations, East-West University, 816 South Michigan Avenue, Chicago, IL 60605. *Phone:* 312-939-0111 Ext. 1818. *Fax:* 312-939-0083. *E-mail:* johnt@eastwood.edu. *Web site:* www.eastwest.edu/.

Illinois College
Jacksonville, Illinois

Sustainability Initiatives Illinois College's president has signed the American College & University Presidents Climate Commitment.

Student Services and Green Events *Sustainability leadership:* sustainability coordinator/director, recycling manager, energy manager, sustainability-focused student government. *Student clubs and activities:* Campus Climate Challenge, outreach materials available about on-campus sustainability efforts. *Housing and facilities:* sustainability-themed housing.

Food Vegan and vegetarian dining options are available for every meal.

Buildings and Grounds *Percentage of institution's eligible buildings as of September 2008 meeting LEED and/or LEED-EB certification criteria: 3%. Renovation and maintenance:* registered for LEED certification for new construction and/or renovation. *Campus grounds care:* uses water conservation devices; employs strategies to reduce light pollution; landscapes with native plant species; protects, restores, and/or creates habitat on campus.

Recycling *Programs and activities:* maintains an on-campus recycling center.

Energy Currently uses or plans to use alternative sources of power and motion, infrared, and/or light sensors to reduce energy uses for lighting. Participates in College & University Green Power Challenge activities.

Purchasing Sustainability criteria used in purchasing include Energy Star (EPA), Green Cleaning Products (Green Seal/Environmental Choice certified), and Forest Stewardship Council (FSC) or American Forest and Paper Association's Sustainable Forestry Initiative (SFI) paper.

Contact Assistant Vice President, Illinois College, 1101 West College Avenue, Jacksonville, IL 62650. *Phone:* 217-245-3162. *E-mail:* amays@ic.edu. *Web site:* www.ic.edu/.

Illinois Institute of Technology
Chicago, Illinois

Sustainability Initiatives Illinois Institute of Technology is a member of the Association for the Advancement of Sustainability in Higher Education (AASHE).

Academics *Sustainability-focused undergraduate major(s):* Environmental Engineering (BS). *Sustainability-focused graduate degree program(s):* Energy, Environment, and Economy (MS/PhD); Environmental Management (MS/MBA). *Sustainability courses and programs:* sustainability-focused course(s) or lecture series, sustainability-focused nonacademic certificate program(s).

Student Services and Green Events *Sustainability leadership:* sustainability coordinator/director, sustainability committee/advisory council, recycling manager, energy manager, sustainability-focused student government. *Student clubs and activities:* student club(s)/group(s) focused on sustainability. *Major sustainability events:* Campus Sustainability Forum series, Sustainable Energy Conference.

Food Sustainable, organic, and/or locally produced foods available in on-campus dining facilities. Fair Trade coffee is used. Vegan and vegetarian dining options are available for every meal.

Transportation Provides free on-campus transportation (bus or other), public transportation access to local destinations, and a car sharing program.

Buildings and Grounds *Percentage of institution's eligible buildings as of September 2008 meeting LEED and/or LEED-EB certification criteria: 2%. Renovation and maintenance:* registered for LEED certification for new construction and/or renovation; uses a Green Seal certified cleaning service. *Campus grounds care:* uses water conservation devices; protects, restores, and/or creates habitat on campus.

Green Jobs for a New Economy

Recycling *Programs and activities:* sustains a computer/technology recycling program; maintains an on-campus recycling center; replaces paper materials with online alternatives. *Campus dining operations:* uses reusable dishware; operates without trays; offers discounts for reusable mugs; uses bulk condiment dispensers and decreased packaging for to-go food service purchases.

Energy Currently uses or plans to use alternative sources of power (solar energy); timers to regulate temperatures based on occupancy hours; motion, infrared, and/or light sensors to reduce energy uses for lighting; and LED lighting.

Purchasing Sustainability criteria used in purchasing include Green Cleaning Products (Green Seal/Environmental Choice certified).

Contact Director of Campus Energy and Sustainability, Illinois Institute of Technology, 100 West 33rd Street, Room 200, Chicago, IL 60616. *Phone:* 312-567-3447. *Fax:* 312-567-3363. *E-mail:* claijos@iit.edu. *Web site:* www.iit.edu/.

Illinois State University
Normal, Illinois

Sustainability Initiatives Illinois State University is a member of the Association for the Advancement of Sustainability in Higher Education (AASHE). This institution's president has signed the American College & University Presidents Climate Commitment. Illinois State University has Green Fees (optional/required) dedicated to sustainability initiatives.

Academics *Sustainability-focused undergraduate major(s):* Environmental Health (BS), Renewable Energy (BS). *Sustainability-focused graduate degree program(s):* Bioenergy Sciences (MS). *Sustainability courses and programs:* sustainability-focused course(s) or lecture series.

Student Services and Green Events *Sustainability leadership:* sustainability coordinator/director, sustainability committee/advisory council, recycling manager, energy manager, sustainability-focused student government. *Student clubs and activities:* Campus Climate Challenge, student club(s)/group(s) focused on sustainability, outreach materials available about on-campus sustainability efforts. *Major sustainability events:* Healthy You Healthy Earth, Focus the Nation, RecycleMania, Earth Day. *Housing and facilities:* sustainability-themed housing.

Food Fair Trade coffee is used. Vegan and vegetarian dining options are available for every meal.

Transportation Provides free on-campus transportation (bus or other), public transportation access to local destinations, a bike loan/rental program, and incentives to carpool or use public transportation.

Buildings and Grounds *Campus grounds care:* uses water conservation devices; employs strategies to reduce light pollution; landscapes with native plant species; protects, restores, and/or creates habitat on campus.

Recycling *Events and organizations:* RecycleMania. *Programs and activities:* sustains a computer/technology recycling program; sustains a pre-consumer food waste composting program; sustains a post-consumer food waste composting program; composts yard waste; replaces paper materials with online alternatives; limits free printing in computer labs and libraries. *Campus dining operations:* uses reusable dishware; operates without trays; offers discounts for reusable mugs; uses bulk condiment dispensers and decreased packaging for to-go food service purchases.

Energy Currently uses or plans to use alternative sources of power (solar energy); timers to regulate temperatures based on occupancy hours; and motion, infrared, and/or light sensors to reduce energy uses for lighting.

Purchasing Sustainability criteria used in purchasing include Energy Star (EPA), Green Cleaning Products (Green Seal/Environmental Choice certified), and Forest Stewardship Council (FSC) or American Forest and Paper Association's Sustainable Forestry Initiative (SFI) paper.

Contact Sustainability Coordinator, Illinois State University, Campus Box 9000, Normal, IL 61790. *Phone:* 309-438-4425. *E-mail:* ecardin@ilstu.edu. *Web site:* www.ilstu.edu/.

Knox College
Galesburg, Illinois

Sustainability Initiatives Knox College is a signatory to the Talloires Declaration. Knox College has Green Fees (optional/required) dedicated to sustainability initiatives.

Academics *Sustainability-focused undergraduate major(s):* Environmental Studies (BA). *Sustainability courses and programs:* sustainability-focused course(s) or lecture series.

Student Services and Green Events *Sustainability leadership:* sustainability committee/advisory council, recycling manager, sustainability-focused student government. *Student clubs and activities:* student club(s)/group(s) focused on sustainability. *Major sustainability events:* Public presentations. *Housing and facilities:* on-campus organic garden for students.

Food Sustainable, organic, and/or locally produced foods available in on-campus dining facilities. Fair Trade coffee is used. Vegan and vegetarian dining options are available for every meal.

Transportation Provides public transportation access to local destinations, a bike loan/rental program, a car sharing program, and incentives to carpool or use public transportation.

Buildings and Grounds *Campus grounds care:* uses water conservation devices; landscapes with native plant species; protects, restores, and/or creates habitat on campus; applies to its grounds only pesticides and fertilizers allowable under the U.S. Department of Agriculture's standards for crop production.

Recycling *Programs and activities:* sustains a computer/technology recycling program; maintains an on-campus recycling center; replaces paper materials with online alternatives; limits free printing in computer labs and libraries. *Campus dining operations:* uses reusable dishware; operates without trays; offers discounts for reusable mugs; uses bulk condiment dispensers and decreased packaging for to-go food service purchases.

Energy Currently uses or plans to use timers to regulate temperatures based on occupancy hours and motion, infrared, and/or light sensors to reduce energy uses for lighting.

Purchasing Sustainability criteria used in purchasing include Energy Star (EPA).

Contact Associate Professor/Chair, Department of Environmental Studies, Knox College, 2 East South Street, Galesburg, IL 61401. *Phone:* 309-341-7142. *E-mail:* pschwart@knox.edu. *Web site:* www.knox.edu/.

North Central College
Naperville, Illinois

Academics *Sustainability courses and programs:* sustainability-focused course(s) or lecture series.

Student Services and Green Events *Sustainability leadership:* sustainability committee/advisory council.

Food Sustainable, organic, and/or locally produced foods available in on-campus dining facilities. Fair Trade coffee is used. Vegan and vegetarian dining options are available for every meal.

Transportation Provides free on-campus transportation (bus or other), a bike loan/rental program, and a car sharing program.

Buildings and Grounds *Renovation and maintenance:* registered for LEED certification for new construction and/or renovation. *Campus grounds care:* uses water conservation devices; landscapes with native plant species.

Recycling *Programs and activities:* reuses surplus department/office supplies; replaces paper materials with online alternatives; limits free printing in computer labs and libraries. *Campus dining operations:* uses reusable dishware; operates without trays; offers discounts for reusable mugs.

Energy Currently uses or plans to use alternative sources of power (geothermal energy) and motion, infrared, and/or light sensors to reduce energy uses for lighting.

Contact North Central College, 30 North Brainard Street, PO Box 3063, Naperville, IL 60566-7063. *Phone:* 630-637-5100. *Web site:* www.noctrl.edu/.

Northwestern University
Evanston, Illinois

Academics *Sustainability-focused undergraduate major(s):* Earth and Planetary Sciences; Environmental Engineering (BS); Environmental Science, Engineering, and Policy (BS). *Sustainability-focused graduate degree program(s):* Earth and Planetary Sciences (PhD), Environmental Engineering and Science (MS, PhD), Environmental Geotechnics (MS, PhD), Plant Biology and Conservation (MS, PhD). *Sustainability courses and programs:* sustainability-focused course(s) or lecture series.

Student Services and Green Events *Sustainability leadership:* sustainability committee/advisory council, recycling manager, energy manager. *Student clubs and activities:* student club(s)/group(s) focused on sustainability, outreach materials available about on-campus sustainability efforts. *Major sustainability events:* Green City Summer Institute, Initiative for Sustainability and Energy at Northwestern (ISEN), ESW Energy Day, Campus Sustainability Lecture and Workshop, Innovating Social Change Conference. *Housing and facilities:* sustainability-themed housing.

Food Sustainable, organic, and/or locally produced foods available in on-campus dining facilities. Fair Trade coffee is used. Vegan and vegetarian dining options are available for every meal.

Transportation Provides free on-campus transportation (bus or other), public transportation access to local destinations, a car sharing program, and incentives to carpool or use public transportation.

Buildings and Grounds *Renovation and maintenance:* registered for LEED certification for new construction and/or renovation; uses a Green Seal certified cleaning service. *Campus grounds care:* uses water conservation devices; employs strategies to reduce light pollution; landscapes with native plant species; protects, restores, and/or creates habitat on campus.

Recycling *Events and organizations:* RecycleMania. *Programs and activities:* sustains a computer/technology recycling program; composts yard waste; reuses surplus department/office supplies; reuses chemicals; replaces paper materials with online alternatives; limits free printing in

computer labs and libraries. *Campus dining operations:* uses reusable dishware; operates without trays; offers discounts for reusable mugs; uses bulk condiment dispensers and decreased packaging for to-go food service purchases.

Energy Currently uses or plans to use timers to regulate temperatures based on occupancy hours; motion, infrared, and/or light sensors to reduce energy uses for lighting; LED lighting; and energy-related performance contracting. Participates in College & University Green Power Challenge activities.

Purchasing Sustainability criteria used in purchasing include Energy Star (EPA) and Forest Stewardship Council (FSC) or American Forest and Paper Association's Sustainable Forestry Initiative (SFI) paper.

Contact Manager of Recycling and Refuse, Northwestern University, Facilities Management, 2020 Ridge Avenue, #200, Evanston, IL 60208. *Phone:* 847-467-1374. *Fax:* 847-491-4269. *E-mail:* j-cahillane@northwestern.edu. *Web site:* www.northwestern.edu/.

Saint Xavier University
Chicago, Illinois

Sustainability Initiatives Saint Xavier University's president has signed the American College & University Presidents Climate Commitment.

Student Services and Green Events *Sustainability leadership:* sustainability coordinator/director, sustainability committee/advisory council, recycling manager, energy manager, sustainability-focused student government. *Student clubs and activities:* student club(s)/group(s) focused on sustainability, outreach materials available about on-campus sustainability efforts. *Major sustainability events:* Smart and Sustainable Campuses Conference, Eastern NACUBO, Mercy Leadership, Farrell Forum, Chicago SCUP, SW Chicago Chamber of Commerce, Lt. Gov. H/E Sustainability Symposium. *Housing and facilities:* sustainability-themed housing, model dorm room that demonstrates sustainable living principles, student-run café that serves environmentally or socially preferable foods.

Food Sustainable, organic, and/or locally produced foods available in on-campus dining facilities. Fair Trade coffee is used. Vegan and vegetarian dining options are available for every meal.

Transportation Provides free on-campus transportation (bus or other), public transportation access to local destinations, a bike loan/rental program, and incentives to carpool or use public transportation.

Buildings and Grounds *Percentage of institution's eligible buildings as of September 2008 meeting LEED and/or LEED-EB certification criteria:* 8%. *Renovation and maintenance:* registered for LEED certification for new construction and/or renovation; uses a Green Seal certified cleaning service. *Campus grounds care:* uses water conservation devices; employs strategies to reduce light pollution; landscapes with native plant species; protects, restores, and/or creates habitat on campus.

Recycling *Events and organizations:* RecycleMania, WasteWise (EPA). *Programs and activities:* sustains a computer/technology recycling program; replaces paper materials with online alternatives; limits free printing in computer labs and libraries. *Campus dining operations:* operates without trays; offers discounts for reusable mugs; uses bulk condiment dispensers and decreased packaging for to-go food service purchases.

Energy Currently uses or plans to use alternative sources of power (biomass energy and wind energy); timers to regulate temperatures based on occupancy hours; motion, infrared, and/or light sensors to reduce energy uses for lighting; LED lighting; and energy-related performance contracting.

Purchasing Sustainability criteria used in purchasing include Energy Star (EPA), Green Cleaning Products (Green Seal/Environmental Choice certified), and Forest Stewardship Council (FSC) or American Forest and Paper Association's Sustainable Forestry Initiative (SFI) paper.

Contact Assistant Vice President for Facilities Management, Saint Xavier University, 3700 West 103rd Street, Chicago, IL 60655. *Phone:* 773-298-3548. *Fax:* 773-298-3263. *E-mail:* pmatthews@sxu.edu. *Web site:* www.sxu.edu/.

Southern Illinois University Carbondale
Carbondale, Illinois

Sustainability Initiatives Southern Illinois University Carbondale is a signatory to the Talloires Declaration.

Academics *Sustainability-focused undergraduate major(s):* Agribusiness Economics—Energy and Environment Policy (BA), Geography and Environmental Resources, Plant Soil Sciences—Environmental Studies (BA). *Sustainability-focused graduate degree program(s):* Advanced Energy and Fuels Management (MA) pending; Environmental Resources and Policy (PhD), Geography and Environmental Resources (MA). *Sustainability courses and programs:* sustainability-focused course(s) or lecture series.

Student Services and Green Events *Sustainability leadership:* sustainability coordinator/director, sustainability committee/advisory council, recycling manager, energy manager. *Student clubs and activities:* Campus Climate Challenge, student club(s)/group(s) focused on sustainability, outreach materials available about on-campus sustainability efforts. *Major sustainability events:* Annual Heartland Bioneers Conference, Center for Delta Studies Climate Change Forum, Changing Climates (League of Women Voters/Sierra Club sponsored forum), Connecting with the Future of Energy (five part symposium series). *Housing and facilities:* sustainability-themed housing.

Food Sustainable, organic, and/or locally produced foods available in on-campus dining facilities. Fair Trade coffee is used. Vegan and vegetarian dining options are available for every meal.

Transportation Provides free on-campus transportation (bus or other), public transportation access to local destinations, a bike loan/rental program, and incentives to carpool or use public transportation.

Buildings and Grounds *Campus grounds care:* uses water conservation devices; landscapes with native plant species; protects, restores, and/or creates habitat on campus.

Recycling *Events and organizations:* RecycleMania. *Programs and activities:* maintains an on-campus recycling center; sustains a pre-consumer food waste composting program; sustains a post-consumer food waste composting program; composts yard waste; reuses surplus department/office supplies; reuses chemicals; replaces paper materials with online alternatives; limits free printing in computer labs and libraries. *Campus dining operations:* uses reusable dishware; operates without trays; offers discounts for reusable mugs; uses bulk condiment dispensers and decreased packaging for to-go food service purchases.

Energy Currently uses or plans to use alternative sources of power (solar energy); timers to regulate temperatures based on occupancy hours; motion, infrared, and/or light sensors to reduce energy uses for lighting; LED lighting; and vending machine motion sensors.

Purchasing Sustainability criteria used in purchasing include Energy Star (EPA) and Green Cleaning Products (Green Seal/Environmental Choice certified).

Contact Assistant Professor, Southern Illinois University Carbondale, Faner Hall MC 4514, Carbondale, IL 62901. *Phone:* 618-453-6024. *E-mail:* therrell@siu.edu. *Web site:* www.siuc.edu.

University of Chicago
Chicago, Illinois

Academics *Sustainability-focused undergraduate major(s):* Environmental Sciences (BS), Environmental Studies (BA), Geophysical Sciences (BA), Geophysical Sciences (BS). *Sustainability-focused graduate degree program(s):* Environmental Science and Policy (MS), Geophysical Sciences (MS), Geophysical Sciences (PhD). *Sustainability courses and programs:* sustainability-focused course(s) or lecture series, noncredit sustainability course(s).

Student Services and Green Events *Sustainability leadership:* sustainability coordinator/director, sustainability committee/advisory council, recycling manager, energy manager, sustainability-focused student government. *Student clubs and activities:* student club(s)/group(s) focused on sustainability. *Major sustainability events:* Earth Week, "Economic Valuation of Ecosystem Services" spring conference. *Housing and facilities:* student-run café that serves environmentally or socially preferable foods, on-campus organic garden for students.

Food Sustainable, organic, and/or locally produced foods available in on-campus dining facilities. Fair Trade coffee is used. Vegan and vegetarian dining options are available for every meal.

Transportation Provides free on-campus transportation (bus or other), public transportation access to local destinations, a car sharing program, and incentives to carpool or use public transportation.

Buildings and Grounds *Renovation and maintenance:* registered for LEED certification for new construction and/or renovation. *Campus grounds care:* landscapes with native plant species; protects, restores, and/or creates habitat on campus.

Recycling *Events and organizations:* RecycleMania. *Programs and activities:* sustains a computer/technology recycling program; sustains a post-consumer food waste composting program; composts yard waste; replaces paper materials with online alternatives; limits free printing in computer labs and libraries. *Campus dining operations:* uses reusable dishware; offers discounts for reusable mugs; uses bulk condiment dispensers and decreased packaging for to-go food service purchases.

Energy Currently uses or plans to use timers to regulate temperatures based on occupancy hours; motion, infrared, and/or light sensors to reduce energy uses for lighting; and LED lighting.

Purchasing Sustainability criteria used in purchasing include Energy Star (EPA), Green Cleaning Products (Green Seal/Environmental Choice certified), and Forest Stewardship Council (FSC) or American Forest and Paper Association's Sustainable Forestry Initiative (SFI) paper.

Contact Director of Sustainability, University of Chicago, 5555 South Ellis Avenue, Chicago, IL 60637. *Phone:* 773-834-8508. *E-mail:* iflanagan@uchicago.edu. *Web site:* www.uchicago.edu/.

University of Illinois at Chicago
Chicago, Illinois

Sustainability Initiatives University of Illinois at Chicago's president has signed the American College & University Presidents Climate Commitment.

Academics *Sustainability-focused graduate degree program(s):* Landscape Ecological and Anthropogenic Processes (LEAP, PhD).

Student Services and Green Events *Sustainability leadership:* sustainability coordinator/director, sustainability committee/advisory council, recycling manager. *Student clubs and activities:* Campus Climate Challenge, student club(s)/group(s) focused on sustainability. *Major sustainability events:* Illinois Sustainable University Symposium; Sustainable Living Roadshow, Sustainability Week, Chicago Wilderness Conference. *Housing and facilities:* on-campus organic garden for students.

Food Fair Trade coffee is used. Vegan and vegetarian dining options are available for every meal.

Transportation Provides free on-campus transportation (bus or other), public transportation access to local destinations, a car sharing program, and incentives to carpool or use public transportation.

Buildings and Grounds *Renovation and maintenance:* registered for LEED certification for new construction and/or renovation. *Campus grounds care:* uses water conservation devices; landscapes with native plant species; protects, restores, and/or creates habitat on campus.

Recycling *Events and organizations:* RecycleMania. *Programs and activities:* sustains a computer/technology recycling program; composts yard waste; reuses surplus department/office supplies; reuses chemicals; replaces paper materials with online alternatives; limits free printing in computer labs and libraries. *Campus dining operations:* uses reusable dishware; offers discounts for reusable mugs.

Energy Currently uses or plans to use alternative sources of power (geothermal energy) and energy-related performance contracting.

Contact Associate Chancellor for Sustainability, University of Illinois at Chicago, Office of Sustainability, MC 996, 1140 South Paulina Street, Chicago, IL 60612. *Phone:* 312-996-3968. *E-mail:* cindy@uic.edu. *Web site:* www.uic.edu/.

University of Illinois at Urbana–Champaign
Champaign, Illinois

Sustainability Initiatives University of Illinois at Urbana–Champaign is a member of the Association for the Advancement of Sustainability in Higher Education (AASHE). This institution's president has signed the American College & University Presidents Climate Commitment. University of Illinois at Urbana–Champaign has Green Fees (optional/required) dedicated to sustainability initiatives.

Academics *Sustainability-focused undergraduate major(s):* Civil Engineering (BS); Earth Systems, Environment, and Society (BS); Environmental Sustainability (BS); Landscape Architecture (BLA); Natural Resources and Environmental Sciences (BS); Urban and Regional Planning (BA). *Sustainability-focused graduate degree program(s):* Civil and Environmental Engineering (MS, PhD), Landscape Architecture (MLA, PhD), Natural Resources and Environmental Science (MS, PhD), Teaching of Earth Science (MS), Urban and Regional Planning (MUP, PhD). *Sustainability courses and programs:* sustainability-focused course(s) or lecture series, noncredit sustainability course(s), sustainability-focused nonacademic certificate program(s).

Student Services and Green Events *Sustainability leadership:* sustainability coordinator/director, sustainability committee/advisory council, recycling manager, energy manager, sustainability-focused student government. *Student clubs and activities:* student club(s)/group(s) focused on sustainability, outreach materials available about on-campus sustainability efforts. *Major sustainability events:* Planet U: The Human Story of Climate Change (conference), E-Waste competition, Innovation Week, Earth Week. *Housing and facilities:* student-run café that serves environmentally or socially preferable foods, on-campus organic garden for students.

Food Sustainable, organic, and/or locally produced foods available in on-campus dining facilities. Fair Trade coffee is used. Vegan and vegetarian dining options are available for every meal.

Transportation Provides free on-campus transportation (bus or other), public transportation access to local destinations, a bike loan/rental program, a car sharing program, and incentives to carpool or use public transportation.

Buildings and Grounds *Percentage of institution's eligible buildings as of September 2008 meeting LEED and/or LEED-EB certification criteria:* 2%. *Renovation and maintenance:* registered for LEED certification for new construction and/or renovation. *Campus grounds care:* uses water conservation devices; landscapes with native plant species; protects, restores, and/or creates habitat on campus.

Recycling *Programs and activities:* sustains a computer/technology recycling program; maintains an on-campus recycling center; sustains a pre-consumer food waste composting program; composts yard waste; reuses surplus department/office supplies; reuses chemicals; replaces paper materials with online alternatives. *Campus dining operations:* uses reusable dishware; operates without trays; offers discounts for reusable mugs; uses bulk condiment dispensers and decreased packaging for to-go food service purchases.

Energy Currently uses or plans to use alternative sources of power (biomass energy and solar energy); timers to regulate temperatures based on occupancy hours; motion, infrared, and/or light sensors to reduce energy uses for lighting; LED lighting; vending machine motion sensors; and energy-related performance contracting.

Purchasing Sustainability criteria used in purchasing include Energy Star (EPA), WaterSense (EPA), Green Cleaning Products (Green Seal/Environmental Choice certified), and Forest Stewardship Council (FSC) or American Forest and Paper Association's Sustainable Forestry Initiative (SFI) paper.

Contact Outreach Coordinator, University of Illinois at Urbana–Champaign, 165 Natural Resource Building, 607 East Peabody, Champaign, IL 61820. *Phone:* 217-244-3436. *Fax:* 217-244-2006. *E-mail:* jcourson@illinois.edu. *Web site:* www.uiuc.edu/.

University of St. Francis
Joliet, Illinois

Sustainability Initiatives University of St. Francis's president has signed the American College & University Presidents Climate Commitment.

Student Services and Green Events *Sustainability leadership:* sustainability committee/advisory council.

Transportation Provides public transportation access to local destinations.

Buildings and Grounds *Campus grounds care:* landscapes with native plant species.

Recycling *Programs and activities:* reuses surplus department/office supplies; replaces paper materials with online alternatives; limits free printing in computer labs and libraries. *Campus dining operations:* uses reusable dishware; offers discounts for reusable mugs; uses bulk condiment dispensers and decreased packaging for to-go food service purchases.

Energy Currently uses or plans to use motion, infrared, and/or light sensors to reduce energy uses for lighting.

Purchasing Sustainability criteria used in purchasing include Energy Star (EPA).

Contact Vice President, Administration and Finance, University of St. Francis, 500 Wilcox Street, Joliet, IL 60432. *Phone:* 815-740-3372. *Fax:* 815-740-5083. *E-mail:* rtenuta@stfrancis.edu. *Web site:* www.stfrancis.edu/.

Indiana

Ball State University
Muncie, Indiana

Sustainability Initiatives Ball State University is a signatory to the Talloires Declaration. This institution's president has signed the American College & University Presidents Climate Commitment.

Academics *Sustainability-focused graduate degree program(s):* Master of Architecture (MArch). *Sustainability courses and programs:* sustainability-focused course(s) or lecture series, noncredit sustainability course(s).

Student Services and Green Events *Sustainability leadership:* sustainability committee/advisory council, recycling manager, energy manager. *Student clubs and activities:* Campus Climate Challenge, student club(s)/group(s) focused on sustainability, outreach materials available about on-campus sustainability efforts. *Major sustainability events:* Greening of the Campus Conference Series 1-8, RecycleMania, Focus the Nation, Architecture 2030 Teach-In, Sustainability Summit for Indiana Colleges and Universities. *Housing and facilities:* sustainability-themed housing.

Food Sustainable, organic, and/or locally produced foods available in on-campus dining facilities. Fair Trade coffee is used. Vegan and vegetarian dining options are available for every meal.

Transportation Provides free on-campus transportation (bus or other), public transportation access to local destinations, and incentives to carpool or use public transportation.

Buildings and Grounds *Percentage of institution's eligible buildings as of September 2008 meeting LEED and/or LEED-EB certification criteria:* 2%. *Renovation and maintenance:* registered for LEED certification for new construction and/or renovation. *Campus grounds care:* uses water conservation devices; employs strategies to reduce light pollution; landscapes with native plant species; protects, restores, and/or creates habitat on campus; applies to its grounds only pesticides and fertilizers allowable under the U.S. Department of Agriculture's standards for crop production.

Recycling *Events and organizations:* RecycleMania. *Programs and activities:* sustains a computer/technology recycling program; composts yard waste; reuses surplus department/office supplies; reuses chemicals; replaces paper materials with online alternatives; limits free printing in computer labs and libraries. *Campus dining operations:* uses reusable dishware; operates without trays; offers discounts for reusable mugs; uses bulk condiment dispensers and decreased packaging for to-go food service purchases.

Energy Currently uses or plans to use alternative sources of power; timers to regulate temperatures based on occupancy hours; motion, infrared, and/or light sensors to reduce energy uses for lighting; and LED lighting.

Purchasing Sustainability criteria used in purchasing include Energy Star (EPA), Green Cleaning Products (Green Seal/Environmental Choice certified), and Forest Stewardship Council (FSC) or American Forest and Paper Association's Sustainable Forestry Initiative (SFI) paper.

Contact Professor and Director, Ball State University, 2000 University Avenue, Muncie, IN 47306-0170. *Phone:* 765-285-1135. *Fax:* 765-285-5622. *E-mail:* rkoester@bsu.edu. *Web site:* www.bsu.edu/.

DePauw University
Greencastle, Indiana

Sustainability Initiatives DePauw University's president has signed the American College & University Presidents Climate Commitment.

Academics *Sustainability-focused undergraduate major(s):* Environmental Geosciences, Individually designed interdisciplinary major. *Sustainability courses and programs:* sustainability-focused course(s) or lecture series, noncredit sustainability course(s).

Student Services and Green Events *Sustainability leadership:* sustainability coordinator/director, sustainability committee/advisory council, recycling manager. *Student clubs and activities:* Campus Climate Challenge, student club(s)/group(s) focused on sustainability. *Major sustainability events:* Focus the Nation, Energy Day, DePauw Discourse entitled "Sustainability and Global Citizenship". *Housing and facilities:* sustainability-themed housing.

Food Sustainable, organic, and/or locally produced foods available in on-campus dining facilities. Fair Trade coffee is used. Vegan and vegetarian dining options are available for every meal.

Transportation Provides public transportation access to local destinations and a bike loan/rental program.

Buildings and Grounds *Percentage of institution's eligible buildings as of September 2008 meeting LEED and/or LEED-EB certification criteria:* 2%. *Renovation and maintenance:* registered for LEED certification for new construction and/or renovation; uses a Green Seal certified cleaning service. *Campus grounds care:* uses water conservation devices; employs strategies to reduce light pollution; landscapes with native plant species; protects, restores, and/or creates habitat on campus.

Recycling *Programs and activities:* sustains a computer/technology recycling program; sustains a pre-consumer food waste composting program; sustains a post-consumer food waste composting program; composts yard waste; reuses surplus department/office supplies; replaces paper materials with online alternatives. *Campus dining operations:* uses reusable dishware; offers discounts for reusable mugs; uses bulk condiment dispensers and decreased packaging for to-go food service purchases.

Energy Currently uses or plans to use timers to regulate temperatures based on occupancy hours; motion, infrared, and/or light sensors to reduce energy uses for lighting; and LED lighting.

Purchasing Sustainability criteria used in purchasing include Energy Star (EPA), Green Cleaning Products (Green Seal/Environmental Choice certified), and Forest Stewardship Council (FSC) or American Forest and Paper Association's Sustainable Forestry Initiative (SFI) paper.

Contact DePauw Sustainability Coordinator, DePauw University, 302A Harrison Hall, 7 East Larabee Street, Greencastle, IN 46135. *Phone:* 765-658-6608. *Fax:* 765-658-4021. *E-mail:* carolsteele@depauw.edu. *Web site:* www.depauw.edu/.

Earlham College
Richmond, Indiana

Sustainability Initiatives Earlham College is a member of the Association for the Advancement of Sustainability in Higher Education (AASHE) and a signatory to the Talloires Declaration.

Buildings and Grounds *Campus grounds care:* uses water conservation devices; landscapes with native plant species.

Recycling *Programs and activities:* sustains a pre-consumer food waste composting program; sustains a post-consumer food waste composting program; composts yard waste.

Energy Currently uses or plans to use motion, infrared, and/or light sensors to reduce energy uses for lighting.

Contact Earlham College, 801 National Road West, Richmond, IN 47374-4095. *Phone:* 765-983-1200. *Web site:* www.earlham.edu/.

Franklin College
Franklin, Indiana

Sustainability Initiatives Franklin College's president has signed the American College & University Presidents Climate Commitment.

Academics *Sustainability-focused undergraduate major(s):* Environmental Studies. *Sustainability courses and programs:* sustainability-focused course(s) or lecture series.

Student Services and Green Events *Sustainability leadership:* sustainability committee/advisory council. *Student clubs and activities:* student club(s)/group(s) focused on sustainability, outreach materials available about on-campus sustainability efforts. *Major sustainability events:* Earth Day displays and events. *Housing and facilities:* student-run café that serves environmentally or socially preferable foods.

Food Sustainable, organic, and/or locally produced foods available in on-campus dining facilities. Fair Trade coffee is used. Vegan and vegetarian dining options are available for every meal.

Transportation Provides public transportation access to local destinations.

Buildings and Grounds *Renovation and maintenance:* registered for LEED certification for new construction and/or renovation; uses a Green Seal certified cleaning service. *Campus grounds care:* uses water conservation devices; landscapes with native plant species; protects, restores, and/or creates habitat on campus.

Recycling *Programs and activities:* sustains a computer/technology recycling program; sustains a pre-consumer food waste composting program; sustains a post-consumer food waste composting program; composts yard waste; reuses surplus department/office supplies; replaces paper materials with online alternatives; limits free printing in computer labs and libraries. *Campus dining operations:* uses reusable dishware; uses bulk condiment dispensers and decreased packaging for to-go food service purchases.

Energy Currently uses or plans to use alternative sources of power; motion, infrared, and/or light sensors to reduce energy uses for lighting; and LED lighting.

Purchasing Sustainability criteria used in purchasing include Energy Star (EPA), Green Cleaning Products (Green

Seal/Environmental Choice certified), and Forest Stewardship Council (FSC) or American Forest and Paper Association's Sustainable Forestry Initiative (SFI) paper.

Contact Project Manager, Franklin College, 101 Branigin Boulevard, Franklin, IN 46131. *Phone:* 317-738-8183. *E-mail:* tpatz@franklincollege.edu. *Web site:* www.franklincollege.edu/.

Hanover College
Hanover, Indiana

Academics *Sustainability courses and programs:* sustainability-focused course(s) or lecture series.

Student Services and Green Events *Sustainability leadership:* sustainability committee/advisory council, recycling manager, sustainability-focused student government. *Student clubs and activities:* student club(s)/group(s) focused on sustainability. *Major sustainability events:* Environmental speakers (such as Ed Begley Jr. and Mia Farrow).

Food Fair Trade coffee is used. Vegan and vegetarian dining options are available for every meal.

Transportation Provides free on-campus transportation (bus or other), public transportation access to local destinations, and a car sharing program.

Buildings and Grounds *Renovation and maintenance:* uses a Green Seal certified cleaning service. *Campus grounds care:* uses water conservation devices; employs strategies to reduce light pollution; landscapes with native plant species; protects, restores, and/or creates habitat on campus; applies to its grounds only pesticides and fertilizers allowable under the U.S. Department of Agriculture's standards for crop production.

Recycling *Programs and activities:* sustains a computer/technology recycling program; maintains an on-campus recycling center; composts yard waste; reuses surplus department/office supplies; replaces paper materials with online alternatives; limits free printing in computer labs and libraries. *Campus dining operations:* uses reusable dishware; uses bulk condiment dispensers and decreased packaging for to-go food service purchases.

Energy Currently uses or plans to use timers to regulate temperatures based on occupancy hours; motion, infrared, and/or light sensors to reduce energy uses for lighting; and LED lighting.

Purchasing Sustainability criteria used in purchasing include Green Cleaning Products (Green Seal/Environmental Choice certified).

Contact Hanover College, PO Box 108, Hanover, IN 47243-0108. *Phone:* 812-866-7000. *Web site:* www.hanover.edu/.

Indiana Wesleyan University
Marion, Indiana

Student Services and Green Events *Sustainability leadership:* sustainability coordinator/director, sustainability committee/advisory council, recycling manager, energy manager.

Food Fair Trade coffee is used. Vegan and vegetarian dining options are available for every meal.

Transportation Provides public transportation access to local destinations and a car sharing program.

Buildings and Grounds *Campus grounds care:* uses water conservation devices; employs strategies to reduce light pollution; landscapes with native plant species; protects, restores, and/or creates habitat on campus; applies to its grounds only pesticides and fertilizers allowable under the U.S. Department of Agriculture's standards for crop production.

Recycling *Programs and activities:* sustains a computer/technology recycling program; maintains an on-campus recycling center; sustains a post-consumer food waste composting program; reuses surplus department/office supplies; replaces paper materials with online alternatives; limits free printing in computer labs and libraries. *Campus dining operations:* uses reusable dishware; uses bulk condiment dispensers and decreased packaging for to-go food service purchases.

Energy Currently uses or plans to use alternative sources of power (geothermal energy); timers to regulate temperatures based on occupancy hours; motion, infrared, and/or light sensors to reduce energy uses for lighting; and LED lighting.

Purchasing Sustainability criteria used in purchasing include Energy Star (EPA) and Green Cleaning Products (Green Seal/Environmental Choice certified).

Contact Vice President for Operations and Facilities Planning, Indiana Wesleyan University, 4201 South Washington Street, Marion, IN 46953. *Phone:* 765-677-2123. *E-mail:* brendan.bowen@indwes.edu. *Web site:* www.indwes.edu/.

Saint Mary-of-the-Woods College
Saint Mary-of-the-Woods, Indiana

Academics *Sustainability-focused graduate degree program(s):* Earth Literacy. *Sustainability courses and programs:* sustainability-focused course(s) or lecture series.

Student Services and Green Events *Sustainability leadership:* sustainability committee/advisory council, recycling manager, energy manager. *Student clubs and activities:* student club(s)/group(s) focused on sustainability. *Major sustainability events:* Focus The Woods symposium.

Food Sustainable, organic, and/or locally produced foods available in on-campus dining facilities. Vegan and vegetarian dining options are available for every meal.

Buildings and Grounds *Renovation and maintenance:* registered for LEED certification for new construction and/or renovation. *Campus grounds care:* landscapes with native plant species.

Recycling *Programs and activities:* replaces paper materials with online alternatives. *Campus dining operations:* uses reusable dishware; uses bulk condiment dispensers and decreased packaging for to-go food service purchases.

Energy Currently uses or plans to use energy-related performance contracting.

Purchasing Sustainability criteria used in purchasing include Green Cleaning Products (Green Seal/Environmental Choice certified).

Contact Vice President for Finance and Administration, Saint Mary-of-the-Woods College, 233 Guerin Hall, St. Mary-of-the-Woods, IN 47876. *Phone:* 812-535-5125. *Fax:* 812-535-1162. *E-mail:* gafdahl@smwc.edu. *Web site:* www.smwc.edu/.

Iowa

Central College
Pella, Iowa

Sustainability Initiatives Central College is a member of the Association for the Advancement of Sustainability in Higher Education (AASHE) and a signatory to the Talloires Declaration. This institution's president has signed the American College & University Presidents Climate Commitment.

Academics *Sustainability-focused undergraduate major(s):* Environmental Studies (BA). *Sustainability courses and programs:* sustainability-focused course(s) or lecture series, noncredit sustainability course(s).

Student Services and Green Events *Sustainability leadership:* sustainability committee/advisory council, energy manager. *Student clubs and activities:* Campus Climate Challenge. *Housing and facilities:* sustainability-themed housing, model dorm room that demonstrates sustainable living principles, on-campus organic garden for students.

Food Sustainable, organic, and/or locally produced foods available in on-campus dining facilities. Fair Trade coffee is used. Vegan and vegetarian dining options are available for every meal.

Buildings and Grounds *Renovation and maintenance:* registered for LEED certification for new construction and/or renovation; uses a Green Seal certified cleaning service. *Campus grounds care:* uses water conservation devices; landscapes with native plant species; protects, restores, and/or creates habitat on campus.

Recycling *Events and organizations:* RecycleMania. *Programs and activities:* sustains a computer/technology recycling program; maintains an on-campus recycling center; sustains a pre-consumer food waste composting program; sustains a post-consumer food waste composting program; composts yard waste; reuses surplus department/office supplies; reuses chemicals; replaces paper materials with online alternatives. *Campus dining operations:* uses reusable dishware; uses bulk condiment dispensers and decreased packaging for to-go food service purchases.

Energy Currently uses or plans to use alternative sources of power (solar energy); timers to regulate temperatures based on occupancy hours; motion, infrared, and/or light sensors to reduce energy uses for lighting; LED lighting; and energy-related performance contracting. Participates in College & University Green Power Challenge activities.

Purchasing Sustainability criteria used in purchasing include Energy Star (EPA) and Green Cleaning Products (Green Seal/Environmental Choice certified).

Contact Central College, 812 University Street, Pella, IA 50219-1999. *Phone:* 641-628-9000. *Web site:* www.central.edu/.

Clarke College
Dubuque, Iowa

Student Services and Green Events *Sustainability leadership:* sustainability committee/advisory council, recycling manager, sustainability-focused student government.

Food Sustainable, organic, and/or locally produced foods available in on-campus dining facilities. Vegan and vegetarian dining options are available for every meal.

Buildings and Grounds *Campus grounds care:* employs strategies to reduce light pollution; landscapes with native plant species; applies to its grounds only pesticides and fertilizers allowable under the U.S. Department of Agriculture's standards for crop production.

Recycling *Programs and activities:* sustains a pre-consumer food waste composting program; sustains a post-consumer food waste composting program; composts yard waste; replaces paper materials with online alternatives. *Campus dining operations:* uses reusable dishware; operates without trays; uses bulk condiment dispensers and decreased packaging for to-go food service purchases.

Energy Currently uses or plans to use motion, infrared, and/or light sensors to reduce energy uses for lighting and energy-related performance contracting.

Purchasing Sustainability criteria used in purchasing include Energy Star (EPA).

Contact Director of Facilities Management, Clarke College, 1550 Clarke Drive, Dubuque, IN 52001. *Phone:* 563-588-8167. *E-mail:* brian.schultes@clarke.edu. *Web site:* www.clarke.edu/.

Coe College
Cedar Rapids, Iowa

Sustainability Initiatives Coe College's president has signed the American College & University Presidents Climate Commitment.

Academics *Sustainability-focused undergraduate major(s):* Environmental Science. *Sustainability courses and programs:* sustainability-focused course(s) or lecture series.

Student Services and Green Events *Sustainability leadership:* sustainability committee/advisory council, recycling manager. *Student clubs and activities:* student club(s)/group(s) focused on sustainability, outreach materials available about on-campus sustainability efforts. *Major sustainability events:* AASHE Conference and Expo, RecycleMania. *Housing and facilities:* on-campus organic garden for students.

Food Sustainable, organic, and/or locally produced foods available in on-campus dining facilities. Fair Trade coffee is used. Vegan and vegetarian dining options are available for every meal.

Transportation Provides free on-campus transportation (bus or other), public transportation access to local destinations, and a bike loan/rental program.

Buildings and Grounds *Renovation and maintenance:* registered for LEED certification for new construction and/or renovation; uses a Green Seal certified cleaning service.

Recycling *Events and organizations:* RecycleMania. *Programs and activities:* sustains a computer/technology recycling program; maintains an on-campus recycling center; sustains a pre-consumer food waste composting program; sustains a post-consumer food waste composting program; composts yard waste; reuses surplus department/office supplies; replaces paper materials with online alternatives; limits free printing in computer labs and libraries. *Campus dining operations:* uses reusable dishware; uses bulk condiment dispensers and decreased packaging for to-go food service purchases.

Energy Currently uses or plans to use timers to regulate temperatures based on occupancy hours.

Purchasing Sustainability criteria used in purchasing include Energy Star (EPA) and Green Cleaning Products (Green Seal/Environmental Choice certified).

Contact Professor of Chemistry/Associate Dean of Faculty, Coe College, 1220 1st Avenue NE, Cedar Rapids, IA 52402. *Phone:* 319-399-8582. *E-mail:* mstclair@coe.edu. *Web site:* www.coe.edu/.

Drake University
Des Moines, Iowa

Sustainability Initiatives Drake University's president has signed the American College & University Presidents Climate Commitment.

Academics *Sustainability-focused undergraduate major(s):* Environmental Policy (BA), Environmental Science (BS). *Sustainability courses and programs:* sustainability-focused course(s) or lecture series.

Student Services and Green Events *Sustainability leadership:* sustainability committee/advisory council. *Student clubs and activities:* student club(s)/group(s) focused on sustainability, outreach materials available about on-campus sustainability efforts. *Housing and facilities:* sustainability-themed housing.

Food Sustainable, organic, and/or locally produced foods available in on-campus dining facilities. Fair Trade coffee is used. Vegan and vegetarian dining options are available for every meal.

Transportation Provides public transportation access to local destinations and incentives to carpool or use public transportation.

Buildings and Grounds *Campus grounds care:* uses water conservation devices; landscapes with native plant species; protects, restores, and/or creates habitat on campus.

Recycling *Programs and activities:* sustains a computer/technology recycling program; reuses surplus department/office supplies; replaces paper materials with online alternatives. *Campus dining operations:* uses reusable dishware; operates without trays; offers discounts for reusable mugs; uses bulk condiment dispensers and decreased packaging for to-go food service purchases.

Energy Currently uses or plans to use motion, infrared, and/or light sensors to reduce energy uses for lighting; LED lighting; vending machine motion sensors; and energy-related performance contracting.

Purchasing Sustainability criteria used in purchasing include Energy Star (EPA) and Green Cleaning Products (Green Seal/Environmental Choice certified).

Contact Director of Communications, Drake University, 2507 University Avenue, Des Moines, IA 50311-4516. *E-mail:* lisa.lacher@drake.edu. *Web site:* www.drake.edu/.

Grinnell College
Grinnell, Iowa

Academics *Sustainability courses and programs:* sustainability-focused course(s) or lecture series.

Student Services and Green Events *Sustainability leadership:* sustainability coordinator/director, sustainability committee/advisory council, recycling manager, sustainability-focused student government. *Student clubs and activities:* student club(s)/group(s) focused on sustainability, outreach materials available about on-campus sustainability efforts. *Major sustainability events:* Bioneers Conference. *Housing and facilities:* sustainability-themed housing, on-campus organic garden for students.

Food Sustainable, organic, and/or locally produced foods available in on-campus dining facilities. Vegan and vegetarian dining options are available for every meal.

Transportation Provides a bike loan/rental program.

Buildings and Grounds *Percentage of institution's eligible buildings as of September 2008 meeting LEED and/or LEED-EB certification criteria:* 33%. *Renovation and maintenance:* registered for LEED certification for new construction and/or renovation. *Campus grounds care:* uses water conservation devices; employs strategies to reduce light pollution; landscapes with native plant species; protects, restores, and/or creates habitat on campus.

Recycling *Events and organizations:* RecycleMania. *Programs and activities:* sustains a computer/technology recycling program; maintains an on-campus recycling center; sustains a pre-consumer food waste composting program; sustains a post-consumer food waste composting program; composts yard waste; reuses surplus department/office supplies; replaces paper materials with online alternatives. *Campus dining operations:* uses reusable dishware; offers discounts for reusable mugs; uses bulk condiment dispensers and decreased packaging for to-go food service purchases.

Energy Currently uses or plans to use alternative sources of power (geothermal energy, solar energy, and wind energy); timers to regulate temperatures based on occupancy hours; motion, infrared, and/or light sensors to reduce energy uses for lighting; LED lighting; and vending machine motion sensors.

Purchasing Sustainability criteria used in purchasing include Energy Star (EPA) and Forest Stewardship Council (FSC) or American Forest and Paper Association's Sustainable Forestry Initiative (SFI) paper.

Contact Environmental and Safety Coordinator, Grinnell College, Grinnell, IA 50112. *Phone:* 641-269-4311. *Fax:* 641-269-4997. *E-mail:* baircr@grinnell.edu. *Web site:* www.grinnell.edu/.

Luther College
Decorah, Iowa

Sustainability Initiatives Luther College is a member of the Association for the Advancement of Sustainability in Higher Education (AASHE). This institution's president has signed the American College & University Presidents Climate Commitment.

Academics *Sustainability courses and programs:* sustainability-focused course(s) or lecture series.

Student Services and Green Events *Sustainability leadership:* sustainability coordinator/director, sustainability committee/advisory council, recycling manager. *Housing and facilities:* on-campus organic garden for students.

Food Sustainable, organic, and/or locally produced foods available in on-campus dining facilities. Fair Trade coffee is used. Vegan and vegetarian dining options are available for every meal.

Transportation Provides a bike loan/rental program.

Buildings and Grounds *Percentage of institution's eligible buildings as of September 2008 meeting LEED and/or LEED-EB certification criteria:* 2%. *Renovation and maintenance:* registered for LEED certification for new construction and/or renovation; uses a Green Seal certified cleaning service. *Campus grounds care:* uses water conservation devices; landscapes with native plant species; protects, restores, and/or creates habitat on campus.

Recycling *Programs and activities:* sustains a computer/technology recycling program; sustains a pre-consumer food waste composting program; sustains a post-consumer food waste composting program; composts yard waste; replaces paper materials with online alternatives. *Campus dining operations:* uses reusable dishware; operates without trays; offers discounts for reusable mugs; uses bulk condiment dispensers and decreased packaging for to-go food service purchases.

Energy Currently uses or plans to use alternative sources of power (geothermal energy); timers to regulate temperatures based on occupancy hours; motion, infrared, and/or light sensors to reduce energy uses for lighting; LED lighting; and energy-related performance contracting.

Purchasing Sustainability criteria used in purchasing include Energy Star (EPA) and Green Cleaning Products (Green Seal/Environmental Choice certified).

Contact Sustainability Coordinator, Luther College, 700 College Drive, Decorah, IA 52101. *Phone:* 563-387-1253. *E-mail:* mattca01@luther.edu. *Web site:* www.luther.edu/.

Maharishi University of Management
Fairfield, Iowa

Sustainability Initiatives Maharishi University of Management is a member of the Association for the Advancement of Sustainability in Higher Education (AASHE). This institution's president has signed the American College & University Presidents Climate Commitment.

Academics *Sustainability-focused undergraduate major(s):* Sustainable Living, Agriculture; Sustainable Living, CSA agriculture; Sustainable Living, Green Building; Sustainable Living, Policy Track; Sustainable Living, Renewable Energy. *Sustainability-focused graduate degree program(s):* Green MBA. *Sustainability courses and programs:* sustainability-focused course(s) or lecture series, sustainability-focused nonacademic certificate program(s).

Student Services and Green Events *Sustainability leadership:* sustainability coordinator/director, sustainability committee/advisory council, recycling manager, energy manager, sustainability-focused student government. *Student clubs and activities:* student club(s)/group(s) focused on sustainability. *Major sustainability events:* Eco Fair. *Housing and facilities:* on-campus organic garden for students.

Food Sustainable, organic, and/or locally produced foods available in on-campus dining facilities. Vegan and vegetarian dining options are available for every meal.

Transportation Provides a bike loan/rental program.

Buildings and Grounds *Percentage of institution's eligible buildings as of September 2008 meeting LEED and/or LEED-EB certification criteria:* 5%. *Campus grounds care:* uses water conservation devices; employs strategies to reduce light pollution; landscapes with native plant species; protects, restores, and/or creates habitat on campus.

Recycling *Programs and activities:* sustains a computer/technology recycling program; maintains an on-campus recycling center; sustains a pre-consumer food waste composting program; sustains a post-consumer food waste composting program; composts yard waste; reuses surplus department/office supplies; reuses chemicals; replaces paper materials with online alternatives. *Campus dining operations:* uses reusable dishware; uses bulk condiment dispensers and decreased packaging for to-go food service purchases.

Energy Currently uses or plans to use alternative sources of power (geothermal energy, solar energy, and wind energy); timers to regulate temperatures based on occupancy hours; and motion, infrared, and/or light sensors to reduce energy uses for lighting.

Purchasing Sustainability criteria used in purchasing include Energy Star (EPA).

Contact Director, Sustainable Living Department, Maharishi University of Management, 1000 North 4th Street, MR 782, Fairfield, IA 52557. *Phone:* 641-472-7000 Ext. 2139. *E-mail:* dfisher@mum.edu. *Web site:* www.mum.edu/.

Mount Mercy College
Cedar Rapids, Iowa

Student Services and Green Events *Sustainability leadership:* sustainability committee/advisory council, recycling manager.

Food Fair Trade coffee is used. Vegan and vegetarian dining options are available for every meal.

Transportation Provides public transportation access to local destinations and a bike loan/rental program.

Buildings and Grounds *Renovation and maintenance:* uses a Green Seal certified cleaning service. *Campus* *grounds care:* landscapes with native plant species; protects, restores, and/or creates habitat on campus.

Recycling *Programs and activities:* sustains a computer/technology recycling program; maintains an on-campus recycling center; composts yard waste; reuses surplus department/office supplies; replaces paper materials with online alternatives. *Campus dining operations:* uses reusable dishware; operates without trays; offers discounts for reusable mugs; uses bulk condiment dispensers and decreased packaging for to-go food service purchases.

Energy Currently uses or plans to use alternative sources of power; timers to regulate temperatures based on occupancy hours; LED lighting; and energy-related performance contracting.

Purchasing Sustainability criteria used in purchasing include Energy Star (EPA), Green Cleaning Products (Green Seal/Environmental Choice certified), and Forest Stewardship Council (FSC) or American Forest and Paper Association's Sustainable Forestry Initiative (SFI) paper.

Contact Director, Advance Program/Chair, Sustainability Committee, Mount Mercy College, 1330 Elmhurst Drive NE, Cedar Rapids, IA 52402. *E-mail:* catkins@mtmercy.edu. *Web site:* www.mtmercy.edu/.

St. Ambrose University
Davenport, Iowa

Student Services and Green Events *Sustainability leadership:* sustainability committee/advisory council, recycling manager, energy manager.

Food Vegan and vegetarian dining options are available for every meal.

Transportation Provides public transportation access to local destinations.

Buildings and Grounds *Campus grounds care:* uses water conservation devices; employs strategies to reduce light pollution; landscapes with native plant species.

Recycling *Programs and activities:* maintains an on-campus recycling center; replaces paper materials with online alternatives. *Campus dining operations:* uses reusable dishware; uses bulk condiment dispensers and decreased packaging for to-go food service purchases.

Energy Currently uses or plans to use timers to regulate temperatures based on occupancy hours; motion, infrared, and/or light sensors to reduce energy uses for lighting; and LED lighting.

Purchasing Sustainability criteria used in purchasing include Energy Star (EPA) and Green Cleaning Products (Green Seal/Environmental Choice certified).

Contact St. Ambrose University, 518 West Locust Street, Davenport, IA 52803-2898. *Phone:* 563-333-6000. *Web site:* www.sau.edu/.

The University of Iowa
Iowa City, Iowa

Academics *Sustainability-focused undergraduate major(s):* Environmental Engineering and Sciences (BS), Environmental Sciences (BS), Environmental Studies in Geography (BA, BS). *Sustainability-focused graduate degree program(s):* Environmental Engineering and Sciences (MS), Environmental Engineering and Sciences (PhD), Geography (MS), Geography (PhD). *Sustainability courses and programs:* sustainability-focused course(s) or lecture series.

Student Services and Green Events *Sustainability leadership:* sustainability coordinator/director, sustainability

committee/advisory council, recycling manager, energy manager, sustainability-focused student government. *Student clubs and activities:* Campus Climate Challenge, Public Interest Research Group (PIRG) chapter on campus, student club(s)/group(s) focused on sustainability, outreach materials available about on-campus sustainability efforts. *Major sustainability events:* Annual Energy Expo, Annual Earth Week events, National Teach-In. *Housing and facilities:* sustainability-themed housing, model dorm room that demonstrates sustainable living principles, on-campus organic garden for students.

Food Sustainable, organic, and/or locally produced foods available in on-campus dining facilities. Vegan and vegetarian dining options are available for every meal.

Transportation Provides free on-campus transportation (bus or other), public transportation access to local destinations, a car sharing program, and incentives to carpool or use public transportation.

Buildings and Grounds *Renovation and maintenance:* registered for LEED certification for new construction and/or renovation. *Campus grounds care:* uses water conservation devices; employs strategies to reduce light pollution; landscapes with native plant species; protects, restores, and/or creates habitat on campus.

Recycling *Programs and activities:* sustains a computer/technology recycling program; sustains a pre-consumer food waste composting program; composts yard waste; reuses surplus department/office supplies; reuses chemicals; replaces paper materials with online alternatives; limits free printing in computer labs and libraries. *Campus dining operations:* uses reusable dishware; offers discounts for reusable mugs; uses bulk condiment dispensers and decreased packaging for to-go food service purchases.

Energy Currently uses or plans to use alternative sources of power (biomass energy and solar energy); timers to regulate temperatures based on occupancy hours; motion, infrared, and/or light sensors to reduce energy uses for lighting; and LED lighting. Participates in College & University Green Power Challenge activities.

Purchasing Sustainability criteria used in purchasing include Energy Star (EPA) and Green Cleaning Products (Green Seal/Environmental Choice certified).

Contact Director, Office of Sustainability, The University of Iowa, 210 University Services Building, Iowa City, IA 52242. *Phone:* 319-355-5500. *E-mail:* elizabeth-christiansen@uiowa.edu. *Web site:* www.uiowa.edu/.

University of Northern Iowa
Cedar Falls, Iowa

Sustainability Initiatives University of Northern Iowa is a member of the Association for the Advancement of Sustainability in Higher Education (AASHE) and a signatory to the Talloires Declaration.

Academics *Sustainability courses and programs:* sustainability-focused course(s) or lecture series, noncredit sustainability course(s).

Student Services and Green Events *Sustainability leadership:* sustainability committee/advisory council, recycling manager, energy manager, sustainability-focused student government. *Student clubs and activities:* Public Interest Research Group (PIRG) chapter on campus, student club(s)/group(s) focused on sustainability, outreach materials available about on-campus sustainability efforts. *Major sustainability events:* Focus the Nation (January), National Wildlife Federation "Chill Out" webcast event in April, Earth

Day. *Housing and facilities:* sustainability-themed housing, student-run café that serves environmentally or socially preferable foods.

Food Sustainable, organic, and/or locally produced foods available in on-campus dining facilities. Fair Trade coffee is used. Vegan and vegetarian dining options are available for every meal.

Transportation Provides free on-campus transportation (bus or other) and public transportation access to local destinations.

Buildings and Grounds *Campus grounds care:* uses water conservation devices; employs strategies to reduce light pollution; landscapes with native plant species; protects, restores, and/or creates habitat on campus; applies to its grounds only pesticides and fertilizers allowable under the U.S. Department of Agriculture's standards for crop production.

Recycling *Programs and activities:* sustains a computer/technology recycling program; maintains an on-campus recycling center; composts yard waste; reuses surplus department/office supplies; reuses chemicals; replaces paper materials with online alternatives. *Campus dining operations:* uses reusable dishware; offers discounts for reusable mugs.

Energy Currently uses or plans to use alternative sources of power (geothermal energy and solar energy); timers to regulate temperatures based on occupancy hours; motion, infrared, and/or light sensors to reduce energy uses for lighting; and LED lighting.

Purchasing Sustainability criteria used in purchasing include Green Cleaning Products (Green Seal/Environmental Choice certified) and Forest Stewardship Council (FSC) or American Forest and Paper Association's Sustainable Forestry Initiative (SFI) paper.

Contact Vice President for Administration and Finance, University of Northern Iowa, 122 Lang Hall, Cedar Falls, IA 50614. *Phone:* 319-273-2382. *E-mail:* tom.schellhardt@uni.edu. *Web site:* www.uni.edu/.

Wartburg College
Waverly, Iowa

Student Services and Green Events *Sustainability leadership:* sustainability coordinator/director, sustainability committee/advisory council, sustainability-focused student government. *Student clubs and activities:* student club(s)/group(s) focused on sustainability. *Major sustainability events:* Go Green Fair, Robert F. Kennedy Jr. Symposia on environmental stewardship, video festival on environmental issues.

Food Sustainable, organic, and/or locally produced foods available in on-campus dining facilities. Fair Trade coffee is used. Vegan and vegetarian dining options are available for every meal.

Transportation Provides a bike loan/rental program.

Buildings and Grounds *Renovation and maintenance:* registered for LEED certification for new construction and/or renovation. *Campus grounds care:* uses water conservation devices; landscapes with native plant species.

Recycling *Programs and activities:* sustains a computer/technology recycling program; maintains an on-campus recycling center; sustains a pre-consumer food waste composting program; replaces paper materials with online alternatives; limits free printing in computer labs and libraries. *Campus dining operations:* uses reusable dishware; operates without trays; offers discounts for reusable mugs; uses bulk condiment dispensers and decreased packaging for to-go food service purchases.

Energy Currently uses or plans to use alternative sources of power (wind energy).

Purchasing Sustainability criteria used in purchasing include Energy Star (EPA) and Green Cleaning Products (Green Seal/Environmental Choice certified).

Contact Campus Sustainability Officer/Assistant Professor of Social Work, Wartburg College, 100 Wartburg Boulevard, Waverly, IA 50677. *Phone:* 319-352-8239. *Fax:* 319-352-8583. *E-mail:* tammy.faux@wartburg.edu. *Web site:* www.wartburg.edu/.

Kansas

MidAmerica Nazarene University
Olathe, Kansas

Student Services and Green Events *Sustainability leadership:* recycling manager. *Housing and facilities:* on-campus organic garden for students.

Food Fair Trade coffee is used. Vegan and vegetarian dining options are available for every meal.

Buildings and Grounds *Campus grounds care:* uses water conservation devices.

Recycling *Programs and activities:* sustains a computer/technology recycling program; maintains an on-campus recycling center.

Contact MidAmerica Nazarene University, 2030 East College Way, Olathe, KS 66062-1899. *Phone:* 913-782-3750. *Web site:* www.mnu.edu/.

Newman University
Wichita, Kansas

Student Services and Green Events *Sustainability leadership:* sustainability coordinator/director, sustainability committee/advisory council, energy manager.

Food Fair Trade coffee is used. Vegan and vegetarian dining options are available for every meal.

Transportation Provides public transportation access to local destinations.

Buildings and Grounds *Campus grounds care:* uses water conservation devices; employs strategies to reduce light pollution; landscapes with native plant species; applies to its grounds only pesticides and fertilizers allowable under the U.S. Department of Agriculture's standards for crop production.

Recycling *Programs and activities:* sustains a computer/technology recycling program; reuses surplus department/office supplies; reuses chemicals; replaces paper materials with online alternatives. *Campus dining operations:* uses reusable dishware; uses bulk condiment dispensers and decreased packaging for to-go food service purchases.

Energy Currently uses or plans to use timers to regulate temperatures based on occupancy hours; motion, infrared, and/or light sensors to reduce energy uses for lighting; LED lighting; and energy-related performance contracting.

Purchasing Sustainability criteria used in purchasing include Energy Star (EPA) and Green Cleaning Products (Green Seal/Environmental Choice certified).

Contact Associate Professor of Chemistry, Newman University, 3100 McCormick, Wichita, KS 67213. *Phone:* 316-942-4291 Ext. 2109. *E-mail:* leybaj@newmanu.edu. *Web site:* www.newmanu.edu/.

Southwestern College
Winfield, Kansas

Sustainability Initiatives Southwestern College's president has signed the American College & University Presidents Climate Commitment.

Academics *Sustainability courses and programs:* sustainability-focused course(s) or lecture series, noncredit sustainability course(s), sustainability-focused nonacademic certificate program(s).

Student Services and Green Events *Sustainability leadership:* sustainability coordinator/director, sustainability committee/advisory council, recycling manager. *Student clubs and activities:* student club(s)/group(s) focused on sustainability. *Major sustainability events:* Kansas Envirothon 2009, RecycleMania.

Buildings and Grounds *Campus grounds care:* uses water conservation devices; landscapes with native plant species.

Recycling *Events and organizations:* RecycleMania. *Programs and activities:* sustains a computer/technology recycling program; maintains an on-campus recycling center; sustains a post-consumer food waste composting program; composts yard waste; replaces paper materials with online alternatives. *Campus dining operations:* uses reusable dishware; uses bulk condiment dispensers and decreased packaging for to-go food service purchases.

Energy Currently uses or plans to use motion, infrared, and/or light sensors to reduce energy uses for lighting.

Purchasing Sustainability criteria used in purchasing include Energy Star (EPA) and Green Cleaning Products (Green Seal/Environmental Choice certified).

Contact Green Team Director, Southwestern College, 100 College Street, Winfield, KS 67156. *Phone:* 620-229-6311. *E-mail:* jason.speegle@sckans.edu. *Web site:* www.sckans.edu/.

The University of Kansas
Lawrence, Kansas

Sustainability Initiatives The University of Kansas is a member of the Association for the Advancement of Sustainability in Higher Education (AASHE). The University of Kansas has Green Fees (optional/required) dedicated to sustainability initiatives.

Academics *Sustainability courses and programs:* sustainability-focused course(s) or lecture series.

Student Services and Green Events *Sustainability leadership:* sustainability coordinator/director, sustainability committee/advisory council, recycling manager, energy manager, sustainability-focused student government. *Student clubs and activities:* student club(s)/group(s) focused on sustainability. *Major sustainability events:* Campus Sustainability Day, Focus the Nation/National Teach-In on Global Warming, KU Energy Fair. *Housing and facilities:* on-campus organic garden for students.

Food Sustainable, organic, and/or locally produced foods available in on-campus dining facilities. Fair Trade coffee is used. Vegan and vegetarian dining options are available for every meal.

Transportation Provides free on-campus transportation (bus or other), public transportation access to local destinations, and incentives to carpool or use public transportation.

Buildings and Grounds *Campus grounds care:* uses water conservation devices; protects, restores, and/or creates habitat on campus.

Recycling *Events and organizations:* RecycleMania. *Programs and activities:* sustains a computer/technology recycling program; maintains an on-campus recycling center; composts yard waste; reuses surplus department/office supplies; reuses chemicals; replaces paper materials with online alternatives; limits free printing in computer labs and libraries. *Campus dining operations:* uses reusable dishware; operates without trays; offers discounts for reusable mugs; uses bulk condiment dispensers and decreased packaging for to-go food service purchases.

Energy Currently uses or plans to use alternative sources of power (geothermal energy); timers to regulate temperatures based on occupancy hours; motion, infrared, and/or light sensors to reduce energy uses for lighting; vending machine motion sensors; and energy-related performance contracting.

Contact Director, The University of Kansas, KU Center for Sustainability, 1246 West Campus Road, Room 301, Lawrence, KS 66045. *Phone:* 785-864-5804. *E-mail:* sustainability@ku.edu. *Web site:* www.ku.edu.

Wichita State University
Wichita, Kansas

Academics *Sustainability courses and programs:* sustainability-focused course(s) or lecture series.

Student Services and Green Events *Sustainability leadership:* recycling manager.

Transportation Provides public transportation access to local destinations.

Buildings and Grounds *Campus grounds care:* uses water conservation devices; landscapes with native plant species.

Recycling *Programs and activities:* sustains a computer/technology recycling program; maintains an on-campus recycling center; composts yard waste.

Energy Currently uses or plans to use motion, infrared, and/or light sensors to reduce energy uses for lighting; LED lighting; vending machine motion sensors; and energy-related performance contracting.

Contact Wichita State University, 1845 North Fairmount, Wichita, KS 67260. *Phone:* 316-978-3456. *Web site:* www.wichita.edu/.

Kentucky

Centre College
Danville, Kentucky

Sustainability Initiatives Centre College's president has signed the American College & University Presidents Climate Commitment. Centre College has Green Fees (optional/required) dedicated to sustainability initiatives.

Academics *Sustainability courses and programs:* sustainability-focused course(s) or lecture series.

Student Services and Green Events *Sustainability leadership:* sustainability committee/advisory council, recycling manager, sustainability-focused student government.

Food Fair Trade coffee is used. Vegan and vegetarian dining options are available for every meal.

Transportation Provides a bike loan/rental program.

Buildings and Grounds *Percentage of institution's eligible buildings as of September 2008 meeting LEED and/or LEED-EB certification criteria:* 6%. *Renovation and maintenance:* registered for LEED certification for new construction and/or renovation. *Campus grounds care:* uses water conservation devices.

Recycling *Events and organizations:* RecycleMania. *Programs and activities:* sustains a computer/technology recycling program; maintains an on-campus recycling center; reuses surplus department/office supplies; replaces paper materials with online alternatives; limits free printing in computer labs and libraries. *Campus dining operations:* operates without trays; offers discounts for reusable mugs; uses bulk condiment dispensers and decreased packaging for to-go food service purchases.

Energy Currently uses or plans to use timers to regulate temperatures based on occupancy hours; motion, infrared, and/or light sensors to reduce energy uses for lighting; LED lighting; and energy-related performance contracting.

Purchasing Sustainability criteria used in purchasing include Energy Star (EPA) and Green Cleaning Products (Green Seal/Environmental Choice certified).

Contact Chair, Presidents Climate Commitment Committee, Centre College, 600 West Walnut, Danville, KY 40422. *Phone:* 859-238-5414. *E-mail:* miles@centre.edu. *Web site:* www.centre.edu/.

Kentucky Wesleyan College
Owensboro, Kentucky

Student Services and Green Events *Sustainability leadership:* sustainability coordinator/director, sustainability committee/advisory council.

Food Vegan and vegetarian dining options are available for every meal.

Transportation Provides public transportation access to local destinations.

Buildings and Grounds *Campus grounds care:* uses water conservation devices; landscapes with native plant species.

Recycling *Programs and activities:* sustains a computer/technology recycling program; maintains an on-campus recycling center; reuses surplus department/office supplies; replaces paper materials with online alternatives; limits free printing in computer labs and libraries. *Campus dining operations:* uses reusable dishware; uses bulk condiment dispensers and decreased packaging for to-go food service purchases.

Energy Currently uses or plans to use timers to regulate temperatures based on occupancy hours; motion, infrared, and/or light sensors to reduce energy uses for lighting; LED lighting; and energy-related performance contracting.

Purchasing Sustainability criteria used in purchasing include Energy Star (EPA) and Green Cleaning Products (Green Seal/Environmental Choice certified).

Contact Director of Facilities, Kentucky Wesleyan College, 3000 Frederica, Owensboro, KY 42301. *Phone:* 270-852-3324. *E-mail:* dknight@kwc.edu. *Web site:* www.kwc.edu/.

Murray State University
Murray, Kentucky

Food Sustainable, organic, and/or locally produced foods available in on-campus dining facilities.

Recycling *Programs and activities:* maintains an on-campus recycling center.

Contact Murray State University, 113 Sparks Hall, Murray, KY 42071. *Phone:* 270-762-3011. *Web site:* www.murraystate.edu/.

University of Kentucky
Lexington, Kentucky

Sustainability Initiatives University of Kentucky has Green Fees (optional/required) dedicated to sustainability initiatives.

Academics *Sustainability-focused undergraduate major(s):* Natural Resource and Conservation Management (BA, BS), Sustainable Agriculture (BS). *Sustainability courses and programs:* sustainability-focused course(s) or lecture series.

Student Services and Green Events *Sustainability leadership:* sustainability committee/advisory council, recycling manager, energy manager, sustainability-focused student government. *Student clubs and activities:* student club(s)/group(s) focused on sustainability. *Major sustainability events:* Big Blue Goes Green: Annual Sustainability Showcase, Earthdays in the Bluegrass, Sustainability Lecture Series. *Housing and facilities:* sustainability-themed housing, on-campus organic garden for students.

Food Sustainable, organic, and/or locally produced foods available in on-campus dining facilities. Fair Trade coffee is used. Vegan and vegetarian dining options are available for every meal.

Transportation Provides free on-campus transportation (bus or other), a bike loan/rental program, and incentives to carpool or use public transportation.

Buildings and Grounds *Renovation and maintenance:* uses a Green Seal certified cleaning service. *Campus grounds care:* uses water conservation devices; employs strategies to reduce light pollution; landscapes with native plant species.

Recycling *Events and organizations:* RecycleMania. *Programs and activities:* sustains a computer/technology recycling program; sustains a pre-consumer food waste composting program; composts yard waste; reuses surplus department/office supplies; reuses chemicals; replaces paper materials with online alternatives; limits free printing in computer labs and libraries. *Campus dining operations:* operates without trays; offers discounts for reusable mugs; uses bulk condiment dispensers and decreased packaging for to-go food service purchases.

Energy Currently uses or plans to use timers to regulate temperatures based on occupancy hours; motion, infrared, and/or light sensors to reduce energy uses for lighting; LED lighting; and energy-related performance contracting.

Purchasing Sustainability criteria used in purchasing include Green Cleaning Products (Green Seal/Environmental Choice certified).

Contact Residence Life Sustainabilty Coordinator, University of Kentucky, 537 Patterson Office Tower, University of Kentucky, Lexington, KY 40506. *Phone:* 859-257-2003. *Fax:* 859-323-0003. *E-mail:* dstedd0@uky.edu. *Web site:* www.uky.edu/.

University of Louisville
Louisville, Kentucky

Sustainability Initiatives University of Louisville's president has signed the American College & University Presidents Climate Commitment. University of Louisville has Green Fees (optional/required) dedicated to sustainability initiatives.

Academics *Sustainability-focused graduate degree program(s):* Biology (PhD), Public Health Sciences (PhD). *Sustainability courses and programs:* sustainability-focused course(s) or lecture series.

Student Services and Green Events *Sustainability leadership:* sustainability coordinator/director, sustainability committee/advisory council, recycling manager, energy manager. *Student clubs and activities:* student club(s)/group(s) focused on sustainability. *Major sustainability events:* Earth Day, environmental awareness fair, Sustainability Day (October).

Food Sustainable, organic, and/or locally produced foods available in on-campus dining facilities. Fair Trade coffee is used. Vegan and vegetarian dining options are available for every meal.

Transportation Provides free on-campus transportation (bus or other), public transportation access to local destinations, and incentives to carpool or use public transportation.

Buildings and Grounds *Percentage of institution's eligible buildings as of September 2008 meeting LEED and/or LEED-EB certification criteria:* 2%. *Renovation and maintenance:* registered for LEED certification for new construction and/or renovation; uses a Green Seal certified cleaning service. *Campus grounds care:* landscapes with native plant species; protects, restores, and/or creates habitat on campus.

Recycling *Events and organizations:* RecycleMania. *Programs and activities:* sustains a computer/technology recycling program; sustains a post-consumer food waste composting program; composts yard waste; reuses surplus department/office supplies; replaces paper materials with online alternatives; limits free printing in computer labs and libraries. *Campus dining operations:* operates without trays.

Energy Currently uses or plans to use alternative sources of power (solar energy); timers to regulate temperatures based on occupancy hours; motion, infrared, and/or light sensors to reduce energy uses for lighting; LED lighting; vending machine motion sensors; and energy-related performance contracting.

Purchasing Sustainability criteria used in purchasing include Energy Star (EPA), Green Electronics Council (GEC) Electronic Product Environmental Assessment Tool (EPEAT) Silver or Gold, Green Cleaning Products (Green Seal/Environmental Choice certified), and Forest Stewardship Council (FSC) or American Forest and Paper Association's Sustainable Forestry Initiative (SFI) paper.

Contact Vice President for Business Affairs, University of Louisville, 108 Grawemeyer Hall, Louisville, KY 40292. *Phone:* 502-852-6163. *E-mail:* larry.owsley@louisville.edu. *Web site:* www.louisville.edu/.

Western Kentucky University
Bowling Green, Kentucky

Sustainability Initiatives Western Kentucky University is a signatory to the Talloires Declaration.

Academics *Sustainability courses and programs:* sustainability-focused course(s) or lecture series.

Student Services and Green Events *Sustainability leadership:* sustainability coordinator/director, sustainability committee/advisory council, recycling manager, energy manager, sustainability-focused student government. *Student clubs and activities:* student club(s)/group(s) focused on sustainability, outreach materials available about on-campus sustainability efforts. *Major sustainability events:* Annual Earth Day Festival, host of Campus Community Partnerships for Sustainability Conference 2009, Focus the Nation National Teach-In.

Food Fair Trade coffee is used. Vegan and vegetarian dining options are available for every meal.

Transportation Provides free on-campus transportation (bus or other), public transportation access to local destinations, a bike loan/rental program, a car sharing program, and incentives to carpool or use public transportation.

Buildings and Grounds *Renovation and maintenance:* registered for LEED certification for new construction and/or renovation; uses a Green Seal certified cleaning service. *Campus grounds care:* protects, restores, and/or creates habitat on campus.

Recycling *Events and organizations:* RecycleMania. *Programs and activities:* maintains an on-campus recycling center; composts yard waste; reuses surplus department/office supplies; replaces paper materials with online alternatives. *Campus dining operations:* uses reusable dishware; operates without trays; offers discounts for reusable mugs; uses bulk condiment dispensers and decreased packaging for to-go food service purchases.

Energy Currently uses or plans to use alternative sources of power; timers to regulate temperatures based on occupancy hours; motion, infrared, and/or light sensors to reduce energy uses for lighting; LED lighting; vending machine motion sensors; and energy-related performance contracting.

Purchasing Sustainability criteria used in purchasing include Green Cleaning Products (Green Seal/Environmental Choice certified).

Contact Sustainability Coordinator, Western Kentucky University, 1906 College Heights Boulevard, #11091, Bowling Green, KY 42101. *Phone:* 270-745-2508. *Fax:* 270-745-6458. *E-mail:* christian.ryan-downing@wku.edu. *Web site:* www.wku.edu/.

Louisiana

Louisiana State University and Agricultural and Mechanical College
Baton Rouge, Louisiana

Academics *Sustainability courses and programs:* sustainability-focused course(s) or lecture series, noncredit sustainability course(s).

Student Services and Green Events *Sustainability leadership:* sustainability coordinator/director, sustainability committee/advisory council, recycling manager, energy manager, sustainability-focused student government. *Housing and facilities:* on-campus organic garden for students.

Food Vegan and vegetarian dining options are available for every meal.

Transportation Provides free on-campus transportation (bus or other), public transportation access to local destinations, and a bike loan/rental program.

Buildings and Grounds *Renovation and maintenance:* uses a Green Seal certified cleaning service.

Recycling *Events and organizations:* RecycleMania. *Programs and activities:* sustains a computer/technology recycling program; composts yard waste; reuses chemicals; replaces paper materials with online alternatives; limits free printing in computer labs and libraries. *Campus dining operations:* uses reusable dishware; offers discounts for reusable mugs; uses bulk condiment dispensers and decreased packaging for to-go food service purchases.

Energy Currently uses or plans to use timers to regulate temperatures based on occupancy hours; motion, infrared, and/or light sensors to reduce energy uses for lighting; LED lighting; and energy-related performance contracting.

Purchasing Sustainability criteria used in purchasing include Green Cleaning Products (Green Seal/Environmental Choice certified).

Contact Manager, Campus Sustainability, Louisiana State University and Agricultural and Mechanical College, Facility Services, Room 130A, Baton Rouge, LA 70803. *Phone:* 225-578-2630. *E-mail:* scribner@lsu.edu. *Web site:* www.lsu.edu/.

Loyola University New Orleans
New Orleans, Louisiana

Sustainability Initiatives Loyola University New Orleans is a signatory to the Talloires Declaration. This institution's president has signed the American College & University Presidents Climate Commitment.

Academics *Sustainability courses and programs:* sustainability-focused course(s) or lecture series.

Student Services and Green Events *Sustainability leadership:* sustainability committee/advisory council, recycling manager, energy manager, sustainability-focused student government. *Student clubs and activities:* Campus Climate Challenge, student club(s)/group(s) focused on sustainability. *Major sustainability events:* Green Salon, Gaia Fest, Hurricane Katrina recovery projects.

Food Sustainable, organic, and/or locally produced foods available in on-campus dining facilities. Fair Trade coffee is used. Vegan and vegetarian dining options are available for every meal.

Buildings and Grounds *Renovation and maintenance:* registered for LEED certification for new construction and/or renovation. *Campus grounds care:* uses water conservation devices; landscapes with native plant species; applies to its grounds only pesticides and fertilizers allowable under the U.S. Department of Agriculture's standards for crop production.

Recycling *Events and organizations:* WasteWise (EPA). *Programs and activities:* reuses chemicals; replaces paper materials with online alternatives. *Campus dining operations:* uses reusable dishware; operates without trays; offers discounts for reusable mugs; uses bulk condiment dispensers and decreased packaging for to-go food service purchases.

Purchasing Sustainability criteria used in purchasing include Energy Star (EPA).

Contact Director, Loyola University New Orleans, Center for Environmental Communication, New Orleans, LA 70118. *Phone:* 504-865-2107. *Fax:* 504-865-2333. *E-mail:* rathomas@loyno.edu. *Web site:* www.loyno.edu/.

Maine

Bates College
Lewiston, Maine

Sustainability Initiatives Bates College's president has signed the American College & University Presidents Climate Commitment.

Academics *Sustainability-focused undergraduate major(s):* Environmental Studies (BA). *Sustainability courses and programs:* sustainability-focused course(s) or lecture series.

Student Services and Green Events *Sustainability leadership:* sustainability coordinator/director, sustainability committee/advisory council. *Student clubs and activities:* student club(s)/group(s) focused on sustainability, outreach materials available about on-campus sustainability efforts. *Major sustainability events:* RecycleMania, Trashion Show, 5th annual Maine State Climate Summit for students. *Housing and facilities:* sustainability-themed housing, on-campus organic garden for students.

Food Sustainable, organic, and/or locally produced foods available in on-campus dining facilities. Fair Trade coffee is used. Vegan and vegetarian dining options are available for every meal.

Transportation Provides public transportation access to local destinations, a bike loan/rental program, and a car sharing program.

Buildings and Grounds *Renovation and maintenance:* uses a Green Seal certified cleaning service. *Campus grounds care:* uses water conservation devices.

Recycling *Events and organizations:* RecycleMania. *Programs and activities:* sustains a pre-consumer food waste composting program; sustains a post-consumer food waste composting program; reuses surplus department/office supplies. *Campus dining operations:* uses reusable dishware; offers discounts for reusable mugs; uses bulk condiment dispensers and decreased packaging for to-go food service purchases.

Energy Currently uses or plans to use motion, infrared, and/or light sensors to reduce energy uses for lighting and vending machine motion sensors.

Purchasing Sustainability criteria used in purchasing include Green Cleaning Products (Green Seal/Environmental Choice certified).

Contact Environmental Coordinator, Bates College, 147 Russell Street, Lewiston, ME 04240. *Phone:* 207-786-8367. *Fax:* 207-786-6026. *E-mail:* jrosenba@bates.edu. *Web site:* www.bates.edu/.

Bowdoin College
Brunswick, Maine

Sustainability Initiatives Bowdoin College's president has signed the American College & University Presidents Climate Commitment.

Academics *Sustainability-focused undergraduate major(s):* Environmental Studies. *Sustainability courses and programs:* sustainability-focused course(s) or lecture series.

Student Services and Green Events *Sustainability leadership:* sustainability coordinator/director, sustainability committee/advisory council, recycling manager. *Student clubs and activities:* Campus Climate Challenge, student club(s)/group(s) focused on sustainability, outreach materials available about on-campus sustainability efforts. *Major sustainability events:* "Polar Extremes: Changes in a Warming World". *Housing and facilities:* student-run café that serves environmentally or socially preferable foods, on-campus organic garden for students.

Food Sustainable, organic, and/or locally produced foods available in on-campus dining facilities. Fair Trade coffee is used. Vegan and vegetarian dining options are available for every meal.

Transportation Provides free on-campus transportation (bus or other), a bike loan/rental program, a car sharing program, and incentives to carpool or use public transportation.

Buildings and Grounds *Renovation and maintenance:* registered for LEED certification for new construction and/or renovation. *Campus grounds care:* uses water conservation devices; employs strategies to reduce light pollution; landscapes with native plant species; protects, restores, and/or creates habitat on campus.

Recycling *Events and organizations:* RecycleMania. *Programs and activities:* sustains a computer/technology recycling program; sustains a pre-consumer food waste composting program; sustains a post-consumer food waste composting program; composts yard waste; reuses surplus department/office supplies; reuses chemicals; replaces paper materials with online alternatives. *Campus dining operations:* uses reusable dishware; operates without trays; offers discounts for reusable mugs; uses bulk condiment dispensers and decreased packaging for to-go food service purchases.

Energy Currently uses or plans to use alternative sources of power (geothermal energy, hydroelectricity/water power, solar energy, and wind energy); timers to regulate temperatures based on occupancy hours; motion, infrared, and/or light sensors to reduce energy uses for lighting; LED lighting; and vending machine motion sensors. Participates in College & University Green Power Challenge activities.

Purchasing Sustainability criteria used in purchasing include Energy Star (EPA) and Green Electronics Council (GEC) Electronic Product Environmental Assessment Tool (EPEAT) Silver or Gold.

Contact Sustainability Coordinator, Bowdoin College, 3800 College Station Facilities Management, Brunswick, ME 04011. *Phone:* 207-725-3086. *Fax:* 207-725-3449. *E-mail:* cpayson@bowdoin.edu. *Web site:* www.bowdoin.edu/.

Colby College
Waterville, Maine

Sustainability Initiatives Colby College's president has signed the American College & University Presidents Climate Commitment.

Academics *Sustainability-focused undergraduate major(s):* Biology—Environmental Studies concentration (BA), Chemistry—Environmental Studies concentration (BA), Environmental Studies Policy (BA), Environmental Studies Science (BA). *Sustainability courses and programs:* sustainability-focused course(s) or lecture series, noncredit sustainability course(s).

Student Services and Green Events *Sustainability leadership:* sustainability committee/advisory council, recycling manager, energy manager. *Student clubs and activities:* Campus Climate Challenge, student club(s)/group(s) focused on sustainability, outreach materials available about on-campus sustainability efforts. *Major sustainability events:* Green Campus Summit, Rachel Carson Celebration, Sustainability Month, Earth Week. *Housing and facilities:* sustainability-themed housing, model dorm room that demonstrates sustainable living principles, on-campus organic garden for students.

Food Sustainable, organic, and/or locally produced foods available in on-campus dining facilities. Fair Trade coffee is used. Vegan and vegetarian dining options are available for every meal.

Transportation Provides free on-campus transportation (bus or other), public transportation access to local destinations, a bike loan/rental program, and a car sharing program.

Buildings and Grounds *Renovation and maintenance:* registered for LEED certification for new construction and/or renovation; uses a Green Seal certified cleaning service. *Campus grounds care:* uses water conservation devices; employs strategies to reduce light pollution; landscapes with native plant species; protects, restores, and/or creates habitat on campus.

Recycling *Events and organizations:* RecycleMania. *Programs and activities:* sustains a computer/technology recycling program; sustains a pre-consumer food waste composting program; sustains a post-consumer food waste composting program; composts yard waste; reuses surplus department/office supplies; replaces paper materials with online alternatives. *Campus dining operations:* uses reusable dishware; operates without trays; offers discounts for reusable mugs; uses bulk condiment dispensers and decreased packaging for to-go food service purchases.

Energy Currently uses or plans to use alternative sources of power (biomass energy, geothermal energy, hydroelectricity/

water power, and wind energy); timers to regulate temperatures based on occupancy hours; motion, infrared, and/or light sensors to reduce energy uses for lighting; LED lighting; vending machine motion sensors; and energy-related performance contracting.

Purchasing Sustainability criteria used in purchasing include Energy Star (EPA) and Green Cleaning Products (Green Seal/Environmental Choice certified).

Contact Environmental Program Manager, Colby College, 4950 Mayflower Hill, Waterville, ME 04901. *Phone:* 207-859-5022. *Fax:* 207-859-5005. *E-mail:* ddeblois@colby.edu. *Web site:* www.colby.edu/.

College of the Atlantic
Bar Harbor, Maine

Sustainability Initiatives College of the Atlantic is a member of the Association for the Advancement of Sustainability in Higher Education (AASHE) and a signatory to the Talloires Declaration. This institution's president has signed the American College & University Presidents Climate Commitment.

Academics *Sustainability-focused undergraduate major(s):* Human Ecology. *Sustainability-focused graduate degree program(s):* Human Ecology (MPhil). *Sustainability courses and programs:* sustainability-focused course(s) or lecture series.

Student Services and Green Events *Sustainability leadership:* sustainability coordinator/director, sustainability committee/advisory council, recycling manager, sustainability-focused student government. *Student clubs and activities:* Campus Climate Challenge, student club(s)/group(s) focused on sustainability, outreach materials available about on-campus sustainability efforts. *Major sustainability events:* Annual statewide Earth Day celebration. *Housing and facilities:* sustainability-themed housing, model dorm room that demonstrates sustainable living principles, student-run café that serves environmentally or socially preferable foods, on-campus organic garden for students.

Food Sustainable, organic, and/or locally produced foods available in on-campus dining facilities. Fair Trade coffee is used. Vegan and vegetarian dining options are available for every meal.

Transportation Provides a bike loan/rental program.

Buildings and Grounds *Percentage of institution's eligible buildings as of September 2008 meeting LEED and/or LEED-EB certification criteria:* 20%. *Campus grounds care:* uses water conservation devices; employs strategies to reduce light pollution; landscapes with native plant species; protects, restores, and/or creates habitat on campus; applies to its grounds only pesticides and fertilizers allowable under the U.S. Department of Agriculture's standards for crop production.

Recycling *Programs and activities:* sustains a computer/technology recycling program; maintains an on-campus recycling center; sustains a pre-consumer food waste composting program; sustains a post-consumer food waste composting program; composts yard waste; reuses surplus department/office supplies; reuses chemicals; replaces paper materials with online alternatives; limits free printing in computer labs and libraries. *Campus dining operations:* uses reusable dishware; operates without trays; offers discounts for reusable mugs; uses bulk condiment dispensers and decreased packaging for to-go food service purchases.

Energy Currently uses or plans to use alternative sources of power (biomass energy, hydroelectricity/water power, and solar energy); timers to regulate temperatures based on occupancy hours; motion, infrared, and/or light sensors to reduce energy uses for lighting; and LED lighting.

Purchasing Sustainability criteria used in purchasing include Energy Star (EPA), Green Cleaning Products (Green Seal/Environmental Choice certified), and Forest Stewardship Council (FSC) or American Forest and Paper Association's Sustainable Forestry Initiative (SFI) paper.

Contact Director of Sustainability, College of the Atlantic, 105 Eden Street, Bar Harbor, ME 04609. *Phone:* 207-288-5015 Ext. 430. *Fax:* 207-288-3780. *E-mail:* tenbroeck@coa.edu. *Web site:* www.coa.edu/.

Unity College
Unity, Maine

Sustainability Initiatives Unity College's president has signed the American College & University Presidents Climate Commitment.

Academics *Sustainability-focused undergraduate major(s):* Agriculture, Food, and Sustainability (BS); Sustainability Design and Technology (BS). *Sustainability courses and programs:* sustainability-focused course(s) or lecture series.

Student Services and Green Events *Sustainability leadership:* sustainability coordinator/director, sustainability committee/advisory council, recycling manager. *Student clubs and activities:* student club(s)/group(s) focused on sustainability. *Major sustainability events:* Teach-In on global warming and energy for the Energy Action Coalition's National Teach-In Day, Environmental Stewardship Fair, Environmental Career Fair, "Art of Stewardship" for sustainability art. *Housing and facilities:* sustainability-themed housing, student-run café that serves environmentally or socially preferable foods, on-campus organic garden for students.

Food Sustainable, organic, and/or locally produced foods available in on-campus dining facilities. Fair Trade coffee is used. Vegan and vegetarian dining options are available for every meal.

Transportation Provides public transportation access to local destinations.

Buildings and Grounds *Renovation and maintenance:* registered for LEED certification for new construction and/or renovation; uses a Green Seal certified cleaning service. *Campus grounds care:* uses water conservation devices; protects, restores, and/or creates habitat on campus.

Recycling *Events and organizations:* RecycleMania. *Programs and activities:* maintains an on-campus recycling center; composts yard waste; replaces paper materials with online alternatives. *Campus dining operations:* uses reusable dishware; operates without trays; offers discounts for reusable mugs; uses bulk condiment dispensers and decreased packaging for to-go food service purchases.

Energy Currently uses or plans to use alternative sources of power (biomass energy, hydroelectricity/water power, and solar energy); timers to regulate temperatures based on occupancy hours; and LED lighting.

Purchasing Sustainability criteria used in purchasing include Energy Star (EPA), Green Cleaning Products (Green Seal/Environmental Choice certified), and Forest Stewardship Council (FSC) or American Forest and Paper Association's Sustainable Forestry Initiative (SFI) paper.

Contact Interim Sustainability Coordinator, Unity College, 90 Quaker Hill Road, Unity, ME 04988. *Phone:* 207-948-3131. *E-mail:* awitham@unity.edu. *Web site:* www.unity.edu/.

University of Maine
Orono, Maine

Sustainability Initiatives University of Maine's president has signed the American College & University Presidents Climate Commitment.

Academics *Sustainability-focused undergraduate major(s):* Ecology and Environmental Science (BS), Forest Ecosystem Science and Conservation (BS), Resource Economics and Policy (BS), Sustainable Agriculture (BS), Wildlife Ecology (BS). *Sustainability-focused graduate degree program(s):* Business Administration Sustainability Focus (MBA), Climate Change Institute (MS), Conservation Biology (MS, PhD), Ecology and Environmental Science (MS, PhD), Forestry (MS, PhD), Peace Studies (MA). *Sustainability courses and programs:* sustainability-focused course(s) or lecture series.

Student Services and Green Events *Sustainability leadership:* sustainability coordinator/director, sustainability committee/advisory council, recycling manager, energy manager. *Student clubs and activities:* Public Interest Research Group (PIRG) chapter on campus, student club(s)/group(s) focused on sustainability, outreach materials available about on-campus sustainability efforts. *Major sustainability events:* CC21: Choices for the 21st Century An Interactive Forum and Environmental Festival. *Housing and facilities:* on-campus organic garden for students.

Food Sustainable, organic, and/or locally produced foods available in on-campus dining facilities. Fair Trade coffee is used. Vegan and vegetarian dining options are available for every meal.

Transportation Provides free on-campus transportation (bus or other), public transportation access to local destinations, a bike loan/rental program, and incentives to carpool or use public transportation.

Buildings and Grounds *Renovation and maintenance:* registered for LEED certification for new construction and/or renovation. *Campus grounds care:* uses water conservation devices; landscapes with native plant species; protects, restores, and/or creates habitat on campus.

Recycling *Events and organizations:* RecycleMania. *Programs and activities:* sustains a computer/technology recycling program; maintains an on-campus recycling center; sustains a pre-consumer food waste composting program; sustains a post-consumer food waste composting program; composts yard waste; reuses chemicals; replaces paper materials with online alternatives. *Campus dining operations:* operates without trays; offers discounts for reusable mugs; uses bulk condiment dispensers and decreased packaging for to-go food service purchases.

Energy Currently uses or plans to use alternative sources of power (hydroelectricity/water power) and motion, infrared, and/or light sensors to reduce energy uses for lighting.

Purchasing Sustainability criteria used in purchasing include Energy Star (EPA).

Contact Sustainability Coordinator, University of Maine, 5703 Alumni Hall, Suite 118, Orono, ME 04469-5703. *Phone:* 207-581-1571. *E-mail:* misa.saros@umit.maine.edu. *Web site:* www.umaine.edu/.

University of Maine at Augusta
Augusta, Maine

Sustainability Initiatives University of Maine at Augusta is a member of the Association for the Advancement of Sustainability in Higher Education (AASHE). This institution's president has signed the American College & University Presidents Climate Commitment.

Academics *Sustainability courses and programs:* sustainability-focused course(s) or lecture series.

Student Services and Green Events *Sustainability leadership:* sustainability committee/advisory council, recycling manager. *Student clubs and activities:* student club(s)/group(s) focused on sustainability, outreach materials available about on-campus sustainability efforts. *Major sustainability events:* Convocation, Energy Forum, academic theme events.

Food Sustainable, organic, and/or locally produced foods available in on-campus dining facilities. Fair Trade coffee is used. Vegan and vegetarian dining options are available for every meal.

Transportation Provides public transportation access to local destinations.

Buildings and Grounds *Campus grounds care:* employs strategies to reduce light pollution; landscapes with native plant species; protects, restores, and/or creates habitat on campus.

Recycling *Programs and activities:* sustains a computer/technology recycling program; maintains an on-campus recycling center; reuses surplus department/office supplies; replaces paper materials with online alternatives; limits free printing in computer labs and libraries. *Campus dining operations:* operates without trays; offers discounts for reusable mugs; uses bulk condiment dispensers and decreased packaging for to-go food service purchases.

Energy Currently uses or plans to use alternative sources of power (biomass energy, hydroelectricity/water power, and wind energy); timers to regulate temperatures based on occupancy hours; motion, infrared, and/or light sensors to reduce energy uses for lighting; LED lighting; and vending machine motion sensors.

Purchasing Sustainability criteria used in purchasing include Energy Star (EPA).

Contact Professor of Natural Science, University of Maine at Augusta, Jewett Hall, University Heights, Augusta, ME 04330. *Phone:* 207-621-3279. *E-mail:* sheilab@maine.edu. *Web site:* www.uma.maine.edu/.

University of Maine at Machias
Machias, Maine

Sustainability Initiatives University of Maine at Machias's president has signed the American College & University Presidents Climate Commitment.

Academics *Sustainability-focused undergraduate major(s):* Biology (BA), Environmental Studies (BS), Marine Biology (BS), Recreation and Tourism Management (BS). *Sustainability courses and programs:* sustainability-focused course(s) or lecture series.

Student Services and Green Events *Sustainability leadership:* sustainability committee/advisory council, recycling manager, sustainability-focused student government. *Student clubs and activities:* student club(s)/group(s) focused on sustainability. *Major sustainability events:* Earth Day Festival and Open House, occasional community workshops. *Housing and facilities:* on-campus organic garden for students.

Food Sustainable, organic, and/or locally produced foods available in on-campus dining facilities. Fair Trade coffee is used. Vegan and vegetarian dining options are available for every meal.

Buildings and Grounds *Renovation and maintenance:* uses a Green Seal certified cleaning service. *Campus grounds care:* uses water conservation devices; landscapes

with native plant species; protects, restores, and/or creates habitat on campus; applies to its grounds only pesticides and fertilizers allowable under the U.S. Department of Agriculture's standards for crop production.

Recycling *Events and organizations:* RecycleMania. *Programs and activities:* sustains a computer/technology recycling program; maintains an on-campus recycling center; sustains a pre-consumer food waste composting program; sustains a post-consumer food waste composting program; composts yard waste; replaces paper materials with online alternatives; limits free printing in computer labs and libraries. *Campus dining operations:* uses reusable dishware; operates without trays; offers discounts for reusable mugs; uses bulk condiment dispensers and decreased packaging for to-go food service purchases.

Energy Currently uses or plans to use alternative sources of power; timers to regulate temperatures based on occupancy hours; and motion, infrared, and/or light sensors to reduce energy uses for lighting.

Purchasing Sustainability criteria used in purchasing include Energy Star (EPA) and Green Cleaning Products (Green Seal/Environmental Choice certified).

Contact Director of Student Life, University of Maine at Machias, Machias, ME 04654. *Phone:* 207-255-1412. *E-mail:* kpage@maine.edu. *Web site:* www.umm.maine.edu/.

University of Southern Maine
Portland, Maine

Sustainability Initiatives University of Southern Maine is a signatory to the Talloires Declaration. This institution's president has signed the American College & University Presidents Climate Commitment.

Academics *Sustainability-focused graduate degree program(s):* Community Planning and Development (MA). *Sustainability courses and programs:* sustainability-focused course(s) or lecture series, sustainability-focused nonacademic certificate program(s).

Student Services and Green Events *Sustainability leadership:* sustainability coordinator/director, sustainability committee/advisory council, recycling manager, energy manager. *Student clubs and activities:* Public Interest Research Group (PIRG) chapter on campus, student club(s)/group(s) focused on sustainability, outreach materials available about on-campus sustainability efforts. *Major sustainability events:* Bicycle Coalition of Maine/USM Annual Bike Swap. *Housing and facilities:* sustainability-themed housing.

Food Fair Trade coffee is used. Vegan and vegetarian dining options are available for every meal.

Transportation Provides free on-campus transportation (bus or other), public transportation access to local destinations, and incentives to carpool or use public transportation.

Buildings and Grounds *Percentage of institution's eligible buildings as of September 2008 meeting LEED and/or LEED-EB certification criteria:* 10%. *Renovation and maintenance:* registered for LEED certification for new construction and/or renovation. *Campus grounds care:* uses water conservation devices; employs strategies to reduce light pollution; landscapes with native plant species; protects, restores, and/or creates habitat on campus.

Recycling *Events and organizations:* RecycleMania. *Programs and activities:* sustains a computer/technology recycling program; sustains a pre-consumer food waste composting program; sustains a post-consumer food waste composting program; composts yard waste; reuses surplus department/office supplies; replaces paper materials with online alternatives; limits free printing in computer labs and libraries. *Campus dining operations:* uses reusable dishware; operates without trays; offers discounts for reusable mugs.

Energy Currently uses or plans to use alternative sources of power (biomass energy, geothermal energy, hydroelectricity/water power, and solar energy); timers to regulate temperatures based on occupancy hours; motion, infrared, and/or light sensors to reduce energy uses for lighting; and LED lighting.

Purchasing Sustainability criteria used in purchasing include Energy Star (EPA), WaterSense (EPA), and Green Electronics Council (GEC) Electronic Product Environmental Assessment Tool (EPEAT) Silver or Gold.

Contact Environmental and Economic Sustainability Coordinator, University of Southern Maine, 96 Falmouth Street, PO Box 9300, Portland, LA 04104-9300. *Phone:* 207-789-4384. *E-mail:* dgreeley@usm.maine.edu. *Web site:* www.usm.maine.edu/.

Maryland

Goucher College
Baltimore, Maryland

Sustainability Initiatives Goucher College is a member of the Association for the Advancement of Sustainability in Higher Education (AASHE). This institution's president has signed the American College & University Presidents Climate Commitment.

Academics *Sustainability courses and programs:* sustainability-focused course(s) or lecture series.

Student Services and Green Events *Sustainability leadership:* sustainability committee/advisory council, recycling manager, energy manager, sustainability-focused student government. *Student clubs and activities:* Campus Climate Challenge, student club(s)/group(s) focused on sustainability, outreach materials available about on-campus sustainability efforts. *Major sustainability events:* Farmers Market and Environmental Resource Fair, Eco Cafe, Earth Day Week events, Guest Thomas Friedman, Climate Change and the Chesapeake Bay panel discussion, Guest Dr. Wangari Muta Maathai, annual campus conversation on sustainability, environmental film series. *Housing and facilities:* sustainability-themed housing, student-run café that serves environmentally or socially preferable foods, on-campus organic garden for students.

Food Sustainable, organic, and/or locally produced foods available in on-campus dining facilities. Fair Trade coffee is used. Vegan and vegetarian dining options are available for every meal.

Transportation Provides public transportation access to local destinations, a car sharing program, and incentives to carpool or use public transportation.

Buildings and Grounds *Percentage of institution's eligible buildings as of September 2008 meeting LEED and/or LEED-EB certification criteria:* 12%. *Renovation and maintenance:* registered for LEED certification for new construction and/or renovation. *Campus grounds care:* uses water conservation devices; employs strategies to reduce light pollution; landscapes with native plant species; protects, restores, and/or creates habitat on campus; applies to its grounds only pesticides and fertilizers allowable under the U.S. Department of Agriculture's standards for crop production.

Recycling *Events and organizations:* RecycleMania. *Programs and activities:* sustains a computer/technology recycling program; sustains a pre-consumer food waste composting program; replaces paper materials with online alternatives; limits free printing in computer labs and libraries. *Campus dining operations:* uses reusable dishware; operates without trays; offers discounts for reusable mugs; uses bulk condiment dispensers and decreased packaging for to-go food service purchases.

Energy Currently uses or plans to use alternative sources of power (solar energy and wind energy); timers to regulate temperatures based on occupancy hours; motion, infrared, and/or light sensors to reduce energy uses for lighting; LED lighting; and vending machine motion sensors.

Purchasing Sustainability criteria used in purchasing include Energy Star (EPA), Green Cleaning Products (Green Seal/Environmental Choice certified), and Forest Stewardship Council (FSC) or American Forest and Paper Association's Sustainable Forestry Initiative (SFI) paper.

Contact Special Assistant to President/Director of Government and Community Relations, Goucher College, 1021 Dulaney Valley Road, Baltimore, MD 21204. *Phone:* 410-337-6042. *Fax:* 410-337-6055. *E-mail:* wendy.litzke@goucher.edu. *Web site:* www.goucher.edu/.

McDaniel College
Westminster, Maryland

Sustainability Initiatives McDaniel College's president has signed the American College & University Presidents Climate Commitment.

Academics *Sustainability-focused undergraduate major(s):* Environmental Policy and Science. *Sustainability courses and programs:* sustainability-focused course(s) or lecture series.

Student Services and Green Events *Sustainability leadership:* sustainability coordinator/director, sustainability committee/advisory council, recycling manager, energy manager.

Food Fair Trade coffee is used. Vegan and vegetarian dining options are available for every meal.

Transportation Provides public transportation access to local destinations.

Buildings and Grounds *Campus grounds care:* uses water conservation devices; protects, restores, and/or creates habitat on campus.

Recycling *Events and organizations:* RecycleMania. *Programs and activities:* sustains a computer/technology recycling program; maintains an on-campus recycling center; reuses surplus department/office supplies; replaces paper materials with online alternatives; limits free printing in computer labs and libraries. *Campus dining operations:* uses reusable dishware; offers discounts for reusable mugs; uses bulk condiment dispensers and decreased packaging for to-go food service purchases.

Energy Currently uses or plans to use alternative sources of power (geothermal energy); timers to regulate temperatures based on occupancy hours; motion, infrared, and/or light sensors to reduce energy uses for lighting; LED lighting; and energy-related performance contracting.

Purchasing Sustainability criteria used in purchasing include Energy Star (EPA) and Green Cleaning Products (Green Seal/Environmental Choice certified).

Contact McDaniel College, 2 College Hill, Westminster, MD 21157-4390. *Phone:* 410-848-7000. *Web site:* www.mcdaniel.edu/.

St. Mary's College of Maryland
St. Mary's City, Maryland

Sustainability Initiatives St. Mary's College of Maryland is a member of the Association for the Advancement of Sustainability in Higher Education (AASHE) and a signatory to the Talloires Declaration. This institution's president has signed the American College & University Presidents Climate Commitment. St. Mary's College of Maryland has Green Fees (optional/required) dedicated to sustainability initiatives.

Academics *Sustainability-focused undergraduate major(s):* Student-Designed major (BA). *Sustainability courses and programs:* sustainability-focused course(s) or lecture series, noncredit sustainability course(s).

Student Services and Green Events *Sustainability leadership:* sustainability coordinator/director, sustainability committee/advisory council, recycling manager, energy manager. *Student clubs and activities:* Campus Climate Challenge, student club(s)/group(s) focused on sustainability, outreach materials available about on-campus sustainability efforts. *Major sustainability events:* National Campus Sustainability Day, Focus The Nation, Polar Bear Splash, Ecofest, RecycleMania. *Housing and facilities:* sustainability-themed housing, model dorm room that demonstrates sustainable living principles, student-run café that serves environmentally or socially preferable foods, on-campus organic garden for students.

Food Sustainable, organic, and/or locally produced foods available in on-campus dining facilities. Fair Trade coffee is used. Vegan and vegetarian dining options are available for every meal.

Transportation Provides public transportation access to local destinations.

Buildings and Grounds *Percentage of institution's eligible buildings as of September 2008 meeting LEED and/or LEED-EB certification criteria:* 10%. *Renovation and maintenance:* registered for LEED certification for new construction and/or renovation; uses a Green Seal certified cleaning service. *Campus grounds care:* uses water conservation devices; employs strategies to reduce light pollution; landscapes with native plant species; protects, restores, and/or creates habitat on campus.

Recycling *Events and organizations:* RecycleMania. *Programs and activities:* sustains a computer/technology recycling program; composts yard waste; replaces paper materials with online alternatives; limits free printing in computer labs and libraries. *Campus dining operations:* uses reusable dishware; operates without trays; offers discounts for reusable mugs.

Energy Currently uses or plans to use alternative sources of power (geothermal energy and solar energy); timers to regulate temperatures based on occupancy hours; motion, infrared, and/or light sensors to reduce energy uses for lighting; vending machine motion sensors; and energy-related performance contracting. Participates in College & University Green Power Challenge activities.

Purchasing Sustainability criteria used in purchasing include Energy Star (EPA) and Green Cleaning Products (Green Seal/Environmental Choice certified).

Contact Facilities Planner/Sustainability Coordinator, St. Mary's College of Maryland, 18952 East Fisher Road, St. Mary's City, MD 20686. *Phone:* 240-895-2093. *E-mail:* cnbornand@smcm.edu. *Web site:* www.smcm.edu/.

Salisbury University
Salisbury, Maryland

Sustainability Initiatives Salisbury University's president has signed the American College & University Presidents Climate Commitment.

Academics *Sustainability-focused undergraduate major(s):* Environmental Issues (BA). *Sustainability courses and programs:* sustainability-focused course(s) or lecture series.

Student Services and Green Events *Sustainability leadership:* sustainability coordinator/director, sustainability committee/advisory council, recycling manager, energy manager. *Student clubs and activities:* student club(s)/group(s) focused on sustainability. *Major sustainability events:* Campus Sustainability Day web conference. *Housing and facilities:* sustainability-themed housing.

Food Vegan and vegetarian dining options are available for every meal.

Transportation Provides free on-campus transportation (bus or other) and public transportation access to local destinations.

Buildings and Grounds *Renovation and maintenance:* registered for LEED certification for new construction and/or renovation. *Campus grounds care:* uses water conservation devices.

Recycling *Events and organizations:* RecycleMania. *Programs and activities:* sustains a computer/technology recycling program; maintains an on-campus recycling center; composts yard waste; reuses surplus department/office supplies; replaces paper materials with online alternatives; limits free printing in computer labs and libraries. *Campus dining operations:* uses reusable dishware.

Energy Currently uses or plans to use alternative sources of power; timers to regulate temperatures based on occupancy hours; motion, infrared, and/or light sensors to reduce energy uses for lighting; vending machine motion sensors; and energy-related performance contracting.

Purchasing Sustainability criteria used in purchasing include Energy Star (EPA).

Contact Salisbury University, 1101 Camden Avenue, Salisbury, MD 21801-6837. *Phone:* 410-543-6000. *Web site:* www.salisbury.edu/.

University of Maryland, Baltimore County
Baltimore, Maryland

Sustainability Initiatives University of Maryland, Baltimore County is a member of the Association for the Advancement of Sustainability in Higher Education (AASHE). This institution's president has signed the American College & University Presidents Climate Commitment.

Academics *Sustainability-focused undergraduate major(s):* Environmental Science (BS), Environmental Studies (BA). *Sustainability-focused graduate degree program(s):* Atmospheric Physics (MS, PhD), Environmental Engineering/Water Resources (MS, PhD), Geography and Environmental Systems (MS, PhD). *Sustainability courses and programs:* sustainability-focused course(s) or lecture series.

Student Services and Green Events *Sustainability leadership:* sustainability coordinator/director, sustainability committee/advisory council, recycling manager, energy manager, sustainability-focused student government. *Student clubs and activities:* Campus Climate Challenge, student club(s)/group(s) focused on sustainability. *Major sustainability events:* Teach-In on Global Warming Solutions, RecycleMania, Power Vote, EcoFest on Earth Day.

Food Sustainable, organic, and/or locally produced foods available in on-campus dining facilities. Fair Trade coffee is used. Vegan and vegetarian dining options are available for every meal.

Transportation Provides free on-campus transportation (bus or other), public transportation access to local destinations, and incentives to carpool or use public transportation.

Buildings and Grounds *Renovation and maintenance:* registered for LEED certification for new construction and/or renovation; uses a Green Seal certified cleaning service. *Campus grounds care:* uses water conservation devices; employs strategies to reduce light pollution; landscapes with native plant species; protects, restores, and/or creates habitat on campus; applies to its grounds only pesticides and fertilizers allowable under the U.S. Department of Agriculture's standards for crop production.

Recycling *Events and organizations:* RecycleMania, Waste-Wise (EPA). *Programs and activities:* sustains a computer/technology recycling program; maintains an on-campus recycling center; reuses surplus department/office supplies; reuses chemicals; replaces paper materials with online alternatives; limits free printing in computer labs and libraries. *Campus dining operations:* uses reusable dishware; offers discounts for reusable mugs; uses bulk condiment dispensers and decreased packaging for to-go food service purchases.

Energy Currently uses or plans to use alternative sources of power; timers to regulate temperatures based on occupancy hours; motion, infrared, and/or light sensors to reduce energy uses for lighting; LED lighting; and energy-related performance contracting.

Purchasing Sustainability criteria used in purchasing include Energy Star (EPA) and Green Cleaning Products (Green Seal/Environmental Choice certified).

Contact University of Maryland, Baltimore County, 1000 Hilltop Circle, Baltimore, MD 21250. *Phone:* 410-455-1000. *Web site:* www.umbc.edu/.

University of Maryland, College Park
College Park, Maryland

Sustainability Initiatives University of Maryland, College Park is a member of the Association for the Advancement of Sustainability in Higher Education (AASHE). This institution's president has signed the American College & University Presidents Climate Commitment. University of Maryland, College Park has Green Fees (optional/required) dedicated to sustainability initiatives.

Academics *Sustainability-focused undergraduate major(s):* Agriculture and Resource Economics, Environmental Science and Policy, Environmental Science and Technology, Natural Resource Management, Natural Resource Sciences. *Sustainability-focused graduate degree program(s):* Agricultural and Resource Economics, Environmental Policy, Marine Environmental Science, Natural Resource Sciences, Sustainable Development and Conservation Biology, Sustainable Energy Engineering. *Sustainability courses and programs:* sustainability-focused course(s) or lecture series, noncredit sustainability course(s).

Student Services and Green Events *Sustainability leadership:* sustainability coordinator/director, sustainability committee/advisory council, recycling manager, energy manager, sustainability-focused student government. *Student clubs and activities:* Campus Climate Challenge, Public Interest Research Group (PIRG) chapter on campus, student club(s)/group(s) focused on sustainability. *Major sus-*

tainability events: National Smart and Sustainable Campuses conferences. *Housing and facilities:* sustainability-themed housing, student-run café that serves environmentally or socially preferable foods, on-campus organic garden for students.

Food Sustainable, organic, and/or locally produced foods available in on-campus dining facilities. Fair Trade coffee is used. Vegan and vegetarian dining options are available for every meal.

Transportation Provides free on-campus transportation (bus or other), public transportation access to local destinations, a car sharing program, and incentives to carpool or use public transportation.

Buildings and Grounds *Renovation and maintenance:* registered for LEED certification for new construction and/or renovation. *Campus grounds care:* uses water conservation devices; employs strategies to reduce light pollution; landscapes with native plant species; protects, restores, and/or creates habitat on campus.

Recycling *Events and organizations:* RecycleMania. *Programs and activities:* sustains a computer/technology recycling program; maintains an on-campus recycling center; sustains a pre-consumer food waste composting program; sustains a post-consumer food waste composting program; composts yard waste; reuses surplus department/office supplies; reuses chemicals; replaces paper materials with online alternatives; limits free printing in computer labs and libraries. *Campus dining operations:* uses reusable dishware; offers discounts for reusable mugs; uses bulk condiment dispensers and decreased packaging for to-go food service purchases.

Energy Currently uses or plans to use alternative sources of power (hydroelectricity/water power, solar energy, and wind energy); timers to regulate temperatures based on occupancy hours; motion, infrared, and/or light sensors to reduce energy uses for lighting; LED lighting; and energy-related performance contracting.

Purchasing Sustainability criteria used in purchasing include Energy Star (EPA), Green Electronics Council (GEC) Electronic Product Environmental Assessment Tool (EPEAT) Silver or Gold, and Green Cleaning Products (Green Seal/Environmental Choice certified).

Contact Campus Sustainability Coordinator, University of Maryland, College Park, 3115 Chesapeake Building, College Park, MD 20742. *Phone:* 301-405-4633. *E-mail:* stewartm@umd.edu. *Web site:* www.maryland.edu/.

University of Maryland University College
Adelphi, Maryland

Sustainability Initiatives University of Maryland University College's president has signed the American College & University Presidents Climate Commitment. University of Maryland University College has Green Fees (optional/required) dedicated to sustainability initiatives.

Academics *Sustainability courses and programs:* sustainability-focused course(s) or lecture series.

Student Services and Green Events *Sustainability leadership:* sustainability coordinator/director, sustainability committee/advisory council, recycling manager. *Student clubs and activities:* student club(s)/group(s) focused on sustainability.

Food Fair Trade coffee is used.

Transportation Provides free on-campus transportation (bus or other), public transportation access to local destinations, a car sharing program, and incentives to carpool or use public transportation.

Buildings and Grounds *Percentage of institution's eligible buildings as of September 2008 meeting LEED and/or LEED-EB certification criteria:* 15%. *Renovation and maintenance:* registered for LEED certification for new construction and/or renovation. *Campus grounds care:* uses water conservation devices; employs strategies to reduce light pollution; landscapes with native plant species; applies to its grounds only pesticides and fertilizers allowable under the U.S. Department of Agriculture's standards for crop production.

Recycling *Programs and activities:* maintains an on-campus recycling center; sustains a pre-consumer food waste composting program; sustains a post-consumer food waste composting program; composts yard waste; reuses surplus department/office supplies; replaces paper materials with online alternatives; limits free printing in computer labs and libraries. *Campus dining operations:* uses reusable dishware; uses bulk condiment dispensers and decreased packaging for to-go food service purchases.

Energy Currently uses or plans to use timers to regulate temperatures based on occupancy hours; motion, infrared, and/or light sensors to reduce energy uses for lighting; LED lighting; and energy-related performance contracting.

Purchasing Sustainability criteria used in purchasing include Energy Star (EPA), Green Cleaning Products (Green Seal/Environmental Choice certified), and Forest Stewardship Council (FSC) or American Forest and Paper Association's Sustainable Forestry Initiative (SFI) paper.

Contact University of Maryland University College, 3501 University Boulevard East, Adelphi, MD 20783. *Phone:* 301-985-7000. *Web site:* www.umuc.edu/.

Washington College
Chestertown, Maryland

Sustainability Initiatives Washington College's president has signed the American College & University Presidents Climate Commitment.

Student Services and Green Events *Sustainability leadership:* sustainability committee/advisory council, recycling manager. *Student clubs and activities:* student club(s)/group(s) focused on sustainability. *Major sustainability events:* George Goes Green, Green Business Seminars, Annual Earth Day events. *Housing and facilities:* model dorm room that demonstrates sustainable living principles.

Food Sustainable, organic, and/or locally produced foods available in on-campus dining facilities. Vegan and vegetarian dining options are available for every meal.

Transportation Provides public transportation access to local destinations.

Buildings and Grounds *Percentage of institution's eligible buildings as of September 2008 meeting LEED and/or LEED-EB certification criteria:* 5%. *Renovation and maintenance:* uses a Green Seal certified cleaning service. *Campus grounds care:* employs strategies to reduce light pollution; landscapes with native plant species.

Recycling *Events and organizations:* RecycleMania. *Programs and activities:* sustains a computer/technology recycling program; sustains a post-consumer food waste composting program; composts yard waste; replaces paper materials with online alternatives; limits free printing in computer labs and libraries. *Campus dining operations:* uses reusable dishware; operates without trays; uses bulk condiment dispensers and decreased packaging for to-go food service purchases.

Energy Currently uses or plans to use alternative sources of power (geothermal energy); timers to regulate temperatures

based on occupancy hours; motion, infrared, and/or light sensors to reduce energy uses for lighting; and LED lighting.

Purchasing Sustainability criteria used in purchasing include Energy Star (EPA) and Green Cleaning Products (Green Seal/Environmental Choice certified).

Contact Climate Action Coordinator, Washington College, Center for Environment and Society, 101 South Water Street, Chestertown, MD 21620. *Phone:* 410-810-7174. *E-mail:* bcunningham3@washcoll.edu. *Web site:* www.washcoll.edu/.

Massachusetts

Amherst College
Amherst, Massachusetts

Academics *Sustainability-focused undergraduate major(s):* Environmental Studies (BA). *Sustainability courses and programs:* sustainability-focused course(s) or lecture series.

Student Services and Green Events *Sustainability leadership:* sustainability coordinator/director, sustainability committee/advisory council, recycling manager, energy manager. *Student clubs and activities:* Public Interest Research Group (PIRG) chapter on campus.

Food Sustainable, organic, and/or locally produced foods available in on-campus dining facilities. Fair Trade coffee is used. Vegan and vegetarian dining options are available for every meal.

Transportation Provides free on-campus transportation (bus or other), public transportation access to local destinations, and a car sharing program.

Buildings and Grounds *Renovation and maintenance:* registered for LEED certification for new construction and/or renovation; uses a Green Seal certified cleaning service. *Campus grounds care:* uses water conservation devices; employs strategies to reduce light pollution; landscapes with native plant species; protects, restores, and/or creates habitat on campus.

Recycling *Events and organizations:* RecycleMania. *Programs and activities:* sustains a computer/technology recycling program; maintains an on-campus recycling center; sustains a pre-consumer food waste composting program; sustains a post-consumer food waste composting program; composts yard waste; reuses chemicals; replaces paper materials with online alternatives. *Campus dining operations:* uses reusable dishware; uses bulk condiment dispensers and decreased packaging for to-go food service purchases.

Energy Currently uses or plans to use timers to regulate temperatures based on occupancy hours; motion, infrared, and/or light sensors to reduce energy uses for lighting; and vending machine motion sensors.

Purchasing Sustainability criteria used in purchasing include Energy Star (EPA) and Green Cleaning Products (Green Seal/Environmental Choice certified).

Contact Amherst College, PO Box 5000, Amherst, MA 01002-5000. *Phone:* 413-542-2000. *Web site:* www.amherst.edu/.

Anna Maria College
Paxton, Massachusetts

Sustainability Initiatives Anna Maria College is a member of the Association for the Advancement of Sustainability in Higher Education (AASHE). This institution's president has signed the American College & University Presidents Climate Commitment.

Academics *Sustainability-focused undergraduate major(s):* Environmental Science (BA). *Sustainability-focused graduate degree program(s):* Occupational and Environmental Health. *Sustainability courses and programs:* sustainability-focused course(s) or lecture series.

Student Services and Green Events *Sustainability leadership:* sustainability committee/advisory council. *Student clubs and activities:* outreach materials available about on-campus sustainability efforts.

Food Sustainable, organic, and/or locally produced foods available in on-campus dining facilities. Fair Trade coffee is used. Vegan and vegetarian dining options are available for every meal.

Transportation Provides free on-campus transportation (bus or other) and incentives to carpool or use public transportation.

Buildings and Grounds *Renovation and maintenance:* registered for LEED certification for new construction and/or renovation; uses a Green Seal certified cleaning service. *Campus grounds care:* uses water conservation devices; employs strategies to reduce light pollution; landscapes with native plant species; protects, restores, and/or creates habitat on campus.

Recycling *Programs and activities:* sustains a computer/technology recycling program; reuses chemicals; replaces paper materials with online alternatives; limits free printing in computer labs and libraries. *Campus dining operations:* uses reusable dishware; operates without trays; uses bulk condiment dispensers and decreased packaging for to-go food service purchases.

Energy Currently uses or plans to use alternative sources of power (wind energy).

Purchasing Sustainability criteria used in purchasing include Energy Star (EPA) and Green Cleaning Products (Green Seal/Environmental Choice certified).

Contact Chair, Climate Committee, Anna Maria College, 50 Sunset Lane, Paxton, MA 01612. *Phone:* 508-849-3382. *Fax:* 508-849-3340. *E-mail:* sswedis@annamaria.edu. *Web site:* www.annamaria.edu/.

Assumption College
Worcester, Massachusetts

Academics *Sustainability-focused undergraduate major(s):* Environmental Science (BA). *Sustainability courses and programs:* sustainability-focused course(s) or lecture series.

Student Services and Green Events *Sustainability leadership:* sustainability coordinator/director, sustainability committee/advisory council, recycling manager, energy manager, sustainability-focused student government. *Student clubs and activities:* student club(s)/group(s) focused on sustainability, outreach materials available about on-campus sustainability efforts. *Major sustainability events:* Hosted campus wide viewing of a national sustainability webinar, Earth Week events. *Housing and facilities:* sustainability-themed housing.

Food Sustainable, organic, and/or locally produced foods available in on-campus dining facilities. Vegan and vegetarian dining options are available for every meal.

Transportation Provides public transportation access to local destinations and a bike loan/rental program.

Buildings and Grounds *Campus grounds care:* uses water conservation devices; landscapes with native plant species; protects, restores, and/or creates habitat on campus.

Recycling *Programs and activities:* sustains a computer/technology recycling program; maintains an on-campus

recycling center; composts yard waste; reuses surplus department/office supplies; reuses chemicals; replaces paper materials with online alternatives; limits free printing in computer labs and libraries. *Campus dining operations:* uses reusable dishware; offers discounts for reusable mugs; uses bulk condiment dispensers and decreased packaging for to-go food service purchases.

Energy Currently uses or plans to use alternative sources of power (solar energy); timers to regulate temperatures based on occupancy hours; motion, infrared, and/or light sensors to reduce energy uses for lighting; LED lighting; and vending machine motion sensors.

Purchasing Sustainability criteria used in purchasing include Energy Star (EPA) and Green Cleaning Products (Green Seal/Environmental Choice certified).

Contact Director of Auxiliary Services, Assumption College, 500 Salisbury Street, Worcester, MA 01606. *Phone:* 508-767-7045. *E-mail:* jlanglois@assumption.edu. *Web site:* www.assumption.edu/.

Babson College
Wellesley, Massachusetts

Sustainability Initiatives Babson College's president has signed the American College & University Presidents Climate Commitment.

Academics *Sustainability courses and programs:* sustainability-focused course(s) or lecture series.

Student Services and Green Events *Sustainability leadership:* sustainability coordinator/director, sustainability committee/advisory council, recycling manager, energy manager. *Student clubs and activities:* student club(s)/group(s) focused on sustainability, outreach materials available about on-campus sustainability efforts. *Major sustainability events:* 3 E Conference, New Business Competition, Sustainable Business Rocket Pitches. *Housing and facilities:* sustainability-themed housing.

Food Sustainable, organic, and/or locally produced foods available in on-campus dining facilities. Fair Trade coffee is used. Vegan and vegetarian dining options are available for every meal.

Transportation Provides free on-campus transportation (bus or other), public transportation access to local destinations, a bike loan/rental program, a car sharing program, and incentives to carpool or use public transportation.

Buildings and Grounds *Renovation and maintenance:* registered for LEED certification for new construction and/or renovation; uses a Green Seal certified cleaning service. *Campus grounds care:* uses water conservation devices; employs strategies to reduce light pollution; landscapes with native plant species; protects, restores, and/or creates habitat on campus; applies to its grounds only pesticides and fertilizers allowable under the U.S. Department of Agriculture's standards for crop production.

Recycling *Events and organizations:* RecycleMania, Waste-Wise (EPA). *Programs and activities:* sustains a computer/technology recycling program; composts yard waste; reuses surplus department/office supplies; replaces paper materials with online alternatives. *Campus dining operations:* uses reusable dishware; operates without trays; offers discounts for reusable mugs; uses bulk condiment dispensers and decreased packaging for to-go food service purchases.

Energy Currently uses or plans to use alternative sources of power (wind energy); timers to regulate temperatures based on occupancy hours; motion, infrared, and/or light sensors to reduce energy uses for lighting; LED lighting; and energy-related performance contracting.

Purchasing Sustainability criteria used in purchasing include Energy Star (EPA), WaterSense (EPA), Green Electronics Council (GEC) Electronic Product Environmental Assessment Tool (EPEAT) Silver or Gold, Green Cleaning Products (Green Seal/Environmental Choice certified), and Forest Stewardship Council (FSC) or American Forest and Paper Association's Sustainable Forestry Initiative (SFI) paper.

Contact Associate Vice President, Facilities, Babson College, 231 Forest Street, Babson Park, MA 02457. *Phone:* 781-239-5840. *Fax:* 781-239-5841. *E-mail:* skaplan1@babson.edu. *Web site:* www.babson.edu/.

Boston Architectural College
Boston, Massachusetts

Academics *Sustainability-focused undergraduate major(s):* Design Studies/Sustainability (BDS). *Sustainability courses and programs:* sustainability-focused course(s) or lecture series, noncredit sustainability course(s), sustainability-focused nonacademic certificate program(s).

Student Services and Green Events *Sustainability leadership:* sustainability committee/advisory council, recycling manager, energy manager, sustainability-focused student government. *Student clubs and activities:* student club(s)/group(s) focused on sustainability, outreach materials available about on-campus sustainability efforts. *Major sustainability events:* Annual Cascieri Lecture/Conference.

Transportation Provides public transportation access to local destinations and incentives to carpool or use public transportation.

Buildings and Grounds *Campus grounds care:* uses water conservation devices; employs strategies to reduce light pollution.

Recycling *Programs and activities:* sustains a computer/technology recycling program; maintains an on-campus recycling center; replaces paper materials with online alternatives; limits free printing in computer labs and libraries.

Energy Currently uses or plans to use timers to regulate temperatures based on occupancy hours and motion, infrared, and/or light sensors to reduce energy uses for lighting.

Purchasing Sustainability criteria used in purchasing include Energy Star (EPA) and Green Cleaning Products (Green Seal/Environmental Choice certified).

Contact Director of Sustainable Design Programs, Boston Architectural College, 320 Newbury Street, Boston, MA 02115. *Phone:* 617-585-0219. *E-mail:* lance.fletcher@the-bac.edu. *Web site:* www.the-bac.edu/.

Boston College
Chestnut Hill, Massachusetts

Academics *Sustainability-focused undergraduate major(s):* Environmental Geosciences (BS). *Sustainability courses and programs:* sustainability-focused course(s) or lecture series.

Student Services and Green Events *Sustainability leadership:* sustainability coordinator/director, recycling manager, energy manager, sustainability-focused student government. *Student clubs and activities:* student club(s)/group(s) focused on sustainability, outreach materials available about on-campus sustainability efforts. *Major sustainability events:* BCisGreen Week. *Housing and facilities:* student-run café that serves environmentally or socially preferable foods, on-campus organic garden for students.

Food Sustainable, organic, and/or locally produced foods available in on-campus dining facilities. Fair Trade coffee is used. Vegan and vegetarian dining options are available for every meal.

Transportation Provides free on-campus transportation (bus or other), public transportation access to local destinations, a car sharing program, and incentives to carpool or use public transportation.

Buildings and Grounds *Renovation and maintenance:* registered for LEED certification for new construction and/or renovation. *Campus grounds care:* uses water conservation devices; employs strategies to reduce light pollution; landscapes with native plant species.

Recycling *Events and organizations:* RecycleMania, WasteWise (EPA). *Programs and activities:* sustains a computer/technology recycling program; maintains an on-campus recycling center; sustains a pre-consumer food waste composting program; sustains a post-consumer food waste composting program; composts yard waste; reuses chemicals; replaces paper materials with online alternatives; limits free printing in computer labs and libraries. *Campus dining operations:* uses reusable dishware; offers discounts for reusable mugs; uses bulk condiment dispensers and decreased packaging for to-go food service purchases.

Energy Currently uses or plans to use alternative sources of power (hydroelectricity/water power and solar energy); timers to regulate temperatures based on occupancy hours; motion, infrared, and/or light sensors to reduce energy uses for lighting; and LED lighting.

Contact Directory of Sustainability and Energy Management, Boston College, 140 Commonwealth Avenue, Chestnut Hill, MA 02467. *Phone:* 617-552-0301. *Fax:* 617-552-0366. *E-mail:* deirdre.manning@bc.edu. *Web site:* www.bc.edu/.

Boston University
Boston, Massachusetts

Academics *Sustainability courses and programs:* sustainability-focused course(s) or lecture series.

Student Services and Green Events *Sustainability leadership:* sustainability coordinator/director, sustainability committee/advisory council, recycling manager, energy manager, sustainability-focused student government. *Student clubs and activities:* student club(s)/group(s) focused on sustainability, outreach materials available about on-campus sustainability efforts. *Major sustainability events:* American Recycling Day, Pardee Center Lecture Series, Department of Geography and Environment lecture series, Earth Day/Earth Week, Clean Energy Initiative, SMG Sustainability forum, RecycleMania. *Housing and facilities:* sustainability-themed housing, on-campus organic garden for students.

Food Sustainable, organic, and/or locally produced foods available in on-campus dining facilities. Fair Trade coffee is used. Vegan and vegetarian dining options are available for every meal.

Transportation Provides free on-campus transportation (bus or other), public transportation access to local destinations, a car sharing program, and incentives to carpool or use public transportation.

Buildings and Grounds *Campus grounds care:* uses water conservation devices; landscapes with native plant species.

Recycling *Events and organizations:* RecycleMania. *Programs and activities:* sustains a computer/technology recycling program; maintains an on-campus recycling center; sustains a pre-consumer food waste composting program; sustains a post-consumer food waste composting program; composts yard waste; reuses surplus department/office supplies; replaces paper materials with online alternatives. *Campus dining operations:* uses reusable dishware; operates without trays; offers discounts for reusable mugs; uses bulk condiment dispensers and decreased packaging for to-go food service purchases.

Energy Currently uses or plans to use alternative sources of power (geothermal energy, solar energy, and wind energy); timers to regulate temperatures based on occupancy hours; motion, infrared, and/or light sensors to reduce energy uses for lighting; LED lighting; and vending machine motion sensors.

Purchasing Sustainability criteria used in purchasing include Energy Star (EPA), WaterSense (EPA), and Green Cleaning Products (Green Seal/Environmental Choice certified).

Contact Director of Sustainability, Boston University, 120 Ashford Street, Boston, MA 02215. *Phone:* 617-358-5596. *Fax:* 617-358-4918. *E-mail:* carlberg@bu.edu. *Web site:* www.bu.edu/.

Brandeis University
Waltham, Massachusetts

Sustainability Initiatives Brandeis University's president has signed the American College & University Presidents Climate Commitment.

Academics *Sustainability-focused undergraduate major(s):* Environmental Studies (BA). *Sustainability-focused graduate degree program(s):* Socially Responsible Business/ Green (MBA), Sustainable International Development (MA). *Sustainability courses and programs:* sustainability-focused course(s) or lecture series.

Student Services and Green Events *Sustainability leadership:* sustainability coordinator/director, sustainability committee/advisory council, recycling manager, energy manager. *Student clubs and activities:* Campus Climate Challenge, student club(s)/group(s) focused on sustainability. *Major sustainability events:* Earthfest.

Food Sustainable, organic, and/or locally produced foods available in on-campus dining facilities. Fair Trade coffee is used. Vegan and vegetarian dining options are available for every meal.

Transportation Provides free on-campus transportation (bus or other), public transportation access to local destinations, a bike loan/rental program, a car sharing program, and incentives to carpool or use public transportation.

Buildings and Grounds *Percentage of institution's eligible buildings as of September 2008 meeting LEED and/or LEED-EB certification criteria:* 5%. *Campus grounds care:* uses water conservation devices; landscapes with native plant species; protects, restores, and/or creates habitat on campus.

Recycling *Events and organizations:* RecycleMania. *Programs and activities:* sustains a computer/technology recycling program; maintains an on-campus recycling center; sustains a pre-consumer food waste composting program; sustains a post-consumer food waste composting program; composts yard waste; reuses surplus department/office supplies; replaces paper materials with online alternatives; limits free printing in computer labs and libraries. *Campus dining operations:* uses reusable dishware; operates without trays; offers discounts for reusable mugs.

Energy Currently uses or plans to use alternative sources of power; timers to regulate temperatures based on occupancy hours; motion, infrared, and/or light sensors to reduce energy uses for lighting; LED lighting; and energy-related performance contracting. Participates in College & University Green Power Challenge activities.

Purchasing Sustainability criteria used in purchasing include Energy Star (EPA).

Contact Sustainability Coordinator, Brandeis University, MS 025 Brandeis University, PO Box 549110, Waltham, MA 02454. *Phone:* 781-736-4194. *E-mail:* jannacr@brandeis. edu. *Web site:* www.brandeis.edu/.

College of the Holy Cross
Worcester, Massachusetts

Sustainability Initiatives College of the Holy Cross's president has signed the American College & University Presidents Climate Commitment.

Academics *Sustainability-focused undergraduate major(s):* Environmental Studies (BA). *Sustainability courses and programs:* sustainability-focused course(s) or lecture series.

Student Services and Green Events *Sustainability leadership:* sustainability committee/advisory council, recycling manager, energy manager, sustainability-focused student government. *Housing and facilities:* on-campus organic garden for students.

Food Sustainable, organic, and/or locally produced foods available in on-campus dining facilities. Fair Trade coffee is used. Vegan and vegetarian dining options are available for every meal.

Transportation Provides free on-campus transportation (bus or other), public transportation access to local destinations, and a car sharing program.

Buildings and Grounds *Renovation and maintenance:* registered for LEED certification for new construction and/or renovation. *Campus grounds care:* uses water conservation devices; employs strategies to reduce light pollution; landscapes with native plant species; protects, restores, and/or creates habitat on campus; applies to its grounds only pesticides and fertilizers allowable under the U.S. Department of Agriculture's standards for crop production.

Recycling *Programs and activities:* sustains a computer/ technology recycling program; composts yard waste; reuses surplus department/office supplies; reuses chemicals; replaces paper materials with online alternatives. *Campus dining operations:* uses reusable dishware; offers discounts for reusable mugs; uses bulk condiment dispensers and decreased packaging for to-go food service purchases.

Energy Currently uses or plans to use alternative sources of power (hydroelectricity/water power, solar energy, and wind energy); timers to regulate temperatures based on occupancy hours; and motion, infrared, and/or light sensors to reduce energy uses for lighting.

Purchasing Sustainability criteria used in purchasing include Energy Star (EPA) and Green Cleaning Products (Green Seal/Environmental Choice certified).

Contact Associate Director of Physical Plant, College of the Holy Cross, 1 College Street, Worcester, MA 01610. *Phone:* 508-793-3025. *Fax:* 508-793-2701. *E-mail:* jcannon@ holycross.edu. *Web site:* www.holycross.edu/.

Emerson College
Boston, Massachusetts

Sustainability Initiatives Emerson College's president has signed the American College & University Presidents Climate Commitment.

Student Services and Green Events *Sustainability leadership:* sustainability coordinator/director, recycling manager, energy manager. *Student clubs and activities:* Campus Climate Challenge, Public Interest Research Group (PIRG) chapter on campus. *Housing and facilities:* sustainability-themed housing, model dorm room that demonstrates sustainable living principles.

Food Sustainable, organic, and/or locally produced foods available in on-campus dining facilities. Fair Trade coffee is used. Vegan and vegetarian dining options are available for every meal.

Transportation Provides free on-campus transportation (bus or other) and public transportation access to local destinations.

Buildings and Grounds *Percentage of institution's eligible buildings as of September 2008 meeting LEED and/or LEED-EB certification criteria:* 20%. *Renovation and maintenance:* registered for LEED certification for new construction and/or renovation; uses a Green Seal certified cleaning service. *Campus grounds care:* uses water conservation devices; employs strategies to reduce light pollution.

Recycling *Programs and activities:* sustains a computer/technology recycling program; maintains an on-campus recycling center; reuses surplus department/office supplies; replaces paper materials with online alternatives. *Campus dining operations:* uses bulk condiment dispensers and decreased packaging for to-go food service purchases.

Energy Currently uses or plans to use timers to regulate temperatures based on occupancy hours; motion, infrared, and/or light sensors to reduce energy uses for lighting; and LED lighting.

Purchasing Sustainability criteria used in purchasing include Energy Star (EPA) and Green Cleaning Products (Green Seal/Environmental Choice certified).

Contact Director, Facilities Management, Emerson College, 120 Boylston Street, Boston, MA 02116-4624. *Phone:* 617-824-8645. *Fax:* 617-824-7859. *E-mail:* neal_lespasio@emerson.edu. *Web site:* www.emerson.edu/.

Fitchburg State College
Fitchburg, Massachusetts

Sustainability Initiatives Fitchburg State College's president has signed the American College & University Presidents Climate Commitment.

Academics *Sustainability-focused undergraduate major(s):* Environmental Biology (BS). *Sustainability courses and programs:* sustainability-focused course(s) or lecture series.

Student Services and Green Events *Sustainability leadership:* sustainability coordinator/director, sustainability committee/advisory council, recycling manager, energy manager, sustainability-focused student government. *Student clubs and activities:* Campus Climate Challenge, Public Interest Research Group (PIRG) chapter on campus, student club(s)/group(s) focused on sustainability. *Major sustainability events:* Northeast Sustainability Symposium. *Housing and facilities:* on-campus organic garden for students.

Food Sustainable, organic, and/or locally produced foods available in on-campus dining facilities. Fair Trade coffee is used. Vegan and vegetarian dining options are available for every meal.

Transportation Provides free on-campus transportation (bus or other), public transportation access to local destinations, and incentives to carpool or use public transportation.

Buildings and Grounds *Renovation and maintenance:* registered for LEED certification for new construction and/or renovation. *Campus grounds care:* uses water conservation devices; employs strategies to reduce light pollution; landscapes with native plant species; protects, restores, and/or creates habitat on campus.

Recycling *Programs and activities:* sustains a computer/technology recycling program; composts yard waste; replaces paper materials with online alternatives. *Campus dining operations:* uses reusable dishware; uses bulk condiment dispensers and decreased packaging for to-go food service purchases.

Energy Currently uses or plans to use timers to regulate temperatures based on occupancy hours and motion, infrared, and/or light sensors to reduce energy uses for lighting.

Purchasing Sustainability criteria used in purchasing include Energy Star (EPA).

Contact Executive Director of Student Auxiliary Services, Fitchburg State College, 160 Pearl Street, Fitchburg, MA 01420. *Phone:* 978-665-4888. *E-mail:* memckenzie@fsc.edu. *Web site:* www.fsc.edu/.

Hampshire College
Amherst, Massachusetts

Sustainability Initiatives Hampshire College's president has signed the American College & University Presidents Climate Commitment.

Academics *Sustainability courses and programs:* sustainability-focused course(s) or lecture series.

Student Services and Green Events *Sustainability leadership:* sustainability committee/advisory council, recycling manager, energy manager. *Housing and facilities:* sustainability-themed housing, on-campus organic garden for students.

Food Sustainable, organic, and/or locally produced foods available in on-campus dining facilities. Fair Trade coffee is used. Vegan and vegetarian dining options are available for every meal.

Transportation Provides public transportation access to local destinations and a bike loan/rental program.

Buildings and Grounds *Renovation and maintenance:* uses a Green Seal certified cleaning service. *Campus grounds care:* uses water conservation devices; employs strategies to reduce light pollution; landscapes with native plant species; protects, restores, and/or creates habitat on campus.

Recycling *Programs and activities:* sustains a computer/technology recycling program; maintains an on-campus recycling center; sustains a pre-consumer food waste composting program; sustains a post-consumer food waste composting program; composts yard waste; reuses surplus department/office supplies; reuses chemicals; replaces paper materials with online alternatives; limits free printing in computer labs and libraries. *Campus dining operations:* uses reusable dishware; offers discounts for reusable mugs; uses bulk condiment dispensers and decreased packaging for to-go food service purchases.

Energy Currently uses or plans to use timers to regulate temperatures based on occupancy hours; motion, infrared, and/or light sensors to reduce energy uses for lighting; and LED lighting.

Purchasing Sustainability criteria used in purchasing include Energy Star (EPA), Green Cleaning Products (Green Seal/Environmental Choice certified), and Forest Stewardship Council (FSC) or American Forest and Paper Association's Sustainable Forestry Initiative (SFI) paper.

Contact Hampshire College, 893 West Street, Amherst, MA 01002. *Phone:* 413-549-4600. *Web site:* www.hampshire.edu/.

Harvard University
Cambridge, Massachusetts

Sustainability Initiatives Harvard University is a member of the Association for the Advancement of Sustainability in Higher Education (AASHE).

Academics *Sustainability-focused undergraduate major(s):* Environmental Engineering (SB), EPS (AB), ESPP (AB). *Sustainability-focused graduate degree program(s):* Environmental Health Doctorate Programs, Environmental Management (MA), Sustainability Science Program. *Sustainability courses and programs:* sustainability-focused course(s) or lecture series, noncredit sustainability course(s).

Student Services and Green Events *Sustainability leadership:* sustainability coordinator/director, sustainability committee/advisory council, recycling manager. *Student clubs and activities:* student club(s)/group(s) focused on sustainability, outreach materials available about on-campus sustainability efforts. *Major sustainability events:* Annual university-wide Sustainability event, Center for the Environment "Future of Energy" lecture series, week-long Earth Day celebration, Sustainable Transportation Orientation Programs, Sustainability Road Shows, Environmental Law Speaker series. *Housing and facilities:* student-run café that serves environmentally or socially preferable foods, on-campus organic garden for students.

Food Sustainable, organic, and/or locally produced foods available in on-campus dining facilities. Fair Trade coffee is used. Vegan and vegetarian dining options are available for every meal.

Transportation Provides free on-campus transportation (bus or other), public transportation access to local destinations, a bike loan/rental program, a car sharing program, and incentives to carpool or use public transportation.

Buildings and Grounds *Renovation and maintenance:* registered for LEED certification for new construction and/or renovation; uses a Green Seal certified cleaning service. *Campus grounds care:* uses water conservation devices; employs strategies to reduce light pollution; landscapes with native plant species.

Recycling *Events and organizations:* RecycleMania. *Programs and activities:* sustains a computer/technology recycling program; maintains an on-campus recycling center; sustains a pre-consumer food waste composting program; sustains a post-consumer food waste composting program; composts yard waste; reuses surplus department/office supplies; replaces paper materials with online alternatives; limits its free printing in computer labs and libraries. *Campus dining operations:* uses reusable dishware; offers discounts for reusable mugs; uses bulk condiment dispensers and decreased packaging for to-go food service purchases.

Energy Currently uses or plans to use alternative sources of power (biomass energy, geothermal energy, hydroelectricity/water power, solar energy, and wind energy); timers to regulate temperatures based on occupancy hours; motion, infrared, and/or light sensors to reduce energy uses for lighting; LED lighting; vending machine motion sensors; and energy-related performance contracting.

Purchasing Sustainability criteria used in purchasing include Energy Star (EPA), WaterSense (EPA), Green Electronics Council (GEC) Electronic Product Environmental Assessment Tool (EPEAT) Silver or Gold, Green Cleaning Products (Green Seal/Environmental Choice certified), and Forest Stewardship Council (FSC) or American Forest and Paper Association's Sustainable Forestry Initiative (SFI) paper.

Contact Harvard University, Cambridge, MA 02138. *Phone:* 617-495-1000. *Web site:* www.harvard.edu/.

Lesley University
Cambridge, Massachusetts

Sustainability Initiatives Lesley University is a signatory to the Talloires Declaration. This institution's president has signed the American College & University Presidents Climate Commitment.

Academics *Sustainability-focused undergraduate major(s):* Environmental Science (BS), Environmental Studies (BS). *Sustainability-focused graduate degree program(s):* Audubon Expedition Institute (MA). *Sustainability courses and programs:* sustainability-focused course(s) or lecture series.

Student Services and Green Events *Sustainability leadership:* sustainability coordinator/director, sustainability committee/advisory council. *Student clubs and activities:* student club(s)/group(s) focused on sustainability. *Major sustainability events:* Fall Sustainability Pledge, Spring Eco-Week, Graduation Pledge. *Housing and facilities:* student-run café that serves environmentally or socially preferable foods.

Food Sustainable, organic, and/or locally produced foods available in on-campus dining facilities. Fair Trade coffee is used. Vegan and vegetarian dining options are available for every meal.

Transportation Provides free on-campus transportation (bus or other), public transportation access to local destinations, a car sharing program, and incentives to carpool or use public transportation.

Buildings and Grounds *Renovation and maintenance:* uses a Green Seal certified cleaning service. *Campus grounds care:* uses water conservation devices; landscapes with native plant species; protects, restores, and/or creates habitat on campus.

Recycling *Events and organizations:* RecycleMania. *Programs and activities:* sustains a computer/technology recycling program; sustains a pre-consumer food waste composting program; sustains a post-consumer food waste composting program; composts yard waste; replaces paper materials with online alternatives; limits free printing in computer labs and libraries. *Campus dining operations:* uses reusable dishware; operates without trays; offers discounts for reusable mugs; uses bulk condiment dispensers and decreased packaging for to-go food service purchases.

Energy Currently uses or plans to use timers to regulate temperatures based on occupancy hours; motion, infrared, and/or light sensors to reduce energy uses for lighting; LED lighting; and vending machine motion sensors.

Purchasing Sustainability criteria used in purchasing include Energy Star (EPA), Green Electronics Council (GEC) Electronic Product Environmental Assessment Tool (EPEAT) Silver or Gold, Green Cleaning Products (Green Seal/Environmental Choice certified), and Forest Stewardship Council (FSC) or American Forest and Paper Association's Sustainable Forestry Initiative (SFI) paper.

Contact Special Projects Manager/Sustainability Coordinator, Lesley University, 29 Everett Street, Cambridge, MA 02138. *Phone:* 617-349-8829. *Fax:* 617-349-8228. *E-mail:* swisniew@lesley.edu. *Web site:* www.lesley.edu/.

Massachusetts Maritime Academy
Buzzards Bay, Massachusetts

Sustainability Initiatives Massachusetts Maritime Academy's president has signed the American College & University Presidents Climate Commitment.

Academics *Sustainability courses and programs:* sustainability-focused course(s) or lecture series.

Student Services and Green Events *Sustainability leadership:* sustainability coordinator/director, sustainability committee/advisory council, recycling manager. *Student clubs and activities:* student club(s)/group(s) focused on sustainability. *Major sustainability events:* CONNECT Sustainability Workshop, Earth Day Concert. *Housing and facilities:* sustainability-themed housing.

Food Sustainable, organic, and/or locally produced foods available in on-campus dining facilities. Vegan and vegetarian dining options are available for every meal.

Transportation Provides public transportation access to local destinations.

Buildings and Grounds *Percentage of institution's eligible buildings as of September 2008 meeting LEED and/or LEED-EB certification criteria:* 5%. *Renovation and maintenance:* registered for LEED certification for new construction and/or renovation; uses a Green Seal certified cleaning service. *Campus grounds care:* uses water conservation devices; employs strategies to reduce light pollution; landscapes with native plant species.

Recycling *Events and organizations:* RecycleMania. *Programs and activities:* sustains a computer/technology recycling program; sustains a pre-consumer food waste composting program; composts yard waste; replaces paper materials with online alternatives; limits free printing in computer labs and libraries. *Campus dining operations:* operates without trays.

Energy Currently uses or plans to use alternative sources of power (solar energy and wind energy); timers to regulate temperatures based on occupancy hours; motion, infrared, and/or light sensors to reduce energy uses for lighting; LED lighting; vending machine motion sensors; and energy-related performance contracting.

Purchasing Sustainability criteria used in purchasing include Energy Star (EPA) and Green Cleaning Products (Green Seal/Environmental Choice certified).

Contact Environmental, Health and Safety Officer, Massachusetts Maritime Academy, 101 Academy Drive, Buzzards Bay, MA 02532. *Phone:* 508-830-5000 Ext. 5235. *E-mail:* kdriscoll@maritime.edu. *Web site:* www.maritime.edu/.

Merrimack College
North Andover, Massachusetts

Sustainability Initiatives Merrimack College is a signatory to the Talloires Declaration.

Academics *Sustainability courses and programs:* sustainability-focused course(s) or lecture series.

Student Services and Green Events *Sustainability leadership:* sustainability coordinator/director, sustainability committee/advisory council, recycling manager, sustainability-focused student government. *Student clubs and activities:* student club(s)/group(s) focused on sustainability, outreach materials available about on-campus sustainability efforts. *Major sustainability events:* Leading the Green Initiative, Wind and Solar Power Technologies.

Food Sustainable, organic, and/or locally produced foods available in on-campus dining facilities. Fair Trade coffee is used. Vegan and vegetarian dining options are available for every meal.

Buildings and Grounds *Renovation and maintenance:* registered for LEED certification for new construction and/or renovation. *Campus grounds care:* uses water conservation devices; employs strategies to reduce light pollution; protects, restores, and/or creates habitat on campus.

Recycling *Programs and activities:* sustains a computer/technology recycling program; maintains an on-campus recycling center; composts yard waste; reuses chemicals; replaces paper materials with online alternatives. *Campus dining operations:* uses reusable dishware; offers discounts for reusable mugs; uses bulk condiment dispensers and decreased packaging for to-go food service purchases.

Energy Currently uses or plans to use alternative sources of power; timers to regulate temperatures based on occupancy hours; motion, infrared, and/or light sensors to reduce energy uses for lighting; and energy-related performance contracting.

Purchasing Sustainability criteria used in purchasing include Green Cleaning Products (Green Seal/Environmental Choice certified) and Forest Stewardship Council (FSC) or American Forest and Paper Association's Sustainable Forestry Initiative (SFI) paper.

Contact Associate Professor of Biology, Merrimack College, Department of Biology, 315 Turnpike Street, N8, North Andover, MA 01845. *Phone:* 978-837-5000 Ext. 4164. *Fax:* 978-837-5180. *E-mail:* lyonj@merrimack.edu. *Web site:* www.merrimack.edu/.

Simmons College
Boston, Massachusetts

Sustainability Initiatives Simmons College's president has signed the American College & University Presidents Climate Commitment.

Academics *Sustainability-focused undergraduate major(s):* Environmental Science. *Sustainability courses and programs:* sustainability-focused course(s) or lecture series.

Student Services and Green Events *Sustainability leadership:* sustainability committee/advisory council, recycling manager, energy manager. *Student clubs and activities:* student club(s)/group(s) focused on sustainability. *Major sustainability events:* Green Jobs and Networking Fair, Fair Trade/Sustainability Clothing Fashion Show.

Food Sustainable, organic, and/or locally produced foods available in on-campus dining facilities. Fair Trade coffee is used. Vegan and vegetarian dining options are available for every meal.

Transportation Provides free on-campus transportation (bus or other), public transportation access to local destinations, a car sharing program, and incentives to carpool or use public transportation.

Buildings and Grounds *Percentage of institution's eligible buildings as of September 2008 meeting LEED and/or LEED-EB certification criteria:* 10%. *Renovation and maintenance:* registered for LEED certification for new construction and/or renovation; uses a Green Seal certified cleaning service. *Campus grounds care:* uses water conservation devices; employs strategies to reduce light pollution; landscapes with native plant species.

Recycling *Events and organizations:* RecycleMania. *Programs and activities:* sustains a computer/technology recycling program; composts yard waste; reuses surplus department/office supplies; limits free printing in computer labs and libraries. *Campus dining operations:* uses reusable dishware; offers discounts for reusable mugs; uses bulk condiment dispensers and decreased packaging for to-go food service purchases.

Energy Currently uses or plans to use timers to regulate temperatures based on occupancy hours; motion, infrared, and/or light sensors to reduce energy uses for lighting; and LED lighting.

Purchasing Sustainability criteria used in purchasing include Energy Star (EPA) and Green Cleaning Products (Green Seal/Environmental Choice certified).

Contact Director of Facilities, Simmons College, 300 The Fenway, Boston, MA 02130. *Phone:* 617-521-2284. *E-mail:* janet.fishstein@simmons.edu. *Web site:* www.simmons.edu/.

Smith College
Northampton, Massachusetts

Sustainability Initiatives Smith College is a member of the Association for the Advancement of Sustainability in Higher Education (AASHE). This institution's president has signed the American College & University Presidents Climate Commitment.

Academics *Sustainability courses and programs:* sustainability-focused course(s) or lecture series.

Student Services and Green Events *Sustainability leadership:* sustainability coordinator/director, sustainability committee/advisory council, recycling manager, energy manager. *Student clubs and activities:* Campus Climate Challenge, Public Interest Research Group (PIRG) chapter on campus, student club(s)/group(s) focused on sustainability. *Major sustainability events:* Focus the Nation. *Housing and facilities:* on-campus organic garden for students.

Food Sustainable, organic, and/or locally produced foods available in on-campus dining facilities. Fair Trade coffee is used. Vegan and vegetarian dining options are available for every meal.

Transportation Provides free on-campus transportation (bus or other), public transportation access to local destinations, a bike loan/rental program, a car sharing program, and incentives to carpool or use public transportation.

Buildings and Grounds *Renovation and maintenance:* registered for LEED certification for new construction and/or renovation. *Campus grounds care:* uses water conservation devices; employs strategies to reduce light pollution; landscapes with native plant species.

Recycling *Events and organizations:* RecycleMania. *Programs and activities:* sustains a computer/technology recycling program; sustains a pre-consumer food waste composting program; sustains a post-consumer food waste composting program; composts yard waste; replaces paper materials with online alternatives; limits free printing in computer labs and libraries. *Campus dining operations:* uses reusable dishware; operates without trays; offers discounts for reusable mugs.

Energy Currently uses or plans to use alternative sources of power (solar energy); timers to regulate temperatures based on occupancy hours; motion, infrared, and/or light sensors to reduce energy uses for lighting; LED lighting; and vending machine motion sensors.

Purchasing Sustainability criteria used in purchasing include Energy Star (EPA), Green Electronics Council (GEC) Electronic Product Environmental Assessment Tool (EPEAT) Silver or Gold, and Green Cleaning Products (Green Seal/Environmental Choice certified).

Contact Environmental Sustainability Director, Smith College, 30 Belmont Avenue, Northampton, MA 01063. *Phone:* 413-585-2427. *E-mail:* dweisbord@smith.edu. *Web site:* www.smith.edu/.

Suffolk University
Boston, Massachusetts

Sustainability Initiatives Suffolk University has Green Fees (optional/required) dedicated to sustainability initiatives.

Academics *Sustainability-focused undergraduate major(s):* Environmental Engineering (BS), Environmental Science (BS), Environmental Studies (BA). *Sustainability courses and programs:* sustainability-focused course(s) or lecture series.

Student Services and Green Events *Sustainability leadership:* sustainability coordinator/director, sustainability committee/advisory council, recycling manager, energy manager, sustainability-focused student government. *Student clubs and activities:* Campus Climate Challenge, student club(s)/group(s) focused on sustainability, outreach materials available about on-campus sustainability efforts. *Major sustainability events:* National Teach-In on Global Warming Solutions, Energy Night, Earth Day Extravaganza, America Recycles Day.

Food Sustainable, organic, and/or locally produced foods available in on-campus dining facilities. Vegan and vegetarian dining options are available for every meal.

Transportation Provides public transportation access to local destinations, a bike loan/rental program, and a car sharing program.

Buildings and Grounds *Percentage of institution's eligible buildings as of September 2008 meeting LEED and/or LEED-EB certification criteria:* 20%. *Renovation and maintenance:* registered for LEED certification for new construction and/or renovation; uses a Green Seal certified cleaning service. *Campus grounds care:* uses water conservation devices; employs strategies to reduce light pollution.

Recycling *Events and organizations:* RecycleMania, WasteWise (EPA). *Programs and activities:* sustains a computer/technology recycling program; sustains a pre-consumer food waste composting program; reuses surplus department/office supplies; reuses chemicals; replaces paper materials with online alternatives. *Campus dining operations:* offers discounts for reusable mugs.

Energy Currently uses or plans to use alternative sources of power; motion, infrared, and/or light sensors to reduce energy uses for lighting; and vending machine motion sensors.

Purchasing Sustainability criteria used in purchasing include Energy Star (EPA), Green Cleaning Products (Green Seal/Environmental Choice certified), and Forest Stewardship Council (FSC) or American Forest and Paper Association's Sustainable Forestry Initiative (SFI) paper.

Contact Campus Sustainability Coordinator, Suffolk University, 8 Ashburton Place, Boston, MA 02108. *Phone:* 617-973-1145. *Fax:* 617-557-1522. *E-mail:* recycle@suffolk.edu. *Web site:* www.suffolk.edu/.

Tufts University
Medford, Massachusetts

Sustainability Initiatives Tufts University is a member of the Association for the Advancement of Sustainability in Higher Education (AASHE) and a signatory to the Talloires Declaration. Tufts University has Green Fees (optional/required) dedicated to sustainability initiatives.

Academics *Sustainability-focused undergraduate major(s):* Biology (BS), Chemistry (BS), Civil and Environmental Engineering (MS), Environmental Engineering (BS), Environmental Studies (BS), International Relations (BS). *Sustainability-focused graduate degree program(s):* Agriculture and Nutrition (MS, PhD), Civil and Environmental Engineering (MS, PhD), International Policy (MA, MALD, PhD), Public Health (MPH), Urban and Environmental Policy and Planning (MA), Veterinary Science and Veterinary Medicine (MS, PhD, DVM). *Sustainability courses and programs:* sustainability-focused course(s) or lecture series, noncredit sustainability course(s), sustainability-focused nonacademic certificate program(s).

Student Services and Green Events *Sustainability leadership:* sustainability coordinator/director, sustainability committee/advisory council, recycling manager, energy manager, sustainability-focused student government. *Student clubs and activities:* student club(s)/group(s) focused on sustainability. *Major sustainability events:* Energy Summit, Climate Fest Focus the Nation, Water and Security, regular speakers, series, and symposium. *Housing and facilities:* student-run café that serves environmentally or socially preferable foods.

Food Sustainable, organic, and/or locally produced foods available in on-campus dining facilities. Fair Trade coffee is used. Vegan and vegetarian dining options are available for every meal.

Transportation Provides free on-campus transportation (bus or other), public transportation access to local destinations, a car sharing program, and incentives to carpool or use public transportation.

Buildings and Grounds *Renovation and maintenance:* registered for LEED certification for new construction and/or renovation; uses a Green Seal certified cleaning service. *Campus grounds care:* uses water conservation devices; employs strategies to reduce light pollution; landscapes with native plant species.

Recycling *Events and organizations:* RecycleMania. *Programs and activities:* sustains a computer/technology recycling program; maintains an on-campus recycling center; sustains a pre-consumer food waste composting program; sustains a post-consumer food waste composting program; composts yard waste; reuses surplus department/office supplies; reuses chemicals; replaces paper materials with online alternatives; limits free printing in computer labs and libraries. *Campus dining operations:* uses reusable dishware; uses bulk condiment dispensers and decreased packaging for to-go food service purchases.

Energy Currently uses or plans to use alternative sources of power (solar energy); timers to regulate temperatures based on occupancy hours; motion, infrared, and/or light sensors to reduce energy uses for lighting; LED lighting; and vending machine motion sensors.

Purchasing Sustainability criteria used in purchasing include Energy Star (EPA) and Green Cleaning Products (Green Seal/Environmental Choice certified).

Contact Director of the Office of Sustainability, Tufts University, Office of Sustainability, Miller Hall, Tufts Institute of the Environment, Medford, MA 02155. *Phone:* 617-627-5517. *Fax:* 617-627-6645. *E-mail:* sarah.creighton@tufts.edu. *Web site:* www.tufts.edu/.

University of Massachusetts Amherst
Amherst, Massachusetts

Sustainability Initiatives University of Massachusetts Amherst's president has signed the American College & University Presidents Climate Commitment.

Academics *Sustainability courses and programs:* sustainability-focused course(s) or lecture series.

Student Services and Green Events *Sustainability leadership:* sustainability committee/advisory council, recycling manager, energy manager, sustainability-focused student government. *Student clubs and activities:* Public Interest Research Group (PIRG) chapter on campus, student club(s)/group(s) focused on sustainability. *Major sustainability events:* Clean Energy Connections Conference, Sustainable Energy Summit. *Housing and facilities:* sustainability-themed housing, model dorm room that demonstrates sustainable living principles, student-run café that serves environmentally or socially preferable foods, on-campus organic garden for students.

Food Sustainable, organic, and/or locally produced foods available in on-campus dining facilities. Fair Trade coffee is used. Vegan and vegetarian dining options are available for every meal.

Transportation Provides free on-campus transportation (bus or other), public transportation access to local destinations, a car sharing program, and incentives to carpool or use public transportation.

Buildings and Grounds *Renovation and maintenance:* uses a Green Seal certified cleaning service. *Campus grounds care:* uses water conservation devices; employs strategies to reduce light pollution; landscapes with native plant species.

Recycling *Events and organizations:* RecycleMania. *Programs and activities:* sustains a computer/technology recycling program; maintains an on-campus recycling center; sustains a pre-consumer food waste composting program; composts yard waste; reuses surplus department/office supplies; reuses chemicals; limits free printing in computer labs and libraries. *Campus dining operations:* offers discounts for reusable mugs; uses bulk condiment dispensers and decreased packaging for to-go food service purchases.

Energy Currently uses or plans to use alternative sources of power (biomass energy, hydroelectricity/water power, and solar energy); timers to regulate temperatures based on occupancy hours; motion, infrared, and/or light sensors to reduce energy uses for lighting; vending machine motion sensors; and energy-related performance contracting.

Purchasing Sustainability criteria used in purchasing include Energy Star (EPA) and Green Cleaning Products (Green Seal/Environmental Choice certified).

Contact EHS Manager, University of Massachusetts Amherst, 102 Draper Hall, Amherst, MA 01003. *Phone:* 413-545-5119. *E-mail:* cruberti@ehs.umass.edu. *Web site:* www.umass.edu/.

University of Massachusetts Boston
Boston, Massachusetts

Sustainability Initiatives University of Massachusetts Boston is a signatory to the Talloires Declaration. This institution's president has signed the American College & University Presidents Climate Commitment. University of Massachusetts Boston has Green Fees (optional/required) dedicated to sustainability initiatives.

Academics *Sustainability-focused undergraduate major(s):* Environmental Studies. *Sustainability-focused graduate degree program(s):* Environmental Sciences and Biology (MS, PhD). *Sustainability courses and programs:* sustainability-focused course(s) or lecture series, noncredit sustainability course(s).

Student Services and Green Events *Sustainability leadership:* sustainability coordinator/director, sustainability committee/advisory council, recycling manager, energy manager. *Student clubs and activities:* Public Interest

Research Group (PIRG) chapter on campus, student club(s)/group(s) focused on sustainability, outreach materials available about on-campus sustainability efforts. *Major sustainability events:* Earth Day, America Recycles Day, Focus the Nation, Conferences by Society for College and University Planning, Massachusetts State Procurement, MASSRecycle.

Food Sustainable, organic, and/or locally produced foods available in on-campus dining facilities. Fair Trade coffee is used. Vegan and vegetarian dining options are available for every meal.

Transportation Provides free on-campus transportation (bus or other), public transportation access to local destinations, and incentives to carpool or use public transportation.

Buildings and Grounds *Renovation and maintenance:* uses a Green Seal certified cleaning service. *Campus grounds care:* uses water conservation devices; employs strategies to reduce light pollution; landscapes with native plant species; protects, restores, and/or creates habitat on campus.

Recycling *Programs and activities:* sustains a computer/technology recycling program; maintains an on-campus recycling center; sustains a pre-consumer food waste composting program; sustains a post-consumer food waste composting program; composts yard waste; replaces paper materials with online alternatives; limits free printing in computer labs and libraries. *Campus dining operations:* uses reusable dishware; operates without trays; offers discounts for reusable mugs; uses bulk condiment dispensers and decreased packaging for to-go food service purchases.

Energy Currently uses or plans to use alternative sources of power; timers to regulate temperatures based on occupancy hours; motion, infrared, and/or light sensors to reduce energy uses for lighting; LED lighting; vending machine motion sensors; and energy-related performance contracting.

Purchasing Sustainability criteria used in purchasing include Energy Star (EPA), Green Cleaning Products (Green Seal/Environmental Choice certified), and Forest Stewardship Council (FSC) or American Forest and Paper Association's Sustainable Forestry Initiative (SFI) paper.

Contact Manager, Sustainability Program, University of Massachusetts Boston, 100 Morrissey Boulevard, Boston, MA 02125. *Phone:* 617-287-5083. *E-mail:* umbe.green@umb.edu. *Web site:* www.umb.edu/.

Westfield State College
Westfield, Massachusetts

Sustainability Initiatives Westfield State College's president has signed the American College & University Presidents Climate Commitment.

Academics *Sustainability-focused undergraduate major(s):* Environmental Science, Geography and Regional Planning. *Sustainability courses and programs:* sustainability-focused course(s) or lecture series.

Student Services and Green Events *Sustainability leadership:* sustainability coordinator/director, sustainability committee/advisory council, recycling manager, energy manager. *Student clubs and activities:* Campus Climate Challenge, Public Interest Research Group (PIRG) chapter on campus. *Housing and facilities:* model dorm room that demonstrates sustainable living principles.

Transportation Provides free on-campus transportation (bus or other) and public transportation access to local destinations.

Buildings and Grounds *Renovation and maintenance:* registered for LEED certification for new construction and/or renovation.

Recycling *Programs and activities:* sustains a computer/technology recycling program; maintains an on-campus recycling center; replaces paper materials with online alternatives.

Energy Currently uses or plans to use alternative sources of power.

Purchasing Sustainability criteria used in purchasing include Energy Star (EPA).

Contact Sustainability Coordinator, Westfield State College, 577 Western Avenue, Westfield, MA 01002. *Phone:* 413-572-5264. *E-mail:* wbickley@wsc.ma.edu. *Web site:* www.wsc.ma.edu/.

Williams College
Williamstown, Massachusetts

Academics *Sustainability-focused undergraduate major(s):* Environmental Studies (BA). *Sustainability courses and programs:* sustainability-focused course(s) or lecture series.

Student Services and Green Events *Sustainability leadership:* sustainability coordinator/director, sustainability committee/advisory council, recycling manager, energy manager. *Student clubs and activities:* Public Interest Research Group (PIRG) chapter on campus, student club(s)/group(s) focused on sustainability, outreach materials available about on-campus sustainability efforts. *Major sustainability events:* Center for Development Economics Conference on the Environment. *Housing and facilities:* student-run café that serves environmentally or socially preferable foods, on-campus organic garden for students.

Food Sustainable, organic, and/or locally produced foods available in on-campus dining facilities. Fair Trade coffee is used. Vegan and vegetarian dining options are available for every meal.

Transportation Provides public transportation access to local destinations and a car sharing program.

Buildings and Grounds *Percentage of institution's eligible buildings as of September 2008 meeting LEED and/or LEED-EB certification criteria:* 2%. *Renovation and maintenance:* registered for LEED certification for new construction and/or renovation; uses a Green Seal certified cleaning service. *Campus grounds care:* uses water conservation devices; employs strategies to reduce light pollution; landscapes with native plant species; protects, restores, and/or creates habitat on campus; applies to its grounds only pesticides and fertilizers allowable under the U.S. Department of Agriculture's standards for crop production.

Recycling *Events and organizations:* RecycleMania. *Programs and activities:* sustains a computer/technology recycling program; sustains a pre-consumer food waste composting program; sustains a post-consumer food waste composting program; composts yard waste; reuses surplus department/office supplies; replaces paper materials with online alternatives; limits free printing in computer labs and libraries. *Campus dining operations:* uses reusable dishware; operates without trays; offers discounts for reusable mugs; uses bulk condiment dispensers and decreased packaging for to-go food service purchases.

Energy Currently uses or plans to use alternative sources of power (hydroelectricity/water power and solar energy); timers to regulate temperatures based on occupancy hours; motion, infrared, and/or light sensors to reduce energy uses for lighting; LED lighting; and vending machine motion sensors. Participates in College & University Green Power Challenge activities.

Purchasing Sustainability criteria used in purchasing include Energy Star (EPA) and Green Cleaning Products (Green Seal/Environmental Choice certified).

Contact Director of the Zilkha Center for Environmental Initiatives, Williams College, PO Box 458, Williamstown, MA 01267. *Phone:* 413-458-5040. *E-mail:* sboyd@williams.edu. *Web site:* www.williams.edu/.

Worcester Polytechnic Institute
Worcester, Massachusetts

Sustainability Initiatives Worcester Polytechnic Institute is a member of the Association for the Advancement of Sustainability in Higher Education (AASHE).

Academics *Sustainability-focused undergraduate major(s):* Environmental Engineering (BS), Environmental Studies (BA). *Sustainability-focused graduate degree program(s):* Environmental Engineering (MEng), Environmental Engineering (MS). *Sustainability courses and programs:* sustainability-focused course(s) or lecture series.

Student Services and Green Events *Sustainability leadership:* sustainability coordinator/director, sustainability committee/advisory council, recycling manager, energy manager. *Student clubs and activities:* student club(s)/group(s) focused on sustainability. *Major sustainability events:* PREcyclemania, RecycleMania, National Teach-In, Earth Day Celebration. *Housing and facilities:* sustainability-themed housing.

Food Sustainable, organic, and/or locally produced foods available in on-campus dining facilities. Fair Trade coffee is used. Vegan and vegetarian dining options are available for every meal.

Transportation Provides free on-campus transportation (bus or other), public transportation access to local destinations, a car sharing program, and incentives to carpool or use public transportation.

Buildings and Grounds *Percentage of institution's eligible buildings as of September 2008 meeting LEED and/or LEED-EB certification criteria:* 7%. *Renovation and maintenance:* registered for LEED certification for new construction and/or renovation; uses a Green Seal certified cleaning service. *Campus grounds care:* uses water conservation devices; landscapes with native plant species; protects, restores, and/or creates habitat on campus.

Recycling *Events and organizations:* RecycleMania. *Programs and activities:* sustains a computer/technology recycling program; sustains a pre-consumer food waste composting program; sustains a post-consumer food waste composting program; reuses surplus department/office supplies; reuses chemicals; replaces paper materials with online alternatives. *Campus dining operations:* uses reusable dishware; operates without trays; offers discounts for reusable mugs; uses bulk condiment dispensers and decreased packaging for to-go food service purchases.

Energy Currently uses or plans to use timers to regulate temperatures based on occupancy hours; motion, infrared, and/or light sensors to reduce energy uses for lighting; and LED lighting.

Purchasing Sustainability criteria used in purchasing include Energy Star (EPA), Green Electronics Council (GEC) Electronic Product Environmental Assessment Tool (EPEAT) Silver or Gold, and Green Cleaning Products (Green Seal/Environmental Choice certified).

Contact Facilities Systems Manager/Sustainability Coordinator, Worcester Polytechnic Institute, 100 Institute Road, Worcester, MA 01609. *Phone:* 508-831-5454. *E-mail:* ltomasz@wpi.edu. *Web site:* www.wpi.edu/.

Worcester State College
Worcester, Massachusetts

Sustainability Initiatives Worcester State College's president has signed the American College & University Presidents Climate Commitment.

Academics *Sustainability-focused undergraduate major(s):* Geography, Environmental Studies concentration (BS). *Sustainability courses and programs:* sustainability-focused course(s) or lecture series.

Student Services and Green Events *Sustainability leadership:* sustainability committee/advisory council, recycling manager. *Student clubs and activities:* Public Interest Research Group (PIRG) chapter on campus, student club(s)/group(s) focused on sustainability. *Major sustainability events:* Sustainability Fair, Sustainability Breakfast.

Food Sustainable, organic, and/or locally produced foods available in on-campus dining facilities. Fair Trade coffee is used. Vegan and vegetarian dining options are available for every meal.

Transportation Provides public transportation access to local destinations.

Buildings and Grounds *Renovation and maintenance:* registered for LEED certification for new construction and/or renovation. *Campus grounds care:* uses water conservation devices; employs strategies to reduce light pollution; landscapes with native plant species; protects, restores, and/or creates habitat on campus.

Recycling *Programs and activities:* sustains a computer/technology recycling program; sustains a post-consumer food waste composting program; composts yard waste; reuses surplus department/office supplies; replaces paper materials with online alternatives; limits free printing in computer labs and libraries. *Campus dining operations:* uses reusable dishware; operates without trays; uses bulk condiment dispensers and decreased packaging for to-go food service purchases.

Energy Currently uses or plans to use alternative sources of power; timers to regulate temperatures based on occupancy hours; motion, infrared, and/or light sensors to reduce energy uses for lighting; and LED lighting.

Purchasing Sustainability criteria used in purchasing include Energy Star (EPA), Green Electronics Council (GEC) Electronic Product Environmental Assessment Tool (EPEAT) Silver or Gold, Green Cleaning Products (Green Seal/Environmental Choice certified), and Forest Stewardship Council (FSC) or American Forest and Paper Association's Sustainable Forestry Initiative (SFI) paper.

Contact Worcester State College, 486 Chandler Street, Worcester, MA 01602-2597. *Phone:* 508-929-8000. *Web site:* www.worcester.edu/.

Michigan

Alma College
Alma, Michigan

Academics *Sustainability-focused undergraduate major(s):* Environmental Science (BA, BS). *Sustainability courses and programs:* sustainability-focused course(s) or lecture series, noncredit sustainability course(s).

Student Services and Green Events *Sustainability leadership:* recycling manager. *Student clubs and activities:* student club(s)/group(s) focused on sustainability, outreach materials available about on-campus sustainability efforts.

Major sustainability events: International DDT Conference on Environment and Health. *Housing and facilities:* sustainability-themed housing.

Food Sustainable, organic, and/or locally produced foods available in on-campus dining facilities. Vegan and vegetarian dining options are available for every meal.

Transportation Provides public transportation access to local destinations, a bike loan/rental program, and incentives to carpool or use public transportation.

Buildings and Grounds *Campus grounds care:* uses water conservation devices; landscapes with native plant species; protects, restores, and/or creates habitat on campus; applies to its grounds only pesticides and fertilizers allowable under the U.S. Department of Agriculture's standards for crop production.

Recycling *Programs and activities:* sustains a computer/technology recycling program; maintains an on-campus recycling center; replaces paper materials with online alternatives; limits free printing in computer labs and libraries. *Campus dining operations:* uses reusable dishware; operates without trays; uses bulk condiment dispensers and decreased packaging for to-go food service purchases.

Energy Currently uses or plans to use alternative sources of power (geothermal energy and solar energy); timers to regulate temperatures based on occupancy hours; motion, infrared, and/or light sensors to reduce energy uses for lighting; LED lighting; and vending machine motion sensors.

Contact Alma College, 614 West Superior Street, Alma, MI 48801-1599. *Phone:* 989-463-7111. *Web site:* www.alma.edu/.

Aquinas College
Grand Rapids, Michigan

Sustainability Initiatives Aquinas College is a member of the Association for the Advancement of Sustainability in Higher Education (AASHE) and a signatory to the Talloires Declaration. This institution's president has signed the American College & University Presidents Climate Commitment.

Academics *Sustainability-focused undergraduate major(s):* Environmental Studies (BA, BS), Sustainable Business (BS). *Sustainability-focused graduate degree program(s):* Master of Management (MM). *Sustainability courses and programs:* sustainability-focused course(s) or lecture series, noncredit sustainability course(s), sustainability-focused nonacademic certificate program(s).

Student Services and Green Events *Sustainability leadership:* sustainability coordinator/director, sustainability committee/advisory council, recycling manager, energy manager, sustainability-focused student government. *Student clubs and activities:* student club(s)/group(s) focused on sustainability, outreach materials available about on-campus sustainability efforts. *Major sustainability events:* Developing a Strategy for Sustainability presentation, Elevating Environmental Integrity presentation, Emerging Energy Strategies presentation, Economicology Conference.

Food Sustainable, organic, and/or locally produced foods available in on-campus dining facilities. Fair Trade coffee is used. Vegan and vegetarian dining options are available for every meal.

Transportation Provides public transportation access to local destinations and incentives to carpool or use public transportation.

Buildings and Grounds *Percentage of institution's eligible buildings as of September 2008 meeting LEED and/or*

LEED-EB certification criteria: 6.5%. *Renovation and maintenance:* registered for LEED certification for new construction and/or renovation. *Campus grounds care:* uses water conservation devices; employs strategies to reduce light pollution; landscapes with native plant species; protects, restores, and/or creates habitat on campus.

Recycling *Events and organizations:* RecycleMania. *Programs and activities:* sustains a computer/technology recycling program; maintains an on-campus recycling center; composts yard waste; reuses surplus department/office supplies; replaces paper materials with online alternatives; limits free printing in computer labs and libraries. *Campus dining operations:* uses reusable dishware; operates without trays; offers discounts for reusable mugs; uses bulk condiment dispensers and decreased packaging for to-go food service purchases.

Energy Currently uses or plans to use alternative sources of power (solar energy); timers to regulate temperatures based on occupancy hours; motion, infrared, and/or light sensors to reduce energy uses for lighting; LED lighting; and energy-related performance contracting.

Purchasing Sustainability criteria used in purchasing include Energy Star (EPA), WaterSense (EPA), Green Cleaning Products (Green Seal/Environmental Choice certified), and Forest Stewardship Council (FSC) or American Forest and Paper Association's Sustainable Forestry Initiative (SFI) paper.

Contact Program Director, Center for Sustainability, Aquinas College, 1607 Robinson Road SE, Grand Rapids, MI 49506-1799. *Phone:* 616-632-1194. *E-mail:* jessica.onan@aquinas.edu. *Web site:* www.aquinas.edu/.

Eastern Michigan University
Ypsilanti, Michigan

Academics *Sustainability courses and programs:* sustainability-focused course(s) or lecture series.

Student Services and Green Events *Sustainability leadership:* sustainability coordinator/director, recycling manager, energy manager. *Student clubs and activities:* student club(s)/group(s) focused on sustainability. *Major sustainability events:* MiAPPA.

Food Sustainable, organic, and/or locally produced foods available in on-campus dining facilities. Fair Trade coffee is used. Vegan and vegetarian dining options are available for every meal.

Transportation Provides free on-campus transportation (bus or other), public transportation access to local destinations, a bike loan/rental program, and a car sharing program.

Buildings and Grounds *Renovation and maintenance:* registered for LEED certification for new construction and/or renovation; uses a Green Seal certified cleaning service. *Campus grounds care:* uses water conservation devices; employs strategies to reduce light pollution; landscapes with native plant species; protects, restores, and/or creates habitat on campus; applies to its grounds only pesticides and fertilizers allowable under the U.S. Department of Agriculture's standards for crop production.

Recycling *Programs and activities:* sustains a computer/technology recycling program; sustains a pre-consumer food waste composting program; composts yard waste; reuses surplus department/office supplies; replaces paper materials with online alternatives; limits free printing in computer labs and libraries. *Campus dining operations:* uses reusable dishware; operates without trays; uses bulk condiment dispensers and decreased packaging for to-go food service purchases.

Energy Currently uses or plans to use alternative sources of power (solar energy); timers to regulate temperatures based on occupancy hours; motion, infrared, and/or light sensors to reduce energy uses for lighting; LED lighting; vending machine motion sensors; and energy-related performance contracting.

Purchasing Sustainability criteria used in purchasing include Energy Star (EPA) and Green Cleaning Products (Green Seal/Environmental Choice certified).

Contact Energy and Sustainability Manager, Eastern Michigan University, 875 Ann Street, Ypsilanti, MI 48197. *Phone:* 734-487-3439. *Fax:* 734-487-8680. *E-mail:* smooreii@ emich.edu. *Web site:* www.emich.edu/.

Grand Valley State University
Allendale, Michigan

Sustainability Initiatives Grand Valley State University is a signatory to the Talloires Declaration. This institution's president has signed the American College & University Presidents Climate Commitment.

Academics *Sustainability courses and programs:* sustainability-focused course(s) or lecture series.

Student Services and Green Events *Sustainability leadership:* sustainability coordinator/director, sustainability committee/advisory council, recycling manager, energy manager, sustainability-focused student government. *Student clubs and activities:* student club(s)/group(s) focused on sustainability, outreach materials available about on-campus sustainability efforts. *Major sustainability events:* Annual Campus Sustainability Week activities in October, annual Student Environmental Awareness week in April, Michigan Student Sustainability Coalition statewide conference, Michigan Higher Education Partnership for Sustainability statewide conference. *Housing and facilities:* sustainability-themed housing, model dorm room that demonstrates sustainable living principles, student-run café that serves environmentally or socially preferable foods, on-campus organic garden for students.

Food Sustainable, organic, and/or locally produced foods available in on-campus dining facilities. Fair Trade coffee is used. Vegan and vegetarian dining options are available for every meal.

Transportation Provides free on-campus transportation (bus or other), public transportation access to local destinations, a car sharing program, and incentives to carpool or use public transportation.

Buildings and Grounds *Renovation and maintenance:* registered for LEED certification for new construction and/or renovation; uses a Green Seal certified cleaning service. *Campus grounds care:* uses water conservation devices; employs strategies to reduce light pollution; landscapes with native plant species; protects, restores, and/or creates habitat on campus.

Recycling *Events and organizations:* RecycleMania. *Programs and activities:* sustains a computer/technology recycling program; maintains an on-campus recycling center; sustains a pre-consumer food waste composting program; composts yard waste; reuses surplus department/office supplies. *Campus dining operations:* uses reusable dishware; operates without trays; offers discounts for reusable mugs; uses bulk condiment dispensers and decreased packaging for to-go food service purchases.

Energy Currently uses or plans to use alternative sources of power (geothermal energy, solar energy, and wind energy); timers to regulate temperatures based on occupancy hours; motion, infrared, and/or light sensors to reduce energy uses for lighting; and LED lighting.

Purchasing Sustainability criteria used in purchasing include Energy Star (EPA), Green Electronics Council (GEC) Electronic Product Environmental Assessment Tool (EPEAT) Silver or Gold, Green Cleaning Products (Green Seal/Environmental Choice certified), and Forest Stewardship Council (FSC) or American Forest and Paper Association's Sustainable Forestry Initiative (SFI) paper.

Contact Director, Sustainable Community Development Initiative, Grand Valley State University, 224 Lake Ontario Hall, 1 Campus Drive, Allendale, MI 49401. *Phone:* 616-331-7461. *Fax:* 616-331-8658. *E-mail:* chrisfn@gvsu.edu. *Web site:* www.gvsu.edu/.

Kalamazoo College
Kalamazoo, Michigan

Sustainability Initiatives Kalamazoo College's president has signed the American College & University Presidents Climate Commitment.

Academics *Sustainability courses and programs:* sustainability-focused course(s) or lecture series.

Student Services and Green Events *Sustainability leadership:* sustainability coordinator/director, sustainability committee/advisory council, recycling manager, energy manager. *Student clubs and activities:* student club(s)/group(s) focused on sustainability. *Major sustainability events:* Dorm Storm, Farms to K Local Food Chef Showdown, Sustainability Guild Workshops, Sustainability Guild Earth Day Festival. *Housing and facilities:* sustainability-themed housing, on-campus organic garden for students.

Food Sustainable, organic, and/or locally produced foods available in on-campus dining facilities. Fair Trade coffee is used. Vegan and vegetarian dining options are available for every meal.

Transportation Provides public transportation access to local destinations, a bike loan/rental program, and a car sharing program.

Buildings and Grounds *Percentage of institution's eligible buildings as of September 2008 meeting LEED and/or LEED-EB certification criteria: 22%. Renovation and maintenance:* registered for LEED certification for new construction and/or renovation; uses a Green Seal certified cleaning service. *Campus grounds care:* uses water conservation devices; employs strategies to reduce light pollution; landscapes with native plant species.

Recycling *Events and organizations:* RecycleMania. *Programs and activities:* sustains a computer/technology recycling program; maintains an on-campus recycling center; composts yard waste; reuses surplus department/office supplies; replaces paper materials with online alternatives; limits free printing in computer labs and libraries. *Campus dining operations:* uses reusable dishware; operates without trays; offers discounts for reusable mugs.

Energy Currently uses or plans to use timers to regulate temperatures based on occupancy hours; motion, infrared, and/or light sensors to reduce energy uses for lighting; and LED lighting.

Purchasing Sustainability criteria used in purchasing include Energy Star (EPA) and Green Cleaning Products (Green Seal/Environmental Choice certified).

Contact Sustainability Coordinator—Intern, Kalamazoo College, 1200 Academy Street, Kalamazoo, MI 49006. *Phone:* 269-806-9827. *Fax:* 269-337-7352. *E-mail:* mpickett@kzoo. edu. *Web site:* www.kzoo.edu/.

Michigan Technological University
Houghton, Michigan

Sustainability Initiatives Michigan Technological University's president has signed the American College & University Presidents Climate Commitment.

Academics *Sustainability-focused undergraduate major(s):* International Sustainable Development. *Sustainability courses and programs:* sustainability-focused course(s) or lecture series, noncredit sustainability course(s).

Student Services and Green Events *Sustainability leadership:* sustainability committee/advisory council, energy manager. *Student clubs and activities:* student club(s)/group(s) focused on sustainability. *Major sustainability events:* Earth Week, Campus Sustainability Week, Annual Sustainability Poster Session, D80 Conference.

Food Fair Trade coffee is used. Vegan and vegetarian dining options are available for every meal.

Transportation Provides public transportation access to local destinations and a bike loan/rental program.

Buildings and Grounds *Renovation and maintenance:* registered for LEED certification for new construction and/or renovation. *Campus grounds care:* uses water conservation devices; employs strategies to reduce light pollution; landscapes with native plant species; protects, restores, and/or creates habitat on campus.

Recycling *Events and organizations:* RecycleMania. *Programs and activities:* sustains a computer/technology recycling program; maintains an on-campus recycling center; reuses surplus department/office supplies; replaces paper materials with online alternatives; limits free printing in computer labs and libraries. *Campus dining operations:* uses reusable dishware; operates without trays; offers discounts for reusable mugs; uses bulk condiment dispensers and decreased packaging for to-go food service purchases.

Energy Currently uses or plans to use alternative sources of power (geothermal energy); timers to regulate temperatures based on occupancy hours; and motion, infrared, and/or light sensors to reduce energy uses for lighting.

Purchasing Sustainability criteria used in purchasing include Energy Star (EPA) and Green Cleaning Products (Green Seal/Environmental Choice certified).

Contact Vice President for Administration, Michigan Technological University, 1400 Townsend Drive, Houghton, MI 49931-1295. *Phone:* 906-487-1737. *E-mail:* eshorsch@mtu.edu. *Web site:* www.mtu.edu/.

Northern Michigan University
Marquette, Michigan

Academics *Sustainability-focused undergraduate major(s):* Earth Science, Earth Science Secondary Education, Ecology, Environmental Conservation, Environmental Science.

Student Services and Green Events *Sustainability leadership:* sustainability coordinator/director, recycling manager, energy manager, sustainability-focused student government. *Student clubs and activities:* student club(s)/group(s) focused on sustainability, outreach materials available about on-campus sustainability efforts. *Major sustainability events:* Earth Day, The Big Green Idea.

Food Sustainable, organic, and/or locally produced foods available in on-campus dining facilities. Fair Trade coffee is used. Vegan and vegetarian dining options are available for every meal.

Transportation Provides free on-campus transportation (bus or other) and public transportation access to local destinations.

Buildings and Grounds *Renovation and maintenance:* registered for LEED certification for new construction and/or renovation. *Campus grounds care:* uses water conservation devices; employs strategies to reduce light pollution; landscapes with native plant species; protects, restores, and/or creates habitat on campus.

Recycling *Programs and activities:* sustains a computer/technology recycling program; composts yard waste; reuses surplus department/office supplies; reuses chemicals; replaces paper materials with online alternatives. *Campus dining operations:* uses reusable dishware; operates without trays; offers discounts for reusable mugs; uses bulk condiment dispensers and decreased packaging for to-go food service purchases.

Energy Currently uses or plans to use alternative sources of power; timers to regulate temperatures based on occupancy hours; motion, infrared, and/or light sensors to reduce energy uses for lighting; vending machine motion sensors; and energy-related performance contracting.

Purchasing Sustainability criteria used in purchasing include Energy Star (EPA) and Green Cleaning Products (Green Seal/Environmental Choice certified).

Contact Owners Representative/Sustainability Coordinator, Northern Michigan University, 1401 Presque Isle Avenue, 136 Services Building, Marquette, MI 49866. *Phone:* 906-227-1446. *E-mail:* brsager@nmu.edu. *Web site:* www.nmu.edu/.

University of Michigan–Flint
Flint, Michigan

Academics *Sustainability-focused undergraduate major(s):* Environmental Chemistry (BS), Environmental Science and Planning (BS), Health Sciences (BS). *Sustainability courses and programs:* sustainability-focused course(s) or lecture series.

Student Services and Green Events *Student clubs and activities:* student club(s)/group(s) focused on sustainability. *Major sustainability events:* Flint River Watershed Coalition.

Food Fair Trade coffee is used. Vegan and vegetarian dining options are available for every meal.

Transportation Provides free on-campus transportation (bus or other), public transportation access to local destinations, a bike loan/rental program, and a car sharing program.

Buildings and Grounds *Campus grounds care:* uses water conservation devices; employs strategies to reduce light pollution.

Recycling *Programs and activities:* sustains a computer/technology recycling program; maintains an on-campus recycling center; composts yard waste; reuses surplus department/office supplies; replaces paper materials with online alternatives. *Campus dining operations:* uses reusable dishware; operates without trays; offers discounts for reusable mugs; uses bulk condiment dispensers and decreased packaging for to-go food service purchases.

Energy Currently uses or plans to use alternative sources of power; timers to regulate temperatures based on occupancy hours; LED lighting; and energy-related performance contracting.

Purchasing Sustainability criteria used in purchasing include Energy Star (EPA), Green Cleaning Products (Green Seal/Environmental Choice certified), and Forest Stewardship Council (FSC) or American Forest and Paper Association's Sustainable Forestry Initiative (SFI) paper.

Contact Environment, Health, and Safety Manager, University of Michigan–Flint, 303 East Kearsley, 204 UPAV, Flint,

MI 48502. *Phone:* 810-766-6763. *Fax:* 810-424-5572. *E-mail:* mjlane@umflint.edu. *Web site:* www.umflint.edu/.

Western Michigan University
Kalamazoo, Michigan

Sustainability Initiatives Western Michigan University is a signatory to the Talloires Declaration.

Academics *Sustainability-focused undergraduate major(s):* Environmental Studies (BS). *Sustainability-focused graduate degree program(s):* Geography (MS), Geosciences (MS), Interdisciplinary Evaluation (PhD). *Sustainability courses and programs:* sustainability-focused course(s) or lecture series, noncredit sustainability course(s).

Student Services and Green Events *Sustainability leadership:* sustainability coordinator/director, sustainability committee/advisory council, recycling manager, energy manager, sustainability-focused student government. *Student clubs and activities:* Campus Climate Challenge, student club(s)/group(s) focused on sustainability, outreach materials available about on-campus sustainability efforts. *Major sustainability events:* Sustainable Business Forum State Conference, Gwen Frostic Lecture/Seminar Series, Best Practices in Sustainability Community Luncheon. *Housing and facilities:* sustainability-themed housing, on-campus organic garden for students.

Food Sustainable, organic, and/or locally produced foods available in on-campus dining facilities. Fair Trade coffee is used. Vegan and vegetarian dining options are available for every meal.

Transportation Provides free on-campus transportation (bus or other), public transportation access to local destinations, and incentives to carpool or use public transportation.

Buildings and Grounds *Percentage of institution's eligible buildings as of September 2008 meeting LEED and/or LEED-EB certification criteria:* 5%. *Renovation and maintenance:* registered for LEED certification for new construction and/or renovation. *Campus grounds care:* uses water conservation devices; employs strategies to reduce light pollution; landscapes with native plant species; protects, restores, and/or creates habitat on campus.

Recycling *Events and organizations:* RecycleMania. *Programs and activities:* sustains a computer/technology recycling program; maintains an on-campus recycling center; composts yard waste; reuses surplus department/office supplies; replaces paper materials with online alternatives; limits free printing in computer labs and libraries. *Campus dining operations:* uses reusable dishware; operates without trays; offers discounts for reusable mugs; uses bulk condiment dispensers and decreased packaging for to-go food service purchases.

Energy Currently uses or plans to use alternative sources of power (geothermal energy, solar energy, and wind energy); timers to regulate temperatures based on occupancy hours; motion, infrared, and/or light sensors to reduce energy uses for lighting; LED lighting; vending machine motion sensors; and energy-related performance contracting.

Purchasing Sustainability criteria used in purchasing include Energy Star (EPA), WaterSense (EPA), Green Cleaning Products (Green Seal/Environmental Choice certified), and Forest Stewardship Council (FSC) or American Forest and Paper Association's Sustainable Forestry Initiative (SFI) paper.

Contact Associate Professor of Environmental Studies, Western Michigan University, Department of Environmental Studies, Kalamazoo, MI 49008. *Phone:* 269-387-2713. *Fax:* 269-387-2272. *E-mail:* harold.glasser@wmich.edu. *Web site:* www.wmich.edu/.

Minnesota

Augsburg College
Minneapolis, Minnesota

Sustainability Initiatives Augsburg College's president has signed the American College & University Presidents Climate Commitment. Augsburg College has Green Fees (optional/required) dedicated to sustainability initiatives.

Academics *Sustainability-focused undergraduate major(s):* Environmental Studies (BA). *Sustainability courses and programs:* sustainability-focused course(s) or lecture series.

Student Services and Green Events *Sustainability leadership:* sustainability coordinator/director, sustainability committee/advisory council, recycling manager, energy manager. *Student clubs and activities:* Public Interest Research Group (PIRG) chapter on campus, student club(s)/group(s) focused on sustainability, outreach materials available about on-campus sustainability efforts. *Major sustainability events:* Neighborhood Sustainability Conference. *Housing and facilities:* on-campus organic garden for students.

Food Sustainable, organic, and/or locally produced foods available in on-campus dining facilities. Fair Trade coffee is used. Vegan and vegetarian dining options are available for every meal.

Transportation Provides free on-campus transportation (bus or other), public transportation access to local destinations, a bike loan/rental program, a car sharing program, and incentives to carpool or use public transportation.

Buildings and Grounds *Campus grounds care:* uses water conservation devices; landscapes with native plant species; protects, restores, and/or creates habitat on campus.

Recycling *Programs and activities:* sustains a computer/technology recycling program; sustains a pre-consumer food waste composting program; sustains a post-consumer food waste composting program; composts yard waste; reuses surplus department/office supplies. *Campus dining operations:* uses reusable dishware; operates without trays; offers discounts for reusable mugs; uses bulk condiment dispensers and decreased packaging for to-go food service purchases.

Energy Currently uses or plans to use alternative sources of power (wind energy); timers to regulate temperatures based on occupancy hours; and motion, infrared, and/or light sensors to reduce energy uses for lighting.

Purchasing Sustainability criteria used in purchasing include Energy Star (EPA) and Green Cleaning Products (Green Seal/Environmental Choice certified).

Contact Custodial Supervisor/Chair Environmental Stewardship Committee, Augsburg College, 2211 Riverside Avenue, Campus Box 67, Minneapolis, MN 55454. *Phone:* 612-330-1641. *Fax:* 612-330-1713. *E-mail:* ruffaner@augsburg.edu. *Web site:* www.augsburg.edu/.

Bemidji State University
Bemidji, Minnesota

Sustainability Initiatives Bemidji State University is a member of the Association for the Advancement of Sustainability in Higher Education (AASHE) and a signatory to the Talloires Declaration. This institution's president has signed the American College & University Presidents Climate Commitment. Bemidji State University has Green Fees (optional/required) dedicated to sustainability initiatives.

Academics *Sustainability-focused undergraduate major(s):* Environmental Studies (BA). *Sustainability-focused gradu-*

ate degree program(s): Environmental Studies (MS). *Sustainability courses and programs:* sustainability-focused course(s) or lecture series.

Student Services and Green Events *Sustainability leadership:* sustainability coordinator/director, sustainability committee/advisory council. *Student clubs and activities:* student club(s)/group(s) focused on sustainability, outreach materials available about on-campus sustainability efforts. *Major sustainability events:* Campus Sustainability Day, Focus the Nation, Home Grown Economy Conference.

Food Sustainable, organic, and/or locally produced foods available in on-campus dining facilities. Fair Trade coffee is used.

Transportation Provides public transportation access to local destinations and incentives to carpool or use public transportation.

Buildings and Grounds *Renovation and maintenance:* uses a Green Seal certified cleaning service. *Campus grounds care:* uses water conservation devices; landscapes with native plant species; protects, restores, and/or creates habitat on campus.

Recycling *Events and organizations:* RecycleMania. *Programs and activities:* sustains a computer/technology recycling program; reuses surplus department/office supplies; replaces paper materials with online alternatives. *Campus dining operations:* uses reusable dishware; operates without trays; offers discounts for reusable mugs; uses bulk condiment dispensers and decreased packaging for to-go food service purchases.

Energy Currently uses or plans to use alternative sources of power (wind energy); timers to regulate temperatures based on occupancy hours; motion, infrared, and/or light sensors to reduce energy uses for lighting; and LED lighting.

Purchasing Sustainability criteria used in purchasing include Green Cleaning Products (Green Seal/ Environmental Choice certified).

Contact Sustainability Coordinator, Bemidji State University, 1500 Birchmont Drive NE, #31, Bemidji, MN 56601. *Phone:* 218-755-2560. *E-mail:* ebaileyjohnson@bemidjistate.edu. *Web site:* www.bemidjistate.edu/.

Carleton College
Northfield, Minnesota

Sustainability Initiatives Carleton College is a member of the Association for the Advancement of Sustainability in Higher Education (AASHE). This institution's president has signed the American College & University Presidents Climate Commitment. Carleton College has Green Fees (optional/required) dedicated to sustainability initiatives.

Academics *Sustainability courses and programs:* sustainability-focused course(s) or lecture series.

Student Services and Green Events *Sustainability leadership:* sustainability committee/advisory council, energy manager, sustainability-focused student government. *Student clubs and activities:* Public Interest Research Group (PIRG) chapter on campus, outreach materials available about on-campus sustainability efforts. *Housing and facilities:* sustainability-themed housing, on-campus organic garden for students.

Food Sustainable, organic, and/or locally produced foods available in on-campus dining facilities. Fair Trade coffee is used. Vegan and vegetarian dining options are available for every meal.

Transportation Provides public transportation access to local destinations, a bike loan/rental program, and incentives to carpool or use public transportation.

Buildings and Grounds *Renovation and maintenance:* registered for LEED certification for new construction and/or renovation. *Campus grounds care:* uses water conservation devices; employs strategies to reduce light pollution; landscapes with native plant species; protects, restores, and/or creates habitat on campus; applies to its grounds only pesticides and fertilizers allowable under the U.S. Department of Agriculture's standards for crop production.

Recycling *Events and organizations:* RecycleMania. *Programs and activities:* sustains a computer/technology recycling program; sustains a post-consumer food waste composting program; composts yard waste; replaces paper materials with online alternatives. *Campus dining operations:* uses reusable dishware; offers discounts for reusable mugs; uses bulk condiment dispensers and decreased packaging for to-go food service purchases.

Energy Currently uses or plans to use alternative sources of power (wind energy); timers to regulate temperatures based on occupancy hours; motion, infrared, and/or light sensors to reduce energy uses for lighting; and LED lighting.

Purchasing Sustainability criteria used in purchasing include Energy Star (EPA), Green Cleaning Products (Green Seal/Environmental Choice certified), and Forest Stewardship Council (FSC) or American Forest and Paper Association's Sustainable Forestry Initiative (SFI) paper.

Contact Educational Associate, Environmental Studies Department, Carleton College, One North College Street, Northfield, MN 55057. *Phone:* 507-222-7018. *E-mail:* ericksoc@carleton.edu. *Web site:* www.carleton.edu/.

Gustavus Adolphus College
St. Peter, Minnesota

Sustainability Initiatives Gustavus Adolphus College is a member of the Association for the Advancement of Sustainability in Higher Education (AASHE). This institution's president has signed the American College & University Presidents Climate Commitment.

Academics *Sustainability-focused undergraduate major(s):* Environmental Studies (BA), Peace Studies (BA). *Sustainability courses and programs:* sustainability-focused course(s) or lecture series.

Student Services and Green Events *Sustainability leadership:* sustainability committee/advisory council, recycling manager. *Student clubs and activities:* student club(s)/group(s) focused on sustainability. *Major sustainability events:* Linnaeus Symposium, Building Bridges, MayDay! Peace Conference, Nobel Conference. *Housing and facilities:* model dorm room that demonstrates sustainable living principles, student-run café that serves environmentally or socially preferable foods, on-campus organic garden for students.

Food Sustainable, organic, and/or locally produced foods available in on-campus dining facilities. Fair Trade coffee is used. Vegan and vegetarian dining options are available for every meal.

Transportation Provides public transportation access to local destinations.

Buildings and Grounds *Renovation and maintenance:* registered for LEED certification for new construction and/or renovation. *Campus grounds care:* uses water conservation devices; protects, restores, and/or creates habitat on campus.

Recycling *Events and organizations:* RecycleMania. *Programs and activities:* sustains a computer/technology recycling program; maintains an on-campus recycling center;

composts yard waste; reuses surplus department/office supplies. *Campus dining operations:* uses reusable dishware; uses bulk condiment dispensers and decreased packaging for to-go food service purchases.

Energy Currently uses or plans to use alternative sources of power and motion, infrared, and/or light sensors to reduce energy uses for lighting.

Purchasing Sustainability criteria used in purchasing include Energy Star (EPA) and Green Cleaning Products (Green Seal/Environmental Choice certified).

Contact Director, Johnson Center for Environmental Innovation, Gustavus Adolphus College, 800 West College Avenue, St. Peter, MN 56082. *Phone:* 507-933-7206. *Fax:* 507-933-6481. *E-mail:* jdontje@gustavus.edu. *Web site:* www.gustavus.edu/.

Hamline University
St. Paul, Minnesota

Academics *Sustainability courses and programs:* sustainability-focused course(s) or lecture series, noncredit sustainability course(s), sustainability-focused nonacademic certificate program(s).

Student Services and Green Events *Sustainability leadership:* sustainability committee/advisory council, recycling manager, energy manager, sustainability-focused student government. *Student clubs and activities:* Public Interest Research Group (PIRG) chapter on campus, outreach materials available about on-campus sustainability efforts.

Food Sustainable, organic, and/or locally produced foods available in on-campus dining facilities. Vegan and vegetarian dining options are available for every meal.

Transportation Provides free on-campus transportation (bus or other) and public transportation access to local destinations.

Buildings and Grounds *Campus grounds care:* uses water conservation devices; landscapes with native plant species.

Recycling *Events and organizations:* RecycleMania. *Programs and activities:* sustains a computer/technology recycling program; sustains a pre-consumer food waste composting program; sustains a post-consumer food waste composting program; composts yard waste; reuses surplus department/office supplies; limits free printing in computer labs and libraries. *Campus dining operations:* uses reusable dishware; operates without trays; offers discounts for reusable mugs; uses bulk condiment dispensers and decreased packaging for to-go food service purchases.

Energy Currently uses or plans to use timers to regulate temperatures based on occupancy hours; motion, infrared, and/or light sensors to reduce energy uses for lighting; LED lighting; and energy-related performance contracting.

Purchasing Sustainability criteria used in purchasing include Energy Star (EPA).

Contact Hamline University, 1536 Hewitt Avenue, St. Paul, MN 55104-1284. *Phone:* 651-523-2800. *Web site:* www.hamline.edu/.

Macalester College
St. Paul, Minnesota

Sustainability Initiatives Macalester College is a member of the Association for the Advancement of Sustainability in Higher Education (AASHE) and a signatory to the Talloires Declaration. This institution's president has signed the American College & University Presidents Climate Commitment.

Academics *Sustainability-focused undergraduate major(s):* Environmental Studies (BA). *Sustainability courses and programs:* sustainability-focused course(s) or lecture series, noncredit sustainability course(s).

Student Services and Green Events *Sustainability leadership:* sustainability coordinator/director, sustainability committee/advisory council, recycling manager, energy manager. *Student clubs and activities:* Campus Climate Challenge, Public Interest Research Group (PIRG) chapter on campus, student club(s)/group(s) focused on sustainability, outreach materials available about on-campus sustainability efforts. *Major sustainability events:* Civic Forum, EnviroThursday, Focus the Nation, Climate Institute, Summer of Solutions. *Housing and facilities:* sustainability-themed housing, on-campus organic garden for students.

Food Sustainable, organic, and/or locally produced foods available in on-campus dining facilities. Fair Trade coffee is used. Vegan and vegetarian dining options are available for every meal.

Transportation Provides public transportation access to local destinations, a bike loan/rental program, a car sharing program, and incentives to carpool or use public transportation.

Buildings and Grounds *Campus grounds care:* uses water conservation devices; landscapes with native plant species; protects, restores, and/or creates habitat on campus.

Recycling *Events and organizations:* RecycleMania. *Programs and activities:* sustains a computer/technology recycling program; maintains an on-campus recycling center; composts yard waste; reuses chemicals; replaces paper materials with online alternatives. *Campus dining operations:* uses reusable dishware; operates without trays; offers discounts for reusable mugs; uses bulk condiment dispensers and decreased packaging for to-go food service purchases.

Energy Currently uses or plans to use alternative sources of power (solar energy and wind energy); timers to regulate temperatures based on occupancy hours; and motion, infrared, and/or light sensors to reduce energy uses for lighting.

Purchasing Sustainability criteria used in purchasing include Energy Star (EPA), Green Electronics Council (GEC) Electronic Product Environmental Assessment Tool (EPEAT) Silver or Gold, and Green Cleaning Products (Green Seal/Environmental Choice certified).

Contact Sustainability Manager, Macalester College, Sustainability Office, 1600 Grand Avenue, St. Paul, MN 55105. *Phone:* 651-696-6019. *E-mail:* shansen2@macalester.edu. *Web site:* www.macalester.edu/.

University of Minnesota, Duluth
Duluth, Minnesota

Sustainability Initiatives University of Minnesota, Duluth's president has signed the American College & University Presidents Climate Commitment.

Academics *Sustainability-focused undergraduate major(s):* Anthropology (BA), Environmental Science (BS), Environmental Studies (BA), Geography (BA), International Studies (BA), Urban and Regional Studies (BA). *Sustainability-focused graduate degree program(s):* Advocacy and Political Leadership (MAPL), Geological Sciences (MS), Integrated Biosciences Program (MS, PhD), Social Work (MSW), Toxicology (MS, PhD), Water Resources Science (MS, PhD), Environmental Health, Environmental Health and Safety (MEHS), Environmental Education (MEd). *Sustainability courses and programs:* sustainability-focused course(s) or lecture series, noncredit sustainability course(s).

Student Services and Green Events *Sustainability leadership:* sustainability coordinator/director, sustainability committee/advisory council, recycling manager, energy manager. *Student clubs and activities:* Public Interest Research Group (PIRG) chapter on campus, student club(s)/group(s) focused on sustainability, outreach materials available about on-campus sustainability efforts. *Major sustainability events:* The Longest Summer Tour (Will Steger),Winter Sustainability Fair, 2009 National Teach-In on Climate Change, 2009 Spring Sustainability Fair.

Food Fair Trade coffee is used.

Transportation Provides public transportation access to local destinations and incentives to carpool or use public transportation.

Buildings and Grounds *Percentage of institution's eligible buildings as of September 2008 meeting LEED and/or LEED-EB certification criteria:* 4%. *Renovation and maintenance:* registered for LEED certification for new construction and/or renovation; uses a Green Seal certified cleaning service. *Campus grounds care:* uses water conservation devices; employs strategies to reduce light pollution; landscapes with native plant species; protects, restores, and/or creates habitat on campus.

Recycling *Events and organizations:* RecycleMania. *Programs and activities:* sustains a computer/technology recycling program; sustains a pre-consumer food waste composting program; sustains a post-consumer food waste composting program; composts yard waste; reuses surplus department/office supplies; reuses chemicals; replaces paper materials with online alternatives; limits free printing in computer labs and libraries. *Campus dining operations:* uses reusable dishware; offers discounts for reusable mugs; uses bulk condiment dispensers and decreased packaging for to-go food service purchases.

Energy Currently uses or plans to use alternative sources of power (solar energy); timers to regulate temperatures based on occupancy hours; motion, infrared, and/or light sensors to reduce energy uses for lighting; LED lighting; and vending machine motion sensors.

Purchasing Sustainability criteria used in purchasing include Green Cleaning Products (Green Seal/Environmental Choice certified).

Contact Sustainability Coordinator, University of Minnesota, Duluth, 241 Darland Administration Building, 1049 University Drive, Duluth, MN 55812. *Phone:* 218-726-8198. *Fax:* 218-726-8127. *E-mail:* mgranley@d.umn.edu. *Web site:* www.d.umn.edu/.

University of Minnesota, Twin Cities Campus
Minneapolis, Minnesota

Sustainability Initiatives University of Minnesota, Twin Cities Campus is a member of the Association for the Advancement of Sustainability in Higher Education (AASHE). This institution's president has signed the American College & University Presidents Climate Commitment.

Academics *Sustainability-focused undergraduate major(s):* Corporate Environmental Management (BS), Environmental Science Policy Management (BS), Global Studies (BA), Sustainability Minor (BA, BS), Sustainable Agriculture (BS), Urban Studies (BA). *Sustainability-focused graduate degree program(s):* Architecture Sustainable Design (MS); Conservation Biology (PhD); Science, Technology, and Environmental Policy (MS-STEP); Sustainable Agriculture Systems (PhD). *Sustainability courses and programs:* sustainability-focused course(s) or lecture series.

Student Services and Green Events *Sustainability leadership:* sustainability coordinator/director, sustainability committee/advisory council, recycling manager, energy manager. *Student clubs and activities:* Campus Climate Challenge, Public Interest Research Group (PIRG) chapter on campus, student club(s)/group(s) focused on sustainability, outreach materials available about on-campus sustainability efforts. *Major sustainability events:* Beautiful U Day, IonE/IREE: E3 Midwest's Premier Energy Economic and Env Conference, Policy @ Humphrey Institute. *Housing and facilities:* sustainability-themed housing, model dorm room that demonstrates sustainable living principles, student-run café that serves environmentally or socially preferable foods, on-campus organic garden for students.

Food Sustainable, organic, and/or locally produced foods available in on-campus dining facilities. Fair Trade coffee is used. Vegan and vegetarian dining options are available for every meal.

Transportation Provides free on-campus transportation (bus or other), public transportation access to local destinations, a bike loan/rental program, a car sharing program, and incentives to carpool or use public transportation.

Buildings and Grounds *Percentage of institution's eligible buildings as of September 2008 meeting LEED and/or LEED-EB certification criteria:* 2%. *Renovation and maintenance:* registered for LEED certification for new construction and/or renovation. *Campus grounds care:* uses water conservation devices; employs strategies to reduce light pollution; landscapes with native plant species; protects, restores, and/or creates habitat on campus.

Recycling *Events and organizations:* RecycleMania, WasteWise (EPA). *Programs and activities:* sustains a computer/technology recycling program; maintains an on-campus recycling center; sustains a pre-consumer food waste composting program; sustains a post-consumer food waste composting program; composts yard waste; reuses surplus department/office supplies; reuses chemicals; replaces paper materials with online alternatives; limits free printing in computer labs and libraries. *Campus dining operations:* uses reusable dishware; operates without trays; offers discounts for reusable mugs; uses bulk condiment dispensers and decreased packaging for to-go food service purchases.

Energy Currently uses or plans to use alternative sources of power (biomass energy); timers to regulate temperatures based on occupancy hours; motion, infrared, and/or light sensors to reduce energy uses for lighting; LED lighting; and vending machine motion sensors.

Purchasing Sustainability criteria used in purchasing include Energy Star (EPA), WaterSense (EPA), Green Electronics Council (GEC) Electronic Product Environmental Assessment Tool (EPEAT) Silver or Gold, Green Cleaning Products (Green Seal/Environmental Choice certified), and Forest Stewardship Council (FSC) or American Forest and Paper Association's Sustainable Forestry Initiative (SFI) paper.

Contact Sustainability Education Coordinator, University of Minnesota, Twin Cities Campus, 200 Hodson Hall, 1980 Folwell Avenue, St. Paul, MN 55108. *Phone:* 612-624-9430. *E-mail:* bethmt@umn.edu. *Web site:* www.umn.edu/tc/.

Winona State University
Winona, Minnesota

Sustainability Initiatives Winona State University's president has signed the American College & University Presidents Climate Commitment.

Academics *Sustainability courses and programs:* sustainability-focused course(s) or lecture series, noncredit sustainability course(s).

Student Services and Green Events *Sustainability leadership:* sustainability coordinator/director, sustainability committee/advisory council, recycling manager, energy manager. *Student clubs and activities:* Campus Climate Challenge, student club(s)/group(s) focused on sustainability. *Major sustainability events:* Annual Energy Summit, Frozen River Film Festival, Annual National Prairie Conference. *Housing and facilities:* on-campus organic garden for students.

Food Sustainable, organic, and/or locally produced foods available in on-campus dining facilities. Fair Trade coffee is used. Vegan and vegetarian dining options are available for every meal.

Transportation Provides free on-campus transportation (bus or other), a car sharing program, and incentives to carpool or use public transportation.

Buildings and Grounds *Percentage of institution's eligible buildings as of September 2008 meeting LEED and/or LEED-EB certification criteria:* 1%. *Renovation and maintenance:* uses a Green Seal certified cleaning service. *Campus grounds care:* uses water conservation devices; employs strategies to reduce light pollution; landscapes with native plant species; protects, restores, and/or creates habitat on campus; applies to its grounds only pesticides and fertilizers allowable under the U.S. Department of Agriculture's standards for crop production.

Recycling *Events and organizations:* RecycleMania, WasteWise (EPA). *Programs and activities:* sustains a computer/technology recycling program; sustains a pre-consumer food waste composting program; sustains a post-consumer food waste composting program; composts yard waste; reuses surplus department/office supplies; reuses chemicals. *Campus dining operations:* uses reusable dishware; operates without trays; offers discounts for reusable mugs; uses bulk condiment dispensers and decreased packaging for to-go food service purchases.

Energy Currently uses or plans to use timers to regulate temperatures based on occupancy hours; motion, infrared, and/or light sensors to reduce energy uses for lighting; LED lighting; and energy-related performance contracting.

Purchasing Sustainability criteria used in purchasing include Energy Star (EPA) and Green Cleaning Products (Green Seal/Environmental Choice certified).

Contact Sustainability Coordinator, Winona State University, 356 Knopp Valley Drive, Winona, MN 55987. *Phone:* 507-454-0810. *E-mail:* cwinbush@hbci.con. *Web site:* www.winona.edu/.

Mississippi

Delta State University
Cleveland, Mississippi

Academics *Sustainability-focused graduate degree program(s):* Community Development—Sustainable Development track (MS). *Sustainability courses and programs:* sustainability-focused course(s) or lecture series.

Student Services and Green Events *Sustainability leadership:* recycling manager, energy manager, sustainability-focused student government. *Housing and facilities:* sustainability-themed housing.

Food Sustainable, organic, and/or locally produced foods available in on-campus dining facilities. Vegan and vegetarian dining options are available for every meal.

Buildings and Grounds *Campus grounds care:* landscapes with native plant species.

Recycling *Programs and activities:* sustains a computer/technology recycling program; reuses chemicals; replaces paper materials with online alternatives; limits free printing in computer labs and libraries. *Campus dining operations:* uses reusable dishware; operates without trays; offers discounts for reusable mugs.

Energy Currently uses or plans to use timers to regulate temperatures based on occupancy hours; motion, infrared, and/or light sensors to reduce energy uses for lighting; and LED lighting.

Purchasing Sustainability criteria used in purchasing include Energy Star (EPA).

Contact Delta State University, Highway 8 West, Cleveland, MS 38733-0001. *Phone:* 662-846-3000. *Web site:* www.deltastate.edu/.

University of Mississippi
Oxford, Mississippi

Sustainability Initiatives University of Mississippi's president has signed the American College & University Presidents Climate Commitment.

Academics *Sustainability courses and programs:* sustainability-focused course(s) or lecture series.

Student Services and Green Events *Sustainability leadership:* sustainability coordinator/director, sustainability committee/advisory council, recycling manager, energy manager, sustainability-focused student government. *Student clubs and activities:* student club(s)/group(s) focused on sustainability. *Major sustainability events:* Green Week—Green Speakers series, outreach/education activities, Green Job Fair.

Food Sustainable, organic, and/or locally produced foods available in on-campus dining facilities. Vegan and vegetarian dining options are available for every meal.

Transportation Provides free on-campus transportation (bus or other), public transportation access to local destinations, and incentives to carpool or use public transportation.

Buildings and Grounds *Renovation and maintenance:* registered for LEED certification for new construction and/or renovation. *Campus grounds care:* protects, restores, and/or creates habitat on campus.

Recycling *Events and organizations:* RecycleMania. *Programs and activities:* sustains a computer/technology recycling program; replaces paper materials with online alternatives. *Campus dining operations:* uses reusable dishware; operates without trays; offers discounts for reusable mugs.

Energy Currently uses or plans to use alternative sources of power (solar energy); timers to regulate temperatures based on occupancy hours; motion, infrared, and/or light sensors to reduce energy uses for lighting; LED lighting; vending machine motion sensors; and energy-related performance contracting.

Purchasing Sustainability criteria used in purchasing include Energy Star (EPA), Green Cleaning Products (Green Seal/Environmental Choice certified), and Forest Stewardship Council (FSC) or American Forest and Paper Association's Sustainable Forestry Initiative (SFI) paper.

Contact Director of Strategic Planning and Campus Sustainability Coordinator, University of Mississippi, Lyceum 224, PO Box 1848, University, MS 38655. *Phone:* 662-915-1678. *Fax:* 662-915-5280. *E-mail:* jwmorris@olemiss.edu. *Web site:* www.olemiss.edu/.

Missouri

Harris-Stowe State University
St. Louis, Missouri

Transportation Provides free on-campus transportation (bus or other).

Buildings and Grounds *Campus grounds care:* uses water conservation devices; protects, restores, and/or creates habitat on campus.

Recycling *Programs and activities:* sustains a computer/technology recycling program; replaces paper materials with online alternatives; limits free printing in computer labs and libraries. *Campus dining operations:* uses reusable dishware; uses bulk condiment dispensers and decreased packaging for to-go food service purchases.

Energy Currently uses or plans to use timers to regulate temperatures based on occupancy hours.

Contact Harris-Stowe State University, 3026 Laclede Avenue, St. Louis, MO 63103-2136. *Phone:* 314-340-3366. *Web site:* www.hssu.edu/.

Lindenwood University
St. Charles, Missouri

Academics *Sustainability courses and programs:* sustainability-focused course(s) or lecture series.

Student Services and Green Events *Sustainability leadership:* sustainability committee/advisory council, sustainability-focused student government. *Student clubs and activities:* outreach materials available about on-campus sustainability efforts.

Food Sustainable, organic, and/or locally produced foods available in on-campus dining facilities. Fair Trade coffee is used. Vegan and vegetarian dining options are available for every meal.

Buildings and Grounds *Campus grounds care:* uses water conservation devices; landscapes with native plant species; protects, restores, and/or creates habitat on campus.

Recycling *Programs and activities:* sustains a computer/technology recycling program; composts yard waste; reuses surplus department/office supplies; replaces paper materials with online alternatives; limits free printing in computer labs and libraries.

Energy Currently uses or plans to use alternative sources of power; timers to regulate temperatures based on occupancy hours; motion, infrared, and/or light sensors to reduce energy uses for lighting; and LED lighting.

Contact Lindenwood University, 209 South Kingshighway, St. Charles, MO 63301-1695. *Phone:* 636-949-2000. *Web site:* www.lindenwood.edu/.

Maryville University of Saint Louis
St. Louis, Missouri

Academics *Sustainability courses and programs:* sustainability-focused course(s) or lecture series.

Student Services and Green Events *Sustainability leadership:* sustainability committee/advisory council, recycling manager, energy manager. *Student clubs and activities:* student club(s)/group(s) focused on sustainability, outreach materials available about on-campus sustainability efforts. *Major sustainability events:* Campus Sustainability Day Conference, Campus Sustainability Day Conference with Saint Louis University. *Housing and facilities:* sustainability-themed housing.

Food Fair Trade coffee is used. Vegan and vegetarian dining options are available for every meal.

Buildings and Grounds *Renovation and maintenance:* registered for LEED certification for new construction and/or renovation. *Campus grounds care:* uses water conservation devices; employs strategies to reduce light pollution; landscapes with native plant species; protects, restores, and/or creates habitat on campus; applies to its grounds only pesticides and fertilizers allowable under the U.S. Department of Agriculture's standards for crop production.

Recycling *Programs and activities:* sustains a computer/technology recycling program; reuses surplus department/office supplies; reuses chemicals; replaces paper materials with online alternatives. *Campus dining operations:* uses reusable dishware; operates without trays; offers discounts for reusable mugs; uses bulk condiment dispensers and decreased packaging for to-go food service purchases.

Energy Currently uses or plans to use timers to regulate temperatures based on occupancy hours; motion, infrared, and/or light sensors to reduce energy uses for lighting; LED lighting; and energy-related performance contracting.

Purchasing Sustainability criteria used in purchasing include Energy Star (EPA) and Green Cleaning Products (Green Seal/Environmental Choice certified).

Contact Maryville University of Saint Louis, 650 Maryville University Drive, St. Louis, MO 63141-7299. *Phone:* 314-529-9300. *Web site:* www.maryville.edu/.

Missouri State University
Springfield, Missouri

Academics *Sustainability courses and programs:* sustainability-focused course(s) or lecture series, noncredit sustainability course(s).

Student Services and Green Events *Sustainability leadership:* sustainability coordinator/director, sustainability committee/advisory council, recycling manager, energy manager. *Student clubs and activities:* student club(s)/group(s) focused on sustainability. *Major sustainability events:* Public Affairs Conference: Sustainable Actions for a Sustainable Future, Recycle Mania, Public Affairs Week. *Housing and facilities:* student-run café that serves environmentally or socially preferable foods.

Food Sustainable, organic, and/or locally produced foods available in on-campus dining facilities. Fair Trade coffee is used. Vegan and vegetarian dining options are available for every meal.

Transportation Provides free on-campus transportation (bus or other) and public transportation access to local destinations.

Buildings and Grounds *Campus grounds care:* landscapes with native plant species; applies to its grounds only pesticides and fertilizers allowable under the U.S. Department of Agriculture's standards for crop production.

Recycling *Events and organizations:* RecycleMania. *Programs and activities:* sustains a computer/technology recycling program; sustains a pre-consumer food waste composting program; sustains a post-consumer food waste composting program; composts yard waste; reuses surplus department/office supplies; reuses chemicals; replaces paper materials with online alternatives. *Campus dining operations:* uses reusable dishware; offers discounts for reusable mugs; uses bulk condiment dispensers and decreased packaging for to-go food service purchases.

Energy Currently uses or plans to use alternative sources of power; timers to regulate temperatures based on occupancy hours; motion, infrared, and/or light sensors to reduce energy uses for lighting; and energy-related performance contracting.

Purchasing Sustainability criteria used in purchasing include Energy Star (EPA).

Contact Sustainability Coordinator, Missouri State University, 901 South National, Springfield, MO 65897. *Phone:* 417-836-8334. *Web site:* www.missouristate.edu/.

University of Central Missouri
Warrensburg, Missouri

Sustainability Initiatives University of Central Missouri's president has signed the American College & University Presidents Climate Commitment. University of Central Missouri has Green Fees (optional/required) dedicated to sustainability initiatives.

Student Services and Green Events *Sustainability leadership:* sustainability committee/advisory council.

Buildings and Grounds *Renovation and maintenance:* registered for LEED certification for new construction and/or renovation. *Campus grounds care:* landscapes with native plant species; protects, restores, and/or creates habitat on campus.

Recycling *Events and organizations:* RecycleMania. *Programs and activities:* sustains a computer/technology recycling program; composts yard waste; reuses surplus department/office supplies; replaces paper materials with online alternatives; limits free printing in computer labs and libraries. *Campus dining operations:* uses reusable dishware; operates without trays; offers discounts for reusable mugs; uses bulk condiment dispensers and decreased packaging for to-go food service purchases.

Energy Currently uses or plans to use alternative sources of power; timers to regulate temperatures based on occupancy hours; motion, infrared, and/or light sensors to reduce energy uses for lighting; and energy-related performance contracting.

Purchasing Sustainability criteria used in purchasing include Energy Star (EPA) and Green Cleaning Products (Green Seal/Environmental Choice certified).

Contact Dean, Science and Technology, University of Central Missouri, 116 West South Street, HUM 225, Warrensburg, MO 64093. *Phone:* 660-543-4450. *E-mail:* greife@ucmo.edu. *Web site:* www.ucmo.edu/.

University of Missouri–Columbia
Columbia, Missouri

Sustainability Initiatives University of Missouri–Columbia's president has signed the American College & University Presidents Climate Commitment.

Academics *Sustainability-focused undergraduate major(s):* Environmental Studies (BA), Environmental Studies (BS). *Sustainability courses and programs:* sustainability-focused course(s) or lecture series.

Student Services and Green Events *Sustainability leadership:* sustainability committee/advisory council, recycling manager, energy manager. *Student clubs and activities:* student club(s)/group(s) focused on sustainability, outreach materials available about on-campus sustainability efforts. *Major sustainability events:* Hazardous Waste Management Summer and Winter Institutes, Community Development Academy Spring and Fall Academy, Missouri Energy Summit, Bio-renewables—Extension, Research, and Technology Conference, Crop Management, Nano and Molecular Medicine. *Housing and facilities:* sustainability-themed housing.

Food Sustainable, organic, and/or locally produced foods available in on-campus dining facilities. Fair Trade coffee is used. Vegan and vegetarian dining options are available for every meal.

Transportation Provides free on-campus transportation (bus or other) and public transportation access to local destinations.

Buildings and Grounds *Campus grounds care:* uses water conservation devices; landscapes with native plant species.

Recycling *Events and organizations:* RecycleMania, WasteWise (EPA). *Programs and activities:* sustains a computer/technology recycling program; maintains an on-campus recycling center; sustains a post-consumer food waste composting program; composts yard waste; reuses surplus department/office supplies; reuses chemicals; replaces paper materials with online alternatives; limits free printing in computer labs and libraries. *Campus dining operations:* uses reusable dishware; offers discounts for reusable mugs; uses bulk condiment dispensers and decreased packaging for to-go food service purchases.

Energy Currently uses or plans to use timers to regulate temperatures based on occupancy hours; motion, infrared, and/or light sensors to reduce energy uses for lighting; and LED lighting.

Contact University of Missouri–Columbia, Columbia, MO 65211. *Phone:* 573-882-2121. *Web site:* www.missouri.edu/.

University of Missouri–St. Louis
St. Louis, Missouri

Sustainability Initiatives University of Missouri–St. Louis's president has signed the American College & University Presidents Climate Commitment.

Academics *Sustainability-focused graduate degree program(s):* Biochemistry (PhD), Ecology (MS), Environmental Studies (PhD), Evolution and Systematics (MS), Molecular Biology and Biotechnology (PhD), Plant Systematics (PhD), Cell and Molecular Biology (MS). *Sustainability courses and programs:* sustainability-focused course(s) or lecture series.

Student Services and Green Events *Student clubs and activities:* student club(s)/group(s) focused on sustainability, outreach materials available about on-campus sustainability efforts. *Major sustainability events:* "What Is a City?—Sustainable Urban Environments".

Food Sustainable, organic, and/or locally produced foods available in on-campus dining facilities. Fair Trade coffee is used. Vegan and vegetarian dining options are available for every meal.

Transportation Provides free on-campus transportation (bus or other) and public transportation access to local destinations.

Buildings and Grounds *Renovation and maintenance:* registered for LEED certification for new construction and/or renovation. *Campus grounds care:* landscapes with native plant species.

Recycling *Programs and activities:* reuses surplus department/office supplies; replaces paper materials with online alternatives. *Campus dining operations:* uses reusable dishware; operates without trays; offers discounts for reusable mugs; uses bulk condiment dispensers and decreased packaging for to-go food service purchases.

Energy Currently uses or plans to use timers to regulate temperatures based on occupancy hours; motion, infrared, and/or light sensors to reduce energy uses for lighting; LED lighting; and vending machine motion sensors.

Purchasing Sustainability criteria used in purchasing include Green Cleaning Products (Green Seal/Environmental Choice certified).

Contact University of Missouri–St. Louis, One University Boulevard, St. Louis, MO 63121. *Phone:* 314-516-5000. *Web site:* www.umsl.edu/.

Westminster College
Fulton, Missouri

Academics *Sustainability-focused undergraduate major(s):* Environmental Science, Environmental Studies, Philosophy. *Sustainability courses and programs:* sustainability-focused course(s) or lecture series.

Student Services and Green Events *Sustainability leadership:* sustainability coordinator/director, sustainability committee/advisory council, recycling manager, energy manager, sustainability-focused student government. *Student clubs and activities:* student club(s)/group(s) focused on sustainability. *Major sustainability events:* Symposium on Democracy, Undergraduate Scholars Forum. *Housing and facilities:* sustainability-themed housing, model dorm room that demonstrates sustainable living principles, on-campus organic garden for students.

Food Sustainable, organic, and/or locally produced foods available in on-campus dining facilities. Fair Trade coffee is used. Vegan and vegetarian dining options are available for every meal.

Buildings and Grounds *Campus grounds care:* uses water conservation devices; landscapes with native plant species.

Recycling *Events and organizations:* WasteWise (EPA). *Programs and activities:* sustains a computer/technology recycling program; composts yard waste; reuses surplus department/office supplies; reuses chemicals; replaces paper materials with online alternatives; limits free printing in computer labs and libraries. *Campus dining operations:* uses reusable dishware; operates without trays; offers discounts for reusable mugs; uses bulk condiment dispensers and decreased packaging for to-go food service purchases.

Energy Currently uses or plans to use timers to regulate temperatures based on occupancy hours; motion, infrared, and/or light sensors to reduce energy uses for lighting; and LED lighting.

Purchasing Sustainability criteria used in purchasing include Energy Star (EPA) and Green Cleaning Products (Green Seal/Environmental Choice certified).

Contact Assistant Professor of Asian Philosophy and Religion, Westminster College, 501 Westminster Avenue, Fulton, MO 65251. *Phone:* 573-592-6229. *Fax:* 573-592-5191. *E-mail:* james.mcrae@westminster-mo.edu. *Web site:* www.westminster-mo.edu/.

William Jewell College
Liberty, Missouri

Academics *Sustainability-focused undergraduate major(s):* Bioethics.

Student Services and Green Events *Sustainability leadership:* sustainability coordinator/director, sustainability committee/advisory council. *Student clubs and activities:* student club(s)/group(s) focused on sustainability, outreach materials available about on-campus sustainability efforts. *Major sustainability events:* Local Action Projects, Campus-wide Awareness Emphasis, Student Project Grant Program.

Food Vegan and vegetarian dining options are available for every meal.

Buildings and Grounds *Renovation and maintenance:* registered for LEED certification for new construction and/or renovation. *Campus grounds care:* uses water conservation devices; landscapes with native plant species.

Recycling *Programs and activities:* sustains a computer/technology recycling program; maintains an on-campus recycling center; composts yard waste; replaces paper materials with online alternatives. *Campus dining operations:* operates without trays; offers discounts for reusable mugs; uses bulk condiment dispensers and decreased packaging for to-go food service purchases.

Energy Currently uses or plans to use timers to regulate temperatures based on occupancy hours; motion, infrared, and/or light sensors to reduce energy uses for lighting; LED lighting; and energy-related performance contracting.

Contact Executive Director, William Jewell College, 500 College Hill, Liberty, MO 64068. *Phone:* 816-415-7557. *Fax:* 816-415-5093. *E-mail:* pratta@william.jewell.edu. *Web site:* www.jewell.edu/.

Montana

The University of Montana
Missoula, Montana

Sustainability Initiatives The University of Montana is a member of the Association for the Advancement of Sustainability in Higher Education (AASHE) and a signatory to the Talloires Declaration. This institution's president has signed the American College & University Presidents Climate Commitment.

Academics *Sustainability-focused undergraduate major(s):* Environmental Studies, Forestry, Resource Conservation. *Sustainability-focused graduate degree program(s):* Community and Environmental Planning (MA), Environmental Studies (MS), EVST Program (JD/MS), Forestry (PhD, MS), Resource Conservation (MS), Wildlife Biology (MS, PhD). *Sustainability courses and programs:* sustainability-focused course(s) or lecture series, noncredit sustainability course(s).

Student Services and Green Events *Sustainability leadership:* sustainability coordinator/director, sustainability committee/advisory council, recycling manager, energy manager, sustainability-focused student government. *Student clubs and activities:* Public Interest Research Group (PIRG) chapter on campus, student club(s)/group(s) focused on sustainability, outreach materials available about on-campus sustainability efforts. *Major sustainability events:* Focus the Nation, Earth Week every April, "Campus Climate Exchange". *Housing and facilities:* sustainability-themed housing, on-campus organic garden for students.

Food Sustainable, organic, and/or locally produced foods available in on-campus dining facilities. Fair Trade coffee is used. Vegan and vegetarian dining options are available for every meal.

Transportation Provides free on-campus transportation (bus or other), public transportation access to local destinations, a bike loan/rental program, a car sharing program, and incentives to carpool or use public transportation.

Buildings and Grounds *Renovation and maintenance:* registered for LEED certification for new construction and/or renovation; uses a Green Seal certified cleaning service. *Campus grounds care:* uses water conservation devices; employs strategies to reduce light pollution; landscapes with native plant species.

Recycling *Programs and activities:* sustains a computer/technology recycling program; maintains an on-campus recycling center; reuses surplus department/office supplies; reuses chemicals. *Campus dining operations:* uses reusable dishware; operates without trays; offers discounts for reusable mugs; uses bulk condiment dispensers and decreased packaging for to-go food service purchases.

Energy Currently uses or plans to use alternative sources of power (geothermal energy, hydroelectricity/water power, solar energy, and wind energy); timers to regulate temperatures based on occupancy hours; motion, infrared, and/or light sensors to reduce energy uses for lighting; LED lighting; vending machine motion sensors; and energy-related performance contracting.

Purchasing Sustainability criteria used in purchasing include Energy Star (EPA) and Green Cleaning Products (Green Seal/Environmental Choice certified).

Contact Sustainability Coordinator, The University of Montana, UM Fac Services, 32 Campus Drive, MS 9288, Missoula, MT 59812. *Phone:* 406-243-6001. *E-mail:* cherie.peacock@mso.umt.edu. *Web site:* www.umt.edu/.

Nebraska

Concordia University, Nebraska
Seward, Nebraska

Sustainability Initiatives Concordia University, Nebraska's president has signed the American College & University Presidents Climate Commitment.

Student Services and Green Events *Sustainability leadership:* sustainability committee/advisory council, energy manager, sustainability-focused student government.

Food Sustainable, organic, and/or locally produced foods available in on-campus dining facilities. Fair Trade coffee is used. Vegan and vegetarian dining options are available for every meal.

Buildings and Grounds *Renovation and maintenance:* uses a Green Seal certified cleaning service. *Campus grounds care:* uses water conservation devices; employs strategies to reduce light pollution; landscapes with native plant species; protects, restores, and/or creates habitat on campus; applies to its grounds only pesticides and fertilizers allowable under the U.S. Department of Agriculture's standards for crop production.

Recycling *Programs and activities:* sustains a computer/technology recycling program; maintains an on-campus recycling center; composts yard waste; reuses surplus department/office supplies; replaces paper materials with online alternatives; limits free printing in computer labs and libraries. *Campus dining operations:* operates without trays; uses bulk condiment dispensers and decreased packaging for to-go food service purchases.

Energy Currently uses or plans to use alternative sources of power; timers to regulate temperatures based on occupancy hours; motion, infrared, and/or light sensors to reduce energy uses for lighting; and LED lighting.

Purchasing Sustainability criteria used in purchasing include Energy Star (EPA), WaterSense (EPA), Green Electronics Council (GEC) Electronic Product Environmental Assessment Tool (EPEAT) Silver or Gold, and Green Cleaning Products (Green Seal/Environmental Choice certified).

Contact Director of Buildings and Grounds, Concordia University, Nebraska, 800 North Columbia Avenue, Seward, NE 67434. *Phone:* 402-643-7415. *Fax:* 402-643-2840. *E-mail:* henderson-bud@aramark.com. *Web site:* www.cune.edu/.

Creighton University
Omaha, Nebraska

Sustainability Initiatives Creighton University is a member of the Association for the Advancement of Sustainability in Higher Education (AASHE).

Academics *Sustainability-focused undergraduate major(s):* Environmental Sciences (BS). *Sustainability courses and programs:* sustainability-focused course(s) or lecture series, noncredit sustainability course(s).

Student Services and Green Events *Sustainability leadership:* sustainability coordinator/director, sustainability committee/advisory council, recycling manager, energy manager. *Student clubs and activities:* student club(s)/group(s) focused on sustainability, outreach materials available about on-campus sustainability efforts. *Major sustainability events:* Sustainability Day events, Earth Day Festivities. *Housing and facilities:* on-campus organic garden for students.

Food Sustainable, organic, and/or locally produced foods available in on-campus dining facilities. Fair Trade coffee is used. Vegan and vegetarian dining options are available for every meal.

Transportation Provides free on-campus transportation (bus or other) and public transportation access to local destinations.

Buildings and Grounds *Percentage of institution's eligible buildings as of September 2008 meeting LEED and/or LEED-EB certification criteria:* 12%. *Renovation and maintenance:* uses a Green Seal certified cleaning service. *Campus grounds care:* uses water conservation devices; employs strategies to reduce light pollution; landscapes with native plant species.

Recycling *Events and organizations:* RecycleMania. *Programs and activities:* sustains a computer/technology recycling program; maintains an on-campus recycling center; reuses surplus department/office supplies; reuses chemicals; replaces paper materials with online alternatives; limits free printing in computer labs and libraries. *Campus dining operations:* uses reusable dishware; operates without trays; offers discounts for reusable mugs; uses bulk condiment dispensers and decreased packaging for to-go food service purchases.

Energy Currently uses or plans to use alternative sources of power (biomass energy); timers to regulate temperatures based on occupancy hours; motion, infrared, and/or light sensors to reduce energy uses for lighting; LED lighting; and energy-related performance contracting.

Purchasing Sustainability criteria used in purchasing include Energy Star (EPA), WaterSense (EPA), Green Cleaning Products (Green Seal/Environmental Choice certified), and Forest Stewardship Council (FSC) or American Forest and Paper Association's Sustainable Forestry Initiative (SFI) paper.

Contact Sustainability Coordinator, Creighton University, 2500 California Plaza, Omaha, NE 68178. *Phone:* 402-546-6404. *E-mail:* mjduda@creighton.edu. *Web site:* www.creighton.edu/.

University of Nebraska at Omaha
Omaha, Nebraska

Academics *Sustainability courses and programs:* sustainability-focused course(s) or lecture series.

Student Services and Green Events *Sustainability leadership:* sustainability committee/advisory council, energy manager. *Student clubs and activities:* outreach materials available about on-campus sustainability efforts.

Food Vegan and vegetarian dining options are available for every meal.

Transportation Provides free on-campus transportation (bus or other).

Buildings and Grounds *Campus grounds care:* uses water conservation devices; landscapes with native plant species.

Recycling *Programs and activities:* sustains a computer/technology recycling program; composts yard waste; reuses surplus department/office supplies; reuses chemicals; replaces paper materials with online alternatives; limits free printing in computer labs and libraries. *Campus dining operations:* uses bulk condiment dispensers and decreased packaging for to-go food service purchases.

Energy Currently uses or plans to use timers to regulate temperatures based on occupancy hours; motion, infrared, and/or light sensors to reduce energy uses for lighting; and LED lighting.

Purchasing Sustainability criteria used in purchasing include Green Cleaning Products (Green Seal/Environmental Choice certified).

Contact Environmental Advocate/Sustainability Champion, University of Nebraska at Omaha, EHS, 6001 Dodge Street, EAB 209, Omaha, NE 68182-0079. *Phone:* 402-554-3921. *E-mail:* pwheeler@unomaha.edu. *Web site:* www.unomaha.edu/.

New Hampshire

Dartmouth College
Hanover, New Hampshire

Academics *Sustainability-focused undergraduate major(s):* Biology—Ecology (BS), Biology—Evolutionary Ecology (BS), Biology—Paleobiology (BS), Engineering (BA), Engineering (BE), Environmental Studies (BA), Geography (BA), Earth Sciences (BA). *Sustainability-focused graduate degree program(s):* Ecology and Evolutionary Biology (PhD), Engineering (MEM, MS, PhD). *Sustainability courses and programs:* sustainability-focused course(s) or lecture series.

Student Services and Green Events *Sustainability leadership:* sustainability coordinator/director, sustainability committee/advisory council, recycling manager, energy manager, sustainability-focused student government. *Student clubs and activities:* Campus Climate Challenge, outreach materials available about on-campus sustainability efforts. *Housing and facilities:* sustainability-themed housing, model dorm room that demonstrates sustainable living principles, student-run café that serves environmentally or socially preferable foods, on-campus organic garden for students.

Food Sustainable, organic, and/or locally produced foods available in on-campus dining facilities. Fair Trade coffee is used. Vegan and vegetarian dining options are available for every meal.

Transportation Provides free on-campus transportation (bus or other), public transportation access to local destinations, a car sharing program, and incentives to carpool or use public transportation.

Buildings and Grounds *Renovation and maintenance:* registered for LEED certification for new construction and/or renovation. *Campus grounds care:* uses water conservation devices; employs strategies to reduce light pollution; landscapes with native plant species; protects, restores, and/or creates habitat on campus.

Recycling *Events and organizations:* RecycleMania. *Programs and activities:* sustains a computer/technology recycling program; sustains a pre-consumer food waste composting program; sustains a post-consumer food waste composting program; composts yard waste; reuses surplus department/office supplies; replaces paper materials with online alternatives. *Campus dining operations:* offers discounts for reusable mugs; uses bulk condiment dispensers and decreased packaging for to-go food service purchases.

Energy Currently uses or plans to use alternative sources of power (biomass energy, geothermal energy, and solar energy); timers to regulate temperatures based on occupancy hours; motion, infrared, and/or light sensors to reduce energy uses for lighting; LED lighting; and energy-related performance contracting.

Purchasing Sustainability criteria used in purchasing include Energy Star (EPA) and Green Cleaning Products (Green Seal/Environmental Choice certified).

Contact Sustainability Manager, Dartmouth College, 63 South Main Street, Room 316, Hanover, NH 03755. *Phone:* 603-646-3532. *Fax:* 603-646-3235. *E-mail:* kathy.lambert@dartmouth.edu. *Web site:* www.dartmouth.edu/.

Granite State College
Concord, New Hampshire

Sustainability Initiatives Granite State College's president has signed the American College & University Presidents Climate Commitment.

Academics *Sustainability courses and programs:* sustainability-focused course(s) or lecture series.

Student Services and Green Events *Sustainability leadership:* sustainability coordinator/director, sustainability committee/advisory council.

Recycling *Programs and activities:* sustains a computer/technology recycling program.

Energy Currently uses or plans to use timers to regulate temperatures based on occupancy hours.

Contact Director of Facilities, Safety, and Sustainability, Granite State College, 8 Old Suncook Road, Concord, NH 03301. *Phone:* 603-513-1382. *Fax:* 603-513-1389. *E-mail:* peter.conklin@granite.edu. *Web site:* www.granite.edu/.

Keene State College
Keene, New Hampshire

Sustainability Initiatives Keene State College is a member of the Association for the Advancement of Sustainability in Higher Education (AASHE). This institution's president has signed the American College & University Presidents Climate Commitment.

Academics *Sustainability-focused undergraduate major(s):* Sustainable Product Design (BS). *Sustainability courses and programs:* sustainability-focused course(s) or lecture series, noncredit sustainability course(s).

Student Services and Green Events *Sustainability leadership:* sustainability coordinator/director, sustainability committee/advisory council, recycling manager, energy manager. *Student clubs and activities:* Campus Climate Challenge, outreach materials available about on-campus sustainability efforts. *Housing and facilities:* sustainability-themed housing.

Food Sustainable, organic, and/or locally produced foods available in on-campus dining facilities. Fair Trade coffee is used. Vegan and vegetarian dining options are available for every meal.

Transportation Provides free on-campus transportation (bus or other), public transportation access to local destinations, a bike loan/rental program, and incentives to carpool or use public transportation.

Buildings and Grounds *Percentage of institution's eligible buildings as of September 2008 meeting LEED and/or LEED-EB certification criteria:* 7%. *Campus grounds care:* uses water conservation devices; employs strategies to reduce light pollution; landscapes with native plant species; protects, restores, and/or creates habitat on campus.

Recycling *Events and organizations:* RecycleMania, Waste-Wise (EPA). *Programs and activities:* sustains a computer/technology recycling program; maintains an on-campus recycling center; sustains a pre-consumer food waste composting program; composts yard waste; reuses surplus department/office supplies; replaces paper materials with online alternatives; limits free printing in computer labs and libraries. *Campus dining operations:* uses reusable dishware; operates without trays; offers discounts for reusable mugs; uses bulk condiment dispensers and decreased packaging for to-go food service purchases.

Energy Currently uses or plans to use alternative sources of power; motion, infrared, and/or light sensors to reduce energy uses for lighting; LED lighting; and vending machine motion sensors.

Purchasing Sustainability criteria used in purchasing include Energy Star (EPA) and Green Cleaning Products (Green Seal/Environmental Choice certified).

Contact Sustainability Coordinator, Keene State College, 229 Main Street, Keene, NH 03435-2502. *Phone:* 603-358-2567. *Fax:* 603-358-2456. *E-mail:* mjensen@keene.edu. *Web site:* www.keene.edu/.

Plymouth State University
Plymouth, New Hampshire

Sustainability Initiatives Plymouth State University's president has signed the American College & University Presidents Climate Commitment.

Academics *Sustainability-focused undergraduate major(s):* Environmental Science and Policy (BS). *Sustainability-focused graduate degree program(s):* Environmental Science and Policy (MS). *Sustainability courses and programs:* sustainability-focused course(s) or lecture series.

Student Services and Green Events *Sustainability leadership:* sustainability coordinator/director, sustainability committee/advisory council, recycling manager, energy manager, sustainability-focused student government. *Student clubs and activities:* Campus Climate Challenge, student club(s)/group(s) focused on sustainability, outreach materials available about on-campus sustainability efforts. *Major sustainability events:* American Institute of Architects IDID Conference, NH Climate Change Policy Task force Meeting, Distributed Heating and Biomass Coalition Working Group, NH Water Conference. *Housing and facilities:* sustainability-themed housing, model dorm room that demonstrates sustainable living principles.

Food Sustainable, organic, and/or locally produced foods available in on-campus dining facilities. Fair Trade coffee is used. Vegan and vegetarian dining options are available for every meal.

Transportation Provides free on-campus transportation (bus or other), public transportation access to local destinations, and a bike loan/rental program.

Buildings and Grounds *Renovation and maintenance:* registered for LEED certification for new construction and/or renovation. *Campus grounds care:* uses water conservation devices; employs strategies to reduce light pollution; landscapes with native plant species; protects, restores, and/or creates habitat on campus; applies to its grounds only pesticides and fertilizers allowable under the U.S. Department of Agriculture's standards for crop production.

Recycling *Events and organizations:* RecycleMania. *Programs and activities:* sustains a computer/technology recycling program; maintains an on-campus recycling center; composts yard waste; reuses surplus department/office supplies; limits free printing in computer labs and libraries. *Campus dining operations:* uses reusable dishware; operates without trays; offers discounts for reusable mugs; uses bulk condiment dispensers and decreased packaging for to-go food service purchases.

Energy Currently uses or plans to use alternative sources of power; motion, infrared, and/or light sensors to reduce energy uses for lighting; and LED lighting.

Purchasing Sustainability criteria used in purchasing include Energy Star (EPA) and Green Cleaning Products (Green Seal/Environmental Choice certified).

Contact Special Assistant to the President and Director of Environmental Sustainability, Plymouth State University, 17 High Street, MSC# 58, Plymouth, NH 03264. *Phone:* 603-535-2306. *E-mail:* bcrangle@plymouth.edu. *Web site:* www.plymouth.edu/.

Southern New Hampshire University
Manchester, New Hampshire

Sustainability Initiatives Southern New Hampshire University's president has signed the American College & University Presidents Climate Commitment.

Academics *Sustainability-focused undergraduate major(s):* Environment, Ethics, and Public Policy (BA). *Sustainability courses and programs:* sustainability-focused course(s) or lecture series, noncredit sustainability course(s).

Student Services and Green Events *Sustainability leadership:* sustainability coordinator/director, sustainability committee/advisory council, recycling manager, energy manager. *Student clubs and activities:* Campus Climate Challenge, student club(s)/group(s) focused on sustainability. *Major sustainability events:* Environmental Sustainability: Making It Work For Your Business.

Food Sustainable, organic, and/or locally produced foods available in on-campus dining facilities. Fair Trade coffee is used. Vegan and vegetarian dining options are available for every meal.

Transportation Provides public transportation access to local destinations, a bike loan/rental program, and incentives to carpool or use public transportation.

Buildings and Grounds *Campus grounds care:* uses water conservation devices; employs strategies to reduce light pollution; landscapes with native plant species; protects, restores, and/or creates habitat on campus.

Recycling *Programs and activities:* sustains a computer/technology recycling program; maintains an on-campus recycling center; replaces paper materials with online alternatives. *Campus dining operations:* uses reusable dishware; offers discounts for reusable mugs; uses bulk condiment dispensers and decreased packaging for to-go food service purchases.

Energy Currently uses or plans to use alternative sources of power (wind energy); timers to regulate temperatures based on occupancy hours; and motion, infrared, and/or light sensors to reduce energy uses for lighting.

Purchasing Sustainability criteria used in purchasing include Energy Star (EPA), Green Cleaning Products (Green Seal/Environmental Choice certified), and Forest Stewardship Council (FSC) or American Forest and Paper Association's Sustainable Forestry Initiative (SFI) paper.

Contact Director, Office for Sustainability, Southern New Hampshire University, PO Box 201, Warner, NH 03278. *Phone:* 603-496-4260. *E-mail:* sustainability@snhu.edu. *Web site:* www.snhu.edu/.

University of New Hampshire
Durham, New Hampshire

Sustainability Initiatives University of New Hampshire is a member of the Association for the Advancement of Sustainability in Higher Education (AASHE) and a signatory to the Talloires Declaration. This institution's president has signed the American College & University Presidents Climate Commitment.

Academics *Sustainability-focused undergraduate major(s):* Classics (BA), Community and Environmental Planning (BS), EcoGastronomy, Environmental Sciences (BS), Health Management and Policy (BS), International and Development Economics (BA). *Sustainability-focused graduate degree program(s):* Environmental Education (MA), Environmental Engineering (MS), Natural Resources and Earth Systems Sciences (PhD), Nutritional Science (MS), Public Health (MPH), Recreation Administration and Management (MS). *Sustainability courses and programs:* sustainability-focused course(s) or lecture series, noncredit sustainability course(s), sustainability-focused nonacademic certificate program(s).

Student Services and Green Events *Sustainability leadership:* sustainability coordinator/director, sustainability committee/advisory council, recycling manager, energy manager. *Student clubs and activities:* Campus Climate Challenge, student club(s)/group(s) focused on sustainability, outreach materials available about on-campus sustainability efforts. *Major sustainability events:* Sustainable Speaker Series, Growing a Green Generation Conference, University-wide dialogues. *Housing and facilities:* sustainability-themed housing, model dorm room that demonstrates sustainable living principles, on-campus organic garden for students.

Food Sustainable, organic, and/or locally produced foods available in on-campus dining facilities. Fair Trade coffee is used. Vegan and vegetarian dining options are available for every meal.

Transportation Provides free on-campus transportation (bus or other), public transportation access to local destinations, a bike loan/rental program, a car sharing program, and incentives to carpool or use public transportation.

Buildings and Grounds *Percentage of institution's eligible buildings as of September 2008 meeting LEED and/or LEED-EB certification criteria: 5%. Renovation and maintenance:* registered for LEED certification for new construction and/or renovation; uses a Green Seal certified cleaning service. *Campus grounds care:* uses water conservation devices; employs strategies to reduce light pollution; protects, restores, and/or creates habitat on campus.

Recycling *Events and organizations:* RecycleMania, Waste-Wise (EPA). *Programs and activities:* sustains a computer/technology recycling program; maintains an on-campus recycling center; sustains a pre-consumer food waste composting program; sustains a post-consumer food waste composting program; composts yard waste; reuses surplus department/office supplies; reuses chemicals; replaces

paper materials with online alternatives; limits free printing in computer labs and libraries. *Campus dining operations:* uses reusable dishware; operates without trays; offers discounts for reusable mugs; uses bulk condiment dispensers and decreased packaging for to-go food service purchases.

Energy Currently uses or plans to use alternative sources of power; timers to regulate temperatures based on occupancy hours; motion, infrared, and/or light sensors to reduce energy uses for lighting; LED lighting; and vending machine motion sensors.

Purchasing Sustainability criteria used in purchasing include Energy Star (EPA), WaterSense (EPA), and Green Cleaning Products (Green Seal/Environmental Choice certified).

Contact Associate Director, University of New Hampshire, 107 Nesmith Hall, 131 Main Street, Durham, NH 03824. *Phone:* 603-862-4088. *Fax:* 603-862-0785. *E-mail:* sustainability.info@unh.edu. *Web site:* www.unh.edu/.

New Jersey

The College of New Jersey
Ewing, New Jersey

Sustainability Initiatives The College of New Jersey's president has signed the American College & University Presidents Climate Commitment. The College of New Jersey has Green Fees (optional/required) dedicated to sustainability initiatives.

Academics *Sustainability courses and programs:* sustainability-focused course(s) or lecture series, noncredit sustainability course(s).

Student Services and Green Events *Sustainability leadership:* sustainability committee/advisory council, recycling manager, energy manager, sustainability-focused student government. *Student clubs and activities:* outreach materials available about on-campus sustainability efforts.

Food Sustainable, organic, and/or locally produced foods available in on-campus dining facilities. Fair Trade coffee is used. Vegan and vegetarian dining options are available for every meal.

Transportation Provides public transportation access to local destinations and incentives to carpool or use public transportation.

Buildings and Grounds *Percentage of institution's eligible buildings as of September 2008 meeting LEED and/or LEED-EB certification criteria: 5%. Campus grounds care:* uses water conservation devices; employs strategies to reduce light pollution; landscapes with native plant species; protects, restores, and/or creates habitat on campus; applies to its grounds only pesticides and fertilizers allowable under the U.S. Department of Agriculture's standards for crop production.

Recycling *Events and organizations:* RecycleMania. *Programs and activities:* sustains a computer/technology recycling program; maintains an on-campus recycling center; sustains a pre-consumer food waste composting program; composts yard waste; reuses surplus department/office supplies; replaces paper materials with online alternatives; limits free printing in computer labs and libraries. *Campus dining operations:* uses reusable dishware; operates without trays; uses bulk condiment dispensers and decreased packaging for to-go food service purchases.

Energy Currently uses or plans to use alternative sources of power (geothermal energy and solar energy); timers to regulate temperatures based on occupancy hours; motion, infrared, and/or light sensors to reduce energy uses for lighting; LED lighting; and energy-related performance contracting.

Purchasing Sustainability criteria used in purchasing include Energy Star (EPA) and Green Cleaning Products (Green Seal/Environmental Choice certified).

Contact Vice President, Facilities Management/ Construction and Campus Safety, The College of New Jersey, PO Box 7718, 2000 Pennington Road, Ewing, NJ 08628. *Phone:* 609-771-3230. *Fax:* 609-637-5150. *Web site:* www.tcnj.edu/.

Drew University
Madison, New Jersey

Sustainability Initiatives Drew University's president has signed the American College & University Presidents Climate Commitment.

Academics *Sustainability-focused undergraduate major(s):* Environmental Studies and Sustainability (BA, BS). *Sustainability-focused graduate degree program(s):* Environmental Ministry (DMin). *Sustainability courses and programs:* sustainability-focused course(s) or lecture series, noncredit sustainability course(s), sustainability-focused nonacademic certificate program(s).

Student Services and Green Events *Sustainability leadership:* sustainability coordinator/director, sustainability committee/advisory council. *Student clubs and activities:* student club(s)/group(s) focused on sustainability, outreach materials available about on-campus sustainability efforts. *Major sustainability events:* Water Conference on Global Water Issues, Campus Sustainability Day, host of Statewide Conference on Diversity Issues in Higher Education. *Housing and facilities:* sustainability-themed housing, student-run café that serves environmentally or socially preferable foods.

Food Sustainable, organic, and/or locally produced foods available in on-campus dining facilities. Fair Trade coffee is used. Vegan and vegetarian dining options are available for every meal.

Transportation Provides public transportation access to local destinations, a bike loan/rental program, and a car sharing program.

Buildings and Grounds *Renovation and maintenance:* registered for LEED certification for new construction and/or renovation. *Campus grounds care:* uses water conservation devices; employs strategies to reduce light pollution; landscapes with native plant species; protects, restores, and/or creates habitat on campus.

Recycling *Events and organizations:* RecycleMania. *Programs and activities:* sustains a computer/technology recycling program; maintains an on-campus recycling center; composts yard waste; reuses surplus department/office supplies; limits free printing in computer labs and libraries. *Campus dining operations:* uses reusable dishware; operates without trays; offers discounts for reusable mugs; uses bulk condiment dispensers and decreased packaging for to-go food service purchases.

Energy Currently uses or plans to use alternative sources of power (geothermal energy); motion, infrared, and/or light sensors to reduce energy uses for lighting; and LED lighting.

Purchasing Sustainability criteria used in purchasing include Energy Star (EPA) and Forest Stewardship Council (FSC) or American Forest and Paper Association's Sustainable Forestry Initiative (SFI) paper.

Contact Campus Sustainability Coordinator, Drew University, Pepin Services Center, 36 Madison Avenue, Madison, NJ 07940. *Phone:* 973-408-3660. *E-mail:* cnotas@drew.edu. *Web site:* www.drew.edu/.

Georgian Court University
Lakewood, New Jersey

Sustainability Initiatives Georgian Court University's president has signed the American College & University Presidents Climate Commitment.

Academics *Sustainability courses and programs:* sustainability-focused course(s) or lecture series.

Student Services and Green Events *Sustainability leadership:* sustainability committee/advisory council. *Student clubs and activities:* student club(s)/group(s) focused on sustainability. *Major sustainability events:* Earth Awareness Week. *Housing and facilities:* student-run café that serves environmentally or socially preferable foods.

Food Sustainable, organic, and/or locally produced foods available in on-campus dining facilities. Fair Trade coffee is used. Vegan and vegetarian dining options are available for every meal.

Transportation Provides free on-campus transportation (bus or other), public transportation access to local destinations, and incentives to carpool or use public transportation.

Buildings and Grounds *Renovation and maintenance:* registered for LEED certification for new construction and/or renovation. *Campus grounds care:* uses water conservation devices; employs strategies to reduce light pollution; landscapes with native plant species; protects, restores, and/or creates habitat on campus.

Recycling *Events and organizations:* RecycleMania, WasteWise (EPA). *Programs and activities:* sustains a computer/ technology recycling program. *Campus dining operations:* uses reusable dishware; operates without trays; offers discounts for reusable mugs; uses bulk condiment dispensers and decreased packaging for to-go food service purchases.

Energy Currently uses or plans to use alternative sources of power (wind energy); timers to regulate temperatures based on occupancy hours; and motion, infrared, and/or light sensors to reduce energy uses for lighting. Participates in College & University Green Power Challenge activities.

Purchasing Sustainability criteria used in purchasing include Energy Star (EPA) and Green Cleaning Products (Green Seal/Environmental Choice certified).

Contact Assistant Vice President, Georgian Court University, 900 Lakewood Avenue, Lakewood, NJ 08701-2697. *Phone:* 732-987-2416. *Fax:* 732-987-2032. *E-mail:* christa@ georgian.edu. *Web site:* www.georgian.edu/.

Montclair State University
Montclair, New Jersey

Sustainability Initiatives Montclair State University's president has signed the American College & University Presidents Climate Commitment.

Academics *Sustainability-focused undergraduate major(s):* Aquatic and Coastal Sciences (BS), Geography with a concentration in Environmental Studies (BA), GeoScience with a concentration in Environmental Science (BS). *Sustainability-focused graduate degree program(s):* Aquatic and Coastal Sciences (MS), Environmental Management (PhD). *Sustainability courses and programs:* sustainability-focused course(s) or lecture series, noncredit sustainability course(s).

Student Services and Green Events *Sustainability leadership:* sustainability coordinator/director, sustainability

Green Jobs for a New Economy

committee/advisory council, recycling manager, energy manager. *Student clubs and activities:* student club(s)/group(s) focused on sustainability. *Major sustainability events:* Earth Day.

Food Sustainable, organic, and/or locally produced foods available in on-campus dining facilities. Fair Trade coffee is used. Vegan and vegetarian dining options are available for every meal.

Transportation Provides free on-campus transportation (bus or other), public transportation access to local destinations, a car sharing program, and incentives to carpool or use public transportation.

Buildings and Grounds *Percentage of institution's eligible buildings as of September 2008 meeting LEED and/or LEED-EB certification criteria:* 10%. *Renovation and maintenance:* registered for LEED certification for new construction and/or renovation. *Campus grounds care:* uses water conservation devices; employs strategies to reduce light pollution; landscapes with native plant species; applies to its grounds only pesticides and fertilizers allowable under the U.S. Department of Agriculture's standards for crop production.

Recycling *Events and organizations:* RecycleMania. *Programs and activities:* sustains a computer/technology recycling program; sustains a pre-consumer food waste composting program; sustains a post-consumer food waste composting program; composts yard waste; reuses surplus department/office supplies; reuses chemicals; replaces paper materials with online alternatives. *Campus dining operations:* uses reusable dishware; operates without trays; offers discounts for reusable mugs; uses bulk condiment dispensers and decreased packaging for to-go food service purchases.

Energy Currently uses or plans to use alternative sources of power (solar energy); timers to regulate temperatures based on occupancy hours; motion, infrared, and/or light sensors to reduce energy uses for lighting; and LED lighting.

Purchasing Sustainability criteria used in purchasing include Energy Star (EPA) and Green Cleaning Products (Green Seal/Environmental Choice certified).

Contact Director of Environmental Health and Safety, Montclair State University, 1 Normal Avenue, Montclair, NJ 07043. *Phone:* 973-655-4367. *Fax:* 973-655-7837. *E-mail:* ferdinanda@mail.montclair.edu. *Web site:* www.montclair.edu/.

Ramapo College of New Jersey
Mahwah, New Jersey

Sustainability Initiatives Ramapo College of New Jersey is a signatory to the Talloires Declaration. This institution's president has signed the American College & University Presidents Climate Commitment.

Academics *Sustainability-focused undergraduate major(s):* Environmental Science (BA), Environmental Science (BS). *Sustainability-focused graduate degree program(s):* Sustainability Studies (MA) in development. *Sustainability courses and programs:* sustainability-focused course(s) or lecture series.

Student Services and Green Events *Sustainability leadership:* sustainability committee/advisory council, sustainability-focused student government. *Student clubs and activities:* Campus Climate Challenge, student club(s)/group(s) focused on sustainability. *Major sustainability events:* Green Meets Green Expo, Climate for Change Conference. *Housing and facilities:* sustainability-themed housing.

Food Fair Trade coffee is used. Vegan and vegetarian dining options are available for every meal.

Transportation Provides public transportation access to local destinations and incentives to carpool or use public transportation.

Buildings and Grounds *Campus grounds care:* landscapes with native plant species; protects, restores, and/or creates habitat on campus.

Recycling *Programs and activities:* replaces paper materials with online alternatives. *Campus dining operations:* uses reusable dishware; operates without trays; offers discounts for reusable mugs.

Energy Currently uses or plans to use alternative sources of power.

Purchasing Sustainability criteria used in purchasing include Energy Star (EPA).

Contact Associate Professor of Environmental Science/Geology, Ramapo College of New Jersey, 505 Ramapo Valley Road, Suite G-418, Mahwah, NJ 07430. *Phone:* 201-684-7209. *E-mail:* erainfor@ramapo.edu. *Web site:* www.ramapo.edu/.

The Richard Stockton College of New Jersey
Pomona, New Jersey

Sustainability Initiatives The Richard Stockton College of New Jersey's president has signed the American College & University Presidents Climate Commitment.

Academics *Sustainability-focused undergraduate major(s):* Environmental Science (BS), Environmental Studies (BA), Environmental Studies/Sustainability and Environmental Policy track (BA), Political Science/Sustainability and Environmental Policy track (BA), Public Health—Environmental Health track. *Sustainability-focused graduate degree program(s):* Environmental Science (PSM). *Sustainability courses and programs:* sustainability-focused course(s) or lecture series, noncredit sustainability course(s), sustainability-focused nonacademic certificate program(s).

Student Services and Green Events *Sustainability leadership:* sustainability coordinator/director, sustainability committee/advisory council, recycling manager. *Student clubs and activities:* student club(s)/group(s) focused on sustainability, outreach materials available about on-campus sustainability efforts. *Major sustainability events:* Harvest Fest, NJHEP Energy Symposium, Campus Earth Day, Annual Environmental Forum, Atlantic County/ACUA, William J. Hughes Public Policy Center, AWA Environmental Conference, Implementing the NJ Energy Plan, ECOSTOCK. *Housing and facilities:* sustainability-themed housing.

Food Sustainable, organic, and/or locally produced foods available in on-campus dining facilities. Fair Trade coffee is used. Vegan and vegetarian dining options are available for every meal.

Transportation Provides free on-campus transportation (bus or other), public transportation access to local destinations, a bike loan/rental program, and incentives to carpool or use public transportation.

Buildings and Grounds *Percentage of institution's eligible buildings as of September 2008 meeting LEED and/or LEED-EB certification criteria:* 5%. *Renovation and maintenance:* registered for LEED certification for new construction and/or renovation; uses a Green Seal certified cleaning service. *Campus grounds care:* uses water conservation devices; landscapes with native plant species; protects, restores, and/or creates habitat on campus.

Recycling *Programs and activities:* sustains a computer/technology recycling program; maintains an on-campus recycling center; reuses surplus department/office supplies; replaces paper materials with online alternatives. *Campus dining operations:* uses reusable dishware; operates without trays; uses bulk condiment dispensers and decreased packaging for to-go food service purchases.

Energy Currently uses or plans to use alternative sources of power (geothermal energy and solar energy); timers to regulate temperatures based on occupancy hours; motion, infrared, and/or light sensors to reduce energy uses for lighting; and LED lighting.

Purchasing Sustainability criteria used in purchasing include Energy Star (EPA) and Green Cleaning Products (Green Seal/Environmental Choice certified).

Contact Dean, School of Natural Sciences and Mathematics, The Richard Stockton College of New Jersey, PO Box 195, Pomona, NJ 08205. *Phone:* 609-652-4548. *E-mail:* dennis.weiss@stockton.edu. *Web site:* www.stockton.edu/.

Rider University
Lawrenceville, New Jersey

Sustainability Initiatives Rider University is a member of the Association for the Advancement of Sustainability in Higher Education (AASHE). This institution's president has signed the American College & University Presidents Climate Commitment.

Academics *Sustainability-focused undergraduate major(s):* Ecobotanical emphasis, Green Entrepreneurialism, Selected Topics: Environment. *Sustainability courses and programs:* sustainability-focused course(s) or lecture series.

Student Services and Green Events *Sustainability leadership:* sustainability coordinator/director, sustainability committee/advisory council. *Student clubs and activities:* student club(s)/group(s) focused on sustainability. *Major sustainability events:* National Campus Sustainability Day, Earth Day, RecycleMania. *Housing and facilities:* on-campus organic garden for students.

Food Sustainable, organic, and/or locally produced foods available in on-campus dining facilities. Fair Trade coffee is used. Vegan and vegetarian dining options are available for every meal.

Transportation Provides free on-campus transportation (bus or other), public transportation access to local destinations, and a car sharing program.

Buildings and Grounds *Renovation and maintenance:* uses a Green Seal certified cleaning service. *Campus grounds care:* uses water conservation devices; employs strategies to reduce light pollution; landscapes with native plant species; protects, restores, and/or creates habitat on campus.

Recycling *Events and organizations:* RecycleMania. *Programs and activities:* sustains a computer/technology recycling program; replaces paper materials with online alternatives. *Campus dining operations:* uses reusable dishware; operates without trays; uses bulk condiment dispensers and decreased packaging for to-go food service purchases.

Energy Currently uses or plans to use alternative sources of power (hydroelectricity/water power and wind energy); timers to regulate temperatures based on occupancy hours; motion, infrared, and/or light sensors to reduce energy uses for lighting; LED lighting; and energy-related performance contracting.

Purchasing Sustainability criteria used in purchasing include Energy Star (EPA) and Green Cleaning Products (Green Seal/Environmental Choice certified).

Contact Sustainability Coordination Manager, Rider University, 2083 Lawrence Road, Lawrenceville, NJ 08690. *Phone:* 609-596-5000 Ext. 7559. *Fax:* 609-896-7707. *E-mail:* megreenberg@rider.edu. *Web site:* www.rider.edu/.

Rutgers, The State University of New Jersey, New Brunswick
Piscataway, New Jersey

Sustainability Initiatives Rutgers, The State University of New Jersey, New Brunswick is a signatory to the Talloires Declaration.

Academics *Sustainability courses and programs:* sustainability-focused course(s) or lecture series.

Student Services and Green Events *Sustainability leadership:* sustainability committee/advisory council, recycling manager, energy manager. *Student clubs and activities:* Campus Climate Challenge, Public Interest Research Group (PIRG) chapter on campus, outreach materials available about on-campus sustainability efforts. *Housing and facilities:* on-campus organic garden for students.

Food Sustainable, organic, and/or locally produced foods available in on-campus dining facilities. Fair Trade coffee is used. Vegan and vegetarian dining options are available for every meal.

Transportation Provides free on-campus transportation (bus or other), public transportation access to local destinations, a car sharing program, and incentives to carpool or use public transportation.

Buildings and Grounds *Campus grounds care:* uses water conservation devices; landscapes with native plant species; protects, restores, and/or creates habitat on campus; applies to its grounds only pesticides and fertilizers allowable under the U.S. Department of Agriculture's standards for crop production.

Recycling *Events and organizations:* RecycleMania, WasteWise (EPA). *Programs and activities:* sustains a computer/technology recycling program; sustains a post-consumer food waste composting program; composts yard waste; reuses chemicals; replaces paper materials with online alternatives; limits free printing in computer labs and libraries. *Campus dining operations:* uses reusable dishware; uses bulk condiment dispensers and decreased packaging for to-go food service purchases.

Energy Currently uses or plans to use timers to regulate temperatures based on occupancy hours and LED lighting.

Purchasing Sustainability criteria used in purchasing include Energy Star (EPA), WaterSense (EPA), Green Electronics Council (GEC) Electronic Product Environmental Assessment Tool (EPEAT) Silver or Gold, Green Cleaning Products (Green Seal/Environmental Choice certified), and Forest Stewardship Council (FSC) or American Forest and Paper Association's Sustainable Forestry Initiative (SFI) paper.

Contact Rutgers, The State University of New Jersey, New Brunswick, 6 Berrue Circle, Piscataway, NJ 08854. *Phone:* 732-445-4117 Ext. 196. *Fax:* 732-445-0404. *E-mail:* mkorntias@facilities.rutgers.edu. *Web site:* www.rutgers.edu/.

New Mexico

New Mexico State University
Las Cruces, New Mexico

Sustainability Initiatives New Mexico State University is a member of the Association for the Advancement of Sustainability in Higher Education (AASHE). This institution's president has signed the American College & University Presidents Climate Commitment.

Academics *Sustainability-focused undergraduate major(s):* Sustainable Development supplemental major (BA). *Sustainability courses and programs:* sustainability-focused course(s) or lecture series.

Student Services and Green Events *Sustainability leadership:* sustainability coordinator/director, sustainability committee/advisory council, recycling manager. *Student clubs and activities:* Public Interest Research Group (PIRG) chapter on campus, student club(s)/group(s) focused on sustainability. *Major sustainability events:* Focus on Energy National Teach-In, World Café, Faculty Panel Workshop on Infusing Sustainability into the Curriculum, Earth Day.

Food Sustainable, organic, and/or locally produced foods available in on-campus dining facilities. Fair Trade coffee is used. Vegan and vegetarian dining options are available for every meal.

Transportation Provides free on-campus transportation (bus or other).

Buildings and Grounds *Renovation and maintenance:* registered for LEED certification for new construction and/or renovation. *Campus grounds care:* uses water conservation devices; employs strategies to reduce light pollution; landscapes with native plant species; protects, restores, and/or creates habitat on campus; applies to its grounds only pesticides and fertilizers allowable under the U.S. Department of Agriculture's standards for crop production.

Recycling *Events and organizations:* RecycleMania, WasteWise (EPA). *Programs and activities:* sustains a computer/technology recycling program; maintains an on-campus recycling center; composts yard waste; replaces paper materials with online alternatives; limits free printing in computer labs and libraries. *Campus dining operations:* uses reusable dishware; operates without trays; uses bulk condiment dispensers and decreased packaging for to-go food service purchases.

Energy Currently uses or plans to use timers to regulate temperatures based on occupancy hours; motion, infrared, and/or light sensors to reduce energy uses for lighting; LED lighting; and energy-related performance contracting.

Purchasing Sustainability criteria used in purchasing include Energy Star (EPA).

Contact Chair, Sustainability and Climate Change Task Force, New Mexico State University, MSC 3BF, PO Box 30003, Las Cruces, NM 88003. *Phone:* 575-646-3125. *Fax:* 575-646-2816. *E-mail:* sloring@nmsu.edu. *Web site:* www.nmsu.edu/.

New York

Adelphi University
Garden City, New York

Student Services and Green Events *Sustainability leadership:* recycling manager, energy manager. *Housing and facilities:* sustainability-themed housing, student-run café that serves environmentally or socially preferable foods.

Food Sustainable, organic, and/or locally produced foods available in on-campus dining facilities. Fair Trade coffee is used. Vegan and vegetarian dining options are available for every meal.

Transportation Provides free on-campus transportation (bus or other), public transportation access to local destinations, and incentives to carpool or use public transportation.

Buildings and Grounds *Renovation and maintenance:* uses a Green Seal certified cleaning service. *Campus grounds care:* uses water conservation devices; employs strategies to reduce light pollution; landscapes with native plant species; protects, restores, and/or creates habitat on campus; applies to its grounds only pesticides and fertilizers allowable under the U.S. Department of Agriculture's standards for crop production.

Recycling *Programs and activities:* sustains a computer/technology recycling program; maintains an on-campus recycling center; composts yard waste; reuses surplus department/office supplies; replaces paper materials with online alternatives; limits free printing in computer labs and libraries. *Campus dining operations:* offers discounts for reusable mugs; uses bulk condiment dispensers and decreased packaging for to-go food service purchases.

Energy Currently uses or plans to use alternative sources of power (geothermal energy); timers to regulate temperatures based on occupancy hours; motion, infrared, and/or light sensors to reduce energy uses for lighting; LED lighting; and energy-related performance contracting.

Purchasing Sustainability criteria used in purchasing include Energy Star (EPA) and Green Cleaning Products (Green Seal/Environmental Choice certified).

Contact Executive Director, Facilities Management, Adelphi University, 1 South Avenue, FAF Building, Garden City, NY 11530. *Phone:* 516-877-3974. *Fax:* 516-877-3991. *E-mail:* kosloski@adelphi.edu. *Web site:* www.adelphi.edu/.

Bard College
Annandale-on-Hudson, New York

Sustainability Initiatives Bard College's president has signed the American College & University Presidents Climate Commitment.

Academics *Sustainability-focused undergraduate major(s):* Environmental Studies (BA). *Sustainability courses and programs:* sustainability-focused course(s) or lecture series.

Student Services and Green Events *Sustainability leadership:* sustainability coordinator/director, sustainability committee/advisory council, recycling manager. *Student clubs and activities:* student club(s)/group(s) focused on sustainability. *Major sustainability events:* Focus the Nation, Global Warming Teach-In 2009. *Housing and facilities:* sustainability-themed housing, student-run café that serves environmentally or socially preferable foods, on-campus organic garden for students.

Food Sustainable, organic, and/or locally produced foods available in on-campus dining facilities. Fair Trade coffee is used. Vegan and vegetarian dining options are available for every meal.

Transportation Provides free on-campus transportation (bus or other) and public transportation access to local destinations.

Buildings and Grounds *Renovation and maintenance:* registered for LEED certification for new construction and/or renovation; uses a Green Seal certified cleaning service. *Campus grounds care:* uses water conservation devices; employs strategies to reduce light pollution; landscapes with native plant species; protects, restores, and/or creates habitat on campus.

Recycling *Events and organizations:* RecycleMania, WasteWise (EPA). *Programs and activities:* sustains a computer/technology recycling program; maintains an on-campus recycling center; sustains a pre-consumer food waste composting program; sustains a post-consumer food waste composting program; composts yard waste; reuses surplus department/office supplies; replaces paper materials with online alternatives. *Campus dining operations:* operates without trays; offers discounts for reusable mugs.

Energy Currently uses or plans to use alternative sources of power (geothermal energy); motion, infrared, and/or light sensors to reduce energy uses for lighting; vending machine motion sensors; and energy-related performance contracting.

Purchasing Sustainability criteria used in purchasing include Energy Star (EPA) and Green Cleaning Products (Green Seal/Environmental Choice certified).

Contact Environmental Resources Auditor, Bard College, PO Box 5000, Annandale, NY 12504-5000. *Phone:* 845-758-7180. *E-mail:* husted@bard.edu. *Web site:* www.bard.edu/.

Brooklyn College of the City University of New York
Brooklyn, New York

Student Services and Green Events *Sustainability leadership:* sustainability committee/advisory council, recycling manager. *Student clubs and activities:* Public Interest Research Group (PIRG) chapter on campus.

Transportation Provides free on-campus transportation (bus or other) and public transportation access to local destinations.

Buildings and Grounds *Campus grounds care:* uses water conservation devices; employs strategies to reduce light pollution; landscapes with native plant species; applies to its grounds only pesticides and fertilizers allowable under the U.S. Department of Agriculture's standards for crop production.

Recycling *Programs and activities:* replaces paper materials with online alternatives; limits free printing in computer labs and libraries. *Campus dining operations:* uses reusable dishware.

Energy Currently uses or plans to use timers to regulate temperatures based on occupancy hours; motion, infrared, and/or light sensors to reduce energy uses for lighting; vending machine motion sensors; and energy-related performance contracting.

Purchasing Sustainability criteria used in purchasing include Energy Star (EPA) and Green Cleaning Products (Green Seal/Environmental Choice certified).

Contact Assistant Vice President, Brooklyn College of the City University of New York, 2900 Bedford Avenue, Brooklyn, NY 11210. *Phone:* 718-951-5867. *E-mail:* czirak@brooklyn.cuny.edu. *Web site:* www.brooklyn.cuny.edu/.

City College of the City University of New York
New York, New York

Sustainability Initiatives City College of the City University of New York's president has signed the American College & University Presidents Climate Commitment.

Academics *Sustainability-focused undergraduate major(s):* Architecture (BArch), Earth System Science/Environmental Engineering (BS), Earth Systems Science (BS), Environmental Earth System Science (BS). *Sustainability-focused graduate degree program(s):* Architecture (MArch, MLA), Earth Systems Science (MA), Sustainability (MS). *Sustainability courses and programs:* sustainability-focused course(s) or lecture series.

Student Services and Green Events *Sustainability leadership:* sustainability coordinator/director, sustainability

committee/advisory council, recycling manager, energy manager. *Student clubs and activities:* Public Interest Research Group (PIRG) chapter on campus.

Food Sustainable, organic, and/or locally produced foods available in on-campus dining facilities. Vegan and vegetarian dining options are available for every meal.

Transportation Provides free on-campus transportation (bus or other), public transportation access to local destinations, and incentives to carpool or use public transportation.

Buildings and Grounds *Renovation and maintenance:* registered for LEED certification for new construction and/or renovation.

Recycling *Programs and activities:* sustains a computer/technology recycling program; composts yard waste. *Campus dining operations:* uses bulk condiment dispensers and decreased packaging for to-go food service purchases.

Energy Currently uses or plans to use alternative sources of power and motion, infrared, and/or light sensors to reduce energy uses for lighting.

Purchasing Sustainability criteria used in purchasing include Energy Star (EPA) and Green Cleaning Products (Green Seal/Environmental Choice certified).

Contact Chief of Staff to the President, City College of the City University of New York, 160 Convent Avenue, A300, New York, NY 10031. *E-mail:* ccnygreen@ccny.cuny.edu. *Web site:* www.ccny.cuny.edu/.

Clarkson University
Potsdam, New York

Academics *Sustainability-focused undergraduate major(s):* Biology (BS), Chemistry (BS), Engineering and Management (BS), Environmental Engineering (BS), Environmental Health Science (BS), Environmental Science and Policy (BS). *Sustainability-focused graduate degree program(s):* Environmental Science and Engineering (MS/PhD). *Sustainability courses and programs:* sustainability-focused course(s) or lecture series.

Student Services and Green Events *Sustainability leadership:* sustainability coordinator/director, sustainability committee/advisory council, recycling manager, energy manager, sustainability-focused student government. *Student clubs and activities:* student club(s)/group(s) focused on sustainability, outreach materials available about on-campus sustainability efforts. *Major sustainability events:* Focus the Nation.

Food Sustainable, organic, and/or locally produced foods available in on-campus dining facilities. Vegan and vegetarian dining options are available for every meal.

Buildings and Grounds *Renovation and maintenance:* registered for LEED certification for new construction and/or renovation. *Campus grounds care:* uses water conservation devices; employs strategies to reduce light pollution; landscapes with native plant species; protects, restores, and/or creates habitat on campus.

Recycling *Programs and activities:* sustains a computer/technology recycling program; maintains an on-campus recycling center; reuses surplus department/office supplies; reuses chemicals; replaces paper materials with online alternatives; limits free printing in computer labs and libraries. *Campus dining operations:* operates without trays; offers discounts for reusable mugs; uses bulk condiment dispensers and decreased packaging for to-go food service purchases.

Energy Currently uses or plans to use alternative sources of power (biomass energy, hydroelectricity/water power, solar energy, and wind energy); timers to regulate temperatures based on occupancy hours; motion, infrared, and/or light sensors to reduce energy uses for lighting; LED lighting; vending machine motion sensors; and energy-related performance contracting.

Purchasing Sustainability criteria used in purchasing include Energy Star (EPA), WaterSense (EPA), and Green Cleaning Products (Green Seal/Environmental Choice certified).

Contact Director of News and Digital Content Services, Clarkson University, PO Box 5535, Potsdam, NY 13699. *Phone:* 315-268-6716. *E-mail:* mgriffin@clarkson.edu. *Web site:* www.clarkson.edu/.

Colgate University
Hamilton, New York

Sustainability Initiatives Colgate University's president has signed the American College & University Presidents Climate Commitment.

Academics *Sustainability-focused undergraduate major(s):* Environmental Studies. *Sustainability courses and programs:* sustainability-focused course(s) or lecture series.

Student Services and Green Events *Sustainability leadership:* sustainability coordinator/director, sustainability committee/advisory council, recycling manager, energy manager, sustainability-focused student government. *Student clubs and activities:* student club(s)/group(s) focused on sustainability. *Major sustainability events:* The Green Summit, Environmental Studies Program. *Housing and facilities:* sustainability-themed housing.

Food Sustainable, organic, and/or locally produced foods available in on-campus dining facilities. Fair Trade coffee is used. Vegan and vegetarian dining options are available for every meal.

Transportation Provides free on-campus transportation (bus or other), public transportation access to local destinations, and a bike loan/rental program.

Buildings and Grounds *Campus grounds care:* uses water conservation devices; landscapes with native plant species; protects, restores, and/or creates habitat on campus.

Recycling *Programs and activities:* sustains a computer/technology recycling program; composts yard waste; reuses surplus department/office supplies; replaces paper materials with online alternatives. *Campus dining operations:* uses reusable dishware; uses bulk condiment dispensers and decreased packaging for to-go food service purchases.

Energy Currently uses or plans to use timers to regulate temperatures based on occupancy hours; motion, infrared, and/or light sensors to reduce energy uses for lighting; and energy-related performance contracting.

Purchasing Sustainability criteria used in purchasing include Energy Star (EPA) and Green Cleaning Products (Green Seal/Environmental Choice certified).

Contact Campus Sustainability Coordinator, Colgate University, 13 Oak Drive, Hamilton, NY 13346-1386. *Web site:* www.colgate.edu/.

The College at Brockport, State University of New York
Brockport, New York

Sustainability Initiatives The College at Brockport, State University of New York has Green Fees (optional/required) dedicated to sustainability initiatives.

Academics *Sustainability-focused undergraduate major(s):* Environmental Science (BS). *Sustainability-focused graduate degree program(s):* Environmental Science (MS). *Sustainability courses and programs:* sustainability-focused course(s) or lecture series.

Student Services and Green Events *Sustainability leadership:* sustainability committee/advisory council, recycling manager, energy manager. *Student clubs and activities:* student club(s)/group(s) focused on sustainability. *Major sustainability events:* Earth Day, Campus Sustainability Day, International Coastal Cleanup event, Campus Cleanups, America Recycles Day, Arbor Day.

Food Sustainable, organic, and/or locally produced foods available in on-campus dining facilities. Fair Trade coffee is used. Vegan and vegetarian dining options are available for every meal.

Transportation Provides public transportation access to local destinations, a bike loan/rental program, and incentives to carpool or use public transportation.

Buildings and Grounds *Percentage of institution's eligible buildings as of September 2008 meeting LEED and/or LEED-EB certification criteria:* 7.15%. *Renovation and maintenance:* registered for LEED certification for new construction and/or renovation; uses a Green Seal certified cleaning service. *Campus grounds care:* uses water conservation devices; employs strategies to reduce light pollution; landscapes with native plant species; protects, restores, and/or creates habitat on campus.

Recycling *Events and organizations:* RecycleMania, WasteWise (EPA). *Programs and activities:* sustains a computer/technology recycling program; maintains an on-campus recycling center; composts yard waste; replaces paper materials with online alternatives; limits free printing in computer labs and libraries. *Campus dining operations:* uses reusable dishware; operates without trays; offers discounts for reusable mugs.

Energy Currently uses or plans to use alternative sources of power (geothermal energy); timers to regulate temperatures based on occupancy hours; motion, infrared, and/or light sensors to reduce energy uses for lighting; LED lighting; vending machine motion sensors; and energy-related performance contracting.

Purchasing Sustainability criteria used in purchasing include Energy Star (EPA) and Green Cleaning Products (Green Seal/Environmental Choice certified).

Contact Sustainability Task Force Chair, The College at Brockport, State University of New York, 350 New Campus Drive, B-45 Lennon Hall, Brockport, NY 14420. *Phone:* 585-395-5966. *Fax:* 585-395-5969. *E-mail:* Hmosher@brockport.edu. *Web site:* www.brockport.edu/.

The College of Saint Rose
Albany, New York

Sustainability Initiatives The College of Saint Rose's president has signed the American College & University Presidents Climate Commitment.

Academics *Sustainability courses and programs:* sustainability-focused course(s) or lecture series.

Student Services and Green Events *Sustainability leadership:* sustainability committee/advisory council.

Food Fair Trade coffee is used. Vegan and vegetarian dining options are available for every meal.

Transportation Provides free on-campus transportation (bus or other), public transportation access to local destinations, and incentives to carpool or use public transportation.

Buildings and Grounds *Renovation and maintenance:* registered for LEED certification for new construction and/or

renovation; uses a Green Seal certified cleaning service. *Campus grounds care:* uses water conservation devices; landscapes with native plant species; protects, restores, and/or creates habitat on campus.

Recycling *Programs and activities:* sustains a computer/technology recycling program; reuses surplus department/office supplies; replaces paper materials with online alternatives; limits free printing in computer labs and libraries. *Campus dining operations:* uses reusable dishware; operates without trays; offers discounts for reusable mugs; uses bulk condiment dispensers and decreased packaging for to-go food service purchases.

Energy Currently uses or plans to use alternative sources of power (geothermal energy and wind energy); timers to regulate temperatures based on occupancy hours; motion, infrared, and/or light sensors to reduce energy uses for lighting; and LED lighting.

Purchasing Sustainability criteria used in purchasing include Energy Star (EPA), Green Cleaning Products (Green Seal/Environmental Choice certified), and Forest Stewardship Council (FSC) or American Forest and Paper Association's Sustainable Forestry Initiative (SFI) paper.

Contact Vice President for Finance and Administration, The College of Saint Rose, 432 Western Avenue, Albany, NY 12203. *Phone:* 518-454-2516. *Fax:* 518-454-2018. *Web site:* www.strose.edu/.

Cornell University
Ithaca, New York

Sustainability Initiatives Cornell University is a member of the Association for the Advancement of Sustainability in Higher Education (AASHE). This institution's president has signed the American College & University Presidents Climate Commitment.

Academics *Sustainability-focused undergraduate major(s):* Sustainable Agriculture (BS). *Sustainability-focused graduate degree program(s):* Sustainable Enterprise (MBA). *Sustainability courses and programs:* sustainability-focused course(s) or lecture series, noncredit sustainability course(s).

Student Services and Green Events *Sustainability leadership:* sustainability coordinator/director, sustainability committee/advisory council, recycling manager, energy manager, sustainability-focused student government. *Student clubs and activities:* student club(s)/group(s) focused on sustainability, outreach materials available about on-campus sustainability efforts. *Major sustainability events:* Net Impact, National Facilitating Sustainable Agriculture Education Conference, Sun Grant Northeast annual conference, Ivy Plus Sustainability Working Group annual meeting. *Housing and facilities:* sustainability-themed housing, model dorm room that demonstrates sustainable living principles, student-run café that serves environmentally or socially preferable foods, on-campus organic garden for students.

Food Sustainable, organic, and/or locally produced foods available in on-campus dining facilities. Fair Trade coffee is used. Vegan and vegetarian dining options are available for every meal.

Transportation Provides free on-campus transportation (bus or other), public transportation access to local destinations, a car sharing program, and incentives to carpool or use public transportation.

Buildings and Grounds *Renovation and maintenance:* uses a Green Seal certified cleaning service. *Campus grounds care:* uses water conservation devices; employs

strategies to reduce light pollution; landscapes with native plant species; protects, restores, and/or creates habitat on campus.

Recycling *Events and organizations:* RecycleMania. *Programs and activities:* sustains a computer/technology recycling program; maintains an on-campus recycling center; sustains a pre-consumer food waste composting program; sustains a post-consumer food waste composting program; composts yard waste; reuses surplus department/office supplies; reuses chemicals; replaces paper materials with online alternatives; limits free printing in computer labs and libraries. *Campus dining operations:* uses reusable dishware; operates without trays; offers discounts for reusable mugs; uses bulk condiment dispensers and decreased packaging for to-go food service purchases.

Energy Currently uses or plans to use alternative sources of power (hydroelectricity/water power and solar energy); timers to regulate temperatures based on occupancy hours; motion, infrared, and/or light sensors to reduce energy uses for lighting; and LED lighting.

Purchasing Sustainability criteria used in purchasing include Energy Star (EPA), Green Electronics Council (GEC) Electronic Product Environmental Assessment Tool (EPEAT) Silver or Gold, Green Cleaning Products (Green Seal/Environmental Choice certified), and Forest Stewardship Council (FSC) or American Forest and Paper Association's Sustainable Forestry Initiative (SFI) paper.

Contact Senior Sustainability Coordinator, Cornell University, 395 Pine Tree Road, Suite 230, Ithaca, NY 14850. *Phone:* 607-255-2757. *E-mail:* drk5@cornell.edu. *Web site:* www.cornell.edu/.

Daemen College
Amherst, New York

Sustainability Initiatives Daemen College is a signatory to the Talloires Declaration.

Academics *Sustainability-focused undergraduate major(s):* Environmental Studies (BA), Environmental Studies (BS). *Sustainability courses and programs:* sustainability-focused course(s) or lecture series.

Student Services and Green Events *Student clubs and activities:* Campus Climate Challenge, student club(s)/group(s) focused on sustainability, outreach materials available about on-campus sustainability efforts. *Major sustainability events:* Annual Environmental Summit, Earth Day Celebration, Focus the Nation Teach-In, Green Jobs Workshops, World on Your Plate Symposium.

Transportation Provides public transportation access to local destinations and incentives to carpool or use public transportation.

Buildings and Grounds *Renovation and maintenance:* registered for LEED certification for new construction and/or renovation. *Campus grounds care:* protects, restores, and/or creates habitat on campus.

Recycling *Events and organizations:* RecycleMania. *Programs and activities:* sustains a computer/technology recycling program; replaces paper materials with online alternatives; limits free printing in computer labs and libraries. *Campus dining operations:* uses reusable dishware.

Energy Currently uses or plans to use alternative sources of power.

Purchasing Sustainability criteria used in purchasing include Energy Star (EPA).

Contact Associate Professor of Biology, Daemen College, 4380 Main Street, Amherst, NY 14226-3592. *Phone:* 716-839-8366. *E-mail:* byoung@daemen.edu. *Web site:* www.daemen.edu/.

D'Youville College
Buffalo, New York

Sustainability Initiatives D'Youville College's president has signed the American College & University Presidents Climate Commitment.

Student Services and Green Events *Sustainability leadership:* recycling manager, energy manager.

Food Vegan and vegetarian dining options are available for every meal.

Transportation Provides public transportation access to local destinations.

Buildings and Grounds *Campus grounds care:* uses water conservation devices.

Recycling *Programs and activities:* sustains a computer/technology recycling program; reuses surplus department/office supplies; replaces paper materials with online alternatives. *Campus dining operations:* uses reusable dishware; operates without trays; uses bulk condiment dispensers and decreased packaging for to-go food service purchases.

Energy Currently uses or plans to use timers to regulate temperatures based on occupancy hours; motion, infrared, and/or light sensors to reduce energy uses for lighting; and energy-related performance contracting.

Purchasing Sustainability criteria used in purchasing include Energy Star (EPA) and Green Cleaning Products (Green Seal/Environmental Choice certified).

Contact D'Youville College, 320 Porter Avenue, Buffalo, NY 14201-1084. *Phone:* 716-829-8000. *Web site:* www.dyc.edu/.

Hobart and William Smith Colleges
Geneva, New York

Sustainability Initiatives Hobart and William Smith Colleges's president has signed the American College & University Presidents Climate Commitment. Hobart and William Smith Colleges has Green Fees (optional/required) dedicated to sustainability initiatives.

Academics *Sustainability-focused undergraduate major(s):* Environmental Studies (BA). *Sustainability courses and programs:* sustainability-focused course(s) or lecture series.

Student Services and Green Events *Sustainability leadership:* sustainability coordinator/director, sustainability committee/advisory council, energy manager. *Student clubs and activities:* student club(s)/group(s) focused on sustainability, outreach materials available about on-campus sustainability efforts. *Major sustainability events:* New England Environmental Studies Conference 2010. *Housing and facilities:* sustainability-themed housing, on-campus organic garden for students.

Food Sustainable, organic, and/or locally produced foods available in on-campus dining facilities. Fair Trade coffee is used.

Transportation Provides free on-campus transportation (bus or other), public transportation access to local destinations, and a bike loan/rental program.

Buildings and Grounds *Campus grounds care:* uses water conservation devices; employs strategies to reduce light pollution; landscapes with native plant species; protects, restores, and/or creates habitat on campus.

Recycling *Events and organizations:* RecycleMania. *Programs and activities:* sustains a computer/technology recycling program; sustains a pre-consumer food waste com-

posting program; sustains a post-consumer food waste composting program; composts yard waste; replaces paper materials with online alternatives; limits free printing in computer labs and libraries. *Campus dining operations:* uses reusable dishware; offers discounts for reusable mugs; uses bulk condiment dispensers and decreased packaging for to-go food service purchases.

Energy Currently uses or plans to use alternative sources of power (geothermal energy, hydroelectricity/water power, solar energy, and wind energy); timers to regulate temperatures based on occupancy hours; motion, infrared, and/or light sensors to reduce energy uses for lighting; vending machine motion sensors; and energy-related performance contracting.

Purchasing Sustainability criteria used in purchasing include Energy Star (EPA) and Green Cleaning Products (Green Seal/Environmental Choice certified).

Contact Sustainability Coordinator, Hobart and William Smith Colleges, 337 Pulteney Street, Geneva, NY 14456. *Phone:* 315-781-4442. *Fax:* 315-781-3654. *E-mail:* landi@hws.edu. *Web site:* www.hws.edu/.

Hofstra University
Hempstead, New York

Sustainability Initiatives Hofstra University is a member of the Association for the Advancement of Sustainability in Higher Education (AASHE).

Academics *Sustainability-focused undergraduate major(s):* Urban Ecology (BA), Urban Ecology (BS). *Sustainability courses and programs:* sustainability-focused course(s) or lecture series, noncredit sustainability course(s).

Student Services and Green Events *Sustainability leadership:* sustainability coordinator/director, sustainability committee/advisory council, recycling manager, energy manager. *Student clubs and activities:* student club(s)/group(s) focused on sustainability, outreach materials available about on-campus sustainability efforts. *Major sustainability events:* "Day of Dialogue" on environmental practices, Focus the Nation, Earth Day events, "National Teach" with climate change lectures, Sustainability Week, "Take Back the Tap" Power vote campaign.

Food Sustainable, organic, and/or locally produced foods available in on-campus dining facilities. Fair Trade coffee is used. Vegan and vegetarian dining options are available for every meal.

Transportation Provides free on-campus transportation (bus or other), public transportation access to local destinations, a car sharing program, and incentives to carpool or use public transportation.

Buildings and Grounds *Renovation and maintenance:* uses a Green Seal certified cleaning service. *Campus grounds care:* uses water conservation devices; employs strategies to reduce light pollution; landscapes with native plant species; protects, restores, and/or creates habitat on campus; applies to its grounds only pesticides and fertilizers allowable under the U.S. Department of Agriculture's standards for crop production.

Recycling *Programs and activities:* sustains a computer/technology recycling program; reuses surplus department/office supplies; replaces paper materials with online alternatives; limits free printing in computer labs and libraries. *Campus dining operations:* uses reusable dishware; operates without trays; offers discounts for reusable mugs; uses bulk condiment dispensers and decreased packaging for to-go food service purchases.

Energy Currently uses or plans to use alternative sources of power; timers to regulate temperatures based on occupancy hours; motion, infrared, and/or light sensors to reduce energy uses for lighting; LED lighting; vending machine motion sensors; and energy-related performance contracting.

Purchasing Sustainability criteria used in purchasing include Energy Star (EPA) and Green Cleaning Products (Green Seal/Environmental Choice certified).

Contact Vice President, Facilities and Operations, Hofstra University, 100 Hofstra University, Hempstead, NY 11549. *Phone:* 516-463-6623. *Fax:* 516-463-5302. *E-mail:* joseph.barkwill@hofstra.edu. *Web site:* www.hofstra.edu/.

Houghton College
Houghton, New York

Sustainability Initiatives Houghton College's president has signed the American College & University Presidents Climate Commitment.

Academics *Sustainability-focused undergraduate major(s):* Biology with Environmental emphasis (BA, BS), Recreation—Outdoor Education (BS). *Sustainability courses and programs:* sustainability-focused course(s) or lecture series.

Student Services and Green Events *Sustainability leadership:* sustainability committee/advisory council, recycling manager, energy manager. *Student clubs and activities:* outreach materials available about on-campus sustainability efforts. *Housing and facilities:* student-run café that serves environmentally or socially preferable foods, on-campus organic garden for students.

Food Fair Trade coffee is used. Vegan and vegetarian dining options are available for every meal.

Transportation Provides public transportation access to local destinations, a bike loan/rental program, and a car sharing program.

Buildings and Grounds *Renovation and maintenance:* registered for LEED certification for new construction and/or renovation. *Campus grounds care:* landscapes with native plant species; protects, restores, and/or creates habitat on campus.

Recycling *Programs and activities:* sustains a computer/technology recycling program; maintains an on-campus recycling center; composts yard waste; reuses surplus department/office supplies; replaces paper materials with online alternatives; limits free printing in computer labs and libraries. *Campus dining operations:* uses reusable dishware; operates without trays; offers discounts for reusable mugs; uses bulk condiment dispensers and decreased packaging for to-go food service purchases.

Energy Currently uses or plans to use alternative sources of power (hydroelectricity/water power); timers to regulate temperatures based on occupancy hours; motion, infrared, and/or light sensors to reduce energy uses for lighting; and LED lighting.

Purchasing Sustainability criteria used in purchasing include Energy Star (EPA), Green Cleaning Products (Green Seal/Environmental Choice certified), and Forest Stewardship Council (FSC) or American Forest and Paper Association's Sustainable Forestry Initiative (SFI) paper.

Contact Chair, Creation Care Task Force, Houghton College, 1 Willard Avenue, Houghton, NY 14744. *Phone:* 585-567-9308. *E-mail:* paul.young@houghton.edu. *Web site:* www.houghton.edu/.

Hunter College of the City University of New York
New York, New York

Academics *Sustainability-focused undergraduate major(s):* Renewable Energy (BA). *Sustainability courses and programs:* sustainability-focused course(s) or lecture series.

Student Services and Green Events *Sustainability leadership:* sustainability coordinator/director, sustainability committee/advisory council, recycling manager, energy manager, sustainability-focused student government. *Student clubs and activities:* Public Interest Research Group (PIRG) chapter on campus, student club(s)/group(s) focused on sustainability, outreach materials available about on-campus sustainability efforts. *Major sustainability events:* CUNY Task Force on Sustainability Conference.

Food Sustainable, organic, and/or locally produced foods available in on-campus dining facilities. Vegan and vegetarian dining options are available for every meal.

Transportation Provides public transportation access to local destinations.

Buildings and Grounds *Renovation and maintenance:* registered for LEED certification for new construction and/or renovation; uses a Green Seal certified cleaning service. *Campus grounds care:* uses water conservation devices.

Recycling *Programs and activities:* sustains a computer/technology recycling program; maintains an on-campus recycling center; reuses surplus department/office supplies; reuses chemicals; replaces paper materials with online alternatives; limits free printing in computer labs and libraries. *Campus dining operations:* uses reusable dishware; offers discounts for reusable mugs.

Energy Currently uses or plans to use motion, infrared, and/or light sensors to reduce energy uses for lighting and energy-related performance contracting.

Purchasing Sustainability criteria used in purchasing include Energy Star (EPA) and Green Cleaning Products (Green Seal/Environmental Choice certified).

Contact Operations Coordinator, Hunter College of the City University of New York, 695 Park Avenue, New York, NY 10021. *Phone:* 212-772-4600. *E-mail:* twilson@hunter.cuny.edu. *Web site:* www.hunter.cuny.edu/.

Ithaca College
Ithaca, New York

Sustainability Initiatives Ithaca College is a member of the Association for the Advancement of Sustainability in Higher Education (AASHE) and a signatory to the Talloires Declaration. This institution's president has signed the American College & University Presidents Climate Commitment.

Academics *Sustainability-focused undergraduate major(s):* Environmental Science (BA), Environmental Studies (BA). *Sustainability courses and programs:* sustainability-focused course(s) or lecture series.

Student Services and Green Events *Sustainability leadership:* sustainability committee/advisory council, recycling manager, sustainability-focused student government. *Student clubs and activities:* Campus Climate Challenge, student club(s)/group(s) focused on sustainability, outreach materials available about on-campus sustainability efforts. *Major sustainability events:* Campus Sustainability Day, Earth Week programming, Sustainability Cafe series, Sustainability speaker series. *Housing and facilities:* sustainability-themed housing, on-campus organic garden for students.

Food Sustainable, organic, and/or locally produced foods available in on-campus dining facilities. Fair Trade coffee is used. Vegan and vegetarian dining options are available for every meal.

Transportation Provides free on-campus transportation (bus or other), public transportation access to local destinations, a car sharing program, and incentives to carpool or use public transportation.

Buildings and Grounds *Percentage of institution's eligible buildings as of September 2008 meeting LEED and/or LEED-EB certification criteria:* 2%. *Renovation and maintenance:* registered for LEED certification for new construction and/or renovation. *Campus grounds care:* uses water conservation devices; employs strategies to reduce light pollution; landscapes with native plant species; protects, restores, and/or creates habitat on campus.

Recycling *Events and organizations:* RecycleMania. *Programs and activities:* sustains a computer/technology recycling program; sustains a pre-consumer food waste composting program; sustains a post-consumer food waste composting program; composts yard waste; reuses surplus department/office supplies; replaces paper materials with online alternatives; limits free printing in computer labs and libraries. *Campus dining operations:* uses reusable dishware; operates without trays; offers discounts for reusable mugs; uses bulk condiment dispensers and decreased packaging for to-go food service purchases.

Energy Currently uses or plans to use alternative sources of power (hydroelectricity/water power); timers to regulate temperatures based on occupancy hours; motion, infrared, and/or light sensors to reduce energy uses for lighting; and LED lighting.

Purchasing Sustainability criteria used in purchasing include Energy Star (EPA), Green Electronics Council (GEC) Electronic Product Environmental Assessment Tool (EPEAT) Silver or Gold, and Green Cleaning Products (Green Seal/Environmental Choice certified).

Contact Special Assistant to the Provost, Ithaca College, Office of the Provost, 953 Danby Road, Ithaca, NY 14850. *Phone:* 607-274-3787. *Fax:* 607-274-3064. *E-mail:* mbrown@ithaca.edu. *Web site:* www.ithaca.edu/.

Manhattanville College
Purchase, New York

Sustainability Initiatives Manhattanville College's president has signed the American College & University Presidents Climate Commitment.

Student Services and Green Events *Sustainability leadership:* sustainability coordinator/director, sustainability committee/advisory council, recycling manager, energy manager, sustainability-focused student government.

Food Sustainable, organic, and/or locally produced foods available in on-campus dining facilities. Fair Trade coffee is used. Vegan and vegetarian dining options are available for every meal.

Transportation Provides free on-campus transportation (bus or other) and public transportation access to local destinations.

Buildings and Grounds *Percentage of institution's eligible buildings as of September 2008 meeting LEED and/or LEED-EB certification criteria:* 4%. *Renovation and maintenance:* registered for LEED certification for new construction and/or renovation; uses a Green Seal certified cleaning service. *Campus grounds care:* uses water conservation devices; landscapes with native plant species; protects, restores, and/or creates habitat on campus.

Recycling *Programs and activities:* sustains a computer/technology recycling program; reuses chemicals; replaces paper materials with online alternatives.

Energy Currently uses or plans to use alternative sources of power (solar energy); motion, infrared, and/or light sensors to reduce energy uses for lighting; and LED lighting.

Purchasing Sustainability criteria used in purchasing include Energy Star (EPA) and Green Cleaning Products (Green Seal/Environmental Choice certified).

Contact Deputy Director, Environmental Health and Safety, Manhattanville College, 2900 Purchase Street, Purchase, NY 10577. *Phone:* 914-323-5227. *Fax:* 914-323-7140. *E-mail:* arnoffs@mville.edu. *Web site:* www.manhattanville.edu/.

New York Institute of Technology
Old Westbury, New York

Academics *Sustainability courses and programs:* sustainability-focused course(s) or lecture series, sustainability-focused nonacademic certificate program(s).

Student Services and Green Events *Sustainability leadership:* sustainability coordinator/director, sustainability committee/advisory council, recycling manager. *Student clubs and activities:* student club(s)/group(s) focused on sustainability, outreach materials available about on-campus sustainability efforts. *Major sustainability events:* Energy Conference.

Transportation Provides free on-campus transportation (bus or other) and public transportation access to local destinations.

Buildings and Grounds *Renovation and maintenance:* uses a Green Seal certified cleaning service. *Campus grounds care:* uses water conservation devices; employs strategies to reduce light pollution; landscapes with native plant species; protects, restores, and/or creates habitat on campus.

Recycling *Programs and activities:* sustains a computer/technology recycling program. *Campus dining operations:* offers discounts for reusable mugs.

Energy Currently uses or plans to use alternative sources of power (solar energy); motion, infrared, and/or light sensors to reduce energy uses for lighting; and energy-related performance contracting.

Contact New York Institute of Technology, PO Box 8000, Old Westbury, NY 11568-8000. *Phone:* 516-686-7516. *Web site:* www.nyit.edu/.

New York University
New York, New York

Sustainability Initiatives New York University is a member of the Association for the Advancement of Sustainability in Higher Education (AASHE). This institution's president has signed the American College & University Presidents Climate Commitment.

Academics *Sustainability-focused undergraduate major(s):* Environmental Studies (BA), Gallatin Individualized Concentrations (BA). *Sustainability-focused graduate degree program(s):* Bioethics (MA, PhD), Environmental Conservation Education (MA), Environmental Law (JD), Gallatin Individualized Concentrations (MA), Strong sustainability focus in Environmental Policy (MPA), Environmental Planning (MA), Interactive Telecommunications (MFA). *Sustainability courses and programs:* sustainability-focused course(s) or lecture series.

Student Services and Green Events *Sustainability leadership:* sustainability coordinator/director, sustainability committee/advisory council, recycling manager, energy manager, sustainability-focused student government. *Student clubs and activities:* student club(s)/group(s) focused on sustainability, outreach materials available about on-campus sustainability efforts. *Major sustainability events:* Global Colloquium of University Presidents on Climate Change, Earth Week, Focus the Nation, Footprint Forward Week. *Housing and facilities:* sustainability-themed housing, on-campus organic garden for students.

Food Sustainable, organic, and/or locally produced foods available in on-campus dining facilities. Fair Trade coffee is used. Vegan and vegetarian dining options are available for every meal.

Transportation Provides free on-campus transportation (bus or other), public transportation access to local destinations, a bike loan/rental program, and incentives to carpool or use public transportation.

Buildings and Grounds *Percentage of institution's eligible buildings as of September 2008 meeting LEED and/or LEED-EB certification criteria:* .1%. *Renovation and maintenance:* registered for LEED certification for new construction and/or renovation; uses a Green Seal certified cleaning service. *Campus grounds care:* uses water conservation devices; employs strategies to reduce light pollution; landscapes with native plant species; protects, restores, and/or creates habitat on campus.

Recycling *Events and organizations:* RecycleMania. *Programs and activities:* sustains a computer/technology recycling program; maintains an on-campus recycling center; sustains a pre-consumer food waste composting program; sustains a post-consumer food waste composting program; composts yard waste; reuses surplus department/office supplies; reuses chemicals; replaces paper materials with online alternatives; limits free printing in computer labs and libraries. *Campus dining operations:* operates without trays; uses bulk condiment dispensers and decreased packaging for to-go food service purchases.

Energy Currently uses or plans to use alternative sources of power; timers to regulate temperatures based on occupancy hours; motion, infrared, and/or light sensors to reduce energy uses for lighting; LED lighting; and vending machine motion sensors. Participates in College & University Green Power Challenge activities.

Purchasing Sustainability criteria used in purchasing include Energy Star (EPA), Green Electronics Council (GEC) Electronic Product Environmental Assessment Tool (EPEAT) Silver or Gold, Green Cleaning Products (Green Seal/Environmental Choice certified), and Forest Stewardship Council (FSC) or American Forest and Paper Association's Sustainable Forestry Initiative (SFI) paper.

Contact Coordinator, NYU Sustainability Task Force, New York University, 740 Broadway, 600C, New York, NY 10003. *Phone:* 212-998-1073. *E-mail:* sustainability@nyu.edu. *Web site:* www.nyu.edu/.

Niagara University
Niagara Falls, New York

Student Services and Green Events *Sustainability leadership:* sustainability coordinator/director, sustainability committee/advisory council, recycling manager, energy manager.

Food Sustainable, organic, and/or locally produced foods available in on-campus dining facilities. Vegan and vegetarian dining options are available for every meal.

Transportation Provides public transportation access to local destinations.

Buildings and Grounds *Percentage of institution's eligible buildings as of September 2008 meeting LEED and/or LEED-EB certification criteria:* 4%. *Campus grounds care:* landscapes with native plant species.

Recycling *Events and organizations:* RecycleMania. *Programs and activities:* sustains a computer/technology recycling program; reuses surplus department/office supplies; replaces paper materials with online alternatives. *Campus dining operations:* uses reusable dishware; offers discounts for reusable mugs.

Energy Currently uses or plans to use alternative sources of power (hydroelectricity/water power); timers to regulate temperatures based on occupancy hours; motion, infrared, and/or light sensors to reduce energy uses for lighting; and LED lighting.

Purchasing Sustainability criteria used in purchasing include Energy Star (EPA).

Contact Niagara University, Niagara Falls, NY 14109. *Phone:* 716-285-1212. *Web site:* www.niagara.edu/.

Paul Smith's College
Paul Smiths, New York

Sustainability Initiatives Paul Smith's College is a member of the Association for the Advancement of Sustainability in Higher Education (AASHE). This institution's president has signed the American College & University Presidents Climate Commitment.

Academics *Sustainability-focused undergraduate major(s):* Environmental Science (BS), Natural Resources (BS), Nature and Culture (BA), Sustainability Studies (BS). *Sustainability courses and programs:* sustainability-focused course(s) or lecture series.

Student Services and Green Events *Sustainability leadership:* sustainability committee/advisory council, energy manager. *Student clubs and activities:* student club(s)/group(s) focused on sustainability. *Major sustainability events:* Step It Up, 350.org climate action.

Food Sustainable, organic, and/or locally produced foods available in on-campus dining facilities. Fair Trade coffee is used. Vegan and vegetarian dining options are available for every meal.

Transportation Provides public transportation access to local destinations and incentives to carpool or use public transportation.

Buildings and Grounds *Campus grounds care:* uses water conservation devices; employs strategies to reduce light pollution; landscapes with native plant species; protects, restores, and/or creates habitat on campus.

Recycling *Events and organizations:* RecycleMania. *Programs and activities:* sustains a computer/technology recycling program; composts yard waste; replaces paper materials with online alternatives. *Campus dining operations:* uses reusable dishware; operates without trays; offers discounts for reusable mugs; uses bulk condiment dispensers and decreased packaging for to-go food service purchases.

Energy Currently uses or plans to use alternative sources of power (wind energy); motion, infrared, and/or light sensors to reduce energy uses for lighting; LED lighting; and vending machine motion sensors. Participates in College & University Green Power Challenge activities.

Purchasing Sustainability criteria used in purchasing include Energy Star (EPA), Green Cleaning Products (Green Seal/Environmental Choice certified), and Forest Stewardship Council (FSC) or American Forest and Paper Association's Sustainable Forestry Initiative (SFI) paper.

Contact Sustainability Council Chairperson, Paul Smith's College, PO Box 265, Paul Smiths, NY 12970. *Phone:* 518-327 6330. *E-mail:* thuber@paulsmiths.edu. *Web site:* www.paulsmiths.edu/.

Pratt Institute
Brooklyn, New York

Sustainability Initiatives Pratt Institute's president has signed the American College & University Presidents Climate Commitment.

Academics *Sustainability-focused graduate degree program(s):* Urban Environmental Systems Management (MS). *Sustainability courses and programs:* sustainability-focused course(s) or lecture series, noncredit sustainability course(s), sustainability-focused nonacademic certificate program(s).

Student Services and Green Events *Sustainability leadership:* sustainability coordinator/director, sustainability committee/advisory council, recycling manager, energy manager, sustainability-focused student government. *Student clubs and activities:* student club(s)/group(s) focused on sustainability, outreach materials available about on-campus sustainability efforts. *Major sustainability events:* National Sustainable Campus Day, Focus the Nation broadcast and events, Green Week/Green Brooklyn Expo. *Housing and facilities:* model dorm room that demonstrates sustainable living principles, on-campus organic garden for students.

Food Sustainable, organic, and/or locally produced foods available in on-campus dining facilities. Fair Trade coffee is used. Vegan and vegetarian dining options are available for every meal.

Transportation Provides public transportation access to local destinations.

Buildings and Grounds *Renovation and maintenance:* registered for LEED certification for new construction and/or renovation; uses a Green Seal certified cleaning service. *Campus grounds care:* uses water conservation devices; employs strategies to reduce light pollution; landscapes with native plant species; protects, restores, and/or creates habitat on campus; applies to its grounds only pesticides and fertilizers allowable under the U.S. Department of Agriculture's standards for crop production.

Recycling *Events and organizations:* RecycleMania, WasteWise (EPA). *Programs and activities:* sustains a computer/technology recycling program; composts yard waste; reuses surplus department/office supplies; reuses chemicals; replaces paper materials with online alternatives; limits free printing in computer labs and libraries. *Campus dining operations:* operates without trays; offers discounts for reusable mugs; uses bulk condiment dispensers and decreased packaging for to-go food service purchases.

Energy Currently uses or plans to use alternative sources of power (hydroelectricity/water power, solar energy, and wind energy); timers to regulate temperatures based on occupancy hours; motion, infrared, and/or light sensors to reduce energy uses for lighting; and energy-related performance contracting.

Purchasing Sustainability criteria used in purchasing include Energy Star (EPA) and Green Cleaning Products (Green Seal/Environmental Choice certified).

Contact Director, Administrative Sustainability, Pratt Institute, 200 Willoughby Avenue, Bklyn, NY 11205. *Phone:* 917-750-6314. *E-mail:* argelber@pratt.edu. *Web site:* www.pratt.edu/.

St. Lawrence University
Canton, New York

Sustainability Initiatives St. Lawrence University's president has signed the American College & University Presidents Climate Commitment.

Academics *Sustainability-focused undergraduate major(s):* Environmental Studies (BA).

Student Services and Green Events *Sustainability leadership:* sustainability coordinator/director, sustainability committee/advisory council, sustainability-focused student government. *Student clubs and activities:* outreach materials available about on-campus sustainability efforts. *Housing and facilities:* sustainability-themed housing.

Food Sustainable, organic, and/or locally produced foods available in on-campus dining facilities. Vegan and vegetarian dining options are available for every meal.

Transportation Provides a bike loan/rental program.

Buildings and Grounds *Renovation and maintenance:* registered for LEED certification for new construction and/or renovation. *Campus grounds care:* protects, restores, and/or creates habitat on campus.

Recycling *Programs and activities:* sustains a computer/technology recycling program; maintains an on-campus recycling center; composts yard waste; reuses surplus department/office supplies. *Campus dining operations:* operates without trays; offers discounts for reusable mugs.

Energy Currently uses or plans to use motion, infrared, and/or light sensors to reduce energy uses for lighting and energy-related performance contracting.

Purchasing Sustainability criteria used in purchasing include Energy Star (EPA).

Contact Associate Vice President of University Relations, St. Lawrence University, Canton, NY 13617. *Phone:* 315-229-5567. *Fax:* 315-229-7422. *E-mail:* lcania@stlawu.edu. *Web site:* www.stlawu.edu/.

State University of New York at Binghamton
Binghamton, New York

Sustainability Initiatives State University of New York at Binghamton's president has signed the American College & University Presidents Climate Commitment.

Academics *Sustainability-focused undergraduate major(s):* Earth Sciences—Natural Resources (BA), Ecosystems (BA), Environmental Economics (BA), Environmental Planning (BA), Environmental Policy and Law (BA), Geological Sciences and Environmental Studies (BA). *Sustainability-focused graduate degree program(s):* Earth Sciences (MA), Environmental Studies (MA). *Sustainability courses and programs:* sustainability-focused course(s) or lecture series.

Student Services and Green Events *Sustainability leadership:* sustainability coordinator/director, sustainability committee/advisory council, recycling manager, energy manager, sustainability-focused student government. *Student clubs and activities:* Campus Climate Challenge, Public Interest Research Group (PIRG) chapter on campus, student club(s)/group(s) focused on sustainability, outreach materials available about on-campus sustainability efforts. *Major sustainability events:* SUNY Sustainability Conference, Bio-Cycle, Food Scrap Management Forums by NYSDEC. *Housing and facilities:* sustainability-themed housing, student-run café that serves environmentally or socially preferable foods, on-campus organic garden for students.

Food Sustainable, organic, and/or locally produced foods available in on-campus dining facilities. Fair Trade coffee is used. Vegan and vegetarian dining options are available for every meal.

Transportation Provides free on-campus transportation (bus or other), public transportation access to local destinations, a car sharing program, and incentives to carpool or use public transportation.

Buildings and Grounds *Percentage of institution's eligible buildings as of September 2008 meeting LEED and/or LEED-EB certification criteria:* 4.3%. *Renovation and maintenance:* registered for LEED certification for new construction and/or renovation; uses a Green Seal certified cleaning service. *Campus grounds care:* uses water conservation devices; employs strategies to reduce light pollution; landscapes with native plant species; protects, restores, and/or creates habitat on campus.

Recycling *Events and organizations:* RecycleMania. *Programs and activities:* sustains a computer/technology recycling program; maintains an on-campus recycling center; sustains a pre-consumer food waste composting program; sustains a post-consumer food waste composting program; composts yard waste; reuses surplus department/office supplies; reuses chemicals; replaces paper materials with online alternatives; limits free printing in computer labs and libraries. *Campus dining operations:* uses reusable dishware; offers discounts for reusable mugs; uses bulk condiment dispensers and decreased packaging for to-go food service purchases.

Energy Currently uses or plans to use alternative sources of power (biomass energy, hydroelectricity/water power, and solar energy); timers to regulate temperatures based on occupancy hours; motion, infrared, and/or light sensors to reduce energy uses for lighting; and LED lighting.

Purchasing Sustainability criteria used in purchasing include Energy Star (EPA) and Green Cleaning Products (Green Seal/Environmental Choice certified).

Contact Acting Vice President for Administration, State University of New York at Binghamton, Administration, PO Box 6000, Binghamton, NY 13902. *Phone:* 607-777-2143. *E-mail:* mmcgoff@binghamton.edu. *Web site:* www.binghamton.edu/.

State University of New York at Fredonia
Fredonia, New York

Sustainability Initiatives State University of New York at Fredonia's president has signed the American College & University Presidents Climate Commitment.

Academics *Sustainability courses and programs:* sustainability-focused course(s) or lecture series.

Student Services and Green Events *Sustainability leadership:* sustainability coordinator/director, sustainability committee/advisory council, recycling manager, energy manager, sustainability-focused student government. *Student clubs and activities:* Campus Climate Challenge, student club(s)/group(s) focused on sustainability. *Major sustainability events:* RecycleMania, Earth Week.

Food Sustainable, organic, and/or locally produced foods available in on-campus dining facilities. Fair Trade coffee is used. Vegan and vegetarian dining options are available for every meal.

Transportation Provides free on-campus transportation (bus or other) and public transportation access to local destinations.

Buildings and Grounds *Renovation and maintenance:* registered for LEED certification for new construction and/or

renovation; uses a Green Seal certified cleaning service. *Campus grounds care:* landscapes with native plant species; protects, restores, and/or creates habitat on campus.

Recycling *Events and organizations:* RecycleMania. *Programs and activities:* sustains a computer/technology recycling program; reuses surplus department/office supplies; replaces paper materials with online alternatives; limits free printing in computer labs and libraries. *Campus dining operations:* uses reusable dishware.

Energy Currently uses or plans to use timers to regulate temperatures based on occupancy hours and motion, infrared, and/or light sensors to reduce energy uses for lighting.

Purchasing Sustainability criteria used in purchasing include Energy Star (EPA) and Green Cleaning Products (Green Seal/Environmental Choice certified).

Contact Regulatory Affairs Specialist, State University of New York at Fredonia, 280 Central Avenue, Fredonia, NY 14063. *Phone:* 716-673-3796. *Fax:* 716-673-4860. *E-mail:* sarah.laurie@fredonia.edu. *Web site:* www.fredonia.edu/.

State University of New York at New Paltz
New Paltz, New York

Sustainability Initiatives State University of New York at New Paltz's president has signed the American College & University Presidents Climate Commitment.

Student Services and Green Events *Sustainability leadership:* sustainability coordinator/director, sustainability committee/advisory council, recycling manager, energy manager. *Student clubs and activities:* Public Interest Research Group (PIRG) chapter on campus, student club(s)/group(s) focused on sustainability. *Major sustainability events:* Sustainability Awareness event.

Food Sustainable, organic, and/or locally produced foods available in on-campus dining facilities. Vegan and vegetarian dining options are available for every meal.

Transportation Provides free on-campus transportation (bus or other), public transportation access to local destinations, and a car sharing program.

Buildings and Grounds *Renovation and maintenance:* registered for LEED certification for new construction and/or renovation. *Campus grounds care:* uses water conservation devices; employs strategies to reduce light pollution; landscapes with native plant species; protects, restores, and/or creates habitat on campus; applies to its grounds only pesticides and fertilizers allowable under the U.S. Department of Agriculture's standards for crop production.

Recycling *Events and organizations:* RecycleMania, WasteWise (EPA). *Programs and activities:* sustains a computer/technology recycling program; maintains an on-campus recycling center; composts yard waste; reuses surplus department/office supplies; replaces paper materials with online alternatives; limits free printing in computer labs and libraries. *Campus dining operations:* uses reusable dishware; offers discounts for reusable mugs; uses bulk condiment dispensers and decreased packaging for to-go food service purchases.

Energy Currently uses or plans to use alternative sources of power (solar energy); timers to regulate temperatures based on occupancy hours; motion, infrared, and/or light sensors to reduce energy uses for lighting; LED lighting; and energy-related performance contracting.

Purchasing Sustainability criteria used in purchasing include Energy Star (EPA), Green Electronics Council (GEC) Electronic Product Environmental Assessment Tool (EPEAT) Silver or Gold, and Green Cleaning Products (Green Seal/Environmental Choice certified).

Contact Director of Facilities Operations/Sustainability Coordinator, State University of New York at New Paltz, 1 Hawk Drive, New Paltz, NY 12561. *Phone:* 845-257-3322. *Fax:* 845-257-3302. *E-mail:* pineb@newpaltz.edu. *Web site:* www.newpaltz.edu/.

State University of New York College at Cortland
Cortland, New York

Sustainability Initiatives State University of New York College at Cortland's president has signed the American College & University Presidents Climate Commitment. State University of New York College at Cortland has Green Fees (optional/required) dedicated to sustainability initiatives.

Student Services and Green Events *Sustainability leadership:* sustainability coordinator/director, sustainability committee/advisory council, recycling manager, energy manager, sustainability-focused student government. *Student clubs and activities:* Campus Climate Challenge, Public Interest Research Group (PIRG) chapter on campus, student club(s)/group(s) focused on sustainability, outreach materials available about on-campus sustainability efforts. *Major sustainability events:* Earth Day, Earthly Matters lecture series.

Food Sustainable, organic, and/or locally produced foods available in on-campus dining facilities. Fair Trade coffee is used. Vegan and vegetarian dining options are available for every meal.

Transportation Provides free on-campus transportation (bus or other), public transportation access to local destinations, a bike loan/rental program, and incentives to carpool or use public transportation.

Buildings and Grounds *Percentage of institution's eligible buildings as of September 2008 meeting LEED and/or LEED-EB certification criteria:* 5%. *Renovation and maintenance:* registered for LEED certification for new construction and/or renovation. *Campus grounds care:* uses water conservation devices; employs strategies to reduce light pollution; landscapes with native plant species; protects, restores, and/or creates habitat on campus.

Recycling *Programs and activities:* composts yard waste; reuses chemicals; replaces paper materials with online alternatives; limits free printing in computer labs and libraries. *Campus dining operations:* uses reusable dishware; operates without trays; uses bulk condiment dispensers and decreased packaging for to-go food service purchases.

Energy Currently uses or plans to use timers to regulate temperatures based on occupancy hours; motion, infrared, and/or light sensors to reduce energy uses for lighting; and energy-related performance contracting.

Purchasing Sustainability criteria used in purchasing include Energy Star (EPA) and Green Cleaning Products (Green Seal/Environmental Choice certified).

Contact Public Relations Director, State University of New York College at Cortland, PO Box 2000, Cortland, NY 13045. *E-mail:* peter.koryzno@cortland.edu. *Web site:* www.cortland.edu/.

State University of New York College at Geneseo
Geneseo, New York

Sustainability Initiatives State University of New York College at Geneseo's president has signed the American College & University Presidents Climate Commitment.

Academics *Sustainability courses and programs:* sustainability-focused course(s) or lecture series.

Student Services and Green Events *Sustainability leadership:* sustainability committee/advisory council. *Student clubs and activities:* student club(s)/group(s) focused on sustainability. *Major sustainability events:* Live Green Expo, Earth Day Celebrations. *Housing and facilities:* on-campus organic garden for students.

Food Sustainable, organic, and/or locally produced foods available in on-campus dining facilities. Fair Trade coffee is used. Vegan and vegetarian dining options are available for every meal.

Transportation Provides free on-campus transportation (bus or other), public transportation access to local destinations, and a bike loan/rental program.

Buildings and Grounds *Campus grounds care:* uses water conservation devices; protects, restores, and/or creates habitat on campus.

Recycling *Events and organizations:* RecycleMania. *Programs and activities:* sustains a pre-consumer food waste composting program; composts yard waste; reuses surplus department/office supplies; reuses chemicals; replaces paper materials with online alternatives; limits free printing in computer labs and libraries. *Campus dining operations:* uses reusable dishware; operates without trays; offers discounts for reusable mugs.

Energy Currently uses or plans to use alternative sources of power (geothermal energy) and motion, infrared, and/or light sensors to reduce energy uses for lighting.

Purchasing Sustainability criteria used in purchasing include Energy Star (EPA).

Contact Co-Chair, Environmental Sustainability Task Force, State University of New York College at Geneseo, 1 College Circle, Geneseo, NY 14454. *E-mail:* gogreen@geneseo.edu. *Web site:* www.geneseo.edu/.

State University of New York College at Potsdam
Potsdam, New York

Sustainability Initiatives State University of New York College at Potsdam's president has signed the American College & University Presidents Climate Commitment.

Academics *Sustainability-focused undergraduate major(s):* Environmental Studies. *Sustainability courses and programs:* sustainability-focused course(s) or lecture series.

Student Services and Green Events *Student clubs and activities:* Campus Climate Challenge, student club(s)/group(s) focused on sustainability. *Housing and facilities:* on-campus organic garden for students.

Food Sustainable, organic, and/or locally produced foods available in on-campus dining facilities. Fair Trade coffee is used. Vegan and vegetarian dining options are available for every meal.

Transportation Provides public transportation access to local destinations and a car sharing program.

Buildings and Grounds *Percentage of institution's eligible buildings as of September 2008 meeting LEED and/or LEED-EB certification criteria:* 20%. *Renovation and maintenance:* registered for LEED certification for new construction and/or renovation. *Campus grounds care:* uses water conservation devices; employs strategies to reduce light pollution; landscapes with native plant species.

Recycling *Programs and activities:* sustains a computer/technology recycling program; reuses surplus department/

office supplies; replaces paper materials with online alternatives; limits free printing in computer labs and libraries. *Campus dining operations:* uses reusable dishware; offers discounts for reusable mugs; uses bulk condiment dispensers and decreased packaging for to-go food service purchases.

Energy Currently uses or plans to use alternative sources of power (hydroelectricity/water power and wind energy); timers to regulate temperatures based on occupancy hours; motion, infrared, and/or light sensors to reduce energy uses for lighting; LED lighting; and energy-related performance contracting.

Purchasing Sustainability criteria used in purchasing include Energy Star (EPA) and Green Cleaning Products (Green Seal/Environmental Choice certified).

Contact Assistant Vice President for Facilities, State University of New York College at Potsdam, 44 Pierrepont Avenue, Potsdam, NY 13676. *Phone:* 315-267-3125. *Fax:* 315-267-2777. *E-mail:* fisherwe@potsdam.edu. *Web site:* www.potsdam.edu/.

State University of New York College of Environmental Science and Forestry
Syracuse, New York

Sustainability Initiatives State University of New York College of Environmental Science and Forestry is a member of the Association for the Advancement of Sustainability in Higher Education (AASHE). This institution's president has signed the American College & University Presidents Climate Commitment.

Academics *Sustainability-focused undergraduate major(s):* Bioprocess Engineering (BS), Conservation Biology (BS), Environmental Engineering (BS), Landscape Architecture (BLA), Natural Resource Management (BS), Wildlife Science (BS). *Sustainability-focused graduate degree program(s):* Environmental Biology (PhD, MS, MPS), Environmental Chemistry (PhD, MS), Environmental Policy (PhD), Environmental/Resource Engineering (PhD, MS, MPS), Forest Resources Management (PhD, MS, MF), Landscape Architecture (MLA, MS). *Sustainability courses and programs:* sustainability-focused course(s) or lecture series, noncredit sustainability course(s).

Student Services and Green Events *Sustainability leadership:* sustainability coordinator/director, sustainability committee/advisory council, recycling manager. *Student clubs and activities:* Public Interest Research Group (PIRG) chapter on campus, student club(s)/group(s) focused on sustainability, outreach materials available about on-campus sustainability efforts. *Major sustainability events:* Annual Earth Week Celebration, Conversations on the Land Conference, Sustainability and Forest Biorefinery Conference, Green Building Conference, Sustainable Use of Renewable Energy, Sustainability and Green Entrepreneurship Conference.

Food Fair Trade coffee is used. Vegan and vegetarian dining options are available for every meal.

Transportation Provides free on-campus transportation (bus or other), public transportation access to local destinations, and a car sharing program.

Buildings and Grounds *Renovation and maintenance:* registered for LEED certification for new construction and/or renovation. *Campus grounds care:* landscapes with native plant species; protects, restores, and/or creates habitat on campus.

Recycling *Programs and activities:* sustains a computer/technology recycling program; maintains an on-campus recycling center; sustains a post-consumer food waste composting program; composts yard waste; reuses surplus department/office supplies; replaces paper materials with online alternatives; limits free printing in computer labs and libraries.

Energy Currently uses or plans to use alternative sources of power (solar energy); timers to regulate temperatures based on occupancy hours; and energy-related performance contracting.

Purchasing Sustainability criteria used in purchasing include Energy Star (EPA), Green Cleaning Products (Green Seal/Environmental Choice certified), and Forest Stewardship Council (FSC) or American Forest and Paper Association's Sustainable Forestry Initiative (SFI) paper.

Contact Associate Dean for Outreach, State University of New York College of Environmental Science and Forestry, 221 Marshall Hall, One Forestry Drive, Syracuse, NY 13210. *Web site:* www.esf.edu/.

State University of New York College of Technology at Delhi
Delhi, New York

Academics *Sustainability-focused undergraduate major(s):* Environmental Studies (AAS). *Sustainability courses and programs:* sustainability-focused course(s) or lecture series, sustainability-focused nonacademic certificate program(s).

Student Services and Green Events *Sustainability leadership:* sustainability committee/advisory council, recycling manager, sustainability-focused student government. *Student clubs and activities:* student club(s)/group(s) focused on sustainability, outreach materials available about on-campus sustainability efforts. *Major sustainability events:* Earth Day Luncheon/Symposium. *Housing and facilities:* sustainability-themed housing.

Food Vegan and vegetarian dining options are available for every meal.

Transportation Provides free on-campus transportation (bus or other) and public transportation access to local destinations.

Buildings and Grounds *Campus grounds care:* uses water conservation devices; employs strategies to reduce light pollution; landscapes with native plant species.

Recycling *Programs and activities:* sustains a computer/technology recycling program; maintains an on-campus recycling center; sustains a post-consumer food waste composting program; composts yard waste; reuses surplus department/office supplies; replaces paper materials with online alternatives. *Campus dining operations:* uses reusable dishware.

Energy Currently uses or plans to use alternative sources of power; timers to regulate temperatures based on occupancy hours; motion, infrared, and/or light sensors to reduce energy uses for lighting; and energy-related performance contracting.

Purchasing Sustainability criteria used in purchasing include Green Cleaning Products (Green Seal/Environmental Choice certified).

Contact Director of Administrative Services, State University of New York College of Technology at Delhi, 2 Main Street, Delhi, NY 13753. *Phone:* 607-746-4498. *E-mail:* martinbg@delhi.edu. *Web site:* www.delhi.edu/.

State University of New York Empire State College
Saratoga Springs, New York

Academics *Sustainability-focused undergraduate major(s):* Environmental Studies. *Sustainability-focused graduate degree program(s):* Liberal Studies (MALS). *Sustainability courses and programs:* sustainability-focused course(s) or lecture series.

Student Services and Green Events *Sustainability leadership:* sustainability committee/advisory council, recycling manager. *Student clubs and activities:* student club(s)/group(s) focused on sustainability, outreach materials available about on-campus sustainability efforts. *Major sustainability events:* All Areas of Study Conference.

Transportation Provides public transportation access to local destinations.

Buildings and Grounds *Percentage of institution's eligible buildings as of September 2008 meeting LEED and/or LEED-EB certification criteria:* 25%. *Renovation and maintenance:* registered for LEED certification for new construction and/or renovation.

Recycling *Programs and activities:* sustains a computer/technology recycling program; maintains an on-campus recycling center; reuses surplus department/office supplies; replaces paper materials with online alternatives.

Energy Currently uses or plans to use alternative sources of power (geothermal energy); timers to regulate temperatures based on occupancy hours; and motion, infrared, and/or light sensors to reduce energy uses for lighting.

Purchasing Sustainability criteria used in purchasing include Energy Star (EPA).

Contact Associate Dean, Center for Distance Learning, State University of New York Empire State College, 111 West Avenue, Saratoga Springs, NY 12866. *Phone:* 518-587-2100 Ext. 2255. *E-mail:* william.ehmann@esc.edu. *Web site:* www.esc.edu/.

State University of New York Upstate Medical University
Syracuse, New York

Sustainability Initiatives State University of New York Upstate Medical University's president has signed the American College & University Presidents Climate Commitment.

Student Services and Green Events *Sustainability leadership:* sustainability coordinator/director, sustainability committee/advisory council, recycling manager, energy manager. *Student clubs and activities:* Campus Climate Challenge, student club(s)/group(s) focused on sustainability, outreach materials available about on-campus sustainability efforts. *Major sustainability events:* Think Green, Management Forum.

Food Vegan and vegetarian dining options are available for every meal.

Transportation Provides free on-campus transportation (bus or other) and public transportation access to local destinations.

Buildings and Grounds *Renovation and maintenance:* registered for LEED certification for new construction and/or renovation. *Campus grounds care:* landscapes with native plant species.

Recycling *Programs and activities:* sustains a computer/technology recycling program; maintains an on-campus recycling center; replaces paper materials with online alternatives.

Energy Currently uses or plans to use alternative sources of power (hydroelectricity/water power and wind energy); timers to regulate temperatures based on occupancy hours; motion, infrared, and/or light sensors to reduce energy uses for lighting; LED lighting; and energy-related performance contracting.

Purchasing Sustainability criteria used in purchasing include Energy Star (EPA).

Contact Assistant Vice President for Facilities and Planning, State University of New York Upstate Medical University, 750 East Adams Street, Syracuse, NY 13210. *Phone:* 315-464-4510. *E-mail:* pelist@upstate.edu. *Web site:* www.upstate.edu/.

Syracuse University
Syracuse, New York

Sustainability Initiatives Syracuse University is a member of the Association for the Advancement of Sustainability in Higher Education (AASHE) and a signatory to the Talloires Declaration. This institution's president has signed the American College & University Presidents Climate Commitment.

Academics *Sustainability-focused undergraduate major(s):* Civil and Environmental Engineering (BS), Environmental Engineering (BS), Public Affairs (BA), Sociology (BA), Supply Chain Management (BS). *Sustainability-focused graduate degree program(s):* Business (MBA), Civil and Environmental Engineering (MS), Civil Engineering (PhD), Environmental Engineering Science (MS), Public Administration (PhD). *Sustainability courses and programs:* sustainability-focused course(s) or lecture series.

Student Services and Green Events *Sustainability leadership:* sustainability coordinator/director, sustainability committee/advisory council, recycling manager, energy manager. *Student clubs and activities:* Public Interest Research Group (PIRG) chapter on campus, outreach materials available about on-campus sustainability efforts. *Housing and facilities:* sustainability-themed housing, student-run café that serves environmentally or socially preferable foods.

Food Sustainable, organic, and/or locally produced foods available in on-campus dining facilities. Fair Trade coffee is used. Vegan and vegetarian dining options are available for every meal.

Transportation Provides free on-campus transportation (bus or other), public transportation access to local destinations, a car sharing program, and incentives to carpool or use public transportation.

Buildings and Grounds *Renovation and maintenance:* registered for LEED certification for new construction and/or renovation; uses a Green Seal certified cleaning service. *Campus grounds care:* uses water conservation devices; employs strategies to reduce light pollution; landscapes with native plant species; protects, restores, and/or creates habitat on campus.

Recycling *Programs and activities:* sustains a computer/technology recycling program; sustains a pre-consumer food waste composting program; reuses surplus department/office supplies; replaces paper materials with online alternatives; limits free printing in computer labs and libraries. *Campus dining operations:* uses reusable dishware; offers discounts for reusable mugs; uses bulk condiment dispensers and decreased packaging for to-go food service purchases.

Energy Currently uses or plans to use alternative sources of power (hydroelectricity/water power); timers to regulate temperatures based on occupancy hours; motion, infrared, and/or light sensors to reduce energy uses for lighting; LED lighting; and vending machine motion sensors.

Purchasing Sustainability criteria used in purchasing include Energy Star (EPA), Green Cleaning Products (Green Seal/Environmental Choice certified), and Forest Stewardship Council (FSC) or American Forest and Paper Association's Sustainable Forestry Initiative (SFI) paper.

Contact Chief Sustainability Officer, Syracuse University, Energy and Computing Management, 621 Skytop Road, Suite 130, Syracuse, NY 13244-5290. *Phone:* 315-443-4993. *Fax:* 315-443-3553. *E-mail:* salloyd@syr.edu. *Web site:* www.syracuse.edu/.

Union College
Schenectady, New York

Sustainability Initiatives Union College is a member of the Association for the Advancement of Sustainability in Higher Education (AASHE). This institution's president has signed the American College & University Presidents Climate Commitment.

Academics *Sustainability-focused undergraduate major(s):* Environmental Studies (BS). *Sustainability courses and programs:* sustainability-focused course(s) or lecture series.

Student Services and Green Events *Sustainability leadership:* sustainability committee/advisory council, recycling manager, energy manager. *Student clubs and activities:* Campus Climate Challenge, student club(s)/group(s) focused on sustainability. *Major sustainability events:* RecycleMania, Environmental Studies Winter Seminar Series, Focus the Nation, Earth Day, Steinmetz Symposia. *Housing and facilities:* sustainability-themed housing, model dorm room that demonstrates sustainable living principles, student-run café that serves environmentally or socially preferable foods, on-campus organic garden for students.

Food Sustainable, organic, and/or locally produced foods available in on-campus dining facilities. Fair Trade coffee is used. Vegan and vegetarian dining options are available for every meal.

Transportation Provides free on-campus transportation (bus or other), public transportation access to local destinations, and a bike loan/rental program.

Buildings and Grounds *Renovation and maintenance:* registered for LEED certification for new construction and/or renovation; uses a Green Seal certified cleaning service. *Campus grounds care:* uses water conservation devices; employs strategies to reduce light pollution; landscapes with native plant species.

Recycling *Events and organizations:* RecycleMania. *Programs and activities:* sustains a computer/technology recycling program; maintains an on-campus recycling center; sustains a pre-consumer food waste composting program; sustains a post-consumer food waste composting program; composts yard waste; replaces paper materials with online alternatives; limits free printing in computer labs and libraries. *Campus dining operations:* uses reusable dishware; operates without trays; offers discounts for reusable mugs; uses bulk condiment dispensers and decreased packaging for to-go food service purchases.

Energy Currently uses or plans to use timers to regulate temperatures based on occupancy hours; motion, infrared, and/or light sensors to reduce energy uses for lighting; LED lighting; and vending machine motion sensors.

Purchasing Sustainability criteria used in purchasing include Energy Star (EPA), WaterSense (EPA), and Green Cleaning Products (Green Seal/Environmental Choice certified).

Contact Vice President, Finance and Administration, Union College, Finance Department, 807 Union Street, Schenectady, NY 12308. *Phone:* 518-388-6104. *Fax:* 518-388-6800. *E-mail:* Blaked@union.edu. *Web site:* www.union.edu/.

University at Albany, State University of New York
Albany, New York

Sustainability Initiatives University at Albany, State University of New York is a member of the Association for the Advancement of Sustainability in Higher Education (AASHE) and a signatory to the Talloires Declaration. This institution's president has signed the American College & University Presidents Climate Commitment.

Academics *Sustainability-focused undergraduate major(s):* Environmental Science (BS). *Sustainability courses and programs:* sustainability-focused course(s) or lecture series.

Student Services and Green Events *Sustainability leadership:* sustainability coordinator/director, sustainability committee/advisory council, energy manager. *Student clubs and activities:* Public Interest Research Group (PIRG) chapter on campus, student club(s)/group(s) focused on sustainability, outreach materials available about on-campus sustainability efforts. *Major sustainability events:* National Teach-In for Global Warming Solutions (February), Earth Day, Sustainability Conference 2009. *Housing and facilities:* sustainability-themed housing.

Food Sustainable, organic, and/or locally produced foods available in on-campus dining facilities. Fair Trade coffee is used. Vegan and vegetarian dining options are available for every meal.

Transportation Provides free on-campus transportation (bus or other), public transportation access to local destinations, a bike loan/rental program, and incentives to carpool or use public transportation.

Buildings and Grounds *Renovation and maintenance:* registered for LEED certification for new construction and/or renovation; uses a Green Seal certified cleaning service. *Campus grounds care:* uses water conservation devices; landscapes with native plant species; protects, restores, and/or creates habitat on campus.

Recycling *Events and organizations:* RecycleMania. *Programs and activities:* sustains a computer/technology recycling program; maintains an on-campus recycling center; replaces paper materials with online alternatives; limits free printing in computer labs and libraries. *Campus dining operations:* operates without trays; offers discounts for reusable mugs.

Energy Currently uses or plans to use timers to regulate temperatures based on occupancy hours; motion, infrared, and/or light sensors to reduce energy uses for lighting; and LED lighting.

Purchasing Sustainability criteria used in purchasing include Energy Star (EPA) and Green Cleaning Products (Green Seal/Environmental Choice certified).

Contact Director of Environmental Sustainability, University at Albany, State University of New York, University Hall 212, Albany, NY 12222. *Phone:* 518-956-8120. *E-mail:* mmallia@uamail.albany.edu. *Web site:* www.albany.edu/.

University of Rochester
Rochester, New York

Sustainability Initiatives University of Rochester is a member of the Association for the Advancement of Sustainability in Higher Education (AASHE).

Academics *Sustainability-focused undergraduate major(s):* Environmental Science (BS), Environmental Studies (BA). *Sustainability-focused graduate degree program(s):* Earth and Environmental Science (MS). *Sustainability courses and programs:* sustainability-focused course(s) or lecture series.

Student Services and Green Events *Sustainability leadership:* sustainability committee/advisory council, recycling manager, energy manager, sustainability-focused student government. *Student clubs and activities:* Campus Climate Challenge, student club(s)/group(s) focused on sustainability. *Major sustainability events:* Mount Trashmore, Campus Sustainability Day, RecycleMania, UR Unplugged, National Teach-In on Global Warming, Local Foods Week, Earth Day. *Housing and facilities:* student-run café that serves environmentally or socially preferable foods, on-campus organic garden for students.

Food Sustainable, organic, and/or locally produced foods available in on-campus dining facilities. Fair Trade coffee is used. Vegan and vegetarian dining options are available for every meal.

Transportation Provides free on-campus transportation (bus or other), public transportation access to local destinations, a bike loan/rental program, a car sharing program, and incentives to carpool or use public transportation.

Buildings and Grounds *Percentage of institution's eligible buildings as of September 2008 meeting LEED and/or LEED-EB certification criteria:* 5%. *Renovation and maintenance:* uses a Green Seal certified cleaning service. *Campus grounds care:* uses water conservation devices; employs strategies to reduce light pollution; landscapes with native plant species; protects, restores, and/or creates habitat on campus.

Recycling *Events and organizations:* RecycleMania, WasteWise (EPA). *Programs and activities:* sustains a computer/technology recycling program; sustains a pre-consumer food waste composting program; sustains a post-consumer food waste composting program; composts yard waste; reuses surplus department/office supplies; reuses chemicals; replaces paper materials with online alternatives; limits free printing in computer labs and libraries. *Campus dining operations:* uses reusable dishware; operates without trays; offers discounts for reusable mugs; uses bulk condiment dispensers and decreased packaging for to-go food service purchases.

Energy Currently uses or plans to use alternative sources of power (hydroelectricity/water power and wind energy); timers to regulate temperatures based on occupancy hours; motion, infrared, and/or light sensors to reduce energy uses for lighting; and LED lighting.

Purchasing Sustainability criteria used in purchasing include Energy Star (EPA), Green Cleaning Products (Green Seal/Environmental Choice certified), and Forest Stewardship Council (FSC) or American Forest and Paper Association's Sustainable Forestry Initiative (SFI) paper.

Contact Senior Associate Provost, University of Rochester, PO Box 270035, Rochester, NY 14627. *Phone:* 585-273-4765. *E-mail:* carol.shuherk@rochester.edu. *Web site:* www.rochester.edu/.

North Carolina

Barton College
Wilson, North Carolina

Student Services and Green Events *Sustainability leadership:* sustainability coordinator/director, sustainability committee/advisory council, recycling manager, energy manager. *Student clubs and activities:* outreach materials available about on-campus sustainability efforts. *Housing and facilities:* student-run café that serves environmentally or socially preferable foods.

Food Sustainable, organic, and/or locally produced foods available in on-campus dining facilities. Fair Trade coffee is used. Vegan and vegetarian dining options are available for every meal.

Buildings and Grounds *Renovation and maintenance:* uses a Green Seal certified cleaning service. *Campus grounds care:* employs strategies to reduce light pollution; landscapes with native plant species; protects, restores, and/or creates habitat on campus.

Recycling *Events and organizations:* RecycleMania. *Programs and activities:* sustains a computer/technology recycling program; maintains an on-campus recycling center; sustains a pre-consumer food waste composting program; replaces paper materials with online alternatives; limits free printing in computer labs and libraries. *Campus dining operations:* uses reusable dishware; operates without trays; uses bulk condiment dispensers and decreased packaging for to-go food service purchases.

Purchasing Sustainability criteria used in purchasing include Energy Star (EPA) and Green Cleaning Products (Green Seal/Environmental Choice certified).

Contact Director of Facilities, Barton College, PO Box 5000, Wilson, NC 27893. *Phone:* 252-399-6557. *Web site:* www.barton.edu/.

Catawba College
Salisbury, North Carolina

Sustainability Initiatives Catawba College's president has signed the American College & University Presidents Climate Commitment.

Academics *Sustainability-focused undergraduate major(s):* Environmental Education (BA), Environmental Science (BS), Environmental Studies (BA), Sustainable Business Community Development (BS). *Sustainability courses and programs:* sustainability-focused course(s) or lecture series, sustainability-focused nonacademic certificate program(s).

Student Services and Green Events *Sustainability leadership:* sustainability coordinator/director, sustainability committee/advisory council, recycling manager, energy manager. *Student clubs and activities:* student club(s)/group(s) focused on sustainability. *Major sustainability events:* Faith and the Environment Conference, symposium with Lester Brown on implementing Plan B 3.0, symposium on Green Restoration and Renovation, NC Clean Air Conference.

Food Sustainable, organic, and/or locally produced foods available in on-campus dining facilities. Fair Trade coffee is used. Vegan and vegetarian dining options are available for every meal.

Transportation Provides public transportation access to local destinations and incentives to carpool or use public transportation.

Buildings and Grounds *Percentage of institution's eligible buildings as of September 2008 meeting LEED and/or LEED-EB certification criteria:* 20%. *Renovation and maintenance:* registered for LEED certification for new construction and/or renovation; uses a Green Seal certified cleaning service. *Campus grounds care:* uses water conservation devices; employs strategies to reduce light pollution; landscapes with native plant species; protects, restores, and/or creates habitat on campus.

Recycling *Events and organizations:* RecycleMania. *Programs and activities:* sustains a computer/technology recycling program; maintains an on-campus recycling center; composts yard waste; reuses surplus department/office supplies; replaces paper materials with online alternatives; limits free printing in computer labs and libraries. *Campus dining operations:* uses reusable dishware; operates without trays; uses bulk condiment dispensers and decreased packaging for to-go food service purchases.

Energy Currently uses or plans to use alternative sources of power (geothermal energy and solar energy); timers to regulate temperatures based on occupancy hours; motion, infrared, and/or light sensors to reduce energy uses for lighting; and LED lighting.

Purchasing Sustainability criteria used in purchasing include Energy Star (EPA), WaterSense (EPA), and Green Cleaning Products (Green Seal/Environmental Choice certified).

Contact Coordinator, Office of Waste Reduction and Recycling, Catawba College, 2300 West Innes Street, Salisbury, NC 28144-2488. *Phone:* 704-637-4242. *Fax:* 704-637-4749. *E-mail:* dnajaria@catawba.edu. *Web site:* www.catawba.edu/.

Davidson College
Davidson, North Carolina

Sustainability Initiatives Davidson College's president has signed the American College & University Presidents Climate Commitment.

Academics *Sustainability-focused undergraduate major(s):* Environmental Studies concentration in place to augment traditional majors. *Sustainability courses and programs:* sustainability-focused course(s) or lecture series.

Student Services and Green Events *Sustainability leadership:* sustainability coordinator/director, sustainability committee/advisory council, recycling manager, sustainability-focused student government. *Housing and facilities:* sustainability-themed housing.

Food Sustainable, organic, and/or locally produced foods available in on-campus dining facilities. Fair Trade coffee is used. Vegan and vegetarian dining options are available for every meal.

Transportation Provides free on-campus transportation (bus or other), public transportation access to local destinations, and a bike loan/rental program.

Buildings and Grounds *Renovation and maintenance:* registered for LEED certification for new construction and/or renovation; uses a Green Seal certified cleaning service. *Campus grounds care:* uses water conservation devices; protects, restores, and/or creates habitat on campus.

Recycling *Events and organizations:* RecycleMania. *Programs and activities:* sustains a computer/technology recycling program; composts yard waste; reuses surplus department/office supplies. *Campus dining operations:* uses reusable dishware; offers discounts for reusable mugs; uses bulk condiment dispensers and decreased packaging for to-go food service purchases.

Energy Currently uses or plans to use alternative sources of power; timers to regulate temperatures based on occupancy hours; motion, infrared, and/or light sensors to reduce energy uses for lighting; and LED lighting.

Purchasing Sustainability criteria used in purchasing include Energy Star (EPA) and Green Cleaning Products (Green Seal/Environmental Choice certified).

Contact Sustainability Fellow, Davidson College, Box 7166, Davidson, NC 28035. *Phone:* 704-894-2388. *E-mail:* kedevoy@davidson.edu. *Web site:* www.davidson.edu/.

Duke University
Durham, North Carolina

Sustainability Initiatives Duke University is a member of the Association for the Advancement of Sustainability in Higher Education (AASHE). This institution's president has signed the American College & University Presidents Climate Commitment.

Academics *Sustainability-focused undergraduate major(s):* Earth and Ocean Sciences (BA, BS), Environmental Science (BS), Environmental Science and Policy (BA), Program II self-designed (BA). *Sustainability-focused graduate degree program(s):* Coastal Environmental Management (MA, PhD), Conservation Science and Policy (MA, PhD), Energy and Environment (MA, PhD), Environmental Economics and Policy (MA, PhD), Environmental Health and Security (MA, PhD), Global Environmental Change (MA, PhD), Joint degree programs for Masters of Environment Management with School of the Environment and Law, Business, Policy and Education. *Sustainability courses and programs:* sustainability-focused course(s) or lecture series, noncredit sustainability course(s).

Student Services and Green Events *Sustainability leadership:* sustainability coordinator/director, sustainability committee/advisory council, recycling manager, energy manager. *Student clubs and activities:* Campus Climate Challenge, student club(s)/group(s) focused on sustainability, outreach materials available about on-campus sustainability efforts. *Major sustainability events:* Earth Month @ Duke, Eco-Olympics, Future of Water in NC conference, FootPrints conference. *Housing and facilities:* on-campus organic garden for students.

Food Sustainable, organic, and/or locally produced foods available in on-campus dining facilities. Fair Trade coffee is used. Vegan and vegetarian dining options are available for every meal.

Transportation Provides free on-campus transportation (bus or other), public transportation access to local destinations, a bike loan/rental program, a car sharing program, and incentives to carpool or use public transportation.

Buildings and Grounds *Percentage of institution's eligible buildings as of September 2008 meeting LEED and/or LEED-EB certification criteria:* 1%. *Renovation and maintenance:* registered for LEED certification for new construction and/or renovation; uses a Green Seal certified cleaning service. *Campus grounds care:* uses water conservation devices; employs strategies to reduce light pollution; landscapes with native plant species; protects, restores, and/or creates habitat on campus.

Recycling *Events and organizations:* RecycleMania, WasteWise (EPA). *Programs and activities:* sustains a computer/technology recycling program; maintains an on-campus recycling center; sustains a pre-consumer food waste composting program; composts yard waste; reuses surplus department/office supplies; reuses chemicals; replaces paper materials with online alternatives; limits free printing in computer labs and libraries. *Campus dining operations:* uses reusable dishware; operates without trays; offers discounts for reusable mugs; uses bulk condiment dispensers and decreased packaging for to-go food service purchases.

Energy Currently uses or plans to use alternative sources of power; motion, infrared, and/or light sensors to reduce energy uses for lighting; LED lighting; and vending machine motion sensors. Participates in College & University Green Power Challenge activities.

Purchasing Sustainability criteria used in purchasing include Energy Star (EPA), Green Electronics Council

(GEC) Electronic Product Environmental Assessment Tool (EPEAT) Silver or Gold, Green Cleaning Products (Green Seal/Environmental Choice certified), and Forest Stewardship Council (FSC) or American Forest and Paper Association's Sustainable Forestry Initiative (SFI) paper.

Contact Sustainability Outreach Coordinator, Duke University, 203 Allen Building, Box 90027, Durham, NC 27708. *Phone:* 919-660-1470. *E-mail:* ryan.powell@duke.edu. *Web site:* www.duke.edu/.

Elon University
Elon, North Carolina

Sustainability Initiatives Elon University is a member of the Association for the Advancement of Sustainability in Higher Education (AASHE).

Academics *Sustainability-focused undergraduate major(s):* Environmental Studies (BA, BS). *Sustainability courses and programs:* sustainability-focused course(s) or lecture series.

Student Services and Green Events *Sustainability leadership:* sustainability coordinator/director, sustainability committee/advisory council, recycling manager. *Student clubs and activities:* student club(s)/group(s) focused on sustainability, outreach materials available about on-campus sustainability efforts. *Major sustainability events:* Fall Environmental Forum, Campus Sustainability Day, Earth Week. *Housing and facilities:* sustainability-themed housing, model dorm room that demonstrates sustainable living principles, on-campus organic garden for students.

Food Sustainable, organic, and/or locally produced foods available in on-campus dining facilities. Fair Trade coffee is used.

Transportation Provides free on-campus transportation (bus or other), public transportation access to local destinations, a bike loan/rental program, and a car sharing program.

Buildings and Grounds *Renovation and maintenance:* registered for LEED certification for new construction and/or renovation. *Campus grounds care:* uses water conservation devices; landscapes with native plant species.

Recycling *Events and organizations:* RecycleMania. *Programs and activities:* sustains a computer/technology recycling program; maintains an on-campus recycling center; sustains a pre-consumer food waste composting program; sustains a post-consumer food waste composting program; composts yard waste; reuses surplus department/office supplies; replaces paper materials with online alternatives; limits free printing in computer labs and libraries. *Campus dining operations:* uses reusable dishware; operates without trays.

Energy Currently uses or plans to use alternative sources of power; timers to regulate temperatures based on occupancy hours; motion, infrared, and/or light sensors to reduce energy uses for lighting; and LED lighting.

Purchasing Sustainability criteria used in purchasing include Energy Star (EPA), Green Cleaning Products (Green Seal/Environmental Choice certified), and Forest Stewardship Council (FSC) or American Forest and Paper Association's Sustainable Forestry Initiative (SFI) paper.

Contact Sustainability Coordinator, Elon University, 2000 Campus Box, 803 West Haggard Avenue, Elon, NC 27244. *Phone:* 336-278-5229. *Fax:* 336-278-5473. *E-mail:* edurr@elon.edu. *Web site:* www.elon.edu/.

Guilford College
Greensboro, North Carolina

Sustainability Initiatives Guilford College is a member of the Association for the Advancement of Sustainability in

Higher Education (AASHE). This institution's president has signed the American College & University Presidents Climate Commitment.

Academics *Sustainability-focused undergraduate major(s):* Environmental Studies (BA). *Sustainability courses and programs:* sustainability-focused course(s) or lecture series.

Student Services and Green Events *Sustainability leadership:* sustainability coordinator/director, sustainability committee/advisory council, recycling manager, energy manager. *Student clubs and activities:* student club(s)/group(s) focused on sustainability, outreach materials available about on-campus sustainability efforts. *Major sustainability events:* Triad Area Sustainability Professionals Conference. *Housing and facilities:* sustainability-themed housing, student-run café that serves environmentally or socially preferable foods, on-campus organic garden for students.

Food Sustainable, organic, and/or locally produced foods available in on-campus dining facilities. Vegan and vegetarian dining options are available for every meal.

Transportation Provides public transportation access to local destinations.

Buildings and Grounds *Percentage of institution's eligible buildings as of September 2008 meeting LEED and/or LEED-EB certification criteria:* 3%. *Renovation and maintenance:* registered for LEED certification for new construction and/or renovation; uses a Green Seal certified cleaning service. *Campus grounds care:* uses water conservation devices; employs strategies to reduce light pollution; landscapes with native plant species; protects, restores, and/or creates habitat on campus.

Recycling *Events and organizations:* RecycleMania. *Programs and activities:* sustains a computer/technology recycling program; maintains an on-campus recycling center; sustains a pre-consumer food waste composting program; composts yard waste; reuses surplus department/office supplies; replaces paper materials with online alternatives; limits free printing in computer labs and libraries. *Campus dining operations:* uses reusable dishware; operates without trays; offers discounts for reusable mugs.

Energy Currently uses or plans to use alternative sources of power (solar energy); timers to regulate temperatures based on occupancy hours; and motion, infrared, and/or light sensors to reduce energy uses for lighting.

Purchasing Sustainability criteria used in purchasing include Energy Star (EPA) and Green Cleaning Products (Green Seal/Environmental Choice certified).

Contact Environmental Sustainability Coordinator, Guilford College, 5800 West Friendly Avenue, Greensboro, NC 27410. *Phone:* 336-316-2923. *Fax:* 336-316-2952. *E-mail:* deesjh@guilford.edu. *Web site:* www.guilford.edu/.

Johnson & Wales University—Charlotte Campus
Charlotte, North Carolina

Academics *Sustainability courses and programs:* sustainability-focused course(s) or lecture series.

Student Services and Green Events *Sustainability leadership:* sustainability committee/advisory council, sustainability-focused student government. *Student clubs and activities:* student club(s)/group(s) focused on sustainability, outreach materials available about on-campus sustainability efforts. *Major sustainability events:* Carolinas Higher Education Sustainable Energy Summit. *Housing and facilities:* student-run café that serves environmentally or socially preferable foods.

Food Sustainable, organic, and/or locally produced foods available in on-campus dining facilities. Vegan and vegetarian dining options are available for every meal.

Transportation Provides free on-campus transportation (bus or other) and public transportation access to local destinations.

Buildings and Grounds *Renovation and maintenance:* uses a Green Seal certified cleaning service. *Campus grounds care:* uses water conservation devices; employs strategies to reduce light pollution; applies to its grounds only pesticides and fertilizers allowable under the U.S. Department of Agriculture's standards for crop production.

Recycling *Programs and activities:* sustains a computer/technology recycling program; maintains an on-campus recycling center; sustains a pre-consumer food waste composting program; sustains a post-consumer food waste composting program; reuses surplus department/office supplies; replaces paper materials with online alternatives; limits free printing in computer labs and libraries. *Campus dining operations:* uses reusable dishware; operates without trays; offers discounts for reusable mugs; uses bulk condiment dispensers and decreased packaging for to-go food service purchases.

Energy Currently uses or plans to use timers to regulate temperatures based on occupancy hours; motion, infrared, and/or light sensors to reduce energy uses for lighting; vending machine motion sensors; and energy-related performance contracting.

Purchasing Sustainability criteria used in purchasing include Energy Star (EPA), WaterSense (EPA), and Green Cleaning Products (Green Seal/Environmental Choice certified).

Contact Director of Facilities Management, Johnson & Wales University—Charlotte Campus, 801 West Trade Street, Charlotte, NC 28202. *Phone:* 980-598-1925. *Fax:* 980-598-1802. *E-mail:* glenn.hamilton@jwu.edu. *Web site:* www.jwucharlotte.org/.

North Carolina State University
Raleigh, North Carolina

Sustainability Initiatives North Carolina State University is a member of the Association for the Advancement of Sustainability in Higher Education (AASHE). This institution's president has signed the American College & University Presidents Climate Commitment.

Academics *Sustainability-focused undergraduate major(s):* Environmental Engineering, Environmental Sciences, Environmental Technology, Natural Resources. *Sustainability-focused graduate degree program(s):* Natural Resources (MNR, MS), Joint degree options. *Sustainability courses and programs:* sustainability-focused course(s) or lecture series, noncredit sustainability course(s), sustainability-focused nonacademic certificate program(s).

Student Services and Green Events *Sustainability leadership:* sustainability coordinator/director, sustainability committee/advisory council, recycling manager, energy manager, sustainability-focused student government. *Student clubs and activities:* student club(s)/group(s) focused on sustainability. *Major sustainability events:* SEE (Society, Environment, Economy) NC State.

Food Fair Trade coffee is used. Vegan and vegetarian dining options are available for every meal.

Transportation Provides free on-campus transportation (bus or other), public transportation access to local destinations, and incentives to carpool or use public transportation.

Buildings and Grounds *Renovation and maintenance:* registered for LEED certification for new construction and/or renovation; uses a Green Seal certified cleaning service. *Campus grounds care:* uses water conservation devices; landscapes with native plant species; protects, restores, and/or creates habitat on campus.

Recycling *Events and organizations:* RecycleMania. *Programs and activities:* sustains a computer/technology recycling program; maintains an on-campus recycling center; composts yard waste; reuses surplus department/office supplies; replaces paper materials with online alternatives; limits free printing in computer labs and libraries. *Campus dining operations:* uses reusable dishware; operates without trays; uses bulk condiment dispensers and decreased packaging for to-go food service purchases.

Energy Currently uses or plans to use alternative sources of power (solar energy); timers to regulate temperatures based on occupancy hours; motion, infrared, and/or light sensors to reduce energy uses for lighting; LED lighting; and energy-related performance contracting.

Purchasing Sustainability criteria used in purchasing include Energy Star (EPA) and Green Cleaning Products (Green Seal/Environmental Choice certified).

Contact Sustainability Outreach Coordinator, North Carolina State University, Campus Box 7536, Raleigh, NC 27695-7536. *Phone:* 919-513-0177. *Fax:* 919-513-1100. *E-mail:* david_dean@ncsu.edu. *Web site:* www.ncsu.edu/.

Roanoke Bible College
Elizabeth City, North Carolina

Student Services and Green Events *Sustainability leadership:* sustainability coordinator/director, sustainability committee/advisory council, recycling manager.

Food Sustainable, organic, and/or locally produced foods available in on-campus dining facilities. Vegan and vegetarian dining options are available for every meal.

Transportation Provides public transportation access to local destinations.

Buildings and Grounds *Campus grounds care:* employs strategies to reduce light pollution; landscapes with native plant species; protects, restores, and/or creates habitat on campus.

Recycling *Programs and activities:* sustains a computer/technology recycling program; composts yard waste; reuses surplus department/office supplies; replaces paper materials with online alternatives. *Campus dining operations:* uses reusable dishware; operates without trays; uses bulk condiment dispensers and decreased packaging for to-go food service purchases.

Energy Currently uses or plans to use alternative sources of power (geothermal energy and solar energy); timers to regulate temperatures based on occupancy hours; motion, infrared, and/or light sensors to reduce energy uses for lighting; and LED lighting.

Purchasing Sustainability criteria used in purchasing include Energy Star (EPA) and Green Cleaning Products (Green Seal/Environmental Choice certified).

Contact Student Life Administrator, Roanoke Bible College, 715 North Poindexter Street, Elizabeth City, NC 27909. *Phone:* 252-334-2073. *E-mail:* ngj@roanokebible.edu. *Web site:* www.roanokebible.edu/.

The University of North Carolina at Charlotte
Charlotte, North Carolina

Sustainability Initiatives The University of North Carolina at Charlotte is a member of the Association for the Advancement of Sustainability in Higher Education (AASHE). The University of North Carolina at Charlotte has Green Fees (optional/required) dedicated to sustainability initiatives.

Academics *Sustainability courses and programs:* sustainability-focused course(s) or lecture series, noncredit sustainability course(s), sustainability-focused nonacademic certificate program(s).

Student Services and Green Events *Sustainability leadership:* sustainability coordinator/director, sustainability committee/advisory council, recycling manager, energy manager, sustainability-focused student government. *Student clubs and activities:* student club(s)/group(s) focused on sustainability, outreach materials available about on-campus sustainability efforts. *Major sustainability events:* Charlotte Regional Indicators Project, Climate Change and Global Health, Its Our Water, Project WET (Water Education for Teachers), Leopold Education Project.

Food Sustainable, organic, and/or locally produced foods available in on-campus dining facilities. Fair Trade coffee is used. Vegan and vegetarian dining options are available for every meal.

Transportation Provides free on-campus transportation (bus or other), public transportation access to local destinations, and incentives to carpool or use public transportation.

Buildings and Grounds *Renovation and maintenance:* registered for LEED certification for new construction and/or renovation; uses a Green Seal certified cleaning service. *Campus grounds care:* uses water conservation devices; employs strategies to reduce light pollution; landscapes with native plant species.

Recycling *Events and organizations:* RecycleMania. *Programs and activities:* sustains a computer/technology recycling program; maintains an on-campus recycling center; sustains a post-consumer food waste composting program; composts yard waste; reuses surplus department/office supplies; reuses chemicals; replaces paper materials with online alternatives; limits free printing in computer labs and libraries. *Campus dining operations:* uses reusable dishware; operates without trays; offers discounts for reusable mugs.

Energy Currently uses or plans to use timers to regulate temperatures based on occupancy hours; motion, infrared, and/or light sensors to reduce energy uses for lighting; and LED lighting.

Purchasing Sustainability criteria used in purchasing include Green Cleaning Products (Green Seal/Environmental Choice certified) and Forest Stewardship Council (FSC) or American Forest and Paper Association's Sustainable Forestry Initiative (SFI) paper.

Contact Sustainability Coordinator, The University of North Carolina at Charlotte, 9201 University City Boulevard, Charlotte, NC 28223. *Phone:* 704-687-2518. *E-mail:* dajones1@uncc.edu. *Web site:* www.uncc.edu/.

Wake Forest University
Winston-Salem, North Carolina

Academics *Sustainability-focused graduate degree program(s):* Environmental Sciences. *Sustainability courses and programs:* sustainability-focused course(s) or lecture series.

Student Services and Green Events *Sustainability leadership:* sustainability coordinator/director, sustainability committee/advisory council, recycling manager, sustainability-focused student government. *Student clubs and activities:* student club(s)/group(s) focused on sustainability. *Major sustainability events:* Earth Day Celebration (April), Sustainability Day Celebration (December). *Housing and facilities:* sustainability-themed housing.

Food Sustainable, organic, and/or locally produced foods available in on-campus dining facilities. Fair Trade coffee is used. Vegan and vegetarian dining options are available for every meal.

Transportation Provides free on-campus transportation (bus or other).

Buildings and Grounds *Renovation and maintenance:* registered for LEED certification for new construction and/or renovation; uses a Green Seal certified cleaning service. *Campus grounds care:* uses water conservation devices; landscapes with native plant species; protects, restores, and/or creates habitat on campus.

Recycling *Programs and activities:* sustains a computer/technology recycling program; maintains an on-campus recycling center; replaces paper materials with online alternatives; limits free printing in computer labs and libraries. *Campus dining operations:* uses reusable dishware; operates without trays; offers discounts for reusable mugs.

Energy Currently uses or plans to use alternative sources of power; timers to regulate temperatures based on occupancy hours; and vending machine motion sensors.

Purchasing Sustainability criteria used in purchasing include Green Cleaning Products (Green Seal/Environmental Choice certified).

Contact Associate Vice President for Facilities and Campus Services, Wake Forest University, 1834 Wake Forest Road, Winston-Salem, NC 27019. *Phone:* 336-758-5679. *E-mail:* altyj@wfu.edu. *Web site:* www.wfu.edu/.

Western Carolina University
Cullowhee, North Carolina

Sustainability Initiatives Western Carolina University is a member of the Association for the Advancement of Sustainability in Higher Education (AASHE).

Academics *Sustainability-focused undergraduate major(s):* Environmental Health Sciences (BS), Environmental Science (BS), Natural Resource Management (BS), Parks and Recreation Management (BS). *Sustainability courses and programs:* sustainability-focused course(s) or lecture series.

Student Services and Green Events *Sustainability leadership:* recycling manager, energy manager, sustainability-focused student government. *Student clubs and activities:* Campus Climate Challenge, student club(s)/group(s) focused on sustainability, outreach materials available about on-campus sustainability efforts. *Major sustainability events:* Earth Day, Focus The Nation, National Teach-In 2009. *Housing and facilities:* sustainability-themed housing, on-campus organic garden for students.

Food Sustainable, organic, and/or locally produced foods available in on-campus dining facilities. Fair Trade coffee is used. Vegan and vegetarian dining options are available for every meal.

Transportation Provides free on-campus transportation (bus or other) and public transportation access to local destinations.

Buildings and Grounds *Renovation and maintenance:* registered for LEED certification for new construction and/or

renovation. *Campus grounds care:* uses water conservation devices; landscapes with native plant species; protects, restores, and/or creates habitat on campus.

Recycling *Events and organizations:* RecycleMania. *Programs and activities:* sustains a computer/technology recycling program; maintains an on-campus recycling center; sustains a pre-consumer food waste composting program; sustains a post-consumer food waste composting program; composts yard waste; reuses surplus department/office supplies; replaces paper materials with online alternatives; limits free printing in computer labs and libraries. *Campus dining operations:* uses reusable dishware; operates without trays; offers discounts for reusable mugs; uses bulk condiment dispensers and decreased packaging for to-go food service purchases.

Energy Currently uses or plans to use alternative sources of power; timers to regulate temperatures based on occupancy hours; motion, infrared, and/or light sensors to reduce energy uses for lighting; and energy-related performance contracting.

Purchasing Sustainability criteria used in purchasing include Energy Star (EPA).

Contact Energy Manager, Western Carolina University, 3476 Old Cullowhee Road, Cullowhee, NC 28723. *Phone:* 828-227-7442. *E-mail:* lbishop@wcu.edu. *Web site:* www. wcu.edu/.

North Dakota

University of North Dakota
Grand Forks, North Dakota

Sustainability Initiatives University of North Dakota's president has signed the American College & University Presidents Climate Commitment.

Academics *Sustainability-focused undergraduate major(s):* Environmental Geoscience, Geography—Environmental. *Sustainability-focused graduate degree program(s):* Earth System Sciences, Environmental Engineering (MS, MEngr). *Sustainability courses and programs:* sustainability-focused course(s) or lecture series.

Student Services and Green Events *Sustainability leadership:* sustainability committee/advisory council, recycling manager, energy manager.

Food Sustainable, organic, and/or locally produced foods available in on-campus dining facilities. Fair Trade coffee is used. Vegan and vegetarian dining options are available for every meal.

Transportation Provides free on-campus transportation (bus or other), public transportation access to local destinations, a bike loan/rental program, and incentives to carpool or use public transportation.

Buildings and Grounds *Campus grounds care:* uses water conservation devices.

Recycling *Events and organizations:* RecycleMania. *Programs and activities:* sustains a computer/technology recycling program; reuses surplus department/office supplies; replaces paper materials with online alternatives. *Campus dining operations:* operates without trays.

Energy Currently uses or plans to use timers to regulate temperatures based on occupancy hours; motion, infrared, and/or light sensors to reduce energy uses for lighting; LED lighting; and energy-related performance contracting.

Contact University of North Dakota, 264 Centennial Drive, Grand Forks, ND 58202. *Phone:* 701-777-2011. *Web site:* www.und.nodak.edu/.

Ohio

Ashland University
Ashland, Ohio

Academics *Sustainability courses and programs:* sustainability-focused course(s) or lecture series.

Student Services and Green Events *Sustainability leadership:* recycling manager, sustainability-focused student government. *Student clubs and activities:* outreach materials available about on-campus sustainability efforts.

Food Sustainable, organic, and/or locally produced foods available in on-campus dining facilities. Fair Trade coffee is used. Vegan and vegetarian dining options are available for every meal.

Transportation Provides public transportation access to local destinations.

Buildings and Grounds *Campus grounds care:* uses water conservation devices; employs strategies to reduce light pollution; landscapes with native plant species; protects, restores, and/or creates habitat on campus.

Recycling *Programs and activities:* sustains a computer/technology recycling program; maintains an on-campus recycling center; reuses surplus department/office supplies; replaces paper materials with online alternatives. *Campus dining operations:* uses reusable dishware.

Energy Currently uses or plans to use alternative sources of power; timers to regulate temperatures based on occupancy hours; motion, infrared, and/or light sensors to reduce energy uses for lighting; LED lighting; and energy-related performance contracting.

Purchasing Sustainability criteria used in purchasing include Green Cleaning Products (Green Seal/Environmental Choice certified).

Contact Ashland University, 401 College Avenue, Ashland, OH 44805-3702. *Phone:* 419-289-4142. *Web site:* www.exploreashland.com/.

Baldwin-Wallace College
Berea, Ohio

Academics *Sustainability-focused undergraduate major(s):* Sustainability (BA). *Sustainability courses and programs:* sustainability-focused course(s) or lecture series, sustainability-focused nonacademic certificate program(s).

Student Services and Green Events *Sustainability leadership:* sustainability committee/advisory council, recycling manager. *Student clubs and activities:* student club(s)/group(s) focused on sustainability, outreach materials available about on-campus sustainability efforts. *Major sustainability events:* Sustainability Symposium.

Food Sustainable, organic, and/or locally produced foods available in on-campus dining facilities.

Transportation Provides public transportation access to local destinations.

Buildings and Grounds *Renovation and maintenance:* uses a Green Seal certified cleaning service.

Recycling *Programs and activities:* sustains a computer/technology recycling program; maintains an on-campus recycling center; sustains a pre-consumer food waste composting program; sustains a post-consumer food waste composting program; composts yard waste; replaces paper materials with online alternatives; limits free printing in computer labs and libraries. *Campus dining operations:* uses reusable dishware.

Energy Currently uses or plans to use alternative sources of power (geothermal energy).

Purchasing Sustainability criteria used in purchasing include Green Cleaning Products (Green Seal/ Environmental Choice certified).

Contact Baldwin-Wallace College, 275 Eastland Road, Berea, OH 44017-2088. *Phone:* 440-826-2900. *Web site:* www.bw.edu/.

Cleveland State University
Cleveland, Ohio

Academics *Sustainability-focused undergraduate major(s):* Environmental Science (BS), Environmental Studies (BA). *Sustainability-focused graduate degree program(s):* Environmental Engineering (MS), Environmental Science (MS). *Sustainability courses and programs:* sustainability-focused course(s) or lecture series.

Student Services and Green Events *Sustainability leadership:* sustainability committee/advisory council, recycling manager, energy manager. *Student clubs and activities:* student club(s)/group(s) focused on sustainability, outreach materials available about on-campus sustainability efforts. *Major sustainability events:* Corporate Roundtable meeting, Symposium on Sustainability, Noon@Nance Sustainability focus. *Housing and facilities:* sustainability-themed housing, model dorm room that demonstrates sustainable living principles.

Food Sustainable, organic, and/or locally produced foods available in on-campus dining facilities. Fair Trade coffee is used. Vegan and vegetarian dining options are available for every meal.

Transportation Provides public transportation access to local destinations and incentives to carpool or use public transportation.

Buildings and Grounds *Percentage of institution's eligible buildings as of September 2008 meeting LEED and/or LEED-EB certification criteria:* 86%. *Renovation and maintenance:* registered for LEED certification for new construction and/or renovation. *Campus grounds care:* uses water conservation devices; employs strategies to reduce light pollution; landscapes with native plant species; protects, restores, and/or creates habitat on campus.

Recycling *Programs and activities:* sustains a computer/ technology recycling program; composts yard waste; replaces paper materials with online alternatives; limits free printing in computer labs and libraries. *Campus dining operations:* uses reusable dishware; operates without trays; uses bulk condiment dispensers and decreased packaging for to-go food service purchases.

Energy Currently uses or plans to use alternative sources of power (geothermal energy); timers to regulate temperatures based on occupancy hours; motion, infrared, and/or light sensors to reduce energy uses for lighting; LED lighting; and energy-related performance contracting.

Purchasing Sustainability criteria used in purchasing include Energy Star (EPA).

Contact Director of Outreach and Business Centers, College of Business, Cleveland State University, 2121 Euclid Avenue, BU 420, Cleveland, OH 44115. *Web site:* www. csuohio.edu/.

The College of Wooster
Wooster, Ohio

Academics *Sustainability courses and programs:* sustainability-focused course(s) or lecture series.

Student Services and Green Events *Sustainability leadership:* sustainability committee/advisory council, recycling manager. *Student clubs and activities:* student club(s)/ group(s) focused on sustainability. *Major sustainability events:* Workshop on integrating sustainability into the curriculum. *Housing and facilities:* sustainability-themed housing.

Food Sustainable, organic, and/or locally produced foods available in on-campus dining facilities. Fair Trade coffee is used. Vegan and vegetarian dining options are available for every meal.

Transportation Provides a bike loan/rental program.

Buildings and Grounds *Campus grounds care:* landscapes with native plant species; protects, restores, and/or creates habitat on campus.

Recycling *Programs and activities:* sustains a computer/ technology recycling program; maintains an on-campus recycling center; sustains a pre-consumer food waste composting program; sustains a post-consumer food waste composting program; composts yard waste; reuses surplus department/office supplies; reuses chemicals; replaces paper materials with online alternatives; limits free printing in computer labs and libraries. *Campus dining operations:* uses reusable dishware; offers discounts for reusable mugs; uses bulk condiment dispensers and decreased packaging for to-go food service purchases.

Energy Currently uses or plans to use timers to regulate temperatures based on occupancy hours; motion, infrared, and/or light sensors to reduce energy uses for lighting; LED lighting; and energy-related performance contracting.

Contact Chair of Environmental Studies, The College of Wooster, 1189 Beall Avenue, Wooster, OH 44691-2363. *Phone:* 330-263-2565. *E-mail:* sclayton@wooster.edu. *Web site:* www.wooster.edu/.

Kent State University
Kent, Ohio

Academics *Sustainability-focused undergraduate major(s):* Architecture (BS), Interior Design (BA). *Sustainability courses and programs:* sustainability-focused course(s) or lecture series.

Student Services and Green Events *Sustainability leadership:* sustainability coordinator/director, sustainability committee/advisory council, recycling manager, energy manager.

Food Sustainable, organic, and/or locally produced foods available in on-campus dining facilities. Fair Trade coffee is used. Vegan and vegetarian dining options are available for every meal.

Transportation Provides free on-campus transportation (bus or other) and public transportation access to local destinations.

Buildings and Grounds *Renovation and maintenance:* registered for LEED certification for new construction and/or renovation; uses a Green Seal certified cleaning service. *Campus grounds care:* uses water conservation devices; employs strategies to reduce light pollution; landscapes with native plant species; protects, restores, and/or creates habitat on campus.

Recycling *Programs and activities:* sustains a computer/ technology recycling program; maintains an on-campus recycling center; composts yard waste; reuses surplus department/office supplies; replaces paper materials with online alternatives. *Campus dining operations:* uses reusable dishware; offers discounts for reusable mugs; uses bulk condiment dispensers and decreased packaging for to-go food service purchases.

Energy Currently uses or plans to use alternative sources of power; timers to regulate temperatures based on occupancy hours; motion, infrared, and/or light sensors to reduce energy uses for lighting; LED lighting; and energy-related performance contracting.

Purchasing Sustainability criteria used in purchasing include Energy Star (EPA) and Green Cleaning Products (Green Seal/Environmental Choice certified).

Contact Kent State University, PO Box 5190, Kent, OH 44242-0001. *Phone:* 330-672-3000. *Web site:* www.kent.edu/.

Kent State University, Stark Campus
Canton, Ohio

Sustainability Initiatives Kent State University, Stark Campus is a member of the Association for the Advancement of Sustainability in Higher Education (AASHE). This institution's president has signed the American College & University Presidents Climate Commitment.

Academics *Sustainability courses and programs:* sustainability-focused course(s) or lecture series.

Student Services and Green Events *Sustainability leadership:* sustainability coordinator/director, sustainability committee/advisory council, recycling manager. *Student clubs and activities:* student club(s)/group(s) focused on sustainability, outreach materials available about on-campus sustainability efforts. *Major sustainability events:* Earth Day/Arbor Day on-campus community activities, Herbert W. Hoover Initiative for Environmental Media Activism, Graduation Pledge, Featured Speaker Series.

Food Vegan and vegetarian dining options are available for every meal.

Transportation Provides public transportation access to local destinations.

Buildings and Grounds *Campus grounds care:* landscapes with native plant species; protects, restores, and/or creates habitat on campus.

Recycling *Events and organizations:* RecycleMania. *Programs and activities:* sustains a computer/technology recycling program; maintains an on-campus recycling center; reuses surplus department/office supplies; replaces paper materials with online alternatives; limits free printing in computer labs and libraries.

Energy Currently uses or plans to use alternative sources of power and motion, infrared, and/or light sensors to reduce energy uses for lighting.

Purchasing Sustainability criteria used in purchasing include Energy Star (EPA).

Contact Director of External Affairs/ACUPCC Government Affairs-Media Relations, Kent State University, Stark Campus, 6000 Frank Avenue NW, North Canton, OH 44720. *Phone:* 330-244-3292. *Fax:* 330-244-3340. *E-mail:* tbiasell@kent.edu. *Web site:* www.stark.kent.edu/.

Marietta College
Marietta, Ohio

Academics *Sustainability courses and programs:* sustainability-focused course(s) or lecture series.

Student Services and Green Events *Sustainability leadership:* recycling manager.

Food Vegan and vegetarian dining options are available for every meal.

Buildings and Grounds *Renovation and maintenance:* uses a Green Seal certified cleaning service.

Recycling *Programs and activities:* sustains a computer/technology recycling program; maintains an on-campus recycling center; reuses chemicals. *Campus dining operations:* uses reusable dishware; operates without trays; offers discounts for reusable mugs.

Energy Currently uses or plans to use motion, infrared, and/or light sensors to reduce energy uses for lighting and LED lighting.

Purchasing Sustainability criteria used in purchasing include Green Cleaning Products (Green Seal/Environmental Choice certified).

Contact Marietta College, 215 Fifth Street, Marietta, OH 45750-4000. *Phone:* 740-376-4000. *Web site:* www.marietta.edu/.

Miami University
Oxford, Ohio

Academics *Sustainability courses and programs:* sustainability-focused course(s) or lecture series, noncredit sustainability course(s).

Student Services and Green Events *Sustainability leadership:* recycling manager, energy manager. *Student clubs and activities:* student club(s)/group(s) focused on sustainability. *Major sustainability events:* Focus the Nation. *Housing and facilities:* sustainability-themed housing.

Food Vegan and vegetarian dining options are available for every meal.

Transportation Provides free on-campus transportation (bus or other).

Buildings and Grounds *Campus grounds care:* uses water conservation devices.

Recycling *Events and organizations:* RecycleMania. *Programs and activities:* sustains a computer/technology recycling program; maintains an on-campus recycling center; composts yard waste. *Campus dining operations:* uses reusable dishware; uses bulk condiment dispensers and decreased packaging for to-go food service purchases.

Energy Currently uses or plans to use timers to regulate temperatures based on occupancy hours; motion, infrared, and/or light sensors to reduce energy uses for lighting; LED lighting; and energy-related performance contracting.

Purchasing Sustainability criteria used in purchasing include Green Cleaning Products (Green Seal/Environmental Choice certified).

Contact Energy Management Engineer, Miami University, Cole Service Building, Oxford, OH 45056. *Phone:* 513-529-3621. *Fax:* 513-529-2482. *E-mail:* ferrarav@muohio.edu. *Web site:* www.muohio.edu/.

Mount Union College
Alliance, Ohio

Sustainability Initiatives Mount Union College's president has signed the American College & University Presidents Climate Commitment.

Academics *Sustainability courses and programs:* sustainability-focused course(s) or lecture series.

Student Services and Green Events *Sustainability leadership:* sustainability coordinator/director, sustainability committee/advisory council, energy manager.

Food Sustainable, organic, and/or locally produced foods available in on-campus dining facilities. Vegan and vegetarian dining options are available for every meal.

Transportation Provides public transportation access to local destinations.

Buildings and Grounds *Renovation and maintenance:* registered for LEED certification for new construction and/or renovation. *Campus grounds care:* uses water conservation devices; landscapes with native plant species.

Recycling *Programs and activities:* sustains a computer/technology recycling program; replaces paper materials with online alternatives; limits free printing in computer labs and libraries. *Campus dining operations:* uses reusable dishware; uses bulk condiment dispensers and decreased packaging for to-go food service purchases.

Energy Currently uses or plans to use alternative sources of power (solar energy); motion, infrared, and/or light sensors to reduce energy uses for lighting; LED lighting; and energy-related performance contracting.

Contact Mount Union College, 1972 Clark Avenue, Alliance, OH 44601-3993. *Phone:* 330-821-5320. *Web site:* www.muc.edu/.

Ohio University
Athens, Ohio

Sustainability Initiatives Ohio University is a member of the Association for the Advancement of Sustainability in Higher Education (AASHE). This institution's president has signed the American College & University Presidents Climate Commitment.

Academics *Sustainability-focused graduate degree program(s):* Environmental Studies (MA). *Sustainability courses and programs:* sustainability-focused course(s) or lecture series, sustainability-focused nonacademic certificate program(s).

Student Services and Green Events *Sustainability leadership:* sustainability coordinator/director, sustainability committee/advisory council, recycling manager, energy manager. *Student clubs and activities:* Campus Climate Challenge, student club(s)/group(s) focused on sustainability, outreach materials available about on-campus sustainability efforts. *Major sustainability events:* Ohio Climate and Energy Workshop, Earth Day week programming. *Housing and facilities:* sustainability-themed housing, on-campus organic garden for students.

Food Sustainable, organic, and/or locally produced foods available in on-campus dining facilities. Fair Trade coffee is used. Vegan and vegetarian dining options are available for every meal.

Transportation Provides free on-campus transportation (bus or other) and public transportation access to local destinations.

Buildings and Grounds *Campus grounds care:* uses water conservation devices; employs strategies to reduce light pollution; landscapes with native plant species; protects, restores, and/or creates habitat on campus.

Recycling *Events and organizations:* RecycleMania, WasteWise (EPA). *Programs and activities:* maintains an on-campus recycling center; sustains a pre-consumer food waste composting program; sustains a post-consumer food waste composting program; composts yard waste; reuses surplus department/office supplies; replaces paper materials with online alternatives; limits free printing in computer labs and libraries. *Campus dining operations:* uses reusable dishware; uses bulk condiment dispensers and decreased packaging for to-go food service purchases.

Energy Currently uses or plans to use alternative sources of power (solar energy); timers to regulate temperatures based on occupancy hours; LED lighting; and vending machine motion sensors.

Purchasing Sustainability criteria used in purchasing include Green Cleaning Products (Green Seal/Environmental Choice certified).

Contact Office of Sustainability Coordinator, Ohio University, 1 Riverside Drive, Athens, OH 45701. *Phone:* 740-593-0460. *E-mail:* marcuss@ohio.edu. *Web site:* www.ohio.edu/.

Shawnee State University
Portsmouth, Ohio

Academics *Sustainability-focused undergraduate major(s):* Environmental/Engineering Technology (BS).

Student Services and Green Events *Sustainability leadership:* sustainability committee/advisory council, recycling manager. *Student clubs and activities:* student club(s)/group(s) focused on sustainability. *Major sustainability events:* Annual Environmental Day for local K–12 schools. *Housing and facilities:* student-run café that serves environmentally or socially preferable foods.

Food Fair Trade coffee is used. Vegan and vegetarian dining options are available for every meal.

Buildings and Grounds *Renovation and maintenance:* uses a Green Seal certified cleaning service. *Campus grounds care:* uses water conservation devices; employs strategies to reduce light pollution; landscapes with native plant species; applies to its grounds only pesticides and fertilizers allowable under the U.S. Department of Agriculture's standards for crop production.

Recycling *Programs and activities:* maintains an on-campus recycling center; replaces paper materials with online alternatives; limits free printing in computer labs and libraries. *Campus dining operations:* uses reusable dishware; uses bulk condiment dispensers and decreased packaging for to-go food service purchases.

Energy Currently uses or plans to use alternative sources of power (geothermal energy); timers to regulate temperatures based on occupancy hours; motion, infrared, and/or light sensors to reduce energy uses for lighting; LED lighting; and energy-related performance contracting.

Purchasing Sustainability criteria used in purchasing include Energy Star (EPA) and Green Cleaning Products (Green Seal/Environmental Choice certified).

Contact Shawnee State University, 940 Second Street, Portsmouth, OH 45662-4344. *Phone:* 740-354-3205. *Web site:* www.shawnee.edu/.

Tiffin University
Tiffin, Ohio

Sustainability Initiatives Tiffin University's president has signed the American College & University Presidents Climate Commitment.

Student Services and Green Events *Sustainability leadership:* sustainability committee/advisory council.

Buildings and Grounds *Percentage of institution's eligible buildings as of September 2008 meeting LEED and/or LEED-EB certification criteria:* 10%. *Renovation and maintenance:* registered for LEED certification for new construction and/or renovation.

Recycling *Programs and activities:* replaces paper materials with online alternatives. *Campus dining operations:* uses bulk condiment dispensers and decreased packaging for to-go food service purchases.

Purchasing Sustainability criteria used in purchasing include Energy Star (EPA).

Contact Associate Professor of Psychology, Tiffin University, Tiffin, OH 44883. *E-mail:* appelj@tiffin.edu. *Web site:* www.tiffin.edu/.

University of Dayton
Dayton, Ohio

Academics *Sustainability-focused undergraduate major(s):* Environmental Biology (BS), Environmental Geology (BS). *Sustainability-focused graduate degree program(s):* Energy Systems, Mechanical Engineering concentration. *Sustainability courses and programs:* sustainability-focused course(s) or lecture series.

Student Services and Green Events *Sustainability leadership:* sustainability coordinator/director, sustainability committee/advisory council, recycling manager, energy manager, sustainability-focused student government. *Student clubs and activities:* student club(s)/group(s) focused on sustainability, outreach materials available about on-campus sustainability efforts. *Major sustainability events:* Stander Symposium. *Housing and facilities:* sustainability-themed housing, student-run café that serves environmentally or socially preferable foods.

Food Sustainable, organic, and/or locally produced foods available in on-campus dining facilities. Fair Trade coffee is used. Vegan and vegetarian dining options are available for every meal.

Transportation Provides public transportation access to local destinations, a car sharing program, and incentives to carpool or use public transportation.

Buildings and Grounds *Renovation and maintenance:* registered for LEED certification for new construction and/or renovation. *Campus grounds care:* uses water conservation devices; landscapes with native plant species.

Recycling *Programs and activities:* sustains a computer/technology recycling program; sustains a pre-consumer food waste composting program; sustains a post-consumer food waste composting program; composts yard waste; replaces paper materials with online alternatives; limits free printing in computer labs and libraries. *Campus dining operations:* uses reusable dishware; offers discounts for reusable mugs; uses bulk condiment dispensers and decreased packaging for to-go food service purchases.

Energy Currently uses or plans to use motion, infrared, and/or light sensors to reduce energy uses for lighting.

Purchasing Sustainability criteria used in purchasing include Energy Star (EPA), Green Cleaning Products (Green Seal/Environmental Choice certified), and Forest Stewardship Council (FSC) or American Forest and Paper Association's Sustainable Forestry Initiative (SFI) paper.

Contact Environmental Sustainability Manager, University of Dayton, 300 College Park, Dayton, OH 45469-2904. *Phone:* 937-229-3087. *E-mail:* hoffmakd@notes.udayton.edu. *Web site:* www.udayton.edu/.

Oklahoma

Oklahoma Christian University
Oklahoma City, Oklahoma

Student Services and Green Events *Sustainability leadership:* sustainability coordinator/director, sustainability committee/advisory council, recycling manager, sustainability-focused student government. *Student clubs and activities:* student club(s)/group(s) focused on sustainability, outreach materials available about on-campus sustainability efforts. *Major sustainability events:* McBride Lecture featuring author Bill McKibben; round table discussion featuring students, area business leaders, Bill McKibben, and OC faculty members. *Housing and facilities:* on-campus organic garden for students.

Food Fair Trade coffee is used.

Transportation Provides a bike loan/rental program.

Buildings and Grounds *Campus grounds care:* uses water conservation devices; landscapes with native plant species.

Recycling *Programs and activities:* sustains a computer/technology recycling program; maintains an on-campus recycling center; sustains a pre-consumer food waste composting program; sustains a post-consumer food waste composting program; composts yard waste; reuses surplus department/office supplies; replaces paper materials with online alternatives; limits free printing in computer labs and libraries. *Campus dining operations:* uses reusable dishware; offers discounts for reusable mugs; uses bulk condiment dispensers and decreased packaging for to-go food service purchases.

Energy Currently uses or plans to use alternative sources of power and motion, infrared, and/or light sensors to reduce energy uses for lighting.

Purchasing Sustainability criteria used in purchasing include Energy Star (EPA).

Contact Executive Director of the Academy of Leadership and Liberty, Oklahoma Christian University, PO Box 11000, Oklahoma City, OK 73136. *Phone:* 405-425-1065. *E-mail:* brian.bush@oc.edu. *Web site:* www.oc.edu/.

Oklahoma City University
Oklahoma City, Oklahoma

Sustainability Initiatives Oklahoma City University is a member of the Association for the Advancement of Sustainability in Higher Education (AASHE).

Academics *Sustainability-focused undergraduate major(s):* Environmental Studies (BS). *Sustainability courses and programs:* sustainability-focused course(s) or lecture series.

Student Services and Green Events *Sustainability leadership:* sustainability committee/advisory council, recycling manager, sustainability-focused student government. *Housing and facilities:* on-campus organic garden for students.

Food Vegan and vegetarian dining options are available for every meal.

Transportation Provides public transportation access to local destinations.

Buildings and Grounds *Renovation and maintenance:* uses a Green Seal certified cleaning service. *Campus grounds care:* employs strategies to reduce light pollution; landscapes with native plant species.

Recycling *Events and organizations:* RecycleMania. *Programs and activities:* sustains a computer/technology recycling program; maintains an on-campus recycling center; sustains a pre-consumer food waste composting program; sustains a post-consumer food waste composting program; composts yard waste. *Campus dining operations:* operates without trays; offers discounts for reusable mugs.

Energy Currently uses or plans to use alternative sources of power (hydroelectricity/water power and wind energy); timers to regulate temperatures based on occupancy hours; motion, infrared, and/or light sensors to reduce energy uses for lighting; and LED lighting.

Purchasing Sustainability criteria used in purchasing include Green Cleaning Products (Green Seal/Environmental Choice certified).

Contact Oklahoma City University, 2501 North Blackwelder, Oklahoma City, OK 73106-1402. *Phone:* 405-208-5000. *Web site:* www.okcu.edu/.

University of Tulsa
Tulsa, Oklahoma

Academics *Sustainability-focused undergraduate major(s):* Environmental Policy (BA, BS). *Sustainability courses and programs:* sustainability-focused course(s) or lecture series.

Student Services and Green Events *Sustainability leadership:* sustainability coordinator/director, sustainability committee/advisory council, recycling manager, energy manager, sustainability-focused student government. *Student clubs and activities:* student club(s)/group(s) focused on sustainability, outreach materials available about on-campus sustainability efforts. *Major sustainability events:* Focus the Nation, Trayless Earth Day, Challenge X National Competition, screening of "Transit Oriented Development", Lecture Series on "Tapped/Bottled Water", Rethinking the Holidays, OK Sustainability Network Conference. *Housing and facilities:* student-run café that serves environmentally or socially preferable foods, on-campus organic garden for students.

Food Sustainable, organic, and/or locally produced foods available in on-campus dining facilities. Fair Trade coffee is used. Vegan and vegetarian dining options are available for every meal.

Transportation Provides free on-campus transportation (bus or other), public transportation access to local destinations, and a bike loan/rental program.

Buildings and Grounds *Campus grounds care:* uses water conservation devices; employs strategies to reduce light pollution; landscapes with native plant species; protects, restores, and/or creates habitat on campus.

Recycling *Events and organizations:* RecycleMania. *Programs and activities:* sustains a computer/technology recycling program; maintains an on-campus recycling center; sustains a pre-consumer food waste composting program; reuses surplus department/office supplies; replaces paper materials with online alternatives. *Campus dining operations:* uses reusable dishware; operates without trays; offers discounts for reusable mugs; uses bulk condiment dispensers and decreased packaging for to-go food service purchases.

Energy Currently uses or plans to use timers to regulate temperatures based on occupancy hours; motion, infrared, and/or light sensors to reduce energy uses for lighting; LED lighting; and energy-related performance contracting.

Purchasing Sustainability criteria used in purchasing include Energy Star (EPA) and Green Cleaning Products (Green Seal/Environmental Choice certified).

Contact Manager of Training and Development/Personnel Services, University of Tulsa, 800 South Tucker Drive, Twin Towers-Human Resources, Tulsa, OK 74104. *Phone:* 918-631-2111. *E-mail:* marty-phillips@utulsa.edu. *Web site:* www.utulsa.edu/.

Oregon

Linfield College
McMinnville, Oregon

Sustainability Initiatives Linfield College's president has signed the American College & University Presidents Climate Commitment.

Academics *Sustainability-focused undergraduate major(s):* Environmental Studies—Policy Focus, Environmental Studies—Science Focus. *Sustainability courses and programs:* sustainability-focused course(s) or lecture series.

Student Services and Green Events *Sustainability leadership:* sustainability coordinator/director, sustainability committee/advisory council, recycling manager, energy manager. *Student clubs and activities:* Campus Climate Challenge, student club(s)/group(s) focused on sustainability. *Major sustainability events:* Focus the Nation. *Housing and facilities:* on-campus organic garden for students.

Food Sustainable, organic, and/or locally produced foods available in on-campus dining facilities. Fair Trade coffee is used. Vegan and vegetarian dining options are available for every meal.

Transportation Provides public transportation access to local destinations.

Buildings and Grounds *Renovation and maintenance:* registered for LEED certification for new construction and/or renovation. *Campus grounds care:* uses water conservation devices; landscapes with native plant species; protects, restores, and/or creates habitat on campus; applies to its grounds only pesticides and fertilizers allowable under the U.S. Department of Agriculture's standards for crop production.

Recycling *Programs and activities:* sustains a computer/technology recycling program; maintains an on-campus recycling center; sustains a pre-consumer food waste composting program; sustains a post-consumer food waste composting program; composts yard waste; reuses surplus department/office supplies; replaces paper materials with online alternatives; limits free printing in computer labs and libraries. *Campus dining operations:* operates without trays; offers discounts for reusable mugs; uses bulk condiment dispensers and decreased packaging for to-go food service purchases.

Energy Currently uses or plans to use alternative sources of power (hydroelectricity/water power and wind energy); timers to regulate temperatures based on occupancy hours; motion, infrared, and/or light sensors to reduce energy uses for lighting; LED lighting; and energy-related performance contracting.

Purchasing Sustainability criteria used in purchasing include Energy Star (EPA) and Green Cleaning Products (Green Seal/Environmental Choice certified).

Contact Director, Capital Planning and Development, Linfield College, 900 SE Baker Street, McMinnville, OR 97128. *Phone:* 503-883-2611. *Fax:* 503-883-2539. *E-mail:* jhall@linfield.edu. *Web site:* www.linfield.edu/.

Oregon Institute of Technology
Klamath Falls, Oregon

Academics *Sustainability courses and programs:* sustainability-focused course(s) or lecture series.

Student Services and Green Events *Sustainability leadership:* sustainability coordinator/director, sustainability committee/advisory council, recycling manager. *Student clubs and activities:* student club(s)/group(s) focused on sustainability, outreach materials available about on-campus sustainability efforts. *Major sustainability events:* Earth Day Fair 2009. *Housing and facilities:* sustainability-themed housing.

Food Fair Trade coffee is used. Vegan and vegetarian dining options are available for every meal.

Transportation Provides free on-campus transportation (bus or other).

Buildings and Grounds *Renovation and maintenance:* registered for LEED certification for new construction and/or

renovation. *Campus grounds care:* applies to its grounds only pesticides and fertilizers allowable under the U.S. Department of Agriculture's standards for crop production.

Recycling *Events and organizations:* RecycleMania. *Programs and activities:* sustains a computer/technology recycling program; maintains an on-campus recycling center.

Energy Currently uses or plans to use alternative sources of power (geothermal energy and solar energy) and LED lighting. Participates in College & University Green Power Challenge activities.

Contact Assistant Professor, Oregon Institute of Technology, 3201 Campus Drive, Klamath Falls, OR 97601. *Phone:* 541-885-1349. *Fax:* 541-885-1687. *E-mail:* carrie.wittmer@ oit.edu. *Web site:* www.oit.edu/.

Oregon State University
Corvallis, Oregon

Sustainability Initiatives Oregon State University's president has signed the American College & University Presidents Climate Commitment. Oregon State University has Green Fees (optional/required) dedicated to sustainability initiatives.

Academics *Sustainability-focused undergraduate major(s):* Bioresource Research (BS, CRED, HBS), Ecological Engineering (BS, CRED, HBS), Environmental Science (BS, CRED, HBS), Forest Management (BS, HBS), Human Development and Family Sciences (BS, HBS), Natural Resources (BS, HBS). *Sustainability-focused graduate degree program(s):* Biological and Ecological Engineering (MEng, MS, PhD), Business Administration (MBA), Environmental Science (MA, MS, PhD), Marine Resource Management (MA, MS), Public Policy (MPP), Water Resources Policy and Management (MS). *Sustainability courses and programs:* sustainability-focused course(s) or lecture series, noncredit sustainability course(s).

Student Services and Green Events *Sustainability leadership:* sustainability coordinator/director, sustainability committee/advisory council, recycling manager, energy manager, sustainability-focused student government. *Student clubs and activities:* Campus Climate Challenge, student club(s)/group(s) focused on sustainability, outreach materials available about on-campus sustainability efforts. *Major sustainability events:* Oregon University System Sustainability Conference, Earth Week at OSU, National Teach-In, Focus the Nation, other professional research and topic-specific conferences. *Housing and facilities:* sustainability-themed housing, model dorm room that demonstrates sustainable living principles, student-run café that serves environmentally or socially preferable foods, on-campus organic garden for students.

Food Sustainable, organic, and/or locally produced foods available in on-campus dining facilities. Fair Trade coffee is used. Vegan and vegetarian dining options are available for every meal.

Transportation Provides free on-campus transportation (bus or other), public transportation access to local destinations, a bike loan/rental program, and incentives to carpool or use public transportation.

Buildings and Grounds *Renovation and maintenance:* registered for LEED certification for new construction and/or renovation. *Campus grounds care:* uses water conservation devices; employs strategies to reduce light pollution; landscapes with native plant species; protects, restores, and/or creates habitat on campus.

Recycling *Events and organizations:* RecycleMania. *Programs and activities:* sustains a computer/technology recy-

cling program; maintains an on-campus recycling center; sustains a pre-consumer food waste composting program; sustains a post-consumer food waste composting program; composts yard waste; reuses surplus department/office supplies; reuses chemicals; replaces paper materials with online alternatives; limits free printing in computer labs and libraries. *Campus dining operations:* uses reusable dishware; offers discounts for reusable mugs; uses bulk condiment dispensers and decreased packaging for to-go food service purchases.

Energy Currently uses or plans to use alternative sources of power (biomass energy, hydroelectricity/water power, solar energy, and wind energy); timers to regulate temperatures based on occupancy hours; motion, infrared, and/or light sensors to reduce energy uses for lighting; LED lighting; and vending machine motion sensors. Participates in College & University Green Power Challenge activities.

Contact Sustainability Coordinator, Oregon State University, 114 Oak Creek Building, Corvallis, OR 97331. *Phone:* 541-737-3307. *E-mail:* brandon.trelstad@oregonstate.edu. *Web site:* www.oregonstate.edu/.

Pacific University
Forest Grove, Oregon

Sustainability Initiatives Pacific University is a signatory to the Talloires Declaration.

Academics *Sustainability-focused undergraduate major(s):* Environmental Science, Sustainable Design. *Sustainability courses and programs:* sustainability-focused course(s) or lecture series, noncredit sustainability course(s), sustainability-focused nonacademic certificate program(s).

Student Services and Green Events *Sustainability leadership:* sustainability committee/advisory council, recycling manager. *Student clubs and activities:* student club(s)/group(s) focused on sustainability, outreach materials available about on-campus sustainability efforts. *Major sustainability events:* Focus the Nation. *Housing and facilities:* sustainability-themed housing, on-campus organic garden for students.

Food Sustainable, organic, and/or locally produced foods available in on-campus dining facilities. Vegan and vegetarian dining options are available for every meal.

Transportation Provides free on-campus transportation (bus or other), public transportation access to local destinations, a bike loan/rental program, and incentives to carpool or use public transportation.

Buildings and Grounds *Percentage of institution's eligible buildings as of September 2008 meeting LEED and/or LEED-EB certification criteria:* 100%. *Renovation and maintenance:* registered for LEED certification for new construction and/or renovation. *Campus grounds care:* uses water conservation devices; employs strategies to reduce light pollution; landscapes with native plant species; protects, restores, and/or creates habitat on campus.

Recycling *Programs and activities:* sustains a computer/technology recycling program; maintains an on-campus recycling center; sustains a pre-consumer food waste composting program; composts yard waste; reuses surplus department/office supplies; replaces paper materials with online alternatives. *Campus dining operations:* operates without trays; offers discounts for reusable mugs; uses bulk condiment dispensers and decreased packaging for to-go food service purchases.

Energy Currently uses or plans to use alternative sources of power (hydroelectricity/water power); timers to regulate temperatures based on occupancy hours; motion, infrared, and/or light sensors to reduce energy uses for lighting; and vending machine motion sensors.

Purchasing Sustainability criteria used in purchasing include Energy Star (EPA), Green Cleaning Products (Green Seal/Environmental Choice certified), and Forest Stewardship Council (FSC) or American Forest and Paper Association's Sustainable Forestry Initiative (SFI) paper.

Contact Pacific University, 2043 College Way, Forest Grove, OR 97116-1797. *Phone:* 503-357-6151. *Web site:* www.pacificu.edu/.

Portland State University
Portland, Oregon

Sustainability Initiatives Portland State University is a member of the Association for the Advancement of Sustainability in Higher Education (AASHE). This institution's president has signed the American College & University Presidents Climate Commitment.

Academics *Sustainability-focused undergraduate major(s):* Community Development (BA), Environmental Studies (BA). *Sustainability courses and programs:* sustainability-focused course(s) or lecture series.

Student Services and Green Events *Sustainability leadership:* sustainability coordinator/director, sustainability committee/advisory council, recycling manager, sustainability-focused student government. *Student clubs and activities:* Campus Climate Challenge, Public Interest Research Group (PIRG) chapter on campus, student club(s)/group(s) focused on sustainability, outreach materials available about on-campus sustainability efforts. *Major sustainability events:* Focus the Nation, Regional Watershed Symposium, Annual Sustainability Conference in School of Business, Urban Ecology Symposium. *Housing and facilities:* student-run café that serves environmentally or socially preferable foods, on-campus organic garden for students.

Food Fair Trade coffee is used. Vegan and vegetarian dining options are available for every meal.

Transportation Provides public transportation access to local destinations and a car sharing program.

Buildings and Grounds *Renovation and maintenance:* registered for LEED certification for new construction and/or renovation. *Campus grounds care:* uses water conservation devices; landscapes with native plant species; protects, restores, and/or creates habitat on campus; applies to its grounds only pesticides and fertilizers allowable under the U.S. Department of Agriculture's standards for crop production.

Recycling *Events and organizations:* RecycleMania. *Programs and activities:* sustains a computer/technology recycling program; sustains a pre-consumer food waste composting program; composts yard waste; reuses surplus department/office supplies; replaces paper materials with online alternatives; limits free printing in computer labs and libraries. *Campus dining operations:* uses reusable dishware; operates without trays; offers discounts for reusable mugs; uses bulk condiment dispensers and decreased packaging for to-go food service purchases.

Energy Currently uses or plans to use alternative sources of power (geothermal energy, solar energy, and wind energy); timers to regulate temperatures based on occupancy hours; motion, infrared, and/or light sensors to reduce energy uses for lighting; and LED lighting.

Purchasing Sustainability criteria used in purchasing include Green Cleaning Products (Green Seal/Environmental Choice certified).

Contact Portland State University, PO Box 751, Portland, OR 97207-0751. *Phone:* 503-725-3000. *Web site:* www.pdx.edu/.

Southern Oregon University
Ashland, Oregon

Sustainability Initiatives Southern Oregon University is a signatory to the Talloires Declaration. This institution's president has signed the American College & University Presidents Climate Commitment. Southern Oregon University has Green Fees (optional/required) dedicated to sustainability initiatives.

Academics *Sustainability-focused undergraduate major(s):* Business (BA), Environmental Studies (BS). *Sustainability-focused graduate degree program(s):* Environmental Education (MS). *Sustainability courses and programs:* sustainability-focused course(s) or lecture series, noncredit sustainability course(s).

Student Services and Green Events *Sustainability leadership:* sustainability committee/advisory council, energy manager, sustainability-focused student government. *Student clubs and activities:* Campus Climate Challenge, Public Interest Research Group (PIRG) chapter on campus, outreach materials available about on-campus sustainability efforts. *Housing and facilities:* sustainability-themed housing, student-run café that serves environmentally or socially preferable foods, on-campus organic garden for students.

Food Sustainable, organic, and/or locally produced foods available in on-campus dining facilities. Fair Trade coffee is used. Vegan and vegetarian dining options are available for every meal.

Transportation Provides a bike loan/rental program and incentives to carpool or use public transportation.

Buildings and Grounds *Percentage of institution's eligible buildings as of September 2008 meeting LEED and/or LEED-EB certification criteria:* 10%. *Renovation and maintenance:* registered for LEED certification for new construction and/or renovation. *Campus grounds care:* uses water conservation devices; landscapes with native plant species.

Recycling *Events and organizations:* RecycleMania. *Programs and activities:* sustains a computer/technology recycling program; sustains a pre-consumer food waste composting program; sustains a post-consumer food waste composting program; composts yard waste; reuses surplus department/office supplies; reuses chemicals; replaces paper materials with online alternatives; limits free printing in computer labs and libraries. *Campus dining operations:* uses reusable dishware; offers discounts for reusable mugs; uses bulk condiment dispensers and decreased packaging for to-go food service purchases.

Energy Currently uses or plans to use alternative sources of power (hydroelectricity/water power, solar energy, and wind energy); timers to regulate temperatures based on occupancy hours; motion, infrared, and/or light sensors to reduce energy uses for lighting; and energy-related performance contracting. Participates in College & University Green Power Challenge activities.

Purchasing Sustainability criteria used in purchasing include Energy Star (EPA) and Green Cleaning Products (Green Seal/Environmental Choice certified).

Contact Vice President for Student Affairs, Southern Oregon University, SU 322, 1250 Siskiyou Boulevard, Ashland, OR 97520. *Phone:* 541-552-6651. *Fax:* 541-552-8324. *E-mail:* eldridgj@sou.edu. *Web site:* www.sou.edu/.

University of Oregon
Eugene, Oregon

Sustainability Initiatives University of Oregon is a member of the Association for the Advancement of Sustainability in Higher Education (AASHE). This institution's president has signed the American College & University Presidents Climate Commitment. University of Oregon has Green Fees (optional/required) dedicated to sustainability initiatives.

Academics *Sustainability-focused undergraduate major(s):* Architecture (BArch), Environmental Studies (BA), Landscape Architecture (BLA). *Sustainability-focused graduate degree program(s):* Architecture (MArch), Business (MBA), Chemistry (PhD), Community and Regional Planning (MCRP), Environmental Studies (MS), Law (JD). *Sustainability courses and programs:* sustainability-focused course(s) or lecture series, noncredit sustainability course(s), sustainability-focused nonacademic certificate program(s).

Student Services and Green Events *Sustainability leadership:* sustainability coordinator/director, sustainability committee/advisory council, recycling manager, energy manager, sustainability-focused student government. *Student clubs and activities:* Public Interest Research Group (PIRG) chapter on campus, student club(s)/group(s) focused on sustainability, outreach materials available about on-campus sustainability efforts. *Major sustainability events:* Annual Public Interest Environmental Law Conference, annual HOPES Conference, Oregon University System Sustainability Conference and Fair, annual Sustainable Business Symposium. *Housing and facilities:* sustainability-themed housing, on-campus organic garden for students.

Food Sustainable, organic, and/or locally produced foods available in on-campus dining facilities. Fair Trade coffee is used. Vegan and vegetarian dining options are available for every meal.

Transportation Provides free on-campus transportation (bus or other), public transportation access to local destinations, a bike loan/rental program, and incentives to carpool or use public transportation.

Buildings and Grounds *Percentage of institution's eligible buildings as of September 2008 meeting LEED and/or LEED-EB certification criteria:* 10.63%. *Renovation and maintenance:* registered for LEED certification for new construction and/or renovation. *Campus grounds care:* uses water conservation devices; employs strategies to reduce light pollution; landscapes with native plant species; protects, restores, and/or creates habitat on campus.

Recycling *Events and organizations:* RecycleMania. *Programs and activities:* sustains a computer/technology recycling program; maintains an on-campus recycling center; sustains a pre-consumer food waste composting program; sustains a post-consumer food waste composting program; composts yard waste; reuses surplus department/office supplies; reuses chemicals; replaces paper materials with online alternatives; limits free printing in computer labs and libraries. *Campus dining operations:* uses reusable dishware; offers discounts for reusable mugs; uses bulk condiment dispensers and decreased packaging for to-go food service purchases.

Energy Currently uses or plans to use alternative sources of power (hydroelectricity/water power, solar energy, and wind energy); timers to regulate temperatures based on occupancy hours; motion, infrared, and/or light sensors to reduce energy uses for lighting; and vending machine motion sensors.

Purchasing Sustainability criteria used in purchasing include Energy Star (EPA) and Green Cleaning Products (Green Seal/Environmental Choice certified).

Contact Sustainability Director, University of Oregon, 145 Columbia Hall, Eugene, OR 97403. *Phone:* 541-346-0709. *E-mail:* smital@uoregon.edu. *Web site:* www.uoregon.edu/.

Western Oregon University
Monmouth, Oregon

Sustainability Initiatives Western Oregon University's president has signed the American College & University Presidents Climate Commitment.

Academics *Sustainability-focused undergraduate major(s):* Earth Science (BA, BS). *Sustainability courses and programs:* sustainability-focused course(s) or lecture series.

Student Services and Green Events *Sustainability leadership:* sustainability committee/advisory council. *Student clubs and activities:* student club(s)/group(s) focused on sustainability. *Major sustainability events:* Green Week 2009. *Housing and facilities:* sustainability-themed housing, student-run café that serves environmentally or socially preferable foods.

Food Sustainable, organic, and/or locally produced foods available in on-campus dining facilities. Fair Trade coffee is used. Vegan and vegetarian dining options are available for every meal.

Transportation Provides public transportation access to local destinations.

Buildings and Grounds *Campus grounds care:* uses water conservation devices.

Recycling *Events and organizations:* RecycleMania. *Programs and activities:* maintains an on-campus recycling center; composts yard waste; reuses surplus department/office supplies; replaces paper materials with online alternatives; limits free printing in computer labs and libraries. *Campus dining operations:* uses reusable dishware; offers discounts for reusable mugs; uses bulk condiment dispensers and decreased packaging for to-go food service purchases.

Energy Currently uses or plans to use motion, infrared, and/or light sensors to reduce energy uses for lighting.

Contact Occupational Environmental Specialist, Western Oregon University, 345 North Monmouth Avenue, Monmouth, OR 97361. *Phone:* 503-838-8156. *E-mail:* risena@wou.edu. *Web site:* www.wou.edu/.

Willamette University
Salem, Oregon

Sustainability Initiatives Willamette University's president has signed the American College & University Presidents Climate Commitment.

Academics *Sustainability-focused undergraduate major(s):* Anthropology (BA), Biology (BA), Economics (BA), Environmental and Earth Science (BA), Politics (BA), Rhetoric and Media Studies (BA). *Sustainability-focused graduate degree program(s):* Sustainability emphasis (MBA), Sustainability Law (JD). *Sustainability courses and programs:* sustainability-focused course(s) or lecture series, noncredit sustainability course(s), sustainability-focused nonacademic certificate program(s).

Student Services and Green Events *Sustainability leadership:* sustainability coordinator/director, sustainability committee/advisory council, recycling manager, energy manager, sustainability-focused student government. *Student clubs and activities:* student club(s)/group(s) focused on sustainability, outreach materials available about on-campus sustainability efforts. *Major sustainability events:* Campus Sustainability Day, Campus Sustainability Month, Focus the Nation Teach-In, Dempsey Environmental Lecture and Conference Series. *Housing and facilities:* sustainability-themed housing, model dorm room that demonstrates sustainable living principles, student-run café that serves environmentally or socially preferable foods, on-campus organic garden for students.

Food Sustainable, organic, and/or locally produced foods available in on-campus dining facilities. Fair Trade coffee is used. Vegan and vegetarian dining options are available for every meal.

Transportation Provides public transportation access to local destinations, a bike loan/rental program, a car sharing program, and incentives to carpool or use public transportation.

Buildings and Grounds *Renovation and maintenance:* registered for LEED certification for new construction and/or renovation; uses a Green Seal certified cleaning service. *Campus grounds care:* uses water conservation devices; employs strategies to reduce light pollution; landscapes with native plant species; protects, restores, and/or creates habitat on campus; applies to its grounds only pesticides and fertilizers allowable under the U.S. Department of Agriculture's standards for crop production.

Recycling *Programs and activities:* sustains a computer/technology recycling program; maintains an on-campus recycling center; sustains a pre-consumer food waste composting program; sustains a post-consumer food waste composting program; composts yard waste; reuses surplus department/office supplies; reuses chemicals; replaces paper materials with online alternatives. *Campus dining operations:* uses reusable dishware; offers discounts for reusable mugs; uses bulk condiment dispensers and decreased packaging for to-go food service purchases.

Energy Currently uses or plans to use alternative sources of power (solar energy); timers to regulate temperatures based on occupancy hours; motion, infrared, and/or light sensors to reduce energy uses for lighting; and LED lighting.

Purchasing Sustainability criteria used in purchasing include Energy Star (EPA), WaterSense (EPA), Green Electronics Council (GEC) Electronic Product Environmental Assessment Tool (EPEAT) Silver or Gold, Green Cleaning Products (Green Seal/Environmental Choice certified), and Forest Stewardship Council (FSC) or American Forest and Paper Association's Sustainable Forestry Initiative (SFI) paper.

Contact Professor/Dempsey Chair/Director, Center for Sustainable Communities, Willamette University, 900 State Street, Salem, OR 97301. *Phone:* 503-370-6820. *E-mail:* jbowerso@willamette.edu. *Web site:* www.willamette.edu/.

Pennsylvania

Bucknell University
Lewisburg, Pennsylvania

Sustainability Initiatives Bucknell University's president has signed the American College & University Presidents Climate Commitment. Bucknell University has Green Fees (optional/required) dedicated to sustainability initiatives.

Academics *Sustainability-focused undergraduate major(s):* Civil and Environmental Engineering (BS), Environmental Studies (BA), Environmental Studies (BS). *Sustainability-focused graduate degree program(s):* Civil and Environmen-

tal Engineering (MS). *Sustainability courses and programs:* sustainability-focused course(s) or lecture series.

Student Services and Green Events *Sustainability leadership:* sustainability coordinator/director, sustainability committee/advisory council, recycling manager, energy manager. *Student clubs and activities:* student club(s)/group(s) focused on sustainability, outreach materials available about on-campus sustainability efforts. *Major sustainability events:* Focus the Nation Climate Change Symposium, Susquehanna River Symposium. *Housing and facilities:* sustainability-themed housing, on-campus organic garden for students.

Food Sustainable, organic, and/or locally produced foods available in on-campus dining facilities. Fair Trade coffee is used. Vegan and vegetarian dining options are available for every meal.

Transportation Provides public transportation access to local destinations and a bike loan/rental program.

Buildings and Grounds *Campus grounds care:* uses water conservation devices; employs strategies to reduce light pollution; landscapes with native plant species; protects, restores, and/or creates habitat on campus.

Recycling *Events and organizations:* RecycleMania. *Programs and activities:* sustains a computer/technology recycling program; maintains an on-campus recycling center; composts yard waste; reuses surplus department/office supplies; replaces paper materials with online alternatives. *Campus dining operations:* uses reusable dishware; operates without trays; offers discounts for reusable mugs; uses bulk condiment dispensers and decreased packaging for to-go food service purchases.

Energy Currently uses or plans to use alternative sources of power (solar energy and wind energy); timers to regulate temperatures based on occupancy hours; motion, infrared, and/or light sensors to reduce energy uses for lighting; and LED lighting.

Purchasing Sustainability criteria used in purchasing include Energy Star (EPA), Green Cleaning Products (Green Seal/Environmental Choice certified), and Forest Stewardship Council (FSC) or American Forest and Paper Association's Sustainable Forestry Initiative (SFI) paper.

Contact Director, Campus Greening Initiative, Bucknell University, Lewisburg, PA 17837. *Phone:* 570-577-1265. *E-mail:* dina.el-mogazi@bucknell.edu. *Web site:* www.bucknell.edu/.

Carnegie Mellon University
Pittsburgh, Pennsylvania

Academics *Sustainability-focused graduate degree program(s):* Environmental Engineering (MS, PhD), Environmental Management and Science (MS, PhD), Sustainable Design (MS). *Sustainability courses and programs:* sustainability-focused course(s) or lecture series.

Student Services and Green Events *Sustainability leadership:* sustainability coordinator/director, sustainability committee/advisory council, recycling manager, sustainability-focused student government. *Student clubs and activities:* student club(s)/group(s) focused on sustainability, outreach materials available about on-campus sustainability efforts. *Major sustainability events:* NRC/CURC Conference and Workshop, ABSIC Meetings, University Lecture Series, International Festival. *Housing and facilities:* sustainability-themed housing.

Food Sustainable, organic, and/or locally produced foods available in on-campus dining facilities. Fair Trade coffee is used. Vegan and vegetarian dining options are available for every meal.

Transportation Provides free on-campus transportation (bus or other), public transportation access to local destinations, a car sharing program, and incentives to carpool or use public transportation.

Buildings and Grounds *Renovation and maintenance:* registered for LEED certification for new construction and/or renovation; uses a Green Seal certified cleaning service. *Campus grounds care:* uses water conservation devices; employs strategies to reduce light pollution; landscapes with native plant species; protects, restores, and/or creates habitat on campus.

Recycling *Events and organizations:* RecycleMania. *Programs and activities:* sustains a computer/technology recycling program; maintains an on-campus recycling center; sustains a pre-consumer food waste composting program; composts yard waste; reuses surplus department/office supplies; reuses chemicals; replaces paper materials with online alternatives; limits free printing in computer labs and libraries. *Campus dining operations:* uses reusable dishware; operates without trays; offers discounts for reusable mugs; uses bulk condiment dispensers and decreased packaging for to-go food service purchases.

Energy Currently uses or plans to use alternative sources of power (biomass energy, hydroelectricity/water power, solar energy, and wind energy); motion, infrared, and/or light sensors to reduce energy uses for lighting; LED lighting; and vending machine motion sensors. Participates in College & University Green Power Challenge activities.

Purchasing Sustainability criteria used in purchasing include Energy Star (EPA), Green Electronics Council (GEC) Electronic Product Environmental Assessment Tool (EPEAT) Silver or Gold, Green Cleaning Products (Green Seal/Environmental Choice certified), and Forest Stewardship Council (FSC) or American Forest and Paper Association's Sustainable Forestry Initiative (SFI) paper.

Contact Executive Director, SEER, Carnegie Mellon University, 5000 Forbes Avenue, Pittsburgh, PA 15213. *Phone:* 412-268-7121. *Fax:* 412-268-7813. *E-mail:* dlange@cmu.edu. *Web site:* www.cmu.edu/.

Chatham University
Pittsburgh, Pennsylvania

Sustainability Initiatives Chatham University is a member of the Association for the Advancement of Sustainability in Higher Education (AASHE). This institution's president has signed the American College & University Presidents Climate Commitment.

Academics *Sustainability-focused undergraduate major(s):* Environmental Science (BS), Environmental Studies (BA), Interior Architecture (BIA), Biology (BS). *Sustainability-focused graduate degree program(s):* Interior Architecture (MSIA), Landscape Architecture (MLA), Landscape Studies (MALS), upcoming Master Arts Liberal Studies (MLS). *Sustainability courses and programs:* sustainability-focused course(s) or lecture series, noncredit sustainability course(s).

Student Services and Green Events *Sustainability leadership:* sustainability coordinator/director, sustainability committee/advisory council, recycling manager. *Student clubs and activities:* student club(s)/group(s) focused on sustainability, outreach materials available about on-campus sustainability efforts. *Major sustainability events:* Rachel Carson Legacy Symposium, Rachel Carson Youth Summit, Western Pennsylvania Landscape Symposium (with Phipps Garden Center, Penn State). *Housing and facilities:* sustainability-themed housing, on-campus organic garden for students.

Food Sustainable, organic, and/or locally produced foods available in on-campus dining facilities. Fair Trade coffee is used. Vegan and vegetarian dining options are available for every meal.

Transportation Provides free on-campus transportation (bus or other), public transportation access to local destinations, and incentives to carpool or use public transportation.

Buildings and Grounds *Renovation and maintenance:* registered for LEED certification for new construction and/or renovation. *Campus grounds care:* uses water conservation devices; employs strategies to reduce light pollution; landscapes with native plant species; protects, restores, and/or creates habitat on campus; applies to its grounds only pesticides and fertilizers allowable under the U.S. Department of Agriculture's standards for crop production.

Recycling *Events and organizations:* RecycleMania. *Programs and activities:* sustains a computer/technology recycling program; sustains a pre-consumer food waste composting program; sustains a post-consumer food waste composting program; composts yard waste; reuses chemicals; replaces paper materials with online alternatives; limits free printing in computer labs and libraries. *Campus dining operations:* uses reusable dishware; operates without trays; offers discounts for reusable mugs; uses bulk condiment dispensers and decreased packaging for to-go food service purchases.

Energy Currently uses or plans to use alternative sources of power and energy-related performance contracting.

Purchasing Sustainability criteria used in purchasing include Energy Star (EPA) and Green Cleaning Products (Green Seal/Environmental Choice certified).

Contact University Sustainability Coordinator, Chatham University, Woodland Road, Pittsburgh, PA 15232. *Phone:* 412-365-1686. *Fax:* 412-365-1691. *E-mail:* mwhitney@chatham.edu. *Web site:* www.chatham.edu/.

Drexel University
Philadelphia, Pennsylvania

Academics *Sustainability-focused undergraduate major(s):* Environmental Engineering (BS), Environmental Science (BS), Urban Environmental Studies (BS). *Sustainability-focused graduate degree program(s):* Environmental Engineering (MS, PhD), Environmental Science (MS, PhD). *Sustainability courses and programs:* sustainability-focused course(s) or lecture series.

Student Services and Green Events *Sustainability leadership:* sustainability coordinator/director, sustainability committee/advisory council, energy manager. *Student clubs and activities:* student club(s)/group(s) focused on sustainability, outreach materials available about on-campus sustainability efforts. *Major sustainability events:* Drexel Community Presentation Series, Global Warming Speakers Series, Fall Sustainability Convocation, Alumni Clean up of Fairmount Park, Earth Week. *Housing and facilities:* sustainability-themed housing.

Food Sustainable, organic, and/or locally produced foods available in on-campus dining facilities. Fair Trade coffee is used. Vegan and vegetarian dining options are available for every meal.

Transportation Provides free on-campus transportation (bus or other), public transportation access to local destinations, a bike loan/rental program, a car sharing program, and incentives to carpool or use public transportation.

Buildings and Grounds *Renovation and maintenance:* registered for LEED certification for new construction and/or

renovation. *Campus grounds care:* uses water conservation devices; employs strategies to reduce light pollution; landscapes with native plant species; protects, restores, and/or creates habitat on campus; applies to its grounds only pesticides and fertilizers allowable under the U.S. Department of Agriculture's standards for crop production.

Recycling *Events and organizations:* RecycleMania. *Programs and activities:* sustains a computer/technology recycling program; maintains an on-campus recycling center; composts yard waste; reuses surplus department/office supplies; reuses chemicals; replaces paper materials with online alternatives; limits free printing in computer labs and libraries. *Campus dining operations:* uses reusable dishware; offers discounts for reusable mugs; uses bulk condiment dispensers and decreased packaging for to-go food service purchases.

Energy Currently uses or plans to use alternative sources of power (geothermal energy and wind energy); timers to regulate temperatures based on occupancy hours; motion, infrared, and/or light sensors to reduce energy uses for lighting; and LED lighting. Participates in College & University Green Power Challenge activities.

Purchasing Sustainability criteria used in purchasing include Energy Star (EPA), Green Electronics Council (GEC) Electronic Product Environmental Assessment Tool (EPEAT) Silver or Gold, Green Cleaning Products (Green Seal/Environmental Choice certified), and Forest Stewardship Council (FSC) or American Forest and Paper Association's Sustainable Forestry Initiative (SFI) paper.

Contact Executive Vice President, Drexel University, Office of the President, 3141 Chestnut Street, Philadelphia, PA 19104. *Phone:* 215-895-2525. *E-mail:* oxholm@drexel.edu. *Web site:* www.drexel.edu/.

East Stroudsburg University of Pennsylvania
East Stroudsburg, Pennsylvania

Sustainability Initiatives East Stroudsburg University of Pennsylvania's president has signed the American College & University Presidents Climate Commitment.

Student Services and Green Events *Sustainability leadership:* sustainability committee/advisory council.

Contact East Stroudsburg University of Pennsylvania, 200 Prospect Street, East Stroudsburg, PA 18301-2999. *Phone:* 570-422-3211. *Web site:* www.esu.edu/.

Franklin & Marshall College
Lancaster, Pennsylvania

Sustainability Initiatives Franklin & Marshall College's president has signed the American College & University Presidents Climate Commitment.

Academics *Sustainability-focused undergraduate major(s):* Environmental Science, Environmental Studies. *Sustainability courses and programs:* sustainability-focused course(s) or lecture series.

Student Services and Green Events *Sustainability leadership:* sustainability coordinator/director, sustainability committee/advisory council, sustainability-focused student government. *Student clubs and activities:* Campus Climate Challenge, student club(s)/group(s) focused on sustainability, outreach materials available about on-campus sustainability efforts. *Major sustainability events:* Sustainability Week. *Housing and facilities:* sustainability-themed housing, student-run café that serves environmentally or socially preferable foods.

Food Sustainable, organic, and/or locally produced foods available in on-campus dining facilities. Vegan and vegetarian dining options are available for every meal.

Transportation Provides free on-campus transportation (bus or other), public transportation access to local destinations, a bike loan/rental program, and incentives to carpool or use public transportation.

Buildings and Grounds *Renovation and maintenance:* registered for LEED certification for new construction and/or renovation; uses a Green Seal certified cleaning service. *Campus grounds care:* uses water conservation devices; landscapes with native plant species.

Recycling *Events and organizations:* RecycleMania. *Programs and activities:* sustains a computer/technology recycling program; reuses surplus department/office supplies; replaces paper materials with online alternatives; limits free printing in computer labs and libraries. *Campus dining operations:* uses reusable dishware; operates without trays; uses bulk condiment dispensers and decreased packaging for to-go food service purchases.

Energy Currently uses or plans to use alternative sources of power.

Purchasing Sustainability criteria used in purchasing include Energy Star (EPA) and Green Cleaning Products (Green Seal/Environmental Choice certified).

Contact Professor of Geosciences, Franklin & Marshall College, PO Box 3003, Lancaster, PA 17604-3003. *E-mail:* carol.dewet@fandm.edu. *Web site:* www.fandm.edu/.

Gettysburg College
Gettysburg, Pennsylvania

Sustainability Initiatives Gettysburg College's president has signed the American College & University Presidents Climate Commitment.

Student Services and Green Events *Sustainability leadership:* sustainability committee/advisory council. *Student clubs and activities:* Campus Climate Challenge. *Housing and facilities:* on-campus organic garden for students.

Food Sustainable, organic, and/or locally produced foods available in on-campus dining facilities. Vegan and vegetarian dining options are available for every meal.

Transportation Provides public transportation access to local destinations and a bike loan/rental program.

Buildings and Grounds *Renovation and maintenance:* registered for LEED certification for new construction and/or renovation. *Campus grounds care:* uses water conservation devices; employs strategies to reduce light pollution; landscapes with native plant species.

Recycling *Events and organizations:* RecycleMania, WasteWise (EPA). *Programs and activities:* sustains a computer/technology recycling program; sustains a pre-consumer food waste composting program; sustains a post-consumer food waste composting program; composts yard waste. *Campus dining operations:* offers discounts for reusable mugs; uses bulk condiment dispensers and decreased packaging for to-go food service purchases.

Energy Currently uses or plans to use motion, infrared, and/or light sensors to reduce energy uses for lighting and LED lighting.

Purchasing Sustainability criteria used in purchasing include Energy Star (EPA) and Green Cleaning Products (Green Seal/Environmental Choice certified).

Contact Gettysburg College, 300 North Washington Street, Gettysburg, PA 17325-1483. *Phone:* 717-337-6000. *Web site:* www.gettysburg.edu/.

Juniata College
Huntingdon, Pennsylvania

Sustainability Initiatives Juniata College is a member of the Association for the Advancement of Sustainability in

Higher Education (AASHE). This institution's president has signed the American College & University Presidents Climate Commitment.

Academics *Sustainability courses and programs:* sustainability-focused course(s) or lecture series, noncredit sustainability course(s).

Student Services and Green Events *Sustainability leadership:* sustainability committee/advisory council. *Housing and facilities:* sustainability-themed housing.

Food Sustainable, organic, and/or locally produced foods available in on-campus dining facilities. Fair Trade coffee is used. Vegan and vegetarian dining options are available for every meal.

Transportation Provides public transportation access to local destinations and a bike loan/rental program.

Buildings and Grounds *Percentage of institution's eligible buildings as of September 2008 meeting LEED and/or LEED-EB certification criteria:* 5%. *Campus grounds care:* uses water conservation devices; employs strategies to reduce light pollution; landscapes with native plant species; protects, restores, and/or creates habitat on campus.

Recycling *Events and organizations:* RecycleMania. *Programs and activities:* sustains a computer/technology recycling program; maintains an on-campus recycling center; reuses surplus department/office supplies; reuses chemicals; replaces paper materials with online alternatives. *Campus dining operations:* uses reusable dishware; operates without trays; offers discounts for reusable mugs; uses bulk condiment dispensers and decreased packaging for to-go food service purchases.

Energy Currently uses or plans to use timers to regulate temperatures based on occupancy hours; motion, infrared, and/or light sensors to reduce energy uses for lighting; and LED lighting.

Purchasing Sustainability criteria used in purchasing include Energy Star (EPA), Green Cleaning Products (Green Seal/Environmental Choice certified), and Forest Stewardship Council (FSC) or American Forest and Paper Association's Sustainable Forestry Initiative (SFI) paper.

Contact Vice President for Finance and Operations, Juniata College, 1700 Moore Street, Huntingdon, PA 16652. *Phone:* 814-641-3707. *E-mail:* yelnosr@juniata.edu. *Web site:* www.juniata.edu/.

Keystone College
La Plume, Pennsylvania

Sustainability Initiatives Keystone College's president has signed the American College & University Presidents Climate Commitment.

Academics *Sustainability-focused undergraduate major(s):* Environmental Resource Management (BS). *Sustainability courses and programs:* sustainability-focused course(s) or lecture series.

Student Services and Green Events *Sustainability leadership:* sustainability committee/advisory council. *Student clubs and activities:* student club(s)/group(s) focused on sustainability. *Major sustainability events:* Keystone College Environmental Education Institute (KCEEI).

Food Sustainable, organic, and/or locally produced foods available in on-campus dining facilities. Fair Trade coffee is used. Vegan and vegetarian dining options are available for every meal.

Transportation Provides free on-campus transportation (bus or other) and incentives to carpool or use public transportation.

Buildings and Grounds *Renovation and maintenance:* uses a Green Seal certified cleaning service. *Campus grounds care:* uses water conservation devices.

Recycling *Events and organizations:* RecycleMania. *Programs and activities:* sustains a computer/technology recycling program; composts yard waste; replaces paper materials with online alternatives. *Campus dining operations:* uses reusable dishware.

Energy Currently uses or plans to use alternative sources of power and LED lighting.

Purchasing Sustainability criteria used in purchasing include Energy Star (EPA) and Green Cleaning Products (Green Seal/Environmental Choice certified).

Contact Keystone College, One College Green, La Plume, PA 18440. *Phone:* 570-945-5141. *Web site:* www.keystone.edu/.

Kutztown University of Pennsylvania
Kutztown, Pennsylvania

Student Services and Green Events *Sustainability leadership:* sustainability committee/advisory council, recycling manager, energy manager, sustainability-focused student government. *Student clubs and activities:* student club(s)/group(s) focused on sustainability. *Major sustainability events:* Earth Day Celebration.

Transportation Provides free on-campus transportation (bus or other).

Buildings and Grounds *Campus grounds care:* uses water conservation devices; employs strategies to reduce light pollution; landscapes with native plant species; protects, restores, and/or creates habitat on campus.

Recycling *Programs and activities:* sustains a computer/technology recycling program; maintains an on-campus recycling center; reuses surplus department/office supplies; replaces paper materials with online alternatives; limits free printing in computer labs and libraries. *Campus dining operations:* uses reusable dishware; operates without trays.

Energy Currently uses or plans to use timers to regulate temperatures based on occupancy hours; motion, infrared, and/or light sensors to reduce energy uses for lighting; and energy-related performance contracting.

Purchasing Sustainability criteria used in purchasing include Green Cleaning Products (Green Seal/Environmental Choice certified).

Contact Kutztown University of Pennsylvania, 15200 Kutztown Road, Kutztown, PA 19530-0730. *Phone:* 610-683-4000. *Web site:* www.kutztown.edu/.

Lehigh University
Bethlehem, Pennsylvania

Sustainability Initiatives Lehigh University has Green Fees (optional/required) dedicated to sustainability initiatives.

Academics *Sustainability-focused undergraduate major(s):* Earth and Environmental Science (BA), Environmental Engineering (BS), Environmental Studies (BA). *Sustainability-focused graduate degree program(s):* Earth and Environmental Science (MS, PhD), Environmental Engineering (MS, PhD), Environmental Policy Design (MA). *Sustainability courses and programs:* sustainability-focused course(s) or lecture series, noncredit sustainability course(s), sustainability-focused nonacademic certificate program(s).

Student Services and Green Events *Sustainability leadership:* sustainability committee/advisory council, recycling manager, sustainability-focused student government. *Student clubs and activities:* student club(s)/group(s) focused on sustainability, outreach materials available about on-campus sustainability efforts. *Major sustainability events:* Focus the Nation, Lehigh Valley Green Expo, Engineers Without Borders. *Housing and facilities:* sustainability-themed housing.

Food Sustainable, organic, and/or locally produced foods available in on-campus dining facilities. Fair Trade coffee is used. Vegan and vegetarian dining options are available for every meal.

Transportation Provides free on-campus transportation (bus or other) and public transportation access to local destinations.

Buildings and Grounds *Renovation and maintenance:* registered for LEED certification for new construction and/or renovation; uses a Green Seal certified cleaning service. *Campus grounds care:* uses water conservation devices; protects, restores, and/or creates habitat on campus; applies to its grounds only pesticides and fertilizers allowable under the U.S. Department of Agriculture's standards for crop production.

Recycling *Programs and activities:* sustains a computer/technology recycling program; maintains an on-campus recycling center; composts yard waste; reuses surplus department/office supplies; reuses chemicals; replaces paper materials with online alternatives. *Campus dining operations:* uses reusable dishware; operates without trays; offers discounts for reusable mugs; uses bulk condiment dispensers and decreased packaging for to-go food service purchases.

Energy Currently uses or plans to use timers to regulate temperatures based on occupancy hours; motion, infrared, and/or light sensors to reduce energy uses for lighting; and LED lighting.

Purchasing Sustainability criteria used in purchasing include Energy Star (EPA), Green Cleaning Products (Green Seal/Environmental Choice certified), and Forest Stewardship Council (FSC) or American Forest and Paper Association's Sustainable Forestry Initiative (SFI) paper.

Contact Lehigh University, 27 Memorial Drive West, Bethlehem, PA 18015-3094. *Phone:* 610-758-3000. *Web site:* www.lehigh.edu/.

Marywood University
Scranton, Pennsylvania

Academics *Sustainability-focused undergraduate major(s):* Environmental Architecture, Interior Design and Architecture. *Sustainability courses and programs:* sustainability-focused course(s) or lecture series.

Student Services and Green Events *Sustainability leadership:* sustainability coordinator/director, sustainability committee/advisory council, recycling manager, energy manager, sustainability-focused student government. *Student clubs and activities:* Campus Climate Challenge, outreach materials available about on-campus sustainability efforts.

Food Sustainable, organic, and/or locally produced foods available in on-campus dining facilities. Fair Trade coffee is used. Vegan and vegetarian dining options are available for every meal.

Transportation Provides public transportation access to local destinations.

Buildings and Grounds *Renovation and maintenance:* registered for LEED certification for new construction and/or renovation; uses a Green Seal certified cleaning service. *Campus grounds care:* uses water conservation devices; employs strategies to reduce light pollution; landscapes with native plant species; protects, restores, and/or creates habitat on campus; applies to its grounds only pesticides and fertilizers allowable under the U.S. Department of Agriculture's standards for crop production.

Recycling *Programs and activities:* sustains a computer/technology recycling program; maintains an on-campus recycling center; replaces paper materials with online alternatives; limits free printing in computer labs and libraries. *Campus dining operations:* uses reusable dishware; operates without trays; uses bulk condiment dispensers and decreased packaging for to-go food service purchases.

Energy Currently uses or plans to use timers to regulate temperatures based on occupancy hours; motion, infrared, and/or light sensors to reduce energy uses for lighting; LED lighting; and energy-related performance contracting.

Purchasing Sustainability criteria used in purchasing include Energy Star (EPA), WaterSense (EPA), and Green Cleaning Products (Green Seal/Environmental Choice certified).

Contact Vice President for Business Affairs and Treasurer, Marywood University, 2300 Adams Avenue, Liberal Arts Building #89, Scranton, PA 18509. *Phone:* 570-348-6222. *Fax:* 570-961-4739. *E-mail:* jxgarvey@marywood.edu. *Web site:* www.marywood.edu/.

Messiah College
Grantham, Pennsylvania

Sustainability Initiatives Messiah College's president has signed the American College & University Presidents Climate Commitment. Messiah College has Green Fees (optional/required) dedicated to sustainability initiatives.

Academics *Sustainability courses and programs:* sustainability-focused course(s) or lecture series.

Student Services and Green Events *Sustainability leadership:* sustainability committee/advisory council, recycling manager. *Student clubs and activities:* student club(s)/group(s) focused on sustainability. *Major sustainability events:* Sustainability Forum, Earth Week activities. *Housing and facilities:* sustainability-themed housing, on-campus organic garden for students.

Food Sustainable, organic, and/or locally produced foods available in on-campus dining facilities. Fair Trade coffee is used. Vegan and vegetarian dining options are available for every meal.

Buildings and Grounds *Campus grounds care:* landscapes with native plant species; protects, restores, and/or creates habitat on campus.

Recycling *Programs and activities:* sustains a computer/technology recycling program; sustains a post-consumer food waste composting program; composts yard waste; limits free printing in computer labs and libraries. *Campus dining operations:* uses reusable dishware; offers discounts for reusable mugs; uses bulk condiment dispensers and decreased packaging for to-go food service purchases.

Energy Currently uses or plans to use alternative sources of power (geothermal energy, hydroelectricity/water power, solar energy, and wind energy); timers to regulate temperatures based on occupancy hours; motion, infrared, and/or light sensors to reduce energy uses for lighting; and LED lighting.

Purchasing Sustainability criteria used in purchasing include Energy Star (EPA) and Forest Stewardship Council

(FSC) or American Forest and Paper Association's Sustainable Forestry Initiative (SFI) paper.

Contact Environmental Health and Safety Manager, Messiah College, Box 3001, One College Avenue, Grantham, PA 17027. *Phone:* 717-691-6011 Ext. 3560. *Fax:* 717-796-5247. *Web site:* www.messiah.edu/.

Philadelphia Biblical University
Langhorne, Pennsylvania

Student Services and Green Events *Student clubs and activities:* outreach materials available about on-campus sustainability efforts.

Food Vegan and vegetarian dining options are available for every meal.

Transportation Provides free on-campus transportation (bus or other).

Buildings and Grounds *Campus grounds care:* uses water conservation devices; landscapes with native plant species.

Recycling *Programs and activities:* sustains a computer/technology recycling program; replaces paper materials with online alternatives; limits free printing in computer labs and libraries. *Campus dining operations:* uses reusable dishware; operates without trays; offers discounts for reusable mugs.

Energy Currently uses or plans to use timers to regulate temperatures based on occupancy hours and motion, infrared, and/or light sensors to reduce energy uses for lighting.

Purchasing Sustainability criteria used in purchasing include Green Cleaning Products (Green Seal/Environmental Choice certified).

Contact Philadelphia Biblical University, 200 Manor Avenue, Langhorne, PA 19047-2990. *Phone:* 215-752-5800. *Web site:* www.pbu.edu/.

Philadelphia University
Philadelphia, Pennsylvania

Sustainability Initiatives Philadelphia University is a signatory to the Talloires Declaration.

Academics *Sustainability-focused undergraduate major(s):* Environmental and Conservation Biology (BS), Environmental Sustainability (BS). *Sustainability-focused graduate degree program(s):* Sustainable Design (MS). *Sustainability courses and programs:* sustainability-focused course(s) or lecture series.

Student Services and Green Events *Sustainability leadership:* sustainability committee/advisory council, recycling manager, energy manager, sustainability-focused student government. *Student clubs and activities:* student club(s)/group(s) focused on sustainability, outreach materials available about on-campus sustainability efforts. *Major sustainability events:* Panel presentation—Inside Philadelphia's Greenest Companies: Sustainability Strategies and "Green Collar Careers". *Housing and facilities:* sustainability-themed housing.

Food Sustainable, organic, and/or locally produced foods available in on-campus dining facilities. Fair Trade coffee is used. Vegan and vegetarian dining options are available for every meal.

Transportation Provides free on-campus transportation (bus or other), public transportation access to local destinations, a bike loan/rental program, and a car sharing program.

Buildings and Grounds *Renovation and maintenance:* uses a Green Seal certified cleaning service. *Campus*

grounds care: uses water conservation devices; employs strategies to reduce light pollution; landscapes with native plant species; protects, restores, and/or creates habitat on campus.

Recycling *Programs and activities:* sustains a computer/technology recycling program; maintains an on-campus recycling center; composts yard waste; reuses chemicals; replaces paper materials with online alternatives. *Campus dining operations:* uses reusable dishware; operates without trays; offers discounts for reusable mugs; uses bulk condiment dispensers and decreased packaging for to-go food service purchases.

Energy Currently uses or plans to use timers to regulate temperatures based on occupancy hours; motion, infrared, and/or light sensors to reduce energy uses for lighting; LED lighting; and energy-related performance contracting.

Purchasing Sustainability criteria used in purchasing include Energy Star (EPA) and Green Cleaning Products (Green Seal/Environmental Choice certified).

Contact Chair, Sustainability Committee/Vice President for Finance and Administration/Treasurer, Philadelphia University, School House Lane & Henry Avenue, Philadelphia, PA 19144. *Phone:* 215-951-2700. *E-mail:* lorantasb@PhilaU.edu. *Web site:* www.philau.edu/.

Rosemont College
Rosemont, Pennsylvania

Sustainability Initiatives Rosemont College is a member of the Association for the Advancement of Sustainability in Higher Education (AASHE). This institution's president has signed the American College & University Presidents Climate Commitment.

Academics *Sustainability-focused undergraduate major(s):* Biology, Chemistry, Ecology, Religious Studies. *Sustainability courses and programs:* sustainability-focused course(s) or lecture series, noncredit sustainability course(s).

Student Services and Green Events *Sustainability leadership:* sustainability coordinator/director, sustainability committee/advisory council, recycling manager, energy manager. *Student clubs and activities:* Campus Climate Challenge, student club(s)/group(s) focused on sustainability, outreach materials available about on-campus sustainability efforts. *Major sustainability events:* Focus the Nation 24-hour Teach-In, National RecycleMania Competition.

Food Sustainable, organic, and/or locally produced foods available in on-campus dining facilities. Vegan and vegetarian dining options are available for every meal.

Transportation Provides free on-campus transportation (bus or other) and public transportation access to local destinations.

Buildings and Grounds *Campus grounds care:* uses water conservation devices; landscapes with native plant species; protects, restores, and/or creates habitat on campus.

Recycling *Events and organizations:* RecycleMania. *Programs and activities:* sustains a computer/technology recycling program; composts yard waste; replaces paper materials with online alternatives. *Campus dining operations:* uses reusable dishware; operates without trays; uses bulk condiment dispensers and decreased packaging for to-go food service purchases.

Energy Currently uses or plans to use alternative sources of power and motion, infrared, and/or light sensors to reduce energy uses for lighting.

Purchasing Sustainability criteria used in purchasing include Energy Star (EPA) and Green Cleaning Products (Green Seal/Environmental Choice certified).

Contact Director of Public Relations, Rosemont College, 1400 Montgomery Avenue, Rosemont, PA 19010. *Phone:* 610-527-0200 Ext. 2967. *Fax:* 610-520-4373. *E-mail:* akropp@rosemont.edu. *Web site:* www.rosemont.edu/.

Saint Joseph's University
Philadelphia, Pennsylvania

Sustainability Initiatives Saint Joseph's University is a member of the Association for the Advancement of Sustainability in Higher Education (AASHE).

Academics *Sustainability-focused undergraduate major(s):* Environmental Science (BS). *Sustainability courses and programs:* sustainability-focused course(s) or lecture series.

Student Services and Green Events *Sustainability leadership:* sustainability coordinator/director, sustainability committee/advisory council, recycling manager. *Student clubs and activities:* student club(s)/group(s) focused on sustainability. *Major sustainability events:* Asia and the Environment Conference 2009.

Food Vegan and vegetarian dining options are available for every meal.

Transportation Provides free on-campus transportation (bus or other), public transportation access to local destinations, a car sharing program, and incentives to carpool or use public transportation.

Buildings and Grounds *Campus grounds care:* uses water conservation devices; landscapes with native plant species; applies to its grounds only pesticides and fertilizers allowable under the U.S. Department of Agriculture's standards for crop production.

Recycling *Events and organizations:* RecycleMania. *Programs and activities:* sustains a computer/technology recycling program; composts yard waste; reuses surplus department/office supplies; replaces paper materials with online alternatives. *Campus dining operations:* operates without trays; uses bulk condiment dispensers and decreased packaging for to-go food service purchases.

Energy Currently uses or plans to use motion, infrared, and/or light sensors to reduce energy uses for lighting and LED lighting.

Purchasing Sustainability criteria used in purchasing include Energy Star (EPA) and Green Cleaning Products (Green Seal/Environmental Choice certified).

Contact Director of Health, Safety, and Environmental Compliance, Saint Joseph's University, 5600 City Avenue, Moore Building, Philadelphia, PA 19131. *Phone:* 610-660-3037. *Fax:* 610-660-3019. *E-mail:* hheim01@sju.edu. *Web site:* www.sju.edu/.

Swarthmore College
Swarthmore, Pennsylvania

Sustainability Initiatives Swarthmore College is a member of the Association for the Advancement of Sustainability in Higher Education (AASHE).

Academics *Sustainability-focused undergraduate major(s):* Environmental Science, special Interdisciplinary major. *Sustainability courses and programs:* sustainability-focused course(s) or lecture series.

Student Services and Green Events *Sustainability leadership:* sustainability committee/advisory council, recycling manager, energy manager. *Student clubs and activities:* student club(s)/group(s) focused on sustainability. *Major sustainability events:* Lax Conference on Entrepreneurship focused on "The Business of Sustainability", frequent lectures. *Housing and facilities:* on-campus organic garden for students.

Food Sustainable, organic, and/or locally produced foods available in on-campus dining facilities. Fair Trade coffee is used. Vegan and vegetarian dining options are available for every meal.

Transportation Provides free on-campus transportation (bus or other), public transportation access to local destinations, a car sharing program, and incentives to carpool or use public transportation.

Buildings and Grounds *Renovation and maintenance:* registered for LEED certification for new construction and/or renovation. *Campus grounds care:* uses water conservation devices; landscapes with native plant species; protects, restores, and/or creates habitat on campus.

Recycling *Programs and activities:* sustains a computer/technology recycling program; sustains a pre-consumer food waste composting program; sustains a post-consumer food waste composting program; composts yard waste; replaces paper materials with online alternatives. *Campus dining operations:* uses reusable dishware; uses bulk condiment dispensers and decreased packaging for to-go food service purchases.

Energy Currently uses or plans to use alternative sources of power (wind energy); timers to regulate temperatures based on occupancy hours; motion, infrared, and/or light sensors to reduce energy uses for lighting; and LED lighting.

Purchasing Sustainability criteria used in purchasing include Energy Star (EPA) and Green Cleaning Products (Green Seal/Environmental Choice certified).

Contact Director of Maintenance/Co-Chair of the Sustainability Committee, Swarthmore College, 500 College Avenue, Swarthmore, PA 19081. *Phone:* 610-328-8278. *Fax:* 610-328-8574. *E-mail:* rthayer1@swarthmore.edu. *Web site:* www.swarthmore.edu/.

Temple University
Philadelphia, Pennsylvania

Sustainability Initiatives Temple University's president has signed the American College & University Presidents Climate Commitment.

Academics *Sustainability-focused undergraduate major(s):* Environmental Studies (BA), Environmental Studies (BS). *Sustainability-focused graduate degree program(s):* Sustainable Community Planning (MS). *Sustainability courses and programs:* sustainability-focused course(s) or lecture series, noncredit sustainability course(s).

Student Services and Green Events *Sustainability leadership:* sustainability coordinator/director, sustainability committee/advisory council, recycling manager, energy manager. *Student clubs and activities:* student club(s)/group(s) focused on sustainability. *Major sustainability events:* Campus Sustainability Day, National Teach-In on Global Warming.

Food Sustainable, organic, and/or locally produced foods available in on-campus dining facilities. Fair Trade coffee is used. Vegan and vegetarian dining options are available for every meal.

Transportation Provides free on-campus transportation (bus or other), public transportation access to local destinations, a car sharing program, and incentives to carpool or use public transportation.

Buildings and Grounds *Campus grounds care:* uses water conservation devices; landscapes with native plant species; protects, restores, and/or creates habitat on campus.

Recycling *Events and organizations:* RecycleMania. *Programs and activities:* sustains a computer/technology recycling program; composts yard waste; reuses chemicals; replaces paper materials with online alternatives; limits free printing in computer labs and libraries. *Campus dining operations:* uses reusable dishware; offers discounts for reusable mugs; uses bulk condiment dispensers and decreased packaging for to-go food service purchases.

Energy Currently uses or plans to use motion, infrared, and/or light sensors to reduce energy uses for lighting.

Purchasing Sustainability criteria used in purchasing include Energy Star (EPA) and Forest Stewardship Council (FSC) or American Forest and Paper Association's Sustainable Forestry Initiative (SFI) paper.

Contact Director of Sustainability, Temple University, 1913 North Broad Street, Mitten Hall, Lower Level, Philadelphia, PA 19122. *Phone:* 215-204-2517. *Fax:* 215-204-3358. *E-mail:* sustainability@temple.edu. *Web site:* www.temple.edu/.

Ursinus College
Collegeville, Pennsylvania

Sustainability Initiatives Ursinus College's president has signed the American College & University Presidents Climate Commitment.

Academics *Sustainability-focused undergraduate major(s):* Environmental Studies (BA, BS). *Sustainability courses and programs:* sustainability-focused course(s) or lecture series.

Student Services and Green Events *Sustainability leadership:* sustainability committee/advisory council, recycling manager, energy manager. *Student clubs and activities:* student club(s)/group(s) focused on sustainability. *Major sustainability events:* Focus the Nation conference, alternative energy conference. *Housing and facilities:* sustainability-themed housing, on-campus organic garden for students.

Food Sustainable, organic, and/or locally produced foods available in on-campus dining facilities. Fair Trade coffee is used. Vegan and vegetarian dining options are available for every meal.

Transportation Provides public transportation access to local destinations, a bike loan/rental program, and a car sharing program.

Buildings and Grounds *Campus grounds care:* uses water conservation devices; employs strategies to reduce light pollution; landscapes with native plant species; protects, restores, and/or creates habitat on campus.

Recycling *Programs and activities:* sustains a computer/technology recycling program; maintains an on-campus recycling center; composts yard waste; replaces paper materials with online alternatives; limits free printing in computer labs and libraries. *Campus dining operations:* uses reusable dishware; operates without trays; offers discounts for reusable mugs; uses bulk condiment dispensers and decreased packaging for to-go food service purchases.

Energy Currently uses or plans to use timers to regulate temperatures based on occupancy hours; motion, infrared, and/or light sensors to reduce energy uses for lighting; and vending machine motion sensors.

Purchasing Sustainability criteria used in purchasing include Energy Star (EPA) and Green Cleaning Products (Green Seal/Environmental Choice certified).

Contact Ursinus College, Box 1000, Main Street, Collegeville, PA 19426-1000. *Phone:* 610-409-3000. *Web site:* www.ursinus.edu/.

Washington & Jefferson College
Washington, Pennsylvania

Sustainability Initiatives Washington & Jefferson College's president has signed the American College & University Presidents Climate Commitment. Washington & Jefferson College has Green Fees (optional/required) dedicated to sustainability initiatives.

Academics *Sustainability-focused undergraduate major(s):* Environmental Studies (BA). *Sustainability courses and programs:* sustainability-focused course(s) or lecture series.

Student Services and Green Events *Sustainability leadership:* sustainability committee/advisory council, recycling manager, sustainability-focused student government. *Student clubs and activities:* student club(s)/group(s) focused on sustainability, outreach materials available about on-campus sustainability efforts. *Major sustainability events:* National Teach-In on Global Warming 2009, host of symposia on coal mining issues. *Housing and facilities:* sustainability-themed housing.

Food Sustainable, organic, and/or locally produced foods available in on-campus dining facilities. Vegan and vegetarian dining options are available for every meal.

Transportation Provides public transportation access to local destinations.

Buildings and Grounds *Renovation and maintenance:* registered for LEED certification for new construction and/or renovation; uses a Green Seal certified cleaning service. *Campus grounds care:* uses water conservation devices; landscapes with native plant species.

Recycling *Events and organizations:* RecycleMania. *Programs and activities:* sustains a computer/technology recycling program; sustains a post-consumer food waste composting program; composts yard waste; replaces paper materials with online alternatives. *Campus dining operations:* uses reusable dishware; offers discounts for reusable mugs; uses bulk condiment dispensers and decreased packaging for to-go food service purchases.

Energy Currently uses or plans to use alternative sources of power (wind energy).

Purchasing Sustainability criteria used in purchasing include Energy Star (EPA) and Green Cleaning Products (Green Seal/Environmental Choice certified).

Contact Associate Professor of Biology, Washington & Jefferson College, 60 South Lincoln Street, Washington, PA 15301. *Phone:* 724-503-1001 Ext. 3358. *E-mail:* reast@washjeff.edu. *Web site:* www.washjeff.edu/.

Puerto Rico

University of Puerto Rico at Bayamón
Bayamón, Puerto Rico

Academics *Sustainability courses and programs:* noncredit sustainability course(s).

Student Services and Green Events *Sustainability leadership:* recycling manager, energy manager.

Food Sustainable, organic, and/or locally produced foods available in on-campus dining facilities.

Transportation Provides public transportation access to local destinations and a car sharing program.

Buildings and Grounds *Renovation and maintenance:* uses a Green Seal certified cleaning service. *Campus grounds care:* uses water conservation devices; employs strategies to reduce light pollution; landscapes with native plant species; protects, restores, and/or creates habitat on campus.

Recycling *Events and organizations:* RecycleMania. *Programs and activities:* sustains a computer/technology recycling program; reuses surplus department/office supplies; replaces paper materials with online alternatives; limits free printing in computer labs and libraries.

Energy Currently uses or plans to use alternative sources of power; timers to regulate temperatures based on occupancy hours; and motion, infrared, and/or light sensors to reduce energy uses for lighting.

Purchasing Sustainability criteria used in purchasing include Energy Star (EPA), Green Cleaning Products (Green Seal/Environmental Choice certified), and Forest Stewardship Council (FSC) or American Forest and Paper Association's Sustainable Forestry Initiative (SFI) paper.

Contact University of Puerto Rico at Bayamón, 170 Carretera 174 Parque Industrial Minillas, Bayamón, PR 00959. *Phone:* 787-786-2885. *Web site:* www.uprb.edu/.

Rhode Island

Roger Williams University
Bristol, Rhode Island

Sustainability Initiatives Roger Williams University's president has signed the American College & University Presidents Climate Commitment.

Academics *Sustainability-focused undergraduate major(s):* Core Concentration Environmental Science, Environmental Chemistry concentration, Environmental Science (BA). *Sustainability courses and programs:* sustainability-focused course(s) or lecture series, noncredit sustainability course(s).

Student Services and Green Events *Sustainability leadership:* sustainability coordinator/director, sustainability committee/advisory council. *Student clubs and activities:* student club(s)/group(s) focused on sustainability, outreach materials available about on-campus sustainability efforts. *Major sustainability events:* RecycleMania and Earth Day activities. *Housing and facilities:* sustainability-themed housing.

Food Sustainable, organic, and/or locally produced foods available in on-campus dining facilities. Fair Trade coffee is used. Vegan and vegetarian dining options are available for every meal.

Transportation Provides free on-campus transportation (bus or other), public transportation access to local destinations, and incentives to carpool or use public transportation.

Buildings and Grounds *Percentage of institution's eligible buildings as of September 2008 meeting LEED and/or LEED-EB certification criteria:* 10%. *Renovation and maintenance:* uses a Green Seal certified cleaning service. *Campus grounds care:* uses water conservation devices; landscapes with native plant species; protects, restores, and/or creates habitat on campus.

Recycling *Events and organizations:* RecycleMania. *Programs and activities:* sustains a computer/technology recycling program; sustains a pre-consumer food waste composting program; sustains a post-consumer food waste composting program; replaces paper materials with online alternatives; limits free printing in computer labs and libraries. *Campus dining operations:* uses reusable dishware; offers discounts for reusable mugs; uses bulk condiment dispensers and decreased packaging for to-go food service purchases.

Energy Currently uses or plans to use motion, infrared, and/or light sensors to reduce energy uses for lighting and LED lighting.

Purchasing Sustainability criteria used in purchasing include Energy Star (EPA) and Green Cleaning Products (Green Seal/Environmental Choice certified).

Contact Dean of School of Art Architecture and Historic Preservation, Roger Williams University, 1 Old Ferry Road, Bristol, RI 02809. *Phone:* 401-254-3607. *E-mail:* swhite@ rwu.edu. *Web site:* www.rwu.edu/.

South Carolina

Coastal Carolina University
Conway, South Carolina

Sustainability Initiatives Coastal Carolina University is a member of the Association for the Advancement of Sustainability in Higher Education (AASHE).

Academics *Sustainability courses and programs:* sustainability-focused course(s) or lecture series.

Student Services and Green Events *Sustainability leadership:* sustainability coordinator/director, sustainability committee/advisory council, sustainability-focused student government. *Student clubs and activities:* Campus Climate Challenge, student club(s)/group(s) focused on sustainability, outreach materials available about on-campus sustainability efforts. *Major sustainability events:* Earth Month.

Food Vegan and vegetarian dining options are available for every meal.

Transportation Provides free on-campus transportation (bus or other), public transportation access to local destinations, and a bike loan/rental program.

Buildings and Grounds *Renovation and maintenance:* registered for LEED certification for new construction and/or renovation; uses a Green Seal certified cleaning service. *Campus grounds care:* uses water conservation devices; landscapes with native plant species; protects, restores, and/or creates habitat on campus.

Recycling *Programs and activities:* maintains an on-campus recycling center; sustains a post-consumer food waste composting program; composts yard waste; replaces paper materials with online alternatives. *Campus dining operations:* uses reusable dishware; operates without trays; offers discounts for reusable mugs; uses bulk condiment dispensers and decreased packaging for to-go food service purchases.

Energy Currently uses or plans to use alternative sources of power (solar energy) and motion, infrared, and/or light sensors to reduce energy uses for lighting.

Contact Sustainability Coordinator, Coastal Carolina University, PO Box 261954, Conway, SC 29528. *Phone:* 843-349-2389. *Fax:* 843-349-2545. *E-mail:* mgmitzne@coastal.edu. *Web site:* www.coastal.edu/.

College of Charleston
Charleston, South Carolina

Sustainability Initiatives College of Charleston's president has signed the American College & University Presidents Climate Commitment.

Student Services and Green Events *Sustainability leadership:* sustainability committee/advisory council, recycling manager. *Housing and facilities:* sustainability-themed housing.

Food Fair Trade coffee is used. Vegan and vegetarian dining options are available for every meal.

Transportation Provides free on-campus transportation (bus or other), public transportation access to local destinations, and incentives to carpool or use public transportation.

Buildings and Grounds *Renovation and maintenance:* registered for LEED certification for new construction and/or renovation.

Recycling *Events and organizations:* RecycleMania. *Programs and activities:* replaces paper materials with online alternatives; limits free printing in computer labs and libraries. *Campus dining operations:* uses reusable dishware; operates without trays; offers discounts for reusable mugs.

Contact Librarian, College of Charleston, Addlestone Library, 66 George Street, Charleston, SC 29424. *Phone:* 843-953-1600. *Fax:* 843-953-8019. *E-mail:* callicottb@cofc.edu. *Web site:* www.cofc.edu/.

Medical University of South Carolina
Charleston, South Carolina

Sustainability Initiatives Medical University of South Carolina's president has signed the American College & University Presidents Climate Commitment.

Student Services and Green Events *Sustainability leadership:* sustainability coordinator/director, recycling manager, sustainability-focused student government. *Student clubs and activities:* outreach materials available about on-campus sustainability efforts.

Food Sustainable, organic, and/or locally produced foods available in on-campus dining facilities. Fair Trade coffee is used. Vegan and vegetarian dining options are available for every meal.

Transportation Provides free on-campus transportation (bus or other), public transportation access to local destinations, and incentives to carpool or use public transportation.

Buildings and Grounds *Renovation and maintenance:* registered for LEED certification for new construction and/or renovation. *Campus grounds care:* uses water conservation devices; landscapes with native plant species; protects, restores, and/or creates habitat on campus.

Recycling *Events and organizations:* RecycleMania, WasteWise (EPA). *Programs and activities:* sustains a computer/technology recycling program; maintains an on-campus recycling center; composts yard waste; reuses surplus department/office supplies; replaces paper materials with online alternatives; limits free printing in computer labs and libraries. *Campus dining operations:* offers discounts for reusable mugs; uses bulk condiment dispensers and decreased packaging for to-go food service purchases.

Energy Currently uses or plans to use alternative sources of power (geothermal energy); timers to regulate temperatures based on occupancy hours; LED lighting; and energy-related performance contracting.

Purchasing Sustainability criteria used in purchasing include Green Cleaning Products (Green Seal/Environmental Choice certified).

Contact Medical University of South Carolina, 97 Jonathan Lucas Street, MSC 190, Charleston, SC 29425. *Phone:* 843-792-9745. *E-mail:* davilac@musc.edu. *Web site:* www.musc.edu/.

University of South Carolina
Columbia, South Carolina

Sustainability Initiatives University of South Carolina's president has signed the American College & University Presidents Climate Commitment.

Academics *Sustainability-focused graduate degree program(s):* Earth and Environmental Resource Management

(MEERM). *Sustainability courses and programs:* sustainability-focused course(s) or lecture series, noncredit sustainability course(s).

Student Services and Green Events *Sustainability leadership:* sustainability coordinator/director, sustainability committee/advisory council, recycling manager, energy manager, sustainability-focused student government. *Student clubs and activities:* Campus Climate Challenge, Public Interest Research Group (PIRG) chapter on campus, student club(s)/group(s) focused on sustainability, outreach materials available about on-campus sustainability efforts. *Major sustainability events:* Earth Summit, Earth Day, Youth Powershift Conference, Sustainability Forum, USGBC Chapter events, Green Movie Series, Move In, Give It Up, RecycleMania. *Housing and facilities:* sustainability-themed housing, model dorm room that demonstrates sustainable living principles, on-campus organic garden for students.

Food Sustainable, organic, and/or locally produced foods available in on-campus dining facilities. Fair Trade coffee is used. Vegan and vegetarian dining options are available for every meal.

Transportation Provides free on-campus transportation (bus or other) and public transportation access to local destinations.

Buildings and Grounds *Renovation and maintenance:* registered for LEED certification for new construction and/or renovation; uses a Green Seal certified cleaning service. *Campus grounds care:* uses water conservation devices; employs strategies to reduce light pollution; landscapes with native plant species; protects, restores, and/or creates habitat on campus.

Recycling *Events and organizations:* WasteWise (EPA). *Programs and activities:* reuses surplus department/office supplies; reuses chemicals; replaces paper materials with online alternatives; limits free printing in computer labs and libraries. *Campus dining operations:* uses reusable dishware; operates without trays; offers discounts for reusable mugs.

Energy Currently uses or plans to use alternative sources of power (biomass energy and solar energy); timers to regulate temperatures based on occupancy hours; motion, infrared, and/or light sensors to reduce energy uses for lighting; LED lighting; vending machine motion sensors; and energy-related performance contracting.

Purchasing Sustainability criteria used in purchasing include Energy Star (EPA), WaterSense (EPA), Green Electronics Council (GEC) Electronic Product Environmental Assessment Tool (EPEAT) Silver or Gold, and Green Cleaning Products (Green Seal/Environmental Choice certified).

Contact Sustainability Coordinator, University of South Carolina, 743 Greene Street, Columbia, SC 29208. *Phone:* 803-777-5428. *E-mail:* koman@sc.edu. *Web site:* www.sc.edu/.

University of South Carolina Beaufort
Beaufort, South Carolina

Sustainability Initiatives University of South Carolina Beaufort's president has signed the American College & University Presidents Climate Commitment.

Student Services and Green Events *Sustainability leadership:* energy manager, sustainability-focused student government.

Food Sustainable, organic, and/or locally produced foods available in on-campus dining facilities. Vegan and vegetarian dining options are available for every meal.

Transportation Provides free on-campus transportation (bus or other).

Buildings and Grounds *Campus grounds care:* uses water conservation devices; employs strategies to reduce light pollution; landscapes with native plant species; protects, restores, and/or creates habitat on campus.

Recycling *Programs and activities:* sustains a computer/technology recycling program; maintains an on-campus recycling center; composts yard waste; reuses surplus department/office supplies; replaces paper materials with online alternatives; limits free printing in computer labs and libraries. *Campus dining operations:* uses reusable dishware; operates without trays; offers discounts for reusable mugs; uses bulk condiment dispensers and decreased packaging for to-go food service purchases.

Energy Currently uses or plans to use alternative sources of power; timers to regulate temperatures based on occupancy hours; motion, infrared, and/or light sensors to reduce energy uses for lighting; and LED lighting.

Contact Director of Facilities, University of South Carolina Beaufort, One University Boulevard, Bluffton, SK 29909. *Phone:* 843-208-8040. *Fax:* 843-208-8015. *E-mail:* rparrot@uscb.edu. *Web site:* www.sc.edu/beaufort/.

Wofford College
Spartanburg, South Carolina

Sustainability Initiatives Wofford College's president has signed the American College & University Presidents Climate Commitment.

Academics *Sustainability-focused undergraduate major(s):* Environmental Studies (BS, BA). *Sustainability courses and programs:* sustainability-focused course(s) or lecture series.

Student Services and Green Events *Sustainability leadership:* sustainability coordinator/director, sustainability committee/advisory council, recycling manager, energy manager. *Student clubs and activities:* student club(s)/group(s) focused on sustainability, outreach materials available about on-campus sustainability efforts. *Major sustainability events:* Global Teach-In.

Food Sustainable, organic, and/or locally produced foods available in on-campus dining facilities. Fair Trade coffee is used. Vegan and vegetarian dining options are available for every meal.

Transportation Provides public transportation access to local destinations and a bike loan/rental program.

Buildings and Grounds *Percentage of institution's eligible buildings as of September 2008 meeting LEED and/or LEED-EB certification criteria:* .01%. *Campus grounds care:* uses water conservation devices; employs strategies to reduce light pollution; protects, restores, and/or creates habitat on campus.

Recycling *Events and organizations:* RecycleMania. *Programs and activities:* sustains a computer/technology recycling program; replaces paper materials with online alternatives. *Campus dining operations:* uses bulk condiment dispensers and decreased packaging for to-go food service purchases.

Purchasing Sustainability criteria used in purchasing include Energy Star (EPA) and Green Cleaning Products (Green Seal/Environmental Choice certified).

Contact Sustainability Coordinator, Wofford College, Wofford College Business Office, 429 North Church Street, Spartanburg, SC 29303. *Phone:* 864-205-2047. *Fax:* 864-597-4237. *E-mail:* allyn.steele@sdsgriffin.org. *Web site:* www.wofford.edu/.

South Dakota

Presentation College
Aberdeen, South Dakota

Student Services and Green Events *Sustainability leadership:* recycling manager.

Food Vegan and vegetarian dining options are available for every meal.

Transportation Provides public transportation access to local destinations.

Buildings and Grounds *Percentage of institution's eligible buildings as of September 2008 meeting LEED and/or LEED-EB certification criteria:* 20%. *Campus grounds care:* employs strategies to reduce light pollution; landscapes with native plant species; applies to its grounds only pesticides and fertilizers allowable under the U.S. Department of Agriculture's standards for crop production.

Recycling *Programs and activities:* sustains a computer/technology recycling program; maintains an on-campus recycling center; reuses surplus department/office supplies; replaces paper materials with online alternatives; limits free printing in computer labs and libraries. *Campus dining operations:* uses reusable dishware; offers discounts for reusable mugs; uses bulk condiment dispensers and decreased packaging for to-go food service purchases.

Energy Currently uses or plans to use alternative sources of power; timers to regulate temperatures based on occupancy hours; and LED lighting.

Purchasing Sustainability criteria used in purchasing include Energy Star (EPA).

Contact Presentation College, 1500 North Main Street, Aberdeen, SD 57401-1299. *Phone:* 605-225-1634. *Web site:* www.presentation.edu/.

Tennessee

Fisk University
Nashville, Tennessee

Student Services and Green Events *Sustainability leadership:* sustainability committee/advisory council. *Student clubs and activities:* outreach materials available about on-campus sustainability efforts.

Recycling *Events and organizations:* WasteWise (EPA). *Programs and activities:* sustains a computer/technology recycling program; replaces paper materials with online alternatives; limits free printing in computer labs and libraries.

Contact Vice President for Institutional Assessment and Research, Fisk University, 1000 17th Avenue North, Nashville, TN 37208. *Phone:* 615-329-8697. *E-mail:* mfleming@fisk.edu. *Web site:* www.fisk.edu/.

Freed-Hardeman University
Henderson, Tennessee

Student Services and Green Events *Sustainability leadership:* sustainability committee/advisory council, recycling manager, energy manager. *Housing and facilities:* student-run café that serves environmentally or socially preferable foods.

Buildings and Grounds *Percentage of institution's eligible buildings as of September 2008 meeting LEED and/or LEED-EB certification criteria:* 5%. *Renovation and maintenance:* uses a Green Seal certified cleaning service. *Cam-*

pus grounds care: uses water conservation devices; landscapes with native plant species; protects, restores, and/or creates habitat on campus.

Recycling *Programs and activities:* sustains a computer/technology recycling program; maintains an on-campus recycling center; reuses surplus department/office supplies; replaces paper materials with online alternatives; limits free printing in computer labs and libraries. *Campus dining operations:* uses reusable dishware; operates without trays; offers discounts for reusable mugs; uses bulk condiment dispensers and decreased packaging for to-go food service purchases.

Energy Currently uses or plans to use timers to regulate temperatures based on occupancy hours and energy-related performance contracting.

Purchasing Sustainability criteria used in purchasing include Energy Star (EPA) and Green Cleaning Products (Green Seal/Environmental Choice certified).

Contact Freed-Hardeman University, 158 East Main Street, Henderson, TN 38340-2399. *Phone:* 731-989-6000. *Web site:* www.fhu.edu/.

Sewanee: The University of the South
Sewanee, Tennessee

Sustainability Initiatives Sewanee: The University of the South is a member of the Association for the Advancement of Sustainability in Higher Education (AASHE) and a signatory to the Talloires Declaration. This institution's president has signed the American College & University Presidents Climate Commitment. Sewanee: The University of the South has Green Fees (optional/required) dedicated to sustainability initiatives.

Academics *Sustainability-focused undergraduate major(s):* Environmental Studies: Ecology and Biodiversity (BA, BS), Environmental Studies: Environmental Chemistry (BA, BS), Environmental Studies: Natural Resources (BA, BS), Environmental Studies: Policy (BA). *Sustainability courses and programs:* sustainability-focused course(s) or lecture series.

Student Services and Green Events *Sustainability leadership:* sustainability coordinator/director, sustainability committee/advisory council, recycling manager, energy manager, sustainability-focused student government. *Student clubs and activities:* student club(s)/group(s) focused on sustainability. *Major sustainability events:* Wind Power Conference, Green Pledge Dinner, ECO-Cup. *Housing and facilities:* sustainability-themed housing, model dorm room that demonstrates sustainable living principles, on-campus organic garden for students.

Food Sustainable, organic, and/or locally produced foods available in on-campus dining facilities. Vegan and vegetarian dining options are available for every meal.

Buildings and Grounds *Percentage of institution's eligible buildings as of September 2008 meeting LEED and/or LEED-EB certification criteria:* 1%. *Renovation and maintenance:* registered for LEED certification for new construction and/or renovation. *Campus grounds care:* uses water conservation devices; employs strategies to reduce light pollution; landscapes with native plant species; protects, restores, and/or creates habitat on campus; applies to its grounds only pesticides and fertilizers allowable under the U.S. Department of Agriculture's standards for crop production.

Recycling *Programs and activities:* sustains a computer/technology recycling program; maintains an on-campus recycling center; sustains a post-consumer food waste composting program; composts yard waste; reuses surplus

department/office supplies. *Campus dining operations:* uses reusable dishware; operates without trays; offers discounts for reusable mugs; uses bulk condiment dispensers and decreased packaging for to-go food service purchases.

Energy Currently uses or plans to use alternative sources of power; timers to regulate temperatures based on occupancy hours; motion, infrared, and/or light sensors to reduce energy uses for lighting; and LED lighting.

Purchasing Sustainability criteria used in purchasing include Energy Star (EPA) and Green Cleaning Products (Green Seal/Environmental Choice certified).

Contact Sustainability Coordinator, Student Affairs, Sewanee: The University of the South, 735 University Avenue, Sewanee, TN 37383. *Phone:* 931-598-2353. *E-mail:* llbutler@sewanee.edu. *Web site:* www.sewanee.edu/.

Union University
Jackson, Tennessee

Academics *Sustainability-focused undergraduate major(s):* Conservation Biology. *Sustainability courses and programs:* sustainability-focused course(s) or lecture series.

Student Services and Green Events *Sustainability leadership:* sustainability coordinator/director, sustainability committee/advisory council, recycling manager. *Student clubs and activities:* student club(s)/group(s) focused on sustainability. *Major sustainability events:* Global Warming Conference, Creation Care Town and Gown Series.

Food Sustainable, organic, and/or locally produced foods available in on-campus dining facilities. Fair Trade coffee is used. Vegan and vegetarian dining options are available for every meal.

Transportation Provides public transportation access to local destinations.

Buildings and Grounds *Percentage of institution's eligible buildings as of September 2008 meeting LEED and/or LEED-EB certification criteria:* 50%. *Campus grounds care:* uses water conservation devices; landscapes with native plant species; protects, restores, and/or creates habitat on campus; applies to its grounds only pesticides and fertilizers allowable under the U.S. Department of Agriculture's standards for crop production.

Recycling *Events and organizations:* RecycleMania, WasteWise (EPA). *Programs and activities:* sustains a computer/technology recycling program; maintains an on-campus recycling center; reuses chemicals; replaces paper materials with online alternatives. *Campus dining operations:* uses reusable dishware; operates without trays; offers discounts for reusable mugs; uses bulk condiment dispensers and decreased packaging for to-go food service purchases.

Energy Currently uses or plans to use timers to regulate temperatures based on occupancy hours; motion, infrared, and/or light sensors to reduce energy uses for lighting; and LED lighting.

Contact Vice President for Student Services/Dean of Students, Union University, 1050 Union University Drive, Jackson, TN 38305-3697. *Phone:* 731-661-5090. *Fax:* 731-661-5017. *E-mail:* kthornbu@uu.edu. *Web site:* www.uu.edu/.

The University of Tennessee
Knoxville, Tennessee

Sustainability Initiatives The University of Tennessee is a member of the Association for the Advancement of Sustainability in Higher Education (AASHE) and a signatory to the Talloires Declaration. This institution's president has signed the American College & University Presidents Climate Commitment. The University of Tennessee has Green Fees (optional/required) dedicated to sustainability initiatives.

Academics *Sustainability-focused undergraduate major(s):* Agricultural Economics (BS); Biosystems Engineering (BS); Environmental and Soil Sciences (BS); Environmental Engineering (BS); Forestry, Wildlife, and Fisheries (BS); Plant Sciences—Bioenergy (BS); Geography (BA); Geology—Environmental Studies specialization (BS). *Sustainability-focused graduate degree program(s):* Agricultural Economics (MS); Biosystems Engineering (MS, PhD); Ecology & Evolutionary Biology (MS, PhD); Environmental Engineering (MS); Environmental Law (JD); Environmental Sociology (MA, PhD); Forestry, Wildlife, and Fisheries (MS); Geography (MS, PhD); STAIR program (PhD). *Sustainability courses and programs:* sustainability-focused course(s) or lecture series.

Student Services and Green Events *Sustainability leadership:* sustainability coordinator/director, sustainability committee/advisory council, recycling manager. *Student clubs and activities:* Campus Climate Challenge, student club(s)/group(s) focused on sustainability, outreach materials available about on-campus sustainability efforts. *Major sustainability events:* Online conference for Tennessee Higher Education Sustainability Association, sustainability-related conference for the Tennessee Association of Physical Plant Administrators. *Housing and facilities:* on-campus organic garden for students.

Food Fair Trade coffee is used. Vegan and vegetarian dining options are available for every meal.

Transportation Provides public transportation access to local destinations and incentives to carpool or use public transportation.

Buildings and Grounds *Campus grounds care:* uses water conservation devices; employs strategies to reduce light pollution; protects, restores, and/or creates habitat on campus.

Recycling *Events and organizations:* RecycleMania. *Programs and activities:* sustains a computer/technology recycling program; maintains an on-campus recycling center; composts yard waste; reuses chemicals; replaces paper materials with online alternatives; limits free printing in computer labs and libraries. *Campus dining operations:* operates without trays; offers discounts for reusable mugs; uses bulk condiment dispensers and decreased packaging for to-go food service purchases.

Energy Currently uses or plans to use alternative sources of power (solar energy and wind energy); timers to regulate temperatures based on occupancy hours; motion, infrared, and/or light sensors to reduce energy uses for lighting; and LED lighting.

Purchasing Sustainability criteria used in purchasing include Energy Star (EPA).

Contact Sustainability Manager, The University of Tennessee, 2233 Volunteer Boulevard, Knoxville, TN 37996-3010. *Phone:* 865-974-7780. *Fax:* 865-974-7786. *E-mail:* gbennet5@utk.edu. *Web site:* www.tennessee.edu/.

Vanderbilt University
Nashville, Tennessee

Academics *Sustainability-focused undergraduate major(s):* Environmental Science (BA), Interdisciplinary (BA). *Sustainability-focused graduate degree program(s):* Environmental Engineering (ME, MS, PhD), Environmental Management (MS, MBA, PhD), Environmental Science (MAT, MS, PhD). *Sustainability courses and programs:* sustainability-focused course(s) or lecture series, noncredit sustainability course(s).

Student Services and Green Events *Sustainability leadership:* sustainability coordinator/director, sustainability committee/advisory council, recycling manager, energy manager, sustainability-focused student government. *Student clubs and activities:* student club(s)/group(s) focused on sustainability, outreach materials available about on-campus sustainability efforts. *Major sustainability events:* Sustainapolooza, EcoSummit, Global Warming Awareness Week, Annual Green St. Patrick's Day paper recycling drive. *Housing and facilities:* sustainability-themed housing.

Food Sustainable, organic, and/or locally produced foods available in on-campus dining facilities. Fair Trade coffee is used. Vegan and vegetarian dining options are available for every meal.

Transportation Provides free on-campus transportation (bus or other), public transportation access to local destinations, a car sharing program, and incentives to carpool or use public transportation.

Buildings and Grounds *Percentage of institution's eligible buildings as of September 2008 meeting LEED and/or LEED-EB certification criteria:* 4.35%. *Renovation and maintenance:* registered for LEED certification for new construction and/or renovation; uses a Green Seal certified cleaning service. *Campus grounds care:* uses water conservation devices; employs strategies to reduce light pollution; landscapes with native plant species; protects, restores, and/or creates habitat on campus.

Recycling *Programs and activities:* sustains a computer/technology recycling program; maintains an on-campus recycling center; sustains a pre-consumer food waste composting program; composts yard waste; reuses surplus department/office supplies; reuses chemicals; replaces paper materials with online alternatives; limits free printing in computer labs and libraries. *Campus dining operations:* uses reusable dishware; offers discounts for reusable mugs; uses bulk condiment dispensers and decreased packaging for to-go food service purchases.

Energy Currently uses or plans to use alternative sources of power (hydroelectricity/water power, solar energy, and wind energy); timers to regulate temperatures based on occupancy hours; motion, infrared, and/or light sensors to reduce energy uses for lighting; and LED lighting.

Purchasing Sustainability criteria used in purchasing include Energy Star (EPA), WaterSense (EPA), Green Cleaning Products (Green Seal/Environmental Choice certified), and Forest Stewardship Council (FSC) or American Forest and Paper Association's Sustainable Forestry Initiative (SFI) paper.

Contact Director, Sustainability and Environmental Management Office, Vanderbilt University, 1161 21st Avenue South, A0201 MCN, Nashville, TN 37232-2665. *Phone:* 615-322-4551. *Fax:* 615-343-4951. *E-mail:* andrea.george@vanderbilt.edu. *Web site:* www.vanderbilt.edu/.

Texas

Huston-Tillotson University
Austin, Texas

Sustainability Initiatives Huston-Tillotson University's president has signed the American College & University Presidents Climate Commitment.

Student Services and Green Events *Sustainability leadership:* sustainability committee/advisory council.

Food Vegan and vegetarian dining options are available for every meal.

Recycling *Programs and activities:* sustains a computer/technology recycling program; maintains an on-campus recycling center; replaces paper materials with online alternatives. *Campus dining operations:* uses reusable dishware.

Energy Currently uses or plans to use timers to regulate temperatures based on occupancy hours.

Purchasing Sustainability criteria used in purchasing include Energy Star (EPA).

Contact Biology Professor, Huston-Tillotson University, 900 Chicon Street, Austin, TX 78702. *Phone:* 512-505-3103. *E-mail:* kwschwab@htu.edu. *Web site:* www.htu.edu/.

Our Lady of the Lake University of San Antonio
San Antonio, Texas

Food Sustainable, organic, and/or locally produced foods available in on-campus dining facilities. Vegan and vegetarian dining options are available for every meal.

Buildings and Grounds *Campus grounds care:* uses water conservation devices; landscapes with native plant species.

Recycling *Programs and activities:* sustains a computer/technology recycling program; maintains an on-campus recycling center.

Contact Director of Institutional Research and Effectiveness, Our Lady of the Lake University of San Antonio, SW 24th Street, San Antonio, TX 78207. *Phone:* 210-434 6711 Ext. 2765. *Fax:* 210-434-6711 Ext. 2798. *E-mail:* wangl@lake.ollusa.edu. *Web site:* www.ollusa.edu/.

Prairie View A&M University
Prairie View, Texas

Academics *Sustainability courses and programs:* sustainability-focused course(s) or lecture series.

Student Services and Green Events *Sustainability leadership:* recycling manager, energy manager, sustainability-focused student government.

Transportation Provides free on-campus transportation (bus or other).

Buildings and Grounds *Renovation and maintenance:* uses a Green Seal certified cleaning service. *Campus grounds care:* uses water conservation devices; employs strategies to reduce light pollution; applies to its grounds only pesticides and fertilizers allowable under the U.S. Department of Agriculture's standards for crop production.

Recycling *Events and organizations:* RecycleMania. *Programs and activities:* maintains an on-campus recycling center; replaces paper materials with online alternatives; limits free printing in computer labs and libraries. *Campus dining operations:* uses reusable dishware; operates without trays; uses bulk condiment dispensers and decreased packaging for to-go food service purchases.

Energy Currently uses or plans to use motion, infrared, and/or light sensors to reduce energy uses for lighting; LED lighting; and energy-related performance contracting.

Purchasing Sustainability criteria used in purchasing include Energy Star (EPA) and Green Cleaning Products (Green Seal/Environmental Choice certified).

Contact Assistant Vice President, Prairie View A&M University, PO Box 519, Prairie View, TX 77446-0519. *Phone:* 936-261-3875. *E-mail:* rcnorton@pvamu.edu. *Web site:* www.pvamu.edu/.

Rice University
Houston, Texas

Sustainability Initiatives Rice University is a member of the Association for the Advancement of Sustainability in Higher Education (AASHE) and a signatory to the Talloires Declaration. This institution's president has signed the American College & University Presidents Climate Commitment.

Academics *Sustainability-focused undergraduate major(s):* Environmental Engineering, Environmental Science, Policy Studies—Environmental option. *Sustainability-focused graduate degree program(s):* Professional Master of Environmental Analysis and Decision Making. *Sustainability courses and programs:* sustainability-focused course(s) or lecture series.

Student Services and Green Events *Sustainability leadership:* sustainability coordinator/director, recycling manager, energy manager, sustainability-focused student government. *Student clubs and activities:* student club(s)/group(s) focused on sustainability, outreach materials available about on-campus sustainability efforts. *Major sustainability events:* Focus the Nation, Sustainability Fair, regular guest speakers hosted by the Center for the Study of Environment and Society, Transforming the Metropolis: Creating Sustainable and Humane Cities Conference. *Housing and facilities:* student-run café that serves environmentally or socially preferable foods, on-campus organic garden for students.

Food Fair Trade coffee is used. Vegan and vegetarian dining options are available for every meal.

Transportation Provides free on-campus transportation (bus or other), public transportation access to local destinations, a car sharing program, and incentives to carpool or use public transportation.

Buildings and Grounds *Renovation and maintenance:* registered for LEED certification for new construction and/or renovation; uses a Green Seal certified cleaning service. *Campus grounds care:* uses water conservation devices; employs strategies to reduce light pollution; landscapes with native plant species; protects, restores, and/or creates habitat on campus.

Recycling *Events and organizations:* RecycleMania. *Programs and activities:* sustains a computer/technology recycling program; composts yard waste; replaces paper materials with online alternatives; limits free printing in computer labs and libraries. *Campus dining operations:* uses reusable dishware; uses bulk condiment dispensers and decreased packaging for to-go food service purchases.

Energy Currently uses or plans to use alternative sources of power (geothermal energy, solar energy, and wind energy); motion, infrared, and/or light sensors to reduce energy uses for lighting; LED lighting; and vending machine motion sensors.

Purchasing Sustainability criteria used in purchasing include Green Cleaning Products (Green Seal/Environmental Choice certified).

Contact Director of Sustainability, Rice University, Facilities Engineering and Planning, PO Box 1892, Mail Stop 312, Houston, TX 77251-1892. *Phone:* 713-348-5003. *Fax:* 713-348-5218. *E-mail:* rrj@rice.edu. *Web site:* www.rice.edu/.

Southwestern University
Georgetown, Texas

Sustainability Initiatives Southwestern University is a signatory to the Talloires Declaration.

Academics *Sustainability-focused undergraduate major(s):* Environmental Studies (BA). *Sustainability courses and programs:* sustainability-focused course(s) or lecture series.

Student Services and Green Events *Sustainability leadership:* sustainability committee/advisory council, recycling manager, energy manager. *Student clubs and activities:* outreach materials available about on-campus sustainability efforts. *Housing and facilities:* sustainability-themed housing, student-run café that serves environmentally or socially preferable foods, on-campus organic garden for students.

Food Sustainable, organic, and/or locally produced foods available in on-campus dining facilities. Fair Trade coffee is used. Vegan and vegetarian dining options are available for every meal.

Transportation Provides a bike loan/rental program.

Buildings and Grounds *Renovation and maintenance:* registered for LEED certification for new construction and/or renovation; uses a Green Seal certified cleaning service. *Campus grounds care:* uses water conservation devices; employs strategies to reduce light pollution; landscapes with native plant species; protects, restores, and/or creates habitat on campus.

Recycling *Programs and activities:* sustains a computer/technology recycling program; reuses surplus department/office supplies; reuses chemicals; replaces paper materials with online alternatives; limits free printing in computer labs and libraries. *Campus dining operations:* uses reusable dishware; operates without trays; uses bulk condiment dispensers and decreased packaging for to-go food service purchases.

Energy Currently uses or plans to use alternative sources of power; timers to regulate temperatures based on occupancy hours; and motion, infrared, and/or light sensors to reduce energy uses for lighting.

Purchasing Sustainability criteria used in purchasing include Energy Star (EPA) and Green Cleaning Products (Green Seal/Environmental Choice certified).

Contact Associate Vice President for Facilities and Campus Services, Southwestern University, 1001 East University Avenue, MAP 103, Georgetown, TX 78626. *Phone:* 512-863-1425. *E-mail:* bmathis@southwestern.edu. *Web site:* www.southwestern.edu/.

Texas Christian University
Fort Worth, Texas

Sustainability Initiatives Texas Christian University's president has signed the American College & University Presidents Climate Commitment.

Academics *Sustainability-focused graduate degree program(s):* Environmental Science, Sustainability Theme, TCU Global Academy. *Sustainability courses and programs:* sustainability-focused course(s) or lecture series.

Student Services and Green Events *Sustainability leadership:* sustainability committee/advisory council, recycling manager, energy manager. *Student clubs and activities:* student club(s)/group(s) focused on sustainability. *Major sustainability events:* Sustainability theme semesters, Sustainability Undergraduate Research Festival, Purple Bike Bike Program Challenge. *Housing and facilities:* sustainability-themed housing.

Food Vegan and vegetarian dining options are available for every meal.

Transportation Provides free on-campus transportation (bus or other), public transportation access to local destinations, a bike loan/rental program, a car sharing program, and incentives to carpool or use public transportation.

Buildings and Grounds *Renovation and maintenance:* registered for LEED certification for new construction and/or renovation; uses a Green Seal certified cleaning service. *Campus grounds care:* uses water conservation devices.

Recycling *Events and organizations:* RecycleMania. *Programs and activities:* sustains a computer/technology recycling program; sustains a post-consumer food waste composting program; composts yard waste; replaces paper materials with online alternatives; limits free printing in computer labs and libraries. *Campus dining operations:* uses reusable dishware; operates without trays; uses bulk condiment dispensers and decreased packaging for to-go food service purchases.

Energy Currently uses or plans to use motion, infrared, and/or light sensors to reduce energy uses for lighting and energy-related performance contracting.

Purchasing Sustainability criteria used in purchasing include Energy Star (EPA), Green Cleaning Products (Green Seal/Environmental Choice certified), and Forest Stewardship Council (FSC) or American Forest and Paper Association's Sustainable Forestry Initiative (SFI) paper.

Contact Sustainability Curriculum Committee Chair, Texas Christian University, TCU Box 298710, Fort Worth, TX 76129. *Phone:* 817-257-5941. *E-mail:* k.whitworth@tcu.edu. *Web site:* www.tcu.edu/.

Texas State University–San Marcos
San Marcos, Texas

Sustainability Initiatives Texas State University–San Marcos has Green Fees (optional/required) dedicated to sustainability initiatives.

Academics *Sustainability courses and programs:* sustainability-focused course(s) or lecture series.

Student Services and Green Events *Sustainability leadership:* sustainability committee/advisory council, recycling manager, energy manager, sustainability-focused student government. *Student clubs and activities:* student club(s)/group(s) focused on sustainability. *Major sustainability events:* Earth Day event, Texas Recycles Day, E-Waste Recycling event. *Housing and facilities:* sustainability-themed housing, on-campus organic garden for students.

Food Vegan and vegetarian dining options are available for every meal.

Transportation Provides free on-campus transportation (bus or other), public transportation access to local destinations, and incentives to carpool or use public transportation.

Buildings and Grounds *Renovation and maintenance:* registered for LEED certification for new construction and/or renovation. *Campus grounds care:* uses water conservation devices; landscapes with native plant species; protects, restores, and/or creates habitat on campus; applies to its grounds only pesticides and fertilizers allowable under the U.S. Department of Agriculture's standards for crop production.

Recycling *Events and organizations:* RecycleMania. *Programs and activities:* sustains a computer/technology recycling program; maintains an on-campus recycling center; sustains a pre-consumer food waste composting program; sustains a post-consumer food waste composting program; replaces paper materials with online alternatives; limits free printing in computer labs and libraries. *Campus dining operations:* offers discounts for reusable mugs.

Energy Currently uses or plans to use timers to regulate temperatures based on occupancy hours; motion, infrared, and/or light sensors to reduce energy uses for lighting; and vending machine motion sensors.

Purchasing Sustainability criteria used in purchasing include Energy Star (EPA) and Green Cleaning Products (Green Seal/Environmental Choice certified).

Contact Associate Vice President, Finance and Support Services Planning, Texas State University–San Marcos, 601 University Drive, San Marcos, TX 78666. *Phone:* 512-245-2244. *Fax:* 512-245-2033. *E-mail:* nnusbaum@txstate.edu. *Web site:* www.txstate.edu/.

Trinity University
San Antonio, Texas

Sustainability Initiatives Trinity University's president has signed the American College & University Presidents Climate Commitment.

Academics *Sustainability courses and programs:* sustainability-focused course(s) or lecture series.

Student Services and Green Events *Sustainability leadership:* sustainability committee/advisory council, recycling manager.

Food Sustainable, organic, and/or locally produced foods available in on-campus dining facilities. Fair Trade coffee is used. Vegan and vegetarian dining options are available for every meal.

Transportation Provides public transportation access to local destinations.

Buildings and Grounds *Percentage of institution's eligible buildings as of September 2008 meeting LEED and/or LEED-EB certification criteria:* 10%. *Renovation and maintenance:* registered for LEED certification for new construction and/or renovation. *Campus grounds care:* uses water conservation devices; landscapes with native plant species.

Recycling *Events and organizations:* RecycleMania. *Programs and activities:* sustains a computer/technology recycling program; sustains a pre-consumer food waste composting program; composts yard waste; reuses surplus department/office supplies; replaces paper materials with online alternatives; limits free printing in computer labs and libraries. *Campus dining operations:* uses reusable dishware; operates without trays; offers discounts for reusable mugs; uses bulk condiment dispensers and decreased packaging for to-go food service purchases.

Energy Currently uses or plans to use alternative sources of power (wind energy) and motion, infrared, and/or light sensors to reduce energy uses for lighting. Participates in College & University Green Power Challenge activities.

Purchasing Sustainability criteria used in purchasing include Energy Star (EPA).

Contact Trinity University, One Trinity Place, San Antonio, TX 78212-7200. *Phone:* 210-999-7011. *Fax:* 210-999-8164. *Web site:* www.trinity.edu/.

University of Houston
Houston, Texas

Academics *Sustainability-focused undergraduate major(s):* Earth Science (BA), Environmental Science (BA). *Sustainability-focused graduate degree program(s):* Atmospheric Science (MS). *Sustainability courses and programs:* sustainability-focused course(s) or lecture series.

Student Services and Green Events *Sustainability leadership:* sustainability committee/advisory council, recycling manager, energy manager. *Student clubs and activities:* student club(s)/group(s) focused on sustainability. *Major sustainability events:* UH Green Day, Green Commuter Fair, RecycleMania, Produce Garden Plantings/weedings, Fair Trade Fridays in October. *Housing and facilities:* student-run café that serves environmentally or socially preferable foods, on-campus organic garden for students.

Food Sustainable, organic, and/or locally produced foods available in on-campus dining facilities. Fair Trade coffee is used. Vegan and vegetarian dining options are available for every meal.

Transportation Provides free on-campus transportation (bus or other), public transportation access to local destinations, and incentives to carpool or use public transportation.

Buildings and Grounds *Percentage of institution's eligible buildings as of September 2008 meeting LEED and/or LEED-EB certification criteria:* 5%. *Campus grounds care:* uses water conservation devices; employs strategies to reduce light pollution; landscapes with native plant species; protects, restores, and/or creates habitat on campus; applies to its grounds only pesticides and fertilizers allowable under the U.S. Department of Agriculture's standards for crop production.

Recycling *Events and organizations:* RecycleMania. *Programs and activities:* sustains a computer/technology recycling program; maintains an on-campus recycling center; sustains a pre-consumer food waste composting program; sustains a post-consumer food waste composting program; composts yard waste; reuses surplus department/office supplies; replaces paper materials with online alternatives; limits free printing in computer labs and libraries. *Campus dining operations:* uses reusable dishware; operates without trays; uses bulk condiment dispensers and decreased packaging for to-go food service purchases.

Energy Currently uses or plans to use alternative sources of power (biomass energy, solar energy, and wind energy); motion, infrared, and/or light sensors to reduce energy uses for lighting; LED lighting; vending machine motion sensors; and energy-related performance contracting.

Contact Auxiliary Customer Service Coordinator, University of Houston, 325 McElhinney Hall, Houston, TX 77204-5011. *Phone:* 713-743-8940. *Fax:* 713-743-5596. *E-mail:* mhoney@central.uh.edu. *Web site:* www.uh.edu/.

University of Houston–Downtown
Houston, Texas

Sustainability Initiatives University of Houston–Downtown's president has signed the American College & University Presidents Climate Commitment.

Student Services and Green Events *Sustainability leadership:* sustainability coordinator/director, sustainability committee/advisory council.

Food Fair Trade coffee is used. Vegan and vegetarian dining options are available for every meal.

Transportation Provides free on-campus transportation (bus or other) and public transportation access to local destinations.

Buildings and Grounds *Campus grounds care:* uses water conservation devices; landscapes with native plant species; protects, restores, and/or creates habitat on campus.

Recycling *Programs and activities:* sustains a computer/technology recycling program; maintains an on-campus recycling center; sustains a pre-consumer food waste composting program; replaces paper materials with online alternatives; limits free printing in computer labs and libraries. *Campus dining operations:* offers discounts for reusable mugs.

Energy Currently uses or plans to use timers to regulate temperatures based on occupancy hours; motion, infrared, and/or light sensors to reduce energy uses for lighting; and LED lighting.

Contact Executive Director, Special Projects, University of Houston–Downtown, One Main Street, Houston, TX 77002. *Phone:* 713-221-8530. *E-mail:* curetonp@uhd.edu. *Web site:* www.uhd.edu/.

Utah

Weber State University
Ogden, Utah

Sustainability Initiatives Weber State University is a member of the Association for the Advancement of Sustainability in Higher Education (AASHE). This institution's president has signed the American College & University Presidents Climate Commitment.

Academics *Sustainability-focused undergraduate major(s):* Geography (BS). *Sustainability courses and programs:* sustainability-focused course(s) or lecture series.

Student Services and Green Events *Sustainability leadership:* sustainability committee/advisory council, sustainability-focused student government.

Transportation Provides free on-campus transportation (bus or other), public transportation access to local destinations, and incentives to carpool or use public transportation.

Buildings and Grounds *Campus grounds care:* employs strategies to reduce light pollution; landscapes with native plant species.

Energy Currently uses or plans to use alternative sources of power (wind energy); vending machine motion sensors; and energy-related performance contracting.

Purchasing Sustainability criteria used in purchasing include Energy Star (EPA).

Contact Professor of Geography, Weber State University, 1210 University Circle, Ogden, UT 84408-1210. *Phone:* 801-626-6944. *E-mail:* bdorsey@weber.edu. *Web site:* www.weber.edu/.

Westminster College
Salt Lake City, Utah

Sustainability Initiatives Westminster College is a member of the Association for the Advancement of Sustainability in Higher Education (AASHE). This institution's president has signed the American College & University Presidents Climate Commitment.

Academics *Sustainability courses and programs:* sustainability-focused course(s) or lecture series.

Student Services and Green Events *Sustainability leadership:* sustainability committee/advisory council, sustainability-focused student government. *Student clubs and activities:* student club(s)/group(s) focused on sustainability. *Major sustainability events:* Bioneers Conference, Green Lunch Series. *Housing and facilities:* on-campus organic garden for students.

Food Sustainable, organic, and/or locally produced foods available in on-campus dining facilities.

Transportation Provides public transportation access to local destinations, a bike loan/rental program, and incentives to carpool or use public transportation.

Buildings and Grounds *Renovation and maintenance:* registered for LEED certification for new construction and/or renovation. *Campus grounds care:* uses water conservation devices; employs strategies to reduce light pollution; landscapes with native plant species; protects, restores, and/or creates habitat on campus.

Recycling *Programs and activities:* sustains a computer/technology recycling program; maintains an on-campus recycling center; composts yard waste; reuses surplus department/office supplies. *Campus dining operations:* uses reusable dishware; offers discounts for reusable mugs.

Energy Currently uses or plans to use alternative sources of power (solar energy and wind energy) and motion, infrared, and/or light sensors to reduce energy uses for lighting.

Purchasing Sustainability criteria used in purchasing include Energy Star (EPA).

Contact Environmental Center Director, Westminster College, 1840 South 1300 East, Salt Lake City, UT 84105. *Phone:* 801-832-2810. *E-mail:* kcase@westminstercollege.edu. *Web site:* www.westminstercollege.edu/.

Vermont

Champlain College
Burlington, Vermont

Student Services and Green Events *Sustainability leadership:* sustainability coordinator/director, sustainability committee/advisory council. *Student clubs and activities:* student club(s)/group(s) focused on sustainability, outreach materials available about on-campus sustainability efforts. *Major sustainability events:* Focus the Nation.

Food Sustainable, organic, and/or locally produced foods available in on-campus dining facilities. Fair Trade coffee is used. Vegan and vegetarian dining options are available for every meal.

Transportation Provides free on-campus transportation (bus or other), public transportation access to local destinations, and incentives to carpool or use public transportation.

Buildings and Grounds *Renovation and maintenance:* registered for LEED certification for new construction and/or renovation. *Campus grounds care:* uses water conservation devices; employs strategies to reduce light pollution; landscapes with native plant species; applies to its grounds only pesticides and fertilizers allowable under the U.S. Department of Agriculture's standards for crop production.

Recycling *Events and organizations:* RecycleMania. *Programs and activities:* sustains a pre-consumer food waste composting program; composts yard waste; reuses surplus department/office supplies; replaces paper materials with online alternatives. *Campus dining operations:* uses reusable dishware; operates without trays; uses bulk condiment dispensers and decreased packaging for to-go food service purchases.

Energy Currently uses or plans to use alternative sources of power (biomass energy and hydroelectricity/water power); timers to regulate temperatures based on occupancy hours; and motion, infrared, and/or light sensors to reduce energy uses for lighting.

Contact Sustainability Coordinator, Champlain College, 212 Battery Street, Burlington, VT 05401. *Phone:* 802-865-5449. *E-mail:* gcalvi@champlain.edu. *Web site:* www.champlain.edu/.

Goddard College
Plainfield, Vermont

Sustainability Initiatives Goddard College's president has signed the American College & University Presidents Climate Commitment.

Academics *Sustainability-focused undergraduate major(s):* Environmental Science, Self-designed programs.

Sustainability-focused graduate degree program(s): Masters in Socially Responsible Business and Sustainable Communities, Self-designed masters program. *Sustainability courses and programs:* sustainability-focused course(s) or lecture series.

Student Services and Green Events *Sustainability leadership:* sustainability coordinator/director, sustainability committee/advisory council, recycling manager, energy manager, sustainability-focused student government. *Student clubs and activities:* Campus Climate Challenge, student club(s)/group(s) focused on sustainability. *Major sustainability events:* Guests speakers as part of the Masters program in socially responsible business and sustainable communities. *Housing and facilities:* student-run café that serves environmentally or socially preferable foods, on-campus organic garden for students.

Food Sustainable, organic, and/or locally produced foods available in on-campus dining facilities. Fair Trade coffee is used. Vegan and vegetarian dining options are available for every meal.

Transportation Provides free on-campus transportation (bus or other), a car sharing program, and incentives to carpool or use public transportation.

Buildings and Grounds *Renovation and maintenance:* registered for LEED certification for new construction and/or renovation; uses a Green Seal certified cleaning service. *Campus grounds care:* employs strategies to reduce light pollution; landscapes with native plant species; protects, restores, and/or creates habitat on campus; applies to its grounds only pesticides and fertilizers allowable under the U.S. Department of Agriculture's standards for crop production.

Recycling *Programs and activities:* sustains a computer/technology recycling program; maintains an on-campus recycling center; sustains a pre-consumer food waste composting program; sustains a post-consumer food waste composting program; composts yard waste; reuses surplus department/office supplies; replaces paper materials with online alternatives; limits free printing in computer labs and libraries. *Campus dining operations:* uses reusable dishware; offers discounts for reusable mugs.

Energy Currently uses or plans to use alternative sources of power and LED lighting.

Purchasing Sustainability criteria used in purchasing include Energy Star (EPA), Green Cleaning Products (Green Seal/Environmental Choice certified), and Forest Stewardship Council (FSC) or American Forest and Paper Association's Sustainable Forestry Initiative (SFI) paper.

Contact Dean of Planning and Assessment, Goddard College, 123 Pitkin Road, Plainfield, VT 05667. *Phone:* 802-454-8311 Ext. 222. *Fax:* 802-454-1174. *E-mail:* judy.fitch@goddard.edu. *Web site:* www.goddard.edu/.

Johnson State College
Johnson, Vermont

Academics *Sustainability courses and programs:* sustainability-focused course(s) or lecture series.

Student Services and Green Events *Sustainability leadership:* sustainability committee/advisory council. *Student clubs and activities:* outreach materials available about on-campus sustainability efforts.

Food Fair Trade coffee is used. Vegan and vegetarian dining options are available for every meal.

Transportation Provides a car sharing program.

Buildings and Grounds *Campus grounds care:* uses water conservation devices; employs strategies to reduce light pol-

lution; landscapes with native plant species; protects, restores, and/or creates habitat on campus; applies to its grounds only pesticides and fertilizers allowable under the U.S. Department of Agriculture's standards for crop production.

Recycling *Programs and activities:* sustains a computer/technology recycling program; sustains a pre-consumer food waste composting program; sustains a post-consumer food waste composting program; composts yard waste; reuses surplus department/office supplies; replaces paper materials with online alternatives; limits free printing in computer labs and libraries. *Campus dining operations:* operates without trays; uses bulk condiment dispensers and decreased packaging for to-go food service purchases.

Energy Currently uses or plans to use alternative sources of power; timers to regulate temperatures based on occupancy hours; motion, infrared, and/or light sensors to reduce energy uses for lighting; LED lighting; and vending machine motion sensors.

Purchasing Sustainability criteria used in purchasing include Energy Star (EPA) and Green Cleaning Products (Green Seal/Environmental Choice certified).

Contact Johnson State College, 337 College Hill, Johnson, VT 05656-9405. *Phone:* 802-635-2356. *Web site:* www.johnsonstatecollege.edu/.

University of Vermont
Burlington, Vermont

Sustainability Initiatives University of Vermont is a member of the Association for the Advancement of Sustainability in Higher Education (AASHE). This institution's president has signed the American College & University Presidents Climate Commitment. University of Vermont has Green Fees (optional/required) dedicated to sustainability initiatives.

Academics *Sustainability-focused undergraduate major(s):* Ecological Agriculture (BS), Environmental Engineering (BS), Environmental Sciences (BS), Environmental Studies (BA, BS), Management and the Environment (BS), Natural Resources (BS), Sustainable Landscape Horticulture (BS). *Sustainability-focused graduate degree program(s):* Field Naturalist (MS), Natural Resources (MS, PhD). *Sustainability courses and programs:* sustainability-focused course(s) or lecture series, noncredit sustainability course(s).

Student Services and Green Events *Sustainability leadership:* sustainability coordinator/director, sustainability committee/advisory council, recycling manager, energy manager, sustainability-focused student government. *Student clubs and activities:* student club(s)/group(s) focused on sustainability, outreach materials available about on-campus sustainability efforts. *Major sustainability events:* Aiken Lectures, Focus the Nation events, EarthFest. *Housing and facilities:* sustainability-themed housing, on-campus organic garden for students.

Food Sustainable, organic, and/or locally produced foods available in on-campus dining facilities. Fair Trade coffee is used. Vegan and vegetarian dining options are available for every meal.

Transportation Provides free on-campus transportation (bus or other), public transportation access to local destinations, a car sharing program, and incentives to carpool or use public transportation.

Buildings and Grounds *Renovation and maintenance:* registered for LEED certification for new construction and/or renovation; uses a Green Seal certified cleaning service. *Campus grounds care:* uses water conservation devices;

employs strategies to reduce light pollution; protects, restores, and/or creates habitat on campus.

Recycling *Programs and activities:* sustains a computer/technology recycling program; sustains a pre-consumer food waste composting program; sustains a post-consumer food waste composting program; composts yard waste; reuses surplus department/office supplies; reuses chemicals; replaces paper materials with online alternatives; limits free printing in computer labs and libraries. *Campus dining operations:* uses reusable dishware; operates without trays; offers discounts for reusable mugs; uses bulk condiment dispensers and decreased packaging for to-go food service purchases.

Energy Currently uses or plans to use alternative sources of power (biomass energy, hydroelectricity/water power, and wind energy); motion, infrared, and/or light sensors to reduce energy uses for lighting; vending machine motion sensors; and energy-related performance contracting.

Purchasing Sustainability criteria used in purchasing include Energy Star (EPA), Green Electronics Council (GEC) Electronic Product Environmental Assessment Tool (EPEAT) Silver or Gold, and Green Cleaning Products (Green Seal/Environmental Choice certified).

Contact Sustainability Director, University of Vermont, Office of Sustainability, 284 East Avenue, Burlington, VT 05405. *Phone:* 802-656-3803. *E-mail:* sustainability@uvm.edu. *Web site:* www.uvm.edu/.

Virginia

The College of William and Mary
Williamsburg, Virginia

Sustainability Initiatives The College of William and Mary has Green Fees (optional/required) dedicated to sustainability initiatives.

Academics *Sustainability-focused undergraduate major(s):* Environmental Policy track, Environmental Science track. *Sustainability courses and programs:* sustainability-focused course(s) or lecture series.

Student Services and Green Events *Sustainability leadership:* sustainability coordinator/director, sustainability committee/advisory council, energy manager, sustainability-focused student government. *Student clubs and activities:* student club(s)/group(s) focused on sustainability, outreach materials available about on-campus sustainability efforts. *Major sustainability events:* "Step it Up" Conference, Virginia Climate Change Conference, National Teach-In on Climate Change. *Housing and facilities:* student-run café that serves environmentally or socially preferable foods, on-campus organic garden for students.

Food Sustainable, organic, and/or locally produced foods available in on-campus dining facilities. Fair Trade coffee is used. Vegan and vegetarian dining options are available for every meal.

Transportation Provides free on-campus transportation (bus or other), public transportation access to local destinations, and a bike loan/rental program.

Buildings and Grounds *Renovation and maintenance:* registered for LEED certification for new construction and/or renovation. *Campus grounds care:* uses water conservation devices; employs strategies to reduce light pollution; landscapes with native plant species; protects, restores, and/or creates habitat on campus; applies to its grounds only pesticides and fertilizers allowable under the U.S. Department of Agriculture's standards for crop production.

Recycling *Events and organizations:* RecycleMania. *Programs and activities:* sustains a computer/technology recycling program; sustains a post-consumer food waste composting program; composts yard waste; reuses surplus department/office supplies; reuses chemicals; replaces paper materials with online alternatives; limits free printing in computer labs and libraries. *Campus dining operations:* uses reusable dishware; operates without trays; offers discounts for reusable mugs; uses bulk condiment dispensers and decreased packaging for to-go food service purchases.

Energy Currently uses or plans to use alternative sources of power; motion, infrared, and/or light sensors to reduce energy uses for lighting; LED lighting; and energy-related performance contracting.

Purchasing Sustainability criteria used in purchasing include Energy Star (EPA) and Green Cleaning Products (Green Seal/Environmental Choice certified).

Contact Director of the Environmental Science and Policy Program, The College of William and Mary, Department of Biology, Williamsburg, VA 23187-8795. *Phone:* 757-221-2553. *E-mail:* jrswad@wm.edu. *Web site:* www.wm.edu/.

Eastern Mennonite University
Harrisonburg, Virginia

Academics *Sustainability-focused undergraduate major(s):* Environmental Studies (BS, BA), Peacebuilding and Development (BS, BA). *Sustainability courses and programs:* sustainability-focused course(s) or lecture series, noncredit sustainability course(s).

Student Services and Green Events *Sustainability leadership:* sustainability committee/advisory council, recycling manager, energy manager. *Student clubs and activities:* outreach materials available about on-campus sustainability efforts. *Housing and facilities:* student-run café that serves environmentally or socially preferable foods, on-campus organic garden for students.

Food Sustainable, organic, and/or locally produced foods available in on-campus dining facilities. Fair Trade coffee is used. Vegan and vegetarian dining options are available for every meal.

Transportation Provides public transportation access to local destinations and a bike loan/rental program.

Buildings and Grounds *Renovation and maintenance:* registered for LEED certification for new construction and/or renovation; uses a Green Seal certified cleaning service. *Campus grounds care:* uses water conservation devices; landscapes with native plant species; protects, restores, and/or creates habitat on campus.

Recycling *Events and organizations:* RecycleMania. *Programs and activities:* sustains a computer/technology recycling program; maintains an on-campus recycling center; sustains a pre-consumer food waste composting program; sustains a post-consumer food waste composting program; composts yard waste; reuses surplus department/office supplies; replaces paper materials with online alternatives. *Campus dining operations:* uses reusable dishware; operates without trays; uses bulk condiment dispensers and decreased packaging for to-go food service purchases.

Energy Currently uses or plans to use timers to regulate temperatures based on occupancy hours.

Purchasing Sustainability criteria used in purchasing include Energy Star (EPA), Green Electronics Council (GEC) Electronic Product Environmental Assessment Tool (EPEAT) Silver or Gold, Green Cleaning Products (Green Seal/Environmental Choice certified), and Forest Stewardship Council (FSC) or American Forest and Paper Association's Sustainable Forestry Initiative (SFI) paper.

Contact Recycling Coordinator, Eastern Mennonite University, 1200 Park Road, Harrisonburg, VA 22802. *Phone:* 540-432-4546. *E-mail:* recycle@emu.edu. *Web site:* www.emu.edu/.

Emory & Henry College
Emory, Virginia

Sustainability Initiatives Emory & Henry College's president has signed the American College & University Presidents Climate Commitment.

Academics *Sustainability-focused undergraduate major(s):* Environmental Studies (BA), Environmental Studies (BS), Geography (BA), Public Policy and Community Service (BA). *Sustainability courses and programs:* sustainability-focused course(s) or lecture series.

Student Services and Green Events *Sustainability leadership:* sustainability committee/advisory council. *Student clubs and activities:* student club(s)/group(s) focused on sustainability. *Major sustainability events:* Winter forum on sustainability with Bill McKibben. *Housing and facilities:* sustainability-themed housing, on-campus organic garden for students.

Food Sustainable, organic, and/or locally produced foods available in on-campus dining facilities. Fair Trade coffee is used. Vegan and vegetarian dining options are available for every meal.

Buildings and Grounds *Percentage of institution's eligible buildings as of September 2008 meeting LEED and/or LEED-EB certification criteria:* 5%. *Renovation and maintenance:* registered for LEED certification for new construction and/or renovation. *Campus grounds care:* uses water conservation devices; protects, restores, and/or creates habitat on campus.

Recycling *Events and organizations:* RecycleMania. *Programs and activities:* sustains a computer/technology recycling program; maintains an on-campus recycling center; replaces paper materials with online alternatives; limits free printing in computer labs and libraries. *Campus dining operations:* uses reusable dishware; operates without trays; uses bulk condiment dispensers and decreased packaging for to-go food service purchases.

Purchasing Sustainability criteria used in purchasing include Energy Star (EPA).

Contact Chair, Climate Working Group, Emory & Henry College, 1 Garnand Drive, PO Box 947, Emory, VA 24327. *Phone:* 276-944-6203. *Fax:* 276-944-6695. *E-mail:* edavis@ehc.edu. *Web site:* www.ehc.edu/.

George Mason University
Fairfax, Virginia

Sustainability Initiatives George Mason University is a member of the Association for the Advancement of Sustainability in Higher Education (AASHE) and a signatory to the Talloires Declaration. This institution's president has signed the American College & University Presidents Climate Commitment.

Academics *Sustainability courses and programs:* sustainability-focused course(s) or lecture series.

Student Services and Green Events *Sustainability leadership:* sustainability coordinator/director, sustainability committee/advisory council, recycling manager, energy manager, sustainability-focused student government. *Housing and facilities:* sustainability-themed housing.

Food Sustainable, organic, and/or locally produced foods available in on-campus dining facilities. Fair Trade coffee is used. Vegan and vegetarian dining options are available for every meal.

Transportation Provides free on-campus transportation (bus or other), public transportation access to local destinations, and incentives to carpool or use public transportation.

Buildings and Grounds *Renovation and maintenance:* registered for LEED certification for new construction and/or renovation. *Campus grounds care:* uses water conservation devices; landscapes with native plant species; protects, restores, and/or creates habitat on campus.

Recycling *Events and organizations:* RecycleMania. *Programs and activities:* sustains a pre-consumer food waste composting program; sustains a post-consumer food waste composting program; reuses surplus department/office supplies; replaces paper materials with online alternatives; limits free printing in computer labs and libraries. *Campus dining operations:* uses reusable dishware; operates without trays; offers discounts for reusable mugs; uses bulk condiment dispensers and decreased packaging for to-go food service purchases.

Energy Currently uses or plans to use timers to regulate temperatures based on occupancy hours; motion, infrared, and/or light sensors to reduce energy uses for lighting; LED lighting; and energy-related performance contracting.

Purchasing Sustainability criteria used in purchasing include Energy Star (EPA), Green Electronics Council (GEC) Electronic Product Environmental Assessment Tool (EPEAT) Silver or Gold, and Green Cleaning Products (Green Seal/Environmental Choice certified).

Contact George Mason University, 4400 University Drive, Fairfax, VA 22030. *Phone:* 703-993-1000. *Web site:* www.gmu.edu/.

Hampden-Sydney College
Hampden-Sydney, Virginia

Academics *Sustainability courses and programs:* sustainability-focused course(s) or lecture series.

Student Services and Green Events *Sustainability leadership:* energy manager.

Food Sustainable, organic, and/or locally produced foods available in on-campus dining facilities. Fair Trade coffee is used. Vegan and vegetarian dining options are available for every meal.

Buildings and Grounds *Renovation and maintenance:* uses a Green Seal certified cleaning service. *Campus grounds care:* uses water conservation devices; landscapes with native plant species; protects, restores, and/or creates habitat on campus.

Recycling *Programs and activities:* sustains a computer/technology recycling program; reuses surplus department/office supplies; reuses chemicals. *Campus dining operations:* uses reusable dishware; offers discounts for reusable mugs; uses bulk condiment dispensers and decreased packaging for to-go food service purchases.

Energy Currently uses or plans to use alternative sources of power (geothermal energy); timers to regulate temperatures based on occupancy hours; motion, infrared, and/or light sensors to reduce energy uses for lighting; LED lighting; vending machine motion sensors; and energy-related performance contracting.

Purchasing Sustainability criteria used in purchasing include Green Cleaning Products (Green Seal/Environmental Choice certified).

Contact Director of Physical Plant, Hampden-Sydney College, PO Box 104, Hampden-Sydney, VA 23943. *Phone:* 434-223-6161. *E-mail:* tgregory@hsc.edu. *Web site:* www.hsc.edu/.

Hollins University
Roanoke, Virginia

Sustainability Initiatives Hollins University's president has signed the American College & University Presidents Climate Commitment. Hollins University has Green Fees (optional/required) dedicated to sustainability initiatives.

Academics *Sustainability-focused undergraduate major(s):* Environmental Studies (BA). *Sustainability courses and programs:* sustainability-focused course(s) or lecture series.

Student Services and Green Events *Sustainability leadership:* sustainability committee/advisory council, recycling manager, sustainability-focused student government. *Student clubs and activities:* student club(s)/group(s) focused on sustainability. *Major sustainability events:* Women in Science and Leadership. *Housing and facilities:* on-campus organic garden for students.

Food Sustainable, organic, and/or locally produced foods available in on-campus dining facilities. Fair Trade coffee is used. Vegan and vegetarian dining options are available for every meal.

Buildings and Grounds *Renovation and maintenance:* registered for LEED certification for new construction and/or renovation; uses a Green Seal certified cleaning service. *Campus grounds care:* uses water conservation devices; employs strategies to reduce light pollution; landscapes with native plant species; protects, restores, and/or creates habitat on campus.

Recycling *Events and organizations:* RecycleMania. *Programs and activities:* sustains a computer/technology recycling program; maintains an on-campus recycling center; sustains a pre-consumer food waste composting program; sustains a post-consumer food waste composting program; composts yard waste; replaces paper materials with online alternatives. *Campus dining operations:* uses reusable dishware; uses bulk condiment dispensers and decreased packaging for to-go food service purchases.

Energy Currently uses or plans to use motion, infrared, and/or light sensors to reduce energy uses for lighting.

Purchasing Sustainability criteria used in purchasing include Energy Star (EPA) and Green Cleaning Products (Green Seal/Environmental Choice certified).

Contact Hollins University, PO Box 9603, Roanoke, VA 24020-1603. *Phone:* 540-362-6000. *Web site:* www.hollins.edu/.

James Madison University
Harrisonburg, Virginia

Sustainability Initiatives James Madison University is a signatory to the Talloires Declaration. This institution's president has signed the American College & University Presidents Climate Commitment.

Academics *Sustainability-focused undergraduate major(s):* Engineering (BSE); Integrated Science and Technology, environment concentration (BS). *Sustainability-focused graduate degree program(s):* Forestry Five Year Dual Degree, Sustainable Environmental Resources Management (MS). *Sustainability courses and programs:* sustainability-focused course(s) or lecture series.

Student Services and Green Events *Sustainability leadership:* sustainability coordinator/director, sustainability committee/advisory council, recycling manager, energy manager. *Student clubs and activities:* student club(s)/group(s) focused on sustainability. *Major sustainability events:* No Drive Day, Campus Sustainability Day, RecycleMania, Earth Day Week. *Housing and facilities:* sustainability-themed housing.

Food Sustainable, organic, and/or locally produced foods available in on-campus dining facilities. Fair Trade coffee is used. Vegan and vegetarian dining options are available for every meal.

Transportation Provides free on-campus transportation (bus or other) and public transportation access to local destinations.

Buildings and Grounds *Renovation and maintenance:* registered for LEED certification for new construction and/or renovation. *Campus grounds care:* uses water conservation devices.

Recycling *Events and organizations:* RecycleMania. *Programs and activities:* maintains an on-campus recycling center; composts yard waste; reuses surplus department/office supplies; replaces paper materials with online alternatives; limits free printing in computer labs and libraries. *Campus dining operations:* operates without trays; offers discounts for reusable mugs.

Energy Currently uses or plans to use timers to regulate temperatures based on occupancy hours; motion, infrared, and/or light sensors to reduce energy uses for lighting; LED lighting; and energy-related performance contracting.

Purchasing Sustainability criteria used in purchasing include Energy Star (EPA), Green Electronics Council (GEC) Electronic Product Environmental Assessment Tool (EPEAT) Silver or Gold, and Green Cleaning Products (Green Seal/Environmental Choice certified).

Contact Executive Director, Institute for Stewardship of the Natural World, James Madison University, Maury 217, MSC 1106, Harrisonburg, VA 22807. *Phone:* 540-568-3202. *E-mail:* brodricj@jmu.edu. *Web site:* www.jmu.edu/.

Longwood University
Farmville, Virginia

Sustainability Initiatives Longwood University is a member of the Association for the Advancement of Sustainability in Higher Education (AASHE) and a signatory to the Talloires Declaration.

Academics *Sustainability courses and programs:* sustainability-focused course(s) or lecture series.

Student Services and Green Events *Sustainability leadership:* sustainability coordinator/director, sustainability committee/advisory council, recycling manager, energy manager. *Student clubs and activities:* student club(s)/group(s) focused on sustainability. *Major sustainability events:* Martin Luther King Symposium and Service Challenge, Globalization and Pluralism, Earthfest, Campus Sustainability Day, 2010 Sustainability Conference.

Food Sustainable, organic, and/or locally produced foods available in on-campus dining facilities. Fair Trade coffee is used. Vegan and vegetarian dining options are available for every meal.

Transportation Provides free on-campus transportation (bus or other) and public transportation access to local destinations.

Buildings and Grounds *Renovation and maintenance:* registered for LEED certification for new construction and/or renovation. *Campus grounds care:* uses water conservation devices; landscapes with native plant species.

Recycling *Events and organizations:* RecycleMania. *Programs and activities:* composts yard waste; reuses surplus department/office supplies; replaces paper materials with online alternatives. *Campus dining operations:* uses reusable dishware; operates without trays; uses bulk condiment dispensers and decreased packaging for to-go food service purchases.

Energy Currently uses or plans to use alternative sources of power (biomass energy and geothermal energy); timers to regulate temperatures based on occupancy hours; motion, infrared, and/or light sensors to reduce energy uses for lighting; LED lighting; and energy-related performance contracting.

Purchasing Sustainability criteria used in purchasing include Energy Star (EPA), Green Electronics Council (GEC) Electronic Product Environmental Assessment Tool (EPEAT) Silver or Gold, and Green Cleaning Products (Green Seal/Environmental Choice certified).

Contact Sustainability Coordinator, Longwood University, 201 High Street, Farmville, VA 23909. *Phone:* 434-395-2572. *Fax:* 434-395-2978. *E-mail:* martinka2@longwood.edu. *Web site:* www.longwood.edu/.

Mary Baldwin College
Staunton, Virginia

Sustainability Initiatives Mary Baldwin College's president has signed the American College & University Presidents Climate Commitment.

Academics *Sustainability-focused undergraduate major(s):* Business Administration (BA, BS). *Sustainability courses and programs:* sustainability-focused course(s) or lecture series.

Student Services and Green Events *Sustainability leadership:* sustainability coordinator/director, sustainability committee/advisory council, recycling manager, sustainability-focused student government.

Food Sustainable, organic, and/or locally produced foods available in on-campus dining facilities. Fair Trade coffee is used. Vegan and vegetarian dining options are available for every meal.

Transportation Provides public transportation access to local destinations.

Buildings and Grounds *Renovation and maintenance:* uses a Green Seal certified cleaning service. *Campus grounds care:* uses water conservation devices; landscapes with native plant species.

Recycling *Events and organizations:* RecycleMania. *Programs and activities:* sustains a computer/technology recycling program; replaces paper materials with online alternatives. *Campus dining operations:* operates without trays.

Energy Currently uses or plans to use timers to regulate temperatures based on occupancy hours and LED lighting.

Purchasing Sustainability criteria used in purchasing include Energy Star (EPA), Green Cleaning Products (Green Seal/Environmental Choice certified), and Forest Stewardship Council (FSC) or American Forest and Paper Association's Sustainable Forestry Initiative (SFI) paper.

Contact Director of Civic Engagement, Mary Baldwin College, Spencer Court, Staunton, VA 24401. *Phone:* 540-887-7111. *E-mail:* sgrance@mbc.edu. *Web site:* www.mbc.edu/.

Radford University
Radford, Virginia

Sustainability Initiatives Radford University is a signatory to the Talloires Declaration.

Academics *Sustainability courses and programs:* sustainability-focused course(s) or lecture series.

Student Services and Green Events *Sustainability leadership:* sustainability coordinator/director, sustainability committee/advisory council, recycling manager, energy manager. *Student clubs and activities:* Campus Climate Challenge, student club(s)/group(s) focused on sustainability. *Major sustainability events:* Appalachian Elements: Speakers, Art Gallery Showing, Panel Discussions, Campus Sustainability Awareness Program, Earth Day events, Mountaintop Removal lectures, Focus the Nation, New River Symposium, Global Climate Change Symposium/Lecture.

Food Sustainable, organic, and/or locally produced foods available in on-campus dining facilities. Fair Trade coffee is used. Vegan and vegetarian dining options are available for every meal.

Transportation Provides free on-campus transportation (bus or other) and public transportation access to local destinations.

Buildings and Grounds *Renovation and maintenance:* registered for LEED certification for new construction and/or renovation. *Campus grounds care:* uses water conservation devices; employs strategies to reduce light pollution; landscapes with native plant species; protects, restores, and/or creates habitat on campus.

Recycling *Events and organizations:* RecycleMania, WasteWise (EPA). *Programs and activities:* sustains a computer/technology recycling program; maintains an on-campus recycling center; composts yard waste; reuses surplus department/office supplies; reuses chemicals; replaces paper materials with online alternatives; limits free printing in computer labs and libraries. *Campus dining operations:* operates without trays; uses bulk condiment dispensers and decreased packaging for to-go food service purchases.

Energy Currently uses or plans to use alternative sources of power (biomass energy); timers to regulate temperatures based on occupancy hours; motion, infrared, and/or light sensors to reduce energy uses for lighting; LED lighting; vending machine motion sensors; and energy-related performance contracting.

Contact Sustainability Coordinator, Radford University, PO Box 6909, Radford, VA 24141. *Phone:* 540-831-7206. *Fax:* 540-831-7783. *E-mail:* wrstephe@radford.edu. *Web site:* www.radford.edu/.

Randolph College
Lynchburg, Virginia

Sustainability Initiatives Randolph College is a member of the Association for the Advancement of Sustainability in Higher Education (AASHE) and a signatory to the Talloires Declaration. This institution's president has signed the American College & University Presidents Climate Commitment.

Academics *Sustainability-focused undergraduate major(s):* Environmental Science (BS), Environmental Studies (BA), Global Studies (BA). *Sustainability courses and programs:* sustainability-focused course(s) or lecture series.

Student Services and Green Events *Sustainability leadership:* sustainability committee/advisory council. *Student clubs and activities:* student club(s)/group(s) focused on sustainability, outreach materials available about on-campus sustainability efforts. *Major sustainability events:* Regular outside speakers on campus sustainability and sustainable development. *Housing and facilities:* sustainability-themed housing, on-campus organic garden for students.

Food Sustainable, organic, and/or locally produced foods available in on-campus dining facilities. Fair Trade coffee is used. Vegan and vegetarian dining options are available for every meal.

Transportation Provides public transportation access to local destinations and a bike loan/rental program.

Buildings and Grounds *Renovation and maintenance:* registered for LEED certification for new construction and/or renovation. *Campus grounds care:* uses water conservation devices; employs strategies to reduce light pollution; landscapes with native plant species; protects, restores, and/or creates habitat on campus.

Recycling *Programs and activities:* sustains a computer/technology recycling program; maintains an on-campus recycling center; sustains a pre-consumer food waste composting program; composts yard waste; reuses surplus department/office supplies; reuses chemicals; replaces paper materials with online alternatives; limits free printing in computer labs and libraries. *Campus dining operations:* uses reusable dishware; operates without trays; uses bulk condiment dispensers and decreased packaging for to-go food service purchases.

Energy Currently uses or plans to use timers to regulate temperatures based on occupancy hours and LED lighting.

Purchasing Sustainability criteria used in purchasing include Energy Star (EPA).

Contact Professor of Psychology and Environmental Studies, Randolph College, 2500 Rivermont Avenue, Lynchburg, VA 24503. *Phone:* 434-947-8546. *Fax:* 434-947-8138. *E-mail:* rbarnes@randolphcollege.edu. *Web site:* www.randolphcollege.edu/.

Shenandoah University
Winchester, Virginia

Sustainability Initiatives Shenandoah University's president has signed the American College & University Presidents Climate Commitment.

Academics *Sustainability-focused undergraduate major(s):* Environmental Studies (BS). *Sustainability courses and programs:* sustainability-focused course(s) or lecture series.

Student Services and Green Events *Sustainability leadership:* sustainability coordinator/director, sustainability committee/advisory council, recycling manager, energy manager.

Food Sustainable, organic, and/or locally produced foods available in on-campus dining facilities. Fair Trade coffee is used. Vegan and vegetarian dining options are available for every meal.

Transportation Provides public transportation access to local destinations.

Buildings and Grounds *Campus grounds care:* uses water conservation devices; employs strategies to reduce light pollution; landscapes with native plant species.

Recycling *Events and organizations:* RecycleMania. *Programs and activities:* sustains a computer/technology recycling program; replaces paper materials with online alternatives. *Campus dining operations:* uses reusable dishware; operates without trays; offers discounts for reusable mugs; uses bulk condiment dispensers and decreased packaging for to-go food service purchases.

Energy Currently uses or plans to use alternative sources of power; timers to regulate temperatures based on occupancy hours; motion, infrared, and/or light sensors to reduce energy uses for lighting; and LED lighting.

Purchasing Sustainability criteria used in purchasing include Energy Star (EPA).

Contact Sustainability Coordinator, Shenandoah University, 1460 University Drive, Winchester, VA 22601. *Phone:* 540-542-6533. *E-mail:* skeenan@su.edu. *Web site:* www.su.edu/.

University of Richmond
Richmond, Virginia

Sustainability Initiatives University of Richmond is a member of the Association for the Advancement of Sustainability in Higher Education (AASHE) and a signatory to the Talloires Declaration. This institution's president has signed the American College & University Presidents Climate Commitment.

Academics *Sustainability-focused undergraduate major(s):* Environmental Sciences (BA), Environmental Sciences (BS), University sponsors a dual-degree program with Duke University in Environmental Management or Forestry earning a bachelor's degree at UR, and a master's degree from Duke. *Sustainability courses and programs:* sustainability-focused course(s) or lecture series, noncredit sustainability course(s).

Student Services and Green Events *Sustainability leadership:* sustainability coordinator/director, sustainability committee/advisory council, recycling manager, energy manager, sustainability-focused student government. *Student clubs and activities:* student club(s)/group(s) focused on sustainability, outreach materials available about on-campus sustainability efforts. *Major sustainability events:* Conferences, symposia, and speakers; annual waste audit; Alternative Energy Festival. *Housing and facilities:* sustainability-themed housing.

Food Sustainable, organic, and/or locally produced foods available in on-campus dining facilities. Vegan and vegetarian dining options are available for every meal.

Transportation Provides free on-campus transportation (bus or other), public transportation access to local destinations, and incentives to carpool or use public transportation.

Buildings and Grounds *Renovation and maintenance:* registered for LEED certification for new construction and/or renovation. *Campus grounds care:* uses water conservation devices; employs strategies to reduce light pollution; landscapes with native plant species; protects, restores, and/or creates habitat on campus.

Recycling *Events and organizations:* RecycleMania. *Programs and activities:* sustains a computer/technology recycling program; maintains an on-campus recycling center; composts yard waste; reuses surplus department/office supplies; reuses chemicals; replaces paper materials with online alternatives; limits free printing in computer labs and libraries. *Campus dining operations:* uses reusable dishware; uses bulk condiment dispensers and decreased packaging for to-go food service purchases.

Energy Currently uses or plans to use timers to regulate temperatures based on occupancy hours and motion, infrared, and/or light sensors to reduce energy uses for lighting.

Purchasing Sustainability criteria used in purchasing include Energy Star (EPA), Green Electronics Council (GEC) Electronic Product Environmental Assessment Tool (EPEAT) Silver or Gold, and Forest Stewardship Council (FSC) or American Forest and Paper Association's Sustainable Forestry Initiative (SFI) paper.

Contact Sustainability Coordinator, University of Richmond, 28 Westhampton Way, Richmond, VA 23173. *Phone:* 804-289-8600. *Web site:* www.richmond.edu/.

University of Virginia
Charlottesville, Virginia

Sustainability Initiatives University of Virginia is a member of the Association for the Advancement of Sustainability in Higher Education (AASHE) and a signatory to the Talloires Declaration. University of Virginia has Green Fees (optional/required) dedicated to sustainability initiatives.

Academics *Sustainability-focused undergraduate major(s):* Civil and Environmental Engineering (BS), Environmental Sciences (BA), Environmental Thought and Practice (BA), Urban and Environmental Planning (BA). *Sustainability-focused graduate degree program(s):* Civil and Environmental Engineering (MS, PhD), Environmental Sciences (MA, MS, PhD), Urban and Environmental Planning (MUP). *Sustainability courses and programs:* sustainability-focused course(s) or lecture series.

Student Services and Green Events *Sustainability leadership:* sustainability coordinator/director, sustainability committee/advisory council, recycling manager, energy manager, sustainability-focused student government. *Student clubs and activities:* student club(s)/group(s) focused on sustainability, outreach materials available about on-campus sustainability efforts. *Major sustainability events:* National Conference on Climate Governance, Virginia Environmental Law Journal Symposium on Green and Sustainable Building, UVA Sustainability and Health Symposium, Greener Grounds: Community Briefing. *Housing and facilities:* on-campus organic garden for students.

Food Sustainable, organic, and/or locally produced foods available in on-campus dining facilities. Fair Trade coffee is used. Vegan and vegetarian dining options are available for every meal.

Transportation Provides free on-campus transportation (bus or other), public transportation access to local destinations, and incentives to carpool or use public transportation.

Buildings and Grounds *Renovation and maintenance:* registered for LEED certification for new construction and/or renovation; uses a Green Seal certified cleaning service. *Campus grounds care:* uses water conservation devices; employs strategies to reduce light pollution; landscapes with native plant species; protects, restores, and/or creates habitat on campus.

Recycling *Events and organizations:* RecycleMania, WasteWise (EPA). *Programs and activities:* sustains a computer/technology recycling program; maintains an on-campus recycling center; sustains a pre-consumer food waste composting program; sustains a post-consumer food waste composting program; composts yard waste; reuses surplus department/office supplies; replaces paper materials with online alternatives; limits free printing in computer labs and libraries. *Campus dining operations:* uses reusable dishware; operates without trays; offers discounts for reusable mugs; uses bulk condiment dispensers and decreased packaging for to-go food service purchases.

Energy Currently uses or plans to use alternative sources of power; timers to regulate temperatures based on occupancy hours; motion, infrared, and/or light sensors to reduce energy uses for lighting; and vending machine motion sensors.

Purchasing Sustainability criteria used in purchasing include Energy Star (EPA), Green Cleaning Products (Green Seal/Environmental Choice certified), and Forest Stewardship Council (FSC) or American Forest and Paper Association's Sustainable Forestry Initiative (SFI) paper.

Contact Sustainability Outreach Coordinator, University of Virginia, PO Box 400726, Charlottesville, VA 22904. *Phone:* 434-243-8594. *E-mail:* lld6b@virginia.edu. *Web site:* www.virginia.edu/.

Virginia Commonwealth University
Richmond, Virginia

Sustainability Initiatives Virginia Commonwealth University is a signatory to the Talloires Declaration. This institution's president has signed the American College & University Presidents Climate Commitment.

Academics *Sustainability courses and programs:* sustainability-focused course(s) or lecture series.

Student Services and Green Events *Sustainability leadership:* sustainability coordinator/director, sustainability committee/advisory council, recycling manager, energy manager, sustainability-focused student government. *Student clubs and activities:* student club(s)/group(s) focused on sustainability. *Major sustainability events:* ACUPCC Climate Leadership Summit, Fundamentals of Carbon Reduction and Certified Carbon Reduction Manager exam, LEED for New Construction Technical Review Workshop, Commonwealth of VA Energy and Sustainability Conference. *Housing and facilities:* sustainability-themed housing.

Food Sustainable, organic, and/or locally produced foods available in on-campus dining facilities. Fair Trade coffee is used. Vegan and vegetarian dining options are available for every meal.

Transportation Provides free on-campus transportation (bus or other), public transportation access to local destinations, and incentives to carpool or use public transportation.

Buildings and Grounds *Renovation and maintenance:* registered for LEED certification for new construction and/or renovation. *Campus grounds care:* uses water conservation devices; employs strategies to reduce light pollution; landscapes with native plant species; protects, restores, and/or creates habitat on campus.

Recycling *Events and organizations:* RecycleMania. *Programs and activities:* sustains a computer/technology recycling program; maintains an on-campus recycling center; reuses surplus department/office supplies; replaces paper materials with online alternatives; limits free printing in computer labs and libraries. *Campus dining operations:* uses reusable dishware; operates without trays; offers discounts for reusable mugs; uses bulk condiment dispensers and decreased packaging for to-go food service purchases.

Energy Currently uses or plans to use alternative sources of power (hydroelectricity/water power and solar energy); timers to regulate temperatures based on occupancy hours; motion, infrared, and/or light sensors to reduce energy uses for lighting; LED lighting; vending machine motion sensors; and energy-related performance contracting.

Purchasing Sustainability criteria used in purchasing include Energy Star (EPA) and Green Cleaning Products (Green Seal/Environmental Choice certified).

Contact Director of Sustainability, Virginia Commonwealth University, 1050 Oliver Hill Way, Room 202, PO Box 980166, Richmond, VA 23298-0166. *Phone:* 804-628-5199. *Fax:* 804-828-2857. *E-mail:* jghosh@vcu.edu. *Web site:* www.vcu.edu/.

Virginia Polytechnic Institute and State University
Blacksburg, Virginia

Academics *Sustainability-focused undergraduate major(s):* Environmental Engineering (BS), Environmental Policy and

Planning (BS), Environmental Science (BS), Humanities Science and Environment (BA), Green Engineering Program, Building Construction Program, Sustainability Energy Solutions for a Global Society. *Sustainability-focused graduate degree program(s):* Environmental Engineering (MS, PhD), Environmental Science (MS, PhD), Urban and Regional Planning (MS). *Sustainability courses and programs:* sustainability-focused course(s) or lecture series, noncredit sustainability course(s).

Student Services and Green Events *Sustainability leadership:* sustainability coordinator/director, sustainability committee/advisory council, recycling manager, energy manager, sustainability-focused student government. *Student clubs and activities:* Campus Climate Challenge, student club(s)/group(s) focused on sustainability. *Major sustainability events:* Virginia Power Shift Conference, Earth Week, Focus the Nation, Sustainability Week, the Arbor Day Foundations Tree Campus USA event. *Housing and facilities:* student-run café that serves environmentally or socially preferable foods.

Food Sustainable, organic, and/or locally produced foods available in on-campus dining facilities. Fair Trade coffee is used. Vegan and vegetarian dining options are available for every meal.

Transportation Provides free on-campus transportation (bus or other), public transportation access to local destinations, and incentives to carpool or use public transportation.

Buildings and Grounds *Percentage of institution's eligible buildings as of September 2008 meeting LEED and/or LEED-EB certification criteria:* 63%. *Renovation and maintenance:* registered for LEED certification for new construction and/or renovation; uses a Green Seal certified cleaning service. *Campus grounds care:* uses water conservation devices; employs strategies to reduce light pollution; landscapes with native plant species; protects, restores, and/or creates habitat on campus.

Recycling *Events and organizations:* RecycleMania. *Programs and activities:* sustains a computer/technology recycling program; composts yard waste; reuses surplus department/office supplies; reuses chemicals; replaces paper materials with online alternatives; limits free printing in computer labs and libraries. *Campus dining operations:* uses reusable dishware; operates without trays.

Energy Currently uses or plans to use timers to regulate temperatures based on occupancy hours; motion, infrared, and/or light sensors to reduce energy uses for lighting; LED lighting; vending machine motion sensors; and energy-related performance contracting.

Purchasing Sustainability criteria used in purchasing include Energy Star (EPA), Green Cleaning Products (Green Seal/Environmental Choice certified), and Forest Stewardship Council (FSC) or American Forest and Paper Association's Sustainable Forestry Initiative (SFI) paper.

Contact Sustainability Program Manager, Virginia Polytechnic Institute and State University, Office of the Associate Vice President for Facilities Services, Sterrett Facilities Complex (Mail Code 0127), Blacksburg, VA 24061. *Phone:* 540-231-5184. *Fax:* 540-231-4745. *E-mail:* denniscc@vt.edu. *Web site:* www.vt.edu/.

Virginia Union University
Richmond, Virginia

Student Services and Green Events *Sustainability leadership:* sustainability committee/advisory council, sustainability-focused student government.

Transportation Provides public transportation access to local destinations.

Contact Virginia Union University, 1500 North Lombardy Street, Richmond, VA 23220-1170. *Phone:* 804-257-5600. *Web site:* www.vuu.edu/.

Washington and Lee University
Lexington, Virginia

Sustainability Initiatives Washington and Lee University is a signatory to the Talloires Declaration. This institution's president has signed the American College & University Presidents Climate Commitment.

Academics *Sustainability-focused undergraduate major(s):* Environmental Studies (BA). *Sustainability courses and programs:* sustainability-focused course(s) or lecture series.

Student Services and Green Events *Sustainability leadership:* sustainability coordinator/director, sustainability committee/advisory council, recycling manager, energy manager. *Student clubs and activities:* student club(s)/group(s) focused on sustainability, outreach materials available about on-campus sustainability efforts. *Major sustainability events:* Campus Sustainability week, monthly lunchtime colloquia. *Housing and facilities:* on-campus organic garden for students.

Food Sustainable, organic, and/or locally produced foods available in on-campus dining facilities. Fair Trade coffee is used. Vegan and vegetarian dining options are available for every meal.

Transportation Provides public transportation access to local destinations and a bike loan/rental program.

Buildings and Grounds *Renovation and maintenance:* registered for LEED certification for new construction and/or renovation. *Campus grounds care:* uses water conservation devices; employs strategies to reduce light pollution; protects, restores, and/or creates habitat on campus.

Recycling *Events and organizations:* RecycleMania, WasteWise (EPA). *Programs and activities:* sustains a computer/technology recycling program; maintains an on-campus recycling center; sustains a pre-consumer food waste composting program; composts yard waste; replaces paper materials with online alternatives; limits free printing in computer labs and libraries. *Campus dining operations:* uses reusable dishware; operates without trays; offers discounts for reusable mugs; uses bulk condiment dispensers and decreased packaging for to-go food service purchases.

Energy Currently uses or plans to use motion, infrared, and/or light sensors to reduce energy uses for lighting and energy-related performance contracting.

Purchasing Sustainability criteria used in purchasing include Energy Star (EPA) and Forest Stewardship Council (FSC) or American Forest and Paper Association's Sustainable Forestry Initiative (SFI) paper.

Contact Environmental Management Coordinator, Washington and Lee University, Facilities Management Department, Denny Circle, Lexington, VA 24450. *Phone:* 540-458-8253. *E-mail:* jwise@wlu.edu. *Web site:* www.wlu.edu/.

Washington

Eastern Washington University
Cheney, Washington

Sustainability Initiatives Eastern Washington University's president has signed the American College & University Presidents Climate Commitment.

Student Services and Green Events *Sustainability leadership:* recycling manager.

Food Sustainable, organic, and/or locally produced foods available in on-campus dining facilities. Fair Trade coffee is used. Vegan and vegetarian dining options are available for every meal.

Transportation Provides public transportation access to local destinations and incentives to carpool or use public transportation.

Buildings and Grounds *Percentage of institution's eligible buildings as of September 2008 meeting LEED and/or LEED-EB certification criteria:* 2%. *Renovation and maintenance:* registered for LEED certification for new construction and/or renovation; uses a Green Seal certified cleaning service. *Campus grounds care:* uses water conservation devices; employs strategies to reduce light pollution; landscapes with native plant species.

Recycling *Events and organizations:* RecycleMania. *Programs and activities:* sustains a computer/technology recycling program; maintains an on-campus recycling center; composts yard waste; replaces paper materials with online alternatives; limits free printing in computer labs and libraries. *Campus dining operations:* uses reusable dishware; offers discounts for reusable mugs.

Energy Currently uses or plans to use alternative sources of power (hydroelectricity/water power); timers to regulate temperatures based on occupancy hours; motion, infrared, and/or light sensors to reduce energy uses for lighting; LED lighting; vending machine motion sensors; and energy-related performance contracting.

Contact Eastern Washington University, 526 5th Street, Cheney, WA 99004-2431. *Phone:* 509-359-6200. *Web site:* www.ewu.edu/.

The Evergreen State College
Olympia, Washington

Sustainability Initiatives The Evergreen State College is a member of the Association for the Advancement of Sustainability in Higher Education (AASHE) and a signatory to the Talloires Declaration. This institution's president has signed the American College & University Presidents Climate Commitment. The Evergreen State College has Green Fees (optional/required) dedicated to sustainability initiatives.

Academics *Sustainability-focused graduate degree program(s):* Environmental Studies (MES), Public Administration (MPA). *Sustainability courses and programs:* sustainability-focused course(s) or lecture series, noncredit sustainability course(s).

Student Services and Green Events *Sustainability leadership:* sustainability coordinator/director, sustainability committee/advisory council, recycling manager, energy manager, sustainability-focused student government. *Student clubs and activities:* Campus Climate Challenge, Public Interest Research Group (PIRG) chapter on campus, student club(s)/group(s) focused on sustainability, outreach materials available about on-campus sustainability efforts. *Major sustainability events:* SYNERGY: The Sustainable Living Conference, Annual Clean Energy Fair, The Rachel Carson Forum. *Housing and facilities:* sustainability-themed housing, model dorm room that demonstrates sustainable living principles, student-run café that serves environmentally or socially preferable foods, on-campus organic garden for students.

Food Sustainable, organic, and/or locally produced foods available in on-campus dining facilities. Fair Trade coffee is used. Vegan and vegetarian dining options are available for every meal.

Transportation Provides free on-campus transportation (bus or other), public transportation access to local destinations, a car sharing program, and incentives to carpool or use public transportation.

Buildings and Grounds *Renovation and maintenance:* registered for LEED certification for new construction and/or renovation; uses a Green Seal certified cleaning service. *Campus grounds care:* uses water conservation devices; employs strategies to reduce light pollution; landscapes with native plant species; protects, restores, and/or creates habitat on campus; applies to its grounds only pesticides and fertilizers allowable under the U.S. Department of Agriculture's standards for crop production.

Recycling *Events and organizations:* RecycleMania. *Programs and activities:* sustains a computer/technology recycling program; maintains an on-campus recycling center; sustains a pre-consumer food waste composting program; sustains a post-consumer food waste composting program; composts yard waste; reuses surplus department/office supplies; replaces paper materials with online alternatives. *Campus dining operations:* uses reusable dishware; operates without trays; offers discounts for reusable mugs; uses bulk condiment dispensers and decreased packaging for to-go food service purchases.

Energy Currently uses or plans to use alternative sources of power (biomass energy and solar energy); motion, infrared, and/or light sensors to reduce energy uses for lighting; LED lighting; and energy-related performance contracting. Participates in College & University Green Power Challenge activities.

Purchasing Sustainability criteria used in purchasing include Energy Star (EPA), Green Electronics Council (GEC) Electronic Product Environmental Assessment Tool (EPEAT) Silver or Gold, Green Cleaning Products (Green Seal/Environmental Choice certified), and Forest Stewardship Council (FSC) or American Forest and Paper Association's Sustainable Forestry Initiative (SFI) paper.

Contact Director of Sustainability, The Evergreen State College, 2700 Evergreen Parkway NW, Olympia, WA 98505. *Phone:* 360-867-6913. *E-mail:* sustainabilitydirector@evergreen.edu. *Web site:* www.evergreen.edu/.

Gonzaga University
Spokane, Washington

Academics *Sustainability-focused undergraduate major(s):* Environmental Studies (BA). *Sustainability courses and programs:* sustainability-focused course(s) or lecture series.

Student Services and Green Events *Sustainability leadership:* sustainability coordinator/director, sustainability committee/advisory council, recycling manager, energy manager, sustainability-focused student government. *Student clubs and activities:* outreach materials available about on-campus sustainability efforts. *Housing and facilities:* sustainability-themed housing, student-run café that serves environmentally or socially preferable foods.

Food Sustainable, organic, and/or locally produced foods available in on-campus dining facilities. Fair Trade coffee is used. Vegan and vegetarian dining options are available for every meal.

Transportation Provides public transportation access to local destinations, a bike loan/rental program, a car sharing program, and incentives to carpool or use public transportation.

Buildings and Grounds *Percentage of institution's eligible buildings as of September 2008 meeting LEED and/or LEED-EB certification criteria:* 5%.

Recycling *Programs and activities:* sustains a computer/technology recycling program; maintains an on-campus recycling center; composts yard waste; reuses surplus department/office supplies; reuses chemicals; replaces paper materials with online alternatives. *Campus dining operations:* offers discounts for reusable mugs.

Energy Currently uses or plans to use alternative sources of power (biomass energy, hydroelectricity/water power, and wind energy); timers to regulate temperatures based on occupancy hours; motion, infrared, and/or light sensors to reduce energy uses for lighting; LED lighting; and vending machine motion sensors.

Purchasing Sustainability criteria used in purchasing include Energy Star (EPA) and Green Cleaning Products (Green Seal/Environmental Choice certified).

Contact Co-Chair, Advisory Council on Stewardship and Sustainability, Gonzaga University, 502 East Boone Avenue, Spokane, WA 99258. *Phone:* 509-313-5885. *E-mail:* sustainability@gonzaga.edu. *Web site:* www.gonzaga.edu/.

Pacific Lutheran University
Tacoma, Washington

Sustainability Initiatives Pacific Lutheran University is a member of the Association for the Advancement of Sustainability in Higher Education (AASHE) and a signatory to the Talloires Declaration. This institution's president has signed the American College & University Presidents Climate Commitment. Pacific Lutheran University has Green Fees (optional/required) dedicated to sustainability initiatives.

Academics *Sustainability courses and programs:* sustainability-focused course(s) or lecture series.

Student Services and Green Events *Sustainability leadership:* sustainability committee/advisory council, recycling manager, sustainability-focused student government. *Student clubs and activities:* Campus Climate Challenge, student club(s)/group(s) focused on sustainability, outreach materials available about on-campus sustainability efforts. *Major sustainability events:* Pierce County Higher Education Sustainability Summit Co-sponsor, Earth Week Program. *Housing and facilities:* on-campus organic garden for students.

Food Sustainable, organic, and/or locally produced foods available in on-campus dining facilities. Fair Trade coffee is used. Vegan and vegetarian dining options are available for every meal.

Transportation Provides free on-campus transportation (bus or other), public transportation access to local destinations, a bike loan/rental program, and incentives to carpool or use public transportation.

Buildings and Grounds *Percentage of institution's eligible buildings as of September 2008 meeting LEED and/or LEED-EB certification criteria:* 12%. *Renovation and maintenance:* registered for LEED certification for new construction and/or renovation; uses a Green Seal certified cleaning service. *Campus grounds care:* uses water conservation devices; employs strategies to reduce light pollution; landscapes with native plant species; protects, restores, and/or creates habitat on campus.

Recycling *Events and organizations:* RecycleMania. *Programs and activities:* sustains a computer/technology recycling program; maintains an on-campus recycling center; sustains a pre-consumer food waste composting program; sustains a post-consumer food waste composting program; composts yard waste; reuses surplus department/office supplies; reuses chemicals; replaces paper materials with online alternatives; limits free printing in computer labs and libraries. *Campus dining operations:* uses reusable dishware; offers discounts for reusable mugs; uses bulk condiment dispensers and decreased packaging for to-go food service purchases.

Energy Currently uses or plans to use alternative sources of power (geothermal energy, hydroelectricity/water power, and wind energy); timers to regulate temperatures based on occupancy hours; motion, infrared, and/or light sensors to reduce energy uses for lighting; and LED lighting. Participates in College & University Green Power Challenge activities.

Purchasing Sustainability criteria used in purchasing include Energy Star (EPA) and Green Cleaning Products (Green Seal/Environmental Choice certified).

Contact Sustainability Committee Chairperson, Pacific Lutheran University, Tacoma, WA 98447. *Phone:* 253-535-8104. *E-mail:* sustain@plu.edu. *Web site:* www.plu.edu/.

Seattle Pacific University
Seattle, Washington

Sustainability Initiatives Seattle Pacific University's president has signed the American College & University Presidents Climate Commitment.

Academics *Sustainability-focused undergraduate major(s):* Biology—Ecology (BS), Engineering—Sustainable and Appropriate Technology (BS), Global Development Studies (BA). *Sustainability courses and programs:* sustainability-focused course(s) or lecture series.

Student Services and Green Events *Sustainability leadership:* sustainability coordinator/director, sustainability committee/advisory council, recycling manager. *Housing and facilities:* student-run café that serves environmentally or socially preferable foods.

Food Sustainable, organic, and/or locally produced foods available in on-campus dining facilities. Fair Trade coffee is used.

Transportation Provides public transportation access to local destinations, a car sharing program, and incentives to carpool or use public transportation.

Buildings and Grounds *Renovation and maintenance:* registered for LEED certification for new construction and/or renovation. *Campus grounds care:* uses water conservation devices; landscapes with native plant species; protects, restores, and/or creates habitat on campus.

Recycling *Events and organizations:* RecycleMania. *Programs and activities:* sustains a computer/technology recycling program; sustains a pre-consumer food waste composting program; sustains a post-consumer food waste composting program; composts yard waste; replaces paper materials with online alternatives; limits free printing in computer labs and libraries. *Campus dining operations:* uses reusable dishware; operates without trays; offers discounts for reusable mugs; uses bulk condiment dispensers and decreased packaging for to-go food service purchases.

Energy Currently uses or plans to use alternative sources of power (hydroelectricity/water power and wind energy); timers to regulate temperatures based on occupancy hours; and motion, infrared, and/or light sensors to reduce energy uses for lighting.

Purchasing Sustainability criteria used in purchasing include Energy Star (EPA) and Green Electronics Council (GEC) Electronic Product Environmental Assessment Tool (EPEAT) Silver or Gold.

Contact Sustainability Coordinator, Seattle Pacific University, 3307 Third Avenue West, Suite 311, Seattle, WA 98119. *Phone:* 206-281-2592. *E-mail:* walrab@spu.edu. *Web site:* www.spu.edu/.

Seattle University
Seattle, Washington

Sustainability Initiatives Seattle University's president has signed the American College & University Presidents Climate Commitment.

Academics *Sustainability-focused undergraduate major(s):* Civil Engineering, Environmental Engineering specialization (BS); Environmental Science (BS); Environmental Studies (BA). *Sustainability-focused graduate degree program(s):* Organization Systems Design and Renewal (MA). *Sustainability courses and programs:* sustainability-focused course(s) or lecture series.

Student Services and Green Events *Sustainability leadership:* sustainability coordinator/director, sustainability committee/advisory council, recycling manager, energy manager. *Student clubs and activities:* student club(s)/group(s) focused on sustainability. *Major sustainability events:* Faculty and Staff Convocation, Working Collaboratively for Sustainability Conference, Focus the Nation, Academic Salon. *Housing and facilities:* sustainability-themed housing, on-campus organic garden for students.

Food Sustainable, organic, and/or locally produced foods available in on-campus dining facilities. Fair Trade coffee is used. Vegan and vegetarian dining options are available for every meal.

Transportation Provides a car sharing program and incentives to carpool or use public transportation.

Buildings and Grounds *Renovation and maintenance:* registered for LEED certification for new construction and/or renovation. *Campus grounds care:* uses water conservation devices; employs strategies to reduce light pollution; landscapes with native plant species; protects, restores, and/or creates habitat on campus.

Recycling *Programs and activities:* sustains a computer/technology recycling program; maintains an on-campus recycling center; sustains a pre-consumer food waste composting program; sustains a post-consumer food waste composting program; composts yard waste; reuses surplus department/office supplies; reuses chemicals; replaces paper materials with online alternatives; limits free printing in computer labs and libraries. *Campus dining operations:* uses reusable dishware; offers discounts for reusable mugs; uses bulk condiment dispensers and decreased packaging for to-go food service purchases.

Energy Currently uses or plans to use alternative sources of power (hydroelectricity/water power and solar energy); timers to regulate temperatures based on occupancy hours; and motion, infrared, and/or light sensors to reduce energy uses for lighting.

Purchasing Sustainability criteria used in purchasing include Energy Star (EPA), WaterSense (EPA), Green Electronics Council (GEC) Electronic Product Environmental Assessment Tool (EPEAT) Silver or Gold, Green Cleaning Products (Green Seal/Environmental Choice certified), and Forest Stewardship Council (FSC) or American Forest and Paper Association's Sustainable Forestry Initiative (SFI) paper.

Contact Campus Sustainability Manager, Seattle University, 901 12th Avenue, PO Box 222000, Seattle, WA 98122. *Phone:* 206-296-6997. *E-mail:* kprice@seattleu.edu. *Web site:* www.seattleu.edu/.

Whitman College
Walla Walla, Washington

Sustainability Initiatives Whitman College has Green Fees (optional/required) dedicated to sustainability initiatives.

Academics *Sustainability-focused undergraduate major(s):* Environmental Studies combined majors. *Sustainability courses and programs:* sustainability-focused course(s) or lecture series.

Student Services and Green Events *Sustainability leadership:* sustainability coordinator/director, sustainability committee/advisory council, recycling manager. *Student clubs and activities:* Campus Climate Challenge, student club(s)/group(s) focused on sustainability. *Major sustainability events:* Campus Sustainability Day, Dining Hall Eat Local Day, Vegetarian and Low Carbon Diet Day. *Housing and facilities:* sustainability-themed housing, on-campus organic garden for students.

Food Sustainable, organic, and/or locally produced foods available in on-campus dining facilities. Fair Trade coffee is used. Vegan and vegetarian dining options are available for every meal.

Transportation Provides public transportation access to local destinations.

Buildings and Grounds *Renovation and maintenance:* uses a Green Seal certified cleaning service. *Campus grounds care:* uses water conservation devices; employs strategies to reduce light pollution; landscapes with native plant species; protects, restores, and/or creates habitat on campus; applies to its grounds only pesticides and fertilizers allowable under the U.S. Department of Agriculture's standards for crop production.

Recycling *Programs and activities:* sustains a computer/technology recycling program; maintains an on-campus recycling center; sustains a pre-consumer food waste composting program; composts yard waste; reuses surplus department/office supplies; reuses chemicals; replaces paper materials with online alternatives. *Campus dining operations:* uses reusable dishware; operates without trays; offers discounts for reusable mugs; uses bulk condiment dispensers and decreased packaging for to-go food service purchases.

Energy Currently uses or plans to use alternative sources of power (geothermal energy, hydroelectricity/water power, solar energy, and wind energy); timers to regulate temperatures based on occupancy hours; motion, infrared, and/or light sensors to reduce energy uses for lighting; LED lighting; and vending machine motion sensors.

Purchasing Sustainability criteria used in purchasing include Energy Star (EPA) and Green Cleaning Products (Green Seal/Environmental Choice certified).

Contact Whitman College, 345 Boyer Avenue, Walla Walla, WA 99362-2083. *Phone:* 509-527-5111. *Web site:* www.whitman.edu/.

West Virginia

American Public University System
Charles Town, West Virginia

Sustainability Initiatives American Public University System's president has signed the American College & University Presidents Climate Commitment.

Academics *Sustainability-focused undergraduate major(s):* Environmental Studies, Environmental Management (BS). *Sustainability-focused graduate degree program(s):* Environmental Management and Policy, Global Environmental Management (MS).

Student Services and Green Events *Sustainability leadership:* sustainability coordinator/director, sustainability committee/advisory council.

Buildings and Grounds *Renovation and maintenance:* registered for LEED certification for new construction and/or renovation. *Campus grounds care:* uses water conservation devices; landscapes with native plant species.

Recycling *Programs and activities:* sustains a computer/technology recycling program; maintains an on-campus recycling center; replaces paper materials with online alternatives.

Energy Currently uses or plans to use timers to regulate temperatures based on occupancy hours; motion, infrared, and/or light sensors to reduce energy uses for lighting; and energy-related performance contracting.

Purchasing Sustainability criteria used in purchasing include Energy Star (EPA), Green Electronics Council (GEC) Electronic Product Environmental Assessment Tool (EPEAT) Silver or Gold, and Green Cleaning Products (Green Seal/Environmental Choice certified).

Contact Administrative Assistant, American Public University System, 111 West Congress Street, Charles Town, WV 25414. *Phone:* 304-885-5250. *Fax:* 304-724-0954. *E-mail:* aadams@apus.edu. *Web site:* www.apus.edu/.

Shepherd University
Shepherdstown, West Virginia

Academics *Sustainability-focused undergraduate major(s):* Environmental Studies (BS). *Sustainability courses and programs:* sustainability-focused course(s) or lecture series.

Student Services and Green Events *Student clubs and activities:* student club(s)/group(s) focused on sustainability, outreach materials available about on-campus sustainability efforts. *Major sustainability events:* Solar Solutions for West Virginia (with West Virginia Division of Energy), Alternative Energy Odyssey Conference (with West Virginia Development Office), Bringing Renewable Energy to West Virginia (with West Virginia Development Office).

Food Sustainable, organic, and/or locally produced foods available in on-campus dining facilities. Fair Trade coffee is used. Vegan and vegetarian dining options are available for every meal.

Transportation Provides free on-campus transportation (bus or other) and public transportation access to local destinations.

Buildings and Grounds *Campus grounds care:* uses water conservation devices; employs strategies to reduce light pollution; landscapes with native plant species; protects, restores, and/or creates habitat on campus.

Recycling *Events and organizations:* RecycleMania. *Programs and activities:* sustains a computer/technology recycling program. *Campus dining operations:* uses reusable dishware; offers discounts for reusable mugs; uses bulk condiment dispensers and decreased packaging for to-go food service purchases.

Energy Currently uses or plans to use motion, infrared, and/or light sensors to reduce energy uses for lighting.

Contact Shepherd University, PO Box 3210, Shepherdstown, WV 25443-3210. *Phone:* 304-876-5000. *Web site:* www.shepherd.edu/.

West Virginia University
Morgantown, West Virginia

Academics *Sustainability-focused undergraduate major(s):* Applied and Environmental Microbiology (BS), Environmental and Natural Resource Economics (BS), Environmental Engineering (BS), Environmental Geoscience (BS), Environ-

mental Protection (BS). *Sustainability-focused graduate degree program(s):* Agricultural and Resource Economics (MS), Environmental Engineering (MS), Resource Management and Sustainable Development (PhD). *Sustainability courses and programs:* sustainability-focused course(s) or lecture series, noncredit sustainability course(s).

Student Services and Green Events *Sustainability leadership:* sustainability coordinator/director, sustainability committee/advisory council, recycling manager, energy manager. *Student clubs and activities:* student club(s)/group(s) focused on sustainability, outreach materials available about on-campus sustainability efforts. *Major sustainability events:* WE CAN Ecolympics, Blue and Gold Mine Sale, Mountaineers Recycle, A-wear-ness Campaign, Sustainable Schools West Virginia Summit, Alternative Transportation Week, Focus the Nation.

Food Sustainable, organic, and/or locally produced foods available in on-campus dining facilities. Fair Trade coffee is used. Vegan and vegetarian dining options are available for every meal.

Transportation Provides free on-campus transportation (bus or other), public transportation access to local destinations, a car sharing program, and incentives to carpool or use public transportation.

Buildings and Grounds *Renovation and maintenance:* registered for LEED certification for new construction and/or renovation; uses a Green Seal certified cleaning service. *Campus grounds care:* uses water conservation devices; protects, restores, and/or creates habitat on campus.

Recycling *Programs and activities:* sustains a computer/technology recycling program; composts yard waste; reuses chemicals; replaces paper materials with online alternatives; limits free printing in computer labs and libraries. *Campus dining operations:* uses reusable dishware; operates without trays; offers discounts for reusable mugs; uses bulk condiment dispensers and decreased packaging for to-go food service purchases.

Energy Currently uses or plans to use timers to regulate temperatures based on occupancy hours; motion, infrared, and/or light sensors to reduce energy uses for lighting; LED lighting; and energy-related performance contracting.

Contact Director of Sustainability, West Virginia University, PO Box 6555, One Waterfront Place, Morgantown, WV 26506. *Phone:* 304-293-7916. *Fax:* 304-293-7156. *E-mail:* csolomon@wvu.edu. *Web site:* www.wvu.edu/.

Wisconsin

Concordia University Wisconsin
Mequon, Wisconsin

Academics *Sustainability-focused undergraduate major(s):* Environmental Studies (BS). *Sustainability-focused graduate degree program(s):* Environmental Education (BSE). *Sustainability courses and programs:* sustainability-focused course(s) or lecture series.

Student Services and Green Events *Sustainability leadership:* sustainability coordinator/director, sustainability committee/advisory council, recycling manager.

Food Sustainable, organic, and/or locally produced foods available in on-campus dining facilities. Fair Trade coffee is used. Vegan and vegetarian dining options are available for every meal.

Transportation Provides a car sharing program.

Buildings and Grounds *Renovation and maintenance:* registered for LEED certification for new construction and/or

renovation; uses a Green Seal certified cleaning service. *Campus grounds care:* uses water conservation devices; employs strategies to reduce light pollution; landscapes with native plant species; protects, restores, and/or creates habitat on campus.

Recycling *Programs and activities:* maintains an on-campus recycling center.

Energy Currently uses or plans to use alternative sources of power; motion, infrared, and/or light sensors to reduce energy uses for lighting; and LED lighting.

Purchasing Sustainability criteria used in purchasing include Energy Star (EPA) and Green Cleaning Products (Green Seal/Environmental Choice certified).

Contact Sustainability Coordinator, Concordia University Wisconsin, 12800 North Lake Shore Drive, Mequon, WI 53097. *Phone:* 262-243-4215. *Fax:* 262-243-4564. *E-mail:* lawrence.sohn@cuw.edu. *Web site:* www.cuw.edu/.

Edgewood College
Madison, Wisconsin

Academics *Sustainability-focused graduate degree program(s):* Individualized Masters in Education program is available in Environmental Studies. *Sustainability courses and programs:* sustainability-focused course(s) or lecture series.

Student Services and Green Events *Sustainability leadership:* sustainability coordinator/director, sustainability committee/advisory council, recycling manager. *Student clubs and activities:* student club(s)/group(s) focused on sustainability, outreach materials available about on-campus sustainability efforts. *Major sustainability events:* Earth Week, Eco-Olympics competition among residence halls. *Housing and facilities:* sustainability-themed housing.

Food Fair Trade coffee is used.

Transportation Provides free on-campus transportation (bus or other), public transportation access to local destinations, and incentives to carpool or use public transportation.

Buildings and Grounds *Percentage of institution's eligible buildings as of September 2008 meeting LEED and/or LEED-EB certification criteria:* 15%. *Renovation and maintenance:* registered for LEED certification for new construction and/or renovation. *Campus grounds care:* uses water conservation devices; employs strategies to reduce light pollution; landscapes with native plant species; protects, restores, and/or creates habitat on campus.

Recycling *Programs and activities:* sustains a computer/technology recycling program; composts yard waste; replaces paper materials with online alternatives. *Campus dining operations:* uses reusable dishware; offers discounts for reusable mugs; uses bulk condiment dispensers and decreased packaging for to-go food service purchases.

Energy Currently uses or plans to use alternative sources of power (wind energy); motion, infrared, and/or light sensors to reduce energy uses for lighting; LED lighting; and vending machine motion sensors.

Purchasing Sustainability criteria used in purchasing include Energy Star (EPA) and Green Cleaning Products (Green Seal/Environmental Choice certified).

Contact Campus Sustainability Coordinator, Edgewood College, 1000 Edgewood College Drive, Madison, WI 53711. *Phone:* 608-663-2254. *Fax:* 608-663-3291. *E-mail:* teandrews@edgewood.edu. *Web site:* www.edgewood.edu/.

Lawrence University
Appleton, Wisconsin

Sustainability Initiatives Lawrence University is a signatory to the Talloires Declaration.

Academics *Sustainability-focused undergraduate major(s):* Environmental Studies (BA). *Sustainability courses and programs:* sustainability-focused course(s) or lecture series.

Student Services and Green Events *Sustainability leadership:* sustainability committee/advisory council, energy manager, sustainability-focused student government. *Student clubs and activities:* student club(s)/group(s) focused on sustainability, outreach materials available about on-campus sustainability efforts. *Major sustainability events:* Earth Week, Yearly Symposium on Environmental Topics, Spoerl Lecture Series. *Housing and facilities:* sustainability-themed housing, on-campus organic garden for students.

Food Sustainable, organic, and/or locally produced foods available in on-campus dining facilities. Fair Trade coffee is used. Vegan and vegetarian dining options are available for every meal.

Transportation Provides public transportation access to local destinations, a bike loan/rental program, and incentives to carpool or use public transportation.

Buildings and Grounds *Renovation and maintenance:* registered for LEED certification for new construction and/or renovation. *Campus grounds care:* uses water conservation devices; landscapes with native plant species; protects, restores, and/or creates habitat on campus.

Recycling *Events and organizations:* RecycleMania. *Programs and activities:* sustains a computer/technology recycling program; sustains a pre-consumer food waste composting program; composts yard waste; replaces paper materials with online alternatives. *Campus dining operations:* operates without trays; offers discounts for reusable mugs; uses bulk condiment dispensers and decreased packaging for to-go food service purchases.

Energy Currently uses or plans to use timers to regulate temperatures based on occupancy hours; motion, infrared, and/or light sensors to reduce energy uses for lighting; and LED lighting.

Purchasing Sustainability criteria used in purchasing include Energy Star (EPA).

Contact Faculty Associate to the President for Sustainability, Lawrence University, 115 South Drew Street, Appleton, WI 54911. *Phone:* 920-832-6733. *Fax:* 920-832-6962. *E-mail:* clarkj@lawrence.edu. *Web site:* www.lawrence.edu/.

Marquette University
Milwaukee, Wisconsin

Academics *Sustainability-focused graduate degree program(s):* Civil Engineering with Environmental focus, Environmental Ethics. *Sustainability courses and programs:* sustainability-focused course(s) or lecture series.

Student Services and Green Events *Sustainability leadership:* sustainability coordinator/director, sustainability committee/advisory council, recycling manager, energy manager, sustainability-focused student government. *Student clubs and activities:* student club(s)/group(s) focused on sustainability, outreach materials available about on-campus sustainability efforts. *Major sustainability events:* Power by the People Concert.

Food Sustainable, organic, and/or locally produced foods available in on-campus dining facilities. Fair Trade coffee is used. Vegan and vegetarian dining options are available for every meal.

Transportation Provides free on-campus transportation (bus or other), public transportation access to local destinations, and incentives to carpool or use public transportation.

Buildings and Grounds *Renovation and maintenance:* registered for LEED certification for new construction and/or

renovation. *Campus grounds care:* uses water conservation devices; employs strategies to reduce light pollution; landscapes with native plant species; protects, restores, and/or creates habitat on campus.

Recycling *Programs and activities:* sustains a computer/ technology recycling program; reuses surplus department/ office supplies; reuses chemicals; replaces paper materials with online alternatives; limits free printing in computer labs and libraries. *Campus dining operations:* uses bulk condiment dispensers and decreased packaging for to-go food service purchases.

Energy Currently uses or plans to use alternative sources of power; motion, infrared, and/or light sensors to reduce energy uses for lighting; LED lighting; and energy-related performance contracting.

Purchasing Sustainability criteria used in purchasing include Energy Star (EPA) and Green Cleaning Products (Green Seal/Environmental Choice certified).

Contact Assistant to the Vice President of Administration, Marquette University, PO Box 1881, 707 North 11th Street, Room 422, Milwaukee, WI 53201-1881. *Phone:* 414-288-1463. *Fax:* 414-288-1451. *E-mail:* mike.whittow@mu.edu. *Web site:* www.marquette.edu/.

Northland College
Ashland, Wisconsin

Sustainability Initiatives Northland College is a member of the Association for the Advancement of Sustainability in Higher Education (AASHE) and a signatory to the Talloires Declaration. This institution's president has signed the American College & University Presidents Climate Commitment. Northland College has Green Fees (optional/ required) dedicated to sustainability initiatives.

Academics *Sustainability-focused undergraduate major(s):* Environmental Chemistry (BS), Environmental Geosciences (BS), Humanity and Nature Studies (BA), Natural Resources (BS), Outdoor Education (BA), Sustainable Community Development (BA). *Sustainability courses and programs:* sustainability-focused course(s) or lecture series, noncredit sustainability course(s), sustainability-focused nonacademic certificate program(s).

Student Services and Green Events *Sustainability leadership:* sustainability coordinator/director, sustainability committee/advisory council, recycling manager, energy manager, sustainability-focused student government. *Student clubs and activities:* student club(s)/group(s) focused on sustainability, outreach materials available about on-campus sustainability efforts. *Major sustainability events:* Energy Awareness Month, Dark Skies Festival, RecycleMania, Northland College Earth Day. *Housing and facilities:* sustainability-themed housing, model dorm room that demonstrates sustainable living principles, on-campus organic garden for students.

Food Sustainable, organic, and/or locally produced foods available in on-campus dining facilities. Fair Trade coffee is used. Vegan and vegetarian dining options are available for every meal.

Transportation Provides free on-campus transportation (bus or other), public transportation access to local destinations, a bike loan/rental program, a car sharing program, and incentives to carpool or use public transportation.

Buildings and Grounds *Renovation and maintenance:* registered for LEED certification for new construction and/or renovation. *Campus grounds care:* uses water conservation devices; employs strategies to reduce light pollution; landscapes with native plant species; protects, restores, and/or creates habitat on campus.

Recycling *Events and organizations:* RecycleMania. *Programs and activities:* sustains a computer/technology recycling program; maintains an on-campus recycling center; sustains a pre-consumer food waste composting program; sustains a post-consumer food waste composting program; composts yard waste; reuses surplus department/office supplies; reuses chemicals; replaces paper materials with online alternatives. *Campus dining operations:* uses reusable dishware; operates without trays; offers discounts for reusable mugs; uses bulk condiment dispensers and decreased packaging for to-go food service purchases.

Energy Currently uses or plans to use alternative sources of power (geothermal energy, solar energy, and wind energy) and motion, infrared, and/or light sensors to reduce energy uses for lighting.

Purchasing Sustainability criteria used in purchasing include Energy Star (EPA), Green Cleaning Products (Green Seal/Environmental Choice certified), and Forest Stewardship Council (FSC) or American Forest and Paper Association's Sustainable Forestry Initiative (SFI) paper.

Contact Campus Sustainability Coordinator, Northland College, 1411 Ellis Avenue, Ashland, WI 54806. *Phone:* 715-682-1492. *E-mail:* chintz@northland.edu. *Web site:* www.northland.edu/.

St. Norbert College
De Pere, Wisconsin

Sustainability Initiatives St. Norbert College's president has signed the American College & University Presidents Climate Commitment.

Academics *Sustainability-focused undergraduate major(s):* Environmental Science. *Sustainability courses and programs:* sustainability-focused course(s) or lecture series.

Student Services and Green Events *Sustainability leadership:* sustainability committee/advisory council, recycling manager, energy manager. *Student clubs and activities:* Campus Climate Challenge, student club(s)/group(s) focused on sustainability, outreach materials available about on-campus sustainability efforts. *Major sustainability events:* National Teach-In Day: Our Carbon Footprint and Global Warming. *Housing and facilities:* sustainability-themed housing.

Food Sustainable, organic, and/or locally produced foods available in on-campus dining facilities. Vegan and vegetarian dining options are available for every meal.

Transportation Provides public transportation access to local destinations.

Buildings and Grounds *Campus grounds care:* uses water conservation devices; employs strategies to reduce light pollution; landscapes with native plant species; applies to its grounds only pesticides and fertilizers allowable under the U.S. Department of Agriculture's standards for crop production.

Recycling *Events and organizations:* RecycleMania. *Programs and activities:* sustains a computer/technology recycling program; maintains an on-campus recycling center; sustains a pre-consumer food waste composting program; sustains a post-consumer food waste composting program; composts yard waste; reuses surplus department/office supplies; reuses chemicals; replaces paper materials with online alternatives; limits free printing in computer labs and libraries. *Campus dining operations:* uses reusable dishware; operates without trays; uses bulk condiment dispensers and decreased packaging for to-go food service purchases.

Energy Currently uses or plans to use alternative sources of power (solar energy); timers to regulate temperatures based on occupancy hours; motion, infrared, and/or light sensors to reduce energy uses for lighting; LED lighting; and vending machine motion sensors.

Purchasing Sustainability criteria used in purchasing include Energy Star (EPA), Green Electronics Council (GEC) Electronic Product Environmental Assessment Tool (EPEAT) Silver or Gold, and Green Cleaning Products (Green Seal/Environmental Choice certified).

Contact St. Norbert College, 100 Grant Street, De Pere, WI 54115-2099. *Phone:* 920-337-3181. *Web site:* www.snc.edu/.

University of Wisconsin–Eau Claire
Eau Claire, Wisconsin

Sustainability Initiatives University of Wisconsin–Eau Claire's president has signed the American College & University Presidents Climate Commitment. University of Wisconsin–Eau Claire has Green Fees (optional/required) dedicated to sustainability initiatives.

Student Services and Green Events *Sustainability leadership:* sustainability coordinator/director, sustainability committee/advisory council, recycling manager, sustainability-focused student government. *Housing and facilities:* on-campus organic garden for students.

Food Sustainable, organic, and/or locally produced foods available in on-campus dining facilities. Fair Trade coffee is used. Vegan and vegetarian dining options are available for every meal.

Transportation Provides free on-campus transportation (bus or other), public transportation access to local destinations, and incentives to carpool or use public transportation.

Buildings and Grounds *Renovation and maintenance:* registered for LEED certification for new construction and/or renovation; uses a Green Seal certified cleaning service. *Campus grounds care:* uses water conservation devices; employs strategies to reduce light pollution; applies to its grounds only pesticides and fertilizers allowable under the U.S. Department of Agriculture's standards for crop production.

Recycling *Events and organizations:* RecycleMania. *Programs and activities:* sustains a computer/technology recycling program; maintains an on-campus recycling center; composts yard waste; reuses surplus department/office supplies; replaces paper materials with online alternatives. *Campus dining operations:* uses reusable dishware; operates without trays; offers discounts for reusable mugs; uses bulk condiment dispensers and decreased packaging for to-go food service purchases.

Energy Currently uses or plans to use alternative sources of power (hydroelectricity/water power and wind energy); timers to regulate temperatures based on occupancy hours; motion, infrared, and/or light sensors to reduce energy uses for lighting; vending machine motion sensors; and energy-related performance contracting.

Purchasing Sustainability criteria used in purchasing include Energy Star (EPA), Green Cleaning Products (Green Seal/Environmental Choice certified), and Forest Stewardship Council (FSC) or American Forest and Paper Association's Sustainable Forestry Initiative (SFI) paper.

Contact Sustainability Fellow, University of Wisconsin–Eau Claire, 405 Hibbard Hall, Eau Claire, WI 54702. *Phone:* 715-836-2761. *E-mail:* halecl@uwec.edu. *Web site:* www.uwec.edu/.

University of Wisconsin–Green Bay
Green Bay, Wisconsin

Sustainability Initiatives University of Wisconsin–Green Bay's president has signed the American College & University Presidents Climate Commitment. University of Wisconsin–Green Bay has Green Fees (optional/required) dedicated to sustainability initiatives.

Academics *Sustainability-focused undergraduate major(s):* Environmental Policy and Planning (BS), Environmental Science (BS). *Sustainability-focused graduate degree program(s):* Environmental Science and Policy (MS). *Sustainability courses and programs:* sustainability-focused course(s) or lecture series.

Student Services and Green Events *Sustainability leadership:* sustainability coordinator/director, sustainability committee/advisory council, sustainability-focused student government. *Student clubs and activities:* student club(s)/group(s) focused on sustainability. *Major sustainability events:* Earth Day, The Cofrin Center for Biodiversity on-going programming related to environmental and ecological issues. *Housing and facilities:* on-campus organic garden for students.

Food Fair Trade coffee is used. Vegan and vegetarian dining options are available for every meal.

Transportation Provides public transportation access to local destinations and incentives to carpool or use public transportation.

Buildings and Grounds *Campus grounds care:* uses water conservation devices; employs strategies to reduce light pollution; landscapes with native plant species; protects, restores, and/or creates habitat on campus.

Recycling *Programs and activities:* sustains a computer/technology recycling program; maintains an on-campus recycling center; composts yard waste; replaces paper materials with online alternatives; limits free printing in computer labs and libraries. *Campus dining operations:* offers discounts for reusable mugs; uses bulk condiment dispensers and decreased packaging for to-go food service purchases.

Energy Currently uses or plans to use alternative sources of power (biomass energy and solar energy); timers to regulate temperatures based on occupancy hours; and motion, infrared, and/or light sensors to reduce energy uses for lighting.

Purchasing Sustainability criteria used in purchasing include Energy Star (EPA) and Green Cleaning Products (Green Seal/Environmental Choice certified).

Contact University of Wisconsin–Green Bay, 2420 Nicolet Drive, Green Bay, WI 54311-7001. *Phone:* 920-465-2000. *Web site:* www.uwgb.edu/.

University of Wisconsin–La Crosse
La Crosse, Wisconsin

Sustainability Initiatives University of Wisconsin–La Crosse is a signatory to the Talloires Declaration. University of Wisconsin–La Crosse has Green Fees (optional/required) dedicated to sustainability initiatives.

Academics *Sustainability-focused undergraduate major(s):* Biology (BS), Chemistry (BS), Geography (BS), Microbiology (BS). *Sustainability courses and programs:* sustainability-focused course(s) or lecture series.

Student Services and Green Events *Sustainability leadership:* sustainability coordinator/director, sustainability committee/advisory council, recycling manager, energy manager, sustainability-focused student government. *Hous-*

ing and facilities: student-run café that serves environmentally or socially preferable foods.

Food Sustainable, organic, and/or locally produced foods available in on-campus dining facilities. Fair Trade coffee is used. Vegan and vegetarian dining options are available for every meal.

Transportation Provides free on-campus transportation (bus or other), public transportation access to local destinations, a bike loan/rental program, and incentives to carpool or use public transportation.

Buildings and Grounds *Renovation and maintenance:* registered for LEED certification for new construction and/or renovation. *Campus grounds care:* uses water conservation devices; landscapes with native plant species.

Recycling *Events and organizations:* RecycleMania. *Programs and activities:* sustains a computer/technology recycling program; maintains an on-campus recycling center; sustains a pre-consumer food waste composting program; composts yard waste; reuses surplus department/office supplies; reuses chemicals; replaces paper materials with online alternatives; limits free printing in computer labs and libraries. *Campus dining operations:* uses reusable dishware; operates without trays; offers discounts for reusable mugs; uses bulk condiment dispensers and decreased packaging for to-go food service purchases.

Energy Currently uses or plans to use alternative sources of power (biomass energy, hydroelectricity/water power, solar energy, and wind energy); timers to regulate temperatures based on occupancy hours; motion, infrared, and/or light sensors to reduce energy uses for lighting; LED lighting; and energy-related performance contracting.

Purchasing Sustainability criteria used in purchasing include Energy Star (EPA) and Green Cleaning Products (Green Seal/Environmental Choice certified).

Contact Professor, University of Wisconsin–La Crosse, 1725 State Street, La Crosse, WI 54601. *Phone:* 608-785-6992. *E-mail:* tyser.robi@uwlax.edu. *Web site:* www.uwlax.edu/.

University of Wisconsin–Stout
Menomonie, Wisconsin

Sustainability Initiatives University of Wisconsin–Stout's president has signed the American College & University Presidents Climate Commitment.

Academics *Sustainability-focused undergraduate major(s):* Applied Science, Environmental Science concentration (BS). *Sustainability courses and programs:* sustainability-focused course(s) or lecture series.

Student Services and Green Events *Sustainability leadership:* sustainability coordinator/director, sustainability committee/advisory council, recycling manager, energy manager. *Student clubs and activities:* student club(s)/group(s) focused on sustainability. *Major sustainability events:* Recyclable Art Competition, Supermileage Challenge, Spring Move-Out, Sustainability Day, Green Commuter Pledge, Residence Hall Energy Competition, RecycleMania, Mission Possible: The Energy Project. *Housing and facilities:* sustainability-themed housing.

Food Fair Trade coffee is used. Vegan and vegetarian dining options are available for every meal.

Transportation Provides incentives to carpool or use public transportation.

Buildings and Grounds *Campus grounds care:* uses water conservation devices; employs strategies to reduce light pollution; protects, restores, and/or creates habitat on campus.

Recycling *Events and organizations:* RecycleMania. *Programs and activities:* sustains a computer/technology recycling program; maintains an on-campus recycling center; reuses surplus department/office supplies; replaces paper materials with online alternatives; limits free printing in computer labs and libraries. *Campus dining operations:* uses reusable dishware; offers discounts for reusable mugs; uses bulk condiment dispensers and decreased packaging for to-go food service purchases.

Energy Currently uses or plans to use timers to regulate temperatures based on occupancy hours; motion, infrared, and/or light sensors to reduce energy uses for lighting; LED lighting; and energy-related performance contracting.

Purchasing Sustainability criteria used in purchasing include Energy Star (EPA) and Green Cleaning Products (Green Seal/Environmental Choice certified).

Contact Vice Chancellor, University of Wisconsin–Stout, PO Box 790, Menomonie, WI 54751. *Phone:* 715-232-1683. *E-mail:* moend@uwstout.edu. *Web site:* www.uwstout.edu/.

University of Wisconsin–Superior
Superior, Wisconsin

Sustainability Initiatives University of Wisconsin–Superior is a member of the Association for the Advancement of Sustainability in Higher Education (AASHE). This institution's president has signed the American College & University Presidents Climate Commitment.

Academics *Sustainability courses and programs:* sustainability-focused course(s) or lecture series.

Student Services and Green Events *Sustainability leadership:* sustainability coordinator/director. *Student clubs and activities:* student club(s)/group(s) focused on sustainability. *Major sustainability events:* Campus Sustainability Day event, National Teach-In on Climate Change, Earth Day event.

Food Sustainable, organic, and/or locally produced foods available in on-campus dining facilities. Fair Trade coffee is used. Vegan and vegetarian dining options are available for every meal.

Transportation Provides public transportation access to local destinations.

Buildings and Grounds *Renovation and maintenance:* registered for LEED certification for new construction and/or renovation.

Recycling *Programs and activities:* sustains a computer/technology recycling program; sustains a pre-consumer food waste composting program; sustains a post-consumer food waste composting program; reuses surplus department/office supplies; replaces paper materials with online alternatives; limits free printing in computer labs and libraries. *Campus dining operations:* uses reusable dishware; uses bulk condiment dispensers and decreased packaging for to-go food service purchases.

Energy Currently uses or plans to use alternative sources of power; motion, infrared, and/or light sensors to reduce energy uses for lighting; and LED lighting.

Purchasing Sustainability criteria used in purchasing include Energy Star (EPA) and Green Cleaning Products (Green Seal/Environmental Choice certified).

Contact Campus Sustainability Coordinator, University of Wisconsin–Superior, Hawkes Hall 309, Superior, WI 54880. *Phone:* 715-394-8444. *E-mail:* jcrede@uwsuper.edu. *Web site:* www.uwsuper.edu/.

University of Wisconsin–Whitewater
Whitewater, Wisconsin

Sustainability Initiatives University of Wisconsin–Whitewater's president has signed the American College & University Presidents Climate Commitment.

Academics *Sustainability courses and programs:* sustainability-focused course(s) or lecture series.

Student Services and Green Events *Sustainability leadership:* sustainability coordinator/director, sustainability committee/advisory council, recycling manager, energy manager. *Student clubs and activities:* student club(s)/group(s) focused on sustainability. *Major sustainability events:* Earth Day, National Teach-In.

Food Fair Trade coffee is used.

Transportation Provides public transportation access to local destinations.

Buildings and Grounds *Campus grounds care:* uses water conservation devices; landscapes with native plant species; protects, restores, and/or creates habitat on campus.

Recycling *Events and organizations:* RecycleMania. *Programs and activities:* sustains a computer/technology recycling program; maintains an on-campus recycling center. *Campus dining operations:* operates without trays; offers discounts for reusable mugs; uses bulk condiment dispensers and decreased packaging for to-go food service purchases.

Energy Currently uses or plans to use timers to regulate temperatures based on occupancy hours; motion, infrared, and/or light sensors to reduce energy uses for lighting; LED lighting; and energy-related performance contracting.

Purchasing Sustainability criteria used in purchasing include Energy Star (EPA).

Contact Professor, Geography, University of Wisconsin–Whitewater, 800 West Main, Whitewater, WI 53190. *Phone:* 262-472-5126. *E-mail:* compase@uww.edu. *Web site:* www.uww.edu/.

Wyoming

University of Wyoming
Laramie, Wyoming

Sustainability Initiatives University of Wyoming is a member of the Association for the Advancement of Sustainability in Higher Education (AASHE). This institution's president has signed the American College & University Presidents Climate Commitment. University of Wyoming has Green Fees (optional/required) dedicated to sustainability initiatives.

Academics *Sustainability courses and programs:* sustainability-focused course(s) or lecture series, noncredit sustainability course(s).

Student Services and Green Events *Sustainability leadership:* sustainability committee/advisory council, recycling manager, energy manager, sustainability-focused student government. *Student clubs and activities:* student club(s)/group(s) focused on sustainability. *Major sustainability events:* C3 Seminar Series, The Good Mule Project 2009, annual Earth Day/Week Celebration. *Housing and facilities:* on-campus organic garden for students.

Food Fair Trade coffee is used. Vegan and vegetarian dining options are available for every meal.

Transportation Provides free on-campus transportation (bus or other), public transportation access to local destinations, and a bike loan/rental program.

Buildings and Grounds *Renovation and maintenance:* registered for LEED certification for new construction and/or renovation. *Campus grounds care:* uses water conservation devices; employs strategies to reduce light pollution; landscapes with native plant species.

Recycling *Events and organizations:* RecycleMania. *Programs and activities:* sustains a computer/technology recycling program; maintains an on-campus recycling center; sustains a pre-consumer food waste composting program; sustains a post-consumer food waste composting program; reuses surplus department/office supplies; reuses chemicals; limits free printing in computer labs and libraries. *Campus dining operations:* uses reusable dishware; offers discounts for reusable mugs; uses bulk condiment dispensers and decreased packaging for to-go food service purchases.

Energy Currently uses or plans to use alternative sources of power (solar energy); motion, infrared, and/or light sensors to reduce energy uses for lighting; and LED lighting.

Purchasing Sustainability criteria used in purchasing include Energy Star (EPA) and Forest Stewardship Council (FSC) or American Forest and Paper Association's Sustainable Forestry Initiative (SFI) paper.

Contact Project Coordinator, ENR Program, University of Wyoming, 1000 East University Avenue, Laramie, WY 82071. *Phone:* 307-766-5146. *Fax:* 307-766-5099. *E-mail:* jillberg@uwyo.edu. *Web site:* www.uwyo.edu/.

CANADA

Dalhousie University
Halifax, Nova Scotia

Sustainability Initiatives Dalhousie University is a signatory to the Talloires Declaration.

Academics *Sustainability-focused undergraduate major(s):* Environment, Sustainability, Society (BA); Environment, Sustainability, Society (BCD); Environment, Sustainability, Society (BMgmt); Environment, Sustainability, Society (BSc). *Sustainability-focused graduate degree program(s):* Interdisciplinary PhD (PhD), Master of Environmental Studies (MES). *Sustainability courses and programs:* sustainability-focused course(s) or lecture series.

Student Services and Green Events *Sustainability leadership:* sustainability coordinator/director, sustainability committee/advisory council, recycling manager, sustainability-focused student government. *Student clubs and activities:* Public Interest Research Group (PIRG) chapter on campus, student club(s)/group(s) focused on sustainability, outreach materials available about on-campus sustainability efforts. *Major sustainability events:* EcoPrise, Eco-efficiency Centre lecture series and events, Elizabeth May Chair annual symposium, Planning and Architecture, Chemistry and Engineering. *Housing and facilities:* model dorm room that demonstrates sustainable living principles, on-campus organic garden for students.

Food Sustainable, organic, and/or locally produced foods available in on-campus dining facilities. Fair Trade coffee is used. Vegan and vegetarian dining options are available for every meal.

Transportation Provides public transportation access to local destinations and a car sharing program.

Buildings and Grounds *Renovation and maintenance:* registered for LEED certification for new construction and/or

renovation; uses a Green Seal certified cleaning service. *Campus grounds care:* uses water conservation devices; employs strategies to reduce light pollution; landscapes with native plant species; protects, restores, and/or creates habitat on campus.

Recycling *Programs and activities:* sustains a computer/technology recycling program; maintains an on-campus recycling center; sustains a pre-consumer food waste composting program; sustains a post-consumer food waste composting program; composts yard waste; reuses surplus department/office supplies; reuses chemicals; replaces paper materials with online alternatives; limits free printing in computer labs and libraries. *Campus dining operations:* uses reusable dishware; operates without trays; offers discounts for reusable mugs; uses bulk condiment dispensers and decreased packaging for to-go food service purchases.

Energy Currently uses or plans to use motion, infrared, and/or light sensors to reduce energy uses for lighting.

Purchasing Sustainability criteria used in purchasing include Energy Star (EPA) and Green Cleaning Products (Green Seal/Environmental Choice certified).

Contact Director of Sustainability, Dalhousie University, 1226 LeMarchant Street, Halifax, NS B3H 3P7, Canada. *Phone:* 902-494-7448. *E-mail:* rjowen@dal.ca. *Web site:* www.dal.ca/.

Nova Scotia Agricultural College
Truro, Nova Scotia

Academics *Sustainability-focused undergraduate major(s):* Bio-environmental Systems Management (BSc), Environmental Sciences (BSc). *Sustainability-focused graduate degree program(s):* Environmental Science, Soil Science and Agricultural Chemistry. *Sustainability courses and programs:* sustainability-focused course(s) or lecture series, noncredit sustainability course(s), sustainability-focused nonacademic certificate program(s).

Student Services and Green Events *Student clubs and activities:* student club(s)/group(s) focused on sustainability, outreach materials available about on-campus sustainability efforts. *Major sustainability events:* Campus-wide audit and implementation of new document management system, Earth Day. *Housing and facilities:* sustainability-themed housing, on-campus organic garden for students.

Food Sustainable, organic, and/or locally produced foods available in on-campus dining facilities. Fair Trade coffee is used. Vegan and vegetarian dining options are available for every meal.

Buildings and Grounds *Campus grounds care:* uses water conservation devices; landscapes with native plant species; protects, restores, and/or creates habitat on campus.

Recycling *Programs and activities:* sustains a computer/technology recycling program; sustains a pre-consumer food waste composting program; sustains a post-consumer food waste composting program; composts yard waste; reuses surplus department/office supplies; reuses chemicals; replaces paper materials with online alternatives; limits free printing in computer labs and libraries. *Campus dining operations:* uses reusable dishware; operates without trays; offers discounts for reusable mugs; uses bulk condiment dispensers and decreased packaging for to-go food service purchases.

Energy Currently uses or plans to use alternative sources of power (biomass energy and wind energy); timers to regulate temperatures based on occupancy hours; and motion, infrared, and/or light sensors to reduce energy uses for lighting.

Purchasing Sustainability criteria used in purchasing include Energy Star (EPA), Green Cleaning Products (Green Seal/Environmental Choice certified), and Forest Stewardship Council (FSC) or American Forest and Paper Association's Sustainable Forestry Initiative (SFI) paper.

Contact Marketing Services Manager, Nova Scotia Agricultural College, PO Box 550, Truro, NS B2N 5E3, Canada. *Phone:* 902-893-6527. *Fax:* 902-897-9399. *E-mail:* smorris@nsac.ca. *Web site:* www.nsac.ns.ca/.

Simon Fraser University
Burnaby, British Columbia

Sustainability Initiatives Simon Fraser University is a signatory to the Talloires Declaration.

Academics *Sustainability-focused undergraduate major(s):* Earth Sciences (BSc), Environmental Education (BEd), Environmental Science (BSc), Geography, Honors Semester in Sustainability (BBA), Undergraduate Semester in Dialogue, Faculty of the Environment (Interdisciplinary undergraduate degrees). *Sustainability-focused graduate degree program(s):* Earth Sciences (MSc), Earth Sciences (PhD), Environmental Education (MEd), Environmental Science (MSc), Resource and Environmental Management (MRM), Resource and Environmental Management (PhD), Faculty of the Environment (interdisciplinary graduate degrees). *Sustainability courses and programs:* sustainability-focused course(s) or lecture series, noncredit sustainability course(s).

Student Services and Green Events *Sustainability leadership:* sustainability coordinator/director, sustainability committee/advisory council, recycling manager, energy manager. *Student clubs and activities:* Public Interest Research Group (PIRG) chapter on campus, student club(s)/group(s) focused on sustainability. *Major sustainability events:* Earth Day, Sustainability Festival, Organic Farmer's Markets. *Housing and facilities:* sustainability-themed housing, model dorm room that demonstrates sustainable living principles, student-run café that serves environmentally or socially preferable foods, on-campus organic garden for students.

Food Sustainable, organic, and/or locally produced foods available in on-campus dining facilities. Fair Trade coffee is used. Vegan and vegetarian dining options are available for every meal.

Transportation Provides public transportation access to local destinations, a car sharing program, and incentives to carpool or use public transportation.

Buildings and Grounds *Percentage of institution's eligible buildings as of September 2008 meeting LEED and/or LEED-EB certification criteria:* 18%. *Campus grounds care:* employs strategies to reduce light pollution; landscapes with native plant species; protects, restores, and/or creates habitat on campus.

Recycling *Programs and activities:* sustains a computer/technology recycling program; maintains an on-campus recycling center; composts yard waste; reuses surplus department/office supplies; replaces paper materials with online alternatives; limits free printing in computer labs and libraries. *Campus dining operations:* uses reusable dishware; offers discounts for reusable mugs; uses bulk condiment dispensers and decreased packaging for to-go food service purchases.

Energy Currently uses or plans to use alternative sources of power (hydroelectricity/water power and solar energy); timers to regulate temperatures based on occupancy hours; motion, infrared, and/or light sensors to reduce energy uses for lighting; and LED lighting.

Purchasing Sustainability criteria used in purchasing include Energy Star (EPA), Green Electronics Council

(GEC) Electronic Product Environmental Assessment Tool (EPEAT) Silver or Gold, Green Cleaning Products (Green Seal/Environmental Choice certified), and Forest Stewardship Council (FSC) or American Forest and Paper Association's Sustainable Forestry Initiative (SFI) paper.

Contact Sustainability Coordinator, Simon Fraser University, 2621 West Mall Complex, 8888 University Drive, Burnaby, BC V5A 1S6, Canada. *Phone:* 778-782-4702. *E-mail:* cbonfield@sfu.ca. *Web site:* www.sfu.ca/.

Université du Québec en Outaouais
Gatineau, Quebec

Student Services and Green Events *Sustainability leadership:* sustainability committee/advisory council.

Food Fair Trade coffee is used. Vegan and vegetarian dining options are available for every meal.

Transportation Provides public transportation access to local destinations.

Recycling *Programs and activities:* sustains a computer/technology recycling program; maintains an on-campus recycling center; replaces paper materials with online alternatives. *Campus dining operations:* offers discounts for reusable mugs.

Contact Université du Québec en Outaouais, Case Postale 1250, Succursale Hull, Gatineau, QC J8X 3X7, Canada. *Phone:* 819-595-3900. *Web site:* www.uqo.ca/.

University of Calgary
Calgary, Alberta

Sustainability Initiatives University of Calgary is a signatory to the Talloires Declaration.

Academics *Sustainability-focused undergraduate major(s):* Bachelor of Science in Engineering (ENEE). *Sustainability-focused graduate degree program(s):* Sustainable Energy Development (MS). *Sustainability courses and programs:* sustainability-focused course(s) or lecture series, noncredit sustainability course(s), sustainability-focused nonacademic certificate program(s).

Student Services and Green Events *Sustainability leadership:* sustainability coordinator/director, sustainability committee/advisory council, recycling manager, energy manager, sustainability-focused student government. *Student clubs and activities:* Campus Climate Challenge, student club(s)/group(s) focused on sustainability, outreach materials available about on-campus sustainability efforts. *Major sustainability events:* Institute for Energy Environment and Economy Distinguished Speakers Series, Student Union: Green Café, Fair Trade: Setting the Standard for a Sustainable Future, Haskayne School of Business: The Changing Climate of the Energy Industry. *Housing and facilities:* sustainability-themed housing.

Food Fair Trade coffee is used. Vegan and vegetarian dining options are available for every meal.

Transportation Provides public transportation access to local destinations, a bike loan/rental program, a car sharing program, and incentives to carpool or use public transportation.

Buildings and Grounds *Renovation and maintenance:* registered for LEED certification for new construction and/or renovation; uses a Green Seal certified cleaning service. *Campus grounds care:* uses water conservation devices; employs strategies to reduce light pollution; landscapes with native plant species.

Recycling *Programs and activities:* sustains a computer/technology recycling program; maintains an on-campus recycling center; sustains a pre-consumer food waste composting program; sustains a post-consumer food waste composting program; composts yard waste; reuses surplus department/office supplies; limits free printing in computer labs and libraries. *Campus dining operations:* uses reusable dishware; offers discounts for reusable mugs; uses bulk condiment dispensers and decreased packaging for to-go food service purchases.

Energy Currently uses or plans to use alternative sources of power (solar energy); LED lighting; and energy-related performance contracting.

Purchasing Sustainability criteria used in purchasing include Energy Star (EPA), Green Cleaning Products (Green Seal/Environmental Choice certified), and Forest Stewardship Council (FSC) or American Forest and Paper Association's Sustainable Forestry Initiative (SFI) paper.

Contact Sustainability Coordinator, University of Calgary, PP127, 2500 University Drive NW, Calgary, AB T2N 1N4, Canada. *Phone:* 403-220-4641. *E-mail:* j.d.wright@ucalgary.ca. *Web site:* www.ucalgary.ca/.

University of Ottawa
Ottawa, Ontario

Sustainability Initiatives University of Ottawa is a signatory to the Talloires Declaration. University of Ottawa has Green Fees (optional/required) dedicated to sustainability initiatives.

Academics *Sustainability courses and programs:* sustainability-focused course(s) or lecture series.

Student Services and Green Events *Sustainability leadership:* sustainability coordinator/director, sustainability committee/advisory council, recycling manager, energy manager, sustainability-focused student government. *Student clubs and activities:* Public Interest Research Group (PIRG) chapter on campus, student club(s)/group(s) focused on sustainability, outreach materials available about on-campus sustainability efforts. *Major sustainability events:* Green Weeks, Sustainable Business Conference, RecycleMania. *Housing and facilities:* student-run café that serves environmentally or socially preferable foods, on-campus organic garden for students.

Food Sustainable, organic, and/or locally produced foods available in on-campus dining facilities. Fair Trade coffee is used.

Transportation Provides free on-campus transportation (bus or other), a bike loan/rental program, and a car sharing program.

Buildings and Grounds *Renovation and maintenance:* registered for LEED certification for new construction and/or renovation. *Campus grounds care:* uses water conservation devices; landscapes with native plant species.

Recycling *Events and organizations:* RecycleMania. *Programs and activities:* sustains a computer/technology recycling program; maintains an on-campus recycling center; sustains a pre-consumer food waste composting program; replaces paper materials with online alternatives; limits free printing in computer labs and libraries. *Campus dining operations:* uses reusable dishware; offers discounts for reusable mugs.

Energy Currently uses or plans to use alternative sources of power; timers to regulate temperatures based on occupancy hours; motion, infrared, and/or light sensors to reduce energy uses for lighting; LED lighting; vending machine motion sensors; and energy-related performance contracting.

Purchasing Sustainability criteria used in purchasing include Energy Star (EPA) and Forest Stewardship Council (FSC) or American Forest and Paper Association's Sustainable Forestry Initiative (SFI) paper.

Contact Sustainable Development Manager, University of Ottawa, 141 Louis Pasteur, Ottawa, ON K1N 6N5, Canada. *Phone:* 613-562-5800 Ext. 2530. *E-mail:* jrausseo@uottawa. ca. *Web site:* www.uottawa.ca/.

University of Prince Edward Island
Charlottetown, Prince Edward Island

Academics *Sustainability courses and programs:* sustainability-focused course(s) or lecture series.

Student Services and Green Events *Sustainability leadership:* sustainability coordinator/director, sustainability committee/advisory council, energy manager. *Housing and facilities:* student-run café that serves environmentally or socially preferable foods.

Food Sustainable, organic, and/or locally produced foods available in on-campus dining facilities. Fair Trade coffee is used. Vegan and vegetarian dining options are available for every meal.

Transportation Provides public transportation access to local destinations.

Buildings and Grounds *Campus grounds care:* uses water conservation devices; landscapes with native plant species; protects, restores, and/or creates habitat on campus.

Recycling *Programs and activities:* sustains a computer/ technology recycling program; maintains an on-campus recycling center; sustains a pre-consumer food waste composting program; sustains a post-consumer food waste composting program; composts yard waste; reuses surplus department/office supplies; reuses chemicals; replaces paper materials with online alternatives; limits free printing in computer labs and libraries. *Campus dining operations:* uses reusable dishware; operates without trays.

Energy Currently uses or plans to use alternative sources of power (biomass energy, geothermal energy, and wind energy); timers to regulate temperatures based on occupancy hours; motion, infrared, and/or light sensors to reduce energy uses for lighting; and LED lighting.

Purchasing Sustainability criteria used in purchasing include Forest Stewardship Council (FSC) or American Forest and Paper Association's Sustainable Forestry Initiative (SFI) paper.

Contact University of Prince Edward Island, 550 University Avenue, Charlottetown, PE C1A 4P3, Canada. *Phone:* 902-566-0439. *Web site:* www.upei.ca/.

The University of Western Ontario
London, Ontario

Sustainability Initiatives The University of Western Ontario is a signatory to the Talloires Declaration.

Academics *Sustainability-focused undergraduate major(s):* Environmental Engineering (BESc), Environmental Science (BA), Environmental Science (BSc), Green Process Engineering (BESc). *Sustainability-focused graduate degree program(s):* Environment and Sustainability (MES), Environment and Sustainability (MS, PhD). *Sustainability courses and programs:* sustainability-focused course(s) or lecture series.

Student Services and Green Events *Sustainability leadership:* sustainability coordinator/director, sustainability committee/advisory council, recycling manager, energy manager, sustainability-focused student government. *Student clubs and activities:* student club(s)/group(s) focused on sustainability. *Major sustainability events:* ENVIRO-WEEK. *Housing and facilities:* student-run café that serves environmentally or socially preferable foods, on-campus organic garden for students.

Food Sustainable, organic, and/or locally produced foods available in on-campus dining facilities. Fair Trade coffee is used.

Transportation Provides public transportation access to local destinations and incentives to carpool or use public transportation.

Buildings and Grounds *Renovation and maintenance:* registered for LEED certification for new construction and/or renovation. *Campus grounds care:* uses water conservation devices; landscapes with native plant species; protects, restores, and/or creates habitat on campus.

Recycling *Programs and activities:* sustains a computer/ technology recycling program; maintains an on-campus recycling center; sustains a pre-consumer food waste composting program; composts yard waste; reuses surplus department/office supplies; reuses chemicals; replaces paper materials with online alternatives. *Campus dining operations:* uses reusable dishware; offers discounts for reusable mugs.

Energy Currently uses or plans to use alternative sources of power (hydroelectricity/water power); timers to regulate temperatures based on occupancy hours; motion, infrared, and/or light sensors to reduce energy uses for lighting; and LED lighting.

Contact Physical Plant Communications Officer, The University of Western Ontario, 1151 Richmond Street, Support Services Building, London, ON N6A 3K7, Canada. *Phone:* 519-661-2111 Ext. 88736. *E-mail:* bwatso5@uwo.ca. *Web site:* www.uwo.ca/.

PART V

APPENDIXES

APPENDIX A

PROFESSIONAL JOBS BY INDUSTRIES

The first job in each job category is the main job title for that broad category. The other jobs are just a sampling of the many job titles that you may find as you check job boards for that broad category. For example, under agricultural engineer, you might find jobs posted for bioresource engineer and environmental engineer. A subsea piping engineer job could be posted under energy as well as transportation. Every job title listed below was found by checking job boards. See "What Does Being Green Mean?" in the front of this guide for more information on job boards.

- Agriculture
  - Agricultural Engineer
    - Agricultural and Biological Engineer
    - Biological Systems Engineer
    - Bioresource Engineer
    - Environmental Engineer
    - Food and Process Engineer
    - Forest Engineer
  - Agricultural Extension Specialist
    - Agricultural Extension Agent
  - Agronomist
    - Agricultural Scientist
- Biotechnology
  - Chemical Engineer
    - Analytical Chemist
    - Biochemical Engineer
    - Chemical Process Engineer
    - Environmental Engineer
    - Process Engineer
  - Microbiologist
    - Bacteriologist
    - Bioprocessing Engineer
    - Clinical Lab Technician (requires a bachelor's degree)
    - Clinical Medical Technician (requires a bachelor's degree)
    - Industrial Microbiologist
    - Quality Assurance Technician (requires a bachelor's degree)
  - Technical and Scientific Sales Representative
    - Account Manager
    - Product Line Sales Manager

- Construction
  - Civil Engineer
    - Aerospace Engineer
    - Architectural Engineer
    - Environmental Engineer
    - Geotechnical Engineer
    - Ocean/Marine Engineer
    - Structural Engineer
    - Traffic Engineer
    - Transportation Engineer
  - Construction Manager
  - Cost Estimator (across many industries)
- Design
  - Architect
    - Architectural Engineer
    - Building Contractor
    - Building Inspector
    - Furniture Designer
    - Interior Designer
    - Marine Architect
    - Urban Planner
  - Landscape Architect
    - Environmental Landscape Architect
    - Landscape Designer
  - Product Designer
    - Commercial Designer
    - Industrial Designer
- Energy
  - Computer Software Applications Engineer
    - Information Technologist
    - Programmer

399

- Software Developer
- Computer Consultant
  o Electrical Engineer
    - Battery Engineer
    - Electrical Engineer Project Manager
    - Electrical Product Engineer
    - Electrical Systems Designer
    - Electro-Mechanical Engineer
    - Electronics Engineer
    - Geothermal Electrical Engineer
    - Hydroelectric Electrical Engineer
    - Power Electronics Engineer
    - Substation Engineer
  o Geoscientist
    - Atmospheric Scientist
    - Economic Geologist
    - Engineering Geologist
    - Environmental Geologist
    - Geochemist
    - Geologist
    - Geophysicist
    - Glacial Geologist
    - Hydrologist
    - Oceanographer
    - Petroleum Geologist
    - Soil Scientist
- Environmental Health
  o Environmental Health Specialist
    - Environmental Protection Officer
    - Health Physicist
    - Industrial Hygienist
    - Occupational Safety and Health Specialist
  o Public Health Nurse
    - Community Health Nurse
    - Statistician
    - Analytics Statistician
    - Applied Statistician
    - Biostatistician
    - Clinical Trials Research Analyst
    - Research Analyst
    - Statistics Analyst
- Natural Resources Management and Conservation
  o Conservation Manager and Forester
    - Environmental Educator
    - Forestry Carbon Scientist
    - Naturalist/Outdoor Educator
    - Range Scientist
    - Soil Conservationist
    - Systems Arborist
    - Utility Arborist
    - Utility Forester
    - Urban Forester
    - Water Conservationist
    - Water Quality Coordinator

- Water Resource Project Manager
  o Environmental Engineer
    - Air Pollution Control Engineer
    - Civil/Environmental Engineer
    - Environmental Hydrogeologist
    - Environmental Scientist
    - Piping Engineer
    - Quality Engineer
    - Remedial Project Engineer
    - Water Resources Engineer
  o Geographic Information Specialist
    - Cartographer
    - Computer Programmer
    - Computer Systems Analyst
    - Database Administrator
    - Database Design Analyst
    - Information Scientist
    - Information Systems Management Specialist
    - Geospatial Information Specialist
    - Photogrammetrist
- Parks, Recreation, and Tourism
  o Conservator and Curator
    - Conservation Administrator
    - Conservation Scientist
    - Conservation Technician (requires a bachelor's degree)
    - Museum Director
    - Museum Technician (requires a bachelor's degree)
    - Preservation Specialist
  o Parks and Recreation Specialist
    - Education Specialist
    - Environmental Education Specialist
    - Interpretive Naturalist
    - Outdoor Education Naturalist
    - Park Activities Coordinator
    - Park Interpretive Specialist
    - Park Manager
    - Park Naturalist
    - Park Ranger
    - Program Manager
  o Turfgrass Manager
    - Athletic Fields Superintendent
    - Buildings and Grounds Supervisor
    - Golf Course Superintendent
    - Grounds Crew Supervisor
    - Grounds Foreman
    - Groundskeeper Supervisor
    - Grounds Maintenance Supervisor
    - Grounds Supervisor
    - Landscape Manager
    - Landscape Supervisor
    - Sod Farm Manager
    - Sports Turf Manager

- Policy, Administration, Analysis, and Advocacy
  - o Environmental Economist
    - Resources Economist
  - o Environmental Scientist
  - o Environmental Technical Writer
    - Environmental Journalist
    - Environmental Reporter
- Transportation
  - o Mechanical Engineer
    - Lead Mechanical Engineer
    - Lead Process Engineer
    - Mechanical Handling Engineer
    - Mechanical Packaging Engineer
    - Piping Inspector
    - Process Design Engineer
    - Projects Control Manager
    - Structural and Piping Designer
    - Subsea Pipeline Engineer
    - Valve Engineer
    - Wells Project Services Engineer
  - o Transportation Engineer
    - Highway Engineer
    - Traffic Engineer
    - Transportation Planning Engineer
  - o Transportation Environmental Planner
    - Aviation Planner
    - Campus Transportation Planner
    - Environmental Planner
    - Transportation Planner
    - Urban and Regional Planner
    - Urban Planner

Because of the number of engineering specialties that cross over industries, all engineering jobs are also collected in the following list. The industry noted in parentheses represents the category under which you will find the job in Chapter 1:

- Aerospace Engineer (Construction)
- Air Pollution Control Engineer (Natural Resources Management and Conservation)
- Agricultural and Biological Engineer (Agriculture)
- Agricultural Engineer (Agriculture)
- Analytical Chemist (Biotechnology)
- Architectural Engineer (Construction, Design)
- Battery Engineer (Energy)
- Biochemical Engineer (Biotechnology)
- Biological Systems Engineer (Agriculture)
- Bioprocessing Engineer (Biotechnology)
- Bioresource Engineer (Agriculture)
- Civil/Environmental Engineer (Natural Resources Management and Conservation)
- Chemical Engineer (Biotechnology)

- Chemical Process Engineer (Biotechnology)
- Civil Engineer (Construction)
- Computer Software Applications Engineer (Energy)
- Electrical Engineer (Energy)
- Electrical Engineer Project Manager (Energy)
- Electrical Product Engineer (Energy)
- Electrical Systems Designer (Energy)
- Electro-Mechanical Engineer (Energy)
- Electronics Engineer (Energy)
- Engineering Geologist (Energy)
- Environmental Engineer (Agriculture, Biotechnology, Construction, Natural Resources Management and Conservation)
- Food and Process Engineer (Agriculture)
- Forest Engineer (Agriculture)
- Geoscientist (Energy)
- Geotechnical Engineer (Construction)
- Geothermal Electrical Engineer (Energy)
- Highway Engineer (Transportation)
- Hydroelectric Electrical Engineer (Energy)
- Lead Mechanical Engineer (Transportation)
- Lead Process Engineer (Transportation)
- Mechanical Engineer (Transportation)
- Mechanical Handling Engineer (Transportation)
- Mechanical Packaging Engineer (Transportation)
- Ocean/Marine Engineer (Construction)
- Piping Engineer (Natural Resources Management and Conservation, Transportation)
- Power Electronics Engineer (Energy)
- Process Design Engineer (Transportation)
- Process Engineer (Biotechnology)
- Projects Control Manager (Transportation)
- Quality Engineer (Natural Resources Management and Conservation)
- Remedial Project Engineer (Natural Resources Management and Conservation)
- Structural and Piping Designer (Transportation)
- Structural Engineer (Construction)
- Subsea Pipeline Engineer (Transportation)
- Substation Engineer (Energy)
- Traffic Engineer (Construction, Transportation)
- Transportation Engineer (Construction, Transportation)
- Transportation Planning Engineer (Transportation)
- Valve Engineer (Transportation)
- Water Resources Engineer (Natural Resources Management and Conservation)
- Wells Project Services Engineer (Transportation)

APPENDIX B

SKILLED JOBS BY INDUSTRIES

The first job in each job category is the main job title for that broad category. The other jobs are just a sampling of the many job titles that you may find as you check job boards for that broad category. For example, under agricultural technician, you might find jobs posted for seed analyst and agricultural extension associate. Some jobs also cross one or more categories. For example, veterinary technologist could be listed under biotechnology jobs as well as natural resources management positions. The job titles listed below were found by checking job boards. See "What Does Being Green Mean?" for more information on job boards.

- Agriculture
  - Agricultural Inspector
    - Seed and Fertilizer Specialist
    - Grain Inspector
    - Meat and Poultry Inspector
    - Food Regulatory Field Supervisor
    - Plant Protection Specialist
    - Plant Pest Inspector
    - Quality Control Specialist
  - Organic Farmer
    - Organic Dairy Farmer
    - Organic Poultry Farmer
    - Organic Livestock Farmer/Rancher
  - Agricultural Technician
    - Agricultural Resources Technician
    - Agricultural Research Technician
    - Agricultural Research Technologist
    - Agricultural Research Associate
    - Seed Analyst
    - County Extension Agent Technician
    - Agricultural Extension Associate
    - Precision Agriculture Technician
- Biotechnology
  - Biological Technician
    - Biological Technologist
    - Biological Science Technician
    - Biologist Aide
    - Environmental Technician
    - Resource Biologist/Fisheries
    - Wildlife Technician
    - Medical Technologist
    - Medical Lab Technician
  - Industrial Engineering Technician
    - Industrial Engineering Analyst
    - Engineering Technician
    - Manufacturing Engineer
    - Manufacturing Technician
    - Process Documentation and Methods Analyst
    - Broadcast and Sound Engineer Technician
    - Radio Operator
    - Quality Control Technician
    - Quality Control Engineering Technician
    - Quality Process Engineer
- Construction
  - Carpenter
  - Construction and Building Inspector
    - Home Inspector
    - Green Building Inspector
    - Electrical Inspector
    - Mechanical Inspector
    - Plumbing Inspector
    - Structural Inspector
    - Public Works Inspector
    - Plan Examiner
    - Specification Inspector
  - Electrician
    - Electrical Engineering Technician
    - Electrical Drafter
    - Motor Repairer
    - Construction and Building Inspector
    - Lineman
  - Heating, Air Conditioning, and Refrigeration (HVAC/R) Technician

- Service Technician
- HVAC Specialist (Heating, Ventilation, and Air Conditioning Specialist)
- HVAC Technician (Heating, Ventilation, and Air Conditioning Technician)
- Air Conditioning Technician (AC Tech)
- HVAC Installer (Heating, Ventilation, and Air Conditioning Installer) Mechanic
- Service Manager
- Refrigeration Mechanic
- Refrigeration Technician
- HVAC/R Service Technician (Heating, Ventilation, and Air Conditioning/Refrigeration)
- Refrigeration Operator
- Commercial Service Technician
- Field Service Technician
- VRT Mechanic (Variable Retention Time Mechanic)

- Design
  - o Architectural and Civil Drafter
    - Drafter
    - Designer
    - Architectural Assistant
    - Technical Illustrator
    - Digital Technician
    - Digital Artist
    - CAD Operator
    - Engineering Technician
    - Facilities Planner
  - o Interior Designer
    - Certified Kitchen Designer
    - Color and Materials Designer
    - Commercial Interior Designer
    - Decorating Consultant
    - Director of Interiors
    - Interior Decorator
    - Interior Design Consultant
    - Interior Design Coordinator
  - o Landscape Designer
    - Landscape Sales
    - Garden Designer
    - Ornamental Garden Designer

- Energy
  - o Electrical and Electronics Engineering Technician
    - Electrical Technician
    - Electrical Field Technician
    - Electrical-Instrument Repairer
    - Electronics Technician
    - Electronics Field Technician
    - Instrument Technician (Utilities)
    - High Voltage Relay Technician
    - Electric Substation Technician—Wind

- Relay Test Technician
- Instrumentation Technician
- Quality Systems Technician
- Quality Systems Analyst
  - o Solar Power Installer
    - Solar Installer
    - Rooftop Solar Installer
    - Solar Project Manager
    - Solar Photovoltaic Installer
    - Solar Thermal Installer
  - o Wind Turbine Fabricator
    - Wind Turbine Machinist
    - Sheet Metal Worker
    - Machinist

- Environmental Health
  - o Environmental Science and Protection Technician
    - Environmental Technician
    - Environmental Specialist
    - Laboratory Technician
    - Laboratory Specialist
    - Process Laboratory Specialist
    - Environmental Health Specialist
    - Sanitarian
    - Public Health Sanitarian
    - Industrial Pretreatment Program Specialist (IPP Specialist)
    - Sanitarian Specialist
    - Associate Environmental Professional
    - Indoor Air Quality Manager
    - Registered Environmental Laboratory Technologist
    - Industrial Environmental Toxicologist
  - o Hazardous Materials (HAZMAT) Specialist
    - Hazardous Materials (HAZMAT) Technician
    - Hazardous Waste Operations and Emergency Response (HAZWOPER) Technician
    - Asbestos Abatement Worker
    - Decontamination/Decommissioning Operator (D & D Operator)
    - Nuclear Waste Handler
    - Radiation Safety Technician
    - Radiological Control and Safety Technician
    - Waste Handling Technician
    - Field Technician
    - Sampler
    - Site Worker
  - o Water and Wastewater Treatment Operator
    - Waste Water Treatment Plant Operator (WWTP Operator)
    - Water Treatment Plant Operator
    - Waste Water Operator
    - Water and Wastewater Laboratory Analyst
    - Water System Operator
    - Industrial Waste Operator

- Process Operator
- Supervisory Control and Data Acquisition (SCADA) Operator
- Plant Maintenance Technologist
- Biosolids Land Applier
- Backflow Prevention Assembly Tester
- Natural Resources Management and Conservation
  - o Conservation and Forest Technician
    - Forest Technician
    - Forestry Technician
    - Wildlife Technician
    - Resource Manager
    - Resource Technician
    - Conservationist
    - Forestry Aide
    - Natural Resources Technician
  - o Environmental Engineering Technician
    - Environmental Technician
    - Environmental Specialist
    - Environmental Engineering Assistant
    - Environmental Field Technician
    - Engineer Technician
  - o Surveying and Mapping Technician
    - Geographical Information System Specialist (GIS Specialist)
    - Geographical Information System Analyst (GIS Analyst)
    - Geographical Information System Technician (GIS Technician)
    - Mapping Technician
    - Stereoplotter Operator
    - Photogrammetric Compilation Specialist
    - Photogrammetric Technician
    - Computer-Aided Design Technician (CAD Technician)
    - Drafter
    - Hydrographic Surveyor
    - Survey Technician
    - Survey Crew Chief
    - Survey Party Chief
    - Field Crew Chief
  - o Veterinary Technologist
    - Veterinary Technician
    - Registered Veterinary Technician
    - Veterinary Assistant
    - Licensed Veterinary Technician
    - Certified Veterinary Technician
    - Veterinary Laboratory Technician
- Parks, Recreation, and Tourism
  - o Outdoor Recreation Specialist
    - Recreation Supervisor
    - Activities Assistant
    - Activity Specialist
    - Activities Coordinator

- Activities Director
- Certified Therapeutic Recreation Specialist (CTRS)
- Recreation Therapist
- Therapeutic Recreation Assistant
- Therapeutic Recreation Leader
- Therapeutic Recreation Director
  - o Restoration Horticulture Specialist
    - Environmental Horticulture Specialist
    - Ecological Restoration Manager
  - o Green Travel Agent
    - Travel Agent
    - Travel Consultant
    - Travel Counselor
- Policy, Administration, Analysis, and Advocacy
  - o Paralegal
    - Legal Assistant
    - Judicial Assistant
  - o Planning Technician
    - Planning Assistant
    - Engineering Technician
    - GIS Technician (Geographic Information Systems)
    - Planning Aide
    - Transportation Planning Assistant
    - Development Technician
    - Code Enforcement Technician
    - Zoning Technician
- Transportation
  - o Bus and Truck Mechanics and Diesel Engine Specialist
    - Aircraft and Avionics Equipment Mechanic
    - Aircraft and Avionics Equipment Service Technician
    - Commercial Transport Mechanic
    - Heavy Equipment Service Technician
    - Heavy Equipment Service Mechanic
    - Heavy Duty Mechanic
    - Mobile Equipment Mechanic
  - o Dispatcher and Telecommunicator
    - Truck Dispatcher
    - Bus Dispatcher
    - Train Dispatcher
    - Aircraft Flight Dispatcher
    - Airline Flight Dispatcher
    - Public Safety Dispatcher
  - o Welder
    - Welding Supervisor
    - Welding Inspector
    - Welder/Solderer
    - Welder/Brazier
    - Welder/Cutter
    - Underwater Welder

APPENDIX C

ENVIRONMENTAL AND ENERGY INSTITUTES AND CENTERS

If you want to find out more about what a particular college or university is doing to support the environment, there is no better place to look than its environmental center or institute. The following list is by no means exhaustive, but it provides a sampling of centers and institutes at two- and four-year institutions in the United States:

Arizona State University
- Center for Environmental Biotechnology
  http://biodesign.asu.edu/centers/eb
- Center for Sustainable Engineering
  (collaboration with Carnegie Mellon
  University and The University of Texas at
  Austin)
  http://www.csengin.org
- Global Institute of Sustainability
  http://sustainability.asu.edu

Boston University
- Center for Energy and Environmental Studies
  (CEES)
  http://www.bu.edu/cees/

Bowdoin College
- Coastal Studies Center
  http://www.bowdoin.edu/csc/index.shtml

Brandeis University
- Arava Institute (collaboration with Brandeis)
  http://www.arava.org

Bronx Community College
- The Center for Sustainable Energy
  http://www.bcc.cuny.edu/
  InstitutionalDevelopment/CSE/

California Institute of Technology
- CalTech Center for Sustainable Energy
  Research
  http://www.ccser.caltech.edu

Carnegie Mellon University
- Green Design Institute
  http://www.ce.cmu.edu/GreenDesign/
  research/sustinf.html
- Center for Sustainable Engineering
  (collaboration with The University of Texas at
  Austin and Arizona State University)
  http://www.csengin.org

City University of New York
- Institute for Sustainable Cities
  http://www.cunysustainablecities.org

Clarkson University
- Center for Sustainable Energy Systems
  http://www.clarkson.edu/cses/

Columbia University
- Center for Energy Marine Transportation and
  Public Policy
  http://www.sipa.columbia.edu/energy/

Cornell University
- Center for a Sustainable Future
  http://www.sustainablefuture.cornell.edu/
  index.php
- Center for Sustainable Global Enterprise
  The Johnson School, Cornell
  http://www.johnson.cornell.edu/sge

Dickinson College
- Center for Environmental and Sustainability
  Education
  http://www.dickinson.edu/
  departments/cese

Duke University
- Nicholas Institute for Environmental Policy Solutions
  http://www.nicholas.duke.edu/institute

Duquesne University
- Center for Environmental Research and Education
  http://www.science.duq.edu/esm/cereabt.html

Georgetown University
- Center for the Environment
  http://www1.georgetown.edu/centers/environment

Grand Valley State University
- Annis Water Resources Institute
  http://www.gvsu.edu/wri/

Harvard University
- Center for the Environment
  http://environment.harvard.edu/index.htm
- Center for International Development Sustainability Science Program
  http://www.cid.harvard.edu/sustsci/grants/index.html
- Office for Sustainability
  http://www.greencampus.harvard.edu/

Hudson Valley Community College
- Center for Energy Efficiency and Building Science in the Workforce Development Institute
  http://www.hvcc.edu/ceebs/about.html

Lane Community College
- Northwest Energy Education Institute
  http://www.nweei.org

Long Beach Community College
- Advanced Transportation Technology Center
  http://attc.lbcc.edu/

Los Angeles Trade-Technical College
- Sustainable Development Education and Training Institute
  http://www.lattc.edu/dept/lattc/REDI/SDETI.html

Mesalands Community College
- North American Wind Research and Training Center
  http://www.mesalands.edu/wind/default.htm

Oklahoma State University
- Building & Environmental Thermal Systems Research Group
  http://www.hvac.okstate.edu/

Oregon State University
- Institute for Water and Watersheds
  http://water.oregonstate.edu

Parsons The New School for Design
- Tishman Environment and Design Center
  http://www.newschool.edu/tedc

Penn State University Park
- Center for Sustainability
  www.cfs.psu.edu
- Shaver's Creek Environmental Center
  www.outreach.psu.edu/shaverscreek

Portland State University
- Center for Sustainable Processes and Practices
  www.pdx.edu/sustainability/about-us-academics

Purdue University
- Center for the Environment
  www.purdue.edu/discoverypark/environment

Princeton University
- Princeton Environmental Institute
  http://web.princeton.edu/sites/PEI/index.html

Red Rock Community College
- Environmental Training Center
  http://www.rrcc.edu/cetc
- Occupational Safety and Health Training Center (Region IV)
  http://www.rrcc.edu/rmec

Rensselaer Polytechnic Institute
- Center for Future Energy Systems
  http://www.rpi.edu/cfes/

Santa Clara University
- Center for Science, Technology and Society
  http://www.scu.edu/sts
- Environmental Studies Institute
  http://www.scu.edu/envs

Santa Fe Community College
- Sustainable Technologies Center
  http://www.sfccnm.edu/

Southern Methodist University
- Institute for the Study of Earth and Man
  http://smu.edu/isem